PUNJABI IDENTITY
IN A GLOBAL CONTEXT

PUNJABI IDENTITY
IN A GLOBAL CONTEXT

edited by
Pritam Singh
Shinder Singh Thandi

OXFORD
UNIVERSITY PRESS

OXFORD
UNIVERSITY PRESS

Oxford University Press is a department of the University of Oxford.
It furthers the University's objective of excellence in research, scholarship,
and education by publishing worldwide. Oxford is a registered trademark of
Oxford University Press in the UK and in certain other countries

Published in India by
Oxford University Press
22 Workspace, 2nd Floor, 1/22 Asaf Ali Road, New Delhi 110002, India

© Oxford University Press 1999

The moral rights of the authors have been asserted

First published by the Association for Punjab Studies (UK) 1996
Second impression 2015

ISBN-13: 978-0-19-564864-5
ISBN-10: 0-19-564864-1

Typeset in Times New Roman
by Bob Pomfret, Educational Media Unit, Oxford Brookes University
Printed at Manipal Technologies Limited, Manipal

To
Sukhjinder, Meena, Amrita, Dilraj, Khushwant and Tanya for their
loving support, patience and understanding

Contents

SECTION III: *Nation States, Punjabis and the New Global Context*

SECTION IV: *International Migration, Globalisation
and Punjabi Diaspora*

PREFACE

Globalisation and its interface with linguistic and regional identity - the theme has never been more important than it is now. Globalised media has heightened our awareness about Quebec, Scotland, Chechnya, the Basque region, Palestine, Kashmir, Karachi, East Timor and Punjab - to name just a few. The process of globalisation by smothering the national sovereignty of the existing nation states has, seemingly paradoxically, triggered off the national aspirations of the regions with strong memories of crystallised identities. Economy, geography, politics, religion, language, music and poetry have played conflicting and complementary roles in consolidating and dissolving the national identities of the regions. This collection of papers is an adventure in the exploration of the vicissitudes of Punjabi identity in a globalised perspective. The existence of three Punjabs - one in India, one in Pakistan and the one in diaspora - promises a fascinating journey into this exploration. This unique and diverse collection embarks on this challenging journey.

ACKNOWLEDGEMENTS

We owe our greatest debt to Meena Dhanda for giving her time generously to improve the quality of this new edition in each of its aspects. In reformatting the manuscript into its final form, Bob Pomfret of the Educational Media Unit, Oxford Brookes University provided prompt and professional assistance. We are extremely thankful to him. The School of Business, Oxford Brookes University and the Coventry Business School, Coventry University provided assistance in many ways in getting this book out, for which we are grateful.

We wish to thank all the authors for contributing their papers and meeting with our demands for corrections and revisions. We especially thank Iftikhar Malik for providing valuable suggestions in editing some of the papers relating to Pakistan. We are deeply indebted to the reviewers of the earlier edition of this book for their encouragement and constructive criticisms.

At Oxford University Press, we owe our gratitude to Rukun Advani for his interest in this project, to Anita Roy for her co-operation and suggestions in the course of its development and to Rasna Dhillon for her patience and valuable support at the final stage.

We hope that this volume will contribute not only to stimulating more quality research on Punjab Studies, but will also help to widen the scope of studies on globalisation, international political economy, colonisation, patterns of agrarian and industrial development in the Third World, regional nationalisms, gender identities in nation formations, religion and ethnicity, South Asian diaspora communities and, yes, on Bhangra music too.

Pritam Singh
Shinder Singh Thandi

CONTRIBUTORS

Roger Ballard
is a Lecturer at the Department of Religions, University of Manchester (UK).

J. S. Grewal
is the Director of the Institute of Punjab Studies, Chandigarh (India) and is a former Vice-Chancellor of Guru Nanak Dev University, Amritsar, Punjab (India) and a former Director of the Indian Institute of Advanced Studies, Shimla, Himachal Pradesh (India).

M. Athar Tahir
is a poet, short story writer and scholar who was educated at Oriel College, Oxford and the University of Pennsylvania. An author and translator of many books on Punjabi literature, he is an elected Fellow of the Royal Asiatic Society of Great Britain.

Darshan Singh
is Professor at the Department of Guru Nanak Sikh Studies, Panjab University, Chandigarh (India).

Lekh Raj Parwana
is Deputy Secretary at the Punjab Legislative Assembly, Chandigarh (India).

Bhupinder Singh
is Professor at the Department of Sociology and Social Anthropology, Panjabi University, Patiala, Punjab (India).

Arvind-pal Singh
is a Research Fellow at the Department of Religion at the School of Oriental and African Studies, University of London and teaches part time at Coventry University, Coventry (UK).

Imran Ali
is Professor at the Lahore University of Management Sciences, Lahore, Punjab (Pakistan).

Masood Zahid
is a Lecturer at the Qaid-i-Azam University, Islamabad, Punjab (Pakistan) and completed his post-graduate research at St. Antony's College, Oxford.

Kamlesh Mohan
is Reader at the Department of History, Panjab University, Chandigarh (India).

Iftikhar Malik
is a Lecturer in international history at the Bath Spa University College (UK) and a former Qaid-i-Azam Fellow at St. Antony's College, Oxford.

Sukhmani Riar
is a Lecturer at the Department of History, Guru Nanak Dev University, Amritsar, Punjab (India).

Indu Banga
is Professor at the Department of History, Panjab University, Chandigarh, Punjab (India).

Nazar Tiwana
lives a retired life in Chicago. He is the son of Khizar Hiyat Khan Tiwana, the last Premier of the United

	Punjab. After his recent conversion to Buddhism, his Buddhist name is Nazram Palden Teo.
Asad Sayeed	is Director Research, Pakistan Institute of Labour Education and Research (PILER), Karachi (Pakistan).
Sucha Singh Gill	is Professor at the Department of Economics, Panjabi University, Patiala, Punjab (India).
Lakhwinder Singh	is a Lecturer at the Department of Economics, Panjabi University, Patiala, Punjab (India).
Chaman Lal	is Professor in Hindi at Panjabi University, Patiala, Punjab (India).
Ikram Ali Malik	retired as a Professor at the Department of History at the University of Punjab, Lahore, Punjab (Pakistan).
Tejwant S. Gill	is Professor at the Department of English at Guru Nanak Dev University, Amritsar, Punjab (India).
Parminder Bhachu	is Henry R. Luce Professor of Cultural Identity and Global Processes at Clark University, Massachusetts (USA).
Arthur Helweg	is Professor at the Department of Anthropology, Western Michigan University, Kalamazoo (USA).
Bruce La Brack	is Professor at the Sociology and Anthropology Department and School of International Studies, University of the Pacific, Stockton, California (USA).
Narindar Singh	is the President of the Canadian Sikhs' Studies Institute, Nepean, Ontario, Canada.
Raminder Kaur	has recently completed her doctorate at the School of Oriental and African Studies, University of London, London (UK).
Virinder Singh Kalra	is a Lecturer in Sociology at the University of Leicester, Leicester (UK).

INTRODUCTION

The Emergence of Punjab Studies

Two apparently contradictory developments seem to have taken place in the broad area of South Asian studies in the last decade and a half: a relative decline in the academic interest in South Asia in the Western world and a significant growth in Punjab Studies. The economic success of Asian Pacific countries, including China, on the one hand and the continuing economic marginalisation of Africa, and especially Sub-Saharan Africa, on the other, have apparently made South Asia a less fascinating place to study for two very different sets of scholars. Those who are looking for success stories in the developing world look towards the Asian Pacific countries and China and those who are appalled by the poverty and human degradation in the Third World find themselves morally impelled to focus their intellectual efforts on studying Africa. The availability of better funding resources for the study of East Asia, Sub-Saharan Africa and Middle East has further contributed to dampening the academic interest in South Asia. In sharp contrast with this declining academic interest in South Asia in general, Punjab Studies have boomed in the last decade and a half. The Indian Punjab had certainly attracted critical intellectual attention in the late 1960s and early 1970s. This attention was almost exclusively focussed on the "Green Revolution" in Punjab - its supporters highlighting its developmental gains and its critics pointing out its inegalitarian consequences. The resurgence of interest in Punjab from mid 1980s onwards is of a qualitatively different kind - it is in the issues of nationalism, ethnicity, language, culture and identity.

Four inter-related sets of developments seem to be responsible for this new turn in Punjab Studies. First, at a global level, the 1980s and the 1990s witnessed the phenomenal growth of identity politics and cultural studies, and Punjab as a region - both in India and Pakistan - got implicated in this global phenomenon. Second, the Indian army's Operation Bluestar action in the Golden Temple at Amritsar in June 1984 had an unprecedented impact in generating academic interest in Punjab Studies from a range of divergent and contesting perspectives. Simply in terms of the quantitative addition to the literature on Punjab Studies, the post-1984 period has been the most remarkable period. A significant number of scholars in India, Pakistan, Europe, North America, Russia and Japan, who had previously taken very little interest in Punjab, participated in the debates on the 'Punjab Question'. One may argue that a society or a community of people can be considered to be truly engaged in a question if the debate on it is not confined only to the academics, but is also joined by other sections of the society. By this criterion, Punjabi society witnessed an unparalleled degree of extensive participation by its different components in the debates on the issues facing Punjab. Not only university academics and journalists, but also police officers, peasant activists, business managers, village priests, administrators, school teachers, retired military men, student leaders, musicians, writers, trade unionists, lawyers, retired judges, engineers, film stars and directors, sports-persons, professional politicians and saints, participated vigorously primarily through the written word. Nationalism, secessionism, religious identity, State repression, terrorist violence, human rights, media control, thought policing and democratisation of elected institutions were some of the issues on which some refreshingly imaginative and some regrettably banal debates brought new dimensions to the literature on Punjab Studies.

Third, the emergence of a new generation of diaspora Punjabi academics in the English speaking world has given a new fillip to Punjab Studies. Most of these young academics come from the second or third generation of the Punjabi immigrant community. The economic success of some sections of this community manifests itself in two forms: the assertion of its self-identity and the aspiration to secure university education for its younger generation. This generation of Punjabi academics has grown up in the Western culture, is trained in Western academic traditions and has a lived experience of dealing with issues of racial, religious, linguistic, cultural and class identities. This generation is making a significant contribution to Punjab Studies through a creative synthesis of their multiple experiences and dialogues. Fourth, the breathtaking developments in telecommunications and information technologies, coupled with the lowering of the costs of air travel in real terms, have speeded up the integration of regions such as Punjab in the globalisation processes. These globalisation processes have enabled the diaspora community to establish more regular economic, social and cultural exchanges with the "homeland", than it would have been possible 20-30 years back. The homeland is now a more accessible part of the global space. This accessibility has the enabling effect of generating a deeper and more sustained interest in the community's own cultural identity than was previously possible.

The institutional manifestations of the growing interest in Punjab Studies have been most obvious in Britain, America and Canada. In America, and to some extent, in Canada, this has resulted in the establishing of Chairs in Punjab and Sikh Studies (and sometimes dismantling them too!) in different universities. Britain, however, has witnessed the most successful and sustained attempt at organisational consolidation of the interest in Punjab Studies. Punjab Research Group (PRG) was launched in 1984 to create a platform for academic discussions on Punjab-related issues. The First International Conference on Punjab Studies was held in June 1994 under the auspices of the Association for Punjab Studies (UK) and resulted in the earlier edition of this book with the title *Globalisation and the Region: Explorations in Punjabi Identity*. The Association's journal *The International Journal of Punjab Studies* was also launched in 1994 and has, since then, played a key role in raising the profile of Punjab Studies. Britain based academics interested in Punjab Studies viz. the editors of this volume, organised panels on Punjab Studies at the last two conferences of the International Congress of Asian and North African Studies held at Hongkong (1993) and Budapest (1997). The Punjab panel has been a regular feature of the European Conferences on Modern South Asian Studies held at Toulouse (1994), Copenhagen (1996) and Prague (1998).

Why a Global Perspective on Punjab Studies?

The title of this book was chosen to suggest the importance of locating the rise of Punjabi identity in a global context and to encourage the perspective on Punjab Studies that we wish to develop. Studying a regional or a linguistic identity from a global perspective is a two-way process. One, a global perspective encourages a scholar to look upon alternative and competing theoretical paradigms. This also encourages the use of insights gained from empirical and theoretical research on other regions in the world to study the specific issues pertaining to the region under study. Two, a global perspective helps to develop a particular habit of thinking i.e. to draw out the general theoretical implications from the study of a specific region. Such a perspective, therefore, helps to enrich the understanding of a region along with the refinement of theoretical tools for regional studies. Both forms of knowledge gains are, potentially, mutually reinforcing and mutually rewarding.

It may be argued that the processes of economic, political, social and cultural change during the colonial and post-colonial phases of Punjab's interaction with the world and the migration of Punjabis to other parts of the world have certain specificities but that those are not unique to Punjab. A global perspective on Punjab Studies is helpful in identifying the differences and similarities of Punjab's experience in comparison with the other regions of the world, which have undergone similar processes of colonial subjection and post-colonial integration into new nation-states. An exercise to draw out the implications of these comparative differences and similarities for theoretical models of regional studies will be of general use.

It may be argued, on fairly strong grounds, that there is no escape from globalisation. However, putting the matter in this way may suggest to some that one has to resign to the reality of the process of globalisation even if one finds it undesirable. That certainly is not our contention. We do look upon globalisation as inevitable, but, precisely because of the inescapability from the process we consider it imperative to underline the necessity of critical dialogue, confrontation and adjustment with it. No doubt, there are some undesirable aspects of globalisation, for example, the potential threat of homogenisation and hegemonisation. The distinction between the two may be a matter of debate but the consequences of both are anti-pluralism, anti-coexistence and anti-egalitarian. In which case, anyone who values pluralism, co-existence of differences and egalitarianism should resist the threatening aspects of globalisation. But the point is that one can resist them only by first acknowledging and recognising the reality of globalisation and not by denying and ignoring it.

This mode of arguing for globalisation can be safely called a weak one, namely, that one should acknowledge one's enemy before one can plan to defeat it. There is, however, a stronger case for advocating a globalisation perspective. The strong case rests upon identification of some desirable aspects of globalisation. Globalisation creates a space for inter-dependence, co-operation, learning from each other's strengths and emulating those strengths (and, of course, learning from each other's weaknesses to avoid them), mutual international understanding, acceptance of difference based on this understanding and international solidarity.

Even those who generally emphasise the negative implications of globalisation cannot fail to notice some of its positive consequences. An interesting paper on this subject by Frances Fox Piven ('Globalizing Capitalism and the Rise of Identity Politics' in Leo Panitch (ed.) *Socialist Register 1995*, Merlin Press, London) could be considered a fairly good representative of such a tendency. We would wish to be excused for a couple of rather lengthy quotations from this study. Frances Piven argues that "instead of wiping out all ancient prejudices, a globalizing capital is prompting a rising tide of fractious racial, ethnic, religious and gender conflict. It is contributing to an identity politics which expresses not only the ancient and venerable prejudices and opinions which were presumably to be swept aside, but the apparently inexhaustible human capacity to create new prejudices and opinions, albeit often in the name of an imagined ancient past" (p.102). But then the author also points out the other aspect of the identity politics generated by globalising capitalism: "All this notwithstanding, identity politics can also be a potentially liberating and even equalizing development, especially among subordinate groups, and the more so in a political culture already dominated by identity politics. This possibility has sometimes been difficult for liberals honed on ideals of universalism to appreciate. Certainly it has been difficult for a Left preoccupied with class to appreciate...identity politics is especially necessary to lower status peoples, to those who are more insecure, and who are more likely to be deprived of recognition and respect by wider currents of culture and social interaction. Subordinate groups try to construct distinctive and sometimes defiant group identities, perhaps to defend themselves against dominant definitions...Moreover, the construction of distinctive identities may be a necessary prelude to self-organisation and political assertion....Indeed, in the cauldron of an American politics based on difference, immigrants who had previously recognised only a village or a locale as their homeland invented new national identities the better to survive and to battle in contests among nationalities. For them, the construction of new identities was a vehicle of at least psychic emancipation, and sometimes of political empowerment as well" (p.106).

Further, the advances made in the environmental and human rights movement in the last decade or so, howsoever limited would not have been made possible without the globalisation of information and networking. If it is accepted, however grudgingly, that the dialectic of the globalisation process generates both some undesirable as well as some desirable consequences, it surely then provides a justifiable ground to argue for a critically acceptable engagement with the process of globalisation. Globalisation is definitely an inescapable process but the form of that globalisation process is not a predetermined one. A critical engagement with the globalisation process affords an opportunity to influence, shape and negotiate the forms of globalisation. As an observer notes: "The counterforce to capitalist globalisation will also be global, but it cannot be global all at once." (Robert Cox, 'Global *Perestroika*' in Ralph Miliband and Leo Panitch (ed.) *Socialist Register 1992*, p.40).

Every word - spoken, written or read - every rupee/dollar/pound - earned, spent, "sent" or saved and every vote - cast or not cast - counts. Therefore, every individual counts. A globally-aware and active individual is more influential in negotiating forms of globalisation than a self-isolated "monk", irrespective of the illusions of self-grandeur such a "monk" may harbour. If every individual is important, certainly a region is more important in negotiating the forms of globalisation. A region, which is globally interactive, is more influential than a region, which is globally isolated. A globally isolated one cannot remain so forever and it will have little power in deciding the forms of ending its isolation when its isolation faces the wrath of the inescapable force of globalisation. Albania, the poorest country in Europe, and Burma, one of the poorest in the world, immediately come to one's mind as examples of an autarkic refusal to come to terms with globalisation. In sharp contrast with these a globally interactive region can select, reject, negotiate and bargain its terms of discourse with the world. South Korea with its fairly successful experience of selective liberalisation is noteworthy in this regard.

Interrogating Punjabi Identity

It is a moot point that had Punjab remained a sovereign state (if the Sikh army had not been defeated in the Anglo-Sikh Wars), its history would have been different. Is it possible to reconstruct the Punjab of pre-1849 and is it even desirable to revert to a monarchy? The fact of the matter is that imperialism has changed the course of world history and it may not be even desirable always to undo all the consequences of colonialism. The future is unpredictable. The process of change is no longer linear and in the modern world it is a 'discontinuous one' - to use the term popularised by Charles Handy, the management guru. A United Punjab may emerge in the future (if the two Germanies can unite and there is a movement to unite the two Koreas, how can the imagination not conjure up images of a united Punjab?), its territorial identity would not be the same as in pre-1849 and it certainly would not be a monarchical Punjab. Punjab or, better still, the Punjabs, at the turn of the next millennium has/ have to define its/their geographical, political and cultural identity/identities in the context of the discourse of the modern world.

This volume as a reader on Punjab Studies

This collection of papers is an attempt to situate the question of the identity of Punjab and Punjabis in the ongoing discourse on regional identity in a global perspective. We believe that this volume fulfils a much-needed gap in Punjab Studies. N.G. Barrier "the internationally recognised doyen of Punjab Studies" (Dulai and Helweg) identified several problems and weaknesses (along with the achievements and successes) in Punjab Studies in an excellent survey he did some years ago. He especially underlined that "The problem is even more serious when viewed from a global perspective" (N. Gerald Barrier "The Evolution of Punjab Studies, 1972-1987", in Surjit Dulai and Arthur Helweg (ed) *Punjab in Perspective: Proceedings of the Research Committee on Punjab Conference*, 1987, South Asia Series Occasional Paper No. 39, Asian Studies Centre, Michigan State University).

Keeping in mind the variety of specialisms covered in these papers, the different geographical locations of the contributors and their differing perspectives and styles of writing, we thought it best to let the contributors speak in their own voice and, hence, made no attempt to impose a uniform style. The book is divided into four sections. Section I deals with pre-colonial Punjab. Section II contains papers that examine issues of Punjabi identity in the early phase of globalisation during the colonial period. Section III has papers which examine Punjab in the new global context of post-colonisation, the emergence of new states and the partitioning of Punjab between two independent nation states of India and Pakistan. Finally, the papers in Section IV, examine Punjabi identity in the context of international migration and the full force of globalisation. Each section is preceded by a brief Editors' Introduction to the set of papers included in that section.

The first paper in the collection, by Roger Ballard, has been located outside the four sections. The main reason for this different position is that it attempts to comprehensively take into account several key issues relating to a trans-regionally and trans-religiously conceived Punjabi identity. Roger Ballard's paper focuses on the question of the religious dimension to Punjabi identity and proposes a framework to analyse its distinct character. The most significant of his efforts is that he has undertaken the challenging task of *naming* Punjabi identity and has dared to call it 'Punjabi religion'. His paper adds a '*kismetic*' dimension to the *panthic, dharamic* and *qaumic* dimensions of 'Punjabi religion' discussed in the existing literature on religions in the Punjab. We hope that this paper helps to highlight the many unifying and common aspects of the many religions of the Punjabi people and, through that, opens up a new dimension to the question of Punjabi identity.

Finally, no collection of papers can discuss all issues pertaining to a theme. However, we feel that this collection of papers has managed to bring together a very wide range of issues from many different perspectives in a way which we can rightly claim to be a new, substantive and, perhaps, unique addition to the literature on Punjab Studies. We hope that this book will serve as a useful reader on Punjab Studies in all the continents of the world where Punjabis and the scholars on Punjab Studies are settled. With this grand hope, we invite the readers to read and reflect on the papers included in this volume.

Pritam Singh
Shinder Singh Thandi

Panth, Kismet, Dharm te Qaum:
Continuity and Change in Four Dimensions of Punjabi Religion

Roger Ballard

Although Punjabi society has long been marked by religious diversity, until little more than a century ago Punjabis of differing religious persuasions lived together in relative peace and harmony. But since then much has changed. With the eruption of religious reform movements explicitly committed to socio-religious differentiation, the former condition of easy-going pluralism was swept away by processes of ever more vigorous polarisation, much to the distress, it must be said, to many of those involved. Yet how can we best explain these extraordinary developments? Why was it that religion suddenly became such a bone of contention that those who differed ceased to respect each other, and instead started to attack each other with such viciousness? Were the underlying tensions between Punjab's various religious traditions so great that the smallest spark was sufficient to precipitate a cataclysm? But if that was really so, why is the current condition of polarisation so unprecedented? Could it then be that far from being an outcome of ancient hatreds, current disjunctions are better understood as a *modern* phenomenon? If so, which aspects of modernity have been most responsible? British colonialism? Christian missionaries? An inadequately developed and/or an insufficiently progressive Independence movement? Stupidity? Democracy? False Consciousness? Fundamentalism?

Although champions for every one of these arguments can easily be found, none seems particularly satisfactory. Despite much spilt ink, no analytical perspective which makes comprehensive sense of Punjab's experience of polarisation has yet to be developed. Nor is this problem in any way specific to Punjab: while similar processes of ethno-religious polarisation can be readily observed in every quarter of the globe, all seem equally intractable – and just as inexplicable. It follows that any lessons we may learn about the nature and dynamics of such processes in a Punjabi context may well be applicable elsewhere, and of course vice-versa.

The intractability of ethnic polarisation

Let us consider for a moment some of the more obvious reasons why ethnic conflicts seem both to be so intractable and so explosive. First, the underlying (and usually mutual) processes of polarisation are invariably accompanied by the development of powerful currents of hostility towards outsiders, together with equally strong feelings of loyalty towards insiders; hence when open conflict does finally erupt, it is often accompanied by a cataclysmic release of violence. In Punjab's case well over 100,000 people lost their lives in 1947, and a further 10 million fled their ancestral homes, never to return. Nor did polarisation end there. Parallel – if so far rather less destructive – disjunctions have since emerged between Hindus and Sikhs in Indian Punjab, as well as between Muslims, Ahmadiyyas and Christians across the border in Pakistan.

A second striking feature of these conflicts is the inability of anyone but the most enthusiastic xenophobes to offer any coherent explanation of their dynamics. Such perplexity is, of course, by no means unique to the Punjab. Western European social science – whether Marxist, Functionalist, Post-modern or Liberal – finds itself just as perplexed by such processes. According to conventional expectations, in a "modern" (or at least "post-modern"), "civilised", and "rational" world, neither xenophobic exclusionism nor its regular partner, fanatical in-group loyalty, should have the popular appeal which they so manifestly do. How, then, can such tendencies be accounted for? One much favoured explanation, particularly in colonial contexts, was that the social and cultural traditions of non-Europeans were so unmodern, so unsophisticated and so irrational that they were left particularly vulnerable to the appeals of parochial tribalism and religious fundamentalism. Yet reassuring however reassuring this view may once have been to its European exponents, after the holocaust in Germany, the collapse of Yugoslavia, let alone the steady growth of inter-racial and inter-ethnic hostility in Europe and North America, there is now so much contemporary evidence to the contrary that it can no longer carry much conviction. Moreover the moment one brings Europe's appalling record of mayhem and slaughter during five centuries of religiously-legitimised Imperial expansion, it becomes clear that the European track-record of ethno-religious savagery is almost certainly a great deal longer than that of anyone else.[1] Thus while ethno-religious polarisation in Punjab is manifestly a product of local contingencies, it is anything but unique.

Against this background my aim in this Chapter is not so much to explore the political dynamics of polarisation in Punjab, but rather to examine its more *religious* dimensions.[2] In so doing I not only wish to consider how, why and what basis religious ideas have proved to be such an effective vehicle for political mobilisation in this context, but also how the whole character of Punjabi religion has been transformed as a result of a century of reformist criticism and mobilisation. Although there is still a strong sense, as we shall see, in which these transformations have been more apparent than real, they have nevertheless been so extensive – or so I shall argue – that the ideas and practices which it is currently conventional to identify as constituting Hindu, Sikh and Muslim orthodoxy are far less ancient than is commonly assumed. On the contrary they are very largely a product of the fertile processes of religious reconstruction which were let loose by nineteenth century reform movements. Hence my central objective in this Chapter is to explore – and also to construct an analytical vocabulary to account for – the radical changes which have taken place in the character of Punjabi religion during the past century.

Reconceptualising Religion in a Punjabi context

As Oberoi comments, religion is a slippery concept at the best of times, and as he goes on to show in his path breaking study *The Construction of Religious Boundaries* (Oberoi 1994), during the early years of British rule very little of what went on in the Punjabi religious arena either conformed to, or could be illuminated by conventional Euro-centric expectations. Nor has the situation improved significantly as a result of subsequent developments. In my view the currently conventional vocabulary for the study of religion remains as misleading as ever, certainly with respect to Punjab, and quite possibly in many other contexts, including Western Europe, as well. It is not hard to see why. Firstly one of the most central assumptions of the European enlightenment was that social progress would necessarily be accompanied by a steady trend towards secularisation, with the result that religion would progressively be restricted to the privacy of the personal and domestic domain – if, indeed, it survived at all; and although this view was also transmitted to elite groups throughout the third world, where it often remains an article of faith amongst "progressive" intellectuals, it is a perspective which empirical developments have now rendered comprehensively threadbare.[3] Secondly, and in consequence, the entrenchment of an impoverished and deeply Euro-centric understanding of what it is that religion might entail has almost wholly obscured the fact that religious experience can include a number of quite different dimensions, each which exert differential levels of interest and attraction over different groups of devotees. Instead Euro-centric assumptions have promoted a much more unitary vision of what religion is all about. Grounded in the spirit of the Protestant reformation, it seeks to reduce all religions to essentialised -isms. Within this framework texts are routinely prioritised over tradition, aspirations to moral and behavioural conformity over spiritual experience, and formal belief over ritual practice. Moreover it is also assumed that only the first half of each of these oppositions is properly "religious". Hence the second is either overlooked, or dismissed as nothing but irrational superstition.

The intellectual hegemony of these philosophical assumptions, as well as of the analytical vocabulary to which they have given rise is in my view thoroughly pernicious. Besides being a major obstacle to the acquisition of a more insightful and illuminating understanding of the role of religion in contemporary Europe, this alien outlook causes even greater confusion in South Asian contexts. If so, it follows that the best way of circumventing the crippling impact of these assumptions is to look elsewhere for theoretical inspiration. Hence even though my own personal roots are thoroughly European, being invited to present the Inaugural Address at the First International Punjab Studies Conference provided me with an excellent opportunity in which to try and throw off those blinkers, and to adopt a more open-minded approach. It follows, therefore, that my use of Punjabi to entitle my address, and my decision to retain it here should not be seen as mere exoticism. Rather it represents a deliberate effort to step beyond the analytical log-jams which are invariably precipitated when Eurocentric conceptual schema is uncritically applied in a Punjabi context.

In doing so I share common ground with Oberoi, who makes exactly the same point in the opening sentence of his book:

> It is all very well for historians to think, speak and write about Islam, Hinduism and Sikhism, but they rarely pause to consider if such clear-cut categories actually found expression in the consciousness, actions, and cultural performances of the actors they describe.... (with respect to historical material from) nineteenth century Punjab I was constantly struck by the brittleness of our textbook classifications. There simply wasn't any one-to-one correspondence between the categories which were supposed to govern religious behaviour on the one hand, and the way in which people actually experienced their everyday lives on the other. (Oberoi 1994: 1-2)

But in taking advantage of the conceptual space which Oberoi has opened up, and especially of his emphasis on the intrinsic clumsiness of the concept of religion, I have also drawn further inspiration from Mark Juergensmeyer's work, and especially from the careful distinction which he sets out between the *panthic, dharmic* and *qaumic* dimensions of religion in his study of the rise of the Ad Dharm movement amongst Punjab's untouchables. In my view Juergensmeyer's conceptual distinction offers a particularly attractive analytical starting point. Precisely because it is grounded in a Punjabi (as opposed to a Latin Christian) philosophical and conceptual universe, this schema enables us to unpack the otherwise undifferentiated phenomenon of religion in a particularly illuminating way.

It would, of course, be quite possible to translate each of Juergensmeyer's concepts into English, and thus into what is widely regarded as a much more universalistic analytical vocabulary. If so, the term *panthic* could be identified as referring to the mystical and spiritual dimension of religious ideas and practice, *dharmic* to its more moral and/or social dimensions, while its *qaumic* dimension highlights the capacity of religious ideas and loyalties to act as a vehicle for ethno-political mobilisation. Finally I have also found it useful to add a fourth dimension, which I have found it convenient to identify as *kismetic*, to Juergensmeyer's scheme. Yet although each of these terms is readily translatable into English, I have nevertheless deliberately avoided doing so. Firstly to keep my analytical categories as congruent as possible with local realities, and secondly in an attempt to guard against the creeping impact of Euro-, and especially Protestanto-centric ideas; and finally because I have found that it enables me to present my central thesis with much greater precision than I could otherwise have hoped for.

As I see it, during the pre-British period the most active features of popular Punjabi religion were concentrated in the *panthic* and *kismetic* domains, to which its *dharmic* dimensions were in many respects quite secondary; meanwhile religion as a *qaumic* phenomenon was almost non-existent. But following the rapid growth of socio-political reform movements from the late nineteenth century onwards, each of Punjab's religious traditions began to organise itself ever more emphatically in *qaumic* terms; as each has done so, each one has steadily reinforced its *dharmic* distinctiveness, but at the cost of ever-growing hostility to the *panthic* and *kismetic* dimensions. Yet despite the increasingly harsh criticism to which both the *panthic* and the *kismetic* components of Punjabi religion have been subjected by the proponents of the new *qaumic* orthodoxies, these dimensions of Punjabi religion are still of immense significance in more personal and private contexts. Although hardly discussed in the literature, and routinely dismissed as misguided, irrational and superstitious by the spokesmen for the new orthodoxies – at least some of whom have imposed their judgements down the barrel of a gun – I would argue that these currently devalued dimensions remain to this day the primary source of spiritual inspiration and personal solace for most Punjabis, and most particularly so in contexts of severe adversity.

The Punjabi context

Yet before I launch into detailed argument, let me first establish just what I mean by Punjab, for I have no intention of restricting myself solely to the much truncated Indian state of Punjab, nor even the rather larger and considerably more populous region across the border in Pakistan. Rather what I have in mind is the fertile plain bounded by the Indus to the west and the Yamuna to the east, rising into the foothills of the Himalayas to the north and tailing off equally fuzzily into the desiccated deserts of Rajasthan to the south. Whilst all the inhabitants of this region will normally (electoral politics apart) readily identify themselves as Punjabis the social and historical specificities of this region are nevertheless worth reviewing before we begin. First of all, it is worth noting that this region had no clear political or administrative identity for at least a millennium. Whilst the greater part of Punjab may have fallen into the *Subeh* of Lahore during the Mughal period, it was nevertheless only a component (albeit one of very considerable importance) in the structure of a much larger Empire. And whilst Maharajah Ranjit Singh successfully incorporated the northern and western parts of the region into his self-established Kingdom, he was nevertheless unable to extend his rule into the cis-Sutlej region, whose rulers – fellow Sikhs though they were – preferred to ally themselves with the British East India Company as a means of avoiding the Maharaja's authority. Yet although Punjab experienced an unprecedented degree of political and administrative coherence during the subsequent period of British rule, that solidarity did not survive Independence.

With the collapse of British rule in 1947 Punjab was divided between India and Pakistan in the midst of an exceedingly vicious process of ethnic cleansing. But those paroxysms did not bring ethno-religious polarisation to a halt. In the aftermath of the sacking of the Golden Temple during the course of Operation Bluestar in 1984, tensions between Punjab's Hindus and Sikhs reached fever pitch. Although a re-run of the events of 1947 seemed for a while to be in prospect, as I write in 1999 all sides seemed to have reached a position of exhaustion. Hence the conflict is currently in abeyance.

Yet despite the depth and strength of these ethno-political disjunctions (to which there are several parallels on the Pakistani side of the border), there can be no dispute that Punjabis share a wide range of social and cultural commonalities. Amongst the most important of these is the Punjabi language. Besides bringing then all together within a single verbal universe, their common tongue also provides the foundations of their distinctive world-view: vigorous, earthy, practical and entrepreneurial, and giving far more respect to iconoclastic humour than to abstract intellectual analysis or philosophical argument. Yet despite the strength of these tendencies, and a consequent reluctance to accept or respect any kind of social, political or clerical hierarchy, the Punjabi tradition is in no way either anti-religious or anti-spiritual. On the contrary the key to Punjabi poetry – and there can be few regions in the world where poetic inspiration is more popular, more respected or more widely appreciated than in Punjab – is the taken-for-granted view that while the ultimate cause of existence is utterly transcendent and in that sense unknowable, that self-same Ultimate (whether conceptualised as Ram, Satnam or Khuda is quite immaterial) is also comprehensively immanent in every aspect of the existent world. It therefore follows that since that Truth enlivens (and is therefore present at the very heart) of every living being, it is also within the grasp of each and everyone – provided that they develop the wit, the sensitivity, the insight and the reflexive determination by means of which to penetrate the self-generated veils of *maya* which obstruct such a realisation.[4]

If so, it follows that in sharp contrast to contemporary processes of religious polarisation, there is a powerful sense in which Punjabi religion has historically manifested itself in a sense of spiritual inspiration which flows freely across current ethnic and religious divisions, and is consequently quite specifically *unbounded*. Nor is this easy-going sense of pluralism confined to the abstract spheres of poetry and spiritual inspiration. In terms of dress, food, music, leisure and entertainment – from games to jokes – a whole range of distinctively Punjabi attitudes, assumptions and practices can readily be discerned. So it is that most Punjabis willingly, and indeed proudly, identify themselves as such, regardless of whether they might otherwise be classified as Hindus, Muslims or Sikhs, and regardless of whether they hold Indian, Pakistani, British, United States, Canadian or any passport. Indeed if cultural distinctiveness was the sole criteria for the construction of a nation-state, Punjab should have so established itself long ago. It is easy to point to many other population groups with far fewer initial commonalities than the Punjabis who have done so with considerable success.

But in fact Punjab's experience has been quite the reverse. Far from undergoing a process of national consolidation, Punjab has been sundered by apparently unstoppable processes of polarisation during the course of the past century. Even though Punjab's common religious, cultural and linguistic heritage provided an excellent vehicle for political consolidation, its potential has been largely eclipsed by the rise of Hindu, Sikh and Muslim revivalism. As a result each group has insisted that its own tradition is wholly autonomous, and has therefore sought to eliminate any sign of possible overlaps between its own tradition and those of its rivals. "Tradition" has been quite shamelessly adjusted to this end. And despite occasional efforts by "leftist" intellectuals to generate a sense of Pan-Punjabi nationalism, religious revivalism has in fact proved to be by far the most effective means of political mobilisation. No-where has this been clearer than amongst the Sikhs. By the late nineteen eighties, hundreds – nay thousands – of idealistic youngsters were felt prepared to lay down their lives to assist in the creation of Khalistan, a comprehensively Sikh nation-state, should the call for self-sacrifice come.

It is developments of this kind that have set my agenda here. How can such outcomes be understood? How and why have such overwhelming processes of polarisation erupted in a region which is otherwise marked by far-reaching cultural and religious continuities? Are current outcomes the inevitable product of intrinsic and inescapable differences between Punjab's three major religious traditions? Or are they, to the contrary, the outcome of new and unprecedented developments in the whole character of those traditions? If so what are those developments, and how are they best understood?

The Religious situation in pre-British Punjab

The religious history of Punjab contains many paradoxes. On the one hand the region has always been a seed-bed of religious innovation. It was here that the initial admixture between the indigenous agricultural civilisations of Harappa and Mohenjdaro and the more nomadic Aryan invaders from central Asia took place more than three and a half millennia ago, and from whose interaction what we now know as classical Hindu civilisation first arose. But whilst Punjab may therefore have been the very cradle of Hindu civilisation, its centre of gravity soon moved off to the east and south. Meanwhile Buddhism became Punjab's pre-eminent religious tradition in the 3rd century BCE, in various forms remained so right up until the arrival of Islam well over a thousand years later. Hence the majority of Punjabi Muslims, and most particularly in the westernmost Pothohar region, were much more Buddhist than Hindu in their beliefs and practices prior to their conversion to Islam. Moreover, despite much mythology about *jihad* playing a significant role in this process, there is little or no evidence to support that view. Far from conversion being precipitated by Hindustan's new rulers unleashing bloodthirsty Muslim warriors on an otherwise defenceless population, the prime movers in this shift in religious affiliation were innumerable charismatic Sufi preachers, whose teachings – which were based on a powerful synthesis between the gnostic theology of Ibn 'Arabi and local traditions of *sahajayana* Buddhism – proved immensely popular.[5] Many of the most successful of these saintly teachers were immigrants from Central Asia, which is where the initial synthesis between these two traditions appears to have taken place. Moreover their tombs – as in the case of Baba Farid Shakarganj in Pakpattan, Datta Ganj Baksh in Lahore and Shaikh Abdul Qadir in Uch, to cite three leading examples – are widely revered to this day, and still attract pilgrims in huge numbers. Last but not least Punjab was the home base of Guru Nanak, whose teachings – grounded in an inspired synthesis between the *nirguna bhakti* devotionalism and the *tantric* philosophy of the Nath yogis – turned out to be equally popular amongst the non-Muslim population of central Punjab a few centuries later.

Yet despite the huge significance of these developments, our current knowledge of just how they occurred and what they entailed remains very limited. Whilst this may in part be a result of the relative paucity of documentary evidence about religious developments in Punjab, it also reflects the long-standing tendency for religious inspiration in this region to place far more emphasis on reporting immediate gnostic experience than on developing formal philosophical arguments. Hence it is poetry, rather than dry textual exegesis, which is, and long has been, the most popular format for literary expression in Punjab. But in addition to all this a further force has been at work since the end of the nineteenth century: the tendency of the vast majority of scholars to assume that each of the region's religious traditions constituted autonomous and free-standing "-isms". If so it followed that the history, demography, and social and cultural experiences of Punjab's Hindu, Sikh and Muslim populations had followed such distinctive trajectories that each could safely be analysed entirely independently of the other two. This left little or no space to consider the significance of the very substantial overlaps between the three traditions, or whether the units of account postulated within such an essentialistic vision actually fitted the empirical task in hand.

But even if it was – and largely still is – assumed that religious history of Punjab could be constructed around separate and largely normative accounts of Hindu, Sikh and Islamic practice, topped off, if necessary, by a straightforward head-count of the size of each group, when the British authorities attempted to carry out just such an exercise in the 1881 Census, they soon discovered that empirical reality simply did not fit this procrustean scheme. This was not because Punjabis lacked religious commitment *per se*, but rather because those commitments were not ordered in such a way as to allow a straightforward categorisation of the population into "Hindus", "Sikhs" and "Muslims". As Ibbetson laments,

> It would hardly be expected that any difficulty or uncertainty
> should be felt in classing the natives of the Province under their
> respective religions. Yet, with the single exception of caste, no
> other one of the details which we have recorded is so difficult
> to fix with exactness, or needs so much explanation and
> limitation before the real value of the figures can be appreciated.
> .... how far they still profess the creed in which they were
> brought up, how far they really believe in what they still profess,
> and what name should be given to their faith, if any, which
> they have substituted for the dogmas they have abandoned ....
> troubles only a few isolated individuals amongst the native
> community. ... it is difficult in many cases to draw the line
> between one Indian creed and another; for distinctions of faith,
> being attended by no deep spiritual conviction, are marked by
> a laxity and catholicity of practice which would be impossible
> to a bigot or an enthusiast. (Ibbetson 1883:101).

Yet despite the immense classificatory difficulties which he encountered,
Ibbetson found plenty of religion: indeed he filled the next fifty quarto pages of his
Census Report with a mass of carefully presented information about popular religious
practice in Punjab, whose empirical detail remains unrivalled to this day. This paradox
clearly raises a very fundamental question. Was it the case, as Ibbetson repeatedly
suggests in the course of his discussion, that his problems arose because the Census
respondents were really so confused and uncertain about the precise character of
their religious commitments? Or did his difficulties arise because the orientalist
conceptual framework within which he was working was largely inappropriate to
the task in hand?

The *panthic* dimension of Punjabi religion

It is, of course, precisely in order to avoid such fallacies that I have sought to develop
less eurocentric conceptual schema, and with that in mind let us begin by exploring
what I have found it convenient to identify as the *panthic* dimension of Punjabi
religion. The term *panth* is of course a familiar term in vernacular Punjabi, where it
is used to identify those who follow a particular spiritual teacher, as in the case of
Nanak-panthi, Kabir-panthi and so forth. Yet although it would be easy enough to
find an English equivalent for the concept of *panth*, I have deliberately avoided
doing so. My preference is not to translate, but instead to continue to utilise the
vernacular term as an analytical category in its own right. This does not obviate the
need for formal definition, however, and with this in mind I shall use the term *panth*
to refer to *a body of people drawn together by their commitment to the teachings of
a specific spiritual master, be he living or (more usually) dead.* Whilst this definition
is somewhat wider in scope than is everyday usage, the expansion is quite deliberate,

since my objective is to establish a categorical term which can be deployed to identify the followers of *any* spiritual teacher, regardless of whether he takes the title Guru, Sant, Yogi, Mahant, Sheikh, Pir or more generic Baba. Thus whilst I am quite aware that the term *panth* is of sanskritic rather of arabic or persian origin, and therefore normally used solely with respect to sectarian groups which are broadly Hindu (or at least non-Muslim) in character, my definition is constructed in such a way that the term becomes applicable across the entire spectrum of religious activity, regardless of conventional distinctions between its Hindu, Sikh and Muslim components.

But having thereby escaped from one set of entanglements it would be idle to become immediately enmeshed in another, so I should immediately emphasise that I am in no way suggesting that each of Punjab's many *panths* constitutes a separate religion. Rather they are much better viewed as variations on a theme. Thus even though the Punjabi religious scene includes a large number of spiritual masters who have gained a *panthic* following, and although each such master teaches in his own distinctive way, virtually all nevertheless share a similar goal: to find some means of penetrating the self-produced veils of ignorance and insensitivity which obstruct our awareness of the ultimate congruence between our individual microcosmic selves and the universal macrocosm. And to the extent that this is so, it follows that the spiritual dimensions of Punjabi religion can usefully be regarded as the contemporary manifestation of a multi-stranded *panthic* tradition which has its roots in the Sahajayana Buddhist tradition which flourished in Punjab over a thousand years ago.[6] Since then further variations have been added to the theme. In particular Sufi Islam has been a major source of further inspiration, but set within a very similar cosmological vision. If so it not only follows that Ustad Nusrat Fateh Ali Khan's *qawwalis* can be regarded as a vivid contemporary representation of the original way in which Baba Nanak originally taught, but that both are also the heirs of a tradition which stretches back to the *dohas* of Kabir and *sahajiya* poets such as Jalandari-pa. However outrageous such a suggestion may seem to those committed to contemporary essentialist understandings, it is nevertheless wholly in keeping with the sensibilities of Punjab's *panthic* tradition. After all if Nanak were still with us to comment on current developments, it is far from unreasonable to suggest that he would wish to add the phrase *koi na Sikh* to his celebrated epigram *koi na Hindu, koi na Musulman*.

This is not, of course, to suggest that there are no significant differences between the Islamic, Sikh and Hindu traditions, or that Punjab's innumerable Babas, Gurus, Sants, Mahants, Pirs and Yogis all preach exactly the same message. Of course not. Each spiritual master develops his own preferred theological synthesis, his own preferred perspective on the human condition, his own preferred method for achieving the ultimate condition of gnosis. That is what inter-*panthic* differences are all about. But whilst these differences are of considerable significance at the level of philosophical debate, Nanak is by no means unusual in suggesting that these are little more than an inevitable consequence of *maya*. Hence the more comprehensively one penetrates its illusory veils, and the more richly one appreciates the Truth which it conceals, the more insignificant such differences become. From this perspective all Punjab's many *panths* emerge as little more than variations on a theme, offering alternative routes to the same ineffable goal. Devotees of the Truth can therefore quite legitimately express themselves in either Muslim, or in Sikh, or in Hindu terms (or in a synthesis of all three) without feeling any sense of contradiction.

The *Kismetic* dimension in Punjabi religion

Yet however rich the mystical dimensions of Punjabi religion may be, it would be a great mistake to assume that all – or even most – of the religious activity precipitated by Punjab's multitude of *panthic* movements are primarily directed at gaining personal gnostic experience. On the contrary, many of the devotees of living Babas, Sants, Pirs and Yogis – and virtually all of those who flock to the shrines of long-dead saints – are primarily concerned with gaining occult assistance in the face of adversity, revealing a further dimension of religious practice which I have found it convenient to identify as *kismetic*. Perhaps other analysts will be able to suggest a more felicitous term, but it seems to me that the concept of *kismet* (fate, in the crudest of terms) provides a convenient umbrella under which to group all those actions and ideological constructions which those who have experienced severe and unexpected adversity – such as death, serious illness, infertility and other forms of personal affliction, or who have found themselves victims of war, flood, famine, and other similar disasters – deploy in an effort to cope with, and above all to make sense of their experience. Whilst some may insist that such adversities are simply the outcome of pure (and therefore quite meaningless) chance, Punjabis are far from alone in rejecting this bleak philosophy, or in seeking to construct a conceptual and religious framework which not only seeks to explain disaster, but also the prospect of reversing (or at least subverting) the malign influences which caused it. Hence what I have in mind as the *kismetic* dimension of religion can be defined as *those ideas, practices and behavioural strategies which are used to explain the otherwise inexplicable, and having done so to turn adversity in its tracks.*[7]

Let us begin by reviewing the various possible causes of adversity which the Punjabi tradition enyisages. First of all, if every event in the existent world is the outcome of the inscrutable will of the Creator, it follows that every single being's *kismet* (or *karma*, if one wishes to render the same sentiment in Hindu or Sikh terms) is underpinned by divine purpose, even if that purpose is by definition beyond human comprehension. The attribution of misfortune to *kismet* in this sense not only provides an answer to the "why me?" question, but also eradicates any sense of personal responsibility – and therefore of guilt – for the event itself. If a disaster was an act of God, it follows that no amount of human intervention could have prevented it. But although such an explanation is a great deal better than nothing is, it only provides a limited degree of psychological satisfaction. If "what is written on one's forehead" is by definition both unknowable and unchangeable, it also follows that there is nothing whatsoever that one can do about it.

So it is that in addition to *kismet*, popular religion suggests that misfortune can also be precipitated by a wide range of other sources, such as the malicious activities of disembodied spirits. Amongst the most important of these are Bhuts, Jinns, Dhags and Churails. Suspended in disembodied limbo, these beings are held to be bitterly jealous of those who have been fortunate enough to enjoy a human birth. As a result they take every opportunity to vent their malevolence on living beings either by causing all manner of accidents, illness or injury, or by entering their victims' very persons as a possessing spirits. Furthermore humans are also regarded as having a capacity to wreak occult havoc on their own account, either as a result of the unconscious impact of envy and jealousy (*nazar*), or through deliberately executed magical practices (*jadoo* and *tuna*).

That these ideas constitute much more than 'superstition' is immediately apparent if we consider the way in which ideas of this kind are deployed by those who have suffered some kind of personal disaster. Not only does it provide them with a much wider set of possible precipitating causes in terms of which to explain their misfortune, but also suggests that if the specific source of disaster can be identified, points in the directions of the counter-measures which it would be appropriate to take to guard against possible future attacks from the same source of malevolence. But just how is that identification to be achieved? It is here that the *panthic* dimension comes firmly to the fore, although on a very different plane from that described earlier.

As everyone familiar with popular religious practice in Punjab will be well aware, guiding devotees towards an ever-richer level spiritual experience is by no means the only – or even the most important – role which Punjab's spiritual masters fulfil. So it is that whilst having (or rather being believed to have) an advanced degree of gnostic awareness is a prerequisite for being accepted in the role of Pir, Sant, Yogi or Baba, the vast majority of those who approach such figures do not seek personal enlightenment, but rather to tap into the occult powers of *siddhi* which all such figures – and especially the shrines of their long-dead predecessors – are popularly held to possess. Such powers are not only perceived as being diagnostic, so enabling them to offer advice on issues of *kismetic* causation, but remedial as well. Hence powerful saints are held to be able to conjure up *siddhic* powers of such intensity that they can put whichever malevolent force is causing the distress to comprehensive flight. So it is that devotees still flock to such figures in huge numbers, searching for remedies for otherwise insuperable difficulties.

How should such activities be adjudged? Most members of Punjab's western-educated elite tend to argue (so long as they themselves are not in the midst of just such troubles) that all such ideas and practices are intrinsically irrational; hence they reject them out of hand as a mass of superstitious mumbo-jumbo. But is such scorn really justified? My own experience suggests that these practices not only have an underlying logic of their own, but that they can also produce some strikingly positive therapeutic outcomes.

In the first place it is worth emphasising that the assumption that spiritual masters – and even more so their tombs – are by definition imbued with *siddhic* powers is a well established component of all of Punjab's *panthic* traditions.[8] Since the central objective of gnostic practice is to rediscover the identity between one's personal being and its universal Source, it follows that the higher the level of spiritual experience which any given Baba, Pir, Yogi, Sant or Guru achieves, the more comprehensive his experience of oneness with – and hence his capacity to share in the powers of – that Source will be; and since Khuda, Allah, Satnam, Ishwar, Paramatma (or whatever epithet one chooses to deploy) is by definition all-seeing and all-powerful, spiritual masters will also begin to acquire these self-same powers. Moreover, since that union becomes even more complete at death – in this case described as *urs*, marriage – it follows that a saint's *mazar*, or tomb, is the site of even more comprehensive *siddhic* powers. Nor are such powers confined solely to tombs. If *siddhi* is an inevitable conjunct of spiritual experience, it follows that all saintly figures will find themselves pursued by devotees seeking assistance in the resolution of their *kismetic* problems; and since those powers are held to directly proportional to the intensity of their spiritual commitment, it follows that the further they retreat to inaccessible deserts, remote jungles or the depths of the Himalayas, the more vigorously sought-after they will tend to become. It is on this basis that wonder-working Pirs and Yogis, as well as the *mazars* and *samadhi*s of their long-dead predecessors, still attract huge flocks of devotees to this very day.

Yet even if these considerations may begin to account for devotees' belief that possessors of *siddhic* powers may have the capacity to assist them with their troubles, sceptics will doubtless still question whether such beliefs and practices can possibly have any kind of beneficial effect. Whilst it would be idle to suggest that such practices *always* have a positive outcome, my experience suggests that they may very often do so; and because analyses of just how this may occur are very rarely articulated, it is worth doing so here.

In the first place, it should be self-evident that having access to a set of ideas and images through which to explain the otherwise inexplicable is deeply reassuring in psychological terms. In the absence of such an explanatory system – and western science offers no such explanations – victims of disaster almost inevitably begin to believe that they must in some way have been personally responsible for causing it, even if there is no rational reason for reaching that conclusion. But if deep-seated feelings of guilt well up to fill the yawning chasm left by an absence of explanation, it follows that an ideological system which contains positive resources for the attribution of meaning can have a very positive therapeutic effect. From this perspective visiting a shrine in search of solace not only amounts to a useful exercise in occupational therapy, but the whole exercise rendered all the more effective to the extent that it is reinforced by a belief that doing so the act itself can trigger off an occult process of distress-relief. Added to this the shrine's officiants often display a considerable degree of psychotherapeutic skill. Having subtly guided supplicants towards a form of causal explanation which is congruent with their immediate personal circumstances, they frequently go on to use this as a means of relieving the real, although for practical reasons often unarticulatable, source of their distress. To take a simple but all too frequent example, a daughter-in-law who finds herself victimised by an unsympathetic and over-exploitative mother-in-law may well become so ill that the wider family concludes that the only cure is to take her on a therapeutic visit to a distant shrine. Whilst the consultation which takes place on her arrival at the shrine may seem at first sight to be nothing more than mumbo-jumbo, closer inspection of the process itself soon reveals otherwise, especially when one realises that the various interpretations which the saintly officiant puts forward can be read as a kind of symbolic algebra through which he begins to explore some much more concrete social processes. For example a discussion as to whether a young woman's aberrant behaviour is the result of involuntary possession by a malevolent agent such as a *bhut* or *churail*, or whether, to the contrary it is the result of unconscious, or worse still of conscious, malevolence by another human being – not least by her mother-in-law – engages very directly with real social issues. When and if a husband can be persuaded to accept that his wife's distress is the result of malfeasance on his mother's part, the effects are dramatic: in doing so he not only accepts his wife's need for greater autonomy, but is implicitly taking his first steps towards partition of the entire extended family. By contrast a finding of malfeasance by some other person is much less serious, and is likely to be remedied by providing the patient a protective *tawiz* (amulet) to keep the hostile forces to which she has hitherto been subjected at bay. There is also third possibility: the attribution of her distress to the presence of a possessing spirit, such as a *bhut*, a *jinn* or a *churail*. This might seem, on the face of it, to dodge the issue entirely – until one notices that such possessing spirits not only routinely "cause" their victims to spit out the otherwise unsayable before they can be persuaded to leave, but that their price for leaving (spirits invariably have to be bought off) requires the victim to be provided with resources which at least temporarily relieve the pressure upon them.

Once we begin to fix our attention on the outcomes of these procedures rather than becoming distracted by the occult character of the local analytical jargon, not only does their underlying rationale become much more comprehensible, but it also becomes possible to distance ourselves from Oberoi's suggestion that all this is located in some kind of enchanted universe. Rather this dimension of Punjabi religion is better understood as being grounded in a highly sophisticated – although manifestly symbolic – conceptual framework, whose central purpose is to make sense of the trials and tribulations of everyday life. It also allows us to recognise that rather than being irrational mumbo-jumbo, the processes of diagnosis and treatment to which it give rise are far from incongruent with more "scientific" forms of psychotherapy.[9] In sum, any suggestion that the *kismetic* dimension is "mere superstition" must be dismissed as both analytically unsustainable and deeply ethnocentric.

Nevertheless these activities have long been a target for ill-informed criticism, not least because they are also because it is strongly gendered in character: whilst officiants in *kismetic* activities are overwhelmingly male, supplicants are predominantly female. The reasons for this are not hard to identify. Besides being exposed to a much greater degree of personal vulnerability in a gender-divided society, women are also expected to shoulder far more responsibility for domestic mishaps than are men. It is precisely because *kismetic* religion answers so directly to female concerns that on any Thursday night women can be seen lighting lamps at a multitude of little shrines across the length and breadth of Punjab, whilst the better known *mazar*s and *samadhi*s draw in crowds of devotees from far and wide. Yet so intense is the prejudice against this dimension of Punjabi religious practice that I cannot point to a single serious contemporary study of such activities. Scholarship appears to have bent to the demands of the formal representatives of Hindu, Sikh and Muslim "orthodoxy", the vast majority of whom not only express extreme hostility towards such practices, unequivocally denounce them as shameful, misguided, irreligious and wrong.

The *dharmic* dimension of Punjabi religion

By contrast with its *panthic* and *kismetic* dimensions, the *dharmic* (or moral) component of Punjabi religion is much less esoteric. Nevertheless a straightforward equation between the Indic concept of *dharma* and the Western concept of morality can be most misleading. In standard Hindu usage, *dharma* refers to all forms of systematic order, whether at a cosmic, a social or a personal level. With this in mind the *dharmic* domain can in my view best be defined as *the divinely established set of rules to which all activities in the existent world, whether amongst humans, animals or even the Gods themselves, should ideally conform*. At first sight, this definition may seem wholly straightforward to western observers. The Christian (and especially Protestant) tradition has always assumed that living in conformity with the scripturally legitimated moral and ethical order is a central prerequisite for salvation, so much so that that is routinely assumed to be the very essence of what religion is all about. But how far is this also true of the Indic context in general, and the Punjabi context in particular? In sharp contrast to Eurocentric expectations, the *panthic* dimension of Punjabi religion puts relatively little emphasis on moral conformity: indeed moral conformity is widely regarded as largely irrelevant to spiritual progress. This is not to suggest that *panthic* domain actively promotes amorality. On the contrary the great majority of Punjab's spiritual masters are – and always have been – highly critical of those who follow the extra-social path of *sannyassic* asceticism, insisting instead that spiritual fulfilment is most richly experienced by those who continued to fulfil their everyday social obligations.[10] Nevertheless they also insist that moral conformity is not, in itself, a route to salvation. Rather the experience of ineffable bliss – *moksha, sahaj* or *ishk* – can only be achieved by those who step way beyond the mundane limitations of the everyday world, to reach a plane of spiritual awareness which rises far above, and which is ultimately at odds with, *samsaric* existence and the *dharmic* order. Indeed it is only at the point of comprehensive and irreversible self-extinction – namely death itself – that the ultimate Truth can be fully experienced.

It is for this reason that the painful paradox of life itself is the central theme in Punjabi poetry. Whilst humans are privileged, thanks to their condition of consciousness, to be in a position to experience that ultimate Truth, that very condition simultaneously distances them – or more accurately still veils them – from realising the immanent presence of the Source in every single fragment of existence. If so it follows that as one's gnostic awareness becomes ever more acute, so the more thrilling – and also the more deeply painful – the very experience of life becomes, for whilst that condition necessarily separates the lover from the Beloved, it is life and consciousness which allows the very experience of *ishk* to occur. As ever, Bulleh Shah catches these contradictions with immense precision when he sings:

> *I'm caught in the mouth of a trap*

> *This passion of ours weighs so mountainously heavy*
> *That just a second's glance can shatter my whole being*
> *Yet still my efforts yield so little – just echoes of your blows!*

> *I'm caught in the mouth of a trap*

> *But as purity makes its own path, you've found your way to me*
> *Enlivening life, shaking me up, and exchanging such*
> *endearments*
> *That sharing in this secret love brings deep savours of*
> *contentment!*

> *I'm caught in the mouth of a trap*

> *Since your resplendent Name illuminates the universe, why*
> *reject my passion?*
> *But keep yourself hidden in the folds of the veil*

> *To grab my handcuffs right in the middle, dangling me upside*
> *down!*
>
> *I'm caught in the mouth of a trap[11]*

Hir Ranjha, Punjab's most popular folktale, makes just the same point. Besides providing endless examples of the ways in which *dharmic* conformity obstructs the experience of *ishk*, the tale's swift and tragic end also demonstrates that such passion can only be fully consummated in death. Waris Shah's epic is therefore wholly congruent with the central theme of Bulleh Shah's poetry: that whilst the exquisitely bittersweet experience of *ishk* is only possible within the context of *samsaric* existence, anxious conformity with *dharmic* conventions means little or nothing to the spiritually committed.[12] This is not to suggest that Punjabi religion lacks a *dharmic* dimension, but rather that morality is not derived from – nor is it of any great significance within – the *panthic* domain of spiritual experience.

But having established what the *dharmic* domain is not, we also need to consider just how it is actually constituted. Although it might seem reasonable to expect that the foundations of this domain would lie in the system of moral and legal rules developed by each of the Punjab's major religious traditions – the Hindu *Dharmashastra*, the Sikh *Rahit* and the Muslim *Shari'a* – we must nevertheless be cautious here. Can we afford to rely solely on textual sources to identify what *dharma* consists of, when the social and moral conventions which Punjabis *actually* follow often differ sharply from those to which Qazis, Pandits and other scholarly experts insist they ought to conform? Asking such questions also seems particularly appropriate in a society where such priestly specialists are routinely dismissed as venial manipulators, constantly inventing spurious rules and regulations to suit their own interests – and pockets! Guru Nanak had a great deal to say about that. So whilst we must undoubtedly take note of the textually grounded moral schemas on which scholarly experts of all kinds routinely rely, I would argue that it is worth paying as much, if not more, attention to the popular social conventions in terms of which Punjabis *actually* organise their everyday lives. Once one does so, the far-reaching differences between Hindu, Sikh and Muslim modes of behaviour on which the textual sources insist begin to shrink quite dramatically.

As soon as one focuses on popular practice, it is immediately apparent that in a very wide range of contexts – including most aspects of family and kinship relations, the ideas and conventions deployed in the preparation and consumption of food, in the maintenance of purity and the avoidance of pollution, and in sustaining a sense of personal dignity or *izzat* (which together constitute the most crucial components of the popular moral order) – almost everyone follows a very similar set of *dharmic* rules and conventions, regardless of which of the three major religious traditions they are formally affiliated. But alongside these substantial continuities there are

also a number of equally crucial diacritica, including
- whether death is followed by cremation or burial
- whether boys are circumcised or not
- whether the meat one eats is *jatka* or *halal*
- whether one's *kesh* (hair) is cut or left uncut
- whether one is vegetarian or non-vegetarian
- whether one smokes tobacco or avoids it

which invariably serve to establish whether the person in question (and his or her entire family) is best identified as Hindu, Muslim or Sikh.

But although this limited range of behavioural markers provides a sufficient basis for religious categorisation in the broadest sense, they are clearly only a component (and a relatively small one at that) of a much larger spectrum of *dharmic* activity. Moreover despite the efforts of reform movements such as the Arya Samaj, the Singh Sabhas and the Jamaat-i-Islami to reinforce mutual differentiation, their excited rhetoric has had relatively little impact on actual practice: everyday Punjabi lifestyles still display a remarkable degree of continuity right across the spectrum of formal religious affiliation. So it is that even though neo-traditionalist movements have put a great deal of effort into widening the political divisions between Punjab's Hindus, Sikhs and Muslims, there is still a strong sense in which members of all three traditions still occupy a common *dharmic* space.

The *Qaumic* dimension of Punjabi religion

Nevertheless the upsurge of ethno-religious nationalism during the course of the past century has led to an increasing degree of *dharmic* differentiation. As a result of the growing influence of religious reform movements, each religious community has made increasingly determined efforts to delineate its boundaries as sharply and as unambiguously as possible. The most dramatic outcome of this kind of process was the comprehensive separation of the region's Muslim population from its Hindu and Sikh components in 1947.[13] Rendered into my own preferred terminology, this can be represented as a process in which the *qaumic* dimension of Punjabi religion gained ever-increasing salience; and as this occurred, its *panthic* and *kismetic* dimensions began to be sidelined, especially in public debate, while its *dharmic* dimension began to be radically transformed in order to support and legitimate an ever-greater tendency towards *qaumic* polarisation. But I must not anticipate myself too much: before proceeding further we must first establish just what the *qaumic* sphere consists of, and how it was organised before processes of ethno-religious polarisation had become so all-consuming as they are today.

In contrast to *panth* and *dharm*, both of which are Sanskritic terms, the word *qaum* (social group or community) like *kismet*, has Arabic and Persian roots. Although widely used in colloquial Punjabi, I shall once again allocate the term a more specific technical meaning, and hence use *qaumic* to refer to *the set of ideas and activities by means of which a body of people set about closing ranks as a community, and to use their enhanced sense of mutual solidarity to advance their collective interests.* It is also worth emphasising that in sharp contrast to the *panthic, kismetic* and *dharmic* domains, *qaumic* activity is by no means necessarily religious in character. *Qaumic* activity in contemporary Punjab may indeed be so organised, but it was not always so. During the early days of the British Raj social and political mobilisation was – as we have seen – much more commonly articulated in terms of solidarities of *zat* or *biraderi*, or in other words through communities which the early British administrators identified as castes and tribes.

From this perspective the social order of pre-modern Punjab can usefully be regarded – at least to a first approximation – as having been constructed around a limited number more or less coherently organised and generally localised *qaumic* communities of this kind. Each such *qaum* was normally associated either with a specific hereditary occupation, and – in the case of peasants and pastoralists – control over a particular territory. The social boundaries of each such group was further reinforced on the one hand by a myth of common descent, and on the other by a commitment to endogamy. The prospect thought that all this maelstrom of *qaumic* groups might be ranked in a single comprehensive hierarchy ranging from the purest of Brahmins at the top to the most polluted sweepers at the bottom has, of course, exercised almost as great a fascination over modern orientalists as it did from nineteenth century British administrators. Nevertheless as Ibbetson himself seems to have been on the point of realising, any attempts to construct a definitive rank order – even on a local basis – turned out to be fruitless. Even though local ideology suggested that the social order was indeed constructed around just such a hierarchy, relative rank has turned out to be a far more fluid phenomenon, and also one which is riddled with many more internal contradictions than essentialist expectations had predicted.

Yet although Denzil Ibbetson's pioneering efforts to conduct such an exercise showed that the questions about religious affiliation, no less than those about relative rank, were surrounded by so much uncertainty that his attempts to represent his findings in numerical terms were – on his own admission – seriously flawed, his questions about *qaum* or *zat* (the terms were deliberately offered as alternatives) yielded a far more coherent and reliable pattern of answers. Not only could most respondents identify quite unambiguously to which local *qaum* or *zat* they belonged, but at least within that local arena there was little dispute about the validity of such claims.[14] This is hardly surprising. As well as being hereditary, endogamous and linked to a specific occupation, these *qaumic* units (as I would prefer to describe them) were self-consciously organised interest groups which formed, amongst other things, the basic collective bargaining units within the local *jajmani* system. Moreover each such *qaum* normally had recourse to its own well-developed means of resolving (or at least attempting to resolve) internal disputes – the *panchayat*.

Yet if the *qaumic* dimension of Punjabi society in this sense was very well organised, what the 1881 Census also revealed was that the great majority of these *zat* and *biraderi* included Hindu, Sikh and Muslim members: in other words these aggregations cut right across the *qaumic* divisions which loom so large in contemporary Punjab. In other words a major change has taken place. During the latter part of the nineteenth century, *qaum* in the sense of *zat* and *biraderi* were the principle vehicles for socio-political mobilisation, the religiously grounded *qaumic* divisions were then a very much more marginal phenomenon. There were other differences too. During the nineteenth century *qaum* in the sense of *zat* and *biraderi* had little or no association with either the *panthic* or the *kismetic* domains, since individual members of any one such *qaum* invariably displayed a wide and disparate range of *panthic* and *kismetic* involvements. By contrast there was a great deal more congruence between the *qaumic* and the *dharmic* domains, for in keeping with the classical concept of *varnadharm*, each local *qaum* not only sustained its own distinctive set of moral rules and conventions, but also a means whereby these could be enforced. If nothing else what all this indicates is that only a century ago the pattern of relationships between the *panthic, kismetic, dharmic* and *qaumic* dimensions of the Punjab's socio-religious order was strikingly different from that which can be witnessed today. Not only was each dimension a good deal more autonomous, but only the first three dimensions were clearly religiously inspired – although in quite different ways. As such they stood in sharp contrast to the bulk of activities in the *qaumic* domain. But above all religion in the contemporary sense was not a particularly significant vehicle for political mobilisation.

Since then much has changed. Although contemporary religious practice in the Punjab is still very much a four-dimensional phenomenon, the balance between its four components has changed substantially, above all because its *qaumic* dimension has undergone a radical shift of character. Hence whilst *zat* and *biraderi* are still very significant vehicles of political mobilisation in local contexts, competition between Hinduism, Sikhism and Islam – understood in each case in wholly *qaumic* terms – now dominates the greater part of political activity in larger-scale arenas. As a result virtually all public discussion, including almost all forms of academic debate, is framed within the context of an assumption not only that one need look no further than these three essentialised entities to understand all aspects of contemporary religious activity, but also that the same set of distinctions can be mapped quite readily onto the past. But however much this historiographical vision may suit current political imperatives, all the empirical evidence indicates that past developments were a great deal more complex than this. Once we break through contemporary reifications, it becomes quite clear that the *qaumic* dimension of religious activity was of much more limited significance in pre-British days, and that since then each tradition has in effect reinvented the greater part of its theological and ideological position, as each formed itself into (or at least represented itself as being) the clearly bounded and essentialised *qaumic* -ism whose existence virtually all contemporary debate and discussion takes for granted.

If, however we regard this state of affairs as being an outcome of a process, and one which is in any event still far less complete than public rhetoric suggests, a much richer field of understanding begins to open up. In particular it allows us to explore the far-reaching impact which increasing salience of *qaumic* activity has had on the status of – if not quite so comprehensively on practice within – the other three domains of activity. In the *dharmic* sphere the emergence of late nineteenth century reform movements – such as the Arya Samaj amongst the Hindus, the Singh Sabhas amongst the Sikhs, and the Ahmadiyyas amongst the Muslims – led to an immense amount of effort being put into the propagation of new (or as those involved insisted, "forgotten") orthodoxies. The Sikh case is particularly instructive in this regard, for as Oberoi has shown, this effectively entailed the construction – virtually *ab initio* – of a new *dharmic* order around which the *qaum* could begin to mobilise itself, whilst the tradition's more plural dimensions in the *panthic* and *kismetic* domains were subjected to ever more vigorous criticism. But these developments were by no means a uniquely Sikh phenomenon. Parallel initiatives, although perhaps rather less dramatic in scale, are easy enough to identify amongst both the Hindus and the Muslims.

Yet however useful this may be as a means of explaining how and why the *panthic* and *kismetic* dimensions of Punjabi religion should have faded so comprehensively into the background, many readers may still be sceptical about my suggestion that religion was of relatively limited significance as a vehicle for *qaumic* terms during the early British and pre-British period. After all the Sikh tradition in general, and Gobind Singh's institution of the Khalsa in particular, appears on the face of it to be a prime examples of a religiously grounded *qaumic* movement. It is to this issue which we must now turn.

The Sikhs as a *Qaum*

While there can be no doubt that in a contemporary Punjabi context the Sikhs do indeed form a *qaum*, was that always so? If we go right back to the beginning, all the evidence suggests that such a prospect would never have crossed Baba Nanak's mind. Whilst he never tired of emphasising the importance of continuing to participate in the everyday social world, the whole objective of his teaching – in true *panthic* style – was to enable his followers to transcend their mundane experience of *samsaric* existence; and because he advocated taking a wholly internal route to *sahaj*, he comprehensively resisted any kind of *qaumic* classification, and was equally disinterested in *dharmic* innovation. But all this soon began to change following Nanak's death, such that Nanak's previously inchoate *panth* began to develop ever more explicit *qaumic* dimensions. Typically enough, his successors' headquarters, first in Goindwal and then in Amritsar, became places of pilgrimage; and as devotees' offerings began to flow into the movement's central exchequer on an ever-increasing scale, the Sikh Gurus' adoption of the deliberately ambiguous title Sachah Padshah gave further emphasis to their steadily increasing political as well as spiritual power. However it was Guru Gobind Singh's creation of a *khalsa* in 1699 – a *qaumic* development if ever there was one – which was the most significant change of all. By requiring all those who accepted the new spiritual discipline to make some very overt, and manifestly *dharmic*, changes in their everyday lifestyles, khalsa membership directly signalled commitment to a new and unmistakably *qaumic* brotherhood. Yet all this established a new and largely unprecedented basis for interpreting what it meant to be a Sikh, we must take care to avoid reaching over-hasty conclusions about the precise significance of these developments. It is all too easy to misread the past by viewing it uncritically through the distorting lenses of contemporary assumptions and expectations, especially when the events in question have become the raw material of contemporary myth makers.

Whilst there can be no doubt that the creation of the Sikh *khalsa* was a highly significant *qaumic* initiative, during Gobind's own lifetime only a minority of Nanak Panthis appear to have accepted the Guru's invitation to join the new movement. Hence in its original form the Khalsa did not include all, or even the majority of those who were inspired by the *panthic* dimensions of Nanak's teaching.[15] But just what was the status of those who did not join Gobind's new regiment of *sant-sipahis*? Nineteenth century reformers had no hesitation in describing the *sahajdharis* (as opposed to the *keshdharis* who joined the new *khalsa*) as "slow-adopters", thereby suggesting that when they eventually gained the courage of their convictions they would find their way into the Khalsa. But just how fair was this judgement? Not only do we need to remember that this usage was coined by reformers who were deeply hostile to *panthic* pluralism on ideological grounds, but that far from being weak-kneed slow-adopters, the *sahajdharis* had good grounds for arguing that the path which they continued to follow was much more congruent with Nanak's own teaching than that of the hirsute *keshdharis*.

Putting all this in historical context, it is worth re-emphasising that Banda Bahadur, Gobind's political (although not his spiritual) successor, was not a Khalsa member, even if subsequent historical revisionists have made strenuous efforts to suggest that he was. Last but not least, the use of the term Khalsa to identify a brotherhood of mystically inspired semi-ascetic military activists is by no means such a uniquely Sikh phenomenon as virtually all extant accounts of Punjabi history tend to assume. As Peter van der Veer relates in his instructive account of the development of the Ramanandi *panth*, not only does this movement still contain a number of loosely aggregated orders of itinerant *sadhus* which are also known as *khalsas*, but during the sixteenth and seventeenth centuries *khalsas* of ascetic warriors (saint-soldiers, indeed!) were a salient feature of both the Shaivite and Vaishnavite traditions in northern India. However they were not holy warriors in the modern sense: members of these *khalsas* fought on a mercenary basis on behalf of a wide variety of rulers, Muslim no less than Hindu (van der Veer 1989: 107-137).

Set in this broader context, Gobind Singh's Khalsa emerges as much less unique than contemporary Sikh myths would have us suppose: in its time it was but one amongst many, even its subsequent history has given it a far greater social and political importance than any of its rivals. It is also worth considering just what these khalsas were *for*, most especially in political terms, since recently constructed myths not only suggest that Gobind's khalsa was unique, but also that it was in essence a *qaumic* vehicle which enabled Punjabi Sikhs (possibly in conjunction with the Punjabi Hindus) to challenge the injustice and exploitation of oppressive Muslim rule. Lectures on this theme can regularly be heard in every contemporary Gurudwara, and they certainly make a good and rousing story. But how congruent are such accounts with historical reality?

Although it is certainly true to say that Gobind Singh pursued an autonomous political agenda for the greater part of his life, and also that his formation of a *khalsa* was manifestly an effort to advance the collective interests of his emergent *qaum*, it is far from easy to specify against whom, and in the face of just what challenges, those interests were being advanced. To argue – as uncritical contemporary commentators all too often suggest – that the Guru's central concern was to counter Muslim oppression is altogether too simplistic. In the first place every one of Gobind Singh's early military exploits brought him into conflict with local *Hindu* hill-rajas, not with the Mughal authorities; and although he and his followers were constantly harried by the Imperial authorities after he had moved his headquarters from sheltered Paonta to more exposed Anandpur, the resulting conflicts are better understood as reflecting the Empire's regional satraps' effort to contain a well-armed local dissident than the outcome of deep-rooted religiously-motivated polarisation within the local Punjabi population. The argument that Gobind was not systematically engaged in religious war is further sustained by the well-attested fact that the Guru employed a number of Pathan (and therefore Muslim) warriors throughout his political career, let alone the further irony that when the Guru met his death in 1708 (at the hands of one of those self-same Pathan servants) in far-off Deccan in 1708, he had left Punjab to offer implicit support to the new Emperor Bahadur Shah's efforts to suppress a rival claimant to the Imperial throne, his brother Kam Baksh.[16]

Hence while Gobind Singh's Khalsa was undoubtedly a *qaumic* development, in the sense that it was a clearly bounded, internally resilient and strongly politically motivated brotherhood, what it quite obviously did *not* do was to unite all those inspired by Nanak's teachings – or in other words Sikhs in the broadest sense – into a single coherent community. Nor did this begin to occur in the immediate aftermath of the Guru's death. Although the khalsa manifestly a potent political symbol for Banda Bahadur, for the late eighteenth century *misldars*, as well as for Maharajah Ranjit Singh – who identified his government as *Sirkar Khalsaji* – between Gobind's death and the imposition of British rule no serious attempt was made to use its ideology as a means of uniting all Sikhs into a socially, culturally and politically coherent community. Although it is at least arguable that members of the Khalsa were rather more committed than most towards attaining such a goal, at least amongst themselves, as Oberoi (1994:24) makes very clear, the Khalsa Sikhs were but one subdivision within a whole series of *panthic* groups which also included Udasis, Nirmalas, Nanak-Panthis, Sahajdharis, Kukas, Nirankaris, Sarvarias and so forth.

While all these issues could easily be discussed at much greater length, enough has been said to underline some basic points about the structure of Punjab's social, political and religious order in the pre-British and early-British period. Firstly while its *panthic* dimension was strong and comparatively well organised, and stretched right across the formal religious spectrum, the *political* significance of such *panthic* movements was relatively limited even when they acquired *qaumic* characteristics. Hence in sharp contrast to developments during the century and a half which has passed since Maharaja Ranjit Singh's death, religious loyalties, however conceptualised, were little used as a vehicle for social and political mobilisation. Hence there was then no sign of the comprehensive polarisation between Hindus, Muslims and Sikhs which has since become such a salient feature Punjab's contemporary socio-political order.

The British Raj and its Impact

While it is easy enough to identify the imposition of British rule as being the principal precipitant of these changes, tracing out the many strands of action and reaction which were set off by the British Raj itself, and which have continued to unfold ever since is such a complex task as to be far beyond the scope of this Chapter, so all I can do is pick out its most crucial dimensions as a precursor to my concluding discussion of their impact on the various dimensions of Punjabi religion.

Following their conquest of the province, Punjab's new rulers saw themselves as having a "civilising mission", so much so that they sought quite unashamedly to impose comprehensive social, political and cultural hegemony over their subjects, making no secret of their view that all things British – whether biological, social, cultural or religious – were by definition comprehensively superior to all things Indian. If Indians were ever to progress to the same level as their rulers, so the new regime insisted, they too would have to learn to be civilised.

Exposure to such an immensely self-confident form of over-rule precipitated very mixed feelings amongst its subjects, and nowhere more so than within Punjab's rising, but overwhelming youthful, new educated elite. On the one hand British disdain precipitated strong feelings of nationalism: to the subjects of this wholly alien Raj, the need to get together to throw out the intruders was self-evident. Yet at the same time they also felt that until they had reformed their own society, and above all had remedied the deficiencies which enabled the British to establish their Raj in the first place, all their efforts would come to nought.

To cut this long story down to a manageable size, let us move straight on to consider by far the most important movement of ideological resistance and reform to emerge in late nineteenth century Punjab: the Arya Samaj. In contrast to all the religious developments we have considered so far, the Samaj owed its existence, and even more so its popularity, to the novel socio-political environment generated by the British Raj;[17] and since one of its principal objectives was political mobilisation, there can be no doubt that it also falls within my definition of a *qaumic* movement. Hence it is useful to consider just whom the Samajis sought to mobilise, on what basis, for what ends. Let me address these in reverse order. The ultimate objective of the Samaj was clearly nationalist: to do away with British rule, and to re-establish India's social, political, and cultural autonomy. The means by which the movement sought to achieve that goal is equally clear. Indian civilisation had lost its autonomy – so the movement's propagandists argued – because the purity and strength of it Aryan heritage had been so seriously weakened by growth of irrelevant and unjustifiable accretions, with the result that it had been unable to resist two successive alien invasions, the first Muslim, and the second British. Given this diagnosis, it followed that without a comprehensive program of social, cultural and above all religious reform, there was no prospect whatsoever of India regaining its lost strength. Hence in their own version of "back to basics", the Arya Samajis insisted that in the interest of national regeneration all diversionary accretions and all foreign imports must be discarded forthwith, so enabling everyone to return to the true values of their tradition as enshrined in the ancient Vedic texts.[18]

Just what moral and social injunctions the Vedas *actually* contain need not detain us for long. Even more so than texts such as the Hebrew Bible, the Vedas have always been open to a wide variety of readings, most particularly because their contents are for the most part so cryptic and obscure that their possible meaning and significance is very much an open question. Indeed if one accepts – as the Hindu tradition has long held – that the Vedas enshrine all possible forms of knowledge, it is quite useful to regard them as a kind of "black box ' within which support for any argument or analysis which one might choose to make can by definition be found. If this is so, the most appropriate way to approach the "Vedic" prescriptions put forward by the Arya Samaj is not through an assessment of the accuracy of Swami Dayananda's interpretations of the textual sources, but rather through an analysis of the meanings which he and his followers chose to assign to them.

The broad outlines of Dayananda's conclusions are well known. Once stripped of its subsequent Hindu accretions, the Aryan religion – so the Swami argued – was a comprehensively monotheistic faith with clearly defined ethical groundings. As opposed to this the whole gamut of popular religion, and most especially practices such as image-worship, *sati*, the veneration of saints and their shrines, and the hereditary ascription of caste status, was dismissed as wholly alien to the faith. Although it is relatively easy to demonstrate that the Vedas themselves offer relatively little support for these conclusions, such criticisms largely miss the point. What matters far more is the consequence of this interpretation, especially in the context of late nineteenth century Punjab, where Christian missionaries were subjecting all aspect of popular religious practice to vitriolic criticism. One of the most important results of the Samaji perspective was that virtually everything with which the missionaries found fault could now be dismissed as an un-Aryan accretion. In ideological terms this was a brilliant move. By surreptitiously adopting the missionaries own agenda, Dayananda's wholly unprecedented reading of the ancient Vedas provided his followers with a vision of Indian civilisation which might well be highly artificial, but which was nevertheless a highly effective means of resisting the denigration to which their involvement in the institutions of the British Raj – in which the missionaries formed the ideological cutting edge – exposed them.

Nor was that all. Dayananda went on to argue not only that the Aryan tradition was more closely congruent with missionaries' ideal of ethical monotheism than trinitarian Christianity, but also that it was far older than, and therefore superior to, all of the three Abrahamic religions, Christianity, Judaism and Islam. Hence a central component in the force of Dayananda's perspective arose from his success in borrowing large chunks of the moral, symbolic and conceptual agenda of the new Raj, and having indigenised his borrowings by presenting them in Vedic clothes, using them to demonstrate that no matter how physically powerful India's arrogant new rulers might be, their own indigenous heritage was in fact far superior to all things European. Hence it is hardly surprising that Dayananda's teachings found a very enthusiastic audience amongst the newly emergent Western-educated elite in the last of India's major provinces to fall under the control of the Raj.

In this respect Swami Dayananda's tour of Punjab in 1879 was particularly well-timed, since it coincided with the emergence of the first set of graduates to have passed right through the new educational system. With few local precedents on which to build, not least because the Brahmo Samaj was perceived as far too much of a Bengali movement to suit Punjabi tastes, these upwardly mobile young graduates had few defences against the poisoned chalice from which they had been forced to sup during the course of their education: no wonder that so many of them became enthusiastic followers of the Arya Samaj. In addition to comprehensively legitimating both their elite status and their "modernity", the Samaj also provided a very effective platform from which to begin to challenge the arrogant Eurocentrism of the colonial regime.

Conclusion: religious reform and its consequences

While the impact which the Arya Samaj and its many successors has had on social, cultural and religious developments throughout the subcontinent is so extensive as to be far beyond the scope of this Chapter, let me draw my argument to a conclusion just by restricting myself to a Punjab context, but also by limiting myself to answering three very specific questions. Firstly just what sorts of people did the Samaj succeed in mobilising within its new ideological framework, and just whom did it alienate? Secondly what kind of agenda for collective mobilisation did its program establish? And thirdly what impact did this have on the four dimensions of Punjabi religion which we have identified?

As far as mobilisation is concerned, the eventual outcome of Samaji nationalism has been deeply contradictory. Although its objective was to unite the entire indigenous population of India, its in-built anti-Islamic polemic was so strong that it alienated – and continues to alienate – the vast majority of Indian Muslims; and although many Punjabi Sikhs were initially attracted to the Samaj because of its capacity to provide a sense of ideological resistance to racism and Eurocentrism, the movement's dismissal of Nanak and his teachings as yet another irrelevant and weakening diversion from Aryan purity soon drove them out again. In other words far from presaging the development of a pan-Indian – or even a pan-Punjabi – nationalism, the Samaj soon put the Punjabi social order onto a track of mutually competitive *qaumic* mobilisation, in which Hindus, Sikhs and Muslims found themselves engaged in a vicious circle of ever-intensifying mutual rivalry.

As commitment to *qaumic* consolidation grew steadily more intense, each group began to follow a similar agenda to that developed by the Arya Samaj. Sikhs and then Muslims also set about establishing unambiguous boundaries around themselves, with the aim of generating the strongest possible sense of moral solidarity amongst those within, the better to resist their rivals. Hence the Sikhs and Muslims followed the Hindus in spawning reform movements whose central aim was to "restore" their tradition to its original condition of pristine purity. So just as Dayananda had systematically reinterpreted the Vedas to generate a novel *dharmic* order which suited the Hindus' *qaumic* objectives, the Tat Khalsa movement "rediscovered" a whole series of social and religious practices (eventually codified in the *rehat maryada*) to which they insisted all Sikhs must now conform. As a result the reform movements which sprang up in all three traditions began to put an ever-increasing emphasis on the need to "restore" *dharmic* conformity. Similar developments also eventually emerged amongst the Muslims, pressed forward by so-called "fundamentalist" groups such as the Jamaat-i-Islami. But whilst these developments were in every case far more novel than their proponents were ever prepared to admit, and although they are far from being fully implemented to this day, they also had far-reaching consequences in other spheres. Not only did each tradition set about revamping and rebuilding its *dharmic* order, but the logic of *qaumic* mobilisation was such that each group also sought comprehensively to homogenise itself, with the result that the "deviant" *panthic* and *kismetic* components of religious practice found themselves subjected to ever more vicious criticism and attack. Quite apart from their allegedly "unmodern" character, the easy-going pluralism which still underpins the greater part of popular belief and practices is wholly antithetical to the dynamics of *qaumic* polarisation, as well as to the politically driven vision of *dharmic* orthodoxy developed within – and still enthusiastically supported by – the greater part of Punjab's western educated urban elite.

But although the *panthic* and *kismetic* dimensions of the Punjabi tradition have consequently been driven to the very margins of public discussion on both sides of the Indo-Pakistani border as well as throughout the diaspora, it would be quite wrong to conclude that such activities have been eclipsed. Quite the reverse. They remain almost as popular as ever, and for very good reasons. Whilst the supporters of publicly conventional neo-orthodoxy may feel very shamefaced about acknowledging any degree of participation in *panthic* and *kismetic* activities – for when the push comes to shove virtually everyone does so – the plain fact is that these dimensions of religious activity provide an opportunity to explore the meaning and purpose of the human condition at a level of sophistication of which the banal certainties of protestantised neo-orthodoxy cannot even begin to conceive. Meanwhile neo-orthodoxy also has a great deal to answer for on its own account. Shameful tragedies such as the bloodbath of 1947, the trauma of Bluestar and its aftermath, and the current persecution of Christians and Ahmadis in Pakistan are in each case a direct consequence of the rise of implacable *qaumic* intransigence. But if these developments are testing the resources of Punjab's *panthic* and *kismetic* traditions virtually to breaking point, those involved would do well to remember that if Nanak, Gorakhnath and Fareed could witness what is currently being done in the name of Truth, all three would share the same feelings of despair at the depth of human folly.

NOTES

1. An argument to this effect is set out in considerable detail in my paper "Islam and the Construction of Europe" (Ballard 1996).

2. In addition to an earlier paper of my own (Ballard 1993), the development of these processes of ethno-religious polarisation has been explored in much greater depth by Kapur (1986).

3. The term secular is understood in a rather different (although in my view no less bankrupt) way in South Asian contexts.

4. Precisely because it explores these themes so graphically as well as so comprehensively, Waris Shah's *Hir Ranjha* (1983) remains an extremely popular source of spiritual inspiration to all Punjabis, whether Hindu, Sikh, Muslim or Christian.

5.   In the Pothohar region, close examination of the physical structure of many of the most noted Sufi shrines suggests that they have been erected right on top of ancient Buddhist stupas.

6.   Although there is no space to explore the matter in detail here, Das Gupta's immensely detailed study (1969) of the Buddhist, Vaishnava and Nath manifestations of the Sahajiya tradition in northern India during the mediaeval period reveals a theological and spiritual universe which displays a remarkable degree of congruence with those which can still be observed in the *panthic* dimension of contemporary Punjabi religion; and whilst White's study of *The Siddha Traditions in Medieval India* is ostensibly focused on the ascetic dimensions of the Nath Yogis, his examination of the logic of their cosmological vision is of much wider relevance, especially in understanding the *kismetic* dimension of Punjabi religion.

7.   As the routine inclusion of a "Your Stars" column in virtually all popular newspapers and magazines published in Western Europe and North America serves to emphasise, *kismetic* religion is by no means a uniquely Punjabi phenomenon.

8.   In more formal terms the idea that *tapas* conveys powers of *siddhi* on the *tapasvi* is a wholly orthodox component of Hindu mythology; such ideas are particularly elaborately developed in the Nath tradition (see White, 1996).

9.   The *kismetic* world contains its fair share of charlatans, as does western psychotherapy and western medicine; but since only those with a positive reputation for effectiveness can expect an expanding customer base, the loop of positive feedback built into such systems tends to weed out the worst offenders.

10. Nanak's concept of *raj men yog* is an excellent example of this view.

11. This represents my own best effort to render Bulleh Shah's words into meaningful English. I have relied on the Punjabi original set out by Taufiq Rafat (1982:83), but the English translation he presents misses many of the poet's more subtle allusions. Puri and Shangari (1986: 177 - 181) present a translation of a longer version of the same *kafi*, set within the midst of a useful commentary on Bulleh Shah's *ouevre*.

12. A very useful commentary on the way in which Bulleh Shah systematically uses the popular folk tale *Hir Ranjha* as a point of reference to reach such conclusions can be found in Matringe (1992); and while Matringe highlights the joint presence of Vaishnavite, Nath and Sufi elements in *Hir*, Puri and Shagari (1986) read just the same material from a Radha Soami Sikh perspective.

13. Significantly enough, there was one component of Punjab's population which was almost entirely unaffected by Partition, for it stood (and to a large extent still stands) right outside this three-way categorisation: the *Dalits* so-called untouchables. Whilst there is no space to explore the issues in detail here, the processes about which Juergensmeyer writes with such insight – and which are also the source of the analytical model deployed in this Chapter – were also developed as means of resistance to the very processes I am seeking to outline.

14. As Ibbetson makes clear in a lengthy commentary (1883: 187-190), the vocabulary in terms of which the question was posed, and especially its efforts to elicit three different segmentary levels of *qaumic* affiliation cause an immense amount of confusion.

15.   Largely because of the immense symbolic importance of the events which took place
       at Anandpur on Baishaki 1699, most recent historiographers of the Sikh tradition have
       covered them with a strong mythical gloss, such that they implicitly suggest that all
       good Sikhs must have promptly joined the Khalsa. However not only did the newswriter
       on the spot report that many of the Brahmins and Khatris explicitly rejected the Guru's
       invitation to do so, but in his careful assessment of the level of support level of support
       enjoyed by the Khalsa in Gobind's lifetime, Grewal (1990: 81) judiciously concludes
       that "it was yet to become the mainstream".

16.   Most Sikh historiographers have sought to cast a veil over these events. So, for example,
       having noted that Gobind Singh attached himself to the Imperial court for more than
       a year, Grewal (1990:79) goes on to suggest that the Guru's sole purpose in doing so
       was to "get Anandpur back". This is most disingenuous. As Banerjee (1972) shows,
       during the last year of his life Gobind and his warriors became Imperial camp followers;
       those seeking favour from the Emperor in such circumstances had no alternative but
       to offer the imperial authorities their implicit allegiance.

17.   Jones (1976) provides an excellent overview of the origins of the Arya Samaj, while
       Graham (1993) explores some of the movements to which it subsequently gave rise.

18.   In his recent and immensely popular polemical essay *The Hindu Phenomenon*, Girilal
       Jain (1994) articulates a very similar perspective.

BIBLIOGRAPHY

Ballard, Roger   "The Politicisation of Religion in Punjab" in Rohit Barot (ed.) *Religion
                    and Ethnicity: Minorities and Social Change in the Metropolis* Kampen:
                    Kok Pharos, 1993.

Ballard, Roger   "Islam and the Construction of Europe" in Shadid and van Koningsveld
                    (eds.) *Islam, Hinduism and Political Mobilisation in Western Europe*
                    Kampen: Kok Pharos, 1996.

Banerjea, Akshya K. *The Philosophy of Gorakhnath* Delhi: Motilal Banarsidass,1983.

Banerjee, Indubhusan *The Evolution of the Khalsa* Calcutta: Mukherjee, 1972.

Das Gupta, Shashibhusan *Obscure Religious Cults* London: Luzac, 1969.

Graham, Bruce   . *Hindu Nationalism and Indian Politics* Cambridge 1993.

Grewal, J. S.   *The New Cambridge History of India, II.3, The Sikhs of Punjab* Cambridge:
                    Cambridge University Press, 1990.

Ibbetson, Denzil *The Panjab Census Report of 1881* Calcutta: Superintendent of
                    Government Printing, 1883.

Jain, Giri Lal   *The Hindu Phenomenon* Delhi: UBS Publishers, 1994.

Jones, W. Kenneth *Arya Dharm: Hindu Conciousness in Nineteenth Century Punjab* Delhi:
                    Manohar, 1976.

Juergensmeyer, Mark *Religion as Social Vision* Berkeley: University of California Press,
                    1982.

Kapur, R.   *Sikh Separatism: The Politics of Faith.* London: Allen and Unwin, 1986.

Matringe, Denis   "Krishnaite and Nath elements in the poetry of eighteenth century Panjabi
                   Sufi Bulleh Shah" in R.S. McGregor (ed.) *Devotional Literature in South
                   Asia* Cambridge: Cambridge University Press, 1992.

Oberoi, Harjot   *The Construction of Religious Boundaries: Culture, Identity and Diversity
                   in the Sikh Tradition* Delhi: Oxford University Press, 1994.

Puri, J.R. and Shagari, J.R. *Bulleh Shah: The Love-intoxicated Iconoclast* Beas: Radha Soami
                   Satsang, 1986.

Rafat, Taufiq (translator) *Bulleh Shah* Lahore: Vanguard, 1982.

Shah, Waris   *The Adventures of Hir and Ranjha,* translated by Charles F.Usborne
                   London: Peter Owen, 1973.

Van der Veer, Peter *Gods on Earth: The management of religious experience and identity in a
                   North India Pilgrimage Centre* London: The Athlone Press, 1988.

White, David Gordon *The Alchemical Body : Siddha Traditions in Medieval* Chicago:
                   University of Chicago Press, 1996.

Section I

Pre-Colonial Punjab

Editors' Introduction

The papers in this section deal primarily with the pre-colonial period in Punjab's history. Pre-colonial period can also be called, with some qualifications, as the pre-globalisation period. The existence of some international exchange during this period can be cited, at best, as an aspect of globalisation in infancy. The more or less autonomous nature of the development process at this stage makes the investigation of the nature of Punjabi identity during this phase rewarding from two angles: one, in terms of providing a long historical gaze at the picture of emerging or not emerging Punjabi identity and two, in terms of providing a comparative perspective to assess the nature of Punjabi identity in the later non-autonomous phases of the development process.

Grewal's paper is an excellent beginning in this direction. It focuses its attention on the pre-colonial phases and then very briefly draws out its implications for the colonial and the post-colonial phases. Athar Tahir's scholarly paper by focusing on the work of Qadiryar, a great Punjabi poet of nineteenth century, not only expands our understanding of the rich and diverse traditions of Islam in the Indian context, it also lays out the complexity and diversity of nineteenth century Punjab. This paper especially highlights Qadiryar's *Var* (Ballad) which celebrates Hari Singh, the Sikh general of the Maharaja of Lahore, Ranjit Singh, who died battling the Afghans in 1837 and *Puran Bhagat*, Qadiryar's *magnum opus* on the romance of a Punjabi Hindu prince. Darshan Singh's paper attempts, by examining Shah Mohammad's poetry, to show how Ranjit Singh's state was seen by Punjabis of different religious backgrounds as a Punjabi State. Parwana's paper on Guru Ravi Dass adds a dimension to the question of Punjabi identity, which has remained largely unexplored viz the identification of the oppressed castes with Punjabi identity.

Bhupinder Singh's paper is a scholarly interpretation of the Sikh theory of religion and politics. His paper needs to be read in conjunction with Roger Ballard's. If Roger Ballard's paper explores the Punjabiness of Hindu, Muslim and Sikh religions as practised by the Punjabis, Bhupinder Singh's expounds on the universal and transcendental dimension of Sikhism. Of particular interest is the formulation that Sikhism stands for multi-central, plural or non-totalitarian society as the normal and natural mode of human social existence.

Punjabi Identity: A Historical Perspective

J. S. Grewal

Geographical regions are older than history. Their influence on economic and social formations in terms of long durations is well recognized. Some of the distinctive features of the life styles, character and mores of peoples inhabiting clearly demarcated regions can be attributed to geographical influences which lend a certain degree of 'objective' reality to regional identities. Such identities are observed and commented upon by outsiders, and they can be studied by social scientists, especially the social anthropologists. Consciousness of regional identity presupposes regional articulation, but it is a product largely of historical processes. This kind of consciousness among the people of the region can also be studied by social scientists, including the historians. The purpose of this paper is not to study empirical realities so much as to present a broad historical perspective on the consciousness of Punjabi identity.

In our search for Punjabi identity we have to search for the Punjab first. For the geographer's Punjab, Spate looks upon the Indo-Gangetic Plains as one of the four basic divisions of the sub-continent. This basic unit is further divided into 'regions'. As a 'region' in the Indo-Gangetic Plains, Spate's 'Punjab' does not include the Bist Jalandhar Doab; nor does it include the Salt Range and the Pothohar. At the same time, his Punjab contains areas outside the rivers Indus and Satlej: the plain areas of Dera Ismail Khan and Dera Ghazi Khan, and a large chunk of Bhawalpur. There is another 'region' of Spate's Indo-Gangetic Plains which is relevant for our present purpose: the Indo-Gangetic Divide, covering the whole of the Bist Jalandhar Doab, the submontane belt from the Satlej to the Jamuna, and the plains upto the ridges of the Aravali near Delhi and the dry bed of the Ghaggar above the Thar Desert. The Indo-Gangetic Divide is a transitional zone between the Punjab and the Upper Ganges Plains, carrying the implication that the area between the river Satlej and the Ghaggar is 'physically' and 'culturally' closer to the 'Punjab', and the area between the Ghaggar and the Jamuna is closer to the Upper Ganges Plains. In *India: A Regional Geography*, edited by Professor R.L. Singh, the Indo-Gangetic Plains form a single macro division of India. But since the book deals only with the Indian Union, the plains of Pakistan are excluded. Nevertheless, the 'Punjab Plains' do figure in this book to cover the states of the Punjab and Haryana, and the Union Territories of Chandigarh and Delhi. The 'Punjab Plains' here are more or less coterminus with the Indo-Gangetic Divide of O.H.K. Spate. Broadly thus, the geographer's Punjab is encompassed by the Himalayas in the north, the Aravali range and the Thar desert in the south, and by the rivers Indus and Jamuna in the west and the east.

Turning to sociologists, cultural anthropologists and historians we come upon titles like the *Castes and Tribes of the Punjab, Legends of the Punjab, The Punjab in Peace and War* and *The Punjab Peasantry in Prosperity and Debt*. Here the Punjab is simply the Punjab province of the British empire. This usage of the concept can be found in some recent works too, as in the *Lions of the Punjab* by Richard Fox. When some of the authors use 'the land of the five rivers' in the titles of their works, as in the *Land of the Five Rivers and Sindh* by David Ross and in *The Land of the Five Rivers: An Economic History of the Punjab* by H.K. Trevaski, 'the land of the five rivers' is simply a metaphor for the British Punjab. This construct of the Punjab was generally accepted by the Indian historians. B.S. Nijjar, for instance, has written a book entitled *The Punjab under the British*. More significantly he has accepted this construct of the Punjab for the pre-British centuries as well in his *Punjab under the Great Mughals* and *The Punjab Under the Sultans*. However, in the work of some other historians, the Punjab is equated with the dominions of Ranjit Singh and his successors, as in the *Punjab as a Sovereign State* by G.L. Chopra and the *Kingdom of the Punjab:1839-45* by B.R. Chopra. Hari Ram Gupta makes a similar use of the term in his *Punjab on the Eve of First Sikh War* (though his map shows the British Punjab, perhaps unconsciously). The equation of 'Punjab' with the dominions of Ranjit Singh was first postulated by the contemporaries of Ranjit Singh.

There are two other uses of the 'Punjab' which we may notice here. Sometimes the term 'land of the five rivers' is taken literally and not as a metaphor. Consequently, one either drops one of the six rivers from the Indus system or equates the Punjab with four *doabs*, rather arbitrarily in both cases, because there is no evidence for any such usage in the past. Romila Thapar, for instance, observes that in one sense 'the Punjab is easy to define. It is the land of five rivers and the interfluvial regions, the Doabs'. If we take the 'five rivers' literally, we can have only four *doabs*. From the very beginning, however, the Punjab was meant to cover five *doabs*. This brings us to the earliest use of the term Punjab.

It is sometimes suggested that the term Pannad can be interpreted as the region of five rivers and equated with the Punjab. A similar suggestion is made about the term Saptasindhu referring to 'the land of seven rivers' as much as to 'seven rivers'. However, this conjectural equation is made possible by familiarity with the Punjab as a region. There was hardly any consciousness of regional identity among those who used these terms. Similarly, the term *madar des* is sometimes taken to mean the same region as the Punjab. But the exact boundaries of *madar des* are nowhere mentioned. By contrast, the Punjab from the very beginning was a politico-administrative unit, used interchangeably with the Mughal province of Lahore. It is significant in this connection that the word Punjab does not occur in the *Tuzk-i Baburi* which contains detailed information on Hindustan, its peoples, its climate, its river systems, its vegetation, its fauna, its geographical regions and its politico-administrative units. In the *Akbarnama*, on the other hand, there are frequent references to the Punjab. This was precisely because Akbar had reorganized the provinces of his empire before the *Akbarnama* was written, and given the name of Punjab to the province of Lahore. At this time the emperor had coined names for the five *doabs* of the province with which we are familiar till today. We may suggest that the term Punjab was meant to refer to the province of five doabs. In any case, if we drop two letters from the phrase *panj-doab*, the letters *dal* and *wao*, we are left with *'Panjab'*. The province of Lahore was the only province of the Mughal empire which had five *doabs*. Even the adjoining province of Multan had four, and later on only three *doabs*. Understandably, this connotation of the Punjab remained current throughout the period of Mughal rule. This connotation was used by Ganesh Das in his *Char Bagh-i Panjab* at the beginning of British rule in the Punjab.

The creation of the Punjab as a politico-administrative unit under Akbar was a necessary cause of Punjabi identity, but it was not a sufficient cause. In addition to geography and politics, social and cultural factors appear to be relevant for regional identity. In this connection we may notice another historical work with the term Punjab in its title: the *Political and Social Movements in Ancient Punjab* by Buddha Prakash. He makes it clear at the outset that his Punjab is coterminus with neither the contemporary Punjab nor the Punjab of the British days. Parts of Afghanistan and Sindh were included in the Punjab of his study. His primary criterion, thus, is neither geographical nor political but socio-cultural. That is why he can say that the 'socio-cultural evolution' of this region transcended the geographic and political boundaries.

The Punjab of Buddha Prakash was marked by significant socio-cultural developments in the post-Vedic period. The earlier cultural synthesis resulting from the interaction between the Aryans and the people of the Indus culture in the Saptasindhu yielded place to another synthesis which was quite distinct and which covered a much larger area. The culture of the Saptasindhu, as reflected in Vedic literature, was marked by the social ideas of *varnashrama*, the ritual of *yajna* and *homa*, the hermitages of the *rishis*, the broad uniformity of manners and moral values, and the common medium of Sanskrit.

However, during the first half of the first millennium before Christ, new tribes poured into the Saptasindhu, gradually obliging the bearers of the Vedic culture to move eastwards, into the Kurukshetra region first and then into the Jamuna-Ganges Doab and the upper Ganges plains. With their rather 'puritanical' values they began to look upon the people of the 'Punjab' as outside the pale of the their culture. Among the peculiarities of the 'Punjabis', it is mentioned that they traded in wool and in horses; they took to sea-voyages; they loved fighting; they ate garlic and onion and they ate the flesh of fowls, sheep, donkeys, pigs, camels and cows: they drank alcohol and their women sang and danced with them in an inebriate state. The tempo of social change was reinforced by the advent of the Greeks, Parthians, Shakas and the Kushanas. Indeed, the Kushana empire became the melting pot of Iranian, Chinese,

Roman and Indian cultures, and almost every aspect of life and culture was 'revolutionized'. The philosophy of Mahayana Buddhism was now expounded in languages other than Sanskrit. Imbibing, assimilating and synthesizing the various cultural trends of Asia, the people of the region developed an elastic and resilient frame of mind.

It is not the accuracy of Buddha Prakash's presentation that concerns us so much as the implication of his conception of regional identity. Can we discern any significant socio-cultural developments in the region called the Punjab under Akbar and Ranjit Singh which had a bearing on Punjabi identity? By the sixteenth century, the demographic composition and distribution in the region had changed since the days of Kanishka due to political changes, peaceful migration, the movement of settlers on land up the river valleys and in the upper parts of the *doabs*. Babur was much impressed by the use of Persian wheel on wells for irrigation as a peculiarity of the Punjab. Abul Fazl comments on the extraordinary populousness and prosperity of the Punjab. Indeed, the number and size of urban centres was beginning to increase, reflecting increase in trade and carrying the implication of relative prosperity. In the sphere of religion, Buddhism had already yielded place to the new faiths of Vaishnavism and Shaivism, which ensured the ascendancy of the Brahman. However, a new movement from within Shaivism was being popularized by the Gorakhnathi Jogis, which was relatively egalitarian and opposed to Brahmanical ritual. The protagonists of Vaishnava Bhakti were beginning to appear on the scene. Islam was represented in the Punjab by both foreign and indigenous people. The countryside as well as the towns were dotted by mosques and *khanqahs*. A revealed book, the Quran, was added to the revealed Vedas, the semi-scriptural Puranas and the semi-sacred Epics. Arabic was added to Sanskrit as another language of elite learning. A popular way of religious life was practised and advocated by the Sufis. A new movement was initiated by Guru Nanak and popularized by his successors during the sixteenth century.

A new language, Persian, had become the language of administration, liberal education, literature and historiography for the upper strata or castes. Meanwhile, the spoken dialects of the common people, in which there was an oral tradition of heroic and love poetry, had begun to acquire the status of a literary language. Much before Amir Khusrau was thinking of Lahauri as the spoken language of the mass of the people, Shaikh Farid of Pakpattan had composed religious poetry in a language associated with the common people of the Multan region. He was not alone among the Sufi Shaikhs to think of addressing the common people in their own language. Shah Husain, a contemporary of Guru Arjan, was writing on a considerable scale after Guru Nanak had made an unprecedented use of the language understood by the common people. Thus, an oral tradition of heroic and love poetry was being reinforced by a literary tradition of religious poetry. A major work of secular poetry in Punjabi was composed by a contemporary or near contemporary of Akbar: the narrative of

Hir and Ranjha by Damodar Gulhati.

Furthermore, the identity given by Akbar to a politico-administrative unit created the possibility of its being extended to the people. It is interesting in this connection to note that Shah Jahan's famous minister Sa'adullah Khan came to be looked upon as a 'Punjabi'. It is most likely, indeed, that members of the Mughal ruling class, due to their long association with the province, came to identify themselves with the region and thus became 'Punjabis'. By the same token, the language in which the people of the province mostly spoke, and composed, came now to be called 'Punjabi'. However, this language was spoken outside the limits of the province of Lahore, which created the possibility of Punjabi identity becoming easily acceptable to the speakers of Punjabi outside the limits of the province of Lahore.

The development of Punjabi literature from the seventeenth to the early nineteenth century came to play an important role in making an increasing number of people conscious of their common culture. Punjabi prose became current on a large scale during the seventeenth century with the compilation of *Janamsakhis*. The genre of narrative poetry popularized by Damodar reached its culmination in the classic treatment of the tale of Hir and Ranjha by Waris Shah in the third quarter of the eighteenth century. He had several predecessors and successors and there were others who wrote on other tales of love. To the tales of love were added the themes of heroism in the late eighteenth and the early nineteenth century. With the emergence of secular literature increased the tendency among creative writers to address themselves to all Punjabis, irrespective of their caste or creed. A certain degree of pride in the Punjabi language began to be expressed by the creative writers, and this was extended to the region, and eventually to Punjabi identity. Waris Shah, for instance, refers to the Punjab, metaphorically, as the ornament on the forehead of Hind. Ahmad Yar expressed his pride in Punjabi and the Punjab quite directly.

Not only the language and literature but also the politics of the times had something to do with this development. The Sikh movement had proved to be the most important of all the new religious movements in the Punjab in terms of its impact on the history of the region. The followers of Guru Gobind Singh established their rule over nearly the whole of the Mughal province of Lahore, and over much more. It was not merely an indigenous rule but also a rule of the ordinary people to whom the epithet of 'Punjabi' applied perhaps more appropriately than to the members of the Mughal ruling class. From the very beginning, the Sikh rulers extended patronage to all Punjabis and associated them with administration. The composition of the ruling class in the kingdom of Ranjit Singh during the early nineteenth century reveals that its members came from all creeds and castes. This led to a certain degree of secularization of politics. Indeed, the secularization of Punjabi literature appears to be the cultural counterpart of this development from the mid-eighteenth to the mid-nineteenth century. Secular literature and secular politics made for a secular regional identity. With this background Shah Muhammad could refer to the war between the East India Company and the ruler of Lahore as a war between 'Hind', and 'Punjab'. He could empathize with the widowed 'Punjabans' who mourned the death of their men on the battle field. He looked upon the British as intruders in a land on which Hindus and Muslims had lived together in peace and comfort. The Punjabi identity came to serve as an arch over cultural diversities.

At this juncture we may turn to Ganesh Das who wrote his history of the Punjab at the end of Sikh rule and the beginning of British rule in the Punjab. His work appears to have a close bearing on Punjabi identity. A great deal of appreciation for the Punjab is built into the title of his work: *Char Bagh-i-Panjab*, which can be rendered into English as 'the garden called the Punjab'. It was meant to illumine the past and the present of the Punjab for the benefit of the British rulers. Ganesh Das expected at the same time to establish his own credentials for possible patronage. In fact, he expected the new rulers to appreciate the contribution made by the Khatris of the Punjab to past administrations. Ganesh Das was acutely conscious of his Khatri identity, feeling rather proud of being a Khatri. The Khatris in his eyes had been important not only in administration but also in soldiering and trade. They were important as landowners in many villages and towns of the Punjab. Ganesh Das himself was an important zamindar of Gujrat where he had served as a *qanungo* under Sikh rule.

There is hardly any doubt that Ganesh Das looked upon himself as a Hindu. He liked to believe that caste order had been instituted by Raja Bharat, the original ancestor of the Khatris. He had divided the society into four *varnas*; the *brahmans*, the *khatris*, the *baishes* and the *shudars*. In fact, Ganesh Das looked upon the *varna* order as the ideal social order. Like a true Khatri again, he upholds the ban on the remarriage of widows. He had a great appreciation for *sati*. He subscribed to the idea that a Hindu who converted to Islam could not be allowed to return to the Hindu fold. Thus, Ganesh Das appears to identify himself with the orthodox among the Hindus. However, he did not think in terms of monolithic Hindu identity. For him, there were several Hindu ways of life. He recognized the distinct existence of Vaishnavas, Shaivas and Shaktas, and their respective places of worship: *thakurdwaras*, *shivalas* and *devidwaras*. He did not appreciate the left-handers among the Shaktas but he had equal regard for Vaishnava *bairagis* and Shaiva *sanniyasis*. He shows greater appreciation for Hindu theists as *sadhs* and *faqirs*. The Hindu identity of Ganesh Das appears to have been less important to him than his Khatri identity. At some places, he tends to equate 'Hindu', with 'Hindi' (Indian), carrying the implication that 'Hindu' for him was not always defined in religious terms. 'Hindi', in any case, is a secular category, like Punjabi.

Ganesh Das reveals great catholicity in his attitude towards other religions. Some descendants of the common ancestor of the Wadera Khatris of the Punjab, of whom Ganesh Das was one, had converted to Islam. Ganesh Das refers to them without hesitation, and without being apologetic. He refers to their achievement in administration, learning and literature rather appreciatively. For the learned of Islam in general, Ganesh Das has nothing but praise, and he refers to a large number of Muslim scholars in the various cities and towns of the Punjab. There was one thing, however, which he did not like about the *'ulama'*, their bigotry. He attributes all past social tension and enmity between Muslims and Hindus, and between Muslims and Sikhs, to the intolerance of the *'ulama'*. By contrast, he has much to say in appreciation of the Sufis and their catholicity. He does not fail to mention the venerable Shaikhs of the past and the present, or their *khanqahs* and *mazars* which were thronged by the common people. Ganesh Das expresses a similar appreciation for Guru Nanak and his followers, looking upon their way of life as one more Hindu or Hindi way of life. However, the Khalsa of Guru Gobind Singh were distinct not only from the Muslims but also from the Hindus of Ganesh Das. They clearly represented a third category. But even they could be regarded as well-meaning arbitrators between Hindus and Muslims *(salis bilkhair)*. On the whole, Ganesh Das appears to subscribe to the idea of cultural co-existence, and to uphold the freedom of conscience.

The ideas and attitudes of Ganesh Das had a bearing on the kind of past he invoked in his *Char Bagh*. First of all, he does not fail to underline the presence and the role of Khatris in the history of the Punjab. However, his identification with the Khatris does not diminish his appreciation for the political achievement of others. Similarly, his identification with Hindus does not stand in his way of appreciating the political achievement of Muslim rulers in India. He does notice that the various categories of Hindus *(tabaqah-i-hunud)* got divorced from the rulership of Hind which passed into the hands of Muslim Sultans. Without any regret or comment, however, he mentions as a fact that the chief of Jammu and Jai Chand of Kanauj were ranged on the side of Shahabuddin Ghuri in the second battle of Taraori in which Prithvi Raj was defeated. What Ganesh Das could not stomach was the fanaticism of a Sultan like Sikandar Lodhi who used to humiliate Hindus, and executed a Brahman for refusing to accept Islam. For Akbar, on the other hand, Ganesh Das had a great admiration. Akbar abolished the *jiziya* on the principle of 'peace with all', or 'total peace' *(sulh-i-kull)*, and he issued orders that whether a Hindu or a Muslim, a Jew or a Christian, all should be allowed the freedom of worship, and none should interfere with others in religious matters. By contrast, Aurangzeb re-imposed the *jiziya*, forced Hindus to convert to Islam, and inflicted punishments on all those men of piety *(darveshes* and *qalandars)* who subscribed to the principle of *sulh-i-kull*. Ganesh Das does not fail to notice that Auranzeb's successor reverted to the policy of Akbar. All those Hindu-like *nau*-Muslims who had been removed from hereditary positions and offices were reinstated by the orders of Bahadur Shah, and they resumed their functions as Qanungos, Chaudharis and Zamindars.

Ganesh Das appreciated Zakariya Khan's treatment of the subject people, and even the attempts of Ahmad Shah Abdali to resettle the country. The association of Khatris with the administration of Muslim rulers was an additional reason for Ganesh Das to appreciate them. Junior partnership in administration was not a thing to be despised. For this reason he could appreciate the Sikh rulers even more. Under their patronage the proportion of Khatris in government and administration became much larger. He had great appreciation for the political success of Ranjit Singh who carried conquest far beyond the limits of the Punjab. The long list of Sardaran-i Kalan under Ranjit Singh clearly demonstrates that they were inducted from different communities and castes of the Punjab. Never before had the Punjab produced an eminent ruler or a shrewd politician like Ranjit Singh. 'During his reign, whatever was, was right'.

The Punjab, according to Ganesh Das, was called *madar des* in older times. But he does not say anything more. That the western boundary of the Punjab was formed by the river Indus is indicated by Ganesh Das in several ways. When Alexander crossed the Indus, he entered 'the Punjab'. The Pothohar was an integral part of 'the Punjab'. The territories of 'the Punjab' extended upto the Indus. In fact, the river Indus marked for Ganesh Das the border between Hindustan and Kabulistan. The Punjab was a part of Hindustan but it was so distinct that Ganesh Das, like Shah Muhammad, can talk of Hind and Punjab as two different entities. The boundary between the two was formed by the river Satlej . On the east of the Satlej was the country of Delhi or Haryana, and on its west was the Punjab. In the south of the Punjab was Multan, and in its north were Jammu and Kashmir. It appears, therefore, that the Punjab for Ganesh Das was virtually the Mughal province of Lahore. Indeed, when he comes to describe the five *doabs* of the Panjab formally in the middle of his book, he describes the former Mughal province of Lahore. As we noticed earlier, the province of Lahore was the only province of the Mughal empire which had five *doabs*. The Punjab was enlarged by the conquests of Ranjit Singh. Ganesh Das has no hesitation in referring to his dominions as 'the kingdom of the Punjab' *(saltnat-i-panjab)*. This can be appreciated if we remember that Ganesh Das was not talking of a geographical region so much as of a politico-administrative unit. Nevertheless, in his search of the past he tended to equate the Punjab with the Mughal province of Lahore. This region was the habitat of peoples professing different creeds and observing different customs and mores; it was the home of peoples divided vertically by ideas and beliefs and horizontally by socio-economic differentiation. The knowledge of the elite languages like Sanskrit, Arabic and Persian was confined practically to men. The majority of the people, both men and women, spoke various dialects of a language to which Ganesh Das refers as the Punjabi language *(zuban-i -panjabi)*. This was the language in which Guru Nanak had composed his hymns.

Ganesh Das was interested in secular rather than religious literature. Much of this literature was in Persian, and Ganesh Das does not fail to mention the works composed in Persian by poets of the Punjab. He also mentions the names of poets who composed in 'Hindi', or Braj Bhasha. In the case of Qadir Bakhsh (Qadir Yar), the author of *Puran Bhagat*, Ganesh Das refers to him as a Hindi poet *(sha'ir-i-hindi)* We know, however, that Qadir Yar wrote his work in Punjabi. In the case of Mian Ahmad Yar, the author of *Kamrup*, there is no mistake: he was a Punjabi poet *(sha'ir-i-panjabi)*. There is a reference also to the Punjabi poet Dayal Singh who wrote a *Siharfi*. Above all, there was Waris Shah whose *Siharfis* were on the lips of the people. He was also the author of *Hir-Ranjha* which treated of a tale of love. This theme had been taken up by Muqbal before Waris and by several others after him. On the whole, thus, Ganesh Das was aware of a good deal of Punjabi literature produced during the late eighteenth and the early nineteenth century. This literature was understood and enjoyed by most of the people of the Punjab, irrespective of their religious affiliation or social position.

Ganesh Das was quite fond of the folklore current in the Punjab during the early nineteenth century. This was another expression of culture which he appreciated. We have already mentioned the tale of Hir and Ranjha, with its locale in the lower Bari Doab, which was perhaps the most popular. Another such tale was that of Sohni and Mahiwal which related to Ganesh Das's own town, Gujrat. Another love tale was placed in the lower Bari Doab, the tale of Mirza and Sahiba. A number of poets wrote about all these tales, and Ganesh Das gives his own versions in the *Char Bagh*. There are two other stories in his work, both of them placed in the Chaj Doab. One of these related to Gujrat itself, the story of Radhi who became a *sati*. Ganesh Das makes a good case for her deliberate sacrifice and does not fail to appreciate that the place of her cremation had become a place of worship. The other story relates to the martyrdom of Haqiqat Rai and Ganesh Das makes a strong case against the fanaticism of the *'ulama'* and their high-handed procedures. The *samadh* of Haqiqat Rai in Sialkot also became a place of worship. Ganesh Das shows commendable restraint in relating the story. Significantly, the martyrdom of Haqiqat Rai would acquire overtly communal tones in the hands of later writers. Ganesh Das appears to have taken his commitment to cultural coexistence rather seriously. His denunciation of fanaticism is intellectual rather than emotional. He had the advantage of having no construct of a communal monolith in his cultural baggage.

Ganesh Das gives no overt expression to Punjabi sentiment, but his appreciation for the region is implicit in his description of the present and his treatment of the past. He is aware of the larger entity of Hind or Hindustan and, at one level, the Punjab is also a part of this entity. However, the Punjab is quite distinct from the rest of the country. For one thing, it was a separate politico-administrative unit, contemporaneously as a state and in the near past as a province. Vaguely, it was also a geographical region. Perhaps the most important reason why Ganesh Das looked upon this region as his own was the fact that for several generations his ancestors, both direct and collateral, had worked as junior partners in the administration of this region, and held lands in this region. Furthermore, the social group with which Ganesh Das identified himself, that is the Khatris, had come to be concentrated in the region and participated in its activities for many centuries in the past in the spheres of politics, administration, soldiering and trade. For him, the past was intimately linked with the present. If the language of his education, his 'father tongue', was Persian, his mother tongue was Punjabi which he shared with the bulk of the people of the region. The literature and folklore of the region was another aspect of the cultural life of the region which he appreciated in common with a large number of people. His religious catholicity enabled him to appreciate cultural coexistence. In the absence of any assumption of communal monoliths, the secular identity of the region could acquire great importance in his eyes. The long tradition of devotional theism in the Punjab, which cut across the formal bounds of religion, was conducive to social as well as religious tolerance. This tradition was much appreciated by Ganesh Das. His Punjabi identity was underpinned by identification with the region, participation in its polity, awareness of links with the past, appreciation for cultural self-expression, and a pronounced interest in matters secular.

British rule in the Punjab came to have important implications for Punjabi identity. In the first place, the area known as the Punjab was extended, covering nearly the whole of the geographical region. Secondly, the impact of western secular and humanistic literature, among several other things, gave rise to new literary forms in the Punjabi language, which strengthened the already increasing interest in secular literature. Thirdly, the possibility of participation in politics in the early twentieth century, especially the politics of the Unionist Party, kept the Punjabi sentiment alive. On the whole, thus, Punjabi identity got extended and reinforced under the British. In the 1940s, a Muslim poet of the Punjab could sing of his pride in the Punjab and its language. Sir Sikandar Hayat Khan could make an appeal in the Legislative Council to the Punjabi sentiment of its members by telling all outsiders to keep their hands off the Punjab.

However, this was not the whole story of colonial rule. The politico-administrative arrangements made by the new rulers and the economic changes brought about by their policies and measures threw up a new middle class which was richer, more numerous, more literate, more influential and more jealous of its interests than ever before in the history of the region. Increasingly with the passage of time, this class assumed the leadership of the Punjabis in social and cultural matters as well as in politics. The colonial rulers, in spite of their professed religious neutrality, thought in terms of religious communities, thereby obliging members of the middle class to think as leaders of religious communities. This in itself might have produced only a mild reaction. But, at the same time, all activities of the Christian missionaries were aggressively geared to the programme of evangelisation. Their frontal attack on all religious traditions of India evoked a reaction on the religious plane.

Movements of reform and revival, led by members of the new middle class, sprang up in the country. Their influence spread to the Punjab, which had its own indigenous movements too. The Hindus, Muslims and Sikhs, all evolved their socio-religious ideologies, which came to influence the attitudes of an increasing number. The question of language and script was raised, and the issue was persistently contested. Punjabi, which had served as the common bond for at least a few centuries, was relegated to a secondary position by the protagonists of Urdu in Persian script and the advocates of Hindi in Devnagri. Those who supported Punjabi came to associate the Gurmukhi script with it for secular as well as religious purposes. Furthermore, the newly sharpened articulation in the professed interest of communities and their culture became the basis increasingly of political articulation. Preoccupation with the interests of one's own community weakened the common Punjabi identity.

When the country was to be partitioned in the interest apparently of one religious community, the other religious communities met the proposal more than half way in getting the province partitioned, a measure that was applied to Bengal as well. After independence, language has been the primary argument for territorial reorganization, but thousands upon thousands of persons whose mother tongue is Punjabi are still outside the Punjab; an equal number, if not more, of Punjabis within the Punjab state refuse to own Punjabi as their mother tongue.

There is one more dimension of the situation, which may be noted for its obvious bearing on Punjabi identity. Historical writing on the Sikhs was already well developed when modest beginnings were made in the field of historiography of the Punjab. The political interest of the East India Company had induced its administrators and diplomats to take notice of the Sikhs as a political power in the late eighteenth century. The ascendancy of Ranjit Singh and his treaties with the East India Company made the Sikhs all the more important in the eyes of the British. A considerable volume of historical literature on the Sikhs was produced, culminating in the classic *History of the Sikhs* by J.D. Cunningham in 1849.

After annexation, the British were not seriously interested in the Sikh past. The tradition of historical writing on the Sikhs now was reinforced by Indian historians. It is interesting to note in this connection that two of the early publications on the subject were based an doctoral theses of two non-Sikh Punjabis : G.C. Narang's *Transformation of Sikhism* and G.L. Chopra's *Punjab as a Sovereign State*. The non-Punjabi 'nationalist' historians too wrote on the Sikhs, like Indubhushan Banerjee with his *Evolution of the Khalsa* and N.K. Sinha with his *Rise of the Sikh Power* and his *Ranjit Singh*. Hari Ram Gupta's voluminous work on Sikh history also belongs to the category of 'nationalist' historiography. Furthermore, interest in Sikh history was an essential part of the Singh Sabha movement. Its lasting influence is reflected in the life-long devotion of Ganda Singh and Harbans Singh to Sikh history. The importance of the Sikhs in the history of the Punjab, and in the history of the country, has thus attracted the attention of both Sikh and non-Sikh historians. Sikh history has become a subject of academic research. At any rate, the tradition of historical writing on the Sikhs has been longer and stronger than the tradition of historical writing on the Punjab. Consequently, many people tend to equate Sikh history with the history of the Punjab, not only those who are rather fond of the Sikh tradition but also those who are not so fond of it. This partial identification with the past militates against regional identity.

In retrospect we can see that the epithet Punjab was initially used for a politico-administrative unit which was marked by certain geographical features but did not constitute a geographical region. This identity was given to a sub-region, at a time when some significant socio-cultural developments were taking place over a larger area. The language spoken by the common people held a crucial importance in these developments, particularly after this language started becoming a literary language. The identity given to the area was extended to its people and their language. The wider frontiers of the language created the possibility of expansion of the 'Punjabi' zone. The acquisition of power by the common people and the character of their polity imparted a new dimension to the situation in which the 'Punjabi' zone was expanding. The combination of these developments made an increasing number of people conscious of their regional identity. The creation of the British Punjab extended the space for both accommodation and definition. The Punjab became coterminus more or less with a geographical region, the area between the Himalayas and the Thar Desert, and between the Indus and the Jamuna. It was not a homogeneous region in socio-cultural terms, but the bulk of its people spoke a common language and accepted a common identity. The Punjab came to serve as a construct for the historians even for the earliest times in the history of the region.

The Punjab, which largely coincided with a fairly well defined geographical region, has been replaced by the states of the Punjab and Haryana, the Union Territory of Chandigarh, parts of Himachal Pradesh and the Punjab of Pakistan. At the same time Punjabi identity has got weakened, if not fractured, by the emergence of highly pronounced communal identities. The politics of recent decades have tended to deepen the grooves created during the previous century. The shattered mirror of Punjabi consciousness reflects tiny images, which refuse to coalesce into a portrait.

BIBLIOGRAPHY

Babur, Zahiruddin Muhammad.
          Babur-Nama (tr. A.S. Beveridge), Oriental Books Reprint Corporation,
          New Delhi, 1970 (reprint).

Banga, Indu.   *Agrarian System of the Sikhs: Late Eighteenth and Early Nineteenth
          Century*, Manohar Publications, New Delhi, 1978.
          "The ruling class in the Kingdom of Lahore", *Journal of Regional History*,

Guru Nanak Dev University, Amritsar, 1982, III, 15-24.

"Formation of a Regional State in Medieval India: A Study of the Punjab under Sikh Rule", *Proceedings of the Indian History Congress*, Kurukshetra, 1982, 823-31.

"Social Structure, Religious Ideology and Political Articulation: The Sikhs of the Punjab", Presidential Address (Modern Section), Indian History Congress, Dharwad, 1988.

"The Emergence of Hindu Consciousness in Colonial Punjab", *Self-Images, Identity and Nationality* (ed. P.C. Chatterji), Indian Institute of Advanced Study, Shimla, 1989, 187-200.

Ganesh Das. *Char Bagh-i-Panjab* (ed. Kirpal Singh), Amritsar Khalsa College, 1965.

Goswamy, B.N. and Grewal, J.S.

The Mughals and the Jogis of Jakbar, Indian Institute of Advanced Study, Shimla, 1967.

The Mughal and Sikh Rulers and the Vaishnavas of Pindori: A Historical Interpretation of 52 Persian Documents, Indian Institute of Advanced Study, Shimla, 1969.

Grewal, J.S. *Muslim Rule in India: The Assessments of British Historians*, Oxford University Press, Calcutta, 1970.

"Cunningham as a Historian of the Sikhs", *From Guru Nanak to Maharaja Ranjit Singh: Essays in Sikh History*, Guru Nanak Dev University, Amritsar, 1972, 123-37 & 188-93.

"The Historian's Punjab", *Miscellaneous Articles*, Guru Nanak Dev University, Amritsar, 1974, 1-10.

"Medieval Punjab and the Historian", Ibid., 11-18.

In the Bye-Lanes of History: Some Persian Documents from a Punjab Town, Indian Institute of Advanced Study, Shimla, 1975.

Medieval India : History and Historians, Guru Nanak Dev University, Amritsar, 1975.

Guru Nanak in History, Punjab University, Chandigarh 1979 (reprint).

"Historical Geography of the Punjab", *Journal of Regional History*, Guru Nanak Dev University, Amritsar, 1980, 1, 1-14.

The Reign of Maharaja Ranjit Singh: Structure of Power, Economy and Society, Punjabi University, Patiala, 1981.

"Literary Evidence: The Case of Hir-Waris", *Journal of Regional History*, Amritsar, 1983, IV, 1-6.

"Business Communities of Punjab", *Business Communities of India* (ed Dwijendra Tripathi) Manohar Publications, New Delhi, 1984, 209-24.

"The Emergence of Punjabi Drama: A Cultural Response to Colonial Rule", *Journal of Regional History*, Amritsar, 1984, V, 115-62.

"The Making of the Sikh Self-Image before Independence", *Self-Images, Identity and Nationality* (ed. P.C. Chatterji), Indian Institute of Advanced Study, Shimla, IL989, 189-200.

    The Sikhs of the Punjab, Cambridge University Press, Cambridge, 1990, (Volume II.3 of *The New Cambridge History of India*).

    Guru Nanak in Western Scholarship, Indian Institute of Advanced Study, Shimla, 1992.

Grewal, J.S. and Indu Banga. (tr. & eds)

    Early Nineteenth Century Panjab: From Ganesh Das's Char Bagh-i-Panjab, Guru Nanak Dev University, Amritsar, 1975.

    (eds) *Maharaja Ranjit Singh and His Times*, Guru Nanak Dev University, Amritsar, 1980

    (tr. & eds) *Civil and Military Affairs of Maharaja Ranjit Singh: A Study of 450 Orders in Persian*, Guru Nanak Dev University, Amritsar, 1987.

Sachdeva, Veena. *Polity and Economy of the Punjab during the Late Eighteenth Century*, Manohar, New Delhi, 1992.

Thapar, Romila.   "Scope and Significance of Regional History", *Ancient Indian Social History: Some Interpretations*, Orient Longman, New Delhi, 1978, 361-76.

A Coat of Many Colours: .
The Problematics in Qadiryar

M Athar Tahir

Qadiryar, who ranks amongst the foremost Punjabi poets, was born as Qadir Bakhsh in the village of Machhike in Pakistani Punjab in 1802 A.D[1]. He adopted the *nom de plume* of Qadiryar during the course of his poetic career. A member of the Sandhu clan of the Jat tribe, distinguished for its martial prowess and agricultural holdings, he was himself a farmer. Qadiryar is reputed to have composed six works, five of which are extant:

1. *The Mi'raj Namah* is based on the Ascension (mi'raj) of Prophet Muhammad (p.b.u.h).
2. The *Var* ("Ballad") celebrates Hari Singh, the Sikh general of the Maharaja Ranjit Singh of Lahore, who died battling the Afghans in 1837.
3. *The Rozah Namah* ("Epistle of Fasting") sings of the virtues and travails of fasting.
4. *Sohni Mahinwal* is the tragic tale of Sohni and her lover, Mahinwal.
5. *Puran Bhagat*, Qadiryar' *magnum opus*, is a Hindu romance about a prince, Puran. It is modelled on the Greek legend of Hippolytus and his stepmother, Phaedra.[2]

In all Punjabi literature, few poets pose as many scholarly problems as Qadiryar. His works are well-known, but little is known of his life, his education, profession and the sequence of composition of his works. What perhaps is even more problematic is that being a Muslim poet he both celebrated a Sikh and composed on a Hindu prince.

This paper is an attempt to piece together the various hints scattered in Qadiryar's poetry for a more comprehensive picture of his life and work. For too long he has been regarded as an "oral poet" in the Milman Parry - Albert Lord sense of the term: illiterate, with good memory and dexterous in composition. He has conveniently been taken at his words and regarded a "farmer, illiterate, poor."[3] It is essential, therefore, to place him in the Punjabi oral tradition and to examine more closely the issue of his reputed illiteracy. Following that, his poetic works will be briefly considered in an effort to determine their chronology. This is crucial because it leads to the final issue of themes : Qadiryar's dramatic shift from composing on a purely Islamic subject, the *mi'raj* of the Prophet, to writing about a Sikh and finally to versifying the legend of Puran, a Hindu.

Albert Lord defines oral poetry as "poetry composed in oral performance by people who cannot read or write."[4] If this definition is accepted, a large body of

Punjabi literature will have to be excluded. Until about a century and a quarter ago, Punjabi poetry was propagated by oral transmission. Only short works, which could be improvised and recited at the spur of the moment, were oral compositions. Larger works were invariably written down before being appropriated by the oral transmitters. At the same time most poetic works in the Punjab were products of literate men. Among the earliest records in Punjabi are the *slokes* of Baba Farid (d. 1265) educated in the Islamic sciences and a famous Sufi master (Shaykh) of his age. The compositions of such luminaries as Shah Husayn (1539 - 1597), Sultan Bahu (1631 - 1691), Bulleh Shah (1680 - 1758), Waris Shah (1722 - 1798) and Qadiryar, among others, give ample evidence of literate minds at work. Many were knowledgeable in matters of Islamic learning while others were literate but turned to more secular disciplines. It was this creative dialogue between the educated poet and the unlettered audience, which gave rise to works at once genuinely popular and genuinely artistic.

Ultimately, there are three ways in which a poem may be called oral: in terms of its composition, its mode of transmission and in its performances.[5] Some Punjabi poetry is oral in all three respects, but by and large, it is oral only in the last two. It is oral simply because it was chanted or declaimed and because its delivery and circulation were oral rather than written. In Qadiryar both the latter aspects find expression. The poet composes for oral delivery and in a "form suitable for performance"[6] as can be seen from his rhymes which are colloquialised to suit oral rendition.[7] That his work found circulation through the oral medium is borne out by the version recorded by R.C. Temple in his seminal *The Legends of the Punjab* (1885): "This is the lay of Puran Bhagat as composed by Qadir Yar. Some sing it in verse, some sing it to drums and fiddles."[8]

Qadiryar's work, then, is oral in its mode of transmission and in its performance. It becomes necessary now to determine the kind of bard or poet he was. For this he needs to be placed in the socio-poetic context of his times. Temple, who collected Punjabi tales and legends in the last quarter of the 19th century, lists six kinds of "bards" or oral poets.[9] For the present purposes these may conveniently be reduced to three often overlapping categories.

Firstly, the institution of "fealty and loyalty of the vassal to their protecting Lords"[10] encouraged the organisation of the professional *ra, bhat or doom*,[11] who recalled in prose or verse or both, the facts, fictions and pedigrees of their lord and his clan. This practice was common throughout the Punjab. The second group was that of the troubadours, travelling comedians, social satirists and entertainers for all occasions of festivity. Since they travelled a good deal, like their counterparts in medieval Europe or the Tartar minstrels of the Central Asian Steppes, their repertoire of poems was greater and more diversified. Their popularity was especially evident at fairs which flourished around shrines of saints at their death anniversary (*'urs*). The compositions, sung, chanted or recited were of religious, martial, romantic or topical interest. The third group consisted of those who were neither preservers of clan heritage nor public reciters. In this group fall the Sufis who used the vernacular for moral and social reform, and those who made a living by other professions but also composed poetry.

For all three groups orality was the main mode of transmitting their works, religious or secular. The currency of the oral rather than the written almost certainly had religious as well as social reasons. Apart from the illiteracy of the general public, there was the religious precedence. Committing the Qur'an and the Traditions of the Prophet *(ahadith)* to memory, remembering hundreds of references in jurisprudence *(fiqh)* was a common practice in early and medieval Muslim learning. Fertile memory, then as now, played a most important role in Muslim education.

Similarly, in the context of Indian religions, teaming numerous mantras, formulae for driving away evil and ushering in gods' graces and larger passages from the *Vedas, Puranas,* Epics and *Sastras* by rote, was an important prerequisite for Brahman pundits, the keepers of Hindu divine scriptures. Writing was held in low regard, even regarded in some aspects as impure. At best written records were merely aids to memory.

The impact of these two traditions was discernible in the life of the Punjabis. Only following the annexation of the Punjab by the British in 1849, did the press and the lithographic process of printing started to make inroads. Parallel to the oral existence of the works, there now emerged the printed texts of circulation. Broadsheets were sold at fairs, markets and gatherings and peddled in villages and towns. The initial distribution and publication was thus "a mixture of print and performance."[12]

These broadsheets, the first printed record of popular culture, were never preserved in libraries. Dismissed by the Arabo-Persian oriented intellectuals of the Punjab as vulgar products of untrained minds, they did not acquire literary status. When Punjabi intellectuals turned their attention to another language, it was to Urdu, modelled on the courtly Persian. The contribution of the Punjabi Muslims and non-Muslims to Urdu forms an important chapter in the evolution and dissemination of that language and its literature. Punjabi literature was kept alive by Sufis and Sikh and Hindu mystics or those who responded to the call of the Muse. Significantly, the most famous version of the romance of Sohni and her Mahinwal was composed by Fazal Shah, a doorman in the office of the Provincial High Court, the romance of Sassi and Punnun by a Sufi Hashim Shah and Puran Bhagat was rendered by Qadiryar, a farmer.

In which of the three categories postulated by Temple then, can Qadiryar be placed? If his ballad on Hari Singh is examined, one may be tempted to place him in the first group, of retainer-poets and *bhats* because the poem celebrates the valour of a Sikh general. The historical evolution of Sikhism may be cited as further evidence. Prior to the partition of British India in 1947, it was a common practice among the Sikhs to employ a Muslim singer in their temples *(gurdawaras)* to sing spiritual hymns and recite passages from the *Guru Granth*. This apparent contradiction of a Muslim's reading out Sikh scriptures was sanctioned in Sikhism because it was modelled on the precedent of Mardana, the Muslim minstrel and constant companion of Guru Nanak, the reputed founder of Sikhism.

There is no external or internal evidence, however, to suggest that Qadiryar was either a retainer-poet of some Sikh chief *(sardar)* or employed in a temple. The ballad on Hari Singh would have provided some evidence if it was commissioned, since it was a common practice to incorporate a few lines praising one's patron, or give some idea of how the work came about. Qadiryar, in his *Sohni Mahinwal*, states that he composed the romance on the insistence of his friends.[13]

Regarding the question of literacy, many critics have taken Qadiryar at his words and stated that he was illiterate.[14] For corroboration his hemistich from *Mi'raj Namah is* quoted.[15] This poem of 1980 lines demonstrates that he was neither unlettered nor only modestly educated. The poem shows an imaginative mind alive to the verses of the *Quran* referring to the Prophet's Night Journey and Ascension as well as to the long debate between early Muslim theologians regarding the exact date of the Ascension. He also shows a preference for the authentic *(sahih)* traditions transmitted by such authorities as Ibn 'Abbas'[16], the Prophet's contemporary. These and similar instances in the text of the poem show a literate mind aware of important theological issues.

Those who have regarded Qadiryar as illiterate have also overlooked the nature of traditional Punjabi village education, which centred around the mosque-schools *(madaris)*. Children were taught to read the *Quran* and write Arabic, to learn the rudiments of Persian and read basic texts. The aim was to impart a certain fundamental facility in handling these two languages, Arabic for its religious pre-eminence and Persian for its literary and administrative importance.

Persian had occupied a position of preference from the end of the 10th century. Sabuktigin and his son, the famous Mahmud of Ghazna, introduced Persian and its highly developed literature to the South Asian subcontinent. With the Slave Dynasty (1186-1289) and later under the Great Mughals (1526-1707), Persian strengthened its foothold in the Punjab. From the land revenue system inherited from the Mughal Emperor Akbar's minister, Todar Mal, the language of transaction continued to be Persian. Even during Ranjit Singh's regime (1799-1839), while Punjabi poets such as Hashim Shah (d. 1823) and Qadiryar were well regarded, the official language continued to be Persian. It became imperative, therefore, for the more enterprising landholders to acquaint themselves with this language in order to keep their land records straight, the frequent machination of the petty revenue official (*patwari*) in check and for interaction at the tahsil and district levels. Furthermore, various quotes in Arabic and Persian and section headings in the *Mi'raj Namah* show Qadiryar's grasp of the two languages. It may be stated with finality that he was neither illiterate nor a travelling bard nor a retainer-poet. Instead he falls into Temple's third category alongside the Sufis and the non-professional composers.

Qadiryar's work provides evidence of familiarity with Sufi concepts such as "dying before death"[17] and the esoteric interpretation of the letter Mim.[18] He is also familiar with Sufi hagiography such as the life of Shaykh Sinan.[19] These concepts are introduced by Qadiryar with an eye to their aesthetic effect rather than in a spirit of reverence typical of the Sufis. However, Qadiryar was almost certainly associated with, if not a member of, the Qadiriyya Order of the Sufis. Textual evidence in his *Rozah Namah* affords one clear hint: "All present themselves at his court, When they hear of the Qadiriyya Order."[20]

The hypothesis is strengthened by the fact that he adopted the *nom de plume* of Qadiryar, friend of Qadir. Qadir most probably refers to Sayyid 'Abd al-Qadir Gilani (d. 1166), the great Sufi master.[21] In the strict sense, the poet was probably not a student (*talib*) or disciple (*murid*) of a teacher (*pir*) or spiritual director (*murshid*). It may be safely postulated that he was an "affiliate", one who paid ritual respect to a holy man, in his case possibly a Qadiri Sufi. There is no hint in any of his extant works that he was initiated formally into the spiritual path (*tariqa*) or was even an aspiring *talib* of some order (*silsilah*). He may have, therefore, been one of the many peasants who resort to *pirs* occasionally in the course of their lives at times of distress or when in want of advice.

We may now address the issue of the sequence of composition of Qadiryar's works. While there is no external evidence available, two historical dates are helpful. *Mi'raj Namah* was certainly the first work. As the poet states, he composed it at a young age in 1829.[22] Besides, he uses both his given name, Qadir Bakhsh[23], and his *nom de plume*, Qadiryar, instead of the shorter Qadira or only Qadiryar as in his other works.

In the *Mi'raj Namah* the finest stanzas are descriptive. The verses which describe the heavenly beast (*buraq*), the ladder leading to the sky, the scenes at each of the seven heavens and the dressing for the Ascension are occasions for the graphic. There is little human action. In some of the minor characters - the Prophet's aunt, Moses and the heavenly beast, one sees Qadiryar's first promising steps towards the characterisation skilfully apparent in *Puran Bhagat*.

The *Mi'raj Namah* is important for the range of its poetic effects and Qadiryar's preoccupation with morality. The audience's attention is never diverted by bizarre spectacles but focused on their moral implications. Not only is technical competence obvious but his dramatic ability makes a hesitant appearance. Considered from the vantage point of *Puran Bhagat,* where the dramatic dominates, the *Mi'raj Namah* seems verbose. And indeed it is. It is the longest and the least successful of his works in terms of poetic conception. But in terms of its didactic content and intent it serves a definite purpose. The mood is one of luxuriance, a medieval almost idyllic luxuriance, whereas in the poems that follow a new complexity emerges, reflecting Qadiryar's grappling with human problems.

The second date, that of Hari Singh's death, is known to be 1837. The *Var* on this general is topical in its subject matter. To wait too long after his death and the incident which is celebrated in the ballad, would be to defeat its purpose. Since by 1839 Maharaja Ranjit Singh had died and by 1849 the British had annexed the Punjab, it is safe to assume that the *Var* was composed soon after Hari Singh's death, probably in late 1837 or in early 1838.

The inclusion of the poet's name in stanzas of a poem is a familiar device. Qadiryar's name figures in his other works regularly and frequently. In the *Var* it is the first word of the seventh line of each stanza. Here it serves several purposes. It identifies the poet with his subject by giving him a role in the narrative. It is also used as a form of address to the listeners, and with the listeners the narrator himself becomes the audience. Finally, it provides an opportunity whereby he can comment on the state of human affairs. This technical device emerges to greater effect in Puran Bhagat. Unlike the *Var* where Qadiryar is the narrator, in the *Rozah Namah* he takes on the persona of a fasting woman waiting for her lover. *Rozah Namah* is a minor masterpiece. It oscillates between the sacred and the profane, for while it sings of the virtues of fasting, it also enumerates the travails inherent in such an ordeal.

Fasting during the month of Ramadhan is one of the five fundamental obligations of every adult, healthy Muslim. Ramadhan is not only a month of physical cleansing but also one, which prompts soul-searching and self-analysis. The soul's struggle for purification is contrasted with the limitations of the flesh. This predicament is the poem's triumph. One is never quite certain whether the spiritual impulse is preferred or the physical accorded approval.

Rozah Namah is strongly influenced by the tradition of folk songs sung by women and girls involved in communal activities such as quern-turning or spinning cotton at the wheel or drawing water at the well. The strong rhythm of the poem lends itself to such choral execution. The poet as a female yearning for her lover, or a God, is a device often resorted to by Sufi poets of various languages.[24] In Punjab, Shah Husayn and Bulleh Shah, among others, have used the female voice to give vent to their spiritual aspirations. A borrowing perhaps from Brij Bhasha and other Bhakti poetic material in which poets as females have longed for the god-lover

Krishna. The ambiguity of mood and technical skill suggests that the *Rozah Namah* followed the *Var.*

While *Puran Bhagat* is Qadiryar's finest work, his *Sohni Mahinwal* is of interest for the technical progress over the previous works. Almost certainly composed before *Puran Bhagat,* it provides the first glimmer of his ability to transcend his focus on individuals and look at human conflict and interaction. The story is so developed as to embody human needs and goals while firmly rooted in the realistic. Despite the almost mythic quality, which surrounded these archetypal stories of lovers, Qadiryar's Sohni and Mahinwal do not become symbolic figures. They embody common predicaments. Only in *Puran Bhagat* is the poet able to synthesise the realistic mode of expression with the mythic and the legend. But in *Sohni Mahinwal* he is able to strike response in the most basic chords that constitute human psyche. The dialogues of the agonising encounter, when the wandering Mahinwal comes begging at the door of the now married Sohni, show Qadiryar at his best.[25] The emotions are handled deftly, concisely. The movement is swift and the impact telling. He has come a good distance from the loose ramblings of the *Mi'raj Namah.* The realistic elements of Qadiryar's art become apparent. Mahinwal is not left to thrive on thin air as other romantic heroes. He is provided for. Fishermen give him from their daily catch, taking him for a holy man.

Although Qadiryar had used the device of dramatic narration in the *Mi'raj Namah, the Var and Sohni Mahinwal,* it is in *Puran Bhagat* that he acquires a maturity comparable with that of Chaucer and the Gawain poet. The narrative moves with classical sense of economy of form and expression. Dramatic scenes are incorporated with an eye for movement rather than for prosy grandeur, as in his first extant work.

The tale (*qissa*)[26] has been defined as a literary genre which narrates "authentic historical or imagined events ... is a harmonious integration of well-knit plot, psychological analysis, fascinating narrative ..." It is a "poetic narration of some length whose theme is derived from events of national scale".[27] In Punjabi literature the *qissa* usually centres around two lovers who fall victim to the oppression of an intolerant society, the active indifference of fate and ends tragically. *Puran Bhagat* is an interesting exception. While linked on the one hand to the cycle of Raja Rasalu legends - the staple theme of ballads - and through it to Hindu myths, on the other hand, the *qissa* owes a good deal to the Arabo-Persian tales of romance.

Of all Punjabi romances *Puran Bhagat* is the only one with a Hindu background. Versified by many Punjabi poets, Qadiryar's rendition remains the most famous.[28] Puran, lesser known than his younger half-brother Rasalu, the great hero of Punjab folk-tales, occupies a central place in the fame of the house of Salivahan,[29] raja of Sialkot.

Briefly, Qadiryar's version is as follows. Puran is born to Salivahan. Following the consultation of the newborn's horoscope by the pundits, the raja sends his son into seclusion. After twelve years Puran returns. In the meantime his father has taken a second wife, Luna, a tanner's daughter. Luna falls in love with Puran who refuses her advances. Rejected, she takes revenge by concocting a tale about Puran's attempt to seduce her. Salivahan is enraged and orders his son's execution. Puran's hands are chopped off and he is thrown in a well. Twelve years later he is rescued by a holy man. Puran becomes the disciple of this guru, Goraknath. For his first test Puran is sent to beg from Sundran, a queen known for her miserliness. The queen on seeing him is infatuated with him. She begs the guru for Puran. Her wish is granted. But in an amusing incident Puran manages to escape. Sundran, grieved by her loss, kills herself. The guru sends Puran to his hometown, Sialkot. There, Puran's fame as a holy man spreads. The raja comes to request the birth of a son since Luna is still childless. Luna is obliged to divulge the truth about Puran and she is granted her wish. Rasalu will be born to her. On seeing his real mother who has gone blind with grief, Puran reveals his identity and restores her sight. The repentant father offers his throne to Puran, but he refuses and returns to his guru.

Structurally, the poem can be neatly divided into three sections corresponding to the Aristotelian Beginning, Middle and End.[30] The first section opens with Puran's birth and closes with his punishment. The second section concerns his rescue by Goraknath, his encounter with Sundran and his spiritual maturation. The last section sees the return of the native for the final resolution.

Without wasting words on a preamble, the poet plunges headlong into the action. Within a few short lines he covers an amazing distance. Puran is born, pundits consulted, future predicted, Puran sent into seclusion, tutors appointed, twelve years pass and Puran is ready to return.[31] This exhilarating pace is maintained throughout the poem. While it displays total command of the subject and the technique, it also shows a certain presumption on the poet's part. He is sure that his audience is familiar with the tale and its undercurrent of symbolism. Accordingly, he does not explicate the symbolic but concentrates on the dramatic presentation of the episodes, as one critic observed.[32]

While *Puran Bhagat* has certain characteristics in common with the epic, it is closer to the romance. The epic invariably celebrates in the form of "a continuous narrative the achievements of one or more heroic personages of history or tradition."[33] *Puran Bhagat* falls short of the scale and scope of such classical epics as the *Iliad*, the *Odyssey,* the *Aeneid* or the Indian *Mahabharata* or *Ramayana*. *Puran Bhagat* is a tale shaped by romantic Sanskrit literature and the preoccupations with tragedy of Arabo-Persian *qissas,* which abound in tales of romance interwoven with "idealism and practical wisdom, and with a passionate longing for spiritual vision."[34] It shares with Western romances the practice of incorporating elements of mystery and fantasy.

As Schlegal and Coleridge recognised, romance expresses "a world permanently within all men: the world of the imagination and of dream."[35] While mystery and fantasy may be convenient devices in Western romances, they are an accepted part of the Eastern ethos. The Punjabi, heir to several cultural currents, was as much at home with the spirituality of the Sufis as the miracle-tales of Buddhist sages and the supernatural exploits of Hindu gods and goddesses. For him the marvellous and the supernatural were and continue to be, accepted, present, palpable. It is a part of his cultural, and to some degree religious, milieu. "Miracles" encountered in life only endorse his inherited beliefs. They require no suspension of disbelief. The survival of Puran in the well, the restoration of his mother's eye-sight, the blooming of the garden when Puran returns to Sialkot and the materialization of the bangle validate Puran's blessedness. Nothing extraordinary, it is the stuff the hallowed are made of. But the unusual does astound even the men of Spirit sometimes.[36] This interplay of the accepted supernatural and the unexpected unusual is a fine comment on the poet's craft. One property of Western romance is the "happy ending."[37] In Punjabi romances the tragic is preferred. Most of the tales of love end in the death of the chief protagonists. *Puran Bhagat* is perhaps the sole exception. Its close is not of pure tragedy, it is closer to Shakespearean comedy with its patterns of "suffering and survival," of "regeneration", where all sufferers "live happily ever after".

Like the writers of medieval Western romances, with the mediating presence of the writer, Qadiryar figures in all his works. *Admiratio* or "admiration," a "central delight" of romance, with its combination of "liberating surprise" and "exhilarating consciousness" of the author's control, is applied to advantage.[38] As in his earlier works, he intervenes to comment and interpret[39] and "absolves us from the need to make full scale interpretations," especially with reference to the role of fate.[40] He changes from dialogue to description, draws us back into the "role of silent spectators and allows our sympathy to shift without pain."[41] He surprises the audience with the various turns in the story. All delightful, liberating.

One is led now to the final area of inquiry. What was it that led the poet to turn from writing on Islamic subjects such as the Prophet's Ascension and fasting during Ramadhan to celebrating a Sikh's death and finally to singing the way to God through *karma* (action)?

The *Var* provides the first notable departure from a Muslim subject. It has been argued above that Qadiryar was not a retainer-poet. There is no evidence to suggest that the *Var* was commissioned for the chief's descendants or written for the pleasure of the Sikh court. Why then a poem in praise of Sikhs? The question becomes of crucial importance when it is known that he had already composed the *Mi'raj Namah,* and it is postulated, was to write the *Rozah Namah.* The following hypothesis is forwarded. Qadiryar focuses on Hari Singh's military adroitness and courage. Surprisingly, he ignores that Hari Singh was tyrannical towards the Afghans and the

Muslims of Kashmir, when he was posted there. Himself a Muslim, Qadiryar could not be totally unaware of this fact. Perhaps his championing the Sikh cause had something to do with his practice of poetry. Having written the long *Mi'raj Namah,* where the movement was slow and the pace ponderous, he turns to a shorter poem. In the *Var* the movement is swift. The poem shifts back and forth between the battle action on the front, the anxieties at the court and the state of affairs in the encampment of the reserve force. Perhaps the *Var* is an exercise in virtuosity or a mere practice in a genre. Though this is possible, it is not plausible. If the *Var* is examined, nowhere does the poet mention the Muslim or Islam. It is the Pathan and the Afghan against the Punjabi. He composed the *Var* neither as a Muslim nor as a Sikh, but as a Punjabi. Hari Singh is written of as a Punjabi battling against the Afghans and the Pathans. The provincial feeling may have been prompted by the political situation prevailing in Ranjit Singh's Punjab. But it may also owe something to being a Jat. Almost all the twelve Sikh *misls* (confederacies) were Jat, and of these at least three, the Kanhia Misl,[42] the Nakai Misl[43] and the Phulkia Misl,[44] with its Jind[45] and Nabha[46] branches were founded by Sandhu Jats. Himself of the Sandhus, even if his hero was not, Qadiryar may have felt the pull of the tribe. And he makes a point of mentioning his clan affiliation in the Var: "Qadir is of Sandhu clan, The house is in Village Machhike."[47]

His shift further away on the religious spectrum towards the polytheistic Hindus poses the other problem. On the surface this is a contradiction. Closer scrutiny however, shows that Puran Bhagat is the product of the same moral sensibility that permeated *the Mi'raj Namah.*

Qadiryar is a moral poet. His morality is not confined to any conventional religion but seizes upon the essential in all. The content of his work remains moral even when garbed in a non-Muslim legend. The preoccupation is apparent in the first poem where morality is inherent in the event itself. In *Puran Bhagat* morality extends towards the human dimension. In the Prophet's celestial journey, moral principles were enacted as abstract, remote. Their manifestation in the human condition has a more potent effect in *Puran Bhagat.* Qadiryar's choice of such a familiar legend of purity at a time when the Punjab was confronted with political and social disintegration and the corruption and decadence of Sikh chiefs, may have been prompted by a personal desire to see sanity prevail. In his guarded manner he may be showing the way out of the morass by composing on the virtues of piety, idealism and spiritualism. By so doing he is at once writing to entertain as well as employing a subtle means of shaping social consciousness. The social role of the *qissa is* strengthened by the preference of the poet for the non-Muslim legend of Puran. Not only is Puran a representative of the Punjabi psyche but is the common hero of all Punjabis: Muslim, Sikh, Hindu. His selection, as the mouthpiece for moral issues has a wider appeal than a figure would from the strictly Arabo-Persian or Sanskrit sources. Qadiryar, through Puran, becomes the citizen of his times.

Puran as a dramatic persona may well be the projection of Qadiryar's individual conviction and commitment. But at a more public level he speaks of the richness of Muslim participation in and contribution to the culture of the Punjab and the whole spectrum of Indian life. Orientalists have tended to treat and project the Muslims as images of exclusiveness. In a multi-religious and multi-ethnic society, such as India's, this impression is particularly pronounced. Historically, the Muslims have neither succumbed, like the Jains, and to some degree the Sikhs, to the larger all-absorbing Hinduism, nor did they, like the Buddhists, prefer other areas outside India. This impression of exclusiveness, perhaps for reasons different than those of the Orientalists, has been encouraged and propagated by the Muslims themselves. But there exists a sizeable area of mutual exchange, an area where various religious strands meet, mix and at times mingle. Historians tend to cite the Mughal Akbar as the "enlightened" emperor of all Indians. Later, his famous descendant Prince Dara Shukoh (d. 1659) is held up as another Muslim who was willing to venture into the Hindu ethos. Apart from these rare persons, occasionally references are made to the Sufis. For Orientalists and scholars of South Asia, there is no other dimension. But it is a creative individual like Qadiryar who obliges one to perceive a third dimension, that of the poets and artists. These poets and the artists are not of the imperial or provincial courts, but, of the people. They show Islam as an interesting human phenomenon in the Indian context as well as lay out the complexity and diversity of nineteenth century Punjab. It is persons like Qadiryar who question the stereotypical images and thereby open a whole range of areas of inquiry.

NOTES

1.   H. S. Hashmi, *Punjabi di Mukhtasar Tarikh*, (p.205) gives his date of birth as 1217 A.H. (1802 A.D.) and date of death as 1309 A.H, (1892 A.D.); M.M.B. Badakhshani, "Si Hart da Fikr te Fun," *Lalan di Pand,* (p.53) gives the date of his death as 1891 A.D.

2.   The sixth work called *Raja Rasalu* is not known. Though several versions of the legend-cycles of Raja Rasalu have been collected by R. C. Temple *Legends of the Punjab* and Charles Swynnerton *The Adventures of the Punjab Hero Raja Rasalu and other Folk-Tales of the Punjab,* 1884, none of them were by Qadiryar. Whether he even wrote this work is open to question. The solitary hint offered is that of intention, at the end of *Puran Bhagat:*
"Then I will relate of Rasalu, for the moment this is enough." (Part V. 1. 75).

3.   *Mi'raj Namah*, lines: 1969.

4.   *The Encyclopedia of Poetry and Poetics*, p. 591.

5.   Ruth Finnegan, *Oral Poetry.* p.17.

6.   Ibid., p. 162.

7.   Random examples: *Ilahi* (Lord) becomes *ilaha* to rhyme with *aya* (came) *Mi'raj Namah, 1.* 1124; Jabbar (mighty) becomes *Jabbari* to rhyme with lachari (helplessness) *Mi'raj Namah 1.* 350, etc.

8.   Lines: 969-70, Vol. ii.

9.   Vol. I. pp. viii-ix.

10.   Diana Laurenson and Alan Swingwood, *The Sociology of Literature*, p. 95.

11.   *Doom:* a caste, "males of which are musicians, and their women singers, dancers and actresses (but they sing and dance etc., in the presence of women only)": J.1. Platts, *A Dictionary of Urdu, Classical Hindi, and English*, p. 569.

12.   Ruth Finnegan, op.cit., p. 162.

13.   Lines: 675-678.

14.   Mohan Singh, *A History of Punjabi Literature;* H. S. Hashmi, *Punjabi di Mukhtasar Tarikh ;* M.M.B. Badakhshani, "Si Harifi da Fikr te Fun", *Lalan di Pand.*

15.   Line : 1969.

16.   Line: 1328.

17.   *Sohni Mahinwal,* lines: 209-210; 664.

18.   Ibid., I: 2.

19.   Ibid., I: 219.

20.   Op. cit., lines: 158-159.

21.   The founder of the Qadiriyya Order. For details see *Encyclopedia of Islam (New),* Vol. 1, pp. 69-70.

22.   Op. cit., I : 1972.

23.   Ibid., lines: 44 and 1240.

24.   See Richard M. Eaton, *Sufis of Bijapur* for discussion on the subject.

25.   Op. cit., lines: 339-342.

26.   We prefer "tale" or "romance" to Serebryakov's "lyrical epic poem" because the *qissa* often neither acquires epic proportions nor quality. Serebryakov, *Punjabi Literature,* p.38.

27.   This, of course, is asking too much of a *qissa.* Though a definition for the ideal, few *qissas* would meet all the conditions. Khanna al-Fahuri, *History of Arab Literature,* Vol. II, p.190, cited by Serebryakov, p. 38.

28.   For details see Taufiq Rafat's English translation of *Puran Bhagat,* pp. 47-48.

29.   Also Shalivakhan, Satavahan: see Serebryakov, p.11. Other variations include Salohan, Salvan, Saluvan, Salhan: see Shafi Aqil's *Punjab Rang,* p. 94.

30.   See Aristotle's *Poetics.*

31.   Part 1, stanzas 1-3.

32.   N.H. Syed, *Recurrent Patterns in Punjabi Poetry,* p. 74.

33.   P. Harvey, *Oxford Companion to English Literature,* p. 27.

34.   Juan Mascaro (tr.), *The Bhagavad Gita,* p. 10.

35.   C. Beer, *The Romance,* p. 7.

36.   *Puran Bhagat,* Part 11, 1: 24.

37.   G. Beer, *The Romance,* p. 19.

38.   N.Frye, *The Anatomy of Criticism,* p.78.

39.   *Puran Bhagat,* Part 1. stanza 28; 11, 20 - 21; Ill, 12; 111, 29.

40.   Ibid., Part 11, 11; 11, 16; III, 6.

41.   N. Frye, *The Anatomy of Criticism,* p. 29.

42.   S.M. Latif, *A History of the Punjab*, p. 104.
43.   Ibid., p.312.
44.   Ibid., p 325.
45.   Ibid., p. 330.
46.   Ibid., p. 332.
47.   Op. cit., lines: 217-218.

BIBLIOGRAPHY

Aqil, Shafil.   *Punjab Rang*, Lahore: Markazi Urdu Board, 1968.

Aristotle   *Poetics* (English translation: S.H. Butcher), New York: Hill and Wang, 1961.

Badakhshani, M.M.B. "Si Harfi da Fikr te Fun," *Lalan di Pand*, Lahore: Aziz Book Depot, 1973.

Beer, G.   *The Romance*, London: Methuens, 1970.

Eaton, R.M.   *Sufis of Bijapur (1300 - 1700)*, Princeton: Princeton University Press, 1978.

Leiden: E. J. Brill. *The Encyclopedia of Islam (New)*.

                   The Encyclopedia of Poetry and Poetics, Princeton: Princeton University Press, 1974.

Finnegan, Ruth.   *Oral Poetry*, Cambridge: Cambridge University Press, 1977.

Frye, N.   *The Anatomy of Criticism*, Princeton : Princeton University Press, 1973.

Grierson, G.A.   *Linguistic Survey of India*, Calcutta: Government Printing Press, 1903.

Griffin, L.H.   *Punjab Chiefs*, Lahore: Government Printing Press, 1940.

Harvey, P.   *Oxford Companion to English Literature*, Oxford: The Clarendon Press, 1967.

Hashmi, H.S.   *Punjabi di Mukhtasar Tarikh*, Lahore: Taj Book Depot, 1977

Jain, B.D.   *Punjabi Zaban te Uhda Literature*, Lahore: Majlis Shah Husayn, 1967.

Khan, Asaf   "Chathiyan di Var," *Lalan di Pand*, Lahore: Aziz Book Depot, 1973.
                   "Introduction," *Jang Hind Panjab*, Lahore: Aziz Book Depot, 1972.
                   "Varan de Pater" *Lalan di Pand*, Lahore: Aziz Book Depot, 1973.

Kushta, M.B.   *Punjabi Shairan da Tazkira*, Lahore: Mian Maula Bakhsh Kushta & Sons,1977.

Latif, S.M.   *A History of the Punjab*, Lahore: People's Publishing House, 1977

Laurenson, L & A. Swingwood *The Sociology of Literature*, London: MacGibbon & Kee, 1971.

Lord, Albert.   *The Singer of Tales*, New York: Atheneum, 1968.

Mascara Juan.   *The Bhagavad Gita*, Harmondsworth: Penguin Books, 1983.

Platts, J.T.   *A Dictionary of Urdu, Classical Hindi and English*, London: Oxford University Press, 1974.

Qadiryar   *Mi'raj Namah*, Lahore: Malik Bashir Ahmad, 1981.
                   Rozah Namah, Lahore: Malik Bashir Ahmad, 1981.
                   Puran Bhagat, Sohni Mahinwal, Hari Singh Nalwa di Var (Editor: Shareef Sabir), Lahore: Panjabi Adabi Markaz, 1978.

	Puran Bhagat, (English translation: Taufiq Rafat), Lahore: Vanguard Books, 1983.
Qurayshi, A.G.	*Punjabi Adab ki Kahani*, Lahore: Aziz Book Depot, 1972.
Rafat, T.	*Puran Bhagat* (English translation), Lahore: Vanguard Books, 1983
Rasalu, Raja	"Punjabi Sha'iri wich Waqia-i Mi'raj Sharif," *The Ravi*, Lahore: Government College, 1980.
Saleem, A.	*Lok Varan*, Islamabad: National Council of the Arts, Folklore Research Centre, 1971.
Serebryakov	*Punjabi Literature*, Lahore: Progressive Books, 1973.
Shackle, C.	*Hasham Shah: Sassi Punnu* (English translation), Lahore: Vanguard Books, 1985.
Singh, Mohan	*A History of Punjabi Literature*, Lahore: Mohan Singh, 1930.
	Gorakhnath and Medieval Hindu Mysticism, Lahore: 1937
	Kabir and the Bhagti Movement, Lahore: Atma Ram & Sons, 1934.
Swynnerton, C.	*The Adventures of the Punjab Hero Raja Rasalu and Other Folk Tales of the Punjab*, Calcutta: W. Newman, 1884.
Syed, N.H.	*Recurrent Patterns in Punjabi Poetry*, Lahore: Panjabi Adabi Markaz, 1978.
Tabassum, S.	*Punjabi ki Shairi par Farsi Rawayat ka Asar*, Lahore: Mahakmah Taluqat-i Amah, Hukumat-i Punjab, 1971.
Tahir, M.A.	"Introduction", *Hasham Shah: Sassi Punnu*, (English translation: Christopher Shackle), Lahore: Vanguard Books, 1985.
Temple, R.C.	*The Indian Antiquity. The Legends of the Punjab*, 2 Vols., Islamabad: Institute of Folk Heritage, 1981.

Shah Mohammad on Punjabi Identity

Darshan Singh

Shah Mohammad was an eminent Punjabi poet. He wrote his war-ballad around the year 1845 A.D. This was very crucial time in terms of its significance for understanding and analysing the issue of Punjabi identity. This issue takes entirely a new turn at this point of the history of Punjab. It narrates the story of what happened with Punjabis after the death of their beloved Maharaja Ranjit Singh. It reflects the difference between the psyche of a victor and that of a vanquished nation. This defeat was not only a defeat of a nation, but it was actually a deathblow to its very existence.

Shah Mohammad's command over the subject and also over the art of poeticising it is par excellence. But it contains a lot more than mere history and poetry. Shah Mohammad's objectivity in depiction is beyond doubt. He had a deep sense of love for Maharaja and the people of Punjab. He enjoys the glory of his people and at the same time laments over their failures. He has a great appreciation for the heroic qualities and the grandeur of the Khalsa army, but at the same time, he ridicules their irresponsible behaviour resulting into their retreat and consequent defeat. He says:

> Brave Singhs when entered the battlefield,
> They killed a large number of white army.
> The brave Singhs killed the army, to finish,
> Which included Indian, Northerns, and Southerns,
> This made the England cry,
> This vacated the four thousand chairs.

In the face of a forceful offensive, the Khalsa army, according to Shah Mohammad, lost no time in leaving the field. He ridicules this unbehoving act of theirs in the words: "Singhs ran away from battle field". He further ridicules "The City of Lahore was living happily. You have handed over the keys of the city to the enemy". He says "O Singhs! the people ask you, what type of performance you have shown".

Thus, Shah Mohammad does not overplay or underplay anyone. He gives the treatment which an individual or a group deserves. This absolutely does not mean that his love and dedication for his country/people is in any way questionable. Shah Mohammad had an immeasurable amount of praise for Maharaja Ranjit Singh. He describes him thus: "The most powerful Ranjit Singh was born to rule the State and to restructure the (map of) the country. He conquered a number of provinces like Multan, Kashmir, Peshawar, Chamba, Jammu, Kangra, and Ladakh right upto China.

The whole of it formed the kingdom of Lahore. Ranjit Singh brought the above together and many more small principalities and united them under one kingdom. Earlier throughout the history of Punjab, it was either ruled by Delhi or by Kabul or partly by both or by a number of small principalities. For the first time in the history of Punjab, the kingdom of Punjab, with Maharaja Ranjit Singh as an independent and sovereign identity, came into being on the map of India/world. According to Shah Mohammad, this was the kingdom of Punjab, government by Punjabis, conquered and sustained by their love and labour. This was an experiment, which had several lessons for the world community to learn. Unfortunately, in the interest of the world community, history could not repeat itself.

Maharaja Ranjit Singh took several steps to strengthen the Punjabi identity. He clearly demonstrated through his policies and actions that kingdom of Punjab belongs to all Punjabis and not to himself or the people of his religion only. He took several unconventional steps to make this perception workable. For example:

1. He belonged to a community, which was severely prosecuted by the earlier rulers of Punjab. His forefathers were subjected to a number of indignities. According to the established legacy of the world from the persecutor, they, with a sense of revenge, persecute their former persecutors. This vicious circle is a permanent part of the order of the world. Sometimes this persecution becomes exemplary. But, Maharaja Ranjit Singh instead of persecuting the earlier persecutors shared power with them. Thus Muslims and their allies, that is Hindus, were made partners in the destiny of the kingdom of Punjab.

2. Thereby contrary to the given legacy, the religious prejudices were unknown in the kingdom of Punjab.

3. So much so that Punjabi language, which was also the religious language of the Sikhs, (because their religious text is written in it), was not made the official language. No doubt, Punjabi remained the cultural language of all Punjabis, it belonged to this land and hence to every inhabitant of Punjab, yet to avoid any mis-understanding on this ground, he allowed Persian to continue as official language. It was simply to avoid any controversy regarding his preferential consideration for any religious group.

4. It is a recorded fact of history that charity was equally distributed for the religious institutions of all the religious groups.

5. Maharaja Ranjit Singh used to run the Government in the name of Khalsa/ Guru/God, showing that the kingdom of God was for all, therefore, so was the Lahore Darbar. It was everyone's ownership because everyone represented Guru/God.[1] It is in this context that Ranjit Singh did not wear a crown, did not sit on a throne[2] and did not issue any coin or seal in his name.[3] The difference between the ruler and the ruled thus stood eliminated.[4] He preferred himself to be called only *Sarkar* (ruler), *Sevadar* (servant) or *Singh Sahib* and not the owner of the kingdom.[5]

This restructuralisation of the power-frame and refashioning of the human psyche helped Maharaja Ranjit Singh to build a vast, strong and viable Punjabi kingdom with a new perception and renewed strength. This experiment proved to be a miracle. Earlier, Punjab was being invaded, captured, truncated and ruthlessly ruled by a number of nations, throughout its eventful existence. It is only at this point of history that Punjab got sovereignty. It was now being ruled by Punjabis, its own people. This realisation of its self-identity harmonised its inner and outer strength, which not only kept itself intact in the face of furious attacks but also began to teach a lesson to the earlier invaders in their own lands. This miracle was the product of the formation and realisation of Punjabi identity.

This cultural consciousness created and nourished by Maharaja Ranjit Singh and its identification with land, instead of a particular group of people, presents an incomparable example in the contemporary history of mankind. This psychologically as well as physically elevated a Punjabi to the highest rank and made him tough and adventurous. The source of the ideological framework which created this temperament, with its full elegance and entirety was best spotted by Professor Puran Singh, a renowned prolific writer of Punjab, He says, "Punjab is neither Hindu nor Musalman; Punjab lives by the name of Gurus".[6] He describes the youth of Punjab as "The elder and younger brothers of Ranjha". He has based his opinion upon the teaching of Sikh Gurus and their historical manifestation through Sikh struggle culminating into a huge Punjabi empire at the hands of Maharaja Ranjit Singh. Sikh Gurus were strictly pro-human, discarding all barriers of caste, colour, sex, religion, area etc. Thus, they propagated through their words and deeds. Their words were put into deed through institutions like *Sangat, Pangat, Langar, Harminder Sahib*, compilation of Guru Granth Sahib etc., which function without any prejudice. These words and deeds had moulded and re-formed the Sikh. Sikh here did not mean a particular people. A Sikh was a remodelled human, and thus, a Sikh and an awakened human were mutually identifiable. Therefore, a Hindu, a Muslim, a Christian or a member of any religion is a Sikh if he follows the principles laid down by the words and deeds of Sikh Gurus.

Thus Sikh psyche or Singh identity meant Punjabi identity, at least Shah Mohammad perceived his contemporary society through this angle. A close study of his text reveals that this was his faith, his conviction and he did not falter in it. For him a Sikh and Punjabi identity were complementary to each other. This is exactly how he has treated the matter in his text.

Shah Mohammad begins his long poem with a sense, which bears direct influence of the ideology of Sikh Gurus. No doubt, the transitoriness of all worldly objects is accepted and preached by all religions, but the way in which Shah Mohammad treats it, it closely resembles the way of the Sikh Gurus. He says, "We must always fear God because he can turn the kings into beggars". This is his typically

Punjabi consciousness cultivated by the Sikh Gurus. Thus the very beginning has its background planted in the soil of the Sikh ethos and hence Punjabi identity.

Shah Mohammad has described the forces of Lahore by a number of names. He calls them *Sikh, Singh, Akali, Khalsa Panth* etc., which to an ordinary man means the army of the Sikhs. Actually it is not so. It means the army of Punjab that is of the Lahore Darbar. Shah Mohammad himself writes that the army of Punjab was not restricted to the Sikhs only. People from all religions joined this army. There were Christian, Muslim and Hindu officers and also Sikh officers and they all joined together to form the army of Lahore. Therefore, the above given names do not mean the army comprised of only the Sikhs. The Sikhs may be more in number, but it was definitely an army in which members of all communities enlisted. Therefore the *Khalsa* army means the army of the Lahore Darbar and hence of all Punjabis.[7] Shah Mohammad writes "the kingdom of Punjab was marching, the number of soldiers was uncountable. None can face them. Singhs will definitely conquer Delhi." Singhs here mean members of the army, which consisted of people drawn from different religious groups.

When Maharani Jindan decided to discuss the "panth" she talked about its bravery. Here "panth" clearly meant the whole corps of army, which included Hindus, Muslims and Sikhs. Therefore, panth in the couplet signifies Punjab and the people of Punjab. This point of view is further strengthened by the poet's words "The whole of the Punjab kingdom (*Badshahi*) started marching". Thus, 'people of Punjab', the 'kingdom of Punjab' and '*panth*' or '*Khalsa*' are mutually identifiable in Shah Mohammad. The poet, while dealing with his subject, presents a unique sense of excellence in correctly and objectively understanding the consolidated image of Punjab identity. This text, from this point of view, is an exemplary treatise on this subject. The poet is so clear and constant about this point of view that it dominates the proceedings throughout his ballad.

Thus Shah Mohammad identifies the mutuality of the kingdom of Punjab and 'Singhs' in the same couplet. The kingdom of Punjab means, as already discussed, a state belonging to everyone who resided in Punjab. Thus a resident of the kingdom of Punjab and a Sikh meant the same for Shah Mohammad. Therefore their identity is same. When Rani Jindan according to Shah Mohammad, out of frustration and anger swore to get the army killed, she says, "I will turn Punjab into a widow" she refers to Punjab, neither to a Sikh nor to a Khalsa. Further she uses the words: "When Panjabna (Punjabi women) become widows". To prove my point, I will take up another stanza expressed by Shah Mohammad. In it he gives a description of a regiment. According to him, the name of the regiment was Akal regiment and it was trained by French Officers. Magar Ali, Magar Khan, Sultan Mohamood, Imam Shah, Ilahi Bux etc. were its generals. Similarly, there were a good number of Hindu generals/officers of high rank[8] like Misar Dewan Chand, Misar Sukhraj, Misar Sawan

Mal, Misar Roop Lal, Misar Bali Ram, Diwan Mool Raj etc. I think these examples clearly prove that *Khalsa* army meant the army of the Punjab. The poet is gently and consistently projecting this image. His main consideration here seems to project the Punjabi identity.

Shah Mohammad has referred to the Anglo-Sikh war as a war between Punjab and Hind (Hindustan). Thus, for him, this war was not a war between the Sikhs and the British. He says, "War between Hind and Punjab is taking place. Armies of both the Kingdoms are expressively strong". This clearly indicates the mind of the poet. He emphatically proves that Punjabi identity had transcended the religious boundaries. The whole of its population took pride in being Punjabi while disowning any other identity. Hissar, Bikaner, Lucknow, Ajmer, Jaipur, were areas across the river Yamuna comprising Hindustan and a Punjabi had no love for that land. In fact, during this battle the people from that land were fighting from the side of the British and against the Punjabis. Thus the participants in this war transcended their religious affiliations and were bound by territorial identity.

During the rule of Maharaja Ranjit Singh, Punjabi identity got firmly consolidated and expressively demonstrated.[9] Shah Mohammad gives an excellent expression to this reality. According to him, the Maharaja was a very powerful and well-accepted ruler. He calls him the most powerful (*mahabali*). This means his writ ran unquestionably. He could easily have built his own religious identity. He could have promoted his religion by making it a state religion and similarly his language as the official language. This he could have imposed upon the other communities. But he did not do so. In fact, such an idea was in direct contradiction to his own culture, the culture given by the Sikh Gurus and nourished by the selfless sacrifices of the Sikh heroes. Instead of promoting communal considerations, he promoted a collective identity, which should be called Punjabi identity.

Shah Mohammad has given a beautiful expression to this aspect of his vision. He says:

> Hindus and Muslims, both were living happily,
> A curse has fallen upon both,
> Never before in Punjab,
> A third community had entered.

According to Shah Mohammad, in Punjab there were only two communities, i.e. Hindus and Muslims. Should this mean that Maharaja Ranjit Singh never promoted the image of Sikh identity? Right from the days of Guru Nanak Sikhism has been presented and grown as a separate and independent religion. It has its own philosophy, ideology, religious customs and concerns and on the whole it's own structure. The Sikh Gurus and Sikh heroes worked very hard for its successful onward growth, fructifying into an alternative order. But, at the same time, they continuously discouraged the growth of any prejudicial tendency among their followers. Indivisible God and indivisible people was their fundamental principle and plank. Therefore, there was no ground for any division resulting into separateness of the human beings. One can have one's feet in the Church but not his head also. Heads and hearts of the people of every religion brought together all the people on this platform and gave them one identity that is Punjabi identity. This means the given reality, as recorded by Shah Mohammad, was such as religion was redefined as culture and hence this perspective was entirely different from the earlier traditional meaning and practice of a religion and culture. As a result of this Shah Mohammad says, "The relationship between Hindus and Muslims is very thick".

There is no doubt that Maharaja Ranjit Singh honestly and sincerely attempted at strengthening the Sikh traditions of mutual brotherhood and common identity. It has a sad part also. Sikhism, right front its inception, vigorously and aggressively supported the cause of the weaker and oppressed section of the society. This was not to the liking of the elite of both the communities. Throughout the Sikh movement, the ruling elite of Hindus and Muslims, both continued to conspire and devise a kind of mechanization through which they could stop its growing influence. Many a times, they even collaborated at crushing it. In fact, this elite was clearly convinced that if this pro-people, particularly pro-oppressed movement succeeded, their interest could be severely jeopardised. Therefore, they left no stone unturned in using all means even unfair ones, to crush it. The arrival of the British, in this context, was a good opportunity for them to revive their subdued urge for the realisation of this self-interest. They immediately stepped in to avail of this opportunity to their maximum gain. Shah Mohammad writes that when the British entered Punjab, as victors, "Pathans came to present their gifts to them. The leaders of all the areas came for this purpose". This class of people who satisfied their own greed sent, through this act, a signal for the ignorant and simple masses who in their utmost simplicity, got trapped by them. They were simple enough not to understand the sophistication of this move. Thus we find that they managed to divide the people into their communal groups.

In this context, Shah Mohammad, attached great value to the struggle of *Khalsa* (Punjabi) in maintaining the grandeur of their exemplary identity both in war and peace. But this well-knit (*Muth-Meeti*) identity of Punjabis was now tactfully assailed and this was a move towards its disintegration. The use of this idiomatic expression clearly indicates this process. Shah Mohammad had an extremely exalted hero in the person of *Khalsa*, which includes every Punjabi. This hero gave a kind of administration, which in real terms, was the government of the people. Therefore, it was known as the Lahore Darbar. It is a wonder of the history that during a long period of half a century of the rule of Khalsa, there was not a single case of discrimination, prejudice or persecution on communal grounds. But, unfortunately, when the *Khalsa* army was defeated, this set in a new trend in the reaction of different communities. Shah Mohammad refers this reality in a very passive mood. He says,

"The future will be determined by the grace of God but at the moment, the authority
of Singhs has been eroded". This erosion of the authority is further expressed again
in a similar mood. Shah Mohammad says, "The land is cut into pieces and has been
changed into the clouds of dust". This means, this was not the land which was cut
into pieces, actually it was the psyche of the people which was divided into narrow
considerations. Unfortunately, the arrival of British was treated as a protective
umbrella and under this protection new tendencies started growing. Realising that
the Lahore Darbar was no more an authority and the real power had passed on to the
British, the local elite, as usual, took no time in changing its mind and stance. Not
only did they change themselves but they were also, again unfortunately, successful
in influencing the respective population by blindly following their unscrupulous new
leaders. The Hindus and the Muslims of Punjab started finding their roots somewhere
else. So much so that their loyalty to their beloved heroes began to disappear fast.
Instead of the local heroes they started identifying themselves with the heroes of the
Arabs and those of the Maharashtra and Rajasthan. (Later on a new class of the elite,
under the garb of proletarianism came into being. They started having their heroes
from Moscow). Therefore, the population of this country unfortunately was divided
into sections and each section started acting in the manner, which suited to the present
rulers, the British. This created a peculiar situation in Punjab and this situation set a
few trends: firstly, the local population started identifying themselves with their earlier
roots. This meant that each community, instead of having faith in the *Khalsa* and the
sacred text of Punjabis, that is, *Shri Guru Granth Sahib*, started looking beyond to
search their roots from the older religious scriptures. Secondly, in their attempt to
please the present ruler, they distanced themselves from everything connected with
the Lahore Darbar. They identified themselves more intensively with their own
Church, their own language, their own way of life. This was a very dangerous trend
which really divided the population into smaller sections. Thus, the power of the
Punjabis seriously suffered. The Government also encouraged this trend
whole-heartedly. These trends resulted in the division of the identity of Punjabis.

Thus, the legacy of this loss of identity has become our heritage. Unfortunately,
we are still suffering from the effects of this legacy. Resultantly, we have closed
minds, closed ears and barren thinking. We are the ones who ourselves are cutting
out roots and squandering away our strength. We are presently living in an area,
where, unfortunately, a large number of the people are not identified with their land.
While the strength of the Lahore Darbar was instrumental in building the Punjabi
identity, the fall of the Lahore Darbar became the ground for disintegrating and
dividing it. Religion, the land, the people of land, all were cut and divided. The earth
under their feet was shaken and their own protective umbrella was torn to pieces.

Shah Mohammad is really a singular authority on this issue. He is very accurate
and forceful in depicting the rise and fall of the Punjabi identity. He clearly says that
when power was with the Lahore Darbar, members of every community shared it

and considered it to be their own power. But when the British came to occupy this land, the local population started looking towards them. He says, "The youngsters now when sit and talk, they talk about having seen the cantonment of the British." The Cantonment (*Chbawni*) is clearly a symbol of power and authority. They had shifted their loyalty from the Lahore Darbar to the ruling British. This change of heart was actually responsible for our prospective maladies. I have no hesitation in saying that this was an occasion of our great misfortune and we are still not out of its clutches.

Thus, Shah Mohammad relates the story of the changing loyalties of Punjabis. When Maharaja Ranjit Singh was ruling, it was a rule of all the Punjabis. But when British occupied the land it became a loss of the Sikh Empire. Shah Mohammad has done a great service by recording our success and failures. We owe a debt to him. This should compel us to realise our strength and folly, to re-think and re-demarcate our concerns and to redirect ourselves, collectively and wholeheartedly, for the projection of Punjabi identity. The real solution, even to the present problem of Punjab, lies in realising and strengthening the cultural nationalism in Punjab. Broadly speaking, this can be a remedy for other states of India also.

NOTES

[All quotations are the author's translations and are taken from *Puran Singh Jeevani te Kavita*, Sahitya Academy, New Delhi, 1976]

1.   The Sovereignty of the Guru Panth Khalsaji, however, did not impose a theocratic character on the state. The Sikhs were not regarded as superior to non-Sikhs simply because the Maharaja hailed from their community. They were on par with the rest of the people. It was not like the medieval Turkish or Mughal state where the followers of Islam were given a status much above the status of those who did not belong to the faith of the rulers.

2.   But even so, had he wanted to sit on the throne, he could have easily had his own throne prepared. But he did not, and this shows that it was not the Mughal throne alone that he did not want to sit on but any throne as he was opposed to doing so as a matter of principle. In the matter of using the chair too, he was not punctilious for there were occasions when he would hold the durbar sitting on a carpet with a velvet cushion at the back. Ranjit Singh's head-dress also was his plain chieftain's turban and there was no special emblem worn as a mark of royalty. Indeed, his dress was extremely simple as compared with the gorgeous dresses of his courtiers. See *Some aspects of State and Society under Ranjit Singh*, Fauja Singh, p.41

3.   The principal coin of Ranjit Singh bore the name of the founder of the Sikh faith and was called *Nanakshahi*. The Persian inscription on it bore the names of both Guru Nanak and Guru Gobind Singh. His official seal no doubt carried his name but in a manner that gave more importance to the Timeless God (Akal) than to him. Ibid., p.56

4.   He believed after the manner of the Sikh Gurus that rulership is a gift from heaven, which a ruler is allowed to have only so long as he deserves it. Ibid, p.42

5.   He liked to be addressed by the plain and simple title of Singh Sahib, a title applicable to any member of the Sikh brotherhood or by the in personal title of Sarkar literally meaning Government. Ibid., p.39

6.   Ranjit Singh's Hindu, Muslim and Sikh subjects equally reciprocated his warm interest in their religions by remembering him in their prayers on important occasions. Ibid, p. 71.

7.   All troops of the state, whether Sikhs, Hindu, Muslim or Gorkha, were known as Khalsa troops. *Some aspects of State and Society under Ranjit Singh*, Fauja Singh, p.61.

8.   In the army there were generals drawn from all communities. *Some aspects of State and Society under Ranjit Singh*, Fauja Singh, p.62

9.   Still another assessment is that he was a leader par excellence of Punjabi nationalism, *Some aspects of State and Society under Ranjit Singh*, Fauja Singh, p.65

Guru Ravi Dass and Punjabi Identity

Lekh Raj Parwana

Punjab is well known in the world for its rich cultural heritage and ancient classical literature. It has provided attractions to foreigners as well as to other states of India. India feels proud of it because of the rich contribution of the Punjab in every sphere of life, particularly in the field of literature, culture and fine arts. Punjab is considered to be the brain of India because it has always taken initiative in launching movements, research, innovations etc. The Punjab became the cultural and civilisational centre of India because educational pursuits and defence devices used to be provided in one form or the other by the Punjabis.

Punjab has undergone several political, social and economic changes, many a time during the last about six thousand years. The present Punjab has become small as a result of political strategies. Even so, it has got the same spirit in it as it had six thousand years ago.

Punjab has given language, civilisation, wisdom, literature and so many gifts not only to India, but also to the whole of the world. It is a matter of sorrow that Punjab was treated mercilessly by invaders and foreigners. They tried to establish their own identity and eliminate the identity of Punjab. They could not succeed in totality because the Punjabis have sufficient strength to withstand the evil forces.

Before I take up the real subject, I would like to make a few observations about the *Bhakti* Movement and the classical background of the Punjabi Heritage prevalent in the then Punjab. It would be a matter of surprise for those who actually do not know the real contribution made by Guru Ravidas to the enhancement and exposition of Punjabi Identity, to *PUNJABIAT*, as we may say in simpler words in Punjabi. During the medieval period, an apple of discord coupled with hatred and discrimination between man and man on the basis of fanatic feelings of religion was in vogue. Imposition thereof on the people was forcibly applied on them without their consent and approval. When we scan this topic historically, socially, economically, politically and psychologically, we may get positive results. In Punjab, before the arrival of Guru Nanak on the forefront with his absolute mission of spreading love, mutual brotherhood, oneness of God and commonness of humanity, the entire society was divided horizontally and socially. Whosoever came to Punjab in the form of invader, looted it, plundered its belongings and murdered those who withstood against them. I cannot help saying that there was an element, that for its own sake in order to serve its own interest, welcomed foreigners, helped them, informed them of the weaknesses of a divided Indian society in particular. That element is the real enemy, which remained hidden, but worked against the country and countrymen. Those who are a part of this element are still there, but democratic forces have subordinated them. However, in order to save the country and the nation, we are required to be very vigilant about their activities. Even today, they remain busy in extending relations illegally with uncalled for and unconcerned forces in order to make money and matter. That element is to be identified and set right.

During his regime, Guru Nanak identified that element and revolted against that, condemned their activities and beautified his Punjabi society by thus spending his precious life. He rekindled the sleeping souls of brave Punjabis, awakened their human sentiments and spoke out: "The service of humanity is the service of God." "The caste of human being is the only one and that should be treated as the only". He launched a move to clean the hearts of unclear minds. He initiated the *Bhakti* Movement of his own style, wherein, recognition and authentication of the Oneness of a Formless God, living in the Abode of truth, omnipresent, omnipotent, hearing every creature - human, sub-human, superhuman, animal or bird, was established. The brightness of Multi-gods and Multi-goddesses, the exclusive representatives of God, was subordinated to his philosophy. All the other nine Gurus followed that movement. Within a span of three hundred years, Ten Masters from Guru Nanak to Guru Gobind Singh pleaded the philosophy of Guru Nanak. They spread his message of love, equality, humanity, coexistence, mutual respect and worship of only one God, who is the creator, who is the destroyer, who plays through Nature his Absolute skill and keeps the machinery of the Universe intact and mobile. This movement brought back the same glitters, psychological prosperity and respect to humanity as it was before the visits of foreign invaders who spoilt the entire identity of Punjabis. The glory of Punjab was an eyesore to foreigners. As a matter of fact, they were not appreciative of it, but matched their intentions and motives to the glory, thus belittling the culture and heritage of Punjab, which was and remained always in paramount and crowned position in the world.

The ancient scholars of Punjab like *MahaRishi* Valmiki gave a true account of the behaviour of Aryans and Non-Aryans in his own style in the *Ramayana* and produced a book of Mother-Philosophy "*Yogvashishta*" consisting of 60,000 *shalokas*. Therein, the concept of the Oneness of God was highlighted by him that was later diluted by Aryan Scholars who wrote the *Upanishads* and other *smritis* and *Shrutis*. Similarly, *Rishi* Vedvyas and his son *Rishi* Sukdev also contributed a lot in the ancient classical literature like the *Mahabharata*, including the *Gita* and the four Vedas. *Rishi* Vedvayas was a Punjabi, who also presented the true picture of the minds of the then Aryans and Non-Aryans. The *karam* philosophy of the *Gita* was enunciated and exposed by *Rishi* Sukdev, who also compiled the Four Vedas with the help of his father *Rishi* Ved Vyas. We, the Indians, feel proud of our classical literature – the *Ramayana*, the *Mahabharata*, the *Yogvashishta*, the *Bhagvad Gita* and the Four Vedas. It is the property of Punjab, the glory of our civilisation, the great height of morality and the paramount truthful philosophy, which we had passed on to our countrymen.

I dare say, Punjab always remained high and glorified in every sphere of life in the country. In other words, Punjab is the brain of India and a storehouse of knowledge of every discipline. That is why we see the devout Punjabi in every country, upholding his sole *Punjabiyat* i.e. "live and let live, love and be loved, respect and be respected". On the basis of my own experience and feelings, I have seen the beauty of the Punjabi in every corner of the World. He lives with dignity, works hard with respectful means, shows sympathy to his friends and relatives. He is kind and disposed well towards humanity. This is the Punjabi identity, which our forefathers in the ancient and medieval period kept high. And even today, in the modern period, Punjab is leading in every discipline of life. This Punjabi identity, the old one, was kept abreast by the Ten Masters (Gurus) in Punjab along with the unstinting help of their devotees, admirers and sympathisers.

The *Bhakti* Movement launched by Guru Nanak did not flow only in Punjab, but it flowed towards other states also. Where Guru Nanak went, the light of knowledge went with him. He was the flambeau of knowledge having the power to mould the hard nuts. Similarly, the philosophy and the movement of the Fifth Guru, Guru Arjan Dev was put to the test. He was treated mercilessly by his contemporary king, but like a true Punjabi, he did not budge an inch from his stand, but kept the dignity of Punjabi very high while sacrificing his life for the sake of humanity. The 9th Master, Guru Tegh Bahadur followed the same path. His power of tolerance and truthfulness of mission was challenged by antihuman forces, but he did not bend before injustice, tyranny, human sufferings and anti-social element. He sacrificed his life for the sake of the Indian people and kept the tradition of morality in Punjab very high. Likewise, Guru Gobind Singh, the 10th Master did whatever remained to be done after his predecessors. He sacrificed his children, his property and valuables during his social resurgence movement. He glorified and embellished the Punjabi identity in the true perspective of the term.

When the fire breaks out, it does destroy the surroundings. The flame of knowledge and the crash programme of Punjabi Gurus, their devotees and disciples, engulfed the dark designs of vested interests and anti-social activities of their contemporaries. It spread like wild fire. The Alvar Saints of South India got awakened with this *Bhakti* cult. The saints of Uttar Pradesh, Madhya Pradesh, Gujarat, Bihar, Maharashtra and Bengal also were positively affected by this casteless and colourless message of the great *Rishis*, Gurus and Saints of Northern India. Guru Nanak travelled far and wide in order to spread the message of his philosophy pertaining to God, humanity and Nature. This enkindled message not only hailed and enthused the Punjabi Mind, but also warranted the attention of wise people living in other states.

The Punjabi character was well known to other Indians and the identity thereof was interwoven in their mental network. The chivalry, bravery, benign attitude, patriotic blend and the recognition of mutual respect for all and sundry of the Punjabis were engraved in the minds of people living in other states. The gifted personality of the Punjabis was the cause of attractions for others. For the sake of inter-communication and mutual benefit to all, the saints of UP, Maharashtra, Gujrat, Bengal, Rajasthan, Madhya Pradesh etc. appeared on the scene and raised their heads for justice, equal respect to all the classes and castes of India. They extended their full co-operation to save the human values at large.

The first batch of UP saints consisting of five saints Ravidas, Kabir, Dhanna, Trilochan and Sadna for the first time visited composite Punjab and met Guru Nanak at *Chuharkana* (now Nankana Sahib, Pakistan) who served them well and gave due respect to all the Saints. Guru Nanak spent the money given to him by his father for business purpose. The business he did, was the business of truth in the service of the saints.

Again the saints came from all over India where Guru Ravidas and Kabir participated in a religious congregation held at Sultanpur Lodhi, District Kapurthala, at *Sant Ghat Gurudwara* about two kilometres away from *Ber Saheb Gurdwara* of Sultanpur Lodhi. Guru Nanak was working there in the storehouse of Lodhi Empire where his brother-in-law (Jai Ram, husband of Bibi Nanaki, Sister of Guru Nanak Dev, was working). For three days, this religious conference continued. Here Guru Nanak composed the *Mool Mantra*, as has been indicated through an exhibit displayed in the said Gurdwara.

Thereafter, Guru Nanak started his travel outside Punjab. The third time, Guru Nanak met *Sant* Ravidas and Kabir was at *Maduadih*, the birthplace of Guru Ravidas, three miles away from the main city of Varanasi (Benaras) and held discussions of mutual interest. *Sant* Ravidas gave due regards to Guru Nanak in the presence of a large number of saints. *Sant* Kabir also took part in spiritual discussions with Guru Nanak. "Guru Ka Bagh" is the place in Benaras where the Saints of importance living in Varanasi used to exchange their views with each other. Guru Nanak and *Sant* Ravidas exchanged their spiritual notes with each other and Bhai Bala who always accompanied Guru Nanak, used to collect the *vani* of the *Sant*s which was written in accordance with the principles laid down by the Gurus and *Sant*s with the mutual consent of each other. The *Vani* was compiled by *Bhai* Bala and the *Vani*s of *Sant* Ravi Das, *Sant* Kabir, Sadna, Sen, Ramanand etc. were included in the *Granth*, namely, "*Pothi Saheb*". When Guru Arjan Dev included the *vanis* of Sri Guru Angad, Guru Amar Das and Guru Ram Dass, he also included in this volume his own *vani* and gave a new caption to "*Pothi Saheb*" as the "*Sri Adi Granth*". When Guru Gobind Singh included the *vani* of his father, Guru Tegh Bahadur, the name of the *Granth* was again changed to "*Sri Guru Granth Sahib*". Meaning thereby, the Tenth Master gave the title of "Guru" to all the saints and *Bhaktas*, whose *vani* finds a place in "*Sri Guru Granth Sahib*". This was the large-heartendness practically of all the Gurus of the Punjab that they placed every human being equal to each other by removing Untouchability and spreading the message of classlessness and castelessness in Indian society. It was the ardent effort of the Punjabi Gurus belonging to the *Khatri* class next in order to the *Brahminic* class who launched the social resurgence movement under the garb of the *Bhakti* Movement. It was the best media acceptable to all the people.

The voices of Guru Ravidas and *Sant* Kabir equally matched with the voice raised by the Sikh Gurus against the social and religious tyrannical order, anti-human elements and fanatic communal forces. The Gurus cleansed the minds of Punjabis and the saints of Uttar Pradesh, Ravidas and Kabir, did the same thing in their State and outside. *Sant* Ravidas toured far and wide. He, along with his disciples, visited Punjab thrice as is evident from the historic record referred to in the foregoing paragraphs. He stayed for a week at *Kharalgarh* in District Hoshiarpur and visited "*Ballan*" in District Jalandhar. Still it requires to be searched out where this great saint spent his precious time. He toured up to Peshawar, Kabul, Kota and Balochistan. He loved the Punjabi culture, Punjab's contribution in religious discipline, its old civilisation and the rich humanistic traditions prevalent in the Punjab State, the then land of five rivers.

The classical scriptures produced by the Punjabis have to be studied in order to defeat the trend of Manuistic caste-ridden traditions, which have divided human community into castes and classes in the name of profession. The Manuistic tradition was loved and adopted by those vested interests who wanted to rule India and keep the serfdom alive for the sake of their own comforts and convenience. The primitive ruled class was enslaved by the Aryans and their interest was to keep them under their strong thumb. Guru Ravidas came to study the existence of apartheid in North India and wanted to draw certain concrete conclusions pertaining to the root cause of the caste system. Having toured and studied, the analyst Ravidas drew some composite conclusions and bricked them in his famous *shaloka* which reflected his religious and political awakening:

> "The City joyful is the name of that City
> Suffering and sorrow abide not there.
> Neither is there any worry of paying taxes
> Nor is held any property.
> Neither fear of punishment for error nor
> of decline.
> This fine place of habitation have I found
> Brother' there will perpetually reign.
> Eternally fixed is the kingship, wherein
> No second or third class citizen exists.

All are like ever fully populated, famous
is that city.
Those abiding therein are prosperous,
The people disport themselves, as they desire.
All are inmates of that mansion
None else has any.
Sayeth Ravidas, the cobbler, freed from all bonds:
Whosoever is citizen of that country, is our friend."

This *shaloka* indirectly reflects the political and social state of mind of Ravidas. He tells the people that there appears to be no discrimination between man and man in God's Abode. He opines that when in God's House there is no discrimination between man and man, why does discrimination prevail in human society. If it is not relevant in God's house, how is it relevant in human existence?

Every Guru and every saint had used the media of religion, in medieval age, for their expressions, may that be political, social, economical or psychological. That media was acceptable to the people at large. They attended the religious congregations with great enthusiasm. They learnt every discipline through this popular media. Ravidas, through the said shaloka expressed his political philosophy i.e. socialist realism or socialist democracy in *Begumpura City Shalok*. He wanted to tell the people to create such a type of society, which is amenable to all, where freedom flows like a river of nectar.

In another *shaloka*, he elevates the human personality to this extent that the stage comes when the difference between men and God eliminates. He with his utter confidence reveals that when there is no difference between man and God then why difference prevails between man and man? "What difference between thee and me and me and thee. No more than between gold and golden bangle. And water and wave."

With the blessing of the Almighty, man is elevated to the highest seat of respect and thus is worshipped by his disciples and admirer. When a man, according to Ravidas, can achieve the equal position by virtue of his meditation, love and blissful truth, how and why can human beings not build up the society of equal opportunities, equal rights and equality before law and God. He raises issues of why the poor are exploited by the rich, why the elite class of society hates the so-called low-born people, why the right to meditation is denied by Brahmins to the other two classes *Vaish* and *Shudra* and, finally, why this caste system and class system exists. Old scholars and saints of pre-Vedic period used to preach equality of man before God and good relations of man with man. Guru Ravidas wanted to establish the same type of society as was before the pre-Vedic period. Vedic and post-Vedic periods did not preserve the truthfulness of the original philosophy, wherein, the relationship between man and man, and, man and God had been founded. Outsiders and invaders spoilt the whole glamorous game of life.

It is a general saying that if you want to finish any community or society, destroy its literature and history, distort the facts and reality of their period. It happened in the case of the aboriginals, i.e. the non-Aryans. They were treated mercilessly. Their properties were usurped and they were denied all rights like equality, fraternity and education. So much so, the status of being citizens in their own state was denied to them.

Persons like Manu degraded them to the lowest ebb. This tyrannical treatment made them feel as if they are *persona non grata*. Psychologically they were pushed to the state of sub-human beings. All this pinched Guru Nanak's pious heart in the Punjab and *Sant* Ravidas' and *Sant* Kabir's in Uttar Pradesh. Guru Nanak initiated the social resurgence movement in the name of the *Bhakti* Movement in the Punjab and *Sant* Ravidas and *Sant* Kabir launched it in UP. This movement became a movement of the masses and the judicious minds supported it through and through.

This was a socio-religious movement having the spirit of political awakening. Rather he revolted against the rule of God. Ravidas also explained the condition of his community in the following words and prayed to the Almighty for relief and solace:

> Our life is like that of frogs, with which the well is full,
> That knoweth not of different lands,
> My mind is by evil passions so gripped,
> That of myself and the Supreme Being
> little sense have I.

When Ravidas came to Punjab and had a chance to listen to the *Vedas*, he felt wonder and stated in his *Vani* as follows:

> By listening to the teaching of *Vedas* and *Puranas*
> Are doubts raised;
> The doubt ever in the heart abides,
> What action rids the self of pride.

In the same *shaloka*, he further rejects the prevalent rituals, which were anti-humanistic:

> Ritual purity is only like the elephant's action of bathing.

Guru Ravidas also toured many states of India for spreading his philosophy & mission. Finally, it may be stated that Guru Ravidas in the real sense of the term, gave due recognition to *Punjabiyat*, i.e. Punjabi identity, and matched his voice with the Gurus' voices. He extended co-operation to the maximum for the acceptance of *Gurumat* and the Guru House gave due regard to Ravidas' philosophy, teachings, mission and movement. The Guru House felt the necessity of Guru Ravidas. The Gurus spent three hundred years to ameliorate the conditions of downtrodden people, the neglected and rejected classes in the Indian society. Had Guru Ravidas and his contemporary saints not extended their co-operation to the Guru House, the movement perhaps would not have fetched the desired goal in the country. The class of Guru Ravidas and Kabir that consisted of the worst of sufferers, had to be lifted up. Guru Ravidas recognised the *Punjabiyat* and got the desired award. Even today, the *Vani* of Ravidas is relevant.

Raj Karega Khalsa: Understanding the Sikh Theory of Religion and Politics

Bhupinder Singh

Introduction: The Litany

Towards the conclusion of the Sikh congregational prayer (*ardas*)[1], a remarkable and central Sikh text, the following verse is recited:

> The Khalsa shall rule and none shall successfully defy them.
> All shall have to petition for their alliance after bitter frustration,
> for the world shall eventually be redeemed through the
> protection that the Order of the Khalsa alone affords.[2]
>
> (Transl. by Kapur Singh 1959: 450)

Obviously, the above averment, repeated ever since Guru Gobind Singh (1675-1708) or at least Banda Singh Bahadur[3] (1670-1716), is of great import and, therefore, it is surprising that little systematic effort has been made by scholars, Sikh or non-Sikh, to draw out its true meaning.

At the popular level, the affirmation is generally interpreted to mean either the capturing of state power by the Sikhs as a specific community or the universal dominion of *dharma* or justice. Apparently, the first interpretation is political (from the standpoint of *miri*) and the second religious (from the stand point of *piri*), although the two are also assumed to somehow imply each other. For some, the non-theocratic *Sarkar-i Khalsa* of Maharaja Ranjit Singh (1799-1839) comes close to fulfilling the ideal of Khalsa raj.

It seems to me that a third interpretation of the litany is possible consistent with the spirit of the Sikh revelation and sublating the insights yielded by popular interpretations.[4]

Sikhism: God, Man and Nature

For understanding the meaning of raj karega Khalsa, it is first necessary to understand the meaning of Sikhism. Every new religion clarifies afresh, in relation to a particular historical context, the relationship between Unity and Variety, Transcendence and Immanence, or between Man, Nature and God. The particular historical context in the case of Sikhism was provided by the antagonism between Hinduism and Islam. A chief task which fell upon Sikhism, therefore, was to mediate[5] between the apparently antagonistic world-views of the Indian and the Semitic religions. And true to its character as a mediation, Sikhism was and is neither and both of Hinduism and Islam at one and the same time. By virtue of its peculiar character, furthermore, Sikhism also successfully resisted being incorporated into the framework of castes versus sects - the two options into which medieval Hinduism forced all dissenting religious and social movements.

. The Sikh Gurus revealed that the relationship between God, man and nature is characterised by identity as well as difference, proximity as well as distance, and complementarity as well as opposition. This is the non-dualist vision of unity in variety and through it the Sikh Gurus dissolved the spurious opposition between monism and monotheism, delinked the Semitic monotheism from the restrictive notions of the chosen people (Judaism), the Messiah (Christianity) and the final revelation (Islam)[6] and redefined and rearranged the different levels of Being and Non-Being, from man and nature to God or the Absolute, recognised in Indian thought, into a new structure and hierarchy.

God as conceived or revealed in Sikhism is in nature as well as in man, that is, immanent, but also transcendent, manifest and unmanifest, personal and impersonal.[7] This yields, inter alia, an interesting cosmology: nature as a theophany or revelation of God to Himself and to man.[8] The implication is that the domains of the temporal and the material, as two aspects of nature, are not to be shunned as in any way unture, unreal, or worthless, but rather integrated with the spiritual. Thus in the view of one scholar, Sikhism invests the virtues of *sannyasa* (spiritual), *grihastha* (material) and *rajya* (temporal) or, which is the same thing, *tariqat, shar'iat* and *hukumat*, conjointly in a single body of faith and conduct.[9] This is manifest, for instance, in the three pairs of symbols, which every Sikh is supposed to wear on his person.

Hair : Comb

: :

Sword : Iron Bangle

: :

(Uncircumcised State) : Shorts

While the first vertical set of three homologous terms, namely, hair sword and uncircumcised state, signifies respectively renunciation, temporal power and procreation (householding), the second similar set of comb, bangle and shorts signifies their control and sublimation. Thus, in India, renunciation was traditionally symbolised by shaven head or unkempt matted hair. Instead, Sikhism recommends growth *and* combing of hair, implying renunciation (hair) as well as its control and sublimation (comb). Sword is an obvious symbol of power (*rajya*), as iron bangle (*dharma chakra*), worn on the right wrist, is that of *dharma* and restraint. Together the sword and the bangle define the theory of *dharma yuddha* meaning the deployment of power in the service of truth and righteousness. The injunction against circumcision is implicit but nonetheless present. The negative injunction signals the approval of procreation and householding, while shorts, once again, symbolise restraint.[10] The Sikh symbols exemplify the dialectical principle of the negation of negation or the unity of opposites - such as *sannyasa* and *grihastha*, *degh* and *tegh*, *miri* and *piri*, *bhakti* and *shakti* - and define the unique Sikh approach to the *homo totus*.

Let us take stock: Sikhism emphasises unity in variety instead of absolute homogeneity or absolute heterogeneity as between God, man and nature. This leads to the recognition of the relevance of political and social variables for "the total human emancipation of religious man" (Uberoi 1969:136):

> "To be able to achieve the integration of temporal and spiritual seems to have been the most significant contribution of Guru Nanak to the totality of the Indian way of life of medieval India. Indeed, he seems to have reared up a new image of a socio-religious community given at once to temporal and spiritual pursuits of life"
>
> (Ray 1975: 59).

> "Sikhism accords to the material universe the same essence of reality as belongs to the ultimately real, though not the same immaculation and intensity. It follows, therefore, according to Sikhism, that there is no true and genuine religious activity except in the socio-political context"
>
> (Kapur Singh 1959:380-81).

Sikhism: God and Religious Diversity

However, there was another, quite a novel question to which Sikhism addressed itself: What is the relation of religions to God? That is, how does the variety of religious forms relate to the unity of God? The Gurus' answer was that all religions as alternative routes to God, who Himself is beyond all religion (*amazhabe* as Guru Gobind Singh said), are equal and true, but also imperfect and, at the esoteric level, intercommunicable and interconvertible. Let me clarify.

There has been a running accent in Sikhism, from Guru Nanak Dev's *Japu* to Guru Gobind Singh's *Jap*, not, only on the unity and sovereignty of God, but also on His ineffable greatness vis-a-vis universe, nature and man; incarnations, prophets and deities or prowers; arts, sciences and religions; and so on. God is inexhaustible by any measure and, therefore, no religion, for instance, whether Hinduism or Islam, could lay exclusive claim to truth. Dilating upon the use of the epithet *amazhabe* by Guru Gobind Singh, Dr. Mohan Singh (1967:257) writes:

"It should not surprise that Guru Gobind Singh who perfected
a new faith lauded his Master with the epithet *amazhabe* , as
the Religion-less One. He says: Thou art, O God, beyond all
religion; thou hast no religion except it be Godliness; Thou has
created one after another all the religious systems and destroyed
them."

In so far as Sikhism knew and enunciated the above truth, it could not just be
another sectarian religion, but a special and higher mediation that harked to what
Schuon (n.d.) calls the transcendent unity of all religions. It also needs reiteration,
although the point has already been made, that the religion of the Gurus was and is
equally close to and/or equally distant from both Hinduism and Islam. If Sikhism
preaches, as is alleged, higher Islam, so it does higher Hinduism:

"Dr. Tara Chand went out of his way in his adventures in history
to allege that Guru Nanak Dev knew more of Islam than of
Hinduism. His allegation was repeated by Sardar Iqbal Ali Shah.
My conclusion is that if there was anyone who knew the whole
of Higher Hinduism and Higher Islam it was Guru Nanak Dev"
                                                    (Diwana 1981:5).

It follows that it was not the intention of the Gurus to displace either Hinduism
or Islam, but to disengage them both from their narrow medieval problematics and
practices and to turn their practitioners to a life full of truth and love of God, man
and nature.[11] All those who chose to follow and defend the new revelation became
Sikhs (Disciples) and eventually the Khalisah or, as in quotidian discourse, Khalsa.

To conclude this brief disquisition: the question of (and answer to) religious
diversity is inscribed within the heart of the Sikh revelation, as is apparent from the
structure of the Granth Sahib and the architecture of the Gurudwara, if we do not
also want to include, in our symbolic reference, the varying costumes of Baba Nanak.[12]
There is unity, the Gurus held, not only in the variety of natural forms, but also of
religious forms. All religions are equally true and truly equal, and also perhaps equally
imperfect. Thus in the formulation of Kapur Singh (1979:27), Sikhism stands for
multicentric, plural, or non-totalitarian society as the normal and natural mode of
human social existence.

In the preceding section, we saw how Sikhism affirms the truth and reality of
nature, history and society, discountenancing individual renunciation or mass desertion
as forms of protest against oppressive society or state. In the present section, we
have seen how Sikhism upholds the principle of religious equality (or freedom) and
plural society. Already we have intimations of the basic axiological principles with
which the ideal or dream of Khalsa raj is woven.

Towards the Formation of the Khalsa Panth: Discourse of History

Perhaps we can close in upon our basic problem by raising some appropriate questions. Who, we may ask, can violate the principle of religious equality and plural society? Obviously, not the humble, the weak, or the dispossessed, but only those who wield power. What is the source of such power? It is the State or the King, above all in the medieval context. Now, what if the State or the King violates the principle and begins to discriminate and oppress?

The Gurus had understood from the very beginning, such an understanding being part of the revelation, that it was not so much religious diversity as unequal power between the rulers and the ruled that was problematical. Therefore, as part of their mission they were required not only to declare the truth about the equality of all religions, but also provide an institutional framework to contain and finally liquidate the asymmetrical power equation. We know the Gurus' ultimate institutional answer: the Khalsa Panth, which joins the axes of *piri* and *miri*, truth and power, religion and politics, or simply theory and practice. But before we turn to the final consummation, the discovery by Sikhism of its perfect exoteric form, let us eavesdrop on the discourse of history.

There are several questions, as yet unsettled, about the pre-British social formation and State in India. However, it is agreed that all the ruling members of the House of Babur (of the Timurind dynasty of Central Asia) after Akbar discriminated, more or less, against the non-Muslims on the lines of the Delhi Sultanate. Looking a little more closely, one discerns three types in the religious and political policies pursued by the Mughals, ruling or non-ruling, in relation to the non-Muslim communities: namely, those of *synthesis* (Akbar), *unity in variety* (Dara Shukoh) and assertion of the *superiority of the Islamic revelation* over others (Aurangzib).

Akbar (1556-1605) followed a consciously syncretist strategy, which culminated in the eclectical *din-ilahi*, a non-starter as everyone knows. Dara Shukoh (1615-1657), a disciple of Sufi saint Mulla Shah and close to Sarmad, stressed the unity underlying various religions, the outstanding testimony being his *Majma al-bohrayan*. In this remarkable work, Dara compared the technical terms of Sufism and Vedanta and came to the conclusion that "there were no differences except purely verbal in the way in which Vedanta and Islam sought to comprehend the Truth" (Satish Chandra 1965: 134-35). Dara also believed, like Akbar, that State should remain above all religions. In contrast, Aurangzib (1658-1707) not only believed in the superiority of Islam over other religions, but also that this fact should reflect in State policies.

"A strong reaction against religious syncretism with the Hindus
asserted itself under Aurangzeb, who of all Mughal Emperors

was the one who gave the most weight to Islamic, specifically
Sunni, legitimation and who was most intransigent in his
ambition to bring the entire subcontinent under the *dar al-Islam*"
                                                    (Wink 1984: 283).

"The legal systems of the late Empires (Ottoman, Safavid and
Mughal), too, were typically reclericalised, religious doctrines
gaining enhanced administrative force over previously casual
secular customs, with the passage of time.... Military rigidity,
ideological zealotry and commercial lethargy thus became the
usual norms of government in Turkey, Persia and India"
                                                    (Anderson 1975: 517).

"But then the tide turned, and during the reigns of Jahangir,
Shahjahan and Aurangzeb, Mughal imperial policy, especially
the policy of these three monarchs towards the Sikhs in general
and the Sikh Gurus in particular, seems to have been definitely
hostile and inimical. The details are too well known to any
student of Indian history, and need not therefore be recounted.
Guru Arjan and Guru Tegh Bahadur fell victims to the general
policy of persecution of the Hindus pursued by Jahangir and
Aurangzeb respectively, though it may be contended that in
each case there seem to have been specific immediate causes
and events that led to the martyrdom of the two Gurus associated
with the meanest and cruellest barbarities of the medieval world"
                                                    (Ray 1975: 24).

Obviously, it was the policy of religion and politics pursued by Aurangzib
and some of his predecessors that served as a catalyst in effecting a formal shift
within Sikhism and paving the way for the formation of the Khalsa Panth.[13] Although
the Khalsa Panth was the entelechy or the logical culmination of Sikhism, its formation
was linked to and mediated by a specific historical conjuncture. At the same time,
however, the Sikh Gurus clearly recognised that the problem of the inequality and
abuse of power was not a conjunctural aberration of sorts, but a structural issue
requiring an institutional solution valid beyond the demands of immediate history.

The Order of the Khalsa, its form and organisation were not born all at once,
but they crystallised over time through a process of evolution, which was perhaps as
necessary as it was drawn out. Guru Nanak Dev (1469-1539), the Founder-Guru,
who laid the foundations of the new faith, also simultaneously laid the foundations
of a critique of tyranny. There was a clear awareness in him that moral order in
human society could not surely subsist without a right kind of political order. Mohan
Singh Diwana (1967: 247-48) has summed up Guru Nanak's critique as follows:

"The Founder-Guru was the first known Indian poet who called India Hindustan, who mentioned all the three conquering Muslim dynasties, Turk, Pathan and Mughal, and who made it clear that their conquests had confronted the goat-hearted Indians not with civilised invaders but with bluerobed barbarians.

He termed the rulers of the age butchers with long knives, agents of darkness engulfing the lights of law and order. As stressed by Guru Nanak Dev, the fivefold challenge of the Muslim was that the subjugated people must: (i) give up Sanskrit learning; (ii) accept conversion, or at any rate, build no new temples and resign themselves to the desecration and destruction of extant temples and idols; (iii) disarm; (iv) tolerate rapine and one way intermarriage; and (v) yield up their savings and a proportion of income in one form or another. The Founder-Guru's initial response was to charge God with having brought to pass this unequal struggle of the carnivorous tiger and the docile goat, permitting mass rape, terrorization, massacre and enslavement; advancing and aggrandizing Khorasan at the expense of Hindustan; and never giving a sign of His compassion and pain at such suffering. Nanak foretold that soon a valiant disciple and protagonist of a fighter Guru would arise to even the scales and exact retribution. He assured those in chain that the doom of the enchainers would be accomplished and at the very hands of the enchained ones."

The next nine Gurus in succession (with the exception of the eighth Guru Harkrishan, who died young) consolidated the political critique as well as the religious doctrine by adopting institutional measures of great symbolic and functional significance. The doctrine was finally consolidated in the form of the *Adi Granth* by Guru Arjan Dev (1581-1606), while the institutional defence against the abuse of state power was consolidated in the form of the Khalsa Panth by Guru Gobind Singh. Guru Gobind Singh later conferred guruship on the Adi Granth and the Khalsa Panth, "thus completing the threefold equation of the godhead, the word as the Guru and the congregation, perhaps recalling the Buddhist trinity of the Buddha, the Dhamma and the Sangha, or the threefold unity of Islam of the godhead (*tanhid*), the scripture (*kalam-i-Allah*) and the community of the faithful (*ummat*)" (Uberoi n.d.: 11).

Let us pause for a while and look back at the thesis stated above. All the Gurus were concerned, in one way or another, with questions of truth and questions of power. However, the first half of the Guru-period, from Guru Nanak to Guru Arjan Dev, was largely taken up with questions of truth and the consolidation of the doctrine. The second half of the Guru period, from Guru Arjan Dev to Guru Gobind Singh, explicitly dealt with questions of power including chiefly the contradiction between the principle of religious equality and plural society, on one side, and the assymetries of power, on the other. It was Guru Arjan Dev indeed who combined the two concerns in equal measure with his pontificate marking the strategic transition from one accent to the other.

Several strategic things seem to have happened during Guru Arjan's time. The influx of the warlike Jat peasantry into the Sikh fold, for instance, is one which has been noted and emphasised. There were, however, more subtle ideological developments within Sikhism, which have escaped the attention of many. The Sikh doctrine had always emphasised the unity and identity of God, Word, Guru and King. It seems that with the compilation of the *Adi Granth* and the institution of hereditary guruship, the kingly, regal, or sovereign aspect of the Guru and God became pronounced. God was Light and Truth (Word), but He was also Power (King) and so was the Guru who thus became the True King.

> "Guru Ramdas who succeeded Guru Amar Das, before he breathed his last, made the institution of Guru hereditary; this decision had also very important political significance and also perhaps important socio-psychological consequences. By the time Guru Arjan was installed as the Guru in full regalia of power and authority and in impressive pomp and splendour, he was declared and accepted by the Sikh Community as *Sacha Padshah*, that is, as their true or real ruler, spiritual and temporal, evidently in contradiction to the false Padshah who was sitting on the throne at Delhi."
>
> (Ray op cit: 25).

Guru Arjan Dev was executed on the orders of Emperor Jahangir in 1606 in accordance with the Mongol law of *yasa*. As narrated in *Tuzk-i Jahangiri*, the Guru was killed partly for his religion and partly for his politics. According to Indubhushan Banerjee (1972: II,3), in addition to the charge of supporting Prince Khusrau, who rebelled against the Emperor:

> "...the charges against the Guru also included the allegation that he called himself the "True King" *(saccha padshah)* that he had established a large organisation with the intention of making war upon the Emperor, and that he had compiled a book which blasphemed both the Hindus and the Mussalmans."

The execution of Guru Arjan Dev moved the succeeding Gurus and the Sikhs from criticism and individual martyrdom to collective armed defence and offence against the Mughal State. Guru Arjan's son, Guru Hargobind, discarded the *seli-topi*, the traditional headgear and the necklace of renunciation, at the time of succession and instead wore two swords of *miri and piri*, of temporal power and spiritual power, as symbols of his indivisible sovereignty. He kept a standing army and built the Akal Takht as the throne of the True King, the Guru and God:

> "Guru Hargobind also fortified Amritsar and built the Akal Takht opposite the Har Mandir, dispensing justice and temporal orders from the former and spiritual guidance from the latter, and living all the time like a king with all the trappings of kingship.

> By the time of Guru Gobind Singh the Sikh community had been all but transformed from a purely religious group to a highly organised body of men and women within a given area, militant in spirit and oriented towards meeting any challenge to their faith and their society, a challenge that came not only from the Mughal emperors and their governors but also from the Hindu rajas of the Punjab Himalayas, more from the latter."

> (Ray op cit : 25).

Guru Hargobind's son and Guru Gobind Singh's father Guru Tegh Bahadur was beheaded in 1675, his execution and martyrdom following the same pattern as that of Guru Arjan Dev. This was the moment, so to speak, of final denouement: the creation of the Khalsa Panth as the perfect form of Sikhism and signifying, in fact, the unity of the temporal and the spiritual, but also of the Guru and the Sikhs.

The Khalsa Panth versus the State

It was on the Baisakhi day in 1699 that Guru Gobing Singh summoned an assembly of his followers at Anandpur Sahib. What happened on that momentous day? W.H. McLeod (1975: 14-15) recapitulates the Sikh tradition in this regard as follows:

> "Summoned from far and wide, his followers had gathered in their thousands at Anandpur Sahib. The Guru had, however, concealed himself in a tent which had been erected on the fair-ground. There he remained in seclusion until the fair was in full swing, when suddenly he emerged before his followers. With fearsome countenance and sword raised aloft he demanded the head of any one of his Sikhs.

> A hush fell upon the mighty concourse and the Guru repeated his demand. Eventually a loyal Sikh came forward and was conducted to the tent. Those who remained outside heard the

thud of a descending sword and observed with horror that the Guru, when he reappeared, bore a blood-stained weapon. Their horror increased when he demanded a second head, and when another Sikh came forward the same process was repeated. Eventually five such volunteers were escorted into the tent. When the Guru reappeared after dispatching his fifth victim he proceeded to draw back the side of the tent. Horror changed to amazement when the gathering observed the five supposed victims alive and well. Beside them lay the corpses of five decapitated goats.

The Guru delivered a sermon. The five who had in loyalty to him volunteered their lives were, he declared, to constitute the nucleus of a new brotherhood, the Khalsa. Those who chose to enlist in the brotherhood were to abandon pride of caste; they were to abandon the old scriptures and places of pilgrimage; and they were to abandon the worship of minor gods and goddesses, and *avatars*. Instead they were to follow only God and the Guru.

Next the Guru prepared *amrit*, or nectar, for a baptismal ceremony. Sweets were mingled with water in an iron bowl and stirred with a two-edged sword. The preparation was administered to the five foundation members who were then instructed to administer the same baptism to the Guru himself. After this all who were willing to join the brotherhood and to accept its discipline were invited to take baptism, and it is said that many thousands of all castes came forward.

Finally, the discipline was promulgated. Five groups of people were to be avoided, all of them either the followers of relatives who had at various times disputed the succession to the Guruship, or else cutters of hair. Various prohibitions were enjoined, notably tobacco, meat from animals slaughtered in the Muslim fashion, and sexual intercourse with Muslim women. And five symbols were to be worn.. the five Ks. All men joined the brotherhood were to add Singh, or Lion, to their given name, and all women were to add Kaur. Thus was the Khalsa Brotherhood... established which in unity, loyalty and courage was to struggle against overwhelming odds, survive the cruellest of persecution, and ultimately rise to supremacy on the ruins of Mughal power and Afghan pretensions."

Guru Gobind Singh created the new Order in a dramatic fashion and laid down its framework and distinct exoteric form. The Khalsa Order was indeed a new institutional structure, but composed of many preexisting elements, the symbols and the instruments, that had evolved in the course of Sikh history.

Now, according to Niharranjan Ray (op. cit.:69), one chief purpose of the Baisakhi of Guru Gobind Singh was to "effect a revolutionary change in the concept of guruhood and in the organisation of that institution and at the same time of the Sikh Society itself":

> "Every step that he took, from the preparation of background and the first call of sacrifice, to his own initiation at the hands of *panj piyaras* and the final step of the declaration of the Khalsa and the Sri Guru Granth Saheb as together replacing the corporeal and hereditary Guru, seems to have been thought out very carefully and worked out very systematically.

> What Guru Gobind Singh did was to my mind, the logical culmination of the process that was started by Guru Nanak himself. Guruhood was meant to be selective; but when Guru Ramdas made it hereditary he introduced a process which contradicted the original principle... Guru Gobind Singh.. abolished altogether the institution of corporeal Guru and installed the Book as the Guru. The organisational and administrative aspects of the institution he chose to vest on a body corporate which he called the Khalsa; its mission was to carry out the spiritual and secular message that resided in the Book"

> (ibid.:69-70).

Let us recall that Sikhism always believed in the equation of God, Guru (=Word) and King (=Sword). To this equation Guru Gobind Singh added the fourth term, the Panth, so that we have the following homologous pairs:

Guru : King
::
Truth : Power
::
Word : Sword
::
Piri : Miri
::
Hari Mandir : Akal Takht
::
Granth : Panth

Sikhism may be defined as the unity of Guru, Granth and Panth. According to the above scheme, the Adi Granth becomes the Guru, the living symbol and instrument of spiritual authority, while the Khalsa Panth assumes kingship becoming the living symbol and instrument of temporal authority.

The Order of the Khalsa is the Order of the Pure (from the Arabic root *Khalis),* but also at the same time the Order of the Sovereign ones (from the well known concept of the *Khalisah lands),* that is, the Guru's and God's very own and directly linked and loyal to Him and to no one else. What could be the political intent and function of such an Order as the Khalsa Confraternity in relation to the State? What could be its politics?

The Khalsa Panth, or Guru Panth, was the final answer to the contradiction between unequal power (e.g. between the rulers and the ruled) and the principle of religious equality and plural society enunciated by the Gurus. It was not a conjunctural response only, as we said earlier, but a structural solution of the problem of the abuse of power. The political intent of the Khalsa, as the Army of God or Dharma was and is to watch over the State and intervene, if necessary through *dharma yuddha,* to influence and correct it. Dharma Yuddha, as an extension of the principle of service (*seva*) indeed, is the political ideal or the ideal praxis of the Khalsa.

If the above is not sufficiently clear, then let me say that it was not the goal of the Khalsa of Guru Gobind Singh to capture state power or to become State-like (State within State) but to serve as a counterweight to State tyranny. Let me quote a remarkable passage from Kapur Singh (1959), who had studied the whole problem of the Sikh theory of religion and politics in great depth. Making an exegesis of a text from Guru Gobind Singh's *Bachitranatak,* he writes:

> "There is no doubt left by the Guru about his meanings... He says that there are two forces which claim allegiance of men's souls on earth, the Truth and Morality as Religion, and the State as embodiment of mere utilitarianism and secular politics. The primary allegiance of man is to the Truth and Morality, and those who fail in this allegiance, suffer under the subjugation of the earthly state, unnourished by the courage and hope which is born through unswerving adherence to their primary allegiance. In this perpetual struggle between the State and Church, for the exclusive possession of the soul of man, a man of culture and religion, shall not lose sight ever of his primary allegiance, and he who does so, does it at his own peril, for by doing so, he helps give birth to times in which everything is force, politics, utility and labour, poverty and hardship, tyranny and slavery, for the religious and moral spirit is suppressed or

destroyed and men become coarse and diabolic. The Guru does not assert that this perpetual dichotomy and antagonism of the Church and the State must be resolved, or even that it is capable of being resolved by the suppression or subjugation of the one by the other; rather, he appears to recognise their eternal antagonism and character and in this antagonism sees the hope and glory of Man, the social and political context in which the Sikh Way of Life is to be practised. The Church must perpetually correct and influence the State without aiming to destroy or absorb it, for, as the History shows the attempt of the one to oust the other meets with no lasting success, and each of the two antagonistic entities arises again and again after having been crushed in vain and both appear anew as if bound together. This is what the Guru means, when he declares in the text, that the "the House of Baba Nanak and the house of Babur, God makesh them both" and "those who repudiate their allegiance to the House of Nanak, suffer grievously, without hope, at the hands of the State".

It is easy, at least for me, to agree with the spirit, if not entirely with the form of the above argument, except in one respect. It seems that the ideal tripartite structure envisaged by Guru Gobind Singh for human society consists of a non-discriminating and non-oppressive State and plural society, both guarded by the Khalsa. But that is in the first or intermediate stage. I believe that the ultimate agenda of the Khalsa is to destroy the State and end the contradiction between State and society, or between state power and people's power, in the long run and move the human society towards some kind of moral self-government. Even if this is held to be utopian, I believe with the great British historian Edward Thompson (1976:83-111) who died recently, that utopiansim has great value in 'educating human desire'.

The Litany Again

Let us return to the litany of raj kerega Khalsa, which was addressed to the Sikhs and the non-Sikhs, the disruptors of the Khalsa within and without and which was couched in terms of the prenationalist discursive opposition of universal dominion versus *fitna* recently studied by Andre Wink, and ask what it finally means. The litany simply means that the institution of Khalsa or the Khalsa Confraternity is the only effective counterweight and protection against the abuse of power by the state and that its truth and power shall prevail in the long run. The litany does not mean that the Khalsa should capture state power and become rulers in the ordinary sense and institute new assymetries of power.

NOTES

1. (i) Etymologically: 'Ardas is a Sanskrit word, from the root *ard*, to ask, to beg, to pray, and *aas* means wish, hope, desire. To ask for what you desire is *ardas*, that is, prayer' (Kapur Singh 1959:437). Kapur Singh obviously follows Bhai Kahn Singh Nabha (1960:61). For an alternative etymology, which traces the origin of *ardas* to the Persian *arzdashta*, see Balbir Singh et al 1975:384.

According to Kapur Singh (ibid.:438-40), as a mode of communion with God, *ardas* is radically distinct from Hindu *yajna*, *puja*, or *prarthana*, Buddhist meditation and Jaina *tapas*. He writes: 'The basic activity of Sikhism is *simrin*, communion with God through the yogic discipline of Name:its obligated and mandatory context is *seva*, loving service of fellow human beings and prayer is the prescribed vitality of this activity. Prayer supports *simrin* which grows and matures in social context. Congregational prayer is, thus, an essentially Sikh institution in India' (p.441).

Apart from its cultic significance, we believe, that the way it brings together religion, politics and history, the real and the ideal, or the concerns of the individual and the concerns of the community and society, a structural study of (the text of) *ardas* can yield not only useful insights into the exoteric form of Sikhism, but also an ideal model for Sikh history and historiography with *dharma-yuddha* as its central focus and organising category.

(ii) The text of ardas, as it stands today, has evolved over time, with more and more of symbolic events in Sikh history getting incorporated into it. Writes Kapur Singh (1959): 'The Sikh congregational prayer is a product of communal composition, which has developed through various stages of the Sikh History quite up to present times, by common consensus of the Sikh community' (p.441). Also see Teja Singh (1938:128-36).

2. (i) Here are a few more translations of the verse:

The Khalsa shall rule, no enemy shall remain.
All those who endure suffering and privation shall be brought to the
safety of the Guru's protection   (McLeod 1984:78).

The Khalsa shall rule. Their enemies shall be scattered.
Only they that seek refuge will be saved
                                                           (Khushwant Singh 1977:90).

The Khalsa shall rule, no hostile refractory shall exist.
Frustrated they shall all submit, and those who come in for shelter
shall be protected   (Ganda Singh 1981:135).

(ii) There is some confusion whether the couplet of raj karega Khalsa is part of ardas. For instance, Puran Singh (1981:123-25) and Teja Singh (1938:21-28) do not include it in their English renderings of the text of the prayer. Similarly, Khushwant Singh writes: 'The lines raj karega Khalsa are not found in the Dasam Granth but are by tradition ascribed to Guru Gobind Singh. They are repeated every time *after* supplicatory prayer, the *ardas* (emphasis added). However, in the view of Kapur Singh (1959:450), the prayer is over only after the recitation of the litanical couplet. We are inclined to follow Kapur Singh. At any rate, the uncertainty as to the exact status of the couplet in relation to *ardas* or its dating (see below) does not really affect the kind of analysis we are undertaking.

3.   The lines (raj karega Khalsa) first occur in the *Tanakhah-nama* (in Punjabi) of Bhai Nandlal Goya (1633?-1713?), a Persian poet and contemporary follower and associate of Guru Gobind Singh. The *Tanakhah-nama* is in question-answer form. The words are uttered by the tenth Guru himself in response to a query from Nandlal.

However, the authorship of the *Tanakhah-nama* has been contested, among others, by Bhai Kahn Singh Nabha. For various details see Ganda Singh (1968). Ganda Singh himself likes to believe that the work (*Tanakhah-nama*) is by Bhai Nandlal Goya. And yet in another piece, he remarks as follows: 'Just as all other historical allusions in the prayer refer to past history, so does this couplet refer to the days of the later Mughals, Bahadurshah to Shah Alam II. It was evidently composed and first sung by the Khalsa during the days of Banda Singh Bahadur (1710-16) who was the first Sikh political leader to declare the independence of his people in the Punjab, (Ganda Singh 1981:135). Other scholars may assign it to a still later date.

4.   Each of the two popular interpretations, the political and the religious, as it stands, is obviously flawed. The former lends support to a strange and asymmetrical power equation as the desired goal of Sikhism:

Sikhs : Non-Sikhs

: :

Rulers : Ruled

This is irreligion. The latter is meaningless because it is non-specific. However, the two interpretations yield crucial variables: namely, those of power and truth, which have to be preserved together in a different and higher synthesis. This is the meaning of sublation.

5. (i) Kapur Singh (1979:27) shares this view: 'The rise of Sikhism synchronised with the advent of the Mughals into this country. The basic problem of the imperial Mughal rule was to consolidate the domination of Islam and the Mughals in India. The basic problem of Sikhism was to determine the grounds for an enduring coordination of the

Semitic ideology and culture with the Aryan spirit and culture' (our translation).

(ii) The notion of mediation should not compromise the status of Sikhism as a fresh and independent revelation, or pretend to exhaust its totality. Perhaps the question was settled long ago. Anyone who has confronted the following hard-hitting words of Mohan Singh Uberoi (1969:1) cannot conceive of Sikhism in terms of vulgar syncretism: 'Nanakism is not a corrupt rustic dialect of Islam nor a far-flung province or an island-colony of the empire of Hinduism. It is not a hangover of Buddhism. It is not a political move masquerading as religious reform, nor an exhibition of change from search for God to search for national integration and universal peace on the battlefield. Nanak is an accusing finger lifted at all contemporary divisors-exploiters, pointing out that their verbal currency has got debased, that their signs have lost the original direction, that there is no grammar in the society, and no syntax in their souls. He was not a beggar setting out to collect crumbs of doctrines and practices. He was not fishing for dialectical victories which the Buddha and Shankara cherished. He had his own God-given pass-word for entering the kingdom of God here and now: "There is nothing else but the one Himself who appears to stage His show for the unlimited exercise of His forgiveness, love, joy and total regard for the all-whole."' All said, however, let us recognise that part of the Sikh Gurus' mission was to reconcile religious diversity with the unity of God: *Ek Khasam do rah*. Thus Puran Singh (1981:234) wrote: 'The Ten Gurus are the first in the history of man to take up the essential idea that later developed as the comparative study of religions, and declared with the emphasis of their distinctive individuality that Ram and Rahim are one and the Feranghi, the Turk, the Hindu and the Muslim are men first.' The notion of mediation has only this much meaning and no more.

6.   On Semitic monotheism and its internal dialectics of thesis (Judaism), anti-thesis (Christianity) and synthesis (Islam), see Schuon (n.d.). For a rounded view of the religions of the Abrahamic family, they should be considered along with their mystical halves - Kabbalah (Judaism), gnosticism (Christianity) and Sufism (Islam) - and various sectarian off-shoots.

7   Sikhism regards the one (mysticism), Absolute (philosophy) and God (religion) as modalities of the same (ultimately) indefinable Reality and Truth. This renders senseless the conventional oppositions of God as spectator and God as actor (theology), creation and emanation (cosmology), faith, ritual and knowledge (epistemology), *dvaita* and *advaita*, *pravritti* and *nivritti* and so on. Sikhism encompasses and depasses the opposing terms.
      In fact, Sikhism has required a new hermeneutics and a new symbolic-conceptual vocabulary at the level of intellectual discourse. The requirement has remained largely unfulfilled.

8.   Sikhism steers clear of the two unacceptable alternatives of pantheism (nature = God)

and Manichaeism (nature = anti-God). Nature is distinct and real, but ultimately subsumed under the God-head.

In a rare piece on Sikh cosmology, Kapur Singh sums up Guru Nanak's concept of nature as follows: 'The religious system and the way of life which Guru Nanak revealed and preached are based on the philosophical doctrines that the Absolute *Purusa* both as self-conscious and unconscious, is the matrix of the world and not simply a term in a confection or admixture, that the world has a Creator, that as created Nature it has no absolute basis or essence independently and apart from this *Purusa*, and last, that the relation between the Creator and the created Nature is not a separate category of existence, but is merely an extension, an emanation of the *Purusa*. This one Absolute *Purusa* is to be contra-distinguished from the *Purusa* of the Vedas... This *Purusa* of the Vedas is not the Creator and Controller of the world but just the neutral stuff of the manifest and the unmanifest worlds, not fundamentally and essentially different from the *Purusa* of the *Samkhya*,'

Introducing his translation of the *Japu* entitled *The mystic ladder*, Dr. Mohan Singh Diwana-Uberoi (1979:3) says: 'Particular attention of the reader is drawn to the revelation that nature directly makes to us. It gives us the essence of truth, it gives us things to hear, see, fear, love, contemplate as essence. While man is limited in his reaches, nature presents unlimited spectacles much closer to its spectator's because man's will in a way puts distance between his maker and himself while there is no distance between God and nature for she is directly His power, His beauty, His sublimity and sails above good and evil. Nature is the very truth of the truth, the visible truth of the invisible formless truth.'

(ii) Nature, body-mind, kingship and woman are modalities of the Divine Power (*qudrat*). Sikhism revalues and revalorises them and regards them as indispensable for human emancipation.

9. The reference is to the work of J.P.S. Uberoi (1969:123-138). Uberoi writes: 'Thus the total ideological and social structure of the medieval Hindu world, including its political institution, rested upon a tripartite division and a system of interrelations among the three worlds symbolised by the King, the *Brahman* and the *Sannyasi*. The domains of *rajya*, *varna grihastha* and of *sannyasa* formed the three sides of the medieval triangle. The same total structure can perhaps be seen in Islamic civilisation of the period in the division and interrelations among the three spheres of *hukumat*, *shar'iat* and *tariqat* or *haqiqat*' (p.134). He continues: 'The new departure of Sikhism, in my interpretation, was that it set out to annihilate the categorical partitions, intellectual and social, of the medieval world. It rejected the opposition of the common citizen or householder versus the renouncer, and of the ruler versus these two, refusing to acknowledge them as separate and distinct modes of existence. It acknowledged the power of the three spheres of *rajya*, *sannyasa* and *grihastha*, but sought to invest

their virtues conjointly in a single body of faith and conduct' (135-36).

10.   The brief exposition of the Sikh symbols, popularly known as the five'Ks', is largely
        based on Uberoi (1969), but also see Kapur Singh (1959:85-107, 137-154). As for the
        injunction against circumcision, Uberoi (ibid.: 132) quotes from M.A. Macauliffe:
        'Ajmer Chand inquired what the marks of the Guru's Sikhs were, that is, how they
        could be recognised. The Guru replied, "My Sikhs shall be in their natural form, that
        is, without the loss of their hair or foreskin, in opposition to ordinances of the Hindus
        and the Muhammadans"'.

        The structural equivalence or homology of circumcision and head-shaving in ritual
        context is well appreciated in anthropological literature. For instance see Leach
        (1976:77-79).

11.   The Sikh Gurus adopted a complex or, if we are allowed the expression, dialectical
        attitude to Hinduism and Islam. They (i) affirmed the essential truth of the revelations
        contained in the *Vedas* and the *Katebas* (sacred Books of the semitic religions: Judaism,
        Christianity and Islam) without ever implying, however, that the divine mysteries
        could be exhausted by either or both of them, (ii) invited the Hindus and the Muslims
        to renew or revitalise the exoteric forms of their respective religions and (iii) came
        down heavily on the disjunction of the spiritual, the temporal and the material in
        medieval Hinduism and medieval Islam.

12.   It is well-known that Guru Granth Sahib contains the hymns of Hindu and Muslim
        saints in addition to those of the Sikh Gurus. For details see Talib (1991).

        As for the architecture of the Gurudwara, Ray (1975:53-54) comments: 'But let us
        enter into a gurdwara. The traditional architectural plan and design of a gurdwara are
        admittedly a result of a creative synthesis of Hindu, Buddhist and Muslim religious
        architecture of the late medieval period, that is, it is Indo-Muslim in character.'
        On Baba's costumes, see, for instance, Bhai Gurdas 91990:16) Archer (1946:75-76)
        writes: 'He sought to reconcile the religions of his day, and even the costume he wore
        in travelling was symbolic of his mission to the larger world. Since garb was a means
        of identifying teachers of religion, his was usually composite. However, further details
        provided by Archer about Baba's composite garb seem rather far-fetched and unreliable.

13.   According to Kapur Singh (1979:32-57), the radical turn in Mughal policy towards
        the non-Muslims took place under the influence of the doctrine of *wahdat-ul-shuhud*
        (unity of appearance) of the Naqashbandi Shaikh Ahmad Sirhindi (1561-1625) put
        forth in opposition to the doctrine of *wahdat-ul-wujud* (unity of existence) followed
        by all other Sufi sects in India including the Qadiris to whom Mian Mir and Dara
        Shukoh belonged. Whatever be the judgement on this aspect of the question, it needs
        to be pointed out that during Guru Gobind Singh's pontificate, Aurangzib constituted

only one half of the provocation, the other being the hill-rajas. Niharranjan Ray (op. cit.) writes: 'One must however recognise that there was a cluster of Hindu chieftains, mainly of Rajput origin, sheltered in the valleys of what was until recently known as the Punjab Himalayas... (From) about the eleventh century onwards, these small feudal citadels of an ossified religion - of Brahminical Hinduism, of orthodoxy and obscurantism - were all but oblivious of the challenges that Hinduism and Hindu society were facing below in the plains (p.1.)'. And further: 'It is curious however that the Hindu *rajas* of the hills were not taken in by this changed attitude of Guru Gobind Singh. They were shrewd and sharp enough to realize what the Guru was invoking Durga or Chandi and the *avataras* of Krishna for, and to know that despite all these the Guru remained the same crusader against Hindu, Smarta-Pauranik Brahmanism and its *jati* system. As a matter of fact, the Hindu *rajas* were sharper and more persistent thorns on the Guru's sides than the Mughals (p. 20-21)'.

BIBLIOGRAPHY

Anderson, P. 1974. *Lineages of the Absolutist State.* London: NLB.

Archer, J.C. 1946. *The Sikhs.* Princeton: Princeton University Press.

Balbir Singh et al (eds.). 1975. *Nirukta Shri Guru Granth Sahib*, Vol II. Patiala: Punjabi University.

Bannerjee, I. 1972. *Evolution of the Khalsa*, Vol II. Calcutta: A. Mukherjee and Co.

Diwana, Mohan Singh. 1981. Guru Nanak looks at the Universes. *The Tribune* (November 8): 5.

Ganda Singh (ed.). 1968. *Bhai Nandlal Granthawali.* Malaysia: Mlacca.

          1981. Raj Karega Khalsa. *The Sikh Review* 328: 135-37.

Gurdas, Bhai. 1990. *Varan Gian Ratnavali.* Sri Amritsar: SGPC.

Kapur Singh. 1959. *Prasharprasna.* Jullundur: Hind Publishers.

          1975. Guru Nanak's Concept of Nature. In Harbans Singh, ed., *Perspectives on Guru Nanak*, pp. 45-46. Patiala: Punjabi University.

          1979. *Sachi Sakhi.* Delhi: Navyug.

Khushwant Singh. 1977. *A History of the Sikhs*, Vol I. Delhi: Oxford University Press.

Leach, E. 1976.   *Culture and communication.* Cambridge: Cambridge University Press.

McLeod, W.H. 1975. *The Evolution of the Sikh community.* Delhi: Oxford University Press. (ed.).

          1984. *Textual Sources for the Study of Sikhism.* Manchester: Manchester University Press.

Mohan Singh. 1967. Arabic-Persian Key-words in Sikhism: Their Origin and Meaning. In *Sikhism and Indian Society*, pp. 247-59. Shimla: Institute of Advanced Study.

Puran Singh. 1981. *Spirit of the Sikh*, Vol II. Patiala: Punjabi University.

Ray, Niharranjan. 1975. *The Sikh Gurus and the Sikh society.* New Delhi: Munshiram Manoharlal.

Satish Chandra. 1965. Dara Shukoh. In B.Lewis et al, eds., *The Encyclopedia of Islam*, pp. 134-135. London: Faber and Faber.

Talib, Gurbachan Singh. 1991. *An Introduction to Guru Granth Sahib*. Patiala: Punjabi University.

Teja Singh. 1938. *Sikhism: Its Ideals and Institutions*. Bombay: Longmans, Green and Co. Ltd.

Thompson, E.P. 1976. Romanticism, Utopianism and Moralism: The Case of William Morris. *New Left Review* 99: 83-III.

Uberoi, J.P.S. 1969. The Five Symbols of Sikhism. In Fauza Singh et al, *Sikhism*, pp. 123-138. Patiala: Punjabi University. *n.d.*

Sikhism and Islam: A Structural Analysis. Unpublished paper.

Uberoi-Diwana, Mohan Singh. 1979. *The Mystic Ladder: English Rendering of the Japu*. Chandigarh: Premjit Niwas.

Wink, A. 1984. Sovereignty and Universal Dominion in South Asia. *The Indian Economic and Social History Review* 3: 264-292.

Section II

Colonial Punjab and the Early Phase of Globalisation

Editors' Introduction

The papers in this section look upon the changes Punjab went through under the impact of colonial integration of Punjab into the global capitalist economy. This period witnesses the dialectical pull of two contradictory tendencies regarding the Punjabi identity. One tendency manifested through the politics of the Unionist party emphasised the unity of Punjabi people so much so that during the early period of Congress-Muslim league conflict, Khizr Hiyat Khan Tiwana went on to assert the distinctiveness of Punjab from the rest of Colonial India. The other tendency - in response to Christian missionaries' proselytising activities - manifested through the rise of revivalist movements among Punjabi Hindus, Muslims and Sikhs, worked to fragment the unified Punjabi identity.

All the papers in this section, except Arvindpal Singh's, fall broadly in the category of 'historical writing'. Arvindpal Singh's paper is a theoretical and methodological paper but we decided to include it in this section because its central thrust is the examination of the question of the relationship between colonialism and cultural identity. The generality of the issues raised in the paper around the question of colonialism, cultural difference and cultural identity make it a better companion, at least in our judgement, to the papers in this section though valid arguments can be advanced to put it in Section IV. By siting this paper as the first one in this section does not suggest any privileging of theory over history as much as placing this as the last one in the section (an alternative we did consider) would not have implied any privileging of history over theory. It is because this paper fits in very well, though from a critical perspective with the overall theme of globalisation and regional/cultural identity, that we thought that it would be more fruitful for the reader to read this before the other papers in this section.

Imran Ali's paper expands on one theme of his earlier pioneering work *Punjab Under Imperialism 1885-1947* which examined the impact of the development of canal colonies on Punjab's political economy. In this paper, Ali highlights the demographic consequences of this policy. The migration of a large number of rural based Sikhs and urban based Hindu traders and professionals from East Punjab to West Punjab during this period of the growth of canal colonies, created the material basis for agriculturally-based Punjabi unity on one hand and the ferocious sectarian violence during the partition period on the other when this unity was broken.

Masood Zahid's and Kamlesh Mohan's are a set of two papers which along with Parminder Bhachu's in Section IV constitute a much needed corrective to gender-bias in Punjab Studies. Masood Zahid's paper explores a rather neglected aspect of gender in social change in Punjab during the colonial rule. His paper shows that the colonial government further perpetuated and reinforced the existing prejudices and institutions against women's education in Punjab. Kamlesh Mohan's paper focuses on the sculpting of gender identities in Punjab in the wider context of colonial integration of Punjab into the global capitalist economy and culture. She examines the discourse of different forms of resistance - nationalist, social reformist, collaborationist, liberal, conservative and communitarian - to colonial economic and cultural hegemony by situating 'the women's question' as a central one in this contest. The paper explores, on one hand, the colonial agenda of moral imperialism in highlighting the oppressed status of women in India and, on the other, the Punjabi elites' adaptation to this onslaught by carefully selected construction of women's moral identity in a patriarchal society. The discussion on the engagement of Arya Samaj and Singh Sabha on the question of 'women's place in society' shows how in the process of responding to the colonial state's constructs of women's role in society, the Punjabi Hindu and Sikh elites incorporated their respective visions of women's role into their conceptions of differentiated Hindu and Sikh identities. The enmeshing of gender identities into regional and religious identities as a response to globalising influences of colonialism created contradictory consequences for women - some autonomy but also the legitimization of the 'household role' of women.

The papers by Iftikhar Malik, Sukhmani Riar and Indu Banga are a set of three papers which provide a historical perspective on the social, political and cultural processes during colonial rule which sharpened the religious cleavages in Punjabi identity. Malik's paper is a detailed analysis of the political process in colonial Punjab which witnessed the rivalry between Punjabi-identity based Unionist Party and the Pan-Muslim identity based Muslim league. His paper captures the two scenarios: first when Punjabi identity was more powerful and later, when it was overcome by Muslim identity.

Sukhmani Riar's paper on the origin of the demand for Khalistan and its pursuit during the period 1940-45 brings to light the collapse of the unified Punjabi identity under the strain of impending partition of India on religious-sectarian grounds and the consequent rise, therefore, of a political tendency among the Sikhs which advocated a separate homeland for the Sikhs.

Indu Banga shows very succinctly that the rise of Arya Samaj by emphasising a Pan-Hindu identity weakened Punjabi Hindus' regional identity as Punjabis. The importance of this paper in throwing light on the nature of fractured Punjabi identity even in the current phase of Punjabi history cannot be over-emphasised.

Nazar Tiwana's personal memoir of his father, Khizr Hayat Khan Tiwana who was the last Premier of the unified Punjab and the leader of the Punjab Unionist

Party from 1942-47, provides us a rare glimpse into the world view of a great Punjabi who opposed the 1947 partition of India from a Punjabi identity perspective and who is reported to have told an informal gathering of friends and family members in London in 1964: "Those of you who do not belong to my generation will live to see Punjabi identity overcome the effects of the religious divide of 1947 and enjoy the fruits of a prosperous and happy Punjab which transcends the limitations of a geographical map."

Writing Otherwise Than Identity:
Translation and Cultural Hegemony

Arvind-pal Singh

Introduction

There is always something rather bizarre about the notion of an Identity (with its capital 'I') that is spoken and written within a context and language that has apparently little to do with its predicate. A conference on 'Punjabi Identity' that takes place in the cosy setting of a western European university, in the language of the ex-coloniser might be just such a case in point. While on the surface such a setting might be a cause for celebration - of having attained to the status of a global identity, 80 million Punjabi speakers world-wide, in all walks of life, transcending religious boundaries etc. - the event of such a conference and the customary publication of a volume such as this, elides the attendant, though unseen, danger posed by the fact that the very question of 'Punjabi Identity', its continuity, change or otherwise, is necessarily linked to its articulation through speech and writing within a global economy of cultural exchange. It is one of the ironies of the colonial and post-colonial legacy that the specifically political economy which regulates cultural exchange also creates a situation where minority cultures construct a 'minor identity' (using Deleuze and Guattari's term) within a major language (English/Hindi/Urdu). Moreover this exchange and construction always occurs as a process which either remains invisible or is itself assimilated to an economy of translation set within the general framework of intercultural exchange, which not surprisingly, follows the division of international labour. The fact that inequality remains the main feature of intercultural exchange is also not surprising considering that the theoretical development of cultural exchange (translation theory included) has relied almost exclusively on the dominant European linguistic and cultural experience, which in turn relies on the implicit postulate of an egalitarian relationship between different linguistic and cultural areas.

In stark contrast, people for whom the articulation of a 'minor identity' is a necessity of their existence within a dominant culture, are faced with the paradoxical choice between (i) the impossibility of *not* writing - thereby not being represented, (ii) the impossibility of writing otherwise than in the dominant language. In other words, the act of writing a 'Punjabi Identity' itself represents the deterritorialisation of the minor language, as well as the connection of what is written to the status of political immediacy. Nevertheless, a 'Punjabi Identity' that is deterritorialised compensates for the loss of its native space by re-territorializing an alternative or marginal space within the dominant language via the agency of a metaphorical transfer of sense/meaning/signification, thus giving the impression of a continuity of essence.

Metaphorology therefore governs the commonly accepted economy of cultural translation.

Under what circumstance, then, can the assertion of something like a 'Punjabi Identity' be positively affirmed? Two examples immediately come to mind, both of which justify what has been stated above. The obvious example is the assertion of 'Punjabiat' by inhabitants of one or other of the Punjabi homelands - Pakistani Punjab and Indian Punjab. The assertion of identity in this case may be seen as a response to demands for the integration of minorities into dominant pan-Hindu or pan-Islamic nationalist cultures. The other example, and one that I shall mainly be concerned with in this essay, concerns the assertion of a collective identity by diaspora Punjabis, which is seen primarily as a response to recent events within Europe such as the disappearance of formerly secure state boundaries, the release of nationalist tensions and an emerging movement towards European unification. The drive towards the unification of Europe is undergirded by the search for a 'European Identity' that has supposedly existed, albeit implicitly, at the subjective and communal level. The whole discussion of what Europe is, is inextricably linked to a specific cultural concept, and therefore a cultural community that shares a common heritage and experience.

Despite the illusion of a vast cultural gulf between 'East' and 'West', there is, it seems, a common and inexorable logic to the South Asian and European movements of unification of the previously dispersed into the one, logic which in the very word unification implies the sense of 'official' and hence uniquely privileged. The logic is one of returning home, going back to origins, to what is authentically and properly European, Indian etc. Yet it is also a logic which in the purity of its idea of identity, refuses to acknowledge the signs of dissent, of the worst violences, of xenophobia and racism, religions and nationalist fanaticism. The commonality notwithstanding, the roots of this logic remain with the tradition of modernism from which the concepts of the sovereign nation state and national identity was conceived, namely, Europe's philosophical, religious and historical heritage. These varied discourses project a European cultural identity based on the idea of Europe as the first world consciousness, the heading or capital of global consciousness. Yet ironically this logic is split at the very moment of its identification, at the moment when origins are posited, due to the existence within Europe of what is not-European, or those to whom the logic of identity, the politics of the proper name, does not apply: immigrants, foreigners, non-European cultures.

This then is the locus of the problem which I hope to elaborate as this essay progresses. The articulation of "minor identity" by minority cultures within Europe and in previously colonised countries, is locked into a circle from which there appears to be no escape. On one level the circle is an economic one, linked to material production and the exchange of commodities. On a less well known level the circle is linked to a semantic crisis involving terms of identity and difference that structure the domain in which cultural discourse is produced. The crisis can be located at the point where notion of exchange-without-loss between different cultures is ruptured; which is tantamount to accepting the fact that translation is neither invisible nor politically neutral. Further, the crisis involves an awareness of the fact that the hegemonic discourse which inscribes the egalitarianism of cultural exchange 'is itself inscribed within a tradition that is already a discourse of the modern Western world.' This discourse is 'the most current and yet it dates back from a moment when Europe sees itself as the horizon'.

As exemplary of all current discourses of modernity it advances itself as the capital for the universal essence of humanity. And not just any modernity but the modernity that inscribes itself as the inscription of the Occident whose example is Europe. This discourse while written primarily within the philosophical/theological tradition of the West has involved an indissoluble relationship to economic and socio-political power. What began as a tentative, even discontinuous relationship between the discourses of philosophy, theology (onto-theo-logy), science, economics, and socio-politics, eventually coalesced into the *episteme* variously called the Enlightenment, the age of reason, or simply bourgeois capitalism. This historical merging bore witness to the currently dominant perceptions of representation, the thinking of being as 'world picture', the sedimentation of metaphysical-rational speculation into the techno-economics of 'enframing' where being is reduced to a mere 'standing reserve'. It is this *episteme* that 'caused' the emergence of the panoptic schemas of visualizing, the microphysics of power that constitutes the sovereign subject, all of which facilitated the achievement of a socio-political consensus i.e. a political identity (at the cost of difference) which was used as a disciplinary instrument for colonising the 'other' of this socio-political identity. Terms such as sovereign subject, capital, onto-theology, humanism, global information culture, universal rationality etc., are therefore means by which the European tradition - and specifically what will henceforth be called the onto-theological tradition - now expresses as the discourse of its cultural identity. What is often overlooked even in the so called emancipatory discourses that try to come to terms with the First World/Third World opposition, is the role of onto-theology in not only determining the essence of the humanism that is now the mark of Western European thinking, *but its role in equally determining the essence of the Third World's response*, often portrayed as a 'weak' or 'minor' language, to the privileged and dominant cultural identity of the West.

In this essay I specifically wish to explore the relationship between cultural identity and onto-theology from within the current historical epoch called the closure, or dislocation of European metaphysics, and to try and see how this dislocation as an event can allow us to glimpse the corresponding emergence of cultural difference from the margins of its own discourse, and by way of this dislocation to question the viability of projects based upon cultural identity in responding to the problem of representation in the text of a dominant culture. From this initial point my concerns will ramify out in two directions: firstly, to interrogate the problem of cultural identity from the perspective of the Punjabi diaspora. How is it that modernist European ideology continues to underpin the intellectual and political framework of South Asian (and particularly Punjabi) politics fifty years after decolonisation, and what consequences does this hold for the political and cultural coherence of diaspora communities in response to the upheavals of European integration? Secondly, to determine how the dominant discourse of the human sciences continues to buttress identity generating networks and discourses by diaspora communities and their countries of origin, thereby helping to retain the binary difference between European and non-European cultures. Does the academic adherence to methodological disciplinarianism hinder the emergence of cultural difference in the ethnographies of non-European cultures? With regard to the specific discourse of onto-theology, I shall begin by focusing attention on recent criticisms of the way in which the Western philosophical tradition has affected the *representation of* and *self-representation by* non-European cultures before, during and after colonialism.

The Ethnocentric Onto-theo-logic of European Cultural Identity

In his recent publication *The Other Heading* one of the foremost critics of Euro-centrism, Jacques Derrida brings the project of 'clotural' reading to bear on the current problems of Europe, particularly the conception of European cultural identity and its responsibility (in view of the Enlightenment's legacy of forgetting) to the 'other'; and specifically to the other 'non-European' cultures that have been suppressed under the dominating logic of metaphysical binary VX that structure the cultural discourse of the West. Derrida's most well known work, *Of Grammatology,* outlines a field of thinking for the future by focusing on some unexamined metaphysical assumptions concerning the practice of *writing*,[4] as well as the first moves towards the dislocation of these assumptions. The aim is to enable the reader to read and write otherwise than in terms of a logic governed purely by identity, thereby opening the reader to a plurality of alterities. This is achieved by directing the reader's attention to the refusal of the suppressed term in a polar set to be dominated by the privileged term; and thus to set the debased term in such a 'structure' where its difference cannot be obscured by its opposite. Derrida's claim here is that writing as a concept has been controlled by a kind of ethnocentrism manifested by the institutions of theology, social history and philosophy in the West; that all three of these institutions disguise this ethnocentrism (what Derrida in *The Other Heading* calls Euro-centrism) as logocentrism where the Word privileged by metaphysics becomes the defining essence of God, Civilization and Philosophy.[5]

One of the most fecund ideas that is brought to light concerns the fact that writing was hampered by a contamination of ideological and theological prejudice because of the link between Judeo-Christianity and the Biblical assumptions about writing. Derrida's conception of ethnocentrism is a subtle combination of (i) the assumption of unique power and authority of European culture, (ii) a projection of desire for metaphysical and theological notions of *presence, totality* and *identity* onto non-European cultures, by the disparagement of what is Western by the Western mind itself. Both (i) and (ii) deny the otherness of the other. The problem resides in the European projection of plenitude in the other - that the other possesses what 'we' lack, and that 'we' must by rights deign to possess - a projection that denies the individuality of the other. Writing, however, resists being encompassed within the natural or human sciences (the 'sciences of man') as it does not assume the underlying metaphysical assumptions that apply to concepts such as 'human' identity or unity. While the metaphysical tradition privileges identity as the assumption of sameness, always and everywhere, writing disrupts this privilege. This disruption of unity and man 'is undoubtedly to renounce the old notion of peoples said to be without writing' and 'without history.'[6] This is a point that I shall take up in relation to colonial discourse later on in this essay.

Derrida's juxtaposing of the following themes: 1) Signs governed by onto- theology; 2) Identity (as expressed in ideas of man, universality, subjectivity etc); 3) Ethnocentrism as a result of privileging the above themes; 4) Writing as the liberation from metaphysical governance of the sign, is fertile not just theoretically, but more so *politically*, especially as a deconstruction of colonialist discourses. Before going on to look at colonial discourses it will be instructive to see how the above notions are actually implemented in decentering the discourse of modernism from its privileged metaphysical foundations, in order to raise the question of writing as a potential force that liberates the other as the other. *Grammatology* announces the liberation of writing from the onto-theological notion of the sign by deconstructing some key concepts of modernism: *self, history* and the *book*. Hence the re-birth of writing coincides with the disappearance of the self, the end of history and the closure of the book.

Modernism began with the Enlightenment project as a contest to master and overturn the hierarchical structures of Western thought and society. This attempt begins with the Oedipal project of mastery: 'the death of God.' The death of God articulated as a humanistic atheism which was the denial of God in the name of man, ironically had its roots in science (influence of nominalism and the privileging of empirical research), theology (Luther's emphasis on *pro nobis,* of individual salvation and the centrality of the self), and philosophy (Descartes' turn to the cogito as the touchstone of certitude and truth).[7] The death of God thus coincided with the birth of the sovereign self. But, driven by pathological doubt and insecurity, the rise of the sovereign self that attends the event of parricide resulted in a ceaseless quest for total control and domination of the earth as the (m)other. According to this psychology of mastery, everything exists only insofar as it is present-at-hand, there to be utilised - man only encounters himself and his need. The encounter with the other is transformed into an encounter with the self. The sovereign subject is guided by a principle of utilitarian consumerism, where otherness is consumed, digested assimilated into identity. This inevitably results in a certain economy: that of domination based on a principle of ownership.

The economy of domination and ownership manifests on both the private (inner) and public (outer) realms. Both realms are in turn governed by a need to satisfy desire for the other, to domesticate the strange or alien: the private satisfied by sexual violence, driven by a phallocentric sexuality; the public satisfied by political violence, manipulation of new markets, colonisation of the alien. The economic logic is simple: if the other fails to mirror the self (us), the other's territory is invaded, colonised and digested. For the sovereign self, the world as other, is the mirror in which the self must be reflected in order to ascertain self-identity.[8] The effort to possess otherness is indirectly an effort to possess the self. This pursuit of selfhood, of becoming an ego (even a God-centred "religious" ego) can only come about by incorporating difference, by excluding difference from identity. Ironically this drive for self-certainty as the goal of modernism, is done in the name of Freedom, Equality and Fraternity - but only of the *same*!

Modernity and identity are inextricably related events. To become a sovereign subject is to possess a proper name and to be possessed by a proper name. The origin of the 'I' is the primal scene of nomination, whereupon the self, by being named, is set apart from others and achieves selfhood by receiving a task for a lifetime. But the name also introduces a paradox. The name gives both   auto-nomy ('I am so and so') and fate. Fate involves a decision: 'How do I become what I am already?' To decide to become what I already am is to acknowledge that I am not, but can become. It is therefore a desire to repeat the origin, the primal scene; an attempt to overcome the splitting of identity (differentiation) at its very origin imposed by time. The self does this by becoming temporal and thereby choosing a fate.[9] Choice necessarily involves becoming authentic. As far as Western theology is concerned the original scene of naming involves the specular relation between God and man. Man is a reflected image of God, and becomes authentic by mimicking, where mimicry involves invocation of God's name. Within the onto-theological tradition, identity is based on the Judeo-Christian God who as the self-centred centre, is the founding principle of cosmic and personal unity. Since God's unity is inseparable from his permanence, time/ plurality/ change and difference is merely illusory - a mere supplement to God's unchanging substance (*ousia*). Hence subjectivity is pure presence, the continuity of substance. Since substance is always present to itself, to its own other, otherness is only illusion. As a pure self-recognition in absolute otherness, subjectivity is a relation manifested in the onto-theological tradition by the noble attributes of love (auto-affection) and knowledge (self-consciousness).

The suppression of difference is clearly demonstrated by the principle tenet of monotheism: that to be is to be one authentic subject. The subject cannot err, be different, for difference would be tantamount to invoking improper name(s), false gods, polytheism. What is most authentic is that which possesses a proper name by which it can be a unique personality. Authentic being, self-presence, self-identity, entails both *oneness* (derived from monotheism) and *ownness* (the psychological root of secular capitalism). Ownness or authenticity draws that which the self claims as its own, in close proximity to it and thereby establishes the authority by which property is owned. As authentic subjectivity and proximity combine into self presence, so monotheism and capitalism are inextricably related. The point to note in this genealogy of onto-theology and identity is that the identification of self-proximity and self-presence absolutises the present now i.e. the subjection of time to the present or the privileging of being as presence. But the paradox of time is not so easily mastered. Even St. Augustine, who in his *Confessions* effectively inaugurates Western onto-theology, found it necessary to posit that the self as well as time is one substance but with three modes. And yet to account for the three-ness of time *and* to retain self-presence, Augustine had to *write* his own recollections in the form of a self-narration or auto-bio-graphy i.e. the putting into words of the self. Thus the role of narration is 'vital' for self-presence. The authentic self is therefore not so much a given fact but a literary construct due to the paradoxical difference that time introduces into the pure now. When the self is narrated as *writing* - rather than voiced narrative - the very event of writing subverts the absolute privilege of presence and discloses the difference within the present. Writing removes not only the purity but the proximity to self that the voice/ breath as spirit has so long privileged. While onto-theology is the ideological privileging of monotheism, writing, by introducing the outside into the inside, is a subversion of the purity and proximity of the specular God-Man mimicry. Since the written mark is external, where voice and breath cannot inspire the body, then writing is the space of impropriety, impurity, supplementarity, plurivocity, inauthenticity.....that is of time, change and difference.

One can see why the post structuralist opposition[10] to the privileging of the sign as pure presence via the transcendental signified and his counter-privileging of the 'dead' written mark, the signifier, is rather like throwing a corpse into a host of angels. The privilege of the sign as transcendental signified (God, self, voice.....) involves a here and now. In the onto-theological tradition, whether this here and now was taken objectively (empirical realism) or subjectively (idealism), its privilege is dispersed at the very moment of its being ex-pressed in language i.e. in the broad sense that Derrida gives to writing. Thus the structure of signification, whether phonetic or written, requires the absence of intuition where intuition is non-other than the purity or 'proper space' of signification in the interiority of the author's mind. Writing is therefore the realisation that nomination as the primal scene of self-identity cannot entail the purity of self-presence or intuition, as pure self-presence can never be realised except as a re-presentation. In other words writing comes before identity and is not supplementary to naming. Correspondingly, representing is the opening of the improper space of writing. It is both a temporalisation and spacing [11] - an irreducible outside as well as an irreducible movement or alterity that is utterly necessary to the structure and process of signification. Presence in its spatialisation and deferral of itself is difference, rather than sameness and identity. Difference in turn is a temporalizing of space and a spatializing of time (not now...): which Derrida combines in his word *difference*. [12] Thus in opposition to the onto-theological tradition, identity is only in becoming, not that which it already is (as difference), other. Only the presence of differance can call identity forth.

In addition to the disappearance of identity in its being written, *Grammatology* signals the end of history and the closure of the book, which are the other pillars of onto-theology. Like God and self history is a theological notion. To have an identity is to have a God; to have a God is to have a history i.e. events connected in a meaningful order. Furthermore to have *one* God (monotheism) is to have *one* history, and this history is both theo- and logo-centric. Its story or narrative thread is the divine *logos* which draws beginning middle and end together to form a coherent totality. Again, what is privileged here is the notion of totality, wholeness or unity which is given to contingent events by an A/author. The narrative function eliminates differences or spaces between contingent events in favour of the security of sameness or meaningful order. This privileged, unified whole, totalised by a divine Author(ity) is the Book. The book, as Derrida explains, is that writing which is totalised by a consciousness which can be human (secular) or divine (theological). In the onto-theological tradition the book is, before all else, God's Book, the Book of Nature in which all mysteries are inscribed. The notions *book, history* and *self*, as theological motifs of totalization, represent the elimination of writing; they are 'the theological presence of a centre,' or the motif of homogeneity, the theological motifs par excellence.' [13] Thus onto-theology pertains to the construction of metaphysical foundations: an origin, end, centre, ground..... and the reason for the post-structuralist insistence on its deconstruction is that these theological notions are inherent, indeed provide models for the newer discourses of secular modernism: namely anthropology as the discourse par excellence pertaining to the ethnography of other, non-European cultures. It is to the promise of writing as liberation of difference, different cultures of writing and therefore to the specific writing of/on others in ethno-graphy as well as related mimicked practises, that I shall turn my attention.

From the foregoing it should be obvious that the post-structuralist emphasis on questioning the discourse of European cultural identity can be regarded as a deconstruction of its founding philosophical-theological concepts through the interrogation of identity, and that its ultimate application is towards the political/ communal realm. And not a rethinking of the political/communal by simply remaining within the narrative of that particular culture, but through the splitting of its fundamentalist assumptions, and by allowing the suppressed, the excluded other, to come in. The reinstatement of writing as the process of primary signification allows us to unravel the narrative of secular modernism. For modernism, the centre or present-now is decisive for the entire temporal process, being the grid through which all experience is filtered and mapped. The temporal now is exemplified by the universal man, today's man, Western rationality, the European (or American), and by implication, Western culture itself. It follows that if the project of identity was a suppression of time through a repression of difference on the individual level, then equally cultural identity, as the basis for political/communal coherence is equally a suppression by the community's political projects of building immortal cultures in order to fight pollution by the alien. History as narrative, always involves a repression of otherness - an otherness that is both within (political totalitarianism) and without (colonisation of the alien).

Colonial Interpretation of Indigenous Cultures and the Construction of Religious Identities

In this section I want to return to the problem of how colonized cultures were written about as opposed to diaspora cultures writing themselves in the textual space of a dominant culture. Recently, cultural theorists like Edward Said and Homi Bhabha have rightly directed our attention towards the post-colonial representation of non-Western cultures through European narrative discourses.[14] In spite of the seminal nature of many of their arguments one of the issues that is hardly raised is how specifically onto-theological or metaphysical assumptions inherited from the West continue to structure the fabric of writing, thinking, socio-political and religious life within South Asia and the diasporas originating from this region. In order to try and address this problem, or at least to put it into a context other than its current representation, I shall focus my attention on the Punjab. The reason for choosing Punjab is valid to this whole debate on identity. Punjab was, and remains, one of the best examples in South Asia of how a dominant European culture shaped and transformed virtually every aspect of life there, including the intellectual and cultural horizons of the native inhabitants, and not least because Punjab was both the barracks of the imperial army as well as the testing ground for colonial administration policy within South Asia.

Punjab eludes a facile interpretation in terms of the well worn pre-modernist/modernist, pre-colonial/colonial structural categories. This region had for many centuries been the battle ground for invaders and new settlers because of its proximity to Afghanistan and therefore the Middle-East and Russia. The pre-colonial culture was largely heterogenous in almost every respect, with ethnic, linguistic and religious disparity and alterity being the norm.[15] Generally speaking, boundaries which would normally be considered to affect inter-subjective praxis - namely religious and linguistic - were highly fluid. This does not mean that there was social chaos. Indeed the socio-political sphere had its own structural grammar, but it was one that tended to remain largely invisible. I shall return to this point later on.

Following the early period of encounter and hostility between indigenous societies and the colonial forces, with the subsequent annexure of kingdoms and territories under the imperial hierarchy, the last quarter of the 19th century ushered in a period of unprecedented change to Punjabi societies. This change was mainly a response to the colonial administration's systemisation of indigenous societies according to its own imperial blue-print. In stark contrast this later period was marked by linguistic, religious and political encounter between the indigenous communities themselves. In order to aid proper governance of the enormous diversity of cultures and traditions the administration helped to bring about the creation of an indigenous class of interpreters or middle-men - mainly civil servants of a professional or pseudo-professional variety. These indigenous elites had to ensure the effective mediation or translation of the imperial codes to their own cultures and communities. [16] It has become a somewhat stereotypical practice to regard these Western-educated elites as the progenitors of the cultural and political changes that have since then marked not only South Asia but other colonised areas.

However this would be to overlook one very important fact, which is that these elite mimick-men inherited the programmatic structure that the Europeans had already set up before they as a class were created. It is important to realise that in the cultural encounter between the Punjab and the West, the first proper contact was made by specially trained scholars/travellers who were essentially the first ethnographers. Acting as probes or receptacles their function was to soak up the indigenous languages and cultures in order to feed them back through the University to their political pay masters. Thus the way that the British eventually organised and administered their rule was dependent almost entirely on what they saw, interpreted and mapped into neatly organised categories. The Europeans' first contact or encounter was visual. The observations interpreted or inferred from this empirical visual data were compared and/or added to their existing databanks on this particular area of knowledge. Hence what they believed they saw in Punjab may not have been the way things actually were but the way that the European mind had been trained to see and judge with a panoptic field of vision. The colonised inhabitants were simply mapped under the epistemic category of *religion*, and the major sub-divisions under this primary category could be identified as Muslim, Hindu and Sikh. We should remember of course that the Europeans felt morally entitled to classify in this manner - moral-value judgement being part of the unique privilege that came with monotheism and Western rationality. Through this crude form of cultural translation, religion became an overdetermined realistic category that gave rise to a multiplicity of easily accessible discourses on the natives, of which the locus or reference point was always religion. The new elites, having been educated and indoctrinated in the Western system, were not immune to this mode of translation. This overdetermination of religion was responsible for the indigenous elites overdetermining their own modes of cultural self-classification. Bhabha and Young in particular have written on the psychological underpinnings of mimicry as a mode of partially offsetting or even usurping authority in the name of the administration itself.[17] While this may well be so, what is of more concern to this essay is that the indigenous elites were imprinted with an identity modelled on their colonial masters. The desire for such an identity was a result of wanting to be recognised as an other, or as Bhabha puts it 'as a subject of difference that is almost the same, but not quite.' [18] Inevitably the desired recognition involved a certain element of misrecognition - or a disturbance in the process of exact mimicking. Even so, insofar as they were imitations of British epistemic judgement, they were nothing less than acquired self-presencings, self-reflections and thus identities in the almost proper sense of the term. In other words they saw themselves, and thereby reproduced their social orders, as the British saw them - through distinct religious categories: Muslim, Sikh, Hindu, each of which was mutually exclusive. In response to hectic proselytisation, not just from Christian missionaries but from each other, the elite groups formed representative political bodies based on these distinctly defined religious identities.[19]

By westernising the educational infrastructure of the indigenous societies the elites groups were responsible for creating social boundaries based primarily on a certain understanding of religion as the cultural signifier. But what is most interesting for the purposes of this essay is how a specifically onto-theological understanding of religion became the foundational principle of their identity. For all three communities, Hindu, Sikh and Muslim, a modern identity was created by appropriating the following key notions: 1) Language: adoption of 'authentic' letters, scripts and a phonetic alphabet as unique to each ethno-religious community; 2) The Book: i.e. canonisation of a primarily oral culture and loose texts into a rigidified and totalised system; 3) History: adoption of a linear view of time, which also entailed an apocalyptic understanding of their historical existence; 4) The Novel: the use of narrative fiction and idealised plots was increasingly used to fix certain ideologies into the community's collective imagination; 5) The Body as a signifier for external identity; 6) Initiation Rites and Social Taboos: as indicators of social and political boundaries marking inside and outside; protection against aliens etc.

What is particularly evident here is the way in which the newly emergent modern identities appropriated and fostered a strongly theological understanding of the written *and* spoken word, indeed of the sign itself. This theologizing of the sign is most evident in the way they represented themselves in their own literature. The following were quite common themes: 'we' have a unique God; access to a unique and rational (not primitive) ideology; a Revealed Scripture (The Book); an authentic history with a venerable originator; a unique World View . . . and so on. But what exactly does the theologizing of the sign mean? It suggests for a start that before contact with print-capitalism the relationship of communities, who previously relied on an oral culture, to language and the sign may have been quite different.[19] The problem is that the essentially Western-humanist bias towards Enlightenment rationality and its norms meant that oral cultures were and still are regarded as backward or primitive, and that the shift away from orality to print culture epitomises the shift into modernism, progress etc. If, on the other hand we accept the implications of recent post-structuralist readings of metaphysical discourses, then this bias cannot be sustained. Oral culture would be regarded as a form of writing - phonetic inscription, where sound is the material signifier. Because of sound's intrinsically temporal and finite nature, the cultural implications of orality are significant: multiple identities or rather a dispersion of identity itself; greater fluidity across linguistic and religious boundaries; 'politics' would be dialogical, face-to-face as it were. In other words oral cultures would tend to favour cultural *difference* rather than a monolithic identity due to the signifier's finite temporal quality. In contrast print-culture's most far reaching effect was to spatialise sacred oral texts into the cold print of books, which had the effect of freezing temporal openness by promoting notions such as permanence, eternal substance etc. Printed texts were models of linearity, uniformity, totalisation; these notions as has been shown are inherently connected to a divine Author or a transcendental signified, thereby paradoxically demoting the physical mark itself.

Inspite of this it is important to add a certain qualifier to what I have said concerning the divide between oral and print cultures. Recent work in the theory and history of religion tends to betray a certain nostalgic desire for a return to oral culture at the expense of jettisoning certain aspects of print culture.[20] What this desire tends to forget, however, is that no matter how open oral cultures may have been, they were still subject to a certain grammar or deep structure; that is, these societies were strictly hierachised by Brahmanic (priestly) domination of the written word as well as caste subdivisions into *biradaries* and kinship structures. They were not coincident with social or political equality in any sense of the Western democratic system, but were nevertheless governed by rigidly metaphysical notions about writing. While print culture did enable oral societies to become politicised around ethno-nationalism,[21] this was infact due to a particular (i.e. onto-theological) appropriation of the written sign, rather than because of writing as such. As mentioned earlier, its primary purpose, in addition to drawing distinct boundaries, was the accumulation of power, authority and centralisation into a particular corporate identity. As in the Western metaphysical tradition, identity, monotheism and capitalism are inextricably intertwined.

It could no doubt be claimed that despite some unforeseen circumstances, the mimicking process was effective in disrupting the cultural and racial suppression that characterised the narcissism of colonial authority, and for claiming equality based on the Europeans' own value system. But the problem and perhaps the misfortune for South Asia today, is that these modern constructed identities which pose as natural and authentic, have not only survived, but simply refuse to die as many postmodern interpreters of South Asian politics would wish. Even the most romantic and superficial observer of India surely cannot fail to see the enormous gulf between the India of the West's imaginings and modern 'democratic' India as it is today with its seething communal tensions, volcanic nationalisms and highly centralized single party state. What is particularly frightening is how communal identities were never defused after 1947 but instead were absorbed by pseudo-secular political parties that not only feed off the communal issue whenever votes are at stake but consistently play the 'national identity' card against minorities. This is not just a problem for South Asia but for other previously colonised nations and their disseminated diasporas. For each of them the post-colonial desire, as the desire for an identity, is articulated through a particular language that can do no other than both mimic and misrecognise, and thus be seen as a shadow of the imperial tongue.

The question of language and the articulation of cultural identity has now become politicized. In this regard one cannot fail to note in current debates on South Asian politics, a discourse that revolves around binary opposites contrasting the *theocratic* nature of politics, literature and culture produced by former colonies with the *secular,* (and by implication progressive) nature of Western politics.[22] The views forwarded by two articulate exponents of this debate - Ashis Nandy and Prakash Chandra Upadhyaya - can be regarded as representative of the two sides of the argument. [23]

The debate is centred around the 'true meaning' of secularism as against the kind of secularism widely espoused in India. Upadhyaya sees a fairly clear cut distinction between what he calls 'genuine secularism' - one that has not really been given the chance to succeed in India - and the Indian version of secularism or what he calls 'majoritarianism.' Majoritarianism is the subordination of genuine secularism to a nationalism of the Hindu majority, where all communities are equal but with 'the Hindu community being more equal than others.' Within this system secularism is reduced to a mere tool of nationalist politics based on the communalization of religions, traditions and cultures. Moreover it has become hegemonic, incorporating the all-inclusive sense of 'Indianness.' It is based on the fact that ethnicity, community, and religious traditions are the "repositories of crucial authentic values," actualized only with the creation in India of a political system built in its own cultural image. This vision is based on an understanding of India as a 'traditional community society' - one that hopes to accommodate the interests of all communities under universal slogans such as *sarvadharma sambhava* or *varnaashrama dharma.* Thus the political scene according to Upadhyaya, rather than being a contest between secularism and traditionalism, is really a hiatus between majority fundamentalism as against many competing minority fundamentalisms. According to Ashis Nandy, on the other hand, 'genuine secularism' espoused by Upadhyaya, is un-Indian, a symptom of the wider diseases of modernity, homogeneity and similarity. What interests Nandy is the authentic, spiritual essence of India, one that can allow 'the recovery of religious tolerance,' which he believes, existed prior to the advent of colonialism.

In a certain sense, Upadhyaya is correct to criticise the covert majoritarianism that seems to be implicit in Nandy's idealistic discourse of authenticity. By means of a clever deconstruction Upadhyaya demonstrates that the discourses of traditionalism operate by employing metaphors peculiar to India's cultural heritage, such as *dharma, Ramrajya,* or *Satya,* which are then translated back into a European framework wherein they become moral unifying factors that can only be understood through metaphysical/onto-theological principles such as universality, uniqueness, identity, nature, natural law, moral and spiritual unity etc. While this mode of cultural translation was initially used effectively by the Arya Samaj, Singh Sabha and other indigenous elites, it was used to even greater effect by Gandhi as the basis of his spiritual nationalism to forge a 'moral unity' of India's social classes - the landed and the landless, rich and poor, privileged and under-privileged - through the deployment of classless metaphors described above. The result was that it allowed the dominant capitalist classes to maintain their position as the weaker classes would accept this dominance with resignation, without envy, and in the name of India's spiritual heritage.

What is effectively involved here is a form of cultural translation, which as described earlier, does not take into account the cultural disparity between the language of Indian traditionalism and the secular onto-theological language of the European tradition. The disparity manifests in a number of ways. Firstly, it ignores the uncritical use and adoption of the term 'religion' as a primary cultural signifier, based as it is in its European context on terms such as morality, faith, ideology etc, all of which are key concepts of Christian-Platonism. Secondly, it ignores the disparity of power relations between the Indian and European contexts. Cultural difference is neutralized by a process of translation, that allows an equalization of cultures under the name of identity by the call to 'revivalism' of authentic cultures. It is this kind of cultural translation - effectively a cultural identification or mimesis - that theologizes cultural signifiers into communalizing principles.

This should not, however, give the impression that Upadhyaya is therefore right to endorse what he calls 'genuine' secularism, whereby it is necessary to base nationalism, democracy and all traditionalisms on purely secular foundations: in other words a clean separation of religion and politics. 'Genuine' secularism would be understood as a process in which religious, ethnic, and traditional ties are transcended, with politics being defined on rationalist and ideological grounds only. This position is just as untenable as that of Nandy. Upadhyaya conveniently forgets that the secularism with which he intends to rationally transcend religion, culture and tradition, is itself a culture in its own right - one that is also based on essentialist metaphysical principles such as Man, Human culture, Universality and ultimately therefore the culture of capitalist techno-economics.

Thus we can see that the opposing arguments of the secularism versus theocracy (traditionalism) debate are in fact two sides of the same coin: one that boils down eventually to the problem of translation as the process of cultural encounter. One side (Nandy) is genealogical. It hearks back to idealistic notions of origin, purity, to a Sanatana tradition which it believes is the true spiritual essence of India and which can be regained in its pristine glory. Ironically these ideas of purity and authenticity are terms of representation which have to be translated into a language that is *not* Indian. Surely the very need to write and represent in English, in an intellectual context that is dominated by a secular scholarship, is itself a mockery of these ideas. The other side (Upadhyaya) is teleological. It looks to an overcoming, or modernizing, of the traditional, cultural, religious spheres which are unfortunate relics of a pre-modern, pre-rational, pre-political age. It does not require any great power of advocacy to argue that both sides of the debate represent the nodal points of European onto-theological metaphysics i.e. *arche* and *telos*.

Translation, as an enactment of the need to articulate in words, impedes the otherwise transparent assimilation of meanings that stand between disparate cultures, under both secular and theological unifying metaphors of 'human' culture. What goes unrecognised by proponents of both genealogical and teleological discourses is that cultural translation exists only as an in-between of different cultures - what Bhabha calls a hybrid culture; and therefore that the culture of South Asia has always been a hybrid culture, that it cannot claim the purity and simplicity in representation that genealogical narratives of nationalism and teleological narratives of secular modernism both claim and take for granted. The question of articulating the hybrid in-betweenness of cultural translation is a question of signification - of the signifier itself. Ever since the need for representing was first realized by the indigenous elites, the basic problem of cultural translation has been put across in terms of a desire to articulate a cultural *identity*: 'the ability to put the right word in the right place.' And yet while it is clear that there has been a failure of cultural translation to be reduced to identity as a mimetic equivalence of different cultures (a desire to be recognized as the same, which becomes at the same time a *mis*recognition of the other), the question has rarely, if ever, been asked as to why this failure occurs. The answer, I suspect, lies in the limits of language, which are at the same time the limits of philosophy as the process that regulates the enactment of translation. Yet these limits far from being respected, have merely been shrugged-off under an attitude of 'ethical naturalism,' a matter of cultural plurality.

But does ethics as an intrinsic part of the western moral and philosophical tradition not seek to apply its principles to the whole world under the guise of universalism? Furthermore, does the articulation of ethics not occur through an epistemology, through the specifically western episteme, and thus through the nature of judgement itself? And must epistemic judgement not ultimately depend on propositions which themselves are linguistic; so that judgement, as the articulation of the episteme, is linked to one particular language and culture, which also happens to be the interpretative grid upon which all so-called ethical judgement is carried out? Neither yesterday's indigenous elites nor today's exponents of pro- or anti-secularism, and pro- or anti- traditionalism (theocracy), have moved away from the ethical-judgemental position of the early orientalist scholars who initially transfixed and mapped out the cultural boundaries, making religion a category of epistemic judgement. Thus articulation of cultural difference as a writing or translation, can begin only by accepting the fact that culture is always becoming hybrid through an acceptance of its intrinsic mortality. In other words, culture is not a static concept but a movement that corresponds to the constant coming and going of human generations, and that with the demise of one generation the temporal distance between succeeding generations forces a hybrid-transformation, a need for re-reading or re-writing i.e. an infinite translation of cultural signifiers.

Thus orientalist scholars and ethnographers who try to explain current ethnic conflicts, the collusion between religion, ethnicity and ethno-nationalism in terms of, economics; or worse still that Eastern cultures have failed to come to terms with modernism; that modernism and liberal democracy is more suited to Western cultures; or that liberal democracy can only be administered by the West, will remain ethnocentric and profoundly mistaken as long as they fail to take note of the onto-theological underpinnings of the language of the formerly colonised nations. On the issue of theocratic politics Edward Said makes a particularly pertinent comment in his recent work *Culture and Imperialism*. Said mentions how during one of his lectures on the nature of politics in recently liberated Middle-Eastern countries given at a university in Lebanon, a young woman draped in the traditional Islamic head-dress asked him in perfect seriousness: 'What about the theocratic alternative?'[24] To Said this comment served as a poignant reminder of the intellectual complacency of Western educated academics involved in judging the post-colonial situation and in particular how Third World intellectuals articulate their own problems in relation to Western discourse. There is however a more sinister aspect to the question of theocratic politics. One cannot help wondering, in view of its domination of the international market and the language of international-*ism* (Americanised English), whether the West has much to gain by keeping theocratic poics and the kind of ethnic nationalism that it engenders alive; or whether Islamic theo-politics, 'fundamentalism' and other such media nasties are not merely enabling the West to redefine its own so security agenda, cultural identity and boundaries in wake of the Soviet Union's demise; and whether so called theocratic nations are not once again the suppressed terms in the polar discourse of Europeanised internationalism: developing/developed, theocratic/secular, theology/anthropology, religion/politics.

Writing-for the Other: Ethnography and the Reification of Cultural

Although postmodernist theories might suggest a weakening and relaxation of objective rigour in studying others, these suggestions have yet to be absorbed by the protagonists of typically modernist discourses for studying the alien, notably ethnography, comparative cultural studies and the social sciences. It seems somewhat surprising that while postmodernist theories have pervaded many areas of intellectual life in Europe, intellectuals from the Third World and the Western diaspora have regarded these new movements with outright hostility or at best with suspicion. Rather than allowing the metaphysical assumptions of their discourse to be undermined, most of these intellectuals have responded by entrenching themselves further in the rhetoric of identity, ideology and forms of religiously inspired ethno-nationalism. That this should happen at all in the postmodernist era is dismaying but not at all surprising when we begin to consider the reasons behind such response.

Much of the blame has to lie with the way that the discourses of the human and cultural 'sciences' such as anthropology, social history and comparative religion have represented marginal diaspora groups. These disciplines appear within the West at the point where theology begins to break down; the rise of universal rational man coincides with the death of God and becomes manifested as a desire for radical alterity in other cultures.[25] The function of these discourses as metaphysical consists in describing the universal structures of the occurrence of the 'human' as a phenomenon in other cultures. As the archetypal ethnographic discipline, cultural anthroplogy aims to represent the radical otherness of the other as an objective mode of cognition. The problem with ethnography is that despite the philosophical upheavals of the 20th century, its basic assumptions have remained rooted within the epistemic paradigm, thus favouring a visual frontal approach to its object of study. The ethnography of the 19th century with its emphasis on empirical realism exemplified by the maxim: 'what you see is what it *is*' was replaced during the 20th century with the increasing assaults on empirical realism/positivism as a mode for studying the other. The linguistic turn in philosophy assured a switch in emphasis from naive categorisation (naming: word/thing correspondence) to a more subtle discourse, exemplified by the linguistic insights of Saussure and Jakobson and the cultural anthropology of Levi-Strauss, known as structuralism. Structuralist discourse has largely characterised modernist ethnography of subject construction, which has aimed to (re)construct the formed identity at a particular time and a particular place in the linear history of a group of people. The driving force behind this project is the drive of the modern first world capitalist economies towards integration and rationalisation of all displacements and differences.

Notwithstanding a few changes, the visually enframing assumptions of the earlier realist ethnography are still apparent within the modern ethnographer's analytical construction of his subjects. Consequently the post-colonial, postmodern and global context has caused a problematisation of this structuralist discourse. Through post-structuralists like Barthes and Derrida, the epistemic realist mode of modernist ethnography is displaced in three ways:[26]
1) By problematising the temporal now in which the other is inscribed.

2) By problematising the spatial here of inscription i.e. the ethnographer's privilege of writing.

3) By depriving the voice of the ethnographer's humanist narrative its usual privilege. As we have seen, writing is capable of problematising the above; it differs the spatial here-ness of inscription; and it removes the privilege of the voice with its proximity to the transcendental signifier i.e. rationality itself.

Because the whole project of anthropology as modelled on the natural sciences was centred around the specifically technical problem of identity formation (or as the eminent modernists Bright and Geyer put it: 'the question of who, or what controls and defines the identity of individuals, social groups, nations and cultures,')[27] there has been, in the face of recent global conflicts, a renewed almost vulture-like interest among anthropologists in questions of ethnicity, racial conflict, and nationalism.[28] Without the exclusive identities that emerge from Third World and diaspora studies, they would have no analytic or descriptive framework to rely on. It is in this context that I would regard a combination of anthropological study and media hyping as complicit in the mis-representation and/or mis-writing of dominated cultures. Of-course ethnographers and comparativists would piously claim that their discipline and its methods defend the authenticity and value system of other cultures; that it represents them as accurately as possible. In this respect they are right; but all this accuracy has done is to privilege a certain metaphysical/onto-theological way of looking at of reading and writing other cultures.

In the previous section I briefly mentioned how, in their desire to articulate a distinct identity, the language of Third World and diaspora intellectuals has largely mimicked the imperial codes of representation and intelligibility. The problem is that Western practitioners of the human sciences, and this goes especially for religious and anthropological studies, have taken these discourses at face value. Since this discourse was expressed to the Western mind through a mode of language that was rational, positivist and transparent i.e. propositional statements through which identities could be asserted: 'I am Muslim' or 'I am Sikh'. Such assertions came to be treated as authentic cultural signifiers in their own right. The problem is that such representations of identity having been authenticated by academia have been mass produced by the media networks with the result that religion as a realistic, phenomenal and overdetermined category has become a facile cultural signifier for the Third World and diaspora groups. These all too literal 'religiously defined' identities have been reified into truth statements, which in turn has privileged the establishment of multi-culturalism or cultural diversity. Not surprisingly these communities have found it difficult to emerge from out of such entrenched positions when faced with significant threats to their social and temporal coherence.

It seems that this problem is centred around the use and abuse of writing. Anthropology as a visual and cognitive study of the other describes what the anthropologist sees. Its writing is *de-scriptive*, a denial of writing, in that the visual aspect - the idea as re-presented on the field of consciousness - is privileged over and above the act of writing itself. Writing that is denied its very physicality is little other than an ideo-logy, an idealisation of the other in front of the mind's eye of the reader - a frontal ontology in the Heideggerian sense. De-scriptive writing de-scribes, un-writes; it is a writing-*for*, on-behalf-of the other who must be represented by the anthropologist. Writing-*for* is essentially a mode of pity ('*we* must speak for *them*'), ethnocentric and a denial of the other's claim to be able to write authentically. At best it is to say: this is how they (the other) would represent themselves if they were able to write.

The crux of this problem therefore is not just the nature of the language employed to represent identity but how language itself is conceived. On the one hand the marginalised other of ethnographical discourse employs a metaphysical notion of the sign to privilege his identity and that of his national group with a strongly onto-theological structure: an origin, authentic History, a sacred Book......etc. Alternatively the ethnographer uses a more secular, humanistic and by implication 'advanced' language which equally petrifies a certain identity as it is then portrayed to the world. Interestingly both deploy writing in a synchronic manner, whereby all events as point now shift into the now of the writer's world, irrespective of whether he is from the First or Third World, with the result that the temporality of the other, i.e. difference, is suppressed. However for both the Western and the diaspora writer the context of language, written and spoken, is the European. Accordingly for both groups the question that remains is how, through what kind of language can cultural difference emerge? The double bind for the Third World/diaspora writer is the he can write, but what he writes is always through translating his culture into the European. He writes his identity in the hope of retaining purity and originality - 'I am Hindu, I am Muslim......' - without realising that these assertions appear on the other side of the language boundary as a mixture of Jew, Greek, European as well as Hindu , Muslim etc. To an audience that already reads and writes in terms of the Jew/Greek/European, this identity appears as more of the 'same' - never in its difference. For his part the ethnographer brings words from the 'other side' into his native European with the result that the other's alterity is defined as an internal aspect of the process of Westernisation and homologation. By the very process of cultural translation the radical alterity of the other is homogenised, made palatable, digestible. It is in effect no different from the process of colon-isation described earlier.

The root of the problem in which cultural difference is suppressed through translation is the scientific/epistemological basis on which this process occurs. According to the current paradigms of language-use, words are merely the exteriorisation of inner thoughts, ideas, self-consciousness. Words are labels for objects 'out there'.[29] Thus if language is merely the external representation of the rational, cognitive process itself, then epistemology is founded on the presupposition that all discourses (as exterior signs) are commensurable with and translatable among each other; since language i.e. the sign as a written mark, is an impure representation of the pure inner process that produces the sign - of the transcendental *logos*, which as the signified for both the Third World and Western writer is onto-theological in origin. The foundation of the truth of these discourses consists precisely in their ability to be translated into a basic language which mirrors facts themselves namely: logic. Hence the aim of cultural translation is clarity, univocity, to minimise the loss of meaning. To summarise: for both Third World and Western ethnographic writing the result is the same: (1) identity can be represented if we use the right words. (2) Writing is denied in favour of idealisation. If language and the way that language has been employed, is the locus of the problem of identity, of seeing the other in terms of the same, of what is familiar and comforting to us at the expense of the alien, then the solution must also lie within this locus. The starting point for a solution is to consider the cultural gap in terms of the failure for difference to emerge from within the language of cultural translation. 'We must begin where we already are,' says Jacques Derrida; and we are always already within language. More to the point we are written within a text that is being written within the European *con*text, since it is the European that dominates global communication. If the text is the problem, then the text must be unravelled and written anew, in a way that writing as the locus of difference can emerge.

Transgressing Identity: Cultural Reception in a Diasporic Context

Cultural translation as the point of contact between Europe and the Punjab first occurred during the period of colonisation with the kind of results that I have already described. Evidently both coloniser and colonised failed to see and translate difference where this difference existed. Ironically, almost a century later, displaced migrants and diaspora groups now face the same situation but in a reverse context. In view of their colonial and post-colonial experience, one of the questions that needs to be raised is: how, from within European cultural domination in almost every sphere, can different cultures emerge as different?

Identity crisis is term that has become a normal part of diaspora culture. Crisis (from the Greek *krinein*) implies a break, a fissure or rupture. In the context of European multi-culturalism or cultural relativism, first generation migrants and others at the margins of European society will not feel any crisis as long as they feel securely bound into a signifying context, culture or tradition which they understand and are thoroughly familiar with. This is the context of what Ricoeur calls the first naivete, where tradition is taken as a pre-given and unquestionable Thou.[30] The problem arises at the stage of handing down; the transmission of traditions and practices, or at the place where a collective identity needs to be represented or narrated to others - i.e. the locus of language. Despite the felt psychological need for cultural identity to be experienced as continuous, authentic, and original, its 'essence' has to be mediated via signs. In order for handing down or passing on to occur the same has to be repeated but in a new context. Culture that is handed down is mediated through signs either orally (phonetic sounds) or via the written mark. Such repetition, however, is always inscribed in temporal flux; it involves a break with the origin and consequently with the idea of a contextless identity.

Furthermore the very inscription of diaspora cultures has shifted from their traditional language into the European. Since all concepts, signs, codes, etc. must therefore be mediated via *other* signs or other cultural codes the problem for second and third generation migrants is more than getting to grips with the technicalities of cultural reception. Rather it resurfaces at a more existential level, where previously unquestioned notions about the origins of individual and collective identity are often shattered. For both the transmitters and receivers of culture the interpretive prerogative has to be radically transformed from the strictly hermeneutic stance concerned with the recuperation of tradition, to one where existence is perceived in terms of a constant negotiation, or a constant translation, *between* different traditions, sign systems and contexts. At stake here is the very notion of what it means to say 'our own' language, or to feel 'at home' within any particular language.

It is the idea of a gap or location that always remains in transition, a continual contestation between different cultures, that disturbs the whole balance of the multi-cultural ethos. This western European form of multiculturalism continues to be underwritten by epistemology, and the primacy of the spectator subject, which as Bhabha rightly says 'seeks to write the totality of different cultures in a narrative of realism....' The point here is that the theories of translation deployed by multiculturalism try to minimize inter-cultural boundaries by its assimalitive metaphors of man, rationality and truth which seek to fill in the gap, or apply band aid to the rupture in trans-cultural (universal) meaning. The problem is perceived as a merely a technical one of putting the right word in the right place at the right time. Which is to say that in its process of translation, the dominant language is able successfully express the sense/meaning of a minor language metaphorically if not literally, and thereby continue the communication of meaning which is perceived to be the function of all languages. In practice this leads to the redundancy and eventually extinction of a minor language. As mentioned previously this entire process is based on the notion of the written sign as exterior and as supplementary. In order for the survival and transmission of minority cultures, the locus of cultural difference as writing must be taken as prior. In other words translation must become the issue of the sign as being re-inscribed within a different context. It is not enough to merely reproduce the figurative aspect of the signs of another culture. The sign as carnal must become anterior to any metaphysical criteria such as "reality", concepts, ideas , meanings etc.

Judging from the literature, it would appear that relatively few diaspora (or 'Third World') academics have begun to question the nature of the language in which their academic discourses are articulated. Fewer still find the need to problematize the process of cultural translation even though it affects virtually all 'disciplines' of the human sciences as well as other contexts of inter-cultural transfer. In another sense it would not be untrue to suggest that there is no boundary between the two cultural spheres, simply because all academic discourse occurs within the Western framework. Ironically, even a conference on 'Punjabi Identity' would be somewhat meaningless due to the fact that all disciplines pertaining to the Punjab could only be articulated through the paradigms currently dominating these disciplines. This is of course to beg the question: what is context? Is there only *one* context - the European? Does the whole question of context not become meaningless?

Diehard disciplinarians and methodological purists will no doubt object that in order to understand things, states of affairs, as they are (note the present tense), i.e. in their proper context or within their own cultural spheres, we as Punjab historians, political scientists, anthropologists etc, are obliged to put things back. This, however, merely emphasises that disciplines and discourses only work from within cultural relativism. For all these disciplines the real occurs in the extra-discursive political, social, historical religious, anthropological...... realms; in other words outside the text of writing itself, such that each discourse pertains to a certain transcendentalism: they apply and refer to the ideal (the object as it should be). And insofar as this ideal is a discursive ideal - a literary norm, a way of speaking about the object of study - one can therefore neither write nor read outside of a particular discipline's context. Exteriority, in other words, is a methodological evil.

Even today for most diaspora and Third World academics the process of translating their tradition-texts as forms of literature, is a case of transparent communication. There is, if procedures and grammars are adhered to, no essential loss of meaning. Inevitably the circle of European metaphysics and onto-theological representation has remained unchallenged. How, then, on what basis, can the texts and literatures of a diaspora culture survive, be transmitted, and translated in the context of the dominant European language that is underpinned by the history of onto-theology/ metaphysics? Should the question of *survival* even be asked? How can the difference of one form of writing (of one language in one context of signification) come to be recuperated through translation? Should one even speak of recuperation?

As shown earlier, translation within a context of multi-culturalist relativism is based on the Platonic tradition: the notion that the word is inextricably linked to the structure of signification which implies the fundamental metaphysical distinction between the sensible and the non-sensible i.e. signifier and signified. The signifier is the written mark (words spoken or written) that points beyond itself to that which it refers or represents i.e. the signified. This signified has been interpreted within the Western tradition in two ways:[31] 1) Realism: where the sign is a real object in the world. 2) Idealism: where the sign is a concept, an idea, or mental image. In both cases however, we try to overcome the real/ideal opposition by assuming that signs carry meanings, which is always somehow transcendent, beyond the mind's grasp. On this assumption, nouns and the act of naming as normative for all languages, i.e. the word and the thing named by the word, are related in a 1:1 correspondence. Thus we have *name/signifier* versus *named/signified*. The latter is always privileged as primary while the former as an inscribed mark, is secondary - the body which merely carries the meaning and is therefore prone to death. This pattern of signification is inherently onto-theological. Within the European context God/Reason is the transcendental signified or as Derrida succinctly puts it, 'the age of the sign is essentially theological...........the sign and divinity have the same time and place of birth.'[32] Thus even if an Eastern language is translated into English, this same system prioritises the signified and so translation ends up being theological in essence. That which is named will be given priority as the transcendental meaning (since it alone is assumed to empower the particular discourse under consideration) over the carnality and arbitrariness on the sign as name.

But writing calls the metaphysical basis of this distinction into question irrespective of the language (system of signs or cultural context) in which writing occurs. The problem with the metaphysical system is that the opposition of sign and signified, whether taken in the realist or idealist sense, is still based upon the paradigm of a field of consciousness. Within the consciousness paradigm the transcendental signified is the measure by which all signs, irrespective of which language they belong to, are measured. Within the writing paradigm the signified is neither independent nor superior to the signifier. The signified is itself a signifier of another signifier and so on; which means that consciousness itself is the particular network of signs within which we work and think, i.e. our linguistic/cultural context, what could at a stretch also be called our tradition. Thus the sign/word is always defined with regard to its difference to other words; in itself the sign or word has no substance or essential meaning. Consciousness is therefore the differential signifying network of signs where meaning is created and destroyed only by differences. In this way language as writing is the movement of differences between signs within a complex web of signs. If writing is governed by movement rather than fixity, by transience of meanings rather than eternal/immutable meaning, then writing cannot privilege any one particular network or context of signification. Thus if language is governed by originary difference, alterity between signs, then the change that occurs when one particular context of signs is placed into another context, should not be bemoaned as an eternal loss of meaning, since the new host text (as a writing) is also a context of differences that does not privilege or impose one 'Eternal Truth.' In both languages, words are the loci of otherness, mystery, difference, and therefore of the inter-play of texts. Since texts do not have fixed boundaries each text is potentially written within every other text; there *are* only *contexts*.

This 'model' of writing, where signs move from one context to another, has important political consequences for translation. Firstly cultural hegemony loosens its stranglehold on the process of translation, since writing removes the ethnocentricity normally associated with individual cultural contexts. Secondly as boundaries break down the notion of 'crossing-over' also becomes less metaphorical and more tangible since boundaries are seen to be metaphysical constructs that allow each culture to contain its signs within an inner region free from invasion from the outside - as well as leakage (dissidency) from the inside out. In other words the gap between two cultures/languages is not so much an exclusive boundary but itself a new signifying context, a place of pure sign movement. Hence the move from one language to another is not so much a loss of meaning or identity, but a new, though transient, space for movement - the creation of new meaning at the same time as the de-structuring of monolithic, 'eternal' meanings i.e. a constant re-writing. Translation is therefore a re-writing in other signs. Loss of identity is always balanced by a gain in difference. Translation is always marked by a non-economy of difference. Such a context of translation can only be practised by those who live within different cultural matrices, where life is never one or the other, but a constant re-writing, a re-forming of words and contexts, a constant re-interpretation. Could, for example, the ligamentous cultural signifier: religion, based as it is on re-*ligare*, be replaced by a more liberated signifier: re-*legere*, based on re-reading and re-writing?   On the other hand for those who prefer the safety of remaining bound into networks of identity based on an exclusion of differences, of others (as in multi-culturalism) translation always involves a loss of sacredness, of meaning, a constant transgression to be avoided. For diasporas the event of translation as transgression should not be taken as an occasion for bewailing the loss of presence, or as a nostalgia for an authentic past, an immutable identity, since their entire context of signification is neither within one nor within the other, but always in-between, on the way, in flux and transient.

In this paper I have tried to reappraise some theoretical issues that govern the representation of cultural identity in the wake of recent developments in post-structuralist theory, and thus to assess its consequences for the cultural and political projects of the Punjab and its diaspora. As against the recent preoccupation with a politics of identity and authenticity which have dominated Indian national politics for the last decade, I have argued for the need to rethink the colonial experience in a radically different way: namely in terms of what remains *unthought* in the process of cultural translation - indeed of translation as an interpretive process - given that language is the site of production of culture as a text. Inspite of the fact that any economy of cultural translation in bound within the general framework of the political economy of globalization and international trade, the emergence of post-colonial literature radically aware of the subversive effects of translation at the close of European metaphysics, will inevitably challenge and redefine hegemonic notions of cultural translation which still continue to be elaborated within the longstanding traditions of the western academy: humanism, universalism and epistemological certainty. Given that the very question of cultural identity itself operates within a paradox - namely that in the current global climate its articulation can only be represented through the language of the politically dominant West whose own cultural logic assumes the role of 'official' - I have attempted to demonstrate the futility of non-engagement with the current phase of 'Western' thinking. Punjab academics across a variety of disciplines need to take heed of the closure of Eurocentric discourses and the possibilities that are opened up for marginal and diasporic cultures, and thus to reappropriate a language of cultural difference as opposed to cultural identity, the former being an intrinsic part of Punjabi culture in its broadest sense prior to the advent of colonialism.

NOTES

1. Jacques Derrida, *L'Autre Cap,* (Minuit, Paris) p6
2. Ibid., p10
3. Ibid., p284. This assertion is based on Derrida's notion of *archi-writing*. With the term archi-writing, Derrida radically extends the traditional concept of writing. Archi-writing is a sort of writing prior to writing that thereby constitutes the functioning of difference within speech or orality. Archi-writing cannot be objectively defined: "It is the very thing that cannot let itself be reduced to the form of a presence...[which] orders all objectivity of the object and all relations of knowledge." (*Of Grammatology*, JHU Press,1976.) All reference (to reality) is predetermined by meaning, and all meaning is predetermined by archi-writing as a differential play of signifiers. Thus language (as the locus of our traditional notions of reality, and as a signifying discourse which defines or explains reality) is to be gathered under the name of writing - indeed, language is a species of writing. Hence there is no linguistic sign (oral or written) before writing as archi-writing. In contradisinction to the Platonic heritage which has promoted the excellence of speech, Derrida isolates the features which have distinguished the traditional concepts of writing (as debased, bastard, parricidal), and than shows that these elements apply equally to the traditional concept of speech and orality as much as to writing.
5. Jacques Derrida, *Of Grammatology*, (Johns Hopkins University Press, 1976) pp3-4
6. Ibid., pp 6-10
7. M.C.Taylor, *Erring: A Postmodern A/Theology*, (Chicago University Press, 1984) pp19-34
8. Jacques Lacan, 'The Mirror Stage as Formative of the I', in *Ecrits*, trans. Alan Sheridan, (Routledge, London, 1989) pp1-7
9. Martin Heidegger, 'Temporality and Historicality,' in *Being and Time*, trans. J. Macquarrie, (Basil Blackwell, London, 1989) pp 424-489
10. See Roland Barthes' 'From Work to Text' in *Textual Strategies.*, ed J.V.Harari, (Methuen and Co. Ltd., London, 1980) and his *Mythologies*, (Hill and Wang, New York, 1972)
11. Jacques Derrida, 'Differance,' in *Speech and Phenomena*, (Northwestern University Press, Evanston, 1973) pp 136-154
12. Ibid, pp 129-161

13. Jacques Derrida, *Of Grammatology*, (Johns Hopkins University Press, Baltimore, 1976) pp 6-10

14. See Edward Said, *Orientalism*, (Penguin, London, 1979) and *Culture and Imperialism*, (Chatto & Windus, London, 1993) or Homi Bhabha, *The Location of Culture*, (Routledge, London, 1993).

15. Harjot Oberoi, *The Construction of Religious Boundaries*, (Oxford University Press, Delhi, 1994)

16. Homi Bhabha, "Of Mimicry and Man", in *The Location of Culture*, (Routledge, London, 1993) pp 85-93

17. Ibid., p 86.

18. See Kenneth Jones, *Arya Dharm: Hindu Consciousness in 19th Century Punjab*, (Berkeley, California, 1976)

19. W.A. Graham, *Beyond the Written Word*, (Cambridge University Press, Cambridge, 1987) p19.

20. See Oberoi.

21. Benedict Anderson, *Imagined Communities: Reflections on the Origin & Spread of Nationalism*, (Verso, London, 1988)

22. One such debate recently broadcast on British television included some interesting exchanges between Salman Rushdie, Mark Tully and Arun Shourie. The backdrop to the debate was the significant shift in Indian Government policy to liberalise its economy in conformity with Western market forces, thereby breaking a 50 year long policy of economic isolation. The question that faced them was whether India in opening itself up to Western capitalism would manage to survive as a nation state, particularly in view of the human carnage caused by serious ethnic-conflicts throughout the sub-continent. The interesting thing about this debate was how Mark Tully and Arun Shourie managed to portray quite accurately the currently opposing trends in S.E.Asian politics. Shourie argued along the lines that a "pure humanist secularism" should provide the fabric of the nation's political and social collectivity - a fabric that would necessarily override the needs and desires of individual cultures and political parties, religious or otherwise; all would be given equal treatment under the aegis of secularism. Tully, ever the romantic dreamer, portrayed what seemed the opposite view: that India needed a strong "cultural identity" in response to the assimilationist threat of Western capitalism, an identity that could only be provided by what he saw the core values enshrined within the religious culture of pan-Hinduism, as championed by the right-wing nationalist BJP. However, when pressed upon the need for national unity in wake of ominous signs of disintegration, both Shourie and Tully managed to agree on the major point that India needed a strong sense of cultural identity around which the nation-state could cohere. For both the most likely candidate for this was provided by the concept "Hindu" which for Shourie was equivalent to secularism, and for Tully was a hazy mixture of the religious-cum-political. In contradistinction to these views Rushdie's remarks represented something of a clean break. Rushdie perceived quite correctly that the binary opposition governing the concepts of cultural identity, secularism versus theocracy, were merely two sides of the same coin, that is, a

suppression of cultura' lifference, in order to maintain the political status-quo represented by either (i) western educated elites whose secular narratives of identity were based upon universalism, progress, unity etc, and (ii) a theocratic nationalism exemplified by the BJP (and other theocratic parties) with its distinctly monotheistic narratives of identity that appeal to One Deity (Ram), One History (based upon the Hindu epics), One Scriptural Authority (Vedic canon), One People (Hindu) etc . [see 'India Week', Channel 4, April 1994]

23.   P.C. Upadhyaya, 'The Politics of Indian Secularism,' *Modern Asian Studies*, 26, 4, (1992) pp815-853. Ashis Nandy, 'The Politics of Secularism' in *Daedalus* 118, (Fall 1989) p4

24.   Edward Said, *Culture & Imperialism*, (Chatto & Windus, London, 1993)

25.   Gianni Vattimo, 'Hermeneutics & Anthroplogy,' in *The End of Modernity*, (Polity Press, London, 1986) pp 145-64

26.   George Marcus, 'Past, Present & Emergent Identities: Requirement For Ethnographies in Late 20th Century Modernity Worldwide,' in *Modernity and Identity*, ed S.Lash and J.Friedman, (Blackwell, Oxford, 1993)

27.   See Marcus p309.

28.   Harry Goulbourne, *Diasporic Politics: Sikhs and the Demand For Khalistan*, (E.S.R.C, Warwick University, 1993)

29.   Richard Rorty, *Philosophy and the Mirror of Nature*, (Blackwell , Oxford, 1993)

30.   Paul Ricoeur, *Interpretation Theory,* (Texas Christian University Press, Fort Worth., 1976) pp43-44

31.   Mark C. Taylor, *Deconstruction in Context*, (Chicago University Press, Chicago, 1986)

32.   Jacques Derrida, *Of Grammatology*, (Johns Hopkins University Press, Baltimore 1976) p75

Sikh Settlers in the Western Punjab during British Rule

Imran Ali

The demography of the Punjab during British rule underwent dramatic changes. The mainspring for these developments was the process of agricultural colonization that opened up the hitherto arid wastes of the western Punjab doabs through the construction of a network of perennial canals. Unlike areas further east, the western Punjab, the region that in 1947 became Pakistani Punjab, failed to receive sufficient monsoonal rainfall to support substantial agricultural production. Some winter rainfall did help to mature the staple foodgrain, wheat, but barani agriculture could at best remain of marginal importance. Well irrigation could be an important source of water, but it could only have localised impact. Dependent on animal power, and prior to the general availability of electrical energy, well irrigation could not support large scale agriculture. Inundation canals were another traditional form of irrigation in western Punjab. But these were seasonal channels, operating only during high water periods. They were also limited to tracts contiguous to rivers, and these tracts were inhabited by settled agricultural communities. These canals were unable to command the somewhat elevated interfluves, which either remained as arid scrub or supported a semi-nomadic pastoral society. The perennial canals constructed by the British from 1885 onwards were spread over these extensive plains. The 'canal colonies', as these tracts came to be called, became a zone of major economic change in this part of British India.[1] The emergent canal network of the Indus basin, spread over Punjab and Sind, became perhaps the largest irrigation system in the world.

In the western Punjab, indigenous population levels were inadequate for opening up the new agrarian frontier. The agricultural communities of the riverain tracts lacked the excess manpower to release to the newly irrigated lands. Indeed, these areas began suffering from labour shortages when tenants and labourers tended to leave for the new tracts.[2] British officials were also reluctant to create disruptions in the landlord-labour nexus of the riverain. Landowners were allocated colony grants to compensate for any disruptions from perennial irrigation.[3] Their proprietary lands also gained greatly in value and productivity wherever they came to be commanded by the new canals.[4] In this period of rapid economic change, the British endeavoured to preserve rather than transform the incumbent agrarian hierarchy of western Punjab.

The other component of the indigenous population were the pastoralists sparsely spread over the areas that eventually obtained perennial irrigation. The British believed that these semi-nomadic tribesmen, collectively known as Janglis, not only lacked the numbers but also the agricultural skills needed for cultivating the cash crops that were necessary for the economic viability of the canal colonies. The Janglis were divided into numerous tribes, the most superior hierarchically being those who owned cattle.[5] The British also refused to recognise the proprietary claims of these Janglis over their extensive pastoral grounds. By tradition, any land not actually cultivated could be claimed by the state. The Janglis were pushed off their pastoral grounds to make way for incoming colony grantees. The consequent dislocation and loss of livelihood led to resentment and protest, inducing the British to allow small grants to Janglis. But only those who were owners of cattle or camels were allotted land, while their underlings had to survive through subtenancies and labour services.[6] Again, the British sought to preserve the preexisting hierarchy.

Thus the land over which perennial irrigation was extended was categorised as Crown (or State) waste land. As its property, the state could thereby dispense with this land in any form or by any method that it wished. Equally importantly, as the proprietor it could grant or sell the land to whoever it wished. Hence 'colonization policy' became a vital accompaniment to canal irrigation: the two processes together created the phenomenon of agricultural colonization in the Punjab. The British made some strategic decisions over the allotment of land. Firstly, they confined land grants to Punjabis rather than to people from other provinces. Secondly, they decided to tap for colonists those parts of the Punjab that had higher population densities.[7] Districts in the central Punjab were said to be suffering most from population pressures. To a lesser extent the *barani* tracts of north-western Punjab had excess numbers that could provide migrants. Political considerations were clearly involved in such decisions. The granting of commercially valuable canal colony land was both an economic and a political process, which created beneficiaries that had acquired landed resources and were thereby beholden to the state. It was no coincidence that the major recruiting grounds of the British Indian army were also the central and northwestern Punjab, the former mainly for Sikhs and the latter for Muslims.

One other consideration in the selection of grantees was that they should be skilful agriculturists. Again, the British believed that the best source for such endowments was amongst the landholding lineages of the central Punjab districts. The all-important strategic decision was made that land allotment to peasant groups be confined to those who already enjoyed a landholding status. After 1900, indeed, the lists of 'agricultural castes' drawn up for each Punjab district under the Alienation of Lands Act were utilised to determine those who could be eligible for land grants in the canal colonies. The poorer, non-landed elements of village society were thereby excluded from proprietary or occupancy access to colony land. The 'service' castes, referred to as 'menials' or kamins, could only benefit from the new lands through employment opportunities as landless labourers and subtenants, a capacity in which they had traditionally remained. Richer nonagriculturists did have the opportunity to purchase canal colony land at auctions; and they were also allotted grants for services in the government. They also stood to benefit from expanded administrative employment, and from profits in agricultural trade, credit and processing. Thus the benefits of agricultural colonization were very largely shared among the already better-off sections of Punjabi society. Among these beneficiaries, the landholding castes of central Punjab were perhaps the most prominent; and a good proportion of these grantees were Sikhs. They belonged especially to the various subsections of the Jat caste.

Sikh settlers were involved with agricultural colonization from its inception. In the earliest project, Sidhnai Colony in Multan District, it was some Sikh Badechah Jats from Amritsar District who in 1886 tried out the soils. When cultivation was found to succeed, the future of the colony was ensured, and there was no shortage of applications for grants.[8] The minimum size of grants in Sidhnai was 50 acres, which was upto four times as large as the smallest grants in later colonies. The reason was that Sidhnai Canal was seasonal rather than perennial. Grantees were required to invest in wells to supplement canal irrigation, and for this they had to be men of some substance. They came from the rich peasant stratum, the British preferring not larger landowners but "small well-do-do agriculturists who will cultivate their own holdings".[9] Of the total land allotted, 80 percent went to Muslims, mostly from Multan, Lahore and Amritsar Districts. The remaining area of 20 percent was allotted to Hindus and Sikhs: disaggregated allotment figures for these two communities were not given. These allottees, numbering around 300 with an area of 57,000 bigahs, came predominantly from Lahore and Multan Districts.[10]

The next project, Sohag Para Colony, was situated in Montgomery District and was settled in 1886-88.[11] Like Sidhnai, this was one of the smaller colonies, with an allotted area of around 90,000 acres. It too was irrigated by an inundation canal that was seasonal rather than perennial. The average size of holdings was around 60 acres, so that the grantees took on subtenancies in addition to being self-cultivators. Jat Sikhs obtained 38 percent of allotted area, or around 29,000 acres. There were 484 such grantees. Thirty-seven Khatri Sikhs from Rawalpindi District were allotted 3,500 acres, or 45 percent of colony land. Their average size of holding was 95 acres, indicating landlord origins. These grants were linked to a very major land grant of 7,800 acres, or 10 percent of colony land, allotted to Baba Sir Khem Singh Bedi, who was also from Rawalpindi. Bedi belonged to a family of Khatri Sikhs claiming descent from Guru Nanak, the founder of the Sikh faith. The British believed that the family's holy status gave it political influence in the Sikh community; and it had also supported them during the struggle of 1857.[12] The extent of this grant made it an exceptional case in the entire history of agricultural colonization. It highlighted the great political value of land grants, as well as the mechanism through which the Punjabi elite moved towards an accommodation with imperialist rule that was to survive the growing claims of nationalism.

Chunian Colony, the next project, was situated in the southern part of Lahore District. It was settled in two stages, between 1896-98 and 1904-06. Like its two predecessors, it was a small colony, with an allotted area of 103,000 acres. It was irrigated by an extension of the Upper Bari Doab Canal, which watered proprietary lands in Amritsar and Lahore Districts. Eighty percent of land was allotted in the form of smallholdings of upto 50 acres, known as 'Peasant' grants.[13] Grantees were predominantly from within Lahore District, among them Jat Sikhs were the best represented. In the area colonised in 1896-98 they comprised around 35 percent of grantees. Apart from peasant colonization, other forms of land utilization were also adopted in Chunian, which were to continue on a much larger scale in later colonies. Around 12,000 acres were sold by auction. For the state auctions were a far quicker method of obtaining returns on investment; but they were without most of the political benefits to be derived from land grants. Also allotted were 5,000 acres in 'civil' grants, ranging in size from 50 - 250 acres. The recipients were retired government officials, rewarded for their administrative services. Also, around 2,000 acres were allotted to military pensioners, whose share was to increase significantly in later colonies. In addition to the 'Peasant' grants, Sikhs obtained land through these other categories as well.

It was with the opening up of Lower Chenab Colony in the Rechna Doab that agricultural colonization assumed significant importance for the recent history of the Punjab. This was the largest of the canal colonies, with an allotted area of over two million acres. Colonised between 1892 and 1905, with further extensions in the late 1910s and 1930s, the colony entirely took up the newly created Lyallpur (now Faisalabad) District, carved out of Gujranwala, Jhang and Lahore Districts. The colony also extended into other contiguous areas in these three districts. The Lower Chenab Canal subdivided into three major networks, those of the Rakh, Jhang and Gugera Branches, which were colonised in sequence.[14] The colony headquarters, Lyallpur, was a completely new town, and in time became an important market centre, overshadowing older towns like Jhang and Chiniot. After 1947 Lyallpur became a major centre for Pakistan's emerging textile industry.

The proprietary claims of the indigenous Jangli population having been discounted, this vast area was categorised as Crown or State Waste land. It was thereby open to the administration to allocate the land as it wished. Three basic types of grants were adopted: Peasant, or *abadkar* (13-50 acres); Yeoman, or *sufedposh* (50-150 acres); and Capitalist, or *rais* (150-600 acres).[15] Peasant grantees received around 80 percent of allotted land, making the colony an area held predominantly by small holders. Yeoman and Capitalist grantees were allowed to acquire proprietary rights, after a qualifying period of five years.

Peasant grantees, however, were intended to remain as occupancy tenants, with the state retaining ownership of these grants. This relationship of owner and tenant was also reflected in a host of contractual regulations concerning a variety of agrarian and civic practices. Examples ranged from regulated inheritance to the proper maintenance of *abadis*, field boundaries and water channels. These 'terms and conditions' were resented by the colonists, who regarded them as arbitrary and unjust, and subject to arbitrariness from the subordinate, native bureaucracy that was responsible for their enforcement. Within a few years of settlement, a political agitation built up in the canal colony villages, with the demand that these tenurial conditions be lifted and proprietary rights allowed to the peasant grantees.[16] The government was not willing to alienate its beneficiaries. After a commission of enquiry, it acceded to these demands.[17] This relapse of the state's interventionist role was embodied in the Colonization of Lands Act of 1912. The grantees became proprietors, they could revert to traditional practices and arrangements (as over inheritance), rather than conform to the many stipulations through which the British had intended to raise them to "a higher level of civilization".

In Lower Chenab Colony, immigrant grantees received almost twice as much land as those indigenous to the Rechna Doab, the proportion being about two-thirds to one-third.[18] Even so, the indigenous and predominantly Muslim Janglis and Hitharis received a substantial amount of land, and to a much greater degree than originally planned. It was the immigrant grantees whom the British expected to be the backbone of the colony. They were to be chosen from among skilled agriculturists belonging to landholding lineages. They were to come from districts suffering from high population densities, and thereby relieve economic pressures in these areas. The British selected seven districts from central Punjab for recruiting such grantees. These were Ambala, Amritsar, Gurdaspur, Hoshiarpur, Jullunder, Ludhiana and Sialkot. Of these Amritsar was the largest recipient, with over 250,000 acres allotted, while Gurdaspur and Sialkot obtained around 150,000 acres, and the others except Ambala got over 100,000 acres each.[19] Other Punjab districts were also allotted smaller areas of land, but over 80 percent of land allocated for immigrant grantees went to the seven selected districts. It was in these districts that the Sikh population was also concentrated.

In terms of the social composition of the grantees, the British kept land allocation almost entirely for the landholding 'agricultural castes'. Richer non-agriculturists could obtain land at auctions or as 'Capitalist' grantees; but the poorer classes were generally excluded from land occupancy. The largest area of land was allotted to immigrant Jats, who got 675,000 acres, of which 230,000 acres went to Muslims and the rest to Hindus and Sikhs. The Arains, who were all Muslims, stood second with around 200,000 acres. Among other Hindu and Sikh castes to receive land (figures were not disaggregated for these two communities), the most prominent were Kambohs, Sainis and Rajputs.[20] Clearly, a very sizeable intake of Sikh settlers from the central Punjab occurred in the Rechna Doab. Whenever possible, grantees from the same caste, or from the same district, were settled in a village. This helped to preserve social cohesion and traditional relationships. Grantees also brought with them their *jajmani* servitors, thus reproducing in the canal colonies the social organization of the older villages. Economic change turned out to be deeply rooted in social continuities.

The access to new and valuable economic resources led to a considerable strengthening of the upper stratum of rural society. There was a consequent weakening in the position of the rural poor and landless. Through the transfer of land, British imperialism was cementing its bonds with, and helping to consolidate the position of, those who were already dominant. Moreover, the central Punjab districts, and even more specifically the castes selected for grantees, were also heavily involved with military recruitment. These castes also formed the backbone of the Sikh component in the British Indian army. Since the major portion of soldiers in the army came from the Punjab, military considerations continued to be an important underlying influence on land utilization in the canal colonies. Indeed, as we shall see, they were also to become a major, overt imperative in colonization policy. In Lower Chenab Colony 15,000 acres were reserved for ex-soldiers on the two earlier branches, the Rakh and Jhang. On the Gugera Branch the amount was raised to 70,000 acres, or almost 10 percent of allotted land on this tract.[21] The military's stake was to grow even further in later colonies.

An intriguing illustration of the link between the military and landed status occurred with the allocation of three villages in Lower Chenab Colony to ex-soldiers of the 23rd, 32nd and 34th Pioneer Regiments. The recipients were not from the agricultural castes, as with other pensioner grants. Instead they were lower caste Mazhbi Sikhs, who had sought service in these regiments. The Mazhbis as a community were regarded by the British as undisciplined and prone to crime. Grants of land to those who had opted for military service was an inducement to other more recalcitrant Mazhbis to reform. In 1911 the Mazhbi grantees were accorded agricultural caste status in Lyallpur and Gujranwala Districts, a status not enjoyed by Mazhbi Sikhs anywhere else in the Punjab.[22]

In the project that followed, Lower Jhelum Colony, the military presence was far more pervasive. Developed between 1902 and 1906, the colony was situated in the Shahpur District, with its headquarters in the newly founded town of Sargodha. Like its predecessors, the colony was originally intended to be settled with civilian colonists, to be drawn from the north-western Punjab, a predominantly Muslim region. The feeling had grown that too much land had passed to the central Punjab and to non-Muslims.[23] The new colony was seen as an opportunity to rectify this imbalance. Grantees had even begun to be selected when a dramatic change in colonization policy occurred. Based on the report in 1901 of a Horse and Mule-breeding Commission, the Government of India demanded that colony grantees should henceforth be required to breed and maintain mules and horses for the military. The report of the commission coincided with the opening up of Lower Jhelum Colony, and this availability of new land came to be regarded as an ideal opportunity to implement the change in policy, towards meeting military goals.[24]

As a result, the original colonization scheme had to be replaced by one that required grantees to possess mares for breeding young stock for the cavalry. Agricultural skills were now secondary, though the grantees still had to come from agricultural castes. In order to retain their viability, the minimum size of Peasant grants was kept at 55 acres, entailing either subtenancies or less intensive land usage. Larger holdings, known as Yeoman Horsebreeding grants, were allotted to members of elite rural families. They were required to maintain several mares, at the rate of 40 acres per mare.[25] Sikhs obtained a number of these grants, though the majority went to Muslim families from contiguous districts. The incursion of horse-breeding did lead to an enlargement of the Sikh component among the Lower Jhelum grantees. Because they had fewer mares at hand, a smaller number of grantees from the submontane districts of Rawalpindi Division were selected than was originally intended. More grantees were chosen from Gujrat, Sialkot and Gujranwala: Sikh agriculturists were better represented in these districts.[26] The colony contained several *mauzas*, or village estates, where land was held exclusively by Sikh grantees.

Grantees in Lower Jhelum Colony could not, however, obtain proprietary rights, as this would have undermined regulated horse-breeding. Succession was also restricted to primogeniture, to prevent subdivision from threatening horse-breeding. This departure from customary law, along with the unrelenting tenurial obligation of maintaining mares and producing foals, led to the Lower Jhelum grantees being more politically restive than other colonists over the years. Agitations demanding the termination of horse-breeding, or at least relief from primogeniture, periodically shook the colony. The growing discontent against horse-breeding was often centred around Sikh villages, where Akali and Congress sentiments found sympathy. But the military prerogative was such that the British held on to horse-breeding, till it was finally abolished in 1940.[27]

In addition to horse-breeding, the military also obtained a far higher share of allotable land for ex-soldiers than in previous colonies. Of an allotted area of 445,000 acres, pensioners received over 75,000 acres. With their presence in the army, Sikhs shared in these grants. Those from cavalry regiments obtained horse-breeding grants. Infantrymen received smaller grants, but these were not subject to horse-breeding tenures. The recipients of these military grants were Punjabis serving in regiments stationed in all five army commands in India: Punjab, Bengal, Bombay, Burma and Madras. Regimental officers rather than civil officials were given the responsibility of selecting these grantees, the choice being determined thus not on agricultural skills but on the nature of service in the army. The indigenous Janglis also received around 60,000 acres of land, on non-horsebreeding conditions and mostly on the periphery of the colony. Along with 'civil' grantees, who were retired government officials, they were the only allottees not involved with military functions in the colony.

The next major colonization project was Lower Bari Doab Colony. Being the only large project developed between 1910 and 1925, colonization policy was framed to serve a number of political and economic needs, though the military interest remained predominant. Horse-breeding was again imposed on civilian peasant grantees, but without such onerous conditions. Compulsion was replaced by competition. Several leaseholds of 25 acres, carrying the horse-breeding tenure, were situated in each village of Peasant grantees, who could compete with each other to obtain them.[28] Horse-breeding would thus be regarded as a valuable additional resource, rather than an imposition whose non-fulfilment threatened the very livelihood of the grantees, as in Lower Jhelum Colony. The ratio of service to ordinary grants varied from village to village, but officials endeavoured to have one for every two grantees. Officials were concerned that this competitive aspect would lead to divisiveness and conflict in villages. These apprehensions were dismissed in view of the perceived strategic value of horse-breeding. This colony remained free of the discontent and the ensuing political protest that Lower Jhelum Colony experienced. The scheme indeed continued till after 1947. The leaseholds were renewable every ten years, and by and large these were continued in favour of incumbents. There were times, however, when the supply of satisfactory applicants from within a village was lacking. The military authorities prevailed upon the government to allow outsiders to obtain these leases, a practice that had earlier been regarded as a potential source of friction.

The horse-breeding leaseholds in Lower Bari Doab Colony came out of an allocation of over 500,000 acres for "Peasant horse-breeders". This included around 180,000 acres reserved for ex-soldiers. Civilian small holders also received grants from the allocation for "Hereditary agriculturists" and "Compensatory grantees", totalling around 100,000 acres.[29] As in the other colonies, Sikh agriculturists were well represented in these allocations, though the actual area allotted by communities is not clear. All these civilian grantees had to belong to agricultural castes: the tradition of excluding the non-landed rural proletariat was continued. The only exception was an allocation of 20,000 acres for "Depressed classes and criminal tribes", made after representations from Christian and other missionary and philanthropic bodies.[30]

The development of Lower Bari Doab Colony coincided with the outbreak of World War I, and this affected the amount of land devoted to military grantees. In the original colonization scheme, 105,000 acres were allocated for military pensioners. With the outbreak of war a further 75,000 acres were added. This decision was taken at a time when all other allocations were being reduced because of the large areas of inferior land encountered in the colony. The British also decided that the allocation should go not to military pensioners, as in previous cases, but instead to military war veterans. This as an inducement to recruitment, and a scale of rewards for war service, that no other province of British India was able to offer. Moreover, in order to help spread recruitment over a wider social base, these grants were opened to men of non-agricultura' castes, but only if they had been actual combatants. The areas eligible for these grants were also expanded. War veterans from any part of the Punjab, as well as from Kashmir, the North-West Frontier Province and the Punjab Native States, could obtain such grants.[31] Sikhs, with their large representation in the army, thereby gained major access to land in Lower Bari Doab Colony.

Elite rural families were catered for in this colony through the allocation of 60,000 acres for "Landed gantry" grants. Eligible for these grants were families mentioned in Griffin and Massy's *Chiefs and Families of Note in the Punjab*, and other prominent divisional and provincial darbari families. These grantees came from all five administrative divisions of the Punjab, though the majority came from western Punjab, because of the higher incidence of larger landholdings there. Services to the administration, war recruitment and help against political agitations, such as the Khilafat and Akali movements, were some of the criteria for making these grants. Another objective was to bolster the fortunes of magnate families that might be suffering from economic pressures. The landlord stratum thus continued to be placated with land, examples from earlier colonies were the 'Capitalist' and 'Yeoman Horse-breeding' grants, and an annual trickle of 'reward' grants for military officers. There were many other examples of more individualised grants. One was the 2,000 acres allotted in Montgomery District to Sardar Jogindra Singh (who in the 1940s became a central minister for railways), on condition that he produce seed and experiment with agricultural machinery.[32] Another was a leasehold of 2,500 acres to Sardar Daljit Singh of Kapurthala, for construction of a network of tubewell.[33] Both men were unable to meet their tenurial conditions. Yet they were allowed to obtain proprietary rights over much of these holdings.

In addition, the British also came to the aid of the larger landed estates when their owners were minors, or in times of adversity, through the mechanism of the Court of Wards.[34] The finances of many estates fell into disarray during the depression years of the 1930s, as agricultural prices and rents collapsed but consumption patterns remained more inelastic. Many elite Sikh families, with substantial canal colony holdings, were thus rescued through the Court of Wards from indigence and possible dissolution. Two examples were the Vahali estate of Jhelum District, which owned 3,300 acres in Chenab Colony alone; and the various holdings of the descendants of the aforementioned Baba Sir Khem Singh Bedi.[35]

A further example of the link between the dispensation of land and political obligation and alignment occurred with various types of 'reward' grants. Areas of 4,000 acres in Upper Jhelum Colony were reserved for those who had helped the administration's fight against crime. The Nili Bar Colony, developed after 1925, also had an allocation of 37,000 acres for 'reward' grants. The Lower Bari Doab Colony and later extensions of Lower Chenab Colony had similar allocations. These grants were utilised liberally for help against political movements.[36] During the 1920s, for example, colony grants were made to those who had worked against the Akali movement. These grants varied in size from 13-100 acres, and were allotted to informers, police and civil officials, local notables, and to families of those killed or severely wounded by the Akalis.[37]

The last major colonization project undertaken during British rule was Nili Bar Colony, situated in the Montgomery and Multan Districts. The scheme covered approximately 800,000 acres of land with perennial irrigation; and 260,000 acres with non-perennial irrigation. The recipients of the latter were predominantly Janglis, or indigenous inhabitants. Colonization commenced in 1925 and continued into the 1940s.[38] Horsebreeding was finally dropped, since enough resources had already been allotted to it. Peasant colonization remained a major feature, with 250,000 acres, or around 30 percent of perennially irrigated land reserved for this purpose. This proportion was much lower than the allocation for Peasant grants in earlier colonies. An area of 75,000 acres was reserved for military pensioners, though ex-soldiers also received land from the allocation for civilian Peasants. Both categories had to belong to 'agricultural castes', denoting once again the exclusion of the non-landowning poor. Grantees were drawn from the central Punjab districts of Amritsar, Ferozepur, Gurdaspur, Jullunder and Ludhiana; and to a lesser extent from some districts in western Punjab. Land was also reserved for those suffering from river action, and the grantees were drawn primarily from central Punjab.

The unique feature of Nili Bar Colony was that over 360,000 acres, or 45 percent of perennially irrigated land, was reserved for sale by auction. This method of land disposal had been adopted for much smaller areas in previous colonies. Only in Lower Bari Doab Colony was the more sizeable area of 70,000 acres reserved for this purpose. Auctions enabled the government to obtain quicker returns on the capital value of the land than settlement by grantees. Also, market values could be realised with auctions, while grantees of land were conceded proprietary rights at highly subsidised rates. The British took this option because of fiscal exigencies: the higher interest rates of the 1920s and the sizeable capital costs of the Sutlej Valley Project, of which Nili Bar Colony was a part. Through auctions richer Punjabis gained access to colony land, even if they did not belong to the 'agricultural castes'. In addition to the landlord and landholding peasant classes, commercial and professional groups could also now obtain further significant landed resources.

The Nili Bar auctions were planned to take place over a number of years, since bringing a surfeit of land on the market would have depressed land prices. The government had initially decided to sell around 15,000 acres per year, and thereby dispose of the land in 20-25 years. The auction process commenced in late 1926; and in the next three years over 40,000 acres were sold.[39] Prices realised were also competitive with current market values. However, the onset of the economic depression created a dramatic reversal. Land prices collapsed, and the government had to discontinue further auctions. Not till 1940 was it able to sell over 5,000 acres per year; and prices did not exceed pre-1930 levels till 1942.

Figures of auction sales reveal that Sikhs were more prominent in purchasing land prior to the economic depression, than after it. This was a pattern also true for agriculturists as opposed to non-agriculturists. Before 1930 the former were buying upto three-quarters of land at the Nili Bar auctions; but of the land sold after 1938, when auctions resumed, they acquired less than half. Of the total land sold till 1944, Sikhs had purchased 30 percent, or 36,000 acres, while Muslims bought 33,000 acres. Hindus purchased 49,000 acres, most of these acquisitions coming consequent to the economic depression, when 'non-agriculturists' were obtaining larger amounts of land.[40] Thus for their numbers Sikhs, as well as Hindus, did obtain a disproportionate amount of land, an indication of their stronger economic standing.

The period of British rule witnessed extensive economic changes and population movements in the Punjab. We have seen above the prominent participation of Sikhs in the utilization of newly developed canal irrigated land in the so-called 'canal colonies', situated in the western *doabs* of prepartition Punjab. The types of landholdings received by Sikhs varied greatly, from grants of several thousand acres to individuals like Baba Sir Khem Singh Bedi and Sardar Jogindra Singh, to 'Peasant' sized holdings of 25 acres. We have emphasised that these landed resources were transferred predominantly to the more 'superior' rural groups: those that were incumbent landholders and were categorised as 'agricultural castes' under the Land Alienation Act. The importance of the military in this province was amply reflected in the large, and indeed disproportionate, areas reserved for military functions and personnel. The social origins of grantees and soldiers were similar: both came from the rural elite and the upper levels of village society.

The strengthening of these groups had a pronounced impact on the political economy of the Punjab. This was indicated by the relative weakness of nationalism, and the continued vibrancy of the British-supported and landlord-led political formation of the Punjab National Unionist Party. Non-landed rural groups also moved to the canal colonies, but they remained as subtenants, labourers or *jajmani* servitors. Commercial groups also obtained major benefits from agricultural colonization, with the substantial increase in trade, agro-processing and agricultural credit. Professional elements also benefitted, from expansion in state employment and increased demand for services. Most of these were non-Muslims, and they emigrated to Indian territory at partition. Sikh and Hindu agricultural owners and workers, largely the families of earlier migrants from the east, also had to move to India. This infusion of human skills must have contributed to the vibrancy of agriculture and the secondary sector in post-1947 north-western India. However, the prospect of losing valuable landed and commercial assets, held by their brethren in western Punjab, must have disconcerted agrarian groups in central Punjab during partition. This feeling of losing such major resources could have been an important factor behind the killings and human suffering that accompanied the division of the province.

NOTES

1.   This process has been studied in greater detail in Imran Ali, "The Punjab Canal Colonies, 1885-1940", Ph.D thesis, Australian National University, 1980; and Imran Ali, *The Punjab Under Imperialism, 1885-1947* (Princeton University Press, Princeton, New Jersey, 1988).

2.   These issues are discussed in: *Report of the Indian Irrigation Commission, 1901-03*, Part II, Ch. 14, p. 31, and "Evidence", vol. 4, Punjab, pp. 3-4. See also Note by Settlement Commissioner, Punjab, 10 May, 1900; in Punjab Revenue and Agriculture Proceedings (Irrigation), July 1900, No. 17.

3.   The Punjab Revenue and Agriculture Proceedings (Irrigation) series for the years 1897-1905 contains copious records on such grants. See also Board of Revenue, Lahore, (hereafter BOR) J/301/619.

4.   See *Punjab Colony Manual* (Lahore, 1936), p.13; and *Chenab Colony Settlement Report* (1915), paras 1 and 84.

5.   For a description of the Janglis, see *Chenab Colony Gazetteer* (1904), pp. 14-24; and *Chenab Colony Settlement Report* (1915), paras 86-93.

6.   For land grants to Jangles in the Rechna Doab, see BOR Files 301/3/17/71 and 301/3/25/217. See also *Chenab Colony Settlement Report* (1915), paras 38-41.

7.   See *Chenab Colony Gazetteer* (1904), p.29; and *Chenab Colony Settlement Report* (1915), para 4.

8.   For colonization proceedings in the Sidhnai Colony, see BOR H/251/3. See also I. Ali, Ph.D. Thesis, pp. 15-22.

9.   Letter of Financial Commissioner, Punjab, to Deputy Commissioners of Lahore, Amritsar, Gurdaspur, Hoshiarpur, and Settlement Officers of Jullunder and Ferozepur, 7 August 1885, in BOR H/251/3 Keep With, p. 4.

10.   See I. Ali, Ph.D. Thesis, Tables 2.2 and 2.3, pp. 20-21.

11.   This process is discussed in *ibid.* pp. 22-26. See also BOR H/251/97; and *Assessment Report of Lower Sohag Para Colony* (1899).

12.   BOR files that covered the grant to Khem Singh Bedi, and subsequent developments, are: J/301/48, 601/1/21/112, 601/1/21/123, 601/1/24/155 and 601/1/24/212.

13.   For land distribution in the Chunian Colony, see I. Ali, Ph.D. Thesis, pp. 27-31. See also BOR H/251/296, H/251/426 and J/301/794.

14.   Some sources for information on the Lower Chenab Colony are: F.P. Young, *Report on the Colonization of the Rakh and Mianali Branches* (Lahore, 1897); *Chenab Colony Gazetteer* (1904); *Chenab Colony Settlement Report* (1915); Dewa Singh, *Colonization of the Rechna Doab* (Lahore, n.d.); and P.W. Paustian, *Canal Irrigation in the Punjab* (New York, 1930).

15.   For a more detailed analysis, see I. Ali, Ph.D. Thesis, pp. 31-55.

16.   *Ibid*, pp. 111-124. See also N.G. Barrier, "The Punjab disturbances of 1907: the response of the British government in India to agrarian unrest", *Modern Asian Studies*, I, 4 (1967), pp. 353-383; and S.R. Sharma, *The Punjab in Ferment* (New Delhi, 1971).

17. See 'Report of the Punjab Colonies Committee, 1907-08' (India Office Records: 10(3514)); and BOR: H/2@1/403 and H/251/416.

18. The BOR contains several files dealing with the colonization in Lower Chenab Colony, two of the largest being H/251/16 A-F and Printed File No. 24, Revenue, vols. I-III.

19. See I. Ali, Ph.D. Thesis, p. 46.

20. *Ibid.*, p.49.

21. For land grants to military pensioners in Lower Chenab Colony, see BOR J/301/431.

22. For information on the Mazhbi settlement in Lower Chenab Colony, see BOR: J/301/3,J/301/1587,301/2/00/205.

23. See especially Note by Financial Commissioner, Punjab, 22 January 1898; in Punjab Revenue and Agriculture Proceedings (Irrigation), April 1898, No. 7.

24. See 'Report of the Horse and Mule-breeding Commission, 1900-01' (IOR: Temporary 544).

25. For a more detailed discussion of the Lower Jhelum colonization, see I. Ali, Ph.D. Thesis, pp. 56-71.

26. The Colonization Officer who was made responsible for selecting grantees was the young W.M. Hailey, later to become an eminent colonial administrator.

27. For an examination of the political and economic aspects of horse-breeding in Lower Jhelum Colony, see *ibid.*, pp. 216-54.

28. For a more detailed analysis, see *ibid.*, pp. 254-64. See also BOR: J/301/1101, J/301/1206,301/2/24/61.

29. See I. Ali, Ph.D. Thesis, pp. 71-89; and BOR: H/251/476, J/301/1185, 301/4/24/9.

30. See I. Ali, Ph.D. Thesis, pp. 157-71. See also BOR: J/301/710, J/301/792, J/301/987, J/301/1179,J/301/1630.

31. See BOR J/301/1178; and I. Ali, Ph.D. Thesis, pp. 191-204.

32. See BOR 301/11/24/18.

33. See BOR: J/301/1055, 301/11/16/11.

34. See I. Ali, Ph.D. Thesis, pp. 133-37.

35. See BOR: 601/1/20/147, 601/1/21/112, 601/1/24/123, 601/1/24/155, 601/1/24/212.

36. See BOR: H/251/475, J/301/1154, 301/14/C9/27.

37. See BOR: 301/3/25/5, 301/3/25/22, 301/3/C9/215, 301/14/00/1, 301/14/00/21.

38. For a more detailed analysis, see I. Ali, Ph.D. Thesis, pp. 92-105; and BOR: 301/1/C9/3-4, 301/2/C9/188.

39. The auction process in Nili Bar Colony was covered in detail in BOR 301/8/C9/47. For the temporary utilization of the lands awaiting auction, see BOR 301/11/C9/51.

40. See I. Ali, Ph.D. Thesis, Appendix I.

Gender Stereotyping and Colonial Schools in the Punjab, 1882-1902

Masood Akhtar Zahid

In the past few decades, a growing concern has been shown by historians, sociologists and other commentators of social phenomena, of the need for an equitable system of resource distribution at the national and international levels. Representing an underprivileged class, women's movements have aimed at a redefinition of women's place in the state and society and the provision of equal opportunities of progress. In its impetuous way, the feminist framework has marked out forces resilient to change in the desired direction. Home, school, colleges, universities and places of work have generally been recognised as communicative agents of gender stereotyping. Seminars, conferences, establishment of departments of women studies, and research projects all point to an awakened worldwide interest and efforts to evolve a gender-free world of equal opportunities. Literacy in general and female literacy in particular has been considered as prerequisite of the desired system. But female illiteracy itself requires further articulation and generous sponsorship before it becomes a powerful ingredient of change.

Within a feminist framework and in relation to Asia and Africa, Nelly P. Stromquest attributes female illiteracy to an interplay of gender-subordination and poverty on the one hand, and the development of a patriarchal theory on the other, which, based on the assumption of women's mental and physical inferiority, confines them to the less critical domestic roles of nurturing and raising children, tending to their husbands and the kindred. Women's supposedly natural ability to serve as mothers, wives and housekeepers has become the cornerstone of the sexual division of labour. She also finds control on women's sexuality as another roadblock to their public participation. Pleased with its continuing erosion in the Western Hemisphere, she attributes to its persistence child marriages and purdah in South Asia. Illiteracy, to her is the plight of the poor and powerless, whereas an educated woman is a threat to those who benefit from her unpaid work and docile attitude.[1]

These variables may have some relevance to the complex social order, which governed the lives of Punjabis nearly a century ago. Despite the growing discourse and decades of socio-economic and religio-political restructuring, the preservation of the male-dominated social order has remained an unwritten agenda of policy making. However, allowances have to be made about the specificity of contexts and traditions before a generalized statement is made about similarities between the old and current norms and forces of resilience. The domestication of women had different connotations, backgrounds and meanings than what one is led to believe from the juvenile literature. Paradoxically, the poverty thesis does not provide a complete explanation, as the isolationist tendencies in the wealthy Punjabis conflicted with the ethos of public and private schools for girls. A regional and periodized approach remains indispensable to any enduring statement about factors contributing to the emergence of a patriarchal society and social order. This paper will highlight the role that was played by the colonial schools in perpetuating that order. It is argued that gender was the underlying theme of educational discourse, development and growth, emanating from shared perceptions of the Europeans and Punjabis.

In perhaps no other sphere of governmental activity was the failure of British policy so pronounced as in women's education. Hunter, the president of the Education Commission of 1882, described the chapter on female education as 'most melancholy of all'. Remorse was also expressed by other officials, who viewed the scale of female illiteracy as a blot on the education system. Manifestation of strong verbal sympathy was often expressed in the form of self-projecting annual education and administration reports. These reports contained separate sections and statistics pertaining to schools for girls, highlighting problems, prospects and progress. They often concluded with self-congratulatory notes and perennial condemnation of the 'native' conservatism. Some lieutenant-governors of Punjab were genuinely interested in improving the lot of the oppressed sections of the population. For example, John Lawrence and Robert Montgomery concerned themselves to alleviating the obvious and grotesque forms of excesses against women. John Lawrence ordered a better organised system of registering births and deaths to control female infanticide and Robert Montgomery launched essay competitions to solicit an informed opinion to work out a strategy to curb this inhuman practice. On the whole, the government's stance was defensive and often triggered by criminal offences. As regards female literacy, it was more or less a confession of failure, an expression of helplessness and a repeat performance of public indifference. Despite his interest in education, even Charles Aitchison, one of the ablest civilians in the province, failed to ensure equal opportunity for women. Reacting to the Hunter Report's emphasis on women's education, Aitchison preferred to wait until the filter-down effect of education among men would have transformed their attitudes towards women's education. It was argued that without educating a sizeable male population, no progress could be made towards the evolution of a judicious system, in which everyone would have a free access to public institutions, regardless of caste, creed and gender. Although filtration theory had failed to encourage education among the masses and was renounced under the 1854 Charles Wood's Despatch, its prevalence was perceptible particularly in relation to women's education.

A cursory reading of the contemporary official records provides a surcharged view of cultural superiority of the Western civilization, as well as an unsavoury impression about the traditions of the colonized. Such a spontaneous as well as pre-rehearsed denigration was central to the so-called reforming mission of the colonizer.

It was a rationale for his 'enlightened' presence in the colonies. The period under study coincided with Victorian England, where public schools promoted special ethos, bravery, manliness and a belief in the white man's duty to rule and where association with women was considered harmful to their upbringing and missions, and horrors of effeminate behaviour were lauded. Many of these young men were destined for service to the Empire, either as army officers or government administrators, and a number of them had relatives serving abroad. Masculine values were systematically ingrained in their receptive minds, for manhood was regarded not as a physical definition but a social construct, nurtured by the social environment and the age. This in view, contact with women was tolerated only out of necessity. It was therefore unlikely for products of those schools to shun their carefully developed disposition and stereotypical images about women even though some early movements towards the equality of educational opportunities at home were being nurtured by reformers such as J.S. Mill and F.D. Maurice. With such upbringing, colonial administrators must have thought, to use Arthur Mahew's words, "that the sex which was marked out by nature to be a domestic ornament in England might safely be left to the same function in India".[2]

It was therefore unnatural for boys trained in the public-school tradition to march against non-egalitarian practices and efface gender-based realms of responsibilities. The colonial system was as patriarchal in outlook and exertions as the system it replaced. To begin with, when Lord Bentinck committed India to English education in 1835, the education of women did not figure on the official agenda. Fourteen years elapsed before a half-hearted attempt was made by Drinkwater Bethune, his Law Member, to establish a state-run school for girls at Calcutta in 1849. Private philanthropy towards women's education was almost non-existent and missionaries were more interested in winning the male converts. Common perceptions between the European officers and indigenous elite, whether English-educated or home-spun, debilitated efforts supportive of female literacy. However, Bethune over-rode his timid colleagues, discounting fears of a social backlash. Together with Ishwar Chander Vidyasagar, the co-founder, he made the School famous all over India. Bethune was struck by the intelligence of Indian girls whom he found as avid learners and intelligent as their European sisters.

Bethune's experience lifted the self-imposed fear of social resistance, and schools for girls were opened in parts of India and the Punjab. Charles Wood's Educational Despatch of 1854 provided a fresh impetus to educational work, with the promise of a better organised educational government and aid. The despatch resulted in the setting up of three universities, Calcutta, Bombay and Madras, and Departments of Public Instruction in each province. At the top of departmental machinery was a director, assisted by circle inspectors, assistant, and district inspectors. This exclusively male club of European officers and their Indian deputies monitored and guided the course of education in the province. The despatch carried a broad outline of education policy, setting priorities and the targets. Future expansion and development of post-secondary education was contemplated on self-help basis, and withdrawal of government was advocated to encourage private enterprise without harming the cause of education. Education of the masses, i.e., primary education, and education of the special classes and women was promised both 'frank and cordial support'.[3]

In 1882, the Hunter Report reviewed the progress of education in India to determine what effect had been given to the Wood's Despatch, as its breaches had been reported by both the General Council of Education in India and leading missionaries. The report shared the apprehensions on fundamental questions of policy which had stressed greater patronage of elementary education in the public sector and the development of grant-in-aid system to promote higher education in the private sector.

It therefore, reaffirmed pursuance of that policy and further expansion of elementary and women's education. Lengthy correspondence ensued between Calcutta and Local Governments. The Punjab government accepted nearly all the recommendations, refusing however to introduce a moral text-book in colleges based on natural religion, lectures on duty of a man and citizen, and special measures to encourage education among Muslims. The Report became a charter of policy directives seeking allegiance to the Despatch, the Magna Carta of Indian education. Changes were introduced in the Punjab Education Code in the light of the Hunter Report. Secondary schools and colleges for boys were not opened in the public sector, in order to economise expenditure and lure the missionaries and indigenous reform organisations, such as Arya Samajes, Muslim Anjumans and Singh Sabhas.

By the turn of the century, the educational landscape in the Punjab revealed some hopeful signs on the score of female literacy. Within two decades from the Hunter Report, the number of girls in government aided and unaided schools was more than doubled. In 1901-02, there were 360 girls' schools with 15,546 pupils. This included 2,849 girls in secondary schools, of which 1,786 were Christian, 691 Hindu, 295 Muslim and 77 Sikh, Parsi and others. Only eleven girls, all Christian, were reported to have reached the collegiate stage.[4] The government considered that level of growth far from satisfactory, but its cause lay in the lukewarm official reception to the noble exhortation of the Hunter Report. Hunter could not avoid the impression that local governments inspired suspicions about the Education Commission's work and indulged in behind-the-scene manipulation to undermine it. On one pretext after another, the Punjab government evaded compliance with its Report, despite Calcutta's occasional reminders and queries.

As for the attitude of educational bureaucracy, the circle inspectors, watchdogs of the system, were often criticised in the press for their inefficiency and lack of interest. The Viceroy, Lord Lansdowne, raised the matter with the Secretary of State, Lord Cross, requesting him to arrange some kind of preliminary training for the educational officers before they assume the charge in India. Lord Cross only agreed to visits by those officers to schools in England to familiarise them with inspection work. Under their contracts of appointment, those officers were required to learn a vernacular language, which would help them with the inspection work, but inspectors were usually regarded as slow learners of the vernacular languages and uninterested in work. Without appreciating the hurdles faced by girls' schools, they would paint a dreary picture about their performance and press for punitive action. Baba Khem Singh Bedi's schools for girls in the central and northern districts would have perished if Charles Aitchison had not disregarded their annihilating reports. Khem Singh, a direct descendent of Guru Nanak, was one of the most influential Punjabis whose involvement in the education of women was seen by Aitchison as a positive influence on the course of literacy. Government grants to aided schools were subject to good reports by the inspectors and often girl's schools found it hard to meet the criteria. In 1889, a female inspectress, Miss Francis, was appointed at half the salary of a male inspector, but, with a province-wide jurisdiction.[5] Her appointment was welcome news, but the sheer size of her responsibility and the hazards of transportation made her work extremely difficult.

The Local Government continued to attribute slow progress of female literacy to the usual source, 'native' conservatism and lack of private philanthropy. It was argued that modern education was against the Eastern ideal of women's life, e.g. 'strict purity, seclusion and domestic duty'.[6] In actual fact, government was equally responsible for their unfulfilled expectations. A concerned Punjabi official, Khan Ahmad Shah, Extra Assistant-Commissioner, Hoshiarpur, complained to the Hunter Commission about the negligence of the Punjab education department to the cause of female education.[7] No bold efforts were made to fight female illiteracy or to popularize English education among the girls. As secular education for girls conflicted with the Indian tradition, the government was determined not to let religion enter the state schools. Both the public and the officials acknowledged the harmful effect of 'godless' education, but it was only non-governmental schools that were given the freedom to make arrangements for religious instruction, if they so wished. Secondly, European inspectors and their Indian deputies became self-appointed agents of women's educational needs and aspirations, and commissions and enquiries heard them as representative of women's viewpoint. Punjab had not yet produced a woman of Pundita Rama Bai's stature who had spoken on behalf of women before the Education Commission at Poona, demanding equal educational opportunities. Purely male influence was discernible in the policy processes and the decisions on mode and content of education among girls' schools. The Punjab Text-Book Committee was filled with male members, officials, missionaries, and Indians reformers. The Committee prepared list of books for schools up to the Middle standard. It often emphasised the streaming of curriculum on the basis of gender with special additional subjects, which would fit a woman for domestic life. Both the Hunter Commission and members of the Text-Book Committee had favoured the inclusion of domestic economy, knitting and sewing as special subjects for girls' schools. As Michelle Maskiell points out, when male reformers promoted women's education it was usually to train women to be better wives and mothers, not to free them from domestic dependency.[8] Miss Francis also advocated that division, thus conceding to the popular demand. Curricula at government, aided and unaided schools was designed to produce better mothers and *sughar bewis* (ideal wives), rather than sharers of public responsibility. Avenues for public participation for women were too limited to train them otherwise.

The recognition of gender was also transparent in the provision of single-sex schools. Echoing public sentiments, Miss Francis feared that no other course would be acceptable to the Punjabis. The scarcity of female teachers had thrown open a debate on what arrangements should be necessary to meet the challenge, for it was not merely a question of good teachers, but of getting any teachers at all.[9] There were no Normal Schools for female teacher-training in the province, except that training classes were attached to a number of ordinary schools. The attendance and quality of those classes was poor and the dropouts rate very high. To Mrs. Steel, who visited these classes in 1882-83, they were a misnomer for Normal Schools.[10] Recruits were almost bribed to join and asked to sign an undertaking to complete the training and join the profession. Situated far away from their permanent abode, Normal Classes did not attract many girls who would have more pressing responsibilities at home, like tending to old parents or grandparents. A teaching career entailed severance of family ties and long absences from home. Monetarily, it was an unattractive proposition with salaries as little as Rs.10 and Rs.3-6-0 in a government and aided primary school, respectively. The plausible alternative of co-educational institutions was not adopted, even though it had been successfully tried in Madras, where more girls were studying in boys' than in single-sex schools.

Gender also determined the type of schools. Just as the birth of a male compared to a female child did not evoke similar gratitude from the family, relatives and the society, their education also revealed discrimination. The birth of a son was often announced with a string of acacia tree leaves hung across the door followed by celebrations and distribution of sweets; that of a girl either passed away unnoticed or registered appropriate words of consolation from the neighbours. Even wealthier classes, which sought the education of sons at prestigious institutions like the Government, Forman Christian and Aitchison Colleges in Lahore, rarely expressed a matching anxiety in the choice of schools for daughters. Thus the initial gap between male and female literacy which was created by the late entry of the state in favour of the latter continued to widen due to social apathy and inadequate support from the government, missionaries and reform organisations. Consequently, Indian men, as O'Malley notes, returned to "unchanged homes" where senior ladies controlled the domestic economy of the household, performed traditional ceremonies and taught traditional culture, but had no knowledge of their men's work and contacts outside.[11]

The purdah system, common among the Muslim *ashraf*, especially in the northern and north-western districts and also among certain Hindus, was one of the major barriers to gender equality. Evolved in India during the Muslim rule, it became a status symbol in the Punjab too. Purdah was intimately connected with ideas of respectability, ownership and inheritance of property, arrangement of marriages, and division of labour. Wealthy Muslim women were secluded in the separate world of *zananah* (the women's part of the household), while Hindu and Sikh high-status women also observed variations of purdah restrictions. Vernacular tracts were published in defence of purdah. Anecdotes and poems, forewarning the dangers of desegregation were read at public meetings. Examples were given of marriage breakups and high divorce rate in Western countries where men and women intermingled freely. Desegregationists were ridiculed as slavish sufferers of an inferiority complex. Purdah enthusiasts found some powerful allies among the leading houses and enlightened Indians of the time. Saiyyid Ahmad Khan, who supported English education for Muslims' emancipation, opposed the same for women, for whom he regarded the traditional home-based education as the right model.[12] In her Urdu work, *Iffat-ul-Muslimat*, Sultan Jahan Begum of Bhopal defended purdah as a symbol of Islamic identity, quoting references from Quran and Hadith. She blamed English-educated husbands of working against a religiously-enjoined practice.[13] Such upper-class defence of women's seclusion was bound to disappoint those who considered its relaxation as essential to women's educational and social progress. Their only ally was a silent change in the attitude of parents, who, faced with the rising demand for educated wives, began to seek Western education for their daughters, too.

In 1886, under the scheme of Local Self-government, schools were transferred to the control of local bodies. Except for the Civil *and Military Gazette,* the move was criticised by the press and the intelligentsia, which doubted the suitability of local bodies for educational government. Partly nominated and partly elected under a limited franchise, with limited funds and power at their disposal, members of the local and district boards were considered a mismatch for the cause of education in general and female education in particular. In most of the thirty-two districts in the province, local and district boards failed to provide the minimum required investment in education. Their stinginess was more marked in relation to schools for girls. According to Miss Francis, they were generally reluctant to give grants-in-aid, and Lahore, Gujrat and Jullundur were particularly obstructive. At times, with the concurrence of district officials, local bodies diverted educational funds to non-educational heads of expenditure like hospitals, police and sanitation works. Barring Amritsar and Gujranwalla, municipal committees turned their back on female education. They often justified their lack of interest by referring to the absence of any pressure from the electorate. In 1890, for instance, the Hoshiarpur district board bragged about the opening of five new primary schools for boys, but refused to open a girls' school without an articulate demand.[14]

As for the missionaries and Indian reformers, they were also driven by considerations other than those which would abolish the manmade division of labour. Very soon the missionaries learnt that uneducated women were one of the major hurdles to their evangelising effort. Freeing men from their counter influence was obligatory. Educated men, no matter how liberal or sympathetic to the Christian faith, would not convert unless the ladies of their household were also educated. The *zanana* visitation by the missionary ladies was prompted by interlinked educational and evangelising motives. The Ludhiana Mission was active in the province since 1830 and was later joined by the Cambridge Mission, and the American Presbyterian Church. Devoting initially to the education of boys, they soon discovered its shortcomings and engaged themselves in the education of women by setting up schools and training teachers. They received liberal aid from the government. Their work inspired envy and emulative efforts by the indigenous reform groups. The period was known for religious controversy, polemical literature and the birth of denominational schools by Muslim Anjumans, Arya Samajes and Singh Sabhas. To safeguard communal interests and religion from the missionary inroads, they offered a blend of secular and religious education at a lesser cost than that in a government or aided institution. They refused to barter their internal freedom with the conditional aid from the government. Like the government and the missionaries, the reform organisations, initially focused on the education of men. And when they entered the sphere of female education, the motivation was not the education of girls in their own right but the creation of a moral mother.

The statistics pertaining to girls' schools and scholars during this period revealed somewhat transformed attitudes towards women's education. However, the trio that co-shared educational responsibility did not reflect a changed vision about the place of women in the state and society. Among them the traditional belief in the manmade division of labour remained as firm as ever. The imperial system and its hierarchies also made no room for public participation of women. The only professions open to women were teaching and medicine, because in both categories the presence of women was regarded as indispensable. In others, women were barred by convention and law. Like many, Gandhi had no qualms in apportioning the greater responsibility for the neglect of women's education to the prejudices and indifference of the Indian men than to the policies of the colonial government.[15] A modification of Gandhi's judgement is essential in the light of equal apathy of the state and the private enterprise in female education. In a system in which men are held supreme, the plight of women, whether Indian or non-Indian, Punjabi or non-Punjabi, was bound to suffer from lethargy, discrimination and the patronising attitude of the rulers. No wonder the male reformers, whether missionaries or Punjabis, failed to make headway in the right direction.

NOTES

1.   Nelly P. Stromquest, "Women And Illiteracy: The Interplay of Gender Subordination
      And Poverty", *Comparative Education* Review, 34, 1, 1990, pp.95-109
2.   Arthur Mahew, *The Education of India,* London, n.d., p. 96
3.   For full text of the Despatch, see S. Satthianadhan, *History of Education in the Madras
      Presidency*, Madras, 1894, Appendix C
4.   *Fourth Quinquennial Review of Education in India*, 1897-98, 1901-02, Calcutta, p.111
5.   *Punjab Education Code,* 1896
6.   A.P. Howell, *Education in British India Prior to 1857 and in 1870-71*, Calcutta, 1872,
      p.50
7.   *Report of the Indian Education Commission*, Calcutta, 1883, Para 677
8.   Michelle Maskiell, "Social Change and Social Control: College-Educated Punjabi
      Women, 1913 to 1960", *Modern Asian Studies* 19, 1, 1985, pp.55-83
9.   *Progress of Education In India*, 1902-07, Vol. I, Calcutta, 1909, p.296
10.   *Report on Popular Education*, 1883-84, p.81
11.   L.S. O'Malley, ed., *Modern India and the West: A Study of the Interaction of their
      Civilizations,* 1968, p. 446
12.   Sheikh Muhammad Ismail Panipati, ed., *Khutbat Sir Sayyid: Speeches of Sir Sayyid,*
      (Urdu), Vol.II, Lahore, 1972, p.65
13.   Sultan Jahan Begum, *Iffat-ul-Muslimat* (Urdu), Agra, 1918, p.4
14.   Deputy-Commissioner, Hoshiarpur, to the Commissioner, Jullundur, 3 September 1890,
      Punjab Home Education Proceedings, February 1891, Proc.6A
15.   Philip Hartog, *Some Aspects of Indian Education Past and Present: Being Three John
      Payne Lectures,* London, 1939, p.53

Clamping Shutters and Valorizing Women:
Tensions in Sculpting Gender-Identities in the Colonial Punjab

Kamlesh Mohan

In the present paper, I propose to explore into the process of gender-identity formation, specifically, the issue of construction of 'new' woman as it had significant bearing on the ongoing search for regional and communal identities from the late 19th century onwards. This was also the time when the status of women in Indian society became a political issue and focus of debate and controversy. Colonial rule, with its moral and civilizing claims, is said to have provided the context for a thoroughgoing re-evaluation of Indian 'tradition' along lines more consonant with the 'modern' economy and society-believed to have been the consequence of India's incorporation into the 'capitalist world system'.[1] The position of women was, in colonial perception, an indicator of the 'modernization' of a country. It also reflected on the ability of its citizens to rule themselves. Lack of 'masculinity' was a cogent argument around which India's unfitness for self-rule and the need for the British rule were justified by colonial rulers. It was in this context that the issue of recasting gender-identities, involving the definition of 'femininity' and 'masculinity', images, roles and relations between man and woman became central to the nationalist discourse and ideologies of social reform movements, particularly, Arya Samaj and Singh Sabha.

The main argument of this paper is that the process of construction of gender-identities especially self-hood, social experience and the roles of women among the enterprising middle classes in the colonial Punjab excluding the Princely states, remained segmented and incomplete. There are two underlying assumptions in my argument. Firstly, the multi-racial and multi-religious character of Punjabi society (as a consequence of its open geographical frontier) had generated socio-cultural tensions and sharpened contradictions in the mindscape of its people despite the broad acceptance of the principle of co-existence in social, political and economic life. Secondly, the overwhelmingly agrarian character of economy of this region had reinforced the persuasive dominance of the patriarchal peasant-culture, which persisted in the social thinking on the issue of gender-identities and role among the urban middle classes, who remained firmly anchored to their moorings in their native village while they were engaged in modernizing themselves.

For the purpose of discussion, the paper shall be divided into five sections: I-Conceptualising the Problem; II-Peasant-ethos, Socio-economic Conditions and Their Implications for Women; III-Social Roots of Middle Classes, Colonial View of Indian Culture and Women, and the Native Response; IV-Sculpting New Gender-Identities: Myths of Past and Contemporary Reality; V-Conclusion.

1. Conceptualising the Problems

It is important to delineate the meanings of several terms that will be employed in the course of our discussion specifically, 'gender', 'gender-identity', 'power', 'authority', 'autonomy' and 'status' formulated by feminist scholarship. For a clear understanding of term 'gender-identity', it is crucial to distinguish between 'sex' and 'gender'. While 'sex' generally carries a biological connotation, 'gender' is a term whose psychological and cultural connotations outweigh the biological component. It refers to social dimensions of one's existence as male and female. 'Gender' usually indicates the degree of conformity of the individual to the standards of femininity and masculinity in various cultures.

The concept of 'gender' can't be fully explicated without reference to the concepts of 'gender-role' and 'gender-identity'. Gender roles may be described in two ways: established gender roles of a culture or gender-roles of an individual.[2] In terms of culture, it may be described as a social norm or standard which summarizes the culturally constructed characteristics for males and females. The characteristics that define 'feminine' and 'masculine' may cover such diverse features as physical attributes, appearances, overt behaviour and covert attributes including feelings, attitudes, motives and beliefs.[3] Gender-roles typically include but are not confined to domestic, vocational, reproductive and erotic roles.[4] 'Gender-identity', broadly speaking, indicates the degree to which an individual regards herself as feminine or masculine. It includes an individual's sense of belonging to one sex or the other (or neither) but is more complicated in that it may include characteristics that are both masculine and feminine by cultural definitions.[5]

A few writers regard 'gender-schema' as crucial to the formation of 'gender-identity'. John Money uses the phrase 'gender-scheme' as basically equivalent to one's sense of gender on the basis of which one's gender identity is formulated.[6] For most individuals, 'gender', 'gender-roles' and 'gender-identity' are almost synonymous, but they can be at variance.[7] There is an imperfect co-relation between possession of gender-role characteristics and one's own sense of gender-identity. Possession of some gender-type characteristic is necessary but not sufficient for a firm gender-identity. Money is insistent that gender identity and gender roles are 'facets of the same entity'. He states that 'gender identity.....is the private experience of gender role; and gender role is the public manifestation of gender identity'.[8] In short, one could not have a gender-identity unless there were gender-roles and one had some attributes of that role; existence of gender-identity ensures the public expression of that identity which in turn ensures the continuance of that role. In order to underscore the integral nature of gender-role and gender-identity we shall hereafter refer to gender-identity as gender identity/role.[9]

Since the construction of gender-identities are formulated within the structure of family and society, it is important to clarify the meaning of the concepts of 'authority' and 'power'. According to Dahl, these are 'influence terms' which define the relationship in which one actor induces other actors to act in a specific way.[10] Influence derived from 'authority' requires cultural legitimation. Defined in this context 'authority' means the right to make a particular decision and to command obedience. Family relations especially daughter-father and husband-wife equations operate on this assumption. 'Power' deals more directly with the instruments that endow the holder with a particular status. While 'status' is a descriptive and ambiguous term, 'power' is an analytical concept, which implies the ability to influence effectively the persons or things, to secure favourable decisions through coercion, persuasion, manipulation of various sorts, bargaining and other forms of influence.

Power-mechanism postulates the superiority of one actor and the inferiority or subordination of the other. Women are subordinated because they lack power to resist injustice, imposition of inequality and exploitation of their sexuality, fertility and labour. Who wields power in society? What are the sources of their power? Which are the institutions that legitimize the subjugation of women? Institutions such as the state, religion and family exercise power in a manner inimical to the well-being and all-round growth of women as autonomous individuals. The legal structure is an example of entrenched power which has apportioned and sanctioned unequal rights between man and woman. Within the family both custom, socialisation process and tradition assign a second class and subordinate role to woman as daughter, sister, wife and mother. It is reinforced by official laws of various kinds. In other words, state, religion and family, being patriarchal institutions glorify the cult of masculinity.

The concept of 'autonomy' also signifies 'power' and is applicable to individual needs. Its basic assumptions is that each individual has the right and opportunity to choose his/her life style, educational prospects, profession, marriage partner, mode of expression of sexuality and control over reproductive functions. As men and women exercise their rights in society and political and economic arena, it is obligatory for them not to infringe or abrogate the rights and freedom of others. 'Status' is a vague term. It may mean demonstration of respect or feeling of being respected at the subjective level. Ironically, symbolic veneration, courtesy or respect may co-exist with deprivation of various sorts and oppression. In the historical context of contemporary social situation, 'status' may also subsume the prevalent religious rituals, customs and practices that had formalized or institutionalized social control, restrictions, oppressions, denial of access to knowledge and economic resources. Its cumulative result may imply damage to physical and psychological components of a woman's personality. The context of 'status' today comprises of a number of development indicators - health levels, education, property, opportunities for use of training and skills that open up chances of employment. It may be pointed out that the concepts of 'power', 'authority' and 'autonomy' are interlinked and useful for conceptualising the 'status' or situation of women in the colonial Punjab as in other regions. These are useful for understanding the issue of gender-relations as these are mediated in the construction of caste, communal, regional and national identities.

II. Peasant-ethos, Socio-economic Conditions: Their Implications for Women

Peasant-ethos

In this section, I have tried to explicate one strand of my argument - incidence of overlapping between the beliefs, attitudes and values with regard to the placement of women in a peasant society and those of the expanding urban-society in the process of recasting socio-economic contours and adjusting with changes brought about by the colonial rule. In the Central and South-east Punjab, where agrarian mode of production formed the basis of economy, the socio-cultural ethos was heavily coloured by the perceptions of the dominant agricultural castes and in particular by the landowning castes. A few empirical details concerning the demography and economy of Punjab will help us in clarifying the argument. In the nineteenth century, Punjab was basically an agrarian society. In 1881, roughly 87.35 per cent of its population lived in the 34,000 villages of the province and only 12.65 per cent in urban centres.[11] In the three largest cities of the state - Lahore, Multan and Amritsar - about a quarter of a million people lived who controlled bulk of the long-distance trade and a part of the small-scale manufacturing industry. There were the smaller towns like Jullundher, Batala, Sialkot and Rawalpindi, each having a population between ten to thirty thousand, which had served as centres of manufacturing. A small number of mercantile families had acquired wealth through the trade in luxury commodities (chiefly woven-gold, silk fabrics, Kashmiri shawls and ivory goods) with central and western Asia and Europe. However, the rulers and their subjects were primarily dependent upon the fruits of the agrarian economy. The economic situation did not change dramatically because of the British policy to retain and reinforce the agrarian character of Punjab's economy. A contemporary English official had noted this point: 'The Punjab can show no vast cities to rival Calcutta and Bombay; no great factories, no varied mineral wealth but the occupations of its people are still not without an interest of their own'.[12] In 1901, about 60 per cent of Punjabis were agriculturists by profession, 20.3 per cent in industries and 6.5 per cent in trade. In the decade 1901-11, while those in agriculture decreased by 2.6 per cent, those dependent on trade and industries increased by 4.5 per cent respectively.[13]

The concept of 'dominant caste', first expounded and applied to a specific region by M N Srinivas[14], is valid for analysing the position of those caste-groups, which had the basic resources, tenacity, drive and aspiration for upward mobility and took advantage of new opportunities created by educational and economic changes under the *raj*.

In the case of the two subregions: central Punjab and South-east Punjab, *Jats* provided the best example of a 'dominant caste' group. Economically and numerically dominant, they had overcome their handicap of a low ritual status by virtue of being landowners as possession of land was regarded as the symbol of a high social status. In the Central Punjab, racially, the *Jats* and *Rajputs* accounted for nearly 28 per cent of population but numerically the *Jat-Rajput* ratio was 3:1[15]. The *Jats* had inhabited the central part of *Bari Doab, Rechna Doab* and *Chaj Doab*. In the south-east Punjab, particularly, Ambala, Gurgaon, Hissar, Karnal and Rohtak, *Jats* formed nearly one third of the local population and held the bulk of agricultural land as peasant-proprietors.

The *Khatris*, who also owned lands but were engaged in shop-keeping like other mercantile classes, constituted about 7 per cent of the total population of the province. *Brahmins*, who enjoyed distinct superiority in social and ritual hierarchy in South India, neither possessed any political authority nor wealth nor learning nor social influence[16] in these two sub-regions. Whatever social and political weightage they had enjoyed in the past (Hill states being the exception), it had been neutralized under the pervasive impact of the new operational values of Sikh religion such as self-respect, dignity of labour, and egalitarianism upon the Punjabi society, particularly, the *Jats* who joined the new brotherhood in large numbers owing to their low standing in the Hindu society. By giving them land-grants and political patronage, Ranjit Singh had further boosted their social and economic status in the Central Punjab in the 19th century.[17]

In the South-east Punjab, propagation and acceptance of Arya Samaj, especially among the land owning *Jats*, led to their emergence as the 'dominant caste'. It is evident from the official observation in the *Census of Punjab, 1901* that 'there is no caste above a Jat'. Such was the dominance of the peasant-model, that majority of the *Brahmins* chose to become cultivators and landowners as priestly castes were not valued. In a turbulent province like Punjab, the *Brahmins* commanded no respect and it was believed that in times of need, 'A dom, a Brahman and a goat were of no avail.'[18] The British, who regarded the *Jats* as the best cultivators and excellent soldiers, reinforced their superiority as a social group over other communities and encouraged their customs and norms for women. With official support combined with their advantages, the *Jats* emerged as a 'dominant caste' in social, economic and numerical terms and they also became a crucial community in the politics of the Central and the South-east Punjab.

Despite internal economic differentiation and disparities, the *Jats* as the single 'dominant caste' became a viable model in shaping the attitudes and customs for social control of women, their placement in kinship structure and their exclusion from social, economic and political power. It was so because transmission of oral culture and customs was mediated through the agency of the second generation which initially went to the neighbouring cities for education and settled down there after getting jobs. However, they retained their links with their native villages.[19]

Socio economic Conditions: Their Implications for Women

Geographically, the British Punjab (including Kashmir lying to its north but excluding Kangra Hills) occupied the extreme North-western corner of India. Its ecology-climate, incidence of rainfall, geographical location of a particular area and the kind of soil-not only determined the patterns of cultivation, labour processes, nature of agrarian relationships and function as well as position of women. It can be divided into three subregions: I-the South-eastern Punjab; II-the Central Punjab; and III-the South-western Punjab. We shall focus our attention on sub-regions II & III. While the Central Punjab possessed the most fertile and intensively cultivated lands, the South-east Punjab was comprised of dry lands but production of millet and grain did not require additional irrigation despite inadequate rainfall. In both these regions, peasant-proprietorship was the prevailing land-ownership pattern. Small landlords co-existed with the peasant-proprietors in the second half of the 19th century.[20] Dependence on family-labour was crucial for producing subsistence crops-wheat and gram in the Central Punjab, millet and gram in the South-east Punjab. Women in the family had to shoulder most of the burden of agricultural work except ploughing. Animal husbandry was their exclusive responsibility.

As the twentieth century began, a new fourth region in the Punjab, known as Canal colonies, was carved. Its distinguishing characteristic was the high productivity of land under canal irrigation, an average of 59 percent in 1902 and nearly 63 percent in 1921. Another salient feature was specialization in the production of export crops, primarily, wheat but cotton also - both indigenous and superior American varieties. This region expanded at a fast pace. In 1901 only one district of Punjab i.e. Lyallpur had more than 55 percent of its land under cultivation but by 1921, there were six. Most of these settlers in the canal colonies were drawn from other parts of Punjab, specifically, from the central districts. The single largest cultivating caste was comprised of the Sikh *Jats*, who made up a quarter of the settlers in the Chenab colony; of these 60 percent were Hindus and 40 percent were Sikhs.

The Canal region, which soon displaced the Central Punjab in the volume of wheat and other crops for export, had grave implications for the migrant women. Without getting any increased access to economic resources of the family, these women were required to work even harder in agricultural operations such as weeding, cotton-picking and sugarcane peeling; their husbands performed back-breaking labour in converting the wild jungles into lush green fields. However, these migrant peasant families could barely earn enough to maintain the family estate and raise the next generation.

Unable to stand the competition from the Canal colonies, the peasant-proprietors in the Central Punjab were forced to become share-croppers or hired out their labour. Hard-pressed by economic necessity, primarily, caused by the realization of escalating land revenue in cash, the family head or adult males went to work in the cities or abroad or joined army and thus leaving womenfolk to push themselves to the extreme limit of physical endurance without any change in their status.[21]

In the South-east Punjab, colonial exploitation had added contradictions and tensions in gender-relations. It also worsened women's daily life and social status. Possessing poor resources as compared with other parts of Punjab, this region remained backward and undeveloped in agriculture under the colonial rule. In addition to its geo-economic handicaps, it suffered from the British policy of excessive investment in Canal colonies and almost total neglect of the interests and needs of agrarian economy in this part of the Punjab. As a result of the official premium on the low value food-cum-fodder crops, the South-east Punjab was condemned to remain as a supplier of draught animals to other parts of this region and provinces of British India.

Notorious for chronic crop-failures, famines and deficit production, agriculture in the South-east Punjab was totally dependent upon family labour and some hired hands. It was not surprising that such economic conditions in an area of inadequate rainfall and poor irrigation facilities reinforced the obsession for sons. It may be inferred that the attitude to women in general and the norms of behaviour prescribed for a mother, in particular are conditioned by the prevailing socio-economic conditions of a particular region. An agriculturally primitive society needs many hands for tilling because it can not always ensure good harvest because of many natural calamities and the use of primitive tools. It also needs sons to inherit property. It needs girls, too, who will marry and bring forth sons and daughters. Thus, huge premium was laid on female fertility, especially, on male lineage. Pride in women's capacity for mothering and ability to get gratification from it are strongly internalised in an agriculture society[22] because no other channels of expression and creativity are available.

The dominant social thinking found expression in popular proverbs and sayings. It was not considered practical to be satisfied with one son as ecological conditions had made agricultural as much dependent on uncertain monsoons as on sturdy and hardworking sons. Thus, the death of an infant daughter was perceived to be a sign of luck for parents and death of a son as a terrible misfortune. The following proverbs show how economic conditions fed the patriarchal biases against the girl child in the South-east Punjab:

> *Chohra mare nirbhag ka,*
> *Chohri mare bhagwan ki.*[23]
> (The one whose son dies is unlucky
> and the one whose daughter dies is lucky).

In the Central Punjab, too, these popular sayings reflected the rural psyche:

Rohi bhaun, sapoot ghar, aur satwanti naar
Ghorian ute charna, chaar surag sansar.[24]
(A heavy soil, a meritorious son in the house-hold, a faithful
and virtuous wife, and the availability of horses for riding are
just four heavens on earth).

The obsession with sons is also illustrated from the blessings often showered by the elderly women upon the young married women:

Budd Suhagin, sat puttari ho![25]
(May you enjoy married status till your old age and be blessed
with seven sons).

Keeping in view the vagaries of monsoon, frequency of famines, chronic crop failures and infertile soil, agriculture was labour intensive. Thus, the birth of a son was as welcome as life-giving rain. It is illustrated by a local saying in Karnal:

Meehin aur bettya to koon dhappya sae.[26]
(Who can be satisfied without rain and son; for cultivation both
are indispensable.)

A number of population censuses, conducted in the colonial Punjab, recorded statistical evidence of the bad consequences of the son-preference value system and adverse female sex-ratio. These attributed the favourable male sex-ratio to a high rate of mortality caused by frequent pregnancies among physically immature girls and their neglect at an advanced stage.

Owing to poor nutrition, women were also more vulnerable than men to recurring famines, droughts and epidemics. Convergence of all these factors lowered the female sex ratio thus giving Punjab the notoriety of having the smallest number of females as compared with the other major provinces of India.[27] In his memoirs, Prakash Tandon described the methods used to kill the infant girls among various social groups in Punjab. The widespread prevalent custom of hypergamy and dowry system also reinforced social and parental bias against girls. An elderly doctor's observations reflected the continuance of the perception of girls as a liability. While pointing towards his little grand-daughter, he remarked:

choti roti khave, vadi boti khave
(While in her childhood, the daughter eats bread, but as a
marriagable girl, she bites into the flesh of her parents.)

Nevertheless, *Jat* women, whom patriarchal values denied autonomy, freedom, public space and access to economic resources, were harnessed to agricultural and domestic labour. A *Jatti* was regarded the most suitable as wife as the following proverb illustrates:

> *Ran Jatti, haur sub chatti.*[28]
> (Only a *Jatti* makes the best wife. All others are drain on one's resources.)

In the popular mind, the image of a Punjabi wife especially *Jatti* was constructed as a sturdy and hard- working woman. The agricultural sayings and proverbs of Punjab celebrate her multiple functions: domestic chores of cooking for the joint family (which gradually became nuclear units) cleaning and scrubbing, nursing the children and extensive animal-husbandry work. Animal-husbandry work which involved tending, feeding, milking the cattle, churning, preparing *ghee* (refined butter oil) was the exclusive responsibility of women and their invisible contribution to the hard-subsistence economy whose backbone was the small peasant-proprietor. Besides, she performed various agricultural operations such as picking cotton, weeding and peeling sugarcane. Two proverbs, couched in local dialect, are equally applicable to both the subregions of Punjab. She is chided for her laxity and dubbed as *Kupatti* (bad and careless women):

> *Mein koli nahin dupatti*
> *Kya chuggegi kupatti.*[29]

> *Kappah guddina dupatti*
> *Tun chuggan ki ayi kupatti.*[30]

Qualities of passivity, docility, submissiveness, pliability, rigid self-restraint, tolerance and readiness for self-sacrifice, suffering and hard-work, valued in a wife by the peasant-society, were grafted in the urban milieu, with cosmetic changes. The agricultural proverbs project these norms:

> *Duman bhala jo bolna*
> *Nuan bhali jo chup*
> *Sawan bhala jo barsana*
> *Jeth bhaleri dhup.*[31]
> (For the bards, it is good to speak and sing; for the daughter-in-law it is proper to be bashful. Rains during the monsoon month of *sawan* (mid-July to mid-August) are good and normal; and the bright and hot sunshine is necessary during the month of Jeth (mid-May to mid-June) to mature to *rabi* crops.)

Paike ne sohrian, vattar na vahian
Sawan ne tarel pai, tenain autar gyian.

(All these things bear no fruit: the life of a girl who did not
cultivate the habit of working in her father's home while
unmarried and also not after marriage in her husband's home;
the labour spent on a field which was not ploughed when in
vattar (the right state of soil-moisture), and the advent of the
monsoon month of *Sawan* (mid-July to mid-August), if it passes
away rainless).

Without having any authority and power to influence decisions of her husband, the
Jatti gave him advice regarding the choice of crops, purchase of animals and timing
of agricultural operations. Some of the proverbs indicate her pragmatic outlook,
keen sense of observation and good judgement, for example:

Chole vadh ke beej de narma
Ae chunan nu main takri.
(My husband sows American cotton after harvesting gram. I
am equal to the task of picking it.)

Na beej nikhatua cheena
Moongla le ke charan lagi
Chittar ho gaya hina.[32]
(O my bad and unsuccessful husband! don't sow the inferior
millet *(cheena)*; I began to pound it in the mortar with a large
pestle. As a result, my buttocks became sore. So arduous is the
job of pounding it).

This proverb expressed her suppressed resentment before her peers instead of chiding
her husband openly. Thus, tension simmered in gender-relations, but the only escape-
route for women was the world of fantasy, woven in their songs.

Some other notions about women in peasant culture also coloured the
perceptions of the Punjabi urban society while reconstructing gender-identities. For
example, the customary law prevailing among the agriculturists regarded the wife
and anything associated with her such as her ornaments, or her earnings (if she was
a wage-earner) as the property of her husband.[33] Her worth was measured in terms
of her parents' social and economic status. It is illustrated by the following two
proverbs:

Janani so jo pakion rani
Zamin so jis de ser te pani,

Uh zamin rani
Jis de ser te pani.[34]

In the peasant culture of the Central Punjab, widow-hood was regarded undesirable and the married state earned social approval, status and respect. To be acceptable in marriage, a girl ought to be beautiful. These find expression in this local proverb:

Dhi Kani, nuan randani, khu di vingi lath
Raste ute kheti, chare chaur chaupat.[35]
(A half-blind daughter, a widowed daughter-in-law, the curved
lath (shaft of the persian wheel) and a crop in a field on the
road-side, all these four are not desirable).

However, widow-remarriage, known as *Karewa* or *Chaddarandezi* was practised among the agricultural castes especially *jats* and the lower castes. *Brahmins* of these two sub-regions, who were land-owners and not priests, followed the dominant social custom of *Karewa* or *Chaddar Andezi*. *Rajputs* were the only exception and looked down upon this custom.[36] The widespread acceptability of widow-remarriage underlined the contradictions in *purdah* culture and *ghunghat* culture, both being distinct from each other. It was not indicative of liberal attitudes but a device for retaining family hold over property through the control and monopoly of a widow's sexuality.

The deep-seated patriarchal urge for the social control of women was rationalized by glorifying chastity and superior worth of a secluded woman. For illustration see three popular proverbs:

Beerbani ghar ki bani.[37]
(A woman who remains at home adorns it.)

The *Multan District Gazetteer* contains another such local saying:

Ander baithi lakh di
Bahr gayi kakh di.[38]

Thus the peasant-ethos of the Central and the South-east Punjab furnished the basic essentials for sculpting gender-identities by the middle classes in urban areas, who borrowed and tried to inculcate some of the qualities of Victorian women in their wives. Prakash Tandon has emphasized this aspect of change in Punjabi society in his comment: 'His (father's) generation founded the new Punjabi middle class and added some modern values to the old Punjabi character, but what they lost in the process was the colour of my grand-uncle and his age.'[39] It may be mentioned that the middle class in Punjab in the early stages of its development was largely rural-based. It was comprised of the small number of the already settled urban professional and trading classes as well as drawn from landed-classes: small land-holders i.e. peasant-proprietors and village literati who sought jobs in the colonial administration and related profession. The British officials, while touring the villages of Punjab, recruited a number of promising young men as *Patwaris* who had no formal educational qualification or degree. In the course of their interaction with their officers and exposure to town or city life, they became ambitious and sent their sons and brothers for education and later on for employment to Lahore and other cities in Punjab. [40]

III. Social Roots of Middle Classes, Colonial View of Indian Culture and Women and The Native Response

Social Roots of Middle Classes

In this section, it is not my intention to examine the causes or factors responsible for the emergence and growth of the middle classes in Punjab but to identify their social roots. I wish to argue that the prevalent social norm of associating land-ownership with high social status in the predominantly agrarian economy of Punjab had tempted the rich urban caste groups other than the notified 'agricultural tribes' to invest safely in the purchase of profitable land property. For example, merchants and money-lenders, who later formed the bulk of commercial middle class in Punjab, owned substantial landed property by the beginning of twentieth century either through purchase of land or through the alienation of land of the heavily indebted peasant. The illiterate peasant, ignorant of law, was compelled to borrow from the village *Sahukar* for the payment of land revenue in cash as required by the total monetization of economy under the *raj*.

According to Fox, 'This process of monetization was accomplished by a combination of British revenue policy and the self-interested actions of indigenous money-lenders and merchants'.[41] From the angle of the social historian, its significance lay in forging links between the social ethos of urban and rural areas. Even a good number of the recruits in the ranks of the rising professional class were drawn from the rich peasant-proprietors or Zamindars (constituting the agrarian middle class) because they prepared their sons to join various professional careers by sending them to new schools and colleges which imparted western education as is evident from Ved Mehta's perceptive portrayal of the fast changes in socio-economic life of Punjabis.[42]

These impressionable boys, conditioned to the values underlying the institutions of marriage, family and property relations, had carried their biases and social experience of gender-identity and roles to the cities where they were exposed to the cultural values of the colonial rulers. Their interaction with their British officers and their admiration for the frank and confident behaviour of English women urged them to discard some of the customs of peasant culture such as seclusion of women and educate their women for 'competent' domesticity.[43] The new elite made lame attempts to westernise their wives by asking them to wear English dress and play harmonium. However, the Punjabi women showed enough attachment to tradition to prevent the change from swamping old values. Commenting upon the complexity of the process of modernisation, Ved Mehta remarked 'Our fathers changed rapidly, our mothers slowly and between them my generation managed to learn the new without entirely forgetting the old.'

The western education affected their thinking process in two ways: (i) the colonisation of their consciousness which aroused their admiration for English education particularly its rationalism and scientific achievements and the democratic institutions leading to imitation of their life-style. (ii) The second response implied their defence of Indian culture especially 'spiritual domain' wherein they were unwilling to acknowledge subjugation and inferiority. On this terrain, the position and status of Indian women became a crucial issue in the wide-ranging debates between the social reformers and the British functionaries/rulers in the late nineteenth and early twentieth century India particularly in the Punjab. In order to understand the parameters of this debate and the Indian response, let us turn to a brief review of the colonial view of Indian society and culture.

Colonial View of Indian Culture and Women and the Native Response

The bulk of colonial writing about India focused on demonstrating the peculiarities of its civilization and barbaric practices relating to women among Hindus, Muslims, and Sikhs especially. The circulation of the damaging negative perception was much wider than the romanticized versions of Orientalist scholarship and preceded and survived their descriptions of India's 'lost glory'. Of those, who built up a systematic indictment of the 'hideous features of Indian society, James Mill is the most representative of this trend of thinking. James Mill's monumental work, *The History of British India* (1840), has been termed as a national balance-sheet of moral lapses and strength of Indian and Western civilizations. He regarded the position of women as the major criteria for evaluating the quality of any civilization. His critique underlined the 'state of dependence' and the 'habitual contempt' of Indian men for their women. As an indicator of their extreme degradation, women were'.... excluded from education and (of a share) in the parental property...That remarkable barbarity, the wife held unworthy to eat with her husband, is prevalent in Hindustan'.[44]

Mill's indictment of degenerate Indian civilization and the abject position of women, who required 'protection' and 'intervention' on humanitarian grounds, was ingrained in the colonial ideology. These two issues became central in the colonial legislation on social issues and politics too. The third issue was the 'effeminacy' of the Hindu men who were unfit to rule themselves. The entire argument was crystallised into a rational justification of the perpetuation of the British rule in India on grounds of moral superiority.

Almost eight decades later, Mill's line of argument would reappear in *Mother India* (1917) whose author Katherine Mayo had drawn a negative portrait of Indian male's personality, characterised by 'inertia, helplessness, lack of initiative, originality and sterility of enthusiasm'.[45] By raising doubts about his flawed 'masculinity' and her harsh criticism of social backwardness, she had reinforced the perceptions of the colonial rulers who had expressed disdain for the weak-kneed Indians especially Bengali men. Resistance of Indian men to the Indian Consent Act 1891, a colonial move towards prohibiting consummation of marriage by Indian men before their wives were twelve years of age, was cited as a proof of their depraved nature, lack of self-restraint and self-discipline.[46] This kind of behaviour, the legislation argued, was associated with 'effeminate' men who were utterly inconsiderate, selfish and inhuman.[47]

The concept of 'motherhood' like that of 'masculinity' had also become the target of ridicule and merciless criticism at the hands of Christian missionaries, foreign medical personnel and the British administrators. The most damaging criticism had appeared in *Mother India* and it aroused vehement nationalist outcry. Early motherhood, the consequence of child marriage, was perceived by the British as one of the major causes of the depraved character of Indian men as opposed to the English 'manly reserve' and 'self-control'. In fact, sexual incontinence was regarded as the basic cause of India's woes - material and spiritual-poverty, sickness, ignorance, political immaturity, depression, ineffectiveness and feeling of inferiority. Commenting upon it, Mayo wrote:

> Force motherhood upon her at the earliest possible moment.
> Rear her son in intensive vicious practices that drain his small
> vitality day by day. Give him no outlet in sports. Give him
> habits that make him by the time he is thirty years of age, a
> decrepit and querulous old wreck and will you ask what has
> sapped the energy of his manhood?[48]

Despite being an exaggeration, this view had an element of truth. It provoked an outcry from the nationalists led by Mahatma Gandhi who dubbed Mayo as a 'Mischief-monger'.[49]

Obviously, the relentless colonial offensive from the third decade of the nineteenth century onwards upon Indian society and culture, with constant focus on the degenerate character of its manhood and their callous neglect and exploitation of women, had generated a complex Indian response. It may be pointed out that the ideologies of social reform and the Indian national movement had gradually grasped the intricacies of the game of moral imperialism wherein women's question, specifically her status and role in Indian society, was used as a crucial tool as well as a psychological ploy to demoralize the subject population and justify their enslavement. However, the emerging Indian intelligentsia from the first half of the nineteenth century onwards, who were involved in resolving the 'crisis' produced by an ideological and cultural encounter between India and England,[50] refused to accept the imperialist projections of the Indian society in *toto*. They gradually developed an obsessive concern with cultural questions while writing a new script for the past. Women's question, especially the reformulation of the concepts of femininity and motherhood, became the crucial component in the process of redrawing the contours of historical consciousness, national and regional identities. Femininity had to be projected in such a way as would facilitate Indian male's efforts to prove his 'masculinity' in the external domain as well as to preserve traditional patriarchal relations within the family and dominance of the male world-view.

In their response to the colonial critique of the degrading position of Indian particularly Hindu women, the middle classes, who had supplied the bulk of the Indian intelligentsia and leadership for movements for social reform and national liberation, were obliged to project the positive aspects of Hindu culture. While asserting the superiority of their culture, the social reformers - Hindu, Muslim and Sikh - made a conscious effort to weed out the dead and outdated elements in their culture and tradition in order to make it more consistent with western ideas of liberalism and humanitarianism. These western values were seen to be a part of the 'material' domain-dominated by western science, technology and method of statecraft. The rival of this domain was 'spiritual' domain and woman was supposed to be its guardian.[51] While the 'material' domain of the non-Europeans had been conquered and monopolised by their colonial masters, the 'spiritual' domain was still under the control of the Indian people, sympathetically interpreted by the Orientalists like William Jones. Hence, the inherent qualities of this realm, representing Indian cultural tradition, values and Indianness, had to be protected. However, this was not possible without sculpting new gender-identities incorporating new ideas of equality and liberalism. Hence, the construction of 'new' woman more than 'new' man engaged the serious attention of the social reformers and the national leadership in the freedom struggle.

IV. Sculpting New Gender-Identities: Myths of Past and Contemporary Reality

In the foregoing discussion, I have shown how the colonial offensive on Indian society and culture had provoked the perceptive social reformers and nationalist leaders to engage in an ideological debate, accompanied by the earnest heart-searching and introspection, with their imperialist adversaries. Its major result was the formulation of a two-pronged strategy; firstly, intellectual defence of the intrinsic superiority and dynamism of Indian culture; secondly, the practical task of reforming those features of social life which they perceived to be the obstacles in the way of the economic and social advancement of the educated middle class. In the course of this process of social-reformation and national identity-formation, a new image of Indian woman had been carved. Herein, woman, as the representative of the 'spiritual' domain, was assigned a central role. Through the construct of 'new' woman, the national leaders, who were constantly accused of their unfitness to rule as a people, sought to prove their manliness as well as superiority of Indian (some times used synonymously with Hindu) culture as compared with alien culture.

In this context, sculpting of new-gender identities, especially, the construct of 'new' woman assumed urgency. Indian women, though not merely passive recipients of this ameliorative activity, were presented with two identities: communitarian (sometimes bordering on communal) and trans-regional or nationalist. The former was more effectively forged at regional level.

Communitarian/Regional Identity

The problem of identity-formation of women from the communitarian perspective in the Punjab was complex as it had no single or coherent model like regenerating the Hindu or the Sikh male from the ignominy of 'effeminacy'. The kind of woman required for the present and future to suit the urges and needs of the western-educated male in the Punjab, who were experiencing the contradictory pulls of the twin forces of cultural marginality and educationally inspired alienation[52] and political subjugation, was to be fashioned in a communitarian/sectarian mould. Punjabi women, who had internalized social subjugation through religious rituals, socialization process in the family and oral culture, were again invoked to become instruments for retrieving religion and culture from abysmal degradation and from the crippling foreign strangle-hold. From the late nineteenth century to the early twentieth century, their social status was made the crucial component of the projects of reforming Hinduism and nature of the Sikh tradition. In other words, the tasks of redefining and reformulating separate religious identities and boundaries focused on the role of women while retaining the existing family-structure, gender-roles and property-relations grounded in the patriarchal ideology. In order to clarify my point, I shall draw my illustrations from Arya Samaj and Singh Sabha ideologies on women's question and their image in social reform literature as the 'semiotic', cultural, affective and territorial universe of the Sikhs and Hindus had remained virtually identical until Kahn Singh Nabha proclaimed separate identity of the *Khalsa* through his Gurmukhi tract *Ham Hindu Nahin* (1897).[53]

These two regional social reform movements, spanning over the last two decades of the nineteenth century and early twenties century, instead of being mere religious manifestations, were an integral component of the socio-cultural complexities which constituted the historical processes during that phase. Being partly a continuation of the ongoing process of socio-cultural rejuvenation and definition of group identities, these movements articulated the fears and anxieties of the small number of the already settled urban professional and trading classes as well as of the first generation of the middle classes (drawn from landed-elites, small land-holders and village literati, who sought jobs in the colonial administration and related professions) regarding their material fortunes in the unfamiliar colonial milieu shaped by the new agrarian, social and educational policies.[54] This hybrid class felt even more insecure and unsure about the preservation of their respective cultural traditions, identities and stability of the institution of family in the face of aggressive evangelicalism often encouraged by the British rulers. The traditional guardians of Hindu and Sikh religious traditions - *Pandits, Babas, Bhais* and *Gyanis* - also experienced an acute sense of insecurity as their vested interests lay in *status quo* rather than in 'inventing' tradition and crafting new and standardized identities - the ambitious project of the restless new elites.[55]

Without going into the detailed history of any of theses movements, I shall focus on the issue why the Arya and Singh Sabha reformers gave centrality to women's question in the course of their quest for new identity. The urgent concern for forging a positive and self-enhancing identity was not peculiar to one socio-religious group. The communal rivalry for image-building had been caused to a great extent by the social forces unleashed by the British colonial expansion into Punjab - communications, commercialization, education, the incorporation of the province into the global economy and the electoral politics. Thus, the Punjab of 1890s, wherein cultural environment underwent radical changes, saw various socio-religious groups locked in a fierce battle with each other,[56] sometimes all of them were ranged against their common enemy - the Christian missionaries. In this battle, the operational tactic adopted by each group seemed to be that the positive quality of one group could only be highlighted when the negative quality of another was juxtaposed. The debates that engaged Hindus, Sikhs and Muslims with the British rulers were focused on two major themes; (i) creation of a 'manly' race (ii) ethics of puritan morality which were subsumed under the banner of a rationalized and purified religion. However, it was Swami Dayanand who endowed the issue of the recovery of Indian 'masculinity'[57] with special significance while expounding his vision of a reformed Hinduism, the Aryan golden age, philosophy and social institutions as embodied in the *Rig-veda*. The crucial point in his thinking was his understanding of the unique role of women in the procreation and rearing of a special breed of men. In his view, motherhood was the sole rationale of a woman's existence. That was why the *Satyarth Prakash* lays downs a variety of rules and regulations for ideal conception, child care and mother care.[58] Dayanand's insistence upon the eugenical perspective led him to advocate the appointment of a wet nurse in order to enable the mother to regain her strength. His concern for racial improvement was further reinforced by his directive to husband and wife to control their passion and preserve their reproductive powers in order to beget children of a 'high mental calibre, strong, energetic and devout'.[59] Thus, Swami Dayanand, while retaining the traditional suspicion of female sexuality, 'transformed it into a force which could be constructively channelized to serve the regeneration of Aryavarta'.

In the historical writings and creative literature, the Aryan theme was developed with reference to the issue of identity unlike Dayanand who linked it with his theory of reformed Hinduism, society, and Indian civilization - its growth, decline and plan for the restoration of its glory. Underlying their task of reconstruction of Aryan 'masculinity', was the consciousness of European representation of the Indians particularly Bengalis as effete, unmanly, slothful and slack people. To refurbish their negative image, the nationalist writers projected heroes from an earlier era. In order to construct an alternative heroic Hindu male identity, elements from history and folklore were borrowed. In there ideal heroes, qualities of pride in Aryan heritage, a strong determination to reassert Hindu identity were combined with the martial qualities associated with particular regions and groups of people such as the Marathas, Rajputs and Sikhs. The process of the reconstruction of the heroic men and women as resisters of foreign rule (earlier Muslims rule) received considerable help from the detailed works of the mid-nineteenth century British writers; Grant Duff on the Marathas, Tod on the Rajputs and Cunningham on the Sikhs.[60] However, it was the more popular historical writings like *Rajasthaner Itihasa*[61] and *Sikh Yudher Itihasa*[62] which created awareness about the chivalric deeds of Rajputs and great battles fought by the Sikhs against the British. Above all, it was Rajani Kanta Gupt's *Arya-kirti*,[63] (reprinted in fifteen editions) containing the sketches of great historical figures of Hindu India among Rajputs, Marathas and Sikhs thus contributing to crystallisation of the ideology of the emerging trend of militant nationalism. Valorization of martial values, perhaps, could be linked to the tradition of according high status to *Kshatriya* values in the ancient social order.

Significance of these writings lay in bringing search for pan-Aryan consciousness and trans-regional unified Hindu identity to a decisive stage. Through his novels, Bankim Chander completed the task of forging a self-enhancing Aryan (used synonymously with national) identity for both men and women characters who combined in their personality - the militancy of the martial groups and spirituality of the *sanyasi*.[64] It is evident from Bankim's *Krishancharita*[65] and *Anandmath*,[66] that the regenerated Hindu 'national' identity excluded the foreigners (Muslims) and the low castes owing to their non-Aryan lineage.

This process of selective reconstitution of communal identities was not peculiar to Hindus, but Sikh and Muslim social-reform ideologues/propagandists and creative writers (also described as cultural nationalists) used the similar *modus operandi* in the nineteenth century. This approach had influenced the reformers in the construction of gender-identity. For example, the Singh Sabha reformers, whose ideology was not expounded by one single charismatic individual like Dayanand but by a diversified leadership - a mix of landed-elite and lower middle class men - belonging to villages or small towns over a period of four decades,[67] had also reflected deep anxiety over the issue of physical degeneracy indirectly while resolving the problem of the rejuvenation of Sikhs as a community. The spokesmen of the Singh Sabha movement, namely Bhai Mohan Singh Vaid and Bhai Vir Singh, had crystallised this concern in a cluster of virtues called *Kshatriya* virtues of fearlessness, courage and physical process underpinned by deep devotion to *Namu* i.e. the Transcendent One. The Sikh heroes and heroines in Bhai Vir Singh's novels personify these virtues while fighting against their Afghan/Mughal persecutors in order to protect and preserve their cultural identity, women's honour, homes and land.[68]

The identity crisis of Sikhs acquired a new dimension with the loss of political power in 1849 when the British annexed the Lahore kingdom. In the hard-pressing and bewildering situation of the Western cultural onslaught on Hindus, Sikhs and Muslims, further complicated by their mutual competition and antagonism, the Singh Sabha reformers perceived the issue of 'manliness' in context with their conscious and concerted drive for Sikhizing the Sikhs and monopolizing the history, imagination and experience of the entire community. Their foremost purpose was to write a separatist Sikh history, reconstitute and demarcate their social universe and tradition from the Hindus, foster and standardise a distinct Sikh identity known as *Tatkhalsa*, distinguished from *Sanatan* Sikhs. The British recognition of their identity as a 'martial' race[69] had made the issue of establishment of the Sikh credentials for physical power less urgent as compared with the Hindus who had been branded as cowardly, weak and impotent. For example, heroic figures in Bhai Vir Singh's novels, especially, *Baba Naudh Singh* (1921), which was set in a contemporary locale, agog with Christian missionary campaign for proselytisation, were not required to prove the physical attributes of courage but the quality of mental and moral resistance. Though not dissimilar in motivation from his earlier novels such as *Sundari*, (1898), *Bijoy Singh*, (1899) and *Satwant Kaur* (1927) *Baba Naudh Singh*, who lived in a Punjab village during settled times, personified the rustic common sense, self-assurance, wit and Sikh virtue and piety. Bhai Vir Singh regarded the British *raj* as a renewed challenge for test of faith. In contrast, qualities of martial valour, physical prowess were ingrained in the lead characters of the three novels set against the backdrop of the fluid political conditions and unsettled social life owing to the impending danger of marauding soldiers in the eighteenth century. While glorifying their chivalrous deeds and relentless struggle against the Afghan Mughal marauders (who captured Punjabi girls and even boys as apart of their booty), Bhai Vir Singh was eager to awaken the sense of pride and self awareness of the Sikhs about their legacy through the exemplary heroes and heroines Sundari, Satwant Kaur and Bijoy Singh. They chose to be initiated into the *Khalsa Panth* and practise its ideals in daily life in all circumstances.

It may be pointed out that Sundari and Satwant Kaur, despite being detached from the domestic boundaries, continued to play their nurturing roles in the form of nursing their wounded brethren or arranging and preparing food for *langar*. However, Bhai Vir Singh did not project motherhood as the sole destiny of Sikh women, the theme often reiterated by Bhai Takht Singh, the Principal of Sikh Kanya Mahavidyalaya, and the Singh Sabha tract-writers. It may be said that the Punjabi spirit of resistance, republicanism and independence provided a common bond for the characters in this historical trilogy[70] which had exhumed the tragic memory of the abducted girls from the historical psyche of the people.

The foregoing discussion has shown that the discourse on the recovery of 'manliness' among the Arya and Singh Sabha reformers, which had aroused similar anxiety in the middle class elites elsewhere in India, was frequently interlaced with concern for restoration of spiritual superiority and moral values. Towards the close of the nineteenth century, there was a distinct shift in the national idiom from exclusive emphasis on *bahubal* (physical power) to the glorification of moral power. With the discovery about the common Aryan origin of Indians and Europeans, there was a resurgence of self-confidence in self-worth and issue of acquiring physical parity with the British rulers was relegated to the second place but not entirely discarded. Later on, Lala Lajpat Rai would take equity of physical vitality and fitness for granted.

The Punjab of 1890s saw the beginnings of this change in the social-reform discourse. Despite the appearance of two pamphlets, Rama Shastri's tract entitled *Intermarriage of Hindus with Europeans and Other Non-Hindu Ladies* (1896) and Bawa Chajju Singh's tract *Brahmachnya Vs. Child-marriage* (1895)[71] about the scientific methods of race-perfection, the nationalists spent more energy in establishing the superiority of Indians in the spiritual-moral sphere in contrast to Western material society. As the issue of the creation of a physically and intellectually virile race had led to the recycling of the ideology of motherhood while retaining the old Indian tradition of deifying mother, similarly, the symbolic value of 'moral' woman was utilized by Hindus, Sikhs and Muslims for constructing their superiority around moral issues.

Among the hotly debated issues which contributed to the creation of a new morality were included vegetarianism vs. non-vegetarianism, idol-worship vs. atheism, kin-killing vs. cow-worshipping, high tradition vs. popular culture and women's question.[72] The issue that generated maximum heat and intra-communal rivalry and factional fights within one reform group was the reconstruction of an ethics of puritan morality to which most middle class groups adhered. The Punjab of 1890s witnessed a fierce competition among these groups to project their own high standard of morality while downgrading the others in the scale.

The colonial state assumed the role of the final arbitrator in the disputes and controversies amongst various groups regarding the morality or immorality of the customs and the health or sickness of a 'religious community'. While doing that, it often laid down the parameters for defining morality. For example, in the *Census of India 1901 for North-West Provinces and Oudh*, the colonial state tried to pass judgement on the moral standards of Hindus:

> the code of morality of the ordinary Hindu is much the same as that of most civilized nations, though, it is nowhere reduced to a code.... The influence of the caste is, however, of the greatest importance here, and some enquiries have expressed their opinion that *the principal sanction attaching to a breach of morality is the fear of caste penalties rather than the dread of divine punishment.* ... Almost any moral law may be broken to save the life of either a Brahman or a cow.[73] (Emphasis is mine).

By expressing its disapproval for the illogical 'religiosity' of every Hindu, the colonial state had constituted one ingredient of the code of morality in terms of Western rationalism.

A perusal of the debates in the social-reform press in Punjab shows that the condition and position of women was used as a measuring rod for the health and morality of a sect, community and nation. How do we explain the middle class social reformers' obsession with creating the 'moral' woman? It is too complex a question to be answered by a mono-casual explanation. Its partial explanation is possible. The first and the foremost is the new elite's growing awareness of the arrogance and contempt of the Europeans particularly the British as a colonizing power, who had developed a comprehensive and damaging critique of social customs, institutions, traditions and 'barbaric' treatment of women in family and society through their systematic ethnographic researches and census reports.[74] It was repeatedly argued that their humane treatment of women proved the British claims of superior morality, integrity and sense of justice. For example, Christian missionaries were proclaimed as 'pioneers of civilization' because they were the first ones to open the eyes of Hindus towards their pernicious social customs like infanticide and *sati.* It was the initiative of missionaries like Alexander Duff that had persuaded the British government to inaugurate a policy of liberal education.[75] This was the standard argument of 'moral imperialism'.

Obviously, the British rulers used the argument of barbarity and social backwardness of Indians for state intervention in the form of legislation for the abolition of some of the social evils in the nineteenth century British India. It may be pointed out that the British administrators and Europeans, despite their deep faith in the *mission civilisatrice*, could not have succeeded in abolishing infanticide legally without the co-operation of those Punjabis (partly influenced by the fast spreading colonial culture and partly by the ongoing process of experimentation and renewal within their won society) who were eager to fabricate a new civil society.[76] Through these forward-looking Punjabis, public opinion had been so strongly mobilized against infanticide that it was discontinued throughout Punjab by 1870s. However, the British rulers did succeed in hammering a sense of inadequacy amongst Punjabis regarding their 'treatment' of women and in launching a Punjabi version of Orientalism through G.W. Leitner - the founder of Anjuman-i-Punjab (1865) in Lahore.[77]

Besides, the British functionaries and administrators utilized ethnography for constructing a selective picture of the organisation and working of native societies in order to underline 'inherent' and 'intrinsic' divisions amongst them. The *raj* created numerous stereotypes about various socio-religious groups and qualified the divisions among them not only in terms of religious but also in terms of their attitudes towards women. The following extract from the *Census of India, 1911* illustrates the point:

> As is well known, the Hindus are less prolific than the
> Muhammadans, Buddhists and Animists, and other
> communities owing mainly to their social customs of early
> marriage and compulsory widow-hood. Girls are commonly
> married long before they reach maturity to men who may be
> much older than themselves, and a very large proportion of
> them lose their husbands while they are still of child-bearing
> age, or even before they have attained it. Apart from this, the
> Hindus have perhaps suffered more than their share from the
> vicissitudes of the decade....In the Punjab they have suffered
> an artificial loss by the removal of the restriction of the term
> Sikh to those who wear the *kes* and observe the other rules of
> conduct ordained by Guru Gobind Singh.[78]

This extract placed Hindus and Muslims in an antagonistic relationship and in a defensive position in relation to the British by constructing two stereotypes at one stroke: child-marrying Hindus and prolific Muslims. These myths were further elaborated. The notion that Hindus were weaklings was linked with the prevalent practice of child-marriage in various parts of India.[79] By using the cliché of 'ignorant' Muslim, the myth of 'multiplying' Muslim was validated.

Sikhs, who were gradually separated from Hindus through the application of arbitrary decisions, were not excepted from this myth-making. Regarding them, two myths were constructed and sustained through almost the entire period of colonial rule in Punjab. While the first projected them as a distinct *panth* and a young nation,[80] the second built their image as a martial race[81] and the British, being convinced of their fighting ability, were keen to utilize them as soldiers in the future imperialist wars as the First and Second World Wars would show. I need not go either into the question of contradictions creeping into the material and data in the official reports vis-a-vis their basic assumptions or into the issue of challenge posed to the colonial stereotypes by various groups. The relevant point for us is how the propagation of these myths by the *raj* created an atmosphere wherein the perception of cultural differences among various groups was sharpened. Its bearing on the process of gender construction was no less significant because growing differentiation of social groups along lines of caste, tribe and religion pushed women's question to the centre-stage and set the tone for its debate.

Such a horrifying picture of the low status and maltreatment of women, believed to be true for the whole of northern India, had a special piquancy for the Punjabi society wherein cultural and moral values were deeply coloured by peasant mentality. In section IV of this paper, an attempt has been made to demonstrate with illustrations from Punjabi agricultural proverbs, sayings and folk-songs that patriarchal values had governed the daily life and role of women. In such a social-set-up, male honour, prestige and happiness were perceived to lie in the control of a woman's sexuality.[82] Protection of the virginity of an unmarried daughter was regarded as a ticklish problem for Hindus, Muslims and Sikhs. Woman's chastity, which has lost none of its value even today, was highly prized in the nineteenth century Punjabi society where bloody feuds over land and women spilled over many generations.[88] Any kind of misbehaviour was interpreted in terms of sexual misbehaviour, lack of character and morality. This is illustrated from the popularity of legends of Heer-Ranjha, Mirza-Sahiban, and Sasi-Punnu[84] whose young heroines are poisoned or forcibly separated from their lovers in the name of family honour, prestige and happiness but dubbed as betrayers by their lovers.

These patriarchal attitudes and notions about the control of women's sexuality prevalent in the contemporary society have been depicted in the memoirs of ambitious brothers and sons of landed elite and rural literatti who had joined the ranks of middle classes and rose to be army officers, bureaucrats, engineers, judges, lawyers, teachers and creative writers. For example, while describing the marriage customs in the nineteenth century Punjab, Prakash Tandon focused on the value attached to a girl's modesty:

> If the boy's family came to suspect that the girl's parents had
> not taken enough care to guard her modesty, or if there was the
> smallest suspicion that the girl was immodest herself, the
> betrothal would immediately be broken off. Such girls brought
> shame upon their families.[85]

Parkash Tandon concedes that illicit sexual relationships were not too many and the society was 'almost puritanical in its morals and conventions, but it was pragmatic in its approach to the odd lapse and infraction'.

The Punjabi society was equally concerned about controlling the sexuality of widows, especially those in the childbearing age. After the death of her husband, a woman was supposed to de-sexualize herself.[86] Young widows were regarded as a problem and burden both by her parents and husband's family. The ritual of *kanyadan* as a part of the marriage ceremony especially among the high caste Hindus seemed to have absolved the married women's parents from any further responsibility. Debarred from pleasures of life, the Hindu widow had to live literally like a bonded slave in her dead husband's family or bow to the custom of self-immolation i.e. *sati*. The rural areas of Central Punjab and South-east Punjab, where the widow-remarriage had social sanction in the form of *Chaddarandezi* or *Karewa* among *Jats*, women had no choice but to marry the elder or younger brother or even the cousins of her husband, in order to avoid division of land and other property. However, no section of the middle classes in this region would accept widow-remarriage at any cost before Arya Samaj ideology had validated it through their re-interpretation of *Vedas*.[87]

Obviously, Dayanand's ideas about the amelioration of women's condition were novel for the Punjabi society wherein social reform activity had remained perfunctory upon 1870s. His formulations about the new role models for women, necessitating education, marriage reforms especially widow-remarriage and *niyoga* (levirate marriage), unleashed long drawn out controversies among Hindus, Sikhs and Muslims in Punjab. They were confronted with the dilemma to choose between two alternatives: whether to protect their honour as Punjabis in the eyes of their tradition-bound *biradari* and to face the ridicule of the colonial officials, Christian missionaries etc. or to modernise themselves. As nationalists, their task was to strike a compromise between tradition and modernity, as both were required by the nationalists, and the social reformers. In such a problematic situation, women became the ideological battleground where these complex issues had to be contested and resolved. It became alarming and demanded immediate attention with the intrusion of active *zenana* missions into Punjabi homes whose stability depended upon women's unquestioning subservience to patriarchal values. As women were perceived to be the most vulnerable part of society, humanising women's life and renewing their commitment to religion, and cultural traditions in the light of elementary knowledge imparted in the two premier Arya and Singh Sabha educational institutions - Kanya Maha Vidyalaya, Jullundher and Sikh Kanya Mahavidyala, Ferozepore - became urgent for the social reformers.

Trans-regional/Nationalist construct

I shall discuss only those features of this construct which are relevant for understanding its linkages with the communitarian constructs of 'new' woman, put forth by Arya Samaj and Singh Sabha reformers, who had reformulated the separate Hindu identity and Sikh identity. Each one of these constructs drew elements from a space inhabited by an urbanised middle-class upper caste Hindu male's perception of the ideal woman. Gandhi had added a dynamic concept - political role - in his model of social role for woman without revolutionizing assumptions on which these middle class reformers had based their construct. He had redefined politics to reconcile it with the space of home.

The Arya Samaj, Singh Sabha and other 19th century reformers had reaffirmed the doctrine of 'separate spheres' rooted in biological differences. Differences between sexes were used to legitimise different social and cultural roles for women in society and prescribe moral code for their interaction with each other. Conceptualisations of these two spheres dichotomised the area of activity for men and women. It implied confinement of woman in private space inside the house and free movement of man in public space but entry into private space according to his need and convenience. While family socialized boys and girls for these gendered roles, marriage as a social institution articulated these differences within an ideological framework. The male was the 'bread winner', the 'provider' and the 'protector' and thus 'superior'; woman was the 'mother' and 'nurturer', the 'giver' and she possessed the quality of tolerance, patience, self-sacrifice, humanity and moral courage; man could be 'selfish', 'possessive,' independent but lacking in real strength and 'intuition'. Thus, language was used as a tool to initiate women into the process of imbibing cultural ideas and values that shaped their images of themselves and inform the visions they entertained about future.[89]

The concepts of femininity and motherhood were given centrality in the construction of modernised version of woman, whose subjugation seemed less galling because of the high projection of her spiritual role. In the Indian tradition of deifying the mother, representations of Durga, Saraswati, Sita and Vaishno as mothers were held up as examples of the deep veneration for women in Indian society. The centrality of *mattabhav* (motherhood)[90] was used to imprint the idea of an ancient, vigorous and superior civilization upon the British mind. In the framework of this definition, 'mother-hood' implied love, caring, suffering, sacrifice for children, moral strength and creative energy. Its major consequence was the formulation of the ideology of motherhood and the crystallisation of the image of a moral, powerful, nurturing and spiritual Mother India - symbolizing the essence of the cultural superiority of Indians.

The eugenical perspective was incorporated in the image of mother who nurtured a race of supermen - physically strong and morally superior. In this ideology of motherhood, procreation was given a place of honour as in the Indian tradition. Idealisation of motherhood in the nationalist construct was shared by the urban reformers. Whereas the utilitarian purpose of nurturing a generation of Indians fit for self-governance was articulated with sophistication by the reformers and national leaders, the peasant society in Central and Southeast Punjab expressed the male-preference through popular sayings in the typical folk-idiom. The overall thrust of these formulations was to emphasize the instrumentality of women in cultural, socio-economic and political life.

The nationalist construct of 'new' woman, which tended to treat gender as a homogeneous category, was based on mythology, history and literature. The mythical figures of Sita, Savitri, Draupadi and Gargi were projected as the epitome of the virtues of Indian womanhood. Uma Chakravarti has rightly commented, 'Women of the past were valorized in two separate ways for their spiritual potential and their role as *Sahadharminis* (partners in religious duties) in ancient times, and as heroic resisters who cheerfully chose death rather than dishonour'.[91] From elements out of history and folklore, representing images of glorious women of the golden past, was fashioned a new identity of women to suit the ends of present and future. The choice of aspects of tradition and the proportion in which these were mixed varied from each reformer to each nationalist leader.[92] However, there was considerable agreement on certain essentials. On the issue of the fundamental characteristics of the Indian woman, more specifically Hindu womanhood, the liberal-revivalist divide was minimal.

Reformers of all hues and the nationalist leadership proposed to enhance the social presence of woman and focus on refashioning their minds and personality. Despite the fierce debate on the content and level of female education, there was no doubt about its efficacy in equipping them with qualities of intelligent comprehension, habits of cleanliness, orderliness and self-discipline. All these virtues were added to the baggage of the traditional womanhood in order to improve family life without threatening patriarchal hierarchy, male control of sexuality and stability of social order.

Both the nationalist construct and the reformers' image of woman gave certain freedom and autonomy to her. In order to qualify this freedom and to contain it within the parameters of patriarchal ideology, the nationalist leadership formulated a 'common' woman construct.[93] This construct covered prostitutes, *nautch* girls, street vendors, fisherman and washerwoman. By projecting them as coarse, vulgar and promiscuous by virtue of being somewhat independent as wage earners, the nationalist leaders had drawn boundaries of moral space for 'new' woman's movement and a code of conduct for her behaviour. This differentiation between the 'common' woman and the much valorized 'new' woman was used as an argument for confining women to spinning and *swadeshi*, later giving reluctant legitimacy to their participation in *dharnas* and processions.

Another interesting and common point in the nationalist and communitarian construct of new woman was the valorization of widowhood which gave social legitimacy to the remarriage of child-widow and thus an oblique approval to peasant custom of widow-remarriage with variations in pragmatic concerns. For example, Gandhi's construct of woman was modelled on the basis of a received notion of the noble qualities of the Hindu widow. Projecting it as Hinduism at its best, Gandhi regarded the '... widow's life as a reflection of Hinduism. When I see a widow, I instinctively bow my head in reverence. Man is but a clod before her. A widow's patient suffering is impossible to rival'.[94] Thus, he had created a god - like woman who was an asset for social welfare and national service.

It may be pointed out that the obsessive concern for women's chastity and honour was shared by reformers, national leaders, high caste Hindus and peasants. Their valorization of widow and their sanction to widow - remarriage with riders were motivated by their keen desire to preserve social order, patriarchal control over female sexuality and monopoly of control over property. However, compromises had visibly been made to make woman's role more valuable in family, society and politics in the colonial milieu.

Did these visions of womanhood constructed by the reformist and nationalist leadership relate to the reality of women's lives, their experiences and actions in contemporary society? There is enough evidence to indicate that many women had internalized the constructed and 'invented' notions of the 'golden' age and believed in the model of superwoman possessing qualities of learning, heroism, spiritual power and high-mindedness of *Sahadharmini* of Vedic times. For the 'new' Singh woman, Sundari was the 'paradigm' of Sikh ethics encapsulated in the maxim - 'Kirat Karni, vand chhakna, te namu japna - to labour for one's keep, to share with others, and to practice the repetition of the Divine name.'[95] As the spokesman of Singh Sabha, Bhai Vir Singh articulated the notion that women were more vulnerable to superstition, idolatry and forgetfulness of the Transcendent One.[96] The ideologies of both the social reform groups shared the belief that rejuvenation of Hindus and Sikhs was possible only through the creation of a 'moral' woman. Thus, they sought to create model women through socialization in schools and homes.

In order to evaluate the extent of their conformity or deviation from the models of "new woman", let us briefly review the career of three women: Sarla Debi Chaudhrani from an urban educated, liberal and highly placed family, Laxmi Arya, from an orthodox and rural background and Rameshwari Nehru, having an aristocratic upbringing.

Sarla Debi Chaudharani[97] (grandniece of Rabindra Nath Tagore and the daughter of a well known former Secretary of the Congress, J. N. Ghoshal and the Bengali novelist Swarna Kumari Debi) has been eulogised by the Bengalis as well as the Punjabis for her contribution to the nationalist movement in both these regions. A cursory glance at her autobiography shows that this had virually ended with her marriage in 1905 to Ram Bhuj Dutt Chaudhari, an Arya Samajist and a nationalist leader. At the age of thirty three, Sarla Debi had been emotionally blackmailed to marry this widower by her mother who pleaded that their high caste family's social prestige would be damaged in case their daughter remained singly. Her conformity with the existing patriarchal norms offers a significant contrast to her behaviour as an unmarried girl.

For example, Sarla Debi had defied her parents by taking a job away from home when she was barely nineteen years old. She had also been actively involved in setting up a secret society *Surhid Samiti* at Mymensingh in 1901. Apart from organising physical training camps for Bengali youth, she had mobilised them for participation in revolutionary activities through her credentials and articles in *Bharati* (earlier edited by her mother). After her marriage in 1905, the centre of her political activities shifted from Bengal to Punjab. Nevertheless, she continued to exert a powerful influence upon the Bengali youth and to co-ordinate their activities from Lahore. Apart from organising the Punjabi women under the banner of Arya Samaj, Sarla Debi was also founder member of the Bharat Stri-Mahamandal. Neither her activities as a Congress worker upto 1945 nor her writings, including patriotic poems, had taken up the issue of womens' rights and problems.

In 1919, Sarla Debi became Gandhi's ardent follower and admirer. Owing to her dynamic personality she became one of the leaders of the *Swadeshi* movement and of the campaign against Dyerism in this region. In the course of their long association, Sarla Debi and Gandhi developed a bond of mutual regard and affection. While the former hailed her mentor as the 'innermost soul of India', the latter regarded his admirer (Sarla Debi) as his 'spiritual wife'[98]. It may be pointed out that their relationship never occasioned any controversy. Besides, the elite response to the entire spell of Sarla Debi's activities illustrated the current perception of gender roles. It is significant that neither the communitarian nor the nationalist construct disapproved of her militancy and high visibility in the mass movement from 1920s to 1940s as it tended to reinforce the 'invented' notion of 'heroic' and 'moral' urban woman.

My second example, Laxmi Arya[99], despite her deviation from the accepted code of conduct for a widow in an orthodox peasant society, has been valorised for her role as a freedom fighter in the form of an award of *Tamra-patra* and a pension by the state government. A brief review of her life story is instructive. Born in December 1893 in a Jat family of a small village Rohra in district Rohtak (south-east Punjab, now known as Haryana), Laxmi Arya became an important participant in the Gandhian movement from 1920s to 1940s. Brought up as an orphan by her grandparents, she became the victim of the then prevalent custom of child-marriage. Married at the age of eleven to Chaudhari Rati Ram, she was ill-treated by her mother-in-law for bringing inadequate dowry. Laxmi Arya, who lost her husband in 1921, had to suffer more humiliation and physical torture at the hands of her mother-in-law. She refused to conform to the normal practice of widow re-marriage in the rural society.

Her brother Balwant Singh who was a staunch Arya Samajist, rescued her from the sad fate of a child widow and urged her to educate herself. Despite stiff opposition from her relatives, Laxmi not only began her self-education from scratch but also joined the *Swadeshi* movement in 1921 along with her brother and adopted *khadder* as her dress. Very soon the villagers began to call her a regular Gandhiite. In 1924, when her brother died, Laxmi was again obliged to carve her own destiny. She decided to join Kanya Maha Vidyalaya in order to continue her education. She lived in *Vidhwa Ashram* (widow's home) which was an integral part of the institution. Owing to economic hardship, she could not continue her education beyond eighth class and took up the job as a teacher in Kanya Gurukul, Khanpur for one year and six months.

From 1930 onwards, when she joined Sabarmati Ashram, Laxmi participated in constructive programme and political activities such as picketing liquor shops, no-tax campaigns, salt *satyagraha* and individual *satyagraha* against India's enforced participation in the Second World War. She suffered imprisonment for varied terms in jails and was fined a number of times as a picketer. Being illiterate, she was given "C" class as a political prisoner. Besides her active participation in the campaign for *Harijan* uplift, Laxmi donated her agricultural land for this cause.

In her own way, Laxmi had worked to redefine women's self image and role in the rural society through her personal conduct. After partition she accompanied Amtu Salam and Laxmi Trikha (ardent disciples of Gandhi) to Pakistan in order to bring back the abducted women as a part of the rehabilitation work. It can be said that these women had become somewhat ambivalent to the prevalent notion of female worth, adjudged in terms of physical chastity which had been violated without their consent.

My third example comes from Rameshwari Nehru's life and career[100]. Her brief life sketch is likely to give us an idea of the process of her transformation from a subdued girl into an articulate and critical woman. Born in 1886, Rameshwari Nehru belonged to a Kashmiri Brahmin family, which had settled in the Punjab during the reign of Maharaja Ranjit Singh. Her father, Raja Narendra Nath, despite his strong inclination towards Arya Samaj, disapproved of its ideal of 'new' woman and its campaign for female education. Obviously, Rameshwari, after being given somewhat informal training in reading and writing but more intensive schooling in domestic arts befitting a *purdah* family, was married to Brijlal Nehru, an officer in the Accounts department. Soon after their marriage, the newly married couple shifted to Ananad Bhavan (Allahabad) where her husband had been brought up by his western-educated and liberal-minded uncle Pandit Motilal Nehru. As a result of her constant exposure to new ideas, discussions about current socio-political trends in Europe and heated debates on the extensive involvement of women in the ongoing national struggle for freedom and as a champion of social classes especially as a founder-editor of *Stree Darpan* (Allahabad), a Hindi magazine for women in north India, her self-image and world-view changed.

As one of the early crusaders for Indian womens' movement, she utilised *Stree Darpan* (started in 1909) for initiating a dialogue between die-hard traditionalists and liberals on vital socio-cultural and political issues[101]. It is not surprising that the journal should have targeted and addressed its message to the bulk of Hindi-knowing middle class women throughout north India. As a social-action journal, it had sought to inculcate a critical temper among its readers and to project a new image of Indian women, which certainly did not resemble the model of an uncompromising rebel as presented by Pandita Rambai. Without disowning their nurturing roles, these sensitive and critical women had argued that they sought to acquire the qualities of alertness, courage, fearlessness, truthfulness, experience in world affairs and an intelligent as well as enlightened outlook in order to perform their nurturing and public roles efficiently. A new sense of self-respect and pride in their identity as women and awareness of their power in their roles as daughters, sisters, mothers and wives had exuded from articles, poems, stories and editorials in the columns of *Stree Darpan*.

Besides, contributors to *Stree Darpan* had demanded the reformulation of a more rational and equitable code of conduct and scrapping of discriminatory social regulations and *shastric* prescriptions regarding the socialisation of male and female children, nature of their education and distribution of socio-economic power among them. As crusaders for social reform and national freedom, they accused Indian men of blatant hypocrisy, which was exposed, by their demand for Home-rule from the British rulers and by their persistent demand for autonomy and human rights to Indian women. It may be pointed out that these women had also urged their sisters to do self-introspection and to liberate themselves from their obsession with ornaments, ignorance, superstitions and blind faith in outdated social customs, rituals and fake religious men.

Keeping in view Rameshwari Nehru's work as a crusader for women's movement both as an editor and an activist in the All India Women's Conference as well as her extensive work for the *Harijan* uplift, should she be categorised as a conformist or a rebel? It may be conceded that she had followed the negotiatory path between the male social reformers' and western feminists' prescriptions for restructuring female lives, ideals for Indian womanhood and their roles on domestic and public terrain. Obviously, she had represented the values of new patriarchy, which advocated mobility within the existing institutional framework but resisted any structural changes. Broadly speaking, the spirit of accommodation shown by her generation had grown out of tactical reasons and not for lack of intelligent awareness of the grim experiential reality of women's lives. Thus, internalisation of values and role models was selective but not mechanical or wholesale.

Rameshwari Nehru was a progressive woman who had effectively used the print-media i.e. *Stree Darpan* for bringing about a qualitative change in the self-image as well as social and intellectual outlook for India's women, particularly Hindi educated women. They were equipped to forge new bonds and loyalties beyond their kinship networks in the course of their interaction through the columns of the journal, which had helped them to carve new spaces and roles for themselves. In fact, Rameshwari Nehru had activated them, to use Herman's phrase, for 'seizing speech' i.e. expressing their anger, silence or gaps in their consciousness. Rameshwari Nehru enabled readers and contributors to *Stree Darpan* to hone and utilise their articulation skills to penetrate the hegemonic male discourse and forced men to listen and respond to their voices. I may add that Sarla Debi and Laxmi Arya, who had neither grappled with the issues of gender subordination and exploitation in writing nor launched campaigns for women's uplift, had experimented with new roles.

Conclusion

As a conclusion to this paper, I wish to underline three points relating to the process of gender construction in the colonial Punjab. Firstly, the bulk of middle classes in this region, having their hearts and minds firmly anchored in peasant-ethos but their material interests tied to the urban colonial world, perhaps, consciously assumed the role of an improvised bridge between the rural and fast expanding urban culture. In their perception of gender - relations, the patriarchal ideology continued to dominate. The institution of patriarchal family, remained a common denominator of the socio-economic and even political networks between rural and urban areas. Similarities in patriarchal practices in rural and urban areas were visible in the maintenance of caste and class basis of marriage as well as norms of sexual morality particularly chastity in the case of woman. In fact, the paradigm of the new 'moral' woman, posited as the opposite of the 'common' woman who was coarse, loud, vulgar, quarrelsome, sexually promiscuous and devoid of superior moral sense, was shared by the 19th century middle class social reformers, Hindu/Sikh landed-elite in this region and the nationalists and it continues to shape the image and consciousness of women.

Secondly, the rural-elites turned-middle classes, who were questioning existing pattern of gender-relations and seeking out solutions to the concrete problems arising out of the rapidly changing external and internal situations, found their answers from a variety of sources. These could be described as reinterpreted classical tradition, modernised folk forms, the legal idea of equality in a liberal democratic state, the utilitarian theory of bureaucratic and industrial practice and the new kind of patriarchy. It is in the context of reconstituting patriarchy, wherein Arya and Singh Sabha's model of 'moral' and 'spiritual' woman (essentially rooted in the values of a peasant society) became relevant. The 'new' woman was subjected to public in addition to family patriarchy. In order to establish a standard pattern of social behaviour for women, the conduct books were published and circulated by the Arya Samaj and Singh Sabha. These books contained guidelines for each aspect of a middle-class woman's life.

A close perusal of the normative literature for women showed that the middle classes had contrived a conscious interlocking of the selective elements of Western and Eastern patriarchy through the sex-differentiated formal education in order to create the model mother and wife to suit the new circumstances and also to absolve themselves from the charge of being primitive, cruel and selfish. Projected as a symbol of cultural superiority, the new image of middle-class woman combined the bourgeois virtues of orderliness, thrift, cleanliness, personal sense of responsibility, literacy, accounting and hygiene with the traditional feminine virtues of chastity, self-sacrifice, service, submissiveness, devotion, patience etc. Complicity not resistance was a desirable attitude. Thus, the most prized component in the standard version of urban 'moral' woman, whether Sikh or Hindu, was her ability to imbibe the ideology of subordination vis-à-vis men. The aim of socialization process in the family and educational programme for men was exactly the opposite: internalization of their hegemonic position and active role in the public domain. In the new patriarchy, however, the ideal of *Sahadharmini* or companion in a monogamous marriage was glorified and thus by implication discarding the prevalent norm of sexual promiscuity in rural society.

In the reconstituted patriarchy, a qualified concept of freedom for woman was propagated. The social reformers and national leaders had reached a tactic agreement on this issue. As long as women demonstrated the so called feminine/ spiritual qualities including submission to the new norms of social behaviour, existing pattern of gender hierarchy and roles, they could go to school, travel in public conveyance, watch public entertainment programmes, participate in nationalist agitations, fund-raising campaigns and take up jobs. However, empowerment of women through education and social and legal reforms was not sought either by the 19th century social reformers or by the nationalist leaders like Lala Lajpat Rai and only to a limited extent by Mahatma Gandhi. The fear that some of these reforms being advocated for women, might eventually lead to their emancipation, made the issue of social reform particularly marriage reforms and higher education as a source of friction and factional disputes among the liberals and conservatives.

Thirdly, the colonial state and the middle classes seemed to share a common terrain but not goals regarding the project of reconstituting patriarchies and reinforcing the subordination and deprivation of women from access to the resources of economic, social and political power. The processes, which made the definition of gender crucial to the formation of class and gender ideologies during the colonial period, were activated in the agrarian economy of Punjab by the British policies. The colonial state had to formulate new land revenue policies for extracting surplus and resort to selective modernisation of economy as exemplified in the Canal colonisation of barren lands in the West Punjab. It had also to create classes and win allies among the landed-elite and peasantry to bolster its image and fight its wars as well as to establish its hegemonic rule in India.

Apart from strengthening the existing unequal gender-relations, these changes were favourable for reconstituting patriarchies, which further helped in the exclusion of women from ownership or control of means of production prevalent in the pre-colonial agrarian structure. Among the measures adopted to ensure this included putting individual property rights primarily in the hands of men with women having only ancillary rights - dependent on their subordinate relationships with men - transforming existing matrilineal systems into patrilineal patterns of succession etc. A further marginalisation of women from public life took place due to the impersonal bureaucratic rule of law and by bringing them under its control, which helped to intensify their dependence on men.

Even through the laws, which were codifications of the customs of the dominant land-owning and other rural groups, juridical sanction was given to certain patriarchal practices regarding marriage, succession and adoption. Thus, the statutory Hindu law was actually a codification of high-caste Hindu norms, which were privileged over customary law. This could only be to the disadvantage of both urban and rural Hindu women.

In the end, it may be stated that the process of construction of gender-identity was suspended before the social and mental personality of 'new' woman and her consciousness could be infused with inner dynamism which would enable her to become autonomous to choose her own destiny. Perhaps, the reason underlying the diversion of the male leadership's attention from women's question was that the emerging middle classes had succeeded in their primary aim of creating a well-defined and strong political identity underpinned by their assertive and separate cultural identities. They had also been able to standardize their distinct identities as religious communities and construct undifferentiated Hindu and Sikh social universe and brotherhood, bound by bonds of a purified or rationalised religion, a set of common *rites de passage* and high tradition of new elite. Put at the centre-stage in the late nineteenth century, the 'new' woman was pushed back to the sanctuary of home when the time came for sharing political, economic and social resources and power after 1947. The new patriarchal approach is crystallised in the comments of the eighty-year-old woman-freedom fighter, Savitri whose husband Comrade Ramkishan became the Chief Minister of Punjab in independent India. She said:

> *Jaloosan wich naare lagaan layi sadi lor si. Jadoan rajnitik takat wandan da waqt aaya sanu kya gya 'tusi tan ghar di rani ho! Iss kichar wich hath gande karan di ki tuq!'*
> (We were useful for raising slogans as volunteers in nationalist agitations. When time came to share political power, our husbands, who remained active in politics, told us 'You are the queen of the domestic realm. Why do you soil your hands in dirty politics!')

NOTES

1.   For a detailed exposition of the theory of capitalist world system, see Immanuel
        Wallerstein, *The Modern World System* (New York): Academic Press, 1974). For its
        interpretation from neo-Marxist or unequal exchange conception of development see
        Samir Amin, *Unequal Development* (New York: Monthly Review Press, 1976); E.
        Laclau. 'Feudalism and Capitalism in Latin America, *New Left Review*, 67 (1971) pp.
        19-38. A. K. Bagchi has argued that colonial rule deindustrialized India. For example
        see his article, 'De-industrialization in India: Some Theoretical Implications'. *Journal
        of Development Studies*, 12(1975-76), pp136-164.
2.   Marilyn French, *Beyond Power: On Men, Women and Morals* (New York: Summit,
        1985). Also Susan Griffin, *Women and Nature: The Roaring Inside Her* (New York:
        Harper Colophon, 1980). There is growing literature challenging the association of
        reason and masculinity see for example Mary Hawkesworth 'Knowers, Knowing,
        Known: Feminist Theory and Claim of Truth' presented at the Women Studies Resource
        Centre, Ontario Institute for Studies in Education, Toronto, Ontario January 12, 1987.
3.   Alison Jagger, *Feminist Politics and Human Nature* (New Jersey: Rowman and Allen
        Helm, 1983), p. 344. Also O'Brien, *The Politics of Reproduction* (London: Routledge
        and Kegan Paul 1983), pp 1-15, 188. Understanding it as the role of individual, John
        Money has described gender-role as everything that a person says and does, to indicate
        to others or to the self the degree in which one is male or female or ambivalent. It
        includes but is not restricted to sexual arousal and response.
4.   John Money and Anke A. Erhardt, *Man & Woman, Boy & Girl: The Differentiation
        and Dimorphism of Gender Identity from Conception to Maturity* (Baltimore: The
        Johns Hopkins University Press, 1972), p.284.
5.   *Ibid.*, p.146.
6.   John Money and Patricia Tucker, *Sexual Signatures: On being a Man or Woman*
        (Toronto: Little Brown & Company, 1975), pp.88.
7.   R.J.Stoller, *Sex and Gender: On the Development of Masculinity and Femininity*
        (London: The Hogarth Press, 1968), p.40. Transvestism is a clear example of this
        mixed-up sense of gender. A man with a sense of being feminine while cross-dressing
        is excitedly aware of being a male.
8.   Money and Erhardt, *Man & Woman, Boy & Girl,* p.146.
9.   *Ibid.* Money laments the 'semantic handicap' of not having a single term to refer to
        'gender-identity-role'. He is concerned that without such a term we may slip into the
        logical and conceptual confusion of thinking that one can juxtapose identity and role.
        The term 'gender-role-identity' has been used in I. Frieze, J. Parsons, P. Johnson, D.
        Ruble and G. Zellman, *Women and Sex Roles* (New York: H H Norton and Company,
        1978).
10.   Robert A Dahl, *Preface to Democratic Theory* (Chicago: The University of Chicago
        Press, 1956), pp.12,13, 79-81.
11.   *Census of Punjab, 1881,* Report (Calcutta: Superintendent of Government of India
        Press, India, 1883), p.17.
12.   *Ibid,* p.2.
13.   *Census of India, 1911,* Report, p.20.
14.   For the exposition of the concept and features of 'dominant caste', see M.N. Srinivas
        'The Dominant Caste in Rampura' *American Anthropologist,* 61, (1959), pp. 1-16. In
        his *Caste in Modern India and Other Essays* (Bombay: Asia Publishing House, 1962,
        p.90, Srinivas specifies *Jats* as the 'dominant caste' in the Central Punjab and South-
        east Punjab (now called Haryana).
15.   Denzil Ibbetson, *Punjab Castes* (First published in 1881. Reprinted, Patiala: Language

Department Punjab, 1970), p.109.

16. Prakash Tandon, *Punjabi Saga:* (1857-1987), pt. I, *Punjabi Century* (1857-1947) (Delhi: Penguin Books, 1988), pp. 73-75.

17. *Census of India 1901*, Report, p.80.

18. Denzil Ibbetson, *Punjab Castes*, p.218.

19. Prakash Tandon, *Punjabi Saga*, p.38.

20. Richard G. Fox 'Urban Class and Communal Consciousness in Colonial Punjab: The Genesis of India's Intermediate Regime', *Modern Asian Studies*, 18.3 (1984), p.465. Also Indu Banga, *Agrarian System of the Sikhs: Late Eighteenth and Early Nineteen Centuries* (New Delhi: Manohar Book Service, 1978).

21. Discussion in the four foregoing paragraphs is based on Richard G. Fox, *Lions of Punjab: Culture in the Making* (New Delhi: Archives Publishers, 1987), pp.56-60.

22. N. Chodorov, *The Reproduction of Mothering: Psychoanalysis and Sociology of Gender*, (California: University of California Press, 1978), pp.38-39.

23. Jainarayan Verma, *Hariyanvi Lokokitiyan: Shastriya Vishleshan* (Delhi: Adarsh Sahitya Prakashan, 1972), p.30.

24. Kishan Singh Bedi, (trans.), *Agricultural Proverbs of the Punjab*, (Chandigarh: Public Relations Department, Punjab), p.19.

25. Informal chat with my grandmother Parmeshwari Devi and her peer group.

26. Jainarayan Verma, *Haryana Ki Lokoktiyan*, p.123.

27. For details of these factors and other contributory causes see *Census of India, 1931 Punjab*, Report, Vol.XVII, pt.1 p.156. Also E. A. Gait, *Census of India, 1911*, Report, Vol. 1 pp 214-9.

28. Kishan Singh Bedi, *Agricultural Proverbs of the Punjab*, p.23.

29. R. Maconachie ed., *Selected Agricultural Proverbs of the Punjab*, (Delhi: Imperial Medical Hall Press, 1870), p.210.

30. Kishan Singh Bedi, *Agricultural Proverbs of the Punjab*, p.55.

31. *Ibid.*, p.77. Two proverbs cited in next three paragraphs have been extracted from the book under reference, pp. 38, 68.

32. *Ibid.*, p.110.

33. H.M. Rattigan, *Digest of Civil Law for the Punjab Chiefly Based on the Customary Law as at Present Ascertained* (First published 1880. Reprinted, Allahabad: The University Book Agency, 1966), p.747.

34. Kishan Singh Bedi, *Agricultural Proverbs of the Punjab*, p.98.

35. *Ibid.*, p.28.

36. For the effects of Customary Law and Hindu Law on widows and the remarriage question see Lucy Carrol, 'Law, Custom and Statutory Social Reform, in *Indian Economic and Social History Review*, 20, 4 October-December (1983), pp.363, 89.

37. Jai Narayan Verma, *Haryana Ki Lokoktiyan*, p.127.

38. *Multan District Gazetteer*, 1901-02, p.98.

39. Prakash Tandon, *Punjabi Saga*, p.38. Also Ved Mehta *Daddyji*, (Delhi: Vikas Publishing House Pvt. Ltd., 1972), p.8.

40. Ved Mehta, *Ibid*, p.10.

41. Richard G. Fox, 'Urban Class and Communal Consciousness in Colonial Punjab', p.465.

42. Ved Mehta, *n*.39, p.40.

43. *Ibid.*, p.56.

44. James Mill, *The History of British India*, with notes by H.H. Wilson, (London: James Madden, 1840), pp.312-13.

45. Katherine Mayo, *Mother India* (London: Howard Baker, 1917), p.16.

46. *Ibid.*, pp.33-55. In these pages, Mayo has reviewed the debates on Indian Consent

Act 1891. Also Mrinalini Sinha. 'Colonial Policy and the Ideology of Moral Imperialism in Late Nineteenth Century Bengal' in M. Kimmel. *Changing Men: New Directions in Research on Men and Masculinity* (New Delhi: Sage Publications, 1987). p.224.

47.   Mrinalini Sinha, *Supra,* p.226.

48.   Katherine Mayo, *n.* 45, p.48.

49.   *Collected Works of Mahatma Gandhi*, Vol. XXXV: 1927-28 (New Delhi: Ministry of Information and Broadcasting, 1969), pp.235, 441. In order to rectify the one-sided picture, containing palpable false-hoods with exaggerations and suppression of facts, he urged U.S. based Dhan Gopal Mukherjee to arrange a lecture tour of Sarojini Naidu. Through her eloquence, the poetess would certainly draw crowds and dispel the wrong impressions created by Mayo's *Mother India.*

50.   Himani Bannerji 'Fashioning a Self: Educational Proposals for and by Women in Popular Magazines in Colonial Bengal', in *Economic and Political Weekly*, 26, 43, 26 October 1991, pp.45-52. In Himani's view, the language of social reform in 19th century and the early years of the 20th century is inscribed with the discourse of 'crisis'. Allusions to 'continuity and change', 'tradition and modernity', all involve the management of gender-roles and division of labour outside and within the family, in terms of the needs of the new times. For example, Tapan Ray Choudhary in *Europe Reconsidered: Perceptions of the West in Nineteenth Century Bengal* (Delhi: Oxford University Press, 1988), pp.ix-x, makes this idea of 'new times' and encounter between' the East' and 'the West', the point of departure of his whole interpretive and historical exercise. The 'encounter', he points out, means 'revolution in their world view'.

51.   Partha Chatterjee, 'The Nationalist Resolution of Women's Question' in Kumkum Sangari and Sudesh Vaid, eds. *Recasting Woman: Essays in Colonial History* (New Delhi: Kali for Women, 1989) pp.238-39.

52.   Kenneth W. Jones, *Arya Dharm: Hindu Consciousness in 19th Century Punjab* (New Delhi: Manohar Publications, 1976), p.314.

53.   For a detailed discussion of the shared cultural tradition, language and social customs, see Harjot S. Oberoi. 'From Ritual to Counter-Ritual: Rethinking the Hindu-Sikh Question 1884-1915 in Joseph T.O'Connell, Milton Israel, Willard G. Oxtoby eds. with W.H. McLeod and J.S. Grewal, visiting eds., *Sikh History and Religion in the Twentieth Century* (Toronto: S. Asia Studies, Univ. of Toronto, 1988), pp.139-147.

54.   Ruchi Ram Sahni, "Self Revelations of an Octogenerian" unpublished manuscript in the possession of Prof. Ashok Sahni, his grandson who is currently teaching in Punjab University, Chandigarh, pp. 127-40. His Memoirs give a fascinating account of the socio-economic changes in Punjab. Also Kenneth W. Jones, *n.* 52, pp.313-15.

55.   Harjot S. Oberoi, *The Construction of Religious Boundaries: Culture, Identity and Diversity in the Sikh Tradition* (Delhi: Oxford University Press, 1994), pp.207-27.

56.   Kenneth W. Jones *n.*52, pp. 16-20, 135-53.

57.   For an excellent elucidation of the concept of 'masculinity' or manliness see J.K. Campbell, *Honour, Family and Patronage: A Study of Institution and Moral Values in a Greek Mountain Community* (New York, Toronto, Bombay: Oxford University Press, 1964), pp.269-70.

58.   Swami Dayanand, *Satyarth Prakash,* trans. Chirajniv Bhardwaj (Agra: Arya Pratinidhi Sabha, 1915), p.22.

59.   Uma Chakravarti, 'Whatever Happened to the Vedic Dasi', in Kumkum Sangari and Sudesh Vaid, *n.*51, p.57. I have borrowed this perspective from Uma Chakravarti.

60.   Grant Duff, *History of Marathas* (London: Longmans Green, 1826); James Tod, *Annals and Antiquities of Rajasthan,* 1828-30, ed. William Crooke (London: Oxford University Press, 1920); J.D. Cunningham, *A History of the Sikhs* (London: John Murray, 1849).

61.   A.R. Malik, 'Modern Historical Writing in Bengali', in C.H. Phillips ed. *Historians of India Pakistan and Ceylon* (London: Oxford University Press, 1961), p.451.

62.   *Ibid.*, p.449.

63.   *Ibid.* The same author wrote a book on the Mutiny entitled *Sipahi Yudher Itihasa* (1876) which glorified Rani of Jhansi, Kunwar Singh and Nana Sahib for their heroic exploits.

64.   T.W. Clark, 'The Role of Bankimchandra in Development of Nationalism', in C.H. Philips, *n* 61, pp. 435-37. In Bankim's view, Indians had been enslaved because they were weak and effeminate and they lacked the consciousness of nationhood. He advocated the creation of a strong militant race. In order to attain this objective, it was essential to restore national unity and pride through a reinterpretation of the past which showed Aryan awareness of nationhood at some stage.

65.   For an interesting analysis of *Krishan Charita* see Sudipto Kaviraj, 'The Myth of Infinity: The Construction of the Figure of Krishna in Krishanchrita', *Occasional Papers* (1987), Nehru Memorial Museum and Library, Delhi.

66.   Josodhara Bagchi, 'Positivism and Nationalism: Womanhood and Crisis in Nationalist Fiction, Bankim Chandra's *Anandmath*', in *Economic and Political Weekly*, 20, 43, 26 October (1985), pp.60-61.

67.   For an excellent analysis of the nature of Singh Sabha leadership and its concerted drive to evolve a separate Sikh identity, universe, tradition and ideology see Harjot S. Oberoi, *n*. 55, pp. 244-52, 286-92, 306-77.

68.   I have based my description and analysis of the Singh reformers' view of 'manliness' on Bhai Vir Singh's novels *Sundari* (1898); *Bejoy Singh* (1899) and *Satwant Kaur* (1927).

69.   Nikky-Guninder Kaur Singh, *The Feminine Principle in the Sikh Vision of the Transcendent* (Cambridge, New York, Cambridge University Press, 1993), p.188.

70.   Harbans Singh, *Bhai Vir Singh* (Delhi: Sahitya Academy, 1972, 1984), p.52.

71.   B. Rama Shastri, *Intermarriage of Hindus with Europeans and Other non-Hindu Ladies* (Lahore: Sant Singh Luther Oriental Press, 1896); Bawa Chajju Singh, *Brahmacharya Vs. Child Marriage* (Lahore: Arorbans Press, 1895).

72.   Kenneth W. Jones, *n* 52, pp. 94-119. For the contest between Popular Culture Vs. High Tradition see Harjot S. Oberoi, *n*. 55, pp. 351-360.

73.   Robert Burn, *Census of India*, 1901, *North-West Provinces & Oudh Report*, Vol. VI, pp.75-6.

74.   For a detailed discussion of this aspect see Kamlesh Mohan, 'Construction of Colonial Ethnography: Imperial Pursuit of Knowledge for Hegemony in British India', in *New Perspectives on Empires and Science* (forthcoming).

75.   *Selections from the Vernacular Newspaper Reports, Punjab, for the year 1899*, (New Delhi: National Archives of India), p.98. *The Nur Afshan* (Ludhiana), 10 February, 1899.

76.   For a first-hand account of the response of young Punjabis to the process of transformation in the Lahore of 1880s see Ruchi Ram Sahni, *n.* 54, pp. 127-40. Also, M. Das., 'The Measures to Abolish Female-infanticide in the North-West Provinces and the Punjab', in *Studies in Economic and Social Development of Modern India* 1854-56 (Calcutta: K.L. Mokhopadhyay, 1959), pp.323-61.

77.   For a detailed study of Punjabi Orientalism see J.P. Perill 'Punjabi Orientalism: The Anjuman-i-Punjab and Punjab University' 1865-68' (Unpublished Ph.D. dissertation, University of Missouri-Columbia, 1976), pt. I, pp. 182-93. Cited in Harjot S. Oberoi, *n*.55, p.223.

78.   E.A. Gait, *Census of India*, 1911, Report, Vol. I, pt. I, p.120. Also *Census of India*, 1901, *n*. 73, pp.116-7.

79.   Khan Ahmad Hasan Khan, *Census of India*, 1931, Punjab Report, Vol. XVII, pt. II, pp.181-5.

80.   J.D. Cunningham, *n*. 60.

81.   Sir George MacMunn, *The Martial Races of India* (Edinburgh, 1912. Reprinted London: Sampson Law, Marston Co., Ltd. 1933), p.254. Also R.W. Falcon, *Handbook on the Sikhs for the Use of Regimental Officers* (Allahabad: Pioneer Press, 1896), p.94.

82.   Prakash Tandon, *Punjabi Saga (1857-1987)*, p. 101.

83.   *Ibid.*, 55.

84.   For the texts of these legends see R.C. Temple, *The Legends of the Punjab*, Vol. I, II & III (Lahore, 1881. Reprinted, Patiala: Department of Languages, Punjab, (1963). also Waris Shah, *Heer Waris*, 1767, ed. Jeet Singh Seetal (Patiala: Pepsu Book Depot, n.d.).

85.   Prakash Tandon, *Punjabi Saga 1857-1987*, p.55.

86.   *Ibid.*, p.102.

87.   *Ibid.*

88.   Sujata Patel, 'Construction and Reconstruction of Women in Gandhi', *Economic and Political Weekly*, 23, 8, 20 February (1988), p.378.

89.   I have borrowed these ideas from Sujata Patel, *Ibid.*, pp. 378-79.

90.   Margaret Cousins, 'Women and Oriental Culture' *The Leader*, 9 January (1930).

91.   Uma Chakravari, 'Whatever Happened to the Vedic Dasi?' in Kumkum Sangari and Sudesh Vaid, *n*. 62, p.52.

92.   *Ibid.*

93.   Suruchi Thapar, 'Women as Activists; Women as Symbols: A Study of the India Nationalist Movement', in *Feminist Review*, 44, Summer (1993).

94.   *Collected Works of Mahatma Gandhi*, Vol. X11, 1924 (New Delhi: Ministry of Information and Broadcasting, 1924), p. 524.

95.   Nikky-Guninder Kaur Singh, *n*, 69. pp. 192-93.

96.   *Ibid.*, p.190.

97.   My observations on Sarla Debi's life and career are based on her autobiography *Jibaner Jhara Pata* (First printed 1922, reprinted, Calcutta, 1925), pp 123-29, 140, 185-86. Also the *Modern Review*, June 1913 and June 1953; Home Department, Political A, Proceedings May 1909, nos. 135-147.

98.   Collected Works of Mahatma Gandhi, vol XIX, pp 138-39.

99.   Personal interview with Laxmi Arya on 14 June 1988.

100. Om Prakash Paliwal, *Rameshwari Nehru: Patriot and Nationalist*, (Delhi: National Book Trust, 1986).

101. For an evaluation of Rameshwari Nehru's contribution to the recasting of women's consciousness see Kamlesh Mohan 'Fashioning Minds and Images: A Case Study of *Stree Darpan* (1909-1928)' in *Contemporary South Asia*, (forthcoming).

Muslim Nationalism and Ethno-regional Postulations: Sir Fazl-i-Husain and Party Politics in the Punjab

Iftikhar H. Malik

The dissolution of the Raj and the emergence of two independent states in South Asia has been a momentous event in recent international history itself heralding a major decolonisation process. It proved to be a culmination point for the complex and multi-faceted battle waged between an institutionalised colonial power and the diverse South Asian communities exhibiting their national constructs through a broad-based appropriation of competitive modernist, primordialist and ethnicist symbols to solidify their claims and counter-claims. While to articulate South Asian Muslims, Pakistan meant a holistic nationalist ideal, to their critics it was merely a communalist impracticality. In the same vein, to the former the demand for a united *national* India simply symbolised majoritarian fascism which will outgrow at the expense of regional and religious minorities in a plural sub-continent. While both the contestants disagreed amongst themselves citing cultural, national, historical and territorial symbols to build up their respective cases, they tended to overlook the inherent cultural and ethnic tensions in their own parallel nationalist espousals. Subsequent to independence in an aura of retrospection and self-assessment, the pluralist forces began to resurface demanding cultural/linguistic, political and economic empowerment as in the former East Pakistan, Tamil Nadu or the Eastern Punjab, but national constructs in their single-mindedness, refused to co-opt them by branding them as separatist and anti-national. Confronted with these challenges between the centripetal and centrifugal forces, it was only at the academic level that the tradition in reinterpreting South Asian history in the diverse perspective of class, culture, caste, gender and region began to emerge.

Like their counterparts in India, Pakistani historians, during the initial stage in history-writing, went out of their way to substantiate their espousal of a *total* nationalism, anchored upon history, religion, ethnicity, culture and territory. Pakistan was perceived as the apex of Muslim trans-territoriality superarching the regional and ethno-lingual diversities. Uniformed Islamic ethos, as perceived and articulated in the Muslim minority province of the UP, was *imagined* to be a trans-regional reality for the entire Muslim sub-continent. Such a superimposition refused to accept pluralism in various provinces like the Punjab and Bengal unleashing its own specific kind of cross-currents. The Pakistan Movement was simplified as a *given* national sentiment that superseded all the 'parochial' traditions by subsuming them under the powerful symbols of Islam and Urdu and was anchored upon a strong centralised state structure that was essentially a colonial legacy and deeply abhorred politicking and constitutionalism. It is in recent years, especially after the evolution of Bangladesh and a persistently turbulent Sindh, that many Pakistani intellectuals have started to recognise the inherent and largely misunderstood and mismanaged pluralism within their country. Pakistani nationalism, in its recent incarnation, is gradually being seen/ idealised as an honest, feasible and voluntary arbiter rather than a unilateral imposition to weed out diversity. However, Pakistanis, like many other similar societies confronted with conflictive pluralism, have still a long way to go to establish a mediatory, trans-regional nationalism. Such an egalitarian consciousness needs to be transmitted through tangible reformative politic-economic measures and by invigorating a moribund civil society suffering at the hands of statist coercion and societal disarray. A rewriting of regional history and a growing acceptance for pluralism in its recent cultural and political context provides a wider arena to deconstruct the *imagined* uniformed national ethos. A fresh consensus through negotiations and appropriate mechanism and institutional support is the only viable strategy to initiate this overdue process. A primordial approach to Pakistani multi-cultural and multi-ethnic experience — from bottom to the top — is not merely an academic notion rather is a national urgency. Similarly, the inter-provincial relationship and centre-province dependency have to be reevaluated so as to minimise inter-regional tensions leading to the peripheralisation of 'smaller' provinces and minorities. Such a back-drop adds pertinence to the review of the historical issues such as the Muslim identity formation in recent Indian history especially in reference to Muslim majority provinces like the Punjab.

The present article, after summarising the historiographical debate, delves into serious questions being raised in intellectual forums across the country regarding the role of regional, religious and national identities. It assumes that the mediation between the three major markers both horizontal and vertical is needed to redefine Pakistani nationalism. Otherwise the acrimonious contestation between the core and peripheries will not allow the evolution of a consensus-based and mutually acceptable nationalism. This thesis is based on the premise that nationalism is not a static thing and does not have to be a monopoly of secular elites[1] or of a powerful middle class, defined as *salariat* by Alavi[2]. In the same vein, one may suggest that difference between community and society as the demarcation point for a nationalism as advocated by Deutsch is euro-centric which, like Kedouri, sees the doctrine only in a modernist perspective[3]. Both Francis Robinson and Paul Brass follow a similar line of the modernists in regionalising and classifying the emergence of Muslim nationalist sentiment and tend to ignore its numerous other denominators which several recent studies seem to be highlighting[4]. It may be emphasised here that Pakistani nationalism as it was being articulated in the 1940s, was combination of a number of complex factors and was a trans-regional, cross-cultural super-ordination, which, rather than rejecting ethnic and regionalist particularisms, volunteered to be a framework to operate as a major articulation against many other competitive and inherently non-Muslim nationalisms. It is in this perspective that a review of Pakistani history in reference to regional traditions is required with the Punjab being a centrepiece in the debate since it proposes to be the flag-carrier for Pakistani nationalism and is increasingly sensitive to criticism from other regional and ethnic groups. In such a discourse, the British Indian Punjab turns out to be quite central not simply as a response to wide-spread 'Punjab bashing' but also because it remains the heartland of Pakistan. Its pre-1947 career with special reference to Muslim party politics revolving around the towering personality of Sir Fazl-i-Husain, despite its apparent 'ruralism' and 'localism' proves to be the epicentre of Pakistan movement in the last decades of the Raj.

The liberal tradition within the imperial context portrayed various Indian communities differently as seen in the writings of the viceroys like Dufferin, Curzon and Minto or by writers like V. Chirol. Carrying the 'white man's burden' in the footsteps of the Utilitarians and imperial historians like Elliot and Dowson, they found India too divisive and in the dire need of imperial benevolence until it was able to stand on its own. Order, development, modernisation and reorganisation were the catch-words. Such historiography found its exponents from amongst the historians like R. Coupland and P. Spear, while its conservative strand was appropriated in the writings of J.A. Gallaghar and Anil Seal, commonly known as the Cambridge School. On the other hand, Indian and Pakistani historians like R.C. Maujamdar, P. Sitaramayya, B.N. Nanda and I. H. Qureshi justified respective nationalism through their historical expositions, considering it to be a straight fight between opposites. Both the schools ignored class, ideology, gender, identity formation and intricate politics of regional and non-elitist groups, which led to the development of Leftist and Subaltern schools. One may dispute their areas of specialisation and emphasis but there is no denying the fact that unlike the imperial school, they grappled with the issues of ordinary South Asians and in contrast with an imaginary consensus of nationalists and that too centred around a handful of personalities or parties, these new groups duly enriched South Asian historiography. The contest between the forces of authority, ideology, ethnicity or between state and civil society has led to growing interest as well as receptivity towards pluralism, regional issues and inter-regional themes, at least at the intellectual level if not among the policy makers. Some other significant disciplines that have enriched South Asian historiography in recent years include peasant studies, studies of diasporic communities and their complex linkages with the main community 'back-home'. While studying recent Muslim experience in South Asia especially in the regions like Punjab, making the most of present-day Pakistan, it is crucial to promote research in these disciplines so as to avoid simplification.

For a long period of time, scholarship on Pakistan Movement has been mainly concentrating on the Muslim identity formation in the United Provinces, somehow underestimating the dynamics and conflicts within the Muslim majority areas and or even the princely states and ignoring their complex and varying inter-*communal*, intra-regional relationships. Eminent historians including I. H. Qureshi, Barbara

Metcalf, David Lelyweld, Mushiral Hasan, Francis Robinson, Paul Brass and Farzana Shaikh have usually sought explanations for Pakistan in reference to Muslim political elite in the U.P. and their symbiotic relationship with a powerful colonial state and other parallel communities active in a rather narrow areas of political and economic opportunities[5]. Such articulate elites were seen to be consciously imagining a super-ordinate *Muslim* identity, banking on *Islamic* cultural symbols and commonalities so as to construct a South Asian Islamic ethos which would guarantee them their 'rightful' position in their competition with the 'others'. Their quest for identity especially during the Later Mughal period coincided with the decline of Muslim political power in a plural, decentralised and growingly Hinduised sub-continent. Even now, it is curious to note that in Pakistani text books, struggle for Pakistan centres on specific regions around Delhi and Oudh with the Punjab, Bengal, NWFP and Sindh joining the bandwagon only at the last moment. As a result of researches by Rafiud Din Ahmed, David Gilmartin, Hamida Khuro, Sarah Ansari, Steve Rittenberg, Ian Talbot and Imran Ali, one does notice a growing interest in the *regional* formation of Pakistani identity.

There are still a number of unanswered questions such as: Was/is there ever a composite Punjabi identity? If there was one, was it simply territorial and culturally *volksgeist?* How did the determinants like religion, religion and language along with a complex relationship with the Raj fragment this identity? Was it the state or the respective elite/helped by *localism* who articulated and politicised fragmented identities or was it a bottom-up situation? How come the synthesised, rural Punjabiat inspired by mystics gave way so quickly to dissensions? Can this process be explained in reference to trans-regional influences (such as Mughals, British, Arya Samajists, Khaksars, Ahrars, or Urdu/Persian/Gurmukhi/Devnagri issues)? or, in its subsequent reformulation, is it to do with a very conscious provincialisation of politics by the state after 1919? Did the divergent identities emerge due to urban/rural chasm or *barani/nehri* divergent economies? Was the Punjabi identity only created/imagined by the Unionists under Sir Husain and others mainly to counter trans-regional influences (League/Congress/Khilafat/Mahasabha), or was it symptomatic of politics of patronage? Why Husain, an otherwise urban statesman, comes to depend on rural lieutenants, yet fails to take the urban Muslim elites along? If there was a rural cohesive *Punjabi* identity, then how come communal riots in 1947 began in Punjab's rural areas unlike the UP but more like Bengal? (A similar process did not take place in Sindh, Balochistan and the NWFP.)

The peasants' revolts characterise a continuum of tradition in the recent history of Punjab and feed into a number of crucial movements like the Ghadr, Akali Dal, Babbar Akalis, Khilafat, Kiriti, Shahidi Jathas, Ahrars, Khaksars and others, yet are again fragmented due to religious particularism leaving Punjabi identity to be a cultural, mystic and territorial identification still unable to mature into a more mundane, negotiable consensus. It appears that the Punjabi identity(ies), like other forms of cultural nationalism, is not static and is being redefined all the time at three places—India, Pakistan and diaspora.

Even to understand Pakistan of today, a proper understanding of the Punjab tradition needs to be recapitulated since it has already matured into an Indus-basin tradition, something that did not take place in the Indian Punjab, where Punjab's role was minimised/contracted unlike its Pakistani counterpart resulting in violence and continued conflictive ethnicity. One may also raise the pertinent issue: Is Punjabi ethnicity just a cultural symbol/ political expediency or result of politico-economic diversity {compare Pothowar with central Punjab and Siraiki-speaking region in Southwestern Punjab}. Similarly, how come Pakistani Punjab, especially its middle class, receives only contempt from its counterparts elsewhere? Curiously, on the one hand, power elites in Pakistan like the Unionists of yesteryears build up a trans-regional alliance, the lower middle class, despite exaggerated pretensions attributed to it, still remains divisive and suspect. In other words, the quest for identity goes on unabated in a diluted form. Could the land reforms and rearrangements of the constituencies aided with diaspora usher a process of percolation eventually leading to some kind of ethnic chauvinism? How come the break-down of political control in the 1940s allows Pakistan movement to overrun Punjab but does not explain Punjab's sudden dominance over the polity strictly from a regionalist bastion to a *national* flagship? Ongoing volatile political activism in the Indian Punjab embodying an armed guerilla warfare, inter-religious dissensions and severe official retaliatory policies, is a microcosm of the pervasive governability crisis in entire South Asia. The dilemma, with all its intensity, is the culmination of various parallel political processes in currency for almost one century. While the state, both colonial and post-colonial, may conveniently and simplistically perceive it as a mere administrative problem or, at the most, an enduring communal disharmony fostered by hazy ideas[6], its very endurance warrants a serious review of numerous crucial denominators. Politicised ethnicity, largely banking on religious and similar other primordial factors, has received added momentum from interaction with a sterilised and elitist state structure in the wake of vital demographic changes and diasporic quest for identity. Neighbouring Pakistani Punjab exhibited a high profile in political defiance for the entire period of Benazir Bhutto's premiership when her Pakistan People's Party (PPP) confronted a formidable opposition from the provincial government of the Islamic Democratic Alliance (IDA/IJI). It eventually catapulted Mian Nawaz Sharif into premiership[7]. Subsequently, Sharif in 1993 faced a revolt from his native Punjab when its chief minister, Manzoor Wattoo, joined hands with the president and Benazir Bhutto to make the prime minister's exit a foregone conclusion. Once again in power, Benazir Bhutto felt uncomfortable with Wattoo and tried to install her PPP administration in the province but was politely rebuked until some rural Wattoo loyalists deserted him in September 1995. Such an increased political activism in the grain basket of the sub-continent may pose a perplexing issue for those to whom the province since early times has been a conformist, centrist and pro-establishment area when it came to its relationship with India-wide movements all the way from the stormy events of 1857 to the 1980s.

The Indian Punjab, after partition and successive administrative redefinition, underwent a radical demographic and political transformation. While in Pakistan, the Punjab, to a substantial extent, has always symbolised the establishment itself, its counterpart in India, despite a major share in the state structure and economy, was turning peripheral. While the Punjabis, both Hindus and Sikhs, became a dominant cultural and economic factor in the Delhi region, within the province itself the embryonic supra-religious identity came under severe strains. With Muslims gone across Wagah as part of the world's largest and perhaps the bloodiest migration, both Sikhs and Hindus, interacted uneasily under the umbrella of a new over-arching Indian identity-itself still a recent reality. The processes let loose by this percolation in the wake of immigration and emigration destabilised the supra-communal Punjabi identity which, was a convergence between the imperial prerogatives and provincial imperatives. It is not to suggest that pre-1947 politics in the province symbolised some commonly-agreed, composite *Punjabiat* as the Unionists would have us believe. The shared Punjabi cultural ethos during the Raj, due to lack of a supra-religious middle class and growing emphasis on religion-based identity, was still short of evolving into a cohesive cultural nationalism. While the Punjabi Muslim refugees were absorbed in Western Punjab, Punjab began to affiliate and then gradually symbolise an over-arching Pakistani nationalism *per se*. Such a new role, lacking egalitarian pluralism, faced growing reaction from the Bengalis and other Pakistanis, causing a serious legitimacy crisis for the state that largely depended on a mutuality carved out by the Urdu-speakers and Punjabi ruling elite. Such an ethnic discreetness duly reflected in the state structure and inherited from the imperial past has been anchored upon an oligarchic triangle of bureaucracy, military and land-owning elite. In retrospect, it might appear as the 'expansion' and 'consolidation' of the Punjabi multiple influences in the young country but certainly not without problems and contradictions. Notwithstanding its larger share in country's population and economy, which itself caused apprehensions in other smaller units in the federation, Punjab became synonymous with the centrist tendencies. Such an inflated role did not help remove the socio-economic diversities and disparities within the province itself. While the Punjabis claimed immense contributions to the national life varying from defence, land reclamation to expatriate labour, they equally felt uneasy at a growing criticism bordering on sheer antagonism from non-Punjabi regional elite. In the process, the Punjabis not only added to apprehensions of the Sindhis and others, even their erstwhile Muhajir partners also began to exhibit non-chalance. Since such a leadership role was mainly coming from the central Punjab representing largest concentration of Pakistan's middle class besides being the core area in national economy, politics and education, the 'hinterlands' within the province such as the southwestern Siraiki-speaking region, felt disenchanted. Faced with such a criticism from various directions and helped by reawakened interest in folk culture during the 1970s, many urban-based intellectuals began to espouse on identity-related issues. Significant developments such as populist politics and the separation of East Pakistan, beckoned a new realism within the Punjabi middle class. While some resented "Punjabi bashing" by the non-Punjabis, others from amongst them vociferously reacted to the denigration of indigenous culture by the cosmopolitan Punjabi elite themselves. Another section counselled for the revival of the Punjabi language and culture in consonance with pluralism in Pakistan without hurting its nationhood[8]. The debate is yet strictly cultural and less ethnic and far from being massive is notably pacifist. It is amazing to see that with all the volatile ethnic movements waging all around it[9], the debate on Punjabi identity in Pakistani Punjab does not entertain any nativist chauvinism. It remains grounded in the forces of moderation and persuasion largely synthesising agrarian, mystical and liberal traditions[10]. It is still early to suggest that a Punjabi consciousness has already evolved in an articulate form, yet one can see growing tolerance for Punjab's indigenous cultural and literary manifestations among its own inhabitants. Religion, geography, shared history, vibrant economy, assimilative cultural values, shared spoken language and assimilative vigour remain the major ingredients in this articulation. In other words, Islamic, Pakistani, South Asian, Punjabi and inter-Punjabi values seem to interact to achieve a synthesised Punjabi identity with wider receptivity and built-in legitimacy, though the recent events in Karachi and Afghanistan raise serious questions about the viability of such a construction. But, on the whole, Punjab remains assimilative, peaceful and still *national* in thinking. Its linguistic, ecological and religious unity—more than anywhere else in Pakistan— allows it to maintain a steady, non-reactive posture, leading to a sustained growth and harmony within the society itself, despite minor linguistic pulls.

In the Indian Punjab, such processes do not seem to have been initiated since with the Muslims gone, the new equation between the Sikhs and Hindus, could not mature into a mutuality. While the Indian Punjab and especially the Sikhs complained of cultural and political marginalisation in a trans-territorial national identification, they became suspicious of the state itself, which to them, appeared to represent only majoritarian interests[11]. As seen in Ayodhya and elsewhere, they are not the only ones to harbour such fears since Muslims, the largest minority in India, equally have been complaining of the systematic "pogroms". [12]

Politics of identity formation

Many of the impediments in achieving a consensus-based Punjabi identity can be seen in its specific history and its interaction with the state and trans-territorial forces in the past. Like in many other cases region, religion and language have been the major markers in Punjab's identity formulation. The role of the state, appropriation of historic symbols, a deeper sense of nativity articulated by diverse elites with varying degree have continuously fed into this process of formulation and redefinition. It must be noted here that sufism, Bhakti movement, evolution of Sikhism and volatile

Sikh-Mughal relationship, British annexation of the Punjab and language controversy, land settlement and canalization, agrarian unrest, reforms of 1919, intricate party politics and the partition are major transforming events in the recent history of the Punjab with their direct bearing on identity formulation, It will be quite useful to reflect upon afore-mentioned major denominators before embarking upon the Muslim party politics in the British Punjab.

Region

Both forms of nationalism—cultural and ethnic—are rooted in territory where an intimate sense of belonging bedrocks the communitarian consciousness. Similarly, a shared geography/ecology causes shared mutuality beside refurbishing economic interdependence. Punjab, both for its inhabitants and outsiders, was and is a geographical expression with salient ecological commonalities. The name itself signifies the explicit role of the river system and almost similar terrain with not that dissimilar ethnic heterogeneity despite the regional/local variations. It has been largely due to its specific geographic features that the Punjab was "imagined" as one major territorial unit where localism permeated. Extra-regional imperial wars, invasions and inter-dynastic feuds over the centuries would cause both integration or fragmentation while the province was identified with major core cities like Lahore and Multan with ever-shifting boundaries. As long as the state in Delhi or in Lahore remained intact the region would escape fragmentation but any metropolitan change would necessitate regional and peripheral disintegration. Personal loyalties solidified by regional divisions and accentuated with religious demarcations in a totally rural, semi-tribal setting would occasionally override the linguistic, cultural (in this case, folk culture) or geographic commonalities. The Raj, while motivated by imperial imperatives and helped by such mutualities, attempted to establish an overarching, supra-communal, Punjabi identity, which would deeply serve its administrative prerogatives. India, or Hindustan as it was called by the Punjab lay beyond the plains of the Punjab though the boundaries in the south— neighbouring present-day Sindh and Balochistan—remained undefined. The Indus river system facilitated greater mobility for the Punjabis towards these regions. With the evolution of Karachi as a major harbour in the late-nineteenth century coinciding with the modernisation and mechanisation of agriculture in the Punjab, an explicit and powerful southward dimension was added to Punjabi ethos. While Sindh was emerging as a new Punjab in the early years of the twentieth century, its economic, cultural and ecological interface with Punjab helped the former's separation from Bombay presidency. Sindh pioneered the movement for Pakistan so as to safeguard its own economic and cultural interest through a trans-regional support. Regional definition of the Punjab, even after several partitions, remains a major denominator for the provincial identity. While in Sindh and Bengal, it was the cultural uniformity operating as the vanguard force in identity formation, in Punjab it was a common territoriality with all its ecological and spatial features.

It is not surprising that the migrants from Indian Punjab into Pakistani Punjab were not perceived as refugees at all. Their assimilation, was comparatively smoother—something that did not take place in Sindh, where the Urdu-speaking refugees persisted with their own separate *Muhajir* identity and even refused to be identified as Sindhis or 'new' Sindhis. {To some analysts, it may be due to the class dimension with Sindh unlike Punjab lacking an assimilative middle class. But such an analysis may be totally misplaced as in Sindh, it is conflictive pluralism of similar (lower middle class) classes, because the very intermediate class itself is ethnicised and lacks a national character.}

Language

It is only in the recent years that historians, ethnicists, political scientists and sociologists, especially in Pakistan, have started looking at the role of language in identity formation/fragmentation. The Bengali-Urdu controversy and more recently Urdu-Sindh dissension have raised the research antenna in this academic realm. In case of Punjab, language played a very curious role all through its history as it both diffused and split the diverse identities. On the one hand, sufi traditions of the Punjabi mystics were appropriated by all the Punjabis irrespective of their religious background, simultaneously in its *written* form it turned out to be a major contestation, hurting the very fibre of trans-communal Punjabiat. In a spoken sense, it was almost the same Punjabi for Hindus, Muslims and Sikhs but when it came to script especially in modern period—with the profusion of print capitalism, evolution of communitarian political sentiments in the wake of economic and cultural competition—language turned out to be a significant differential. Ranjeet Singh had depended on Persian, the lingua franca of literary and official Indians, but a few years after him, the displacement of Persian with English and especially the growing popularity of Urdu, proved a major turning point.

The Punjabi Muslims, pursuing the traditional Persian/Arabic script of Punjabi, comfortably accepted Urdu with a closer similarity to Punjabi in vocabulary, script and syntax. Urdu, after Persian, began to symbolise Muslim glory whereas Punjabi for them remained a spoken mother tongue. A cluster of various dialects, Punjabi was still the language of Punjab, though in his survey, Grierson defined its varieties in the western regions as 'Lahnda'—the sunset region.[13] The emphasis on Devnagri and Gurmukhi scripts—mildly akin to Hindi-Urdu controversy in the UP—only fragmented the trans-communal ethos which had been operative in the recent past. The growth of vernacular languages, as is emphasised by Benedict Anderson, turns out to be the major departure point and the Punjabis started redefining their identities *separate* from each other. Other denominators like region and religion were used as claims and counter-claims only to widen the ever-increasing engulfment, which in the twentieth century resulted into extreme form of communalisation and ethnic cleansing.

Even in post-1947 years, the tensions on the basis of linguistic particularism, remain unabated. The movement for Punjabi Suba, separation of Harayna or the cultural form of Siraiki dissent against the Punjabi cultural domination {in this case central Punjab} exhibit an ongoing process in self-redefinition. Siraiki is similar to Punjab and most of Punjabi mystic literature is in Siraiki but the accent on its separatism especially mingled with the demand for a separate Siraiki province is an ongoing debate. Siraiki may not be so different from Punjabi or akin to Sindhi, but its very politicisation in regions like Bahawalpur is rooted in recent demographic changes. The migration of east Punjabis into this region in 1947 in large numbers {for instance, in early years of Pakistan, 43% of Multan's population consisted of refugees} and their economic hold has caused a cultural rethink among lower middle class Siraiki-speaking intellectuals[14]. It is interesting to note that Urdu was the official and literary language of the state of Bahawalpur during the British period and the recent articulation of Siraiki-based political separatism appears misplaced. In addition, the way some of these intellectuals are literally rewording Siraiki is making it extremely unintelligible for many other Siraiki speakers. Their linguistic version is akin to the language of upper Sindh but it appears as if their reservations against central Punjab are pushing them southwards, which might have its own portents in subsequent years. Siraiki is used by the Sunni and Shia *ulema* in their sermons and *zikr* and is thus a lingua franca but its confinement to territorial specificity and too much literalisation for the sake of substantiating its separatism from Punjabi as such may not prove after all positive for the language and its rich cultural heritage itself.

Religion

In the absence of a uniformed religion but with an intense religious factor in the daily lives of the Punjab, it is no wonder that the mystics and intellectuals yearned for tolerance and sought folk-based commonality. They abhorred religious particularism of clergy which remained a powerful reality. On the one hand, Punjabi Muslims especially in rural areas felt uneasy with the Deobandis perceived as Wahabis, while simultaneously they accepted the parallel Brelvi tradition from the same UP which they found akin to their values. Similar tensions existed within the Hindu and Sikhs communities where scriptural and mystic traditions remained polarised. However, in all the forms clerical establishments did remain powerful as was the case with the *Sajjada nishin* or *piri silsillas*. The arrival of the missionaries and the profusion of printed religious literature further regimented religion-based identification. Whereas the Arya Samaj and Sangathan communalized many Hindus, Tabligh equally intensified Muslimness. Such processes of intense religious debates increased political awareness and added to cultural separateness of the major communities in the province. In addition, within the communities they caused sectarianism as was the case with Mirza Ghulam Ahmed of Qadian, who as a devout Muslim *maulvi* engaged himself in *mazakras* with the missionaries in the late-nineteenth century and in the process established his own Ahmadiyya sect, commonly denounced by all other Muslim sects.

The religio-political parties like the Ahrars or others nearer to a similar programme like the Khaksars played dual role of increasing the political awareness but within a religious context, which helped strengthen religion-based organisation of the Muslim community. Similarly, the issue of Shahidganj deeply politicised the Sikhs but in the process deeply communalized them. Religious definition or religion-based organisation of a community is not a static process as one sees in case of Shia-Sunni flare-ups in Pakistani Punjab, which otherwise is overwhelmingly Muslim. However, with Islam acquiring a more pronounced place in communitarian life, Punjabi identity was overwhelming overshadowed by trans-regionalism of 'Pakistan'. based on Islamic symbols, Muslim nationalism provided the major vehicle for political articulation to Indian Muslims including the Punjabis as has been observed by Gilmartin: "The movement for the creation of Pakistan was the first and perhaps the most successful of those twentieth-century Islamic movements that sought to bring about an Islamic transformation of the post-colonial state"[15]. It was by aligning with the *Mashaikh* and *silsillas* that the urban Muslims were able to gather Punjabi support behind Pakistan. However, Gilmartin fails to make a difference between "Islam" and "Muslim" like many other scholars as such an interpretation suffers from a typical reductionism, without taking into account the complex economic, cultural and ethnic movements at operation at smaller levels across India. As a consequence, pluralism turning more and more conflictive any trans-regional alliance became highly desirable.

The Raj, while helping to construct and solidify a rural-based political elite, left religion to its own course without any apparent fondness for it. It obtained official attention only when it posed any threat to the status-quo. While the rural elite immersed themselves in religious and communal matters on personal and private basis, their approach as a pressure group, largely reflected their supra-communal prerogatives. Like India-wide political parties, religious parties turned out to be rabble-rousers in the mofussil areas. It is educative to note that all the revivalist and reformist movements in the Punjab since 1857 were deeply steeped in religious idiom, a by-product of the 'worldly' processes unleashed by the state. To a large extent, political and religious activism remained confined to urban areas and that too on a limited scale given the thin nature of a middle class. The state's preferential polices towards rural elite and administrative priorities vetoing the legislative and political imperatives, had slowed down the growth of an urban middle class. While rural elite espoused supra-communal rhetoric as late as 1947, the infantile urban middle class suffered from religious/ideological schisms. Thus, in a sense, localism added with personality-based cliche, characterised Punjab's politics well until the 1940's. Such a scenario, avoiding the parallel of the UP, Bombay or Bengal, served the colonial interests but hindered any tangible political articulation that could threaten the status-quo or could translate itself into a tangible, cohesive political creed. The Muslim politics, for a long time, reflected these divisive patterns, where rural/urban chasm added with divisive personal/regionalist loyalties in the absence of a unanimous ideal helped reinforce fragmentation. Such a deadlock was broken only with the introduction of 'Pakistan' as an ultimate, supra-regional ideal with a massive appeal. The weakening of the Raj during the War and a growing urban-based activism added to the breakdown of that static equilibrium that had earlier kept Punjab encapsulated from such a politicking.

One cannot look at these determinants in isolation to understand the political debates and complex identity formation of pre-1947 Punjab. The policies of the state and various other important developments immediately in the province and elsewhere in South Asia played crucial role in ever-changing politics of identities. Significant official policies including land settlement, irrigation schemes, population transfers, military recruitment, expansion of educational and communication facilities done mainly in the public sector unleashed a series of processes. While the colonial government initiated its far-reaching policies it equally avoided upsetting age-old rural set-up. Besides strengthening the agrarian sector, it reinvigorated the rural elite with a new leash of life. By bestowing magisterial powers and extensive land grants, the families of regional influentials were transformed into a strong class of subordinate, faithful allies. These intermediaries guaranteed status-quo in their respective areas and proved strong arm during the urgencies and emergencies acting as pillars of stability. With the reforms of 1919, these landed elites were inducted into legislative ("responsible") politics through a restrictive mechanism lacking any electoral agenda. A very specific, limited and largely docile role was expected of these largely apolitical and non-ideological elite, whose loyalties totally lay with their self-interests. This *enhanced* political role added to their laurels within their constituencies simultaneous with providing a buffer to organised, assertive, supra-individual politicking which could have threatened the Raj. Even while Sir Fazl-i-Husain and Sir Chhotu Ram rallied them together as the Unionist Party, the personal and local loyalties were not ruled out. The government had been able to construct a Punjabi supra-communal, political identity, intrinsically steeped in ruralism and localism, counterbalancing any party-, urban- or mass-based political movements espousing supra-regional or ideological causes as was the case with the Indian National Congress (INC), All-India Muslim League (AIML), and the Communist Party (CP).[16]

Politics in the British Punjab

Specific political patterns carved out in the Punjab under the Raj allowed restrictive politicisation in the province without helping the evolution of a mass-based, supra-communal, trans-territorial Punjabi identity. Even long after independence, both religion and region, with varying emphasis, have remained transcendant factors in determining the course of events in the Punjab and similar other places[17]. Whereas in Pakistani Punjab the *ulema* always opposed territorial, ethnic and cultural nationalism, in India, religion has played a pronounced role in the various forms of politicised manifestations of nationalism. While in the British Punjab, the three major religious communities pursued parallel religio-ethnic politics, in both the independent countries *Punjabiat* has its own critics from amongst the religious and nationalist elite.

Despite some visible lacunae in its political career causing inconsistencies in its political career, Punjab's case has not been so unique if compared with other provinces in the Empire. In addition, as mentioned above, certain sets of factors advertently hindered the political development which eventually led to a stigma of Punjab-bashing by ultra-nationalists or similar other groups. The paper briefly looks at such roadblocks in terms of official policies like bureaucratization, competition among various communities/groups within the Punjab and, most of all, the inherent contradictions between the rural and urban party politics as persistently reflected in the Muslim Punjab. Needless to say, at least in Pakistani national experience, it is not totally untrue to claim that to understand post-independence Pakistani politics one has to grasp the pre-1947 political career of the Punjab. In the same vein, it is impossible to comprehend the inherent unevenness in Pakistani political spectrum without understanding the growth and prevalence of the Unionist Party as a permeating tradition through its eventual amalgamation into other Pakistani parties without the transformation of basic elitist socio-economic and political infra-structure[18]. In other words, the Punjab tradition—rather Indus basin tradition— has triumphantly continued to dominate the post-partition Pakistani history.[19]

The Unionists pretended to have evolved a cohesive, all-encompassing identity through their "ruralism" without any secularist claims but the issues like Shahidganj or later growing support for Pakistan besides their essentially anti-urban bias, exposed their inherent contradictions. Their clientele relationship with the state in the wake of their non-mandatory role and non-ideological politicking smacked more of interests rather than of some declared ideals. Even after independence, such a mutually advantageous role has remained persistent.Similarly, like the topography and languages, the religious make-up of the populace before 1947 was evidently diversified and one does not need to be reminded that religion, region, language, caste/*biradari* (forming primordial ethnic identification) and economics (professional background) have been key-elements in South Asian history. In the same context, the canal-fed areas, even after almost a century, have remained totally different in their economy and resultant outlook from the *barani* region where people have generally opted for soldiery and similar other professions. Myths of Punjabi prosperity and 'domination' do not reflect at all in the *barani* areas. Industrial and urban development has been equally confined to certain specific regions leading to a number of grievances from western and northern Punjab, along with retarding the urban-based mainstream political movements. Historically speaking, the provincial boundaries, at different times, remained overlapping, intermittently reaching Jalalabad in Afghanistan or Delhi for that matter in nineteenth century British India. Lahore and Multan usually symbolized two separate provinces while Pothowar and southwestern regions witnessed tribal suzerainty under the Ghakkars, Hindu Shahis or Baluch tribes in the south. Under the British, to suit the administrative imperatives, the 'modern' Punjab emerged where experimentation in canalization, colonization and consolidation of Raj in collaboration with the feudatory families took place with political initiative being transferred from urban to rural areas[20]. The Punjab turned out to be mainly agrarian and predominantly rural in political ethos with industry, educational, judicial and media-related institutions concentrated largely in Lahore and any effort to upset the feudatory preferences for status quo was systematically thwarted. From the British to the Muslim League and ever-since the rural pressure groups maintain the hereditary mainstay in the political squabbling rendering the politics a very one-dimensional affair[21]. The collaboration between the landed aristocracy (more sophisticated and well-tuned to modern exigencies now) and services sometime masterminded by the latter or by some urban maverick, still sets the rules of governance in the country at large. Such a collaboration, worked successfully as long as it was confined to the provincial politics, but given post-1947 multiple, competitive identities, it has already generated serious resentment among the non-Punjabis who questioned its political, moral and ethnic legitimacy.

Muslim Politics in British Punjab

Following a policy of cooption, *biradari*-based chieftains like the Mazaris, Legharis, Mamdots, Khans of Kasur, Noons, Maliks, Khattars, Syeds, Qureshis, Gilanis, Gardezis, Qizilbashis, Khars, Daultanas, Gurmanis, Raos, Chhathas, Cheemas and Tiwanas were all tempted to offer their allegiance to the Raj[22]. Following the events of 1857, "some of the more powerful chiefs were given jagirs, and later on were invested with magisterial powers in their respective estates; and so by a diplomatic stroke of policy, they were turned from foes to friends"[23]. The new rulers valued deeply the timely support from the Punjabi landed aristocrats who had "responded with laudable alacrity and their men proved most useful"[24]. The Punjabi chiefs' loyalty to their British masters made them the most powerful pressure group both in provincial politics and administration[25]. Equipped with this wherewithal, they quarantined the province against the nationalist and peasant movements from making inroads and gained further benefits accruing from dependency relationship[26]. The lack of educational and political institutions, along with the peasants' total dependence upon the landlords, proved a lasting hinderance in the evolution of political consciousness among the ordinary Punjabis. Even the small-town economy did not offer any extra-local political acumen. With its peculiarity as the most bureaucratised province in India, Punjab, for a long time, was seen only through the prisms of administrative imperatives. A few urban academic institutions, established by the missionaries, voluntary organisations or government, mainly catered to the affluent families. For instance, Punjab Chiefs' College was established in 1866 as "a sort of Punjab Eton", two years after Government College, Lahore had been founded[27]. The Lahore Veterinary School and the Punjab Public Library came into being in 1882. The earliest school to impart modern education to the pupils was opened in Lahore in 1847 by the American Presbyterian missionaries. It subsequently came to be known as Forman-Christian College[28]. Similar other missionary schools and colleges followed in Sialkot, Gujranwala and Rawalpindi. These missionaries had already pioneered the first regular press in Ludhiana in 1836, which published *Ludhiana Akhbar,* a weekly in Persian.[29] Although moneyed Muslim families had begun to send their sons to the Aligarh College in the 1880s, their number remained very meagre. The Anjuman-i-Islamiya was the first notable organisation to be established in 1869 purported to the socio-religious uplift of the Punjabi Muslims. It was originally "set up to take over and maintain the Badshahi Mosque which had been converted, during the Sikh rule, into a magazine for storage of gunpowder, etc., but was being restored to the Muslims by the British"[30.] The Anjuman also supported Sir Syed Ahmed Khan's activities in the Punjab. In 1884, in Lahore, a number of concerned Muslims established the well-known Anjuman-i-Himayat-i-Islam (Society of the Supporters of Islam) to advocate modern education among Punjabi Muslims. Certain noted personalities financed the activities of the Anjuman which besides establishing schools undertook a number of other welfare projects in and around Lahore. The Anjuman's annual sessions turned out to be distinct rallies and Allama Iqbal held his poetry recitals at such functions[31]. In addition to these two major organisations, the urban Muslims had established *biradari*-based *tanzims* in cities like Lahore mostly led by the Kashmiri and Arai families. The Muslims in rural Punjab largely depended on *madrassa*-based localised religious education. The Hindus and the Sikhs, in major urban centres, had their own schools and colleges to look after the educational needs of their communities, but in rural Punjab, their educational and publishing activities, like those of the Muslims, remained minimal. Fragmentation, in other words, was the order of the day. Divisive political 'power' was the prerogative of the far-fetched *mofussil* areas whereas the prospective urban 'leadership' lay in disarray. "The Punjab", as Azim Husain commented much later, "has never had a settled government for any length of time, such as would have enabled it to develop a tradition and a culture of its own like those of Oudh, Bengal or Maharashtra. Apart frow a lack of cultural tradition, the religious background has been confused. Old nomad tribalism, Hinduism, Brahminism, Buddhism, Islamism (sic.) and Sikhism, all throughout Punjabi history, counteracted one another and none of them could become strong enough to be a decisive influence in the life of the province. Perhaps this is the reason why the Punjab has been such a fertile ground for new faiths". [32]

The induction of the Land Alienation Act of 1901 and the agrarian unrest of 1907 in the Punjab heralded a new political era dominated by leaders like Lala Lajpat Rai, Sir Mohammad Shafi and Sir Fazl-i-Husain. It equally symbolised a new phase in agitational politics. Lajpat Rai,[33] a prominent reformer and ideologue had to leave India like his contemporary Har Dayal[34] with both ending up in the United States after travels and political publicising at various places. With a visible Sikh majority, the Ghadr Party spearheaded its propaganda movement in North America, Europe

and Asia to be eventually banned, and prosecuted in the San Francisco Trial and the
Lahore Trial of 1916-17. A number of arms caches and the abortive attempts for
armed revolts by the Punjabi soldiers were preempted and a chapter in Punjabi activist
tradition was closed[35]. The Ghadrites subsequently infiltrated various other movements
in South Asia and maintained their international connections all through the successive
decades. During the Ghadr revolt, in many areas of the Punjab including the western
districts, a number of incidents creating law and order situation occurred[36]. It is
interesting to note that the Ghadrites, to a limited extent, were able to forge a supra-
communal Punjabi identity in diaspora though it suffered strains due to inter-personal
rivalries in the wake of official coercion and temptation.

The vernacular press of the Punjab, until a much later phase, did not exhibit
any vocal espousal of long-term alternatives. In the second decade of the twentieth
century, a number of English and Urdu newspapers from outside the province,
influenced Muslim opinion on contemporary issues such as the Balkan crisis and the
future of the Ottoman Khilafat. These included *Comrade, Hamdard*, edited and owned
by the Ali Brothers in addition to *Al-Hilal*, edited by Maulana Abul Kalam Azad.
The leading contemporary English daily, *The Civil and Military Gazette*, Lahore, of
Kiplingsque fame, followed a calculated conservative editorial policy. It was
subsequently joined by *The Punjab Tribune,* an influential paper with strong political
persuasion, which after partition moved across the new borders. The *Zamindar* of
Lahore had emerged as a leading Muslim paper in Urdu during early years, enjoying
an unprecedented circulation, but was closed down during the First World War. In
later years, it experienced similar frequent closures and confiscation of deposit money.
Edited by a fiery speaker and poet, Maulana Zafar Ali Khan, it continued its
publication well after independence.

In 1915, a system of voluntary censorship was adopted in the Punjab which
further circumscribed the freedom of the press to a great extent[37]. However, the *Haq*,
with its wide circulation and a number of other papers that continued to appear during
the time did put forward different viewpoints on provincial and India-wide issues.
There were Urdu, Gurmukhi and English editions of the *Haq*, and in 1918, its
circulation was about 77,000 and its price was one paisa per copy. The *Paisa Akhbar*
of Lahore, a popular contemporary paper, had lost much of its early vigour, yet
commanded sufficient respect. *The Tribune, Ahsaan, Tehzeeb-i-Naswan, Inquilab*
and *The Eastern Times* were some other known Punjabi papers to have appeared
subsequently usually supporting particular Muslim viewpoints on issues. *Ahsaan*
supported the policies of Sir Fazl-i-Husain and his political successor, Sir Sikandar
Hayat Khan, while *Inquilab*, during the 1940s, supported the AIML. *Tehzeeb-i-
Niswan* was edited and published by Imtiaz Ali Taj, the famous Urdu playwright and
devoted itself to women-related issues. *The Eastern Times* was brought out by Malik
Barkat Ali, the veteran Muslim Leaguer and was looked after by his son, Malik
Maratib Ali. But it had to discontinue its publication within the three years of its

inception. By late-1940s, *Dawn* had achieved the status of the official and authentic mouthpiece of the AIML besides other Urdu papers like *Nawa-i-Waqt*, which ideologically supported movement for Pakistan. Newspapers and periodicals published in other South Asian urban centres were also read by the Punjabi elites in the early decades of the present century, only after they had escaped the strict censorship. The rural Punjabis remained almost uninfluenced by the press given their economic plight, dismal rate of literacy and an isolated existence in the throes of an overpowering feudalism.

Politics of Parties or Personalities?

Following the Act of 1861, legislative councils had been established in all parts of British India except the Punjab which formed its first council only in 1897. All the nine members of the Punjab Legislative Council were selected by the Lieutenant-Governor, including the usual names like Sir Behram Khan, Nawab Muhammad Hayat Khan, Malik Muhammad Amin Khan and Malik Khuda Bakhsh Khan were nominated from amongst the Muslims time and again[38]. The Minto-Morley Reforms gave Punjab a sort of constitutional parity with Assam, quite asymmetrical with its population. Consequently, Punjab was allocated only thirty seats on the Imperial Legislative Council. In terms of contemporary Muslim leadership, Mian Fazl-i-Husain, Mian Mohammad Shafi, Mian Shah Din, Zafar Ali Khan, Ghazanfar Ali, Lal Khan, Barkat Ali and, of course, Allama Iqbal were the familiar names. Fazl-i-Husain entered active politics in 1904, and, at a time, held dual membership of the INC and AIML. Gradually, he began to focus on provincial politics. During the First World War, in a session of the Punjab Provincial Conference, held in October 1917, he deplored the official policies in the Punjab where "at every step one feels that it is the worst treated province in India". Not only, as he noted, did it have no Executive Council, it lacked its own High Court and its representation on the Imperial Council was both inadequate and ineffective[39]. His interest in establishing a separate provincial political party stemmed from *realpolitik* as he felt that given the weak party-politics at the country-level, the best course was to reorganise the provincial political contours. The reforms of 1919 had made such a shift possible given the increased significance of the provincial politics. Realizing the backwardness of his province he rose to the occasion and built up the Unionist Party into the most influential political organisation in the province. As the founder of the Punjab Unionist Party, Sir Husain proved to be the most influential politician in the province who did not shirk even from challenging Jinnah when the later tried to popularize the Muslim League in the province in 1936. His provincial role did not lessen his espousal of federal arrangement for India with maximum provincial autonomy.

Another noted Punjabi Muslim leader to rise to an all-India stature was Sir Mohammad Shafi, another Lahorite who began his political career in 1907 and then presided over the League's Lucknow session in 1913. Dissenting with the AIML's decision to cooperate with the INC under the Lucknow Pact, he resigned from the AIML and formed his own All-India Muslim Association, of which he became the General Secretary. He served in both the Punjab Provincial Council and the Imperial Legislative Council for some time, until in July 1919, he was appointed on the viceroy's executive council looking after the education portfolio. Later on, he became the law member and the vice-president of the council, which, in those days, was exceedingly important position for an Indian. For a time, Sir Shafi had competed with Sir Husain for the political leadership of the Punjab and differences between them would come into open in the annual sessions of the League. Leading a 'progressive' group of the Muslim Leaguers, Fazl-i-Husain tried to maintain an edge over Sir Shafi[40]. When Mian Husain engaged himself in the Unionist politics in the 1920s, Mian Shafi reactivated his League-related politics. His daughter, Jahan Ara Shah Nawaz, continued to play an active political career in the province until, like many other Unionists, she joined the AIML and worked for Pakistan.[41]

Justice Shah Din, another eminent Punjabi Muslim from Lahore's Arain family, had been a member of the Simla Deputation of October 1906 and, became the President of the Punjab Provincial Muslim League in December 1907. Mian Shah Din was closely associated with the Anglo-Muhammadan Association of Upper India in his capacity as one of its founding members. He was an admirer and supporter of Syed Amir Ali and Syed Ahmed Khan and worked for similar programs in the Punjab. By that time, Sir Muhammad Iqbal had begun taking an active interest in politics and his poems were inspiring Indian Muslims with a new dynamic self-consciousness. He based his ideas and philosophy on the resurgence of Islam that would become boundless and timeless in its ultimate realisation. Initially, he joined Sir Husain's 'progressive' group along with Malik Barkat Ali and Taj-ud-Din but, subsequently turned a devout Leaguer following Jinnah. After Sikandar-Jinnah Pact of 1937, Iqbal turned a vocal critical of Unionists' politics in the province as he genuinely felt that the former ultimately desired hijacking the League so as to neutralise its chance. Barkat Ali, the only Leaguer elected for the Punjab Legislative Assembly in the late-1930s and early 1940s, tried to publicize the League's cause and brought out his *Eastern Times* to project the policies of the Muslim League[42]. He was supported by Ashiq Batalvi[43] and the Punjab Muslim Students Federation who shared their distrust of the Unionists[44]. Like many other leaders, Raja Ghazanfar Ali Khan had begun his political career with the Khilafat movement and after a brief encounter with the League, rejoined the Unionist Party in 1937, which he again left for the AIML to work for Pakistan.

After completing his education in London, Fazl-i-Husain, on his return in 1904, initially joined the Anjuman-i-Himayat-i-Islam whose members came from a cross-section of urban Muslim community. The Anjuman discouraged political activities and mainly concerned itself with social and educational programmes though Husain tried to persuade its leaders to adopt a more active and assertive role. His forward-looking ideas were opposed by a section within the Anjuman led by Sir Shafi. This conflict led to the bifurcation of the Anjuman and Sir Husain, leading his group of enthusiasts formed what he called the Muslim League, thus for the first time the name being applied to a Muslim organization in the sub-continent.[45] To counteract Fazl-i-Husain and his group, Sir Shafi established his Muslim Association. Shortly afterwards, the AIML came into existence in Dacca with its first session being held in Karachi in 1907. Both Sir Husain and Sir Shafi, while leading their respective groups participated in the League's session with the expectation to be affiliated with India-wide body. To meet the expectations of both the leaders, the League leadership advised dissolution of their respective groups to be instead redesigned as the Punjab Branch of the Muslim League. Accordingly, Shah Din was appointed the President of the Punjab Muslim League with Sir Shafi and Sir Husain being assigned the offices of Secretary and Joint Secretary respectively. Initially, the pro-government Shafi group dominated the Punjab Muslim League, while Fazl-i-Husain and his colleagues advocated closer cooperation with the INC. Fazl-i-Husain's influence in the AIML became more visible when, in 1913, under his persuasion the League adopted attainment of self-government as its ultimate objective. Sir Husain was concurrently the Secretary of the INC in the Punjab and had tried to establish its branches in various districts. At the Lucknow session of the Muslim League in 1916 Shafi group was formally dissolved with Husain emerging as the de facto leader of the Muslim Punjab. The League's decision in Lucknow to cooperate with the Congress had deeply dismayed Sir Shafi who instead believed in closer cooperation with the government. During the Khilafat movement, Sir Husain like Jinnah, stayed aloof from mass politics and tried to concentrate on building his career in the Punjab. Further parting of the way came with the establishment of the Unionist Party and its cooperation with the Simon Commission. Even some other avowed Leaguers in the Punjab preferred to cooperate with the Simon Commission making Jinnah disaffiliate the rebels-led Punjab Muslim League. Though Sir Husain remained a potential leader on all-India basis and held important positions on the viceroy's executive council from time to time, all through the 1920s and 1930s, Punjab's politics remained his focal point. His ventures like the establishment of All-India Muslim Conference reconfirmed his country-wide political stature yet the Unionist politics never disappeared from his attention.

The Unionist Politics

With the implementation of the Reforms of 1919 political spectrum in India weighed heavily in favour of the provincial/regional politics, eroding the *national* basis of trans-regional movements. Such a parochialism and regionalisation of politics mostly revolving around the personalities rather than ideas suited the Raj and in areas like Punjab it operated more in favour of the dynastic feudatory politics[46]. Fazl-i-Husain's special concern for the rural people and his desire to play a more effective role from an institutional base led him to think in terms of organizing a party to contain the urban biases against them[47]. The contemporary Punjabi Muslim landlords, like their urban counterparts, were divided into many factions that represented variations in personal/clannish interests more than basic ideological differences. One such faction included Shahab-ud-Din, Mian Ahmed Yar Khan Daultana and their cohorts while another consisted of the Noons, Tiwanas and their friends. The latter group, mostly comprising of young enthusiasts, was supported by Muharram Ali Chishti of Lahore and Pir Mohammad Husain Shah of Sahiwal and volunteered to follow Sir Husain. Since neither the League nor the Congress then advocated pro-rural policies in a non-communal nomenclature, Fazl-i- Husain felt that he could provide an alternative. In 1921, the Punjab Legislative Council, of which Sir Husain was a member, stood as follows:

Nominated:		23
Elected:		
	Muslims	35
	Sikhs	15
	Hindus & others	21
Total		94

Muslim MLAs being in a majority held the balance of power in the Council and rural colleagues from amongst them organised a Rural Block, which became the Rural Party under the leadership of Fazl-i-Husain. The guiding principles for the Rural Party were: to be open to all communities; to work for the uplift of backward rural areas; and to sponsor programmes and measures to protect the backward people of the Punjab. It was from the Rural Party of the Muslim zamindars that the Punjab Unionist Party emerged bringing together members of the landed aristocracy from all the communities. Even so, Muslim MLAs formed a majority in the Unionist Party and Fazl-i-Husain provided a direction by enunciating programme of the rural uplift in addition to solidifying his personal political stature in the sub-continental politics. A decade later, some non-Muslim Unionists were feeling uneasy with Husain's unilateral powers as they suspected a definite pro-Muslim bias in his policies. Such elements, with the secret support from some Muslim colleagues, as we shall see later, even began courting Sir Sikandar Hayat Khan as a substitute for Fazl-i-Husain.[48]

The Unionist Party stipulated the following main objectives:
a)   to attain dominion status within the British Commonwealth by constitutional means;
b)   to demonstrate that Indians are capable of assuming increasing responsibilities of self-government;
c)   to provide equal opportunities for all, and to provide special government assistance to backward classes and rural areas;
d)   to secure a fair distribution of taxes between agricultural and urban areas;
e)   to check exploitation of economically backward classes by economically dominant classes;

f)   to provide indigenous industry;
g)   to encourage and undertake social measures such as literacy, education, suppression of corruption, etc.

As is obvious, the main objective of the Party was to save rural agriculturalists from the money lenders, traders and industrialists, and, thus, in a way, was further fanning of rural versus urban sentiments in the Punjab as one notices the emphasis on "backward classes", a slogan which still reverberates on both sides of the borders. However, it operated as the major ideological convergence which provided rationale and cohesion to the Unionist Party all through the twenty-four years of its existence. Sir Maclagan, the then Lieutenant-Governor of the Punjab, recognised the Unionist Party officially and reappointed Fazl-i-Husain as the minister for education, the later recommending Lal Chand for the portfolio of agriculture. The Hindu opposition protested against the selection of a rural Jat as minister. Subsequently, Chaudhary Chhotu Ram, a co-founder of the party and a Jat, replaced Lal Chand. During its early formative years, the party included Muslim notables like Sir Iqbal, Mir Maqbool Mahmood, Shaikh Din Mohammad and Sir Abdul Qadir. Sir Qadir, a close friend of Sir Iqbal, an impressive speaker and versatile writer, retained the office of the Vice-President of the Party.

Malcolm Hailey, the new chief executive in Lahore, resented Husain's growing influence in provincial politics construing it as an irksome interference in his administration. Sir Husain, confident of his wider support and political credentials, did not budge and his party continued to gain further strength. Given the fact that both the AIML and INC were confined to a few urban-based individuals, and additionally suffered from factional politics, Husain's party kept on growing. It deeply appealed to influential rural elements and manifested electoral, supra-communal credentials no matter how limited they might be. When Sir Husain took up his new assignment as the Revenue Member, Sir Chhotu Ram attended to the party business as his faithful lieutenant. Although he had to stay away from the Punjab from 1930 to 1935 to occupy a seat on the viceroy's executive council, he kept himself in close contact with all the political developments in his native province. During this period, he largely reposed his confidence in Sikandar Hayat for leading the party. Once, when in 1930, a dispute developed between Chaudhary Zafrullah Khan and Firoz Khan Noon over a ministerial position, Fazl-i-Husain asked Sikandar Hayat to arrange a truce between the two colleagues. When the office of the Revenue Minister fell vacant with Husain's departure to join the viceroy's executive council, certain senior Unionists began vying for it. A tussle ensued between the Maliks and Sikandar Hayat and it was only with Husain's support that Sikandar Hayat finally replaced him without causing any breach in the party's ranks.

Sir Fazl-i-Husain did not want to get embroiled in the Shahidganj issue and was already looking ahead at the forthcoming elections for the Punjab Legislative

Assembly under the auspices of the Act of 1935. His main preoccupation was to keep the India-wide parties like the League and Congress out of the Punjab by maintaining a united front of the Unionists. Such a policy also proved a major obstacle in his finding a meeting ground with Jinnah for whom the problem of the Indian Muslims had changed from a mere communal to a national dimension. The Unionists stressed on maintaining a homogenous political policy for a heterogenous society without any strong ideological moorings except for open pro-rural bias by cashing on the British sensitivities towards the landed gentry. Husain openly differed with the Quaid-i-Azam when the later tried to establish Muslim League Parliamentary Board in the province[49]. This infuriated Iqbal, Barkat Ali and other Leaguers in the Punjab who felt that the Unionist politics was proving a hinderance in the mass-based Muslim political development in the province.

Jinnah fully realised that Sir Husain was a power to be reckoned with in the Punjab and tried to bring him into the League. Sir Husain was requested by Jinnah to preside over the 24th annual session of the AIML being held in April 1936 at Bombay. The invitation was repeated through the offices of Sir Aga Khan and Ahmed Yar Khan Daultana but the Mian politely refused. After the session Jinnah came to Lahore and saw Sir Husain who had just reorganised his party. Jinnah suggested to him that the Muslim candidates from the province should contest the election as Leaguers not as Unionists, but Sir Husain did not accept it. At this juncture, differences between Sikandar Hayat and Sir Husain came out into open temporarily though they were quickly patched up through the efforts of Daultana and Shahab-ud-Din. It was reported that Sikandar Hayat wanted to establish a party of his own to lead the next provincial cabinet and the speculation received strength with criticism levelled against Sir Husain by some Hindu politicians like Gulshan Rai, who wrote to Husain: "The impression I have gathered during the last few months is that the Europeans want Sir Sikandar, and not you to form the first Ministry of the autonomous Punjab..."[50] But, the fact remains that many non-Muslim Unionists like Sir Ram, Sir Roberts Owen and many of their Muslim colleagues remained very close and faithful to Sir Husain. On the eve of the elections, Chhotu Ram and Daultana brought out a pamphlet, *Punjab Politics*, and asked Fazl-i-Husain to write a `Foreword' to it. In his remarks, Mian Fazl-i-Husain, while dilating on his ideas, modestly refused to take the credit for dynamic political activities in the Punjab and pleaded for a united stance.[51]

In April 1936, the office of the Central Committee of the Unionist Party was set up at No. 14-C Davis Road Lahore, under the chairmanship of Ahmad Yar Khan Daultana, while Sardar Habibullah, Ghulam Muhy-ud-Din, Syed Afzal Ali Hasni and Shah Nawaz of Mamdot held other important offices. Amir-ud-Din was appointed the Private Secretary of the leader of the Party, and Maqbool Mahmood was designated as its Propaganda Secretary. Fazl-i-Husain had successfully held together different elements and did "all the necessary spadework for giving the Unionist Party a good start under the new constitution" so that the fruits of his labour were reaped by Sir

Sikandar Hayat Khan.[52] When Sir Husain died on July 9, 1936, the Central Committee of the Unionist Party appointed Sikandar Hayat as the new party chief. Sir Sikandar Hayat, at the time, was the Deputy Governor of the Reserve Bank of India, a post he had acquired on a recommendation from Sir Husain.

With the demise of Sir Husain in 1936 a long, stable and equally decisive period in Punjabi politics ended. His successor, belonging to the Hayat family of Wah and an industrialist with real estate interests, became the first Chief Minister of the Punjab under the India Act of 1935. While the province entered a new phase in its politics the Punjab tradition went on triumphantly. However, the new premier had to face a more formidable force in the form of a reinvigorated AIML which had begun concentrating on Muslim majority provinces to enlist wider support. Sikandar-Jinnah Pact of 1937 during the Lucknow session of the AIML was a breakthrough for the League which could have not happened during the life-time of Sir Husain yet, still many urban Leaguers like Barkat Ali never trusted the Unionists.[53]

Within less than three years of signing of the Sikandar-Jinnah Pact, Jinnah was able to rally South Asian Muslims around the political creed of an independent nation-state with *Muslim* providing a larger and cohesive identity to them. The League's session at Lahore in 1940 decided for separate political redefinition which brought the Muslim masses into political spectrum for the first time in the history of the Punjab. Witnessing this major transformation, many of the former Unionists joined the League in the mid-1940s along with the *Sajjada nishin* families intermingling with both urban and rural elites as well as the masses from amongst the Punjabi Muslims[54]. It even politicised a large section of urban women for whom otherwise politics had remained an all-male domain[55]. The other parties of the 1930s, like the Khaksars and the Ahrars, could not come up with a similar cohesive political destination that the League had carved out and were thus swept along. Both the Khaksars and the Ahrars were led by religio-political elites with urban, lower middle class background but their vacillation on sub-national issues or confrontation with the government had already weakened them. It is not to deny them their role in creating some degree of consciousness on certain contemporary issues among the common Muslims, yet such movements generally proved to be localized emotional outbursts. The Majlis-i-Ahrar-i-Islam was founded in 1929 with the avowed aim of establishing an Islamic state in the sub-continent and its membership came from the cadres that had lost hope in the League, Khilafatists and the Congress. Some of these people were enthused by the Russian Revolution of 1917. The Ahrars formally met in their first session on December 29, 1929, under the chairmanship of Afzal Haq. Ataaullah Shah Bokhari, Abu Saeed Anwar, Mazhar Ali Azhar, Shorish Kashmiri and Maulvi Gul Sher Khan were some of the other known pioneer Ahrars whereas Zafar Ali Khan left them in the 1930s to form his own Ittehad-i-Millat Party. The Ahrars took an active stand against the policies of the Maharajah of Kashmir in the 1930s by sponsoring marches into the state, advocated Muslim possession of the

Shahidganj and constantly protested against the Ahmadis[56]. The Tehrik-i-Khaksar of Allama Inayatullah Khan Mashriqi came into existence in April 1931 at Lahore and some four months later, on August 25, 1931, its first regular contingent organised a parade at Panduki, near Lahore. Allama Mashriqi, a mathematician of excellent calibre, began the Khaksars as a non-communal party but gradually it turned out to be a total Muslim organisation spearheading activism on a number of socio-economic and political issues. Its engagement on too many fronts dissipated its energies and vigour. It tried to resolve Shia-Sunni differences in a rather unique manner through rallies and defiantly challenged Sikandar Hayat's government on March 19, 1940, resulting in quite a few deaths. Like the Ahrars, the Khaksars had their heyday in the 1930s but their confrontations with the Unionist hierarchy and emotional outbursts left them weakened.[57]

Postscript

Given a complex plethora of several conflictive identities, it is still perplexing to explain the major shift in Punjabi Muslim opinion vis-a-vis Pakistan movement in the crucial 1940s. While Paul Brass, Francis Robinson and Mushirul Hasan, owing to their largely UP-related researches might find it difficult to accept a 'communitarian' Muslim feeling cutting across the sectarian and regional loyalties, some analysts might still accredit the British factor for such a transformation.[58] But it is only desirable and not imperative that well-knit communitarian identity must precede the attainment of a sovereign nationhood. State, like in many European countries, itself can be instrumental in such a formative process. But even then, many cases such as Canada, United Kingdom or former Soviet Union are still groping for a mutually-agreed, all-encompassing identity.

Some historians attribute the major transformation of Muslim public opinion in favour of Pakistan to the departure of powerful regional/provincial leaders that the League was finally able to make inroads in Muslim majority provinces such as Punjab and Bengal[59]. But such an interpretation does not hold "the whole-truth" since same powerful non-League elite held the sway in Muslim majority provinces like the NWFP yet Pakistan turned out to be an overarching programme beyond any regional containment. In addition, such an argument, while relegating Pakistan to a mere incident of history, totally ignores the ideological and religious factor in the South Asian Muslim politics. The Pakistani intellectual historians would explain this major shift in context of trans-territorial loyalties of the South Asian Muslims based on a long-standing historical experience, without excepting the Punjabis, owing to their altitude towards League's credentials as a supra-regional Muslim party (two-nation concept)[60]. The Indian historians have usually felt comfortable in relegating evolution of Pakistan to an imperial policy of divide and rule made further convenient by the strategic blunders on the part of the Congress[61]. For some historians of the Punjab, the shift in political attitudes came about due to the ascendancy of the indigenous factors within the province[62]. For expatriate Muslim historians, witnessing emergent revivalist movements within the Muslim societies in the 1980s, the evolution of Pakistan as a common political creed can be understood only in context of Islamic concept of political community, not simply in terms of composite arithmetical democracy.[63]

To sum up, Punjab's politics well until mid-1940s, presented a faction-ridden, regionalised spectrum while a vigilant British administration, through far-reaching policies had been able to co-opt the rural, land-based elite. The emphasis on administration rather than on governance hampered the development of a cohesive Punjabi political tradition. Primordial and rural/urban loyalties resulted into added fissures in the body-politic with groups falling back on sectarian, clannish and regional affinities. The country-wide political movements, lacking a superordinate ideological substitute to the primordial identities, could not develop their roots in the province where local loyalties superseded trans-territorial idealism. Muslim religio-political parties suffered from similar ideological problems and depended on emotional rhetoric which fizzled out with the lapse of time. And, when the League came out with a more super-ordinate idealism in the form of Pakistan, it equally felt the urgency of co-opting the rural powerful elite from amongst the Punjabi Muslims. This double-pronged strategy proved successful as the Unionists feared a more overpowering Congress on the march which had already established its ministries in most of the provinces. Like Bengali leadership, the Punjabi Muslim leadership joined hands with the League in October 1937 which worked usefully for both until the demand for Pakistan seemed to overtake the rural-based provincial 'separatism'. The Unionists, especially, after the death of Fazl-i-Husain, could not sustain a policy of quarantining their province from outside influences as Pakistan had become a common mystique. Yet, once having obtained the country they, depending on their long-standing experience in politicking as intermediaries, struck back as the assertive ruling elite in the young country along with the expatriates from the UP. But the Punjab tradition was not going to work for long in a country with equally strong and mutually competitive multiple regionalist identities. The Bengalis, Pushtuns, Sindhis and subsequently even the Muhajireen started resenting 'the Punjabi domination'. Once again, many Punjabi intellectuals find themselves in a quandary in this musical chairs of clashing identities.

NOTES

1.   To Kedourie, nationalism is basically a political sentiment which is essentially formulated by the new secular intellectual, hostile to the traditional dynastic and religious order. Problems with this definition is that it refuses to take into account the role of religion and traditional elite in the formulation of the doctrine as the case with Zionism or similar other nationalisms (Irish for instance) into account. See Elie Kedourie, *Nationalism*, London, 1966, pp. 49-50.

2.   Hamza Alavi appears to see a modernist, ambitious middle class enjoying its 'traditional' hold over the Muslim political destiny. To him this *salariat* solidifies its interests by imagining, creating and then ruling Pakistan

3.   As quoted in Malcolm Yapp, "Language, Religion and Political Identity: A general Framework" in David Taylor and Malcolm Yapp (eds), *Political Identity in South Asia*, London, 1979, p. 12.

4.   In addition to the valuable volumes by these two South Asianists, see their debate in Taylor and Yapp, *op.cit.*

5.   These and other works are mentioned in subsequent references. Also, see Iftikhar H. Malik, "Identity Formation and Muslim Party Politics in the Punjab, 1897-1936: A Retrospective Analysis", *Modern Asian Studies*, 29, 2 (1995).

6.   The vexing problem of mutually antagonistic and volatile identity was extremely confusing to the British especially in the closing days of the Raj. The gubernatorial reports, at the most, found, tensions and dissension "very confusing". For instance, see *Report on the Situation in the Punjab for Second Half of September, 1944*, L/P&J/ 5/247, India Office Library and Records (IOL&R); and Sir Jenkins (Governor of Punjab) to Lord Wavell, May 31, 1946, and, Jenkins to Wavell, September 14, 1946, *Fortnightly Governor's Reports*, L/P&J/5/249, IOL&R.

7.   Benazir Bhutto became the Prime Minister in December 1988 after a plural electoral verdict which enabled Nawaz Sharif to establish provincial government in the Punjab. Bhutto's government was dismissed through a presidential order on August 6, 1990, following which provincial government in the Punjab resigned as well. During these eighteen months, Pakistan experienced a very nerve-breaking bi-polarisation between the centre and the province on almost every policy matter besides "horse trading" among the legislators. Such a plural system, if allowed to operate with open-mindedness, could have suited the country the most with its built-in checks and balances, but the high-handedness based on personal loyalties in the absence of programme-oriented politicking made it suffer from bi-polarity.

8.   In an international conference on such Punjab-related themes in Lahore, many speakers urged fellow Punjabis not to shun their own mother-tongue besides reiterating their appeal to make Punjabi as a medium of instruction in the schools. For details, see *The Daily Jang*, (London), January 4, 1993.

9.   Many Punjabis are deeply shocked the way the Kabul regime has been manhandling their diplomats in Afghanistan. In early 1995, Pakistani embassy was stormed by 5,000 protestants who killed a diplomat beside injuring many others seriously. Eventually, the mission was closed. There was a mixed anger and shock over such a reaction from the people whom Pakistanis had looked after for so long during their long ordeal against the former Soviet Union. The situation seems to have changed since the Taliban's takeover of Kabul.

10.   In Karachi several Punjabi policemen, rickshaw drivers, paramilitary personnel and labourers have been killed over the past many years, largely by the militant groups

within the Muhajir Qaumi Movement (MQM). On November 2, 1995, 16 unskilled labourers from Dera Ghazi Khan in southwestern Punjab were rounded up. They were lined up by the militants belonging to the Muhajir Tiger Force of the MQM and were shot dead mercilessly. While 15 were killed on the spot, the sixteenth escaped as he fell under the dead bodies and miraculously escaped bullets raining all over from such a close range inside a small room. The injured survivor cried for help in the neighbourhood, but out of fear none came to his rescue largely out of fear. The terrorists left a message with the dead bodies for Naseerullah Babar, the PPP interior minister, stating: "Gift for Naseerullah Babar". These workers like many others have been the victim of a strong anti-Punjabi, anti-establishment crusade unleashed by the MQM in Karachi. For details, see *The Daily News* (London). November 3, 1995.

Last year, 35 funerals took place on the same day in Quetta, Balochistan, of Balochi/ Pushtun workers who fell victim to a similar discretionary attack.

11.   It appears that the uneasy majority-minority relationship in India, a historical problem indeed, remains unresolved. While ethnicity may be a similar 'prop' for activism, basic differentiation of the community still largely harbours on religious identification. Excepting supra-religious elites, Hindu-Muslim, Hindu-Sikh, or caste-based polarisation (traditionally viewed as religious identification) keep on vetoing the evolution of any cross-communal equation. Ethnicity is solidified by religious divide while ethnicity itself does not play any role in this inter-communal dichotomy. Punjabi Hindus and Punjabi Sikhs kill one another the way Bomabyites, both Hindu and Muslim, fall upon each other. It is more similar to contemporary situation in former Yugoslavia or Northern Ireland. Religion, in other words, still holds the vetoing power. To the leaders of the BJP, VHP and Shiv Sena, regional or lingual commonalities are irrelevant since, to them, Indian nationalism must be redefined as a majoritarian creed with Hinduism providing the core ethos. To them, Indian Muslims (and other non-Hindus) are non_Indian, as long as they remain non-Hindus. See Ball Thackeray's interview in *Time International*, January 25, 1993.

12.   "Anger Rising in Bombay. 'It's a Pogrom', The Muslims Say", *International Herald Tribune*, January 16-17, 1993; also, ""Homeless Muslims try to flee Bombay", *The Times*, January 13, 1993; and, "Might vs. Right", *Time International*, January 18, 1993.

13.   For relevant section, see vol. ix, part I, *Western India and Panjab* (Calcutta, 1916) and vol. viii, part I of *Sindhi and Lahnda* (Calcutta, 1919).

14.   For a useful discussion, see C. Shackle, "Cultural Identity in Pakistan Panjab" in G. Krishna (ed) *Contributions in South Asian Studies*, vol. I, Delhi, 1979.

15.   David Gilmartin, *Empire and Islam: Punjab and the Making of Pakistan*, London, 1988, p.1.

16.   For a relevant discussion, see Imran Ali, "The Punjab and the Retardation of Nationalism", in D. A. Low, ed., *The Political Inheritance of Pakistan*, London, 1991.

17.   Quite a few writers awoke to the cause of *Punjabiat* during the 1980s coming to the defence of the province in terms of resistance and revolution. For instance, see Hanif

Ramay, *Punjab Ka Muqqaddima,* (Urdu) Lahore, 1987. During Benazir Bhutto's premiership, the opposition-led Punjab witnessed a campaign based on slogans like *Jaag Punjabi, Jaag* (Wake up Punjabi, Wake up!). Some observers have attributed such slogans to Pakistani intelligence agencies trying to destabilise Benazir Bhutto's government. See, Maleeha Lodhi & Zahid Hussain, "The Invisible Government", *The News* in *The Jang,* September 30, 1992.

18.   Pakistani polity, like many other developing countries, suffers from elitist exclusivity as the pervasive influence of the feudatory, bureaucratic (both civil and military) and industrial elite monopolise the decision-making processes and institutions. In ideological sense, dissensions between the reformist/modernist and traditional elites further play inhibitive role in the development of responsive and accountable political system. For a theoretical and historical analysis, see Asaf Hussain, *Elite Politics in an Ideological State: The Case of Pakistan,* London, 1979. Alavi feels that in Pakistan, it is the bourgeois elites—the *Salariat*—who, in collaboration with traditional elites, monopolise the politic-economic institutions. See Hamza Alavi, "Pakistan and Islam: Ethnicity and Ideology", in Fred Halliday and Hamza Alavi, eds., *State and Ideology in the Middle East and Pakistan,* London, 1987, pp.64-110.

19.   For further discussion on the subject see, P. M. H. van den Dungen, *The Punjab Tradition: Influence and Tradition in Nineteenth Century India,* London, 1972.

20.   Such significant developments including the settlement of the 'new' Punjab, according to a recent study, stemmed from the imperial rationale of the administrators and eventually turned out to be a major retarding factor in the development of a cohesive political tradition. See Imran Ali, *The Punjab Under Imperialism, 1885-1947,* Princeton, 1987. On may easily extend the same argument to any part of the sub-continent under the Raj. The British, like other colonials, were in the sub-continent mainly to rule and would certainly not go out of their way to inculcate the political traditions and institutions that could eventually lead them out.

21.   On the element of continuity, see Craig Baxter, "The People's Party Vs. the Punjab Feudalists", in J. Henry Corson and et. al., eds., *Contemporary Problems of Pakistan,* Leiden, 1974, pp. 6-29.

22.   For further details, see Andrew J. Major, "The Punjabi Chieftains and the Transition from Sikh to British Rule", in Low, *op. cit.*

23.   Krishna Kapur, *A History of Development of Judiciary in the Punjab, 1884-1926,* Lahore, 1928, p. 26.

24.   *Selections From the Public Correspondence for the Affairs of the Punjab,* Vol. IV, Lahore, 1859, p. 170. It was further observed in the report: "The chiefs who remained either with feudal possessions or with independent powers were on our side to a man". *Ibid.,* p. 188.

25.   Such a well-planned policy with clear 'bias' for executive naturally has had its results both for India and Pakistan. The events in Indian Punjab "the roots of Sikh separatism

can be traced to the unintended consequences of British rule....In the latter [Pakistan], political instability has been rooted in the conscious policy of British officials. They determined that the Punjab should become a major centre of army recruitment. In order to legitimize their rule in the region, they bolstered parochial loyalties and the influence of the landowners. These legacies frustrate the foundations of a Pakistani nationalism grounded in the establishment of a system of Islamic social justice". Ian Talbot, "British Rule in the Punjab, 1849-1947", *The Journal of Imperial and Commonwealth History*, XIX, No. 2. p. 218.

26.   Andrew J. Major, *op. cit.*, p. 80.

27.   S. M. Latif, *The History of the Panjab: From the Remotest Antiquity to the Present Time*, Lahore, 1891, p. 590.

28.   "India, Ancient and Modern", *New Englander*, 15, 1856, p. 494.

29.   For details, see Iftikhar H. Malik, *US-South Asia Relations, 1784-1940: A Historical Perspective*, Islamabad, 1987, pp. 42-43.

30.   S. M. Ikram, *Modern Muslim India and the Birth of Pakistan*, Lahore, 1969, p. 203.

31.   For more on its activities see, Mian Amir-ud-Din, *Yaad-i-Ayyam*, (Urdu), Lahore, 1983.

32.   Azim Husain, *Fazl-i-Husain. A Political Biography*, Bombay, 1946, p. 71.

33.   Rai published his monthly *Young India* while based in New York at a time when the Ghadrites had come under official scrutiny. An author of a number of valuable works, Rai lived an active, mobile life which came to an end in anti-Simon Commission agitation in 1927. For his views, see *Unhappy India, (Calcutta*, 1928), his last and massive volume in India written in response to Katherine Mayo's *Mother India*. Also, Naeem Gul Rathore, "Indian Nationalist Agitation in the United States. A Study of Lala Lajpat Rai and the India Home Rule League of America, 1914-1920", a Ph. D. dis...ertation, Columbia University, New York, 1965.

34.   Har Dayal, after a teaching and active career in the USA and Europe as an Indian nationalist died in Philadelphia in 1939 as a Hindu visionary.See his "India in America",*Modern Review*, July 1911 and, *Forty-Four Months in Germany and Turkey*, London, 1924. Also, C. Emily Brown, *Har Dayal: Hindu Revolutionary and Rationalist*, Tucson, 1975.

35.   For a detailed account of the Punjabi migrations to Canada and the United States, the local reaction, the Ghadr interlude and the eventual transformation of the Ghadrites, see Iftikhar H. Malik, *op. cit.*, pp.93-258.

36.   For official records, see M. S. Leigh, *The Punjab and the War*, Lahore, 1922, p. 22-23; also, Michael O'Dwyer, *India As I Knew It: 1885-1925*, London, 1926, pp. 183-188.

37.   For contemporary statistics and policies, see Information Division, Government of

Punjab, *Statement of Newspapers and Periodicals Published in the Punjab during the year 1917,* Allahabad, 1917.

38. "From 1910-1919 the Punjab was administered by a Lieutenant-Governor who had the assistance of a small Advisory Council of about a dozen people. They were the most loyal, elderly men belonging to the well-to-do class, who had rendered political and administrative services to the British Government and they had no political opinions except those which the British liked. They were not elected because they were brilliant orators, nor because they had attained high degrees. They were elected or nominated for their common sense which they could bring to bear on their country's problems. They were well-to-do people who were in a position to help people, to approach government officials". Firoz Khan Noon, *From Memory,* Lahore, 1966, p. 83-84.

39. *Ibid.,* p. 89.

40. For more biographical details on Sir Shafi, see Jahan Ara Shah Nawaz, *Father and Daughter,* Lahore, 1971.

41. For further details, see *ibid.*

42. For a comprehensive biography on Malik Barkat Ali, see M. Rafique Afzal, *Malik Barkat Ali: His Life and Writings,* Lahore, 1969.

43. See, Ashiq Husain Batalvi, *Iqbal Kay Akhiri Do Saal,* (Urdu), Lahore, 1961; *Hamari Qaumi Jido-Jihd,* 3 volumes, Lahore, 1966,1968, 1975.

44. For more on student politics, see Sarfaraz Hussain Mirza, ed., *The Punjab Muslim Students Federation: An Annotated Documentary Survey,* Lahore, 1978; *Tasawwur-i-Pakistan say Qararadad-i-Pakistan Tak,* (Urdu), Lahore, 1983.

45. Leon B. Poullada, "Contemporary Political Parties in the Punjab", Master's thesis, University of Pennsylvania, 1954, p. 13.

46. On the historical interpretation of this viewpoint, see David Page, *The Prelude to Partition: The Indian Muslims and the Imperial System of Control, 1920-1932,* Delhi, 1982, pp. 46-58 and 46-72.

47. Syed Nur Ahmad, *Mian Fazl-i-Husain. A Review of His Life and Work,* Lahore, 1936, p. 40. In a speech before the Punjab Legislative Council in 1923 he claimed to believe in " the principle of helping the backward communities irrespective of their religion, be they Muslim, Hindu or Sikh". *Punjab Legislative Council Debates,* Vol. IV, March 15, 1923, p. 1318.

48. For more on Sikandar Hayat, see Iftikhar H. Malik, *Sikandar Hayat Khan: A Political Biography,* Islamabad, 1985; also, see Syed Nur Ahmad, *op. cit.*

49. He wrote to Sikandar Hayat: "Jinnah's move in establishing a Central Parliamentary Board of the League was wrong move, detrimental to the Indian Muslim interest. We have taken the right line...Miscellaneous urbanites like Iqbal, Shuja, Tajuddin, Barkat

Ali, have naturally been trying to make something out of it...So the scheme is purely a paper one".

Sikandar Hayat held a similar view as he observed: "His activities during the past few weeks, judging from the press reports, are contrary to his professions...If he meddles, he would only be encouraging fissiparous tendencies already painfully discernible in a section of Punjabi Muslims, and might burn his fingers; and in any case, we cannot possibly allow 'provincial autonomy' to be tampered with in any sphere, and by anybody, be he a nominee of the powers who have given us the autonomy or a President of the Muslim League or any other association or body". Fazl-i-Husain to Sikandar Hayat, May 6, 1936; and, Sikandar Hayat to Fazl-i-Husain, May 1, 1936. For details see, Waheed Ahmad, ed., *Letters of Mian Fazl-i-Husain,* Lahore, 1977.

50.   Quoted in Azim Husain, *op. cit.,* p. 336-337.

51.   Waheed Ahmad, *op. cit.,* p. 346.

52.·   S. M. Ikram, *op. cit.,* p. 233.

53.   For more on this topic, see M. Rafique Afzal, *Guftar-i-Iqbal,*(Urdu), Lahore, 1969.

54.   For a recent study, see David Gilmartin, *Empire and Islam: Punjab and the Making of Pakistan,* London, 1988.

55.   See, Sarfaraz Hussain Mirza, *Muslim Women's Role in the Pakistan Movement,* Lahore, 1969.

56.   For further details, see Afzal Haq, *Tarikh-i-Ahrar,* (Urdu) Lahore, n.d.; Janbaz Mirza, *Karvan-i-Ahrar,* (Urdu), 2 Vols., Lahore, 1975; Shorish Kashmiri, *Pass-i-Diwar-i-Zindan,* (Urdu), Lahore, 1971; and, Ikram Ali Malik,"Pakistan Resolution and Unionist Party", in K. F. Yusuf, et. al., eds., *Pakistan Resolution Revisited,* Islamabad, 1990, pp. 347-366.

57.   See Safdar Saleemi, *Khaksar Tehrik Ki Sola Sala Jiddo-Jihd,* (Urdu), Lahore, n.d.; Allama Mashriqi, *Qaul-i-Faisal,* (Urdu), Lahore, 1935; *Maulvi Ka Ghalat Mazhab, No. 4,* (Urdu), Lahore, 1937; *Al-Islah,* (Lahore), October 20, 1939 to March 15, 1940; and, Abdullah Malik, *Punjab Ki Siyasi Tehrikain,* (Urdu), Lahore, 1971. For British official view on the Khaksars, see, *John Morton Collection,* MSS. Eur. D. 1003, and, *Indian Police Collection,* MSS. Eur. F. 161, IOR&L.

58.   Such a school includes quite a few famous Western scholars conveniently grouped as Cambridge school along with some South Asian historians: Paul Brass, *Language, Religion and Politics in North India,* Cambridge, 1974; Peter Hardy, *The Muslims of British India,* Cambridge, 1972; David Page, *op. cit.;* Francis Robinson, *Separatism Among Indian Muslims. The Politics of the United Provinces' Muslims 1860-1923.* Cambridge, 1974; and, Mushirul Hasan, *Nationalism and Communal Politics in India, 1916-1928,* Delhi, 1978. In the context of the Punjab, a recent study claims that it was merely the break-down of the status quo in the 1940s earlier fiercely maintained by

the British in the province that let the trans-territorial forces like the League break the provincial isolationism. See Ian Talbot, *Punjab and the Raj, 1849-1947,* Delhi, 1988.

59.   See Ayesha Jalal, *The Sole Spokesman: Jinnah, the Muslim League and the Demand for Pakistan,* Cambridge, 1985.

60.   The leading spokesman of this school was Aziz Ahmad whose *Studies in Islamic Culture in the Indian Environment* (Oxford, 1964) followed by *Islamic Modernism in India and Pakistan, 1857-1964,* (Oxford, 1967) turned out to be pioneering works. Along with K. K. Aziz, Khalid B. Sayeed and Hafeez Malik, Ahmad turned out to be a permeating influence on a generation of scholars like Gail Minault, Barbara Metcalf, Rafiuddin Ahmed and Farzana Shaikh.

61.   For instance, see Anita Inder Singh, *The Origins of the Partition of India, 1936-1947,* Delhi, 1987.

62.   David Gilmartin, *Islam and Imperialism,* London, 1989.

63.   Farzana Shaikh, *Community and Consensus in Islam. Muslim Representation in Colonial India, 1860-1947,* Cambridge, 1989.

Khalistan: The Origins of the Demand and Its Pursuit Prior to Independence, 1940-45

Sukhmani Riar

Khalistan was first asked for the Sikhs by a medical doctor, Dr. V.S. Bhatti of Ludhiana immediately after the All India Muslim League had passed its 'Lahore Resolution' on March 23, 1940. Dr. Bhatti had demanded it in a brochure of less than forty printed pages entitled *Khalistan*. He demanded it on the presumption that Pakistan was bound to be established sooner or later and since it was to be a theocratic state of the Muslims, it was likely to be an unfriendly neighbour of 'Independent India'. Dr. Bhatti proposed the Khalistan of his conception to act as a buffer between two unfriendly independent states.

The Khalistan so proposed and demanded for the Sikhs was meant to include three areas. In the first place it was to include the central districts of Punjab Province of the then directly administered 'British Empire' in India. The districts mentioned by Bhatti were Ludhiana, Jalandhar, Ambala, Ferozpur, Lahore, Amritsar, Layallpur, Gujranwala, Sheikhupura, Montgomery, Hissar, Rohtak and Karnal. Secondly it was to include the princely states of the 'Cis-Satluj' lying between Satluj and Jamuna whose administration was supervised by the Governor of the Punjab as 'Regent, viz. Nabha, Patiala, and, Faridkot, Kalsia and Malerkotla. And lastly, it was to include the 'Shimla Group' of states whose supervision was done by the Deputy commissioner of Shimla with the title of 'Superintendent'. The head of the proposed Khalistan was to be the Maharaja of Patiala. This Khalistan according to Bhatti was to be a theocratic state and administered by its head with the aid of a cabinet consisting of representative of federating units.[1]

We can easily see that Dr. Bhatti's demand for Khalistan, was a counterblast to the Muslim League Lahore Resolution. It aimed at pitching Sikh communalism against Muslim communalism likely to be worked up by Jinnah all over India by categorizing Indian Muslims as a nation than a minority. That this was the intention of Bhatti is evident from the fact that the territory sought for Khalistan in Bhatti's brochure included an important part of the proposed sovereign state of the Muslims either as a distinct entity in the North-Western India or part of one entity, including Muslim majority areas to the East of India but as sovereign separate state separate from India. It would be worth noting that in term of political geography of present day sub-continent of India the proposed Khalistan was to be not only the whole of the 'Punjabi Suba' including the union territory of Chandigarh, of the districts, Hiassar, Rohtak, Karnal and Ambala of Haryana and the whole of Himachal Pardesh in the present day but also parts of the Pakistan with important areas covered by the districts of Lahore, Sheikhupur, Gujranwala, Layallpur and Montgomery districts, Bhatti's Khalistan demand did not end there. It went on to demand also "a corridor consisting of thin strips of Sind, Bahawalpur and Rajputana enabling the Sikhs to have an outlet to the Gulf of Cutch, for without a sea port they will be bottled up and dependent on others for trade".[2]

The Khalistan demand proposed by Bhatti, appealed to a section of anti-Akali Sikhs in and out of the Punjab Congress, for its possibility of becoming an effective counter campaign likely to be waged by Jinnah and his Muslim League. It particularly appealed to Baba Gudit Singh of *Komagata Maru* fame. Baba had attained fame as a great freedom fighter in 1914 for exposing the discriminatory attitude of an important dominion of the British Commonwealth against the Indians and the refusal of both the Government of Great Britain and that of India to back the Indians in asking for the rights of migration to the dominions of the British Commonwealth. He had added to his fame during the First World War and for a couple of years later by leading an underground life of nearly six years till 1920 when on the advise of Mahatma Gandhi he surrendered to the police and underwent an imprisonment of 5-years.[3] After his release he became an enthusiastic congressman. In August, 1937, he formed an independent Congress Party in the Punjab to help Pandit Nehru in his forthcoming election tours to fight the Punjab elections in December-January, 1936-37 and showed great scepticism into Dr. Gopi Chand Bhargav's understanding with the Akalis for fighting the elections.[4] The understanding was effected between Dr. Gopi Chand Bhargav and Master Tara Singh on November 17, 1936 to fight the Khalsa National Party.[5] Under the terms of this agreement Sikh Congressmen were to contest in ten of the twenty four Sikh seats. The rest were to be fought by Shromani Akali Dal. The Akalis stuck to this agreement except on two seats. One of these two seats on which Akalis backed out from this agreement was allotted to Gurdit Singh. Here he was opposed by an Akali who won by a substantial number of more votes than obtained by Baba Gurdit Singh. The defeat did not make Gurdit Singh give up his congress membership but it did make him a frustrated congressman.[6] Maybe it was this frustration that was at the back of his giving a slogan which might rehabilitate him in the eyes of the leadership of the organization to which he had stuck in spite of the latter's failure to force the Akalis not to help his candidature against one who had chosen to oppose him in the election in 1937. It is difficult to be sure but in all probability it was he who might have encouraged Bhatti in publishing his monograph while the year long discussion was being carried out among All India muslim circles on the final form to be given to the muslims's place in the future constitutional setup of India.[7] But even if that might not be the case he had called a convention on May 19, 1940 in association with Ranjodh Singh Tarsikka and Jagjit Singh, editor of *Khalsa Sevak*[8] Jagjit Singh's association with him in all probability was dictated by Giani Sher Singh, his predecessor in the editorial chair of *Khalsa Sevak*.[9] It is difficult to say what motivated Ranjodh Singh Tarsikka for the simple reason that very little is known aboout the background of Tarsikka and even less being is known about his politics. In all probability he was an activist of either the Central Akali Dal or of the Punjab Congress.

Whatever the motivation of Ranjodh Singh Tarsikka, we can presume that Baba Gurdit Singh seem to have chosen to regain his old position in Sikh politics by becoming an advocate of Khalistan. That he was most enthusiastic on doing that at this stage was evident from the fact that simultaneously with his convention of May 19 he had organized another convention on a wider scale than the one held on May 10. This larger convention which was organized by Gurdit Singh in association with Jagjit Singh, the editor of *Khalsa Sevak* was attended by 126 Sikh Delegate claiming to represent all Sikh organizations in the Punjab. They gathered together and deliberated on Khalistan. The convention gave precise details of the territory proposed to be included in it. They were apparently different from the ones in Bhatti's Khalistan and extended the boundaries of Khalistan to the North-East of the then British Punjab to include Jammu, then as now as a part of Jammu & Kashmir and the North-West Frontier Province upto Jamrud, the last British post of the British Empire in India. It was argued that this was as much a part of the territory between Satluj and Chenab as the one constituting a large part of Khalistan in Bhatti's pamphlet, "which Maharaja Dalip singh gave as *Amanat'* (Trust) to the British".[10] Obviously while arguing that way the convention had the treaty of Bharowal in mind. It was signed as far back as December 1846 between Sir Fredrick Currie and a council of regency of eight Sardars as the representative of the East India Company and the Lahore Government headed at least formally by Maharaja Dalip Singh respectively.[11] The convention obviously did not use the same argument as the one on which the All India Muslim League had based its arguments for the right to have independent separate states in the areas of India over which they were in a majority.[12] Nor did the convention leaders claimed that the Sikhs were a nation, an important claim made by Jinnah while justifying the All India Muslim League demand of Independent Sovereign state for the Muslims of India.[13] The demand for Khalistan was sought to be achieved according to the decision of the two conventions inspired by Baba Gurdit Singh through an organization established at the second convention which claimed to represent " All Sikh organizations". The new organization was significantly named Guru Raj Darbar Khalsa Board with powers to add ten or more members to launch a propaganda campaign for Khalistan.[14] Obviously the intention was to set up Khalistan as a theocratic Sikh state.

Neither Bhatti's pamphlet nor the two conventions bore much fruits among the Sikhs in general inspite of the great excitement created among the Sikhs by the resolution of All India Muslim League at Lahore on March 23, 1940. To a great extent that was because both the top leaders of the Shromani Akali Dal and those of the Indian National Congress openly came out against the demand of Khalistan made on behalf of the Sikhs. Master Tara Singh who was then not only the president of Shromani Akali Dal but also a member of the working committee of the Punjab

Provincial Congress and All India Congress Committee strongly ran down the Khalistan as spelled out by Bhatti. In fact he had expressed immediate anger against Bhatti's brochure in a pamphlet meant to be widely circulated. He observed in this pamphlet 'While opposing the Pakistan scheme some Sikhs have lost their heads and they are preaching the establishment of Sikh rule. This will simply be adding to the confusion already created by the Muslim League. Swaraj is the only solution of our county's misfortune.'[15] That was of course before the two conventions of May 1940 inspired and organized by the hero of Kamagatamaru and before some conferences organized by "hot headed Sikhs", particularly in the Eastern parts of the Punjab where the Muslims were in minority. One such conference was held at Jagraon on May 24, 1940. In this conference it was stated that the Sikhs of Malwa would like to see the establishment of Khalistan in case Pakistan was created by the British Raj.[16] That was on the very day that a Muslim member of the Provincial Congress working committee was putting forth a representation to the then congress president, Maulana Abdul Kalam Azad alleging that some Akalis were mis-using the Congress platform to propagate the Sikh Raj in the name of scuttling the Pakistan scheme.[17] It deserves to be noticed that intelligence agencies of the Government of India were then pointing out that the scheme of Pakistan had revived the Sikh memories of the muslim rule in the eighteenth century and oppression of Muslim rulers over the Sikhs in that period.[18]

In August 1940 the opposition of both the Shromani Akali Dal and Panjab Congress literally ended the Khalistan demand and its place was taken by the demand for Azad Punjab. It remained at least the Akali demand throughout the turbulence created amongst the Sikhs by the August offer of Lintithgow, the then 'conservative' Governor General of India in 1940, the Rajagopalachariya's supporting offer to Jinnah through the British Government subsequently in the same year accepted the resignation of Master Tara Singh from the Congress. He remained out of Congress throughout the individual Satyragraha led by Gandhiji in 1941, during the great concession made to the Muslim majority provinces by Cripps in March-April 1942 to obtaining Pakistan, and also when the 'Quit India' movement was at its height and the Azad Punjab continued to be the demand of Shromani Akali Dal. That remained the Sikh demand as voiced by Shromani Akali Dal even when 'Quit India' movement of the Congress was at its high between August 1942 and March 1943. It continued to be demanded by the Shromani Akali Dal till May 1944.

In May 1944, the Shromani Akali Dal by now out of the Indian National Congress and running the administration of Punjab in collaboration with the Unionist Ministry began under playing the demand for Azad Punjab and started hobnobbing with the demand for Khalistan that its leader Master Tara Singh had opposed in 1940. The rationale of this new attitude of the Akali Dal was provided by the release of Gandhiji on May 6, 1944. They began moves to win over Jinnah to help force the British Government to promise leaving India on the close of the war and establish a

National Government at the centre in the immediate future on the basis of Raja Ji's formula spelled out publicly after the release of Gandhiji.[19] The Akali Dal suddenly began underplaying its demand for Azad Punjab and started hobnobbing with the demand for Khalistan. It sought to commit the entire Sikh community behind this demand by organizing an All Party Sikh Conference at Amritsar in August 1944, where strong speeches were made against Mahatma Gandhi and for the first time Master Tara Singh stated that the Sikhs were a separate nation.[20] The conference demanded an independent Sikh state and authorized Master Tara Singh to go into the question of taking suitable steps to have such a state. Master Tara Singh set the tone for doing that by declaring that the Sikhs who were a Nation would see that if and when India was divided, the Sikhs should not be made slaves either of Pakistan or Hindustan.[21] The leaders of the Akalis in the conference had made no secret of the fact that now the Dal preferred Khalistan to the Azad Punjab. In doing that they fought shy of using the expression Khalistan and instead of Khalistan they spoke of 'Independent Sikh State' for the Sikhs. When Mangal Singh Gill moved a resolution in this conference which demanded Azad Punjab, Mohinder Singh, a close associate of Master Tara Singh, moved an 'amendment' to the resolution. Mohinder Singh's amendment asked for an independent Sikh State. Giani Kartar Singh supported Mohinder Singh's amendment. He argued, "if Pakistan was to be formed, why not give an independent state to the Sikhs too".[22]

Unmindful of the new twist that Akali Dal had now given to the 'Sikh Politics' Gandhi went ahead with the meeting agreed upon by Jinnah. He seems to have convinced himself before that meeting through a quick exchange of letters with Wavell who had succeeded Lintithgow as the Governor General and the Viceroy on October 20, 1943.[23] and apparently taken the initiative in releasing him on May 10, 1944.[24] The politician in Gandhi, however, sought to take advantage of Wavell's announcement that prevented the British Government from declaring India completely independent, though, he was willing to consider the formation of a `National Government' at the centre. Gandhi declared on August 18, 1944, that it was clear that the British were not prepared to give their power to India unless India develops the strength to wrest it from them.[25] Maybe he believed India could be made to develop that strength through some understanding with Jinnah on the basis of the Raja Ji's Formula, which he had proposed discussing in his meeting with Jinnah scheduled to begin two days later. Inspite of the best wishes of Gandhi[26] the talks between him and Jinnah failed, but as long as they were carried on, the Shromani Akali Dal felt extremely agitated. Its leaders went to the extent of sending their volunteers to picket the venue of Gandhi-Jinnah talks on September 24, 1944.[27] The failure of the talks did not quite satisfy them because Jinnah and Gandhi sought to give an impression they might begin again.[28] The Shromani Akali Dal held the fifth session of the All India Akali Conference at Lahore on October 14, 1944, a little over a fortnight after the breakdown of Gandhi-Jinnah talks. It did that under the presidentship of Jathedar Pritam Singh Gojran.[29] While unfurling the Sikh Flag at the conference, Master Tara Singh warned the Sikhs of not only the danger from communists who had by now prevailed upon themselves to support the Muslim League demand spelled out in Lahore resolution of March 23, 1940,[30] but also from Mahatma Gandhi and Jinnah.[31] He added that the Sikhs were determined to fight the British who had denied them their freedom; they were equally determined not to submit to the dictates of Jinnah and Gandhi, both of whom according to him wanted to impose Hindu and Muslim domination on the Sikhs by dividing India.[32] He insisted that Gandhi's discussing of the Rajaji Formula with Jinnah amounted to the Congress not keeping the promise it had made to the Sikhs in 1929 that they would be consulted whenever any communal and political settlement was negotiated.[33]

Master Tara Singh's criticism in these strong words activated non-Akali Sikhs. Durlab Singh, Secretary of Central Sikh Youth League and the Progressive Akali Dal wrote to Mahatma Gandhi asking him to remove the "misunderstanding the Akalis had created among the Sikhs against the Congress."[34] Gandhi responded to Durlab Singh's demand on him by assuring Durlab Singh that Sikh interests and the interests of the nationalists were safe in his hands and those of the Congress: "My association with Rajaji in his formula could not effect the Sikh position in the slightest degree even if Quaid-i-Azam had accepted the formula. The Lahore Resolution of the Congress referred to by you stands. The result of Quaid-i-Azam Jinnah's acceptance would have been that both of us would have approached the Sikhs and others effected to secure their acceptance. I had made this clear in my letter to Master Ji."[35]

Gandhiji's explanation added to the tension already brewing between the two groups in the Dal, one that of Master Tara Singh with Giani Kartar Singh as his active supporter then, and the other of those who had first joined Gandhi in his 'Individual Satyragraha' in 1940-1941 and then the 'Quit India' movement between August, 1942 and February, 1943.[36] The latter released in early 1944 included Udham Singh Nagoki, Ishar Singh Majhail and Partap Singh Kairon. They had watched carefully in prison, the politics of the Dal conducted by Tara Singh with dismay and now when out of prison they were almost itching to criticize Master Tara Singh for accepting the 'Sikander -Baldev Singh pact of June 1942 and hobnobbing with Jinnah's Muslim League in forming a Muslim ministry in North-West Frontier.[37] Released almost simultaneously in October 1944, they supported Gandhi's move to normalize Indian politics including an understanding, if possible, with Jinnah on latter's demand for Pakistan. Ishar Singh Majhail, for example declared at All India Jubilee Akali Conference held at Jandiala in Jalandhar district on November 25, 1944 "that the Dal will continue to stand by the Congress in every struggle launched to achieve India's freedom as it did in the past." [38] He criticized severely the communists and the 'Raja Ji's Formula', but unlike Kartar Singh's group he did not criticise the Congress.[39]

The inter party Akali conflict did not assume a bitter form because soon after the end of Akali-Jinnah talks and the Udham Singh group beginning to criticize Tara Singh's politics, a few non party public men in the country decided to form a committee to devise ways and means for an agreed constitution.[40] Known as the 'Sapru Committee', it issued a questionnaire towards the end of 1944 to a good number of political parties soliciting their views on fundamental rights, representation of communities in the services, Pakistan issue, territorial adjustment and alternative to Pakistan. The questionnaire united the two camps of the Akali Dal and then they asked a number of non-Akali Sikhs to join the Dal in preparing the memorandum for Sapru Committee. The memorandum so prepared was signed by thirty prominent Sikh leaders and legislators including Master Tara Singh, Giani Kartar Singh, Sampuran Singh Layallpuri, Surjit Singh Majithia, Bhai Jodh Singh, Swaran Singh, Ujjal Singh, and Ishar Singh Majhail.[41] In this memorandum which was by no means only an Akali Dal memorandum, though submitted to the Sapru Commute by it, the signatories insisted that "the Sikhs were opposed to the Pakistan scheme, but if it was indeed agreed upon the Sikhs will like to have a 'Sikh State'.[42] The memorandum described the Pakistan scheme as "unnatural, reactionary and opposed to the best interests of the country as it litigated against the lessons of history and requirements of geography" and because it signed the 'Death Warrant' of the future of the Sikh Community as a whole.[43] The scheme, the memorandum felt was based upon the false presumption that the Punjab was the homeland of the Muslims only.[44] The memorandum demanded that "In case Pakistan was created 'the Sikhs' would insist on the creation of 'Sikh State' which would include a substantial majority of Sikh population and their important shrines, historic Gurudwaras and places, with provision for transfer and exchange of population and property."[45]

The Sapru Committee submitted its report in March, 1945. The report rejected Pakistan and removed the *raisen detre* to the Sikh demand for independent Sikh State as enunciated by the Shromani Akali Dal on behalf of the Sikhs. The memorandum submitted by the Shromani Akali Dal on behalf of Sikhs and the demand for independent Sikh State ceased to be the demand of any section of the Sikhs. It ceased to be the Sikh demand at least temporarily so in March, 1945, but only for a while. The demand was revived soon after a few months when Lord Wavell, the Governor General took the initiative to resolve the political deadlock in India on May 6, 1945. On returning back from England, Wavell started preparing for a meeting of the leaders of the political parties in India. He got in touch with Gandhi, Jinnah and Rajgopalachariya by June 16, 1945, released the members of the Congress working committee and invited an All Parties Meeting beginning at Shimla on June 25, 1945. In all he invited twenty one members to this meeting including Gandhi, who came in his personal capacity.[46]

The conference which came to be called the 'First Shimla Conference' met from June 25, 1945 to July 14, 1945 and was attended by all those who were invited to it. They included premiers of the provinces where the popular ministries were functioning, the ex-premiers of the provinces ruled by the Governor under the act of 1935, the presidents of the Congress and the Muslim League, the deputy leaders of the League party in the legislative assembly and the Congress and League leaders in the council of states, the leaders of the Nationalist party and of European Group in the assembly, one representative of the scheduled castes and one of the Sikhs. In all twenty five members attended the meeting if we exclude Gandhi. Though present at Shimla, Gandhi did not attend the conference.[47]

The Viceroy inaugurated the conference with a short speech after welcoming the invitees and explaining the purpose of the meeting. He said "It is not a constitutional settlement, it is not a final solution of India's complex problems that is proposed. But if it succeeds, I am sure it will pave the way towards the settlement and will bring it nearer."[48]

At this stage we must examine the role played by Master Tara Singh in the First Shimla Conference, between June 21 and July 14, 1945. Before doing that we must note that Tara Singh was invited by Wavell to represent the Sikhs in the conference after some hesitation. Tara Singh claimed to represent at Shimla deliberations not the Shromani Akali Dal as much as the entire Sikh Community.[49] Master Tara Singh was neither the president of Shromani Akali Dal nor of the Shromani Gurudwara Prabandhak Committee, when invited to the Shimla conference. Both the positions were then held by his rivals in Sikh politics. The president of the Shromani Akali Dal at that time was Babu Labh Singh[50] and of the S.G.P.C., Jathedar Mohan Singh Nagoki, both active members of Udham Singh Nagoki group in the Shromani Akali Dal that was very near the Indian National Congress and had participated in both Gandhi's individual 'Satyragraha'-1941 and the 'Quit India Movement' of 1942.[51] It must be further noted that in playing the role that he did at the conference, Master Tara Singh had kept himself in constant touch with Baldev Singh,[52] a member of the Punjab Ministry then lead by Malik Khizar Hayat Khan Tiwana, who was, like Master Tara Singh, the only other Punjabi participating in the Shimla Conference. Khizar Hayat Khan who was at the conference as the then chief Minister of Punjab was in fact to become a key figure in the conference. It was Wavell's insistence on including him in the proposed provisional government at the centre. That was one of the main objective for which Wavell had called the conference and provided Jinnah the main pretext to wreck the conference.[53]

Claiming as he did that he was the sole spokesman of the Sikhs, Master Tara Singh did three things at the conference. The first of them was to categorically state that the Sikhs did not identify themselves with either the Indian National Congress or the Muslim League. In the second place he stated that what really the Sikhs wanted was a part of the overall provisions under which they would like the British to transfer power to Indian hands. Lastly he submitted that the Sikh attitude was for the formation of the provisional government at the centre in the immediate future.

He performed the first task easily or so he felt when he categorically stated that the 'Sikhs' did not identify themselves with the demands of the Indian National Congress though they were in complete sympathy with the Indian National congress' demand of independence.[54] He of course went on to state that the Sikhs were opposed completely to the Pakistan demand made by the All India Muslim League. He observed that the Sikhs were totally opposed to the formation of Pakistan, because "Pakistan was a greater danger" to the Sikhs "than to other communities."[55] What the Sikhs wanted he categorically stated was Khalistan.[56] In stating the Sikh demand, in the second of the three tasks, he demanded Khalistan. He however made the Sikh demand conditional which made it appear far too flexible than that of Jinnah, to the Governor General, to the Viceroy and also to the representatives of the Congress at the conference. Possibly they appreciated Tara Singh doing that.

On the formation of interim government the primary and the immediate objective of the conference, Master Tara Singh's stand was in tune on the long term constitutional setup. It was not a pro-Congress stand. In one of the earlier meetings of the conference he had stated that the 'Sikhs' were not with the Congress, though they were for independence. At the end of the conference he made a speech in Shimla that he was prepared to agree to the formation of the Pakistan if Jinnah would agree to the separate state for the Sikhs.[57]

He was taking a stand which was neither pro-Congress nor pro-League in the first week of July 1945.[58] Wavell had proposed on June 25, 1945, that "The party leaders should send a panel of names to me, and I should try to form an acceptable council for them,"[59] which as suggested by Jinnah would consists five Hindus, five Muslims, one Sikh and one scheduled caste,[60] in addition to the Governor General and the Commander-in-Chief. Master Tara Singh met Wavell on July 6, 1945 and agreed to join the interim government himself much to the dislike of Wavell who felt he "would be a poor member of the council."[61] Wavell would have liked to have either Sardar Baldev Singh or Sir Datar Singh. When however he asked Tara Singh to suggest one of these two names the latter did not do so. He might well have then reacted with the observation that "Baldev Singh could not be spared from Punjab and that Datar Singh although honest and capable would not be acceptable as he belonged to a non-agricultural tribe and was not an Akali.[62]

Master Tara Singh at the conference obviously was working in unison with the Punjab Premier, Sir Khizer Hayat Khan neither popular with the Congress leader nor with the Muslim Leaguers attending the conference. Wavell on the other hand was most keen in having Khizar in the council that he proposed forming. That is what Master Tara Singh would have liked Wavell to do. It is significant that in his autobiography Master Tara Singh observed that at Shimla Conference he had met Sikander some what intimately and formed a much higher opinion of the latter than he had earlier.[63]

Unfortunately for Tara Singh, as indeed for Wavell and the Congress leadership, the Shimla conference failed but from the point of view of the role played by Tara Singh a few further comments deserve to be noted in addition to those already made. We have already noted that he did three things in this Conference but what needs to be said in addition particularly on the new prospect that he came to now have on the 'Sikh Demand' of Khalistan. Among them an important one which is not discernible in the edited version of *Wavell's Journal* deserves mention. It was that while arguing for Khalistan, he emphasized a proviso which was not explicitly stated in the demands for Khalistan made earlier and put forth a new argument as much as for the Sikhs demanding it as also for the British who were yet to take a decision on it. The proviso that he emphasized now stated that Sikhs be granted Khalistan if the British agreed to concede Pakistan to Muslims even if they did not have a majority in any part of the Punjab. Tara Singh now emphasized this proviso probably to bring round the Indian National Congress to support the Sikhs when they demanded Khalistan. He must have felt necessary to win the Congress support to fight the Muslim League that had gained rapid strength in the Punjab since November 1944 when Daniyal Latifi, a former communist, who had become the office secretary of the Punjab Muslim League Headquarters at Lahore, in June 1944, drafted the election manifesto of the Punjab Muslim League. For some by-elections in Muslim seats, Sajjad Zaheer was an activist of the Communist Party in India earlier. He had 'wrapped up' this manifesto "in phraseology which is popular among the professed adherents of Communism."[64] which had helped Mohammed Khan Daultana and Mohammed Shah Nawaz Mamdot, sons of two prominent Unionists under Sir Sikandar Hayat Khan's leadership,[65] to build up Muslim League branches all over the Punjab. The death of Sir Chottu Ram in January 1945[66] had further led to the growth of Muslim League influence and the decline of Khizar Hayat Khan's and his unionist party's influence in the Punjab. Master Tara Singh under the circumstances was most keen on both getting on the right side of the Congress and win over the support of the Sikhs demanding Khalistan. His emphasis on the Sikhs getting Khalistan only if Muslim League was conceded Pakistan was thus naturally aimed at humouring the Congress.

Master Tara Singh, in giving a new argument in favour of Khalistan, had wider objective. It was to put the British Government and the Muslim League in the wrong and appeal to the thinking public opinion in the country that Sikhs could be granted Khalistan even if they do not have a majority anywhere in the Punjab but in the two tahsils of Taran Taran and Moga. The argument was that the British had created the Jewish State of Israel in Palestine, the Jews had in it lesser number than even Christians, a little to say of the Arab Muslims whose number was much greater.[67]

NOTES

1.   Rajindra Prasad, '*India Divided*', 3rd. edition. Bombay, 1947, p 254.
2.   V.S. Bhatti. *op. cit.*, p.4.
3.   S.P. Sen (ed). *Dictionary of National Biography*, Vol-2 , Calcutta, 1983, p.123.

4. Baba Gurdit Singh to the secretary AICC, File No. E-17/1937 lying at Nehru Memorial Museum and Library. New Delhi (hereafter quoted as NMML). See also Kirpal C. Yadav, *Elections in Punjab*, p.95.
5. *The Tribune*, November 18, 1936.
6. Baba Gurdit Singh went in for an election petition against the successful Akali Partap Singh Kairon. He lost the petition on July 19, 1937. See K.C. Yadav. *op. cit.* p.98.
7. For almost a year between March 1939 and March 1940, a sub committee appointed by Muhammad Ali Jinnah as the president of All India Muslim League had discussed numerous schemes proposed by important Muslims and Muslim organizations on the goal to be adopted by the Muslim League as the objective to be pursued by the Muslim League of India. For details, see Ayesha Jalal, *The Sole Spokesman: Jinnah, Muslim League and the Demand for Pakistan*, Cambridge, 1984, pp.53, 54.
8. *The Tribune*, May 21, 1940.
9. Giani Sher Singh, a Dhaliwal Jat, veteran of the Gurdwara Reform Movement became the moving spirit behind Sardar Mehtab Singh group in 1926-27. He remained a bitter opponent of Master Tara Singh till November 15, 1941 when he entered in compromise with 'Master' and joined the Akali Dal. That was when Tara Singh had left Congress and began demanding 'Azad Punjab'. In 1944, he became an advocate of Khalistan. Giani Sher Singh died in the first week of October 1944. Giani Sher Singh was born in the first week on January 1890 at Thikri Wala. At the age of two he lost his eye-sight but that did not prevent his educating himself in Gurmukhi, Urdu, Hindi, Sanskrit and Persian. Later he obtained proficiency in English also. He earned fame as a newspaper man by 1935 which enabled him to undergo the publication of a daily *Khalsa Sevak*. Giani Gurcharan Singh, *Giani Sher Singh: Jeevan ate Liktan'*, Delhi 1988, p.3.
10. *The Tribune*, May 21, 1940.
11. For details of how and why this treaty of Bharowal was signed see S.S. Bal, *British Policy towards the Punjab 1844-45*, Calcutta pp.84, 85.
12. *The Tribune*, May 29, 1940.
13. For Jinnah's arguments see Jinnah's Presidential Address at the 27th. Annual Session of the Muslim League, at Lahore. See Syed Shrifudden Pirzada, Foundations of Pakistan: All India Muslim League Documents. Vol-2. Indian Edition. Delhi, 1982, pp.332, 339.
14. *Tho Tribune*, May 29, 1940.
15. *The Tribune*, April 18, 1940.
16. *The Tribune*, May 29, 1940.
17. *The Tribune*, May 29, 1940.
18. Home Department (Political) Government of India. Proceedings File No. 4/I/1940 and 18/6/1940, National Archives of India, New Delhi.
19. Mitra, Narander Nath (ed.) *The Indian Annual Register* Vol-2. Bombay, 1943, p.6.
20. Khushwant Singh, *A History of the Sikhs*, Vol-2. Delhi, 1978, p.253.
21. Mitra, Narender Nath (ed.) *The Indian Annual Registar* Vol-2, Bombay, 1944, p.212.
22. *The Tribune*, August 21, 1944.
23. Penderal Moon (ed.) *Wavell: The Viceroy's Journal*, New Delhi, reprint 1973, p.34.
24. Ibid, p.71.
25. *A Centenary History of the Indian National Congress*, Vol-3, p.618.
26. Stanely Wolpert, *Jinnah of Pakistan*, Delhi. 1983, pp. 230-236.
27. *The Tribune*, September 25, 1944.
28. See. *The Collected Works of Mahatma Gandhi*, Vol-LXVIII. Appendix 12, p.418, Stanley Wolpert, *op. cit.* p.235.
29. Kailash Chander Gulati, *The Akalis Past and Present*. New Delhi, 1974, p.104.
30. David Gilmartin, *Empire and Islam: Punjab and the Making of Pakistan* (Oxford University Press), 1989, pp.196-197.

31. *Mitra's Register*, (1944), Vol-11, p.218; *The Tribune*, October 16, 1944 and October 17, 1944.
32. Gulati, *op. cit.*, p.104.
33. Gulati, *op. cit.*, p.104.
34. Mitra N., *Indian Annual Register*, 1944, Vol-2, p. 218; *The Tribune*, November 15, 1944.
35. Ibid. pp.221-222. *The Tribune* November 15, 1944. 'Text of correspondence between Gandhi and Durlab Singh.'
36. *A Centenary History of The Indian National Congress*, vol.3.
37. Gulati, *op. cit.*, p106.
38. Mitra N, *Indian Annual Register*, 1944, Vol-2, p.223. *The Tribune*, November 27, 1944, *Akali Patrika*, November 27, 1944.
39. Gulati, *op. cit.*, p.106.
40. Mitra N, *Indian Annual Register*, 1945, Vol-2, p.33.
41. *The Tribune*, February 24, 1945 : 'Punjab Home Land of Sikhs And Not of Muslims'.
42. *The Tribune*, February 24, 1945.
43. *Civil and Military Gazette*, Lahore, 1945, p.77; Harnam Singh, 'Punjab The Homeland of The Sikhs'.
44. Ibid., pp.78-79.
45. Ibid., p.79.
46. Sarojni Regani, 'The Nation In Ferment', Chapter 7, in *Centenary History of Indian National Congress*, Vol-3, Delhi, 1985, p.632.
47. For names see '*Wavell-The Viceroy's Journal, op. cit.*, pp.147-148.
48. Mitra N, *Indian Annual Register*, 1945, Vol-1, p.239.
49. Ibid. p.239.
50. Gobinder Singh, *Religion and Politics in Punjab*, New Delhi, 1986, Appendix III, p.322. See also *Ajit*, February 1986.
51. *A Centenary History of the Indian National Congress*, Vol-3, pp.564-574.
52. See *Wavell-The Viceroy's Journal*, p.146.
53. Ibid. p.148.
54. V.P. Menon, *The Transfer of Power in India*, pp.303-304.
55. Minutes of the meeting of The Simla Conference on July 14, 1945. Nicholson Manergh (editor-in-chief), *The Transfer of Power, 1942-1947*, Vol-5, document 603, p.1246.
56. Ibid. p.1246.
57. V.P. Menon, *The Transfer of Power in India*, pp.306, 307.
58. See entries June 27, in Wavell's *The Viceroy's Journal*, p.149.
59. Ibid. p.150.
60. Ibid. p.149.
61. Ibid. p.152.
62. Ibid. p.153.
63. Jaswant Singh (ed.), Master Tara Singh: *Jivan Sangharsh te Udesh*, Amritsar, 1972, p.194.
64. Punjab Fortnightly Report for the Second Half of July 1944. Home Political File No. 18/7/44., National Archives of India, New Delhi.
65. *The Tribune*, November 8, 1944.
66. They were Mian Mumtaz Daultana, son of Mian Ahamad Yar Khan Daultana and Iftikhar Hussain Mamdot, son of Mohammad Shah Nawaz Mamdot.
67. The data as given in Ashok Mehta and Achyut Patwardhan, *Communal Triangle*, Bombay, 1945, pp.50, 51.

Arya Samaj and Punjabi Identity

Indu Banga

In the early nineteenth century, the Punjab had a distinct politico-administrative set up, a characteristic pattern of economic organization and a somewhat distinct socio-cultural life. As a part of the South-Asian subcontinent and North Indian polity, economy and society, it had its core area and subregions, marked by boundaries which were not exactly sharp on all sides, but clear enough to give a sense of identity to its ruling class and its poets and writers. In the 1840s, in the process of its conquest by the British, the consciousness of Punjabi regional identity was expressed by the writers of the Punjab irrespective of their religious or sub-regional affiliation. In the 1940s, when India was nearing independence from British rule, the native bureaucracy, politicians and the intelligentsia of the Punjab worked hard for its partition. Their religious affiliation, with all its cultural adjuncts appeared to them to be far more important and meaningful than their attachment to 'the land of five rivers'.

Obviously, during the hundred years of British rule in the Punjab regional identity was relegated to the background or even replaced by a new identity. The urban middle class Hindus experienced probably the maximum transformation to espouse an aggressive communal articulation. In the process, an over-arching Hindu identity emerged as the strongest identity, with a pan-Indian identity as the adjunct. The Arya Samaj made a substantial contribution towards this communalization of consciousness and the erosion of secular regional identity. Though founded outside the Punjab and by a non-Punjabi, the ideology of the Arya Samaj had a profound bearing on the ideas, attitudes and priorities of the upwardly mobile urban middle class Hindus in the Punjab. For subjective and objective reasons, their ideas and attitudes did not remain static; they underwent significant transformations.

For a study of the transformation which took place among the urban middle class Hindus under British rule we propose to analyse the writings of three important figures: Ganesh Das, who wrote his history of the Punjab at the very beginning of British rule, in 1849; Swamy Dayanand Saraswati, the founder of the Arya Samaj, who wrote the final version of his *Satyartha Prakash* in 1883; and Lajpat Rai who started writing for the press and the platform in the 1880s and continued to do so until 1928, the year of his death. To all these writers we propose to pose questions regarding their self-identification and their conception of the country and the region. This analysis may provide a glimpse of the process by which important shifts of emphasis were taking place in terms of self-identity.

Ganesh Das, a Wadera Khatri and a hereditary *qanungo* of Gujrat in the Punjab, wrote his *Char Bagh-i Panjab* at the behest of the new rulers. As a comprehensive account of the region in Persian, covering more than four hundred pages in print, his work throws light on its history, topography, administrative arrangements and cultural life. He dilates upon matters falling within the range of his personal interests, including the history of his family and that of the Khatris in general. On the whole, he is a fair representative of the educated Hindu middle class of the Punjab during the early nineteenth century.

Ganesh Das looked upon himself as a 'Hindu', a term which appears to refer to Indians who were not Muslim. He had no conception of 'Hinduism' as a single religious phenomenon. He refers to different systems of religious belief and practice such as Shaiva, Vaishnava and Shakta, disapproving only of the left-hand worship of the Goddess. In social matters Ganesh Das identifies himself with the Brahmanic orthodoxy, upholding the *varna* order, extolling the practice of *sati,* and disapproving of reconversion of Hindu converts to Islam. He includes the Nanakpanthis among 'Hindus', but looks upon the Khalsa of Guru Gobind Singh as distinct from both Hindus and Muslims and as arbiters between the two. He refers to the Muslim converts (*nau*-Muslims) among his ancestors without any rancour, noting their achievements with a certain degree of pride. He appreciates Sufi beliefs and practices, Sufi liberality and Islamic learning. He has nothing but admiration for Akbar for his liberal attitude, and he denounces Sikandar Lodhi and Aurangzeb for their bigotry. He observes restraint in narrating Haqiqat Rai's execution which in his view had been caused by the bigotry of the *ulema*. On the whole, Ganesh Das subscribes to the idea of cultural coexistence, with different religious communities living peacefully together.

Ganesh Das appears to attach great importance to his identity as a Khatri of the sub-caste Wadera. He traces with some pride the history of his ancestors who had come to the Punjab from Gujarat in Western India sometime during the fifteenth century. They got employment in the revenue administration as *qanungos, amils* and *diwans*. Some of them became traders and proprietors of land, and acquired bases in both urban and rural life of the region. Ganesh Das refers to scores of other well-placed Khatri families and traces their descent from the legendary Raja Bharat. They got concentrated in the Punjab. For rather recent times, he records with satisfaction the important positions held by Khatris under the Afghan, the Mughal and the Sikh rulers. The royal patrons are appreciated for recognizing the merit of Khatris, irrespective of the former's religious affiliation. Under the Sikh rulers in general and Ranjit Singh in particular, Khatris were able substantially to improve their position to become members of the ruling class. Ganesh Das has the greatest appreciation for Ranjit Singh among the patrons of the Khatris, which was in strict proportion to their induction in the civil and military administration at higher levels. The Khatris thus gained much from the indegenization of polity in the early nineteenth century.

Ganesh Das had a catholic attitude towards language and learning. He notices with appreciation the achievement of many men, and a few women, in different branches of Hindu learning, Islamic theology, jurisprudence, historiography, poetry and medicine. Persian was his 'father tongue' in the sense that he was formally educated in Persian for a career in administration. It stands distinguished from his mother tongue, Punjabi, which was the language of communication for him as for most other people in the region. For the past several hundred years it had been the medium of creative expression. Ganesh Das refers to the language of Guru Nanak's compositions as *'zuban-i-Panjabi'*. This was also the language in which Ahmad Yar, Qadir Yar, Muqbal, Waris Shah and several other poets composed their works. Ganesh Das does not mention the script in which Punjabi was written, but we know that the scripts in use were Persian and Devnagri as well as Gurmukhi.

Ganesh Das was conscious of the entity of Hindustan of which the Punjab was a part, but quite a distinct part. It was a politico-administrative unit under the Mughals and an independent entity since the late eighteenth century. The core of the region was constituted by the area covered by all the five *doabs* between the Indus and the Sutlej, or the area covered by the Mughal province of Lahore. This is the region he describes in detail, *doab* by *doab*, talking of the courses of the rivers, the cities and towns and important villages, the men of learning and the men of piety, and the elite. He does not forget to relate the folk tales current in the Punjab. His appreciation for the Punjab is built into the title of the work which alludes to the region as a beautiful garden.

Swamy Dayanand came to the Punjab in 1877, and established eleven *Arya Samajes* during his stay of about fifteen months in the province. By the time of his death in 1883, thirty-seven *samajs* had come up in the cities and towns of the Punjab. Within two decades the number of Arya *Samajes* shot up to two hundred, leaving the United Provinces far behind though it had been the main theatre of Swamy Dayanand's activities. His ideology appears to have had a special appeal for the urban educated Hindus of the Punjab so much so that the Arya Samaj came to be regarded as essentially a Punjabi movement.

The self-identification of Swamy Dayanand rested on a set of inter-related ideas. He looked upon himself as an 'Arya' and a follower of the Vedas which were used by him as a touchstone for assessing the value of all philosophical and religious ideas. He believed that the noble and the learned among mankind were called 'Arya'. The four Vedas were revealed by God to their sages after their migration from Tibet to 'Aryavarta'. Their faith thus was the oldest in the history of mankind. As the revealed word of God, the Vedas are believed to be eternal and infallible; they are the source of all true knowledge and they possess universal validity. There was a time when the whole world believed in the Vedas, and this was also the time when the whole world was under the imperial sway of the 'Aryas'. This situation lasted till the Mahabharata war. Swamy Dayanand cherished the vision of a return of that pre-Mahabharat golden age when true religion will prevail again and the Aryas will re-establish their political supremacy. There was a close correspondence between religion and polity in the vision of Swamy Dayanand. The revival of Vedic religion was meant to ensure the good of mankind through right knowledge, good moral conduct, self-effort, and social responsibility.

Although Swamy Dayanand was addressing himself primarily to the literate Hindus from the three upper castes (*dwijas*), he was averse to using the label 'Hindu' because it had originated outside India and carried the stigma of 'slavery'. Hence, all those who looked upon themselves as 'Hindu', must reform their beliefs and practices in accordance with the Vedas and become 'Aryas'. In the longest chapter in the *Satyartha Prakash*, the Swamy denounces the Brahmanical and other sects for what he broadly regards as perverse falsity and immorality. In four chapters he dwells at lengths on exposing the false beliefs and irrational practices of all religions prevalent in India ('Purani, Jaini, Kirani and Kurani') so that the discerning persons may see for themselves that the path of the Vedas was the most rational, and therefore, superior to all. In a chapter on the hollowness of the Bible and its God, he refers to the Christians as 'barbarians' (*jungli*) and denounces the racial and discriminatory policies of the state, equating British rule with Christianity and patriotism with opposition to Christianity. His severest condemnation is directed against Islam and Muslims. Apart from being barbarian they were unclean (*malechha*); their religion was not only false, it sanctified war, plunder, slaughter, and demolition of temples. However, denunciation (k*handan*) was meant to pave the way for propagation (*mandan*), reform and education.

Swamy Dayanand approved of the learning of foreign languages for service, travel and trade, but he regarded Sanskritic education as the essential foundation for character building and for the reestablishment of the supremacy of the Vedic religion. Since the sages like Kabir and Nanak were ignorant of the divine language Sanskrit, they could not possibly propagate the true religion. On this assumption, the Swamy exclusively used Sanskrit for his early writings, speeches and debates. During his visit to Calcutta in 1872-73, however, he realized that Hindi could be more effective as the language of communication and cultural self-expression among non-Muslims. This realization synchronized with the controversy then current over the use of Hindi vs Urdu for administration and education at lower rungs. The Swamy now began to look upon Hindi as 'Arya-Bhasha' whereas in his earlier writings it was merely called Devangri, Prakrit or Bhasha. He mobilized his Aryas even from the non-Hindi speaking areas of the Punjab, Gujarat and Maharashtra to learn to use Hindi and to collect signatures and send memorials to the Hunter Commission on Education in support of Hindi. Twelve out of twenty-nine memorials sent by the Aryas came from the Punjab. Lajpat Rai, then a young man, got his 'first' lesson in 'Hindu nationalism' through the movement for Hindi, though he did not yet know the

Devnagri alphabet.

Swamy Dayanand saw Hindi as the basis for cultural as well as political
unity of the 'Aryavarta', which, in his view, encompassed 'the best land mass' in the
world extending from the river Attock (Indus) to the Brahmaputra in the east and the
Vindhya mountains in the south. There are indications in his letters towards the end
of his life that he was contemplating going across the Vindhyas. At any rate, no
particular region appears to be important to him, not even the Punjab - the land in
which the Rigveda was composed. Ironically, several important developments in
the Arya Samaj during and after the Swamy's life time - *shudras* being allowed to
read the Vedas, *shuddhi* being used for reconversion and purification, Sanskritic and
Anglo-Vedic education, higher education for girls, and the apparatus for propagation
- originated in the Punjab, but it did not figure in any significant manner in his
scheme of things. In fact, all parts of North India where he travelled to propagate his
ideas, merely remained provinces or states of Aryavarta to be united for common
action by the over-arching religio-social identity of his conception. Rather, Swamy
Dayanand oriented the Punjabi Hindus away from the region and its culture by
stressing on the unity of religion, language and politics. Together, the trinity of
Aryavarta, Arya Dharma and Arya-Bhasha thus subverted the secular regional identity
cherished by the Punjab Hindus only about a generation earlier.

Lajpat Rai had a great admiration for Swamy Dayanand who successfully
met the cumulative challenge from Islam, Christianity and secularization:

> For the first time in the history of Hindustan since its fall, a
> Hindu scholar, born of Brahmin parents, opened the sealed gate
> of Hinduism to the rest of mankind. This followed as a logical
> consequence of his position in relation to the Vedas. The Vedas
> were the Word of God; they had been revealed in the beginning
> of creation, for the good of the race; they alone were the primal
> revelation.

The Arya Samaj for Lajpat Rai was intended to be and was, 'essentially, a
Hindu organization'. He liked to believe that the future of the Arya Samaj was
'practically the future of Hinduism'. The Samaj did not aim at any future 'outside
and beyond the pale of Hinduism'. An important aspect of the Arya Samaj was its
proselytizing character which was meant to meet the challenge from Christianity
and Islam. It was meant to transform the character of Hinduism. Thus, the Arya
Samaj was 'one of the most potent nationalizing forces'. It aimed at the formation of
'a new national character'. The programme of *shuddhi*, literally purification, was
meant to bring the Hindu converts back from Islam or Christianity. More than that it
was meant to raise the status of the depressed classes by reclaiming them as Aryas.
The depressed classes for Lajpat Rai were 'Hindu', but if they were not thus reclaimed

they could very well go over to Christianity or Islam. The removal of untouchability could promote communal efficiency. 'Every untouchable is a Hindu and for all civil purposes as good a Hindu as a Brahmin. His position as a member of the Hindu community, possessing all the civil rights of a Hindu, must be secured for him'. To educate the untouchables was to 'enrich your community and your country'.

The 'greatest strength' of the Hindus lay in their numbers. No other community could share this 'power' with them. Therefore, Lajpat Rai had no hesitation in telling others that they could have their respective religions and serve their communities to the best of their abilities. He often addressed 'my Hindu countrymen' on their interests as a community. 'I adore Hindu culture', he says at one place. 'I shall at all times be prepared not only to serve the Hindus but to sacrifice all that is near and dear to me if such a sacrifice may be necessary for its protection from danger'. He did not relish the idea of Hindus being subservient to non-Hindus, whether Muslims or Europeans. Therefore, he wanted the Hindus 'to continue to fight for liberty even under a sense of sole responsibility. March they must towards the goal of Swaraj, shoulder to shoulder with others if possible, and by themselves, if necessary'.

Lajpat Rai liked to believe that 'Hindu nationalism' had existed in ancient India. The Vedas provided the basis of 'the unity of Hinduism'. The fact that the foreigners used the term 'Hindu' for the people of ancient India was indicative of the existence of Hindu nationality. The people of ancient India did not refer to themselves as Hindus but as Aryas, but they had a common religion, a common language and common interests. Lajpat Rai exhorted the contemporary Hindus to have a common name and to realize that they had a common ancestry, a common history, a common religion, a common language and a common future.

Through the movement for Hindu Organization (Sangathan) Lajpat Rai wanted to translate this idea into reality. It was considered necessary also as a counterpoise to the evil effects of communal representation given to Muslims and Sikhs. As the president of the Hindu Mahasabha in 1925, he stressed the importance of organization which meant 'power, influence and prestige'. He wanted the Hindus 'to move every nerve to be communally efficient and united' unless they wished 'to commit political *hara-kiri*'. In view of the growing tension with Muslims, he asked the Hindus to prepare themselves to face 'the British machine guns and the Muslim *lathis*'. He appealed to the Hindu electorates 'to send genuine nationalist stern patriots and firm Hindus' who would not 'endanger the position of the Hindu community'.

Lajpat Rai had great appreciation for the educational institutions established by the Arya Samaj. Informed by the 'national character' of the Arya Samaj and deriving inspiration from the Vedas, the Arya institutions were 'national' also because they did not depend on the government for financial support and they did not employ non Aryas, particularly Europeans. The Anglo-Vedic education in the D.A.V.

institutions in Lahore, and elsewhere, was meant to encourage the study of English literature, science and technology as well as Hindu literature, classical Sanskrit and the Vedas. However, he disapproved of the stress exclusively on Sanskrit and oriental learning and isolation from society which were the hallmark of the Gurukal Kangri system of education, devised along the lines suggested by Swamy Dayanand. In his own conception of 'national education' he would rather give the place of pride to Hindi and modern Indian languages. In his later years, Lajpat Rai came to subscribe to the idea of women having access to a similar kind of education as men so that women could become equally useful members of the society. In this respect too his ideas were more advanced than those of Swamy Dayanand.

Unlike the Swamy, Lajpat Rai is far more conscious of the Punjab as the main arena of his political activity, meaningful social action and successful professional life. He refers to the Punjab, the people of the Punjab and the Punjabis. He was instrumental in starting the paper *Panjabee*. He could address himself to 'my countrymen in the Punjab', and to the 'educated community of the Punjab'. He refers to the 'manly races' of the Punjab demoralized by British rule; to lack of political consciousness among the people of the Punjab; or to the beginning of political awakening among them. He regrets that all three communities of the province were kept in separate water-tight compartments by the bureaucracy. They had communal representation, communal colleges, communal schools and communal clubs. The springs of national solidarity were poisoned by communal differences. Lajpat Rai is grateful to friends, leaders and countrymen of the 'other provinces' who espoused the cause of *his* province. On the whole, however, the Punjab for Lajpat Rai was nothing more than the British province of the Punjab. It is a convenient label for a well marked territorial unit within the 'motherland'. The concern for the country and the pan-Indian-community reinforced each other to weaken the hold of '*Panjabiat*' on the emotions and sentiments of the '*Sher-i-Punjab*'. It is not surprising that because of its communal underpinnings, he was deeply moved by the partition of Bengal, but to secure the dominance of Hindus he himself proposed the partitioning of the Punjabi-speaking areas nearly twenty five years before the Punjab was actually partitioned in 1947.

In Lajpat Rai the three identities - Arya, Hindu and Indian stood enmeshed in such a way that there was no room left for any emotional identification with the region. He was not alone. Under the influence of the collective programmes, structured organizations, educational and social welfare institutions of the Arya Samaj, the middle class Hindus of the Punjab by and large came to share his outlook and concerns. They tended to equate class interests with communitarian interests and communitarian interests with national interests. The ideology of Swamy Dayanand was partly inverted or transformed in the process of adjustment with the dictates and demands of the changing situation. The Arya Dharm of the Swami's conception had little in common with the existing systems of religious belief and practice, whether

Christian, Muslim, Sikh, Buddhist, Jain or 'Hindu'. His concealed hostility towards all these systems made them equally bad in the eyes of the Aryas. With the passage of time, and in the face of the obtrusive presence of the Christian missionaries, Muslims and Sikhs, the Aryas would be willing to overlook their religious differences with the 'Hindus'. On the issue of language and script, they would stick to their preference for Hindi in Devnagri script. For the country as a whole they would come to look upon the subcontinent as the Aryavarta. Thus, the three major planks of Arya ideology would move in the direction of aggressive patriotic 'Hindu' nationalism. In all this programme there was little room left for Punjabi sentiments, regional language or regional identity.

SELECT BIBLIOGRAPHY

Banga, Indu   'The Emergence of Hindu Consciousness in Colonial Punjab' in *Self-Images, Identity and Nationality*, Ed. P.C. Chatterjee, Shimla: Indian Institute of Advanced Study, 1989.

'The Ideology of Swami Dayanand' *Cultural Reorientation in Modern India*, Eds. Indu Banga and Jaidev, Shimla: IIAS, in press.

Grewal, J.S. and Indu Banga, Trs and Eds. *Early Nineteenth Century Panjab* (from Ganesh Das's *Char Bagh-I-Panjab)*, Amritsar: Guru Nanak (Dev) University, 1975.

Jones, Kenneth W. *Arya Dharm, Hindu Consciousness in 19th Century Punjab*, First South Asian edn., New Delhi: Manohar, 1976.

Jordens, J.T.F.   *Dayananda Sarasvati: His Life and Ideas*, 2nd imp. Delhi: Oxford University Press, 1979.

Joshi, Vijay Chandra *Lala Lajpat Rai, Writings and Speeches,* Vol 1. 1905-1919, Vol 2. 1929 -1928, 1st edn.: Delhi: University Publishers, 1966.

Rai, Lajpat   *A History of the Arya Samaj* (First Published 1915). Rev. and Ed. Sri Ram Sharma, Bombay: Orient Longman, 1967.

Unhappy India, Calcutta: Banna Publishing Co., 5th reprint, 1928.

Saraswati, Dayanand *Dayanandiya Laghu-grantha Sangraha* (Hindi), Ed. Yudhishter Mimansak, Bahalgarh, Sonipat: Ramlal Kapur Trust, 1975.

Samskar-Vidhi (Hindi), 25th imp. Ajmer: Vedic Yantralaya, 1968.

Satyartha Prakash (Hindi), 36th edn. Delhi: Arsh Sahitya Prachar Trust, 1988.

Unionism in the British Punjab:
A Personal Memoir

Nazar Tiwana

There has recently been much written on the history of the Punjab Unionist Party and its struggle with the Muslim League during the period leading up to Partition. Indeed, distinguished authors in this field such as Imran Ali, Iftikhar Malik and Ian Talbot are attending this conference. David Gilmartin and Craig Baxter, long term friends of mine have also made considerable contributions. This presentation is not intended to go over this well trodden ground once more, but rather to present a previously unrecorded melange of observations, impressions and anecdotes relating to my late father, Khizr Hayat Tiwana who was the last Premier of the British Punjab and the leader of the Punjab Unionist Party from 1942-7.

Sir Khizr opposed the Two Nation Theory and clashed with Jinnah, the leader of the Muslim League over the future of the Punjab region. Until his final days he profoundly believed that the partition was a *mistake* and could not ultimately survive. I clearly recall him saying to an informal gathering of friends and family members in London in 1964, 'those of you who do not belong to my generation will live to see Punjabi identity overcome the effects of the religious divide of 1947 and enjoy the fruits of a prosperous and happy Punjab which transcends the limitations of a geographical map.'

Before going on to present some more of my father's views on Jinnah, the Muslim League and the causes of the Partition, it is perhaps in order to say a little about myself in order to set them in context. I was born at the Tiwana family estate at Kalra, now in Sargodha district, Pakistan in 1927. This was one of the largest estates in the West Punjab and had been greatly built up during the minority of my grandfather, Sir Umar Hayat Tiwana. It was irrigated by a series of private canals which had been constructed by my great grandfather, Malik Sahib Tiwana who had fought alongside the British in 1857. I was Sir Khizr's eldest son. He regarded me as his political heir, just as he had been Sir Umar's heir before him. He thus took me into his confidence to a remarkable extent for one so young. I frequently accompanied him to political meetings, when I was on vacation from Aitchison College, Lahore. I also stayed with him in the house which we rented in Simla East each summer from Rai Bahadur Jodha Mall. I was present at the time of the 1945 Simla Conference in which Khizr stood up to Jinnah regarding Unionist membership of the Viceroy's Executive Council. I also accompanied him to Bombay early in September 1943 when he visited Jinnah in an endeavour to remove the ambiguities which surrounded the relationship between the Unionist Party and the Muslim League. Indeed, he dictated a summary of the talks to me and this text formed the basis of his report to the Punjab Governor Glancy on his return to Simla.

All this can be authenticated by Dr. Ian Talbot who is working on my father's biography. The point I wish to make is that I am representing here a first hand account of Sir Khizr's views, some of which have never been made public. They should therefore be of considerable interest to academic researchers and to those in search of the true Punjabi identity, whether by looking at the past, the present or into the future.

In this section I wish to add to the historical record of two key periods in my father's clash with Jinnah over the future of the Punjab. The first concerns his July 1943 meeting with him. The second the much more publicised Khizr-Jinnah Talks of March/April 1944. After looking at these specific episodes, I wish to conclude by talking briefly about my father's general approach to politics and views on the Partition.

As I have already indicated, I accompanied my father on his visit to Bombay in the late summer of 1943. The background to this was the growing pressure on the Muslim Unionists to come directly under the AIML control. This pressure was coming both from the AIML and Muslim League activists in the Punjab. My father made his stand on the autonomy given to the Muslim Unionists under the terms of the Jinnah-Sikander Pact of 1937. The historical record we now have is based on the press releases and the British accounts which have been subsequently made available to scholars. You will recall that my father dictated to me his recollection of the discussions. Contained in this is an issue which to the best of my knowledge has been neglected by all historians. This concerns the issue of factionalism being the result of a reactivation of the Punjab Muslim League as Jinnah wished.

My father pointed out that there was a strong possibility of a conflict of interest between the President of the Muslim League organisation and the leader of a new Muslim League Assembly Party. Jinnah disregarded this as an argument for maintaining the Unionist status quo, despite my father's view that similar personality clashes had developed between Congress organisation Presidents and Parliamentary leaders. This was of course not central to his argument for maintaining the existing arrangements. It centred around the need for communal harmony and stability in a region which was crucial to the War effort. But it does show his political acumen and foresight. The Aurangzeb Khan Muslim League Government in the Frontier was to be wrecked by precisely such conflicts of interests.

Regarding the March/April 1944 Jinnah Khizr talks, I would like to add just one fact to the historical record. Standard accounts fail to take into significance the illness and death of General Umar Hayat Tiwana during these crucial negotiations. My father was a very emotional and sensitive man who was greatly affected by this tragic loss. Jinnah's dignified response to his personal bereavement momentarily softened his attitude. Indeed, I know that in the second round of discussions my father was ready to compromise, but Jinnah ultimately rejected this because of the pressure by such politicians as Mian Mumtaz Daultana and Shaukat Hayat. It served their ambitions to have an open breach between the Unionists and the Muslim League. Daultana used Sikander's son Shaukat in the attempt to bring down my father's government. My father could in fact have become leader of the Muslim League in the Punjab if he had buckled down to Jinnah's demands. But he was a man of principle and refused to take this easy way of it. In the end the League had to hound him from office, denouncing him as a *kafir*. When his ministry was finally broken in March 1947, the cost was the division of the Punjab and untold human suffering. The Unionist-Akali Congress coalition which had taken office after the 1946 elections had secured peace in the Punjab despite the terrible sufferings ill Calcutta and Bihar. It was only after its collapse that the so-called 'communal war of succession' got underway.

But all this was of course in the future in the Spring of 1944. My father still had confidence then that the British would not leave the Punjab in chaos. He was aware that serious repercussions might result from his standing up to Jinnah, but he had only an inkling of the dangers which lay ahead for himself and his family, but more importantly for the Punjab itself. I can still remember vividly the scene at my father's 22 Queen's Road residence, when he received the call from Jinnah which represented the final ultimatum to abandon the Unionist Party name and form a Government which was unmistakably of Muslim League hue.

In this section I wish to conclude my presentation by recalling my late father's general approach to politics, and Punjabi identity. Sir Khizr as I have indicated regarded the Muslim League demand for Pakistan as a total disaster for the Punjab. He warned British officials repeatedly that it would result in civil war. The Punjab Governor, Sir Betrand Glancy took these warnings to heart, but they were ignored in New Delhi. My father also had serious misgivings about the longer term cultural and economic consequences of a likely partition of the Punjab. He always envisaged a united Punjab as a thriving economic unit. He also adhered to a view of a composite Punjabi culture which excluded no one on the basis of religion. He had acquired this attitude not only from the educational experience at Aitchison but the knowledge that there were Sikh and Hindu as well as Muslim branches of the Tiwana tribe. Indeed on one occasion he used the latter fact to deny the two nation theory to Jinnah's face.

I know for certain that my father believed that Partition would sunder the fabric of Punjabi society and destroy a whole way of life. He regarded the Muslim League's demands as based on the hatred of the non-Muslim. He maintained that there was nothing in the Koran that made the creation of Pakistan a sacred act. On the contrary the Partition was profoundly un-Islamic in the true sense of the faith. His personal distaste for Jinnah arose from the latter's hypocracy in using religion for his own political interests, when he possessed only a rudimentary knowledge of Islam himself and did not practice it in a ritual sense.

My father always maintained that the Muslim League movement could have been stopped in its tracks if the British had pressed Jinnah for the meaning and geographical extent of the Pakistan demand. He personally sought clarification on a number of occasions but to no avail. I know for a fact that it was discussed at the July 1943 Bombay meeting but Jinnah hedged.

Jinnah answered on that occasion that he could not at this stage possibly define Pakistan in a geopolitical sense as the demand itself had not been accepted by either the Congress or the British. He said he could talk about it at a later date. My father pointed out that the reaction of his non-Muslim Cabinet colleagues vis-a-vis Pakistan could not be gauged as this would depend on how it influenced the boundaries and population of the Punjab. Jinnah then replied that in trying to allay their fears my father was putting the cart before the horse. His riposte was that the Punjabi Unionist breed was averse to wearing 'blinkers' or being blindfolded into an uncertain future.

To the end of his life my father felt badly let down by the British over their handling of Jinnah, especially at the Simla Conference and over the timing of the transfer of power. He felt that their actions made his position in the Punjab untenable. I recall that he undoubtedly hoped for more support from them because of the Unionist Party's endeavours during the War effort. It did not occur to him that political self-interest counted for more than loyalty in the closing months of British rule. He still however retained good personal friendships with former officials after Partition. I particularly think of his relationship with Stuart Abbott and Bertrand Glancy in this respect. Sir Winston Churchill once singled him out for praise at a luncheon at his Chartwell home. Churchill shared the view with my father that Attlee had badly handled the transfer of power in 1947.

My father argued for a radical decentralisation of power within a United India. He at first even wondered whether the Cabinet Mission proposals of 1946 were too centralising. Towards the end of his tenure of office, he floated the idea that the Punjab should become a self-governing dominion within the British Empire. This can be documented from the official records, although the British ignored this proposal because it did not suit their strategic purpose.

These beliefs were maintained in private by my father during his long retirement from public life. In January 1975, whilst in California a week before his death, he expressed the view that before the end of the century some kind of new geo-socio-political order would emerge in the subcontinent which would transcend the artificial 1947 Partition. It would restore the common cultural and economic ties which had been surrendered in the name of religion.

Section III

Nation States, Punjabis and the New Global Context

Editors' Introduction

The papers in this section deal with the changes in the two Punjabs after the emergence of the independent Nation States - India and Pakistan - in the new global context of decolonisation in the Third World. The papers by Asad Sayeed and Ikram Ali Malik deal with the Punjab in Pakistan and the rest of the papers with the Punjab in India.

Asad Sayeed's paper examines the impact of the integration of Punjab into the global capitalist economy, through the British canal colony policy, on the emergence of middle class in Punjab, the subsequent dislocations of this class after the 1947 Partition and the role this class played in dislodging Ayub from power in Pakistan. The continuing importance of this class in Bhutto era, Zia period, Nawaz Sharif phase and the current political scene is hinted.

The two papers by Sucha Singh Gill and Lakhwinder Singh examine some aspects of the changes in the Punjab economy. There is a complementarity between these two papers. Lakhwinder Singh argues for setting up large-scale industrial units in Punjab as the only way to increase industrial competitiveness of Punjab both nationally (within India) as well as globally. Sucha Singh Gill argues that a higher degree of industrialisation of Punjab economy accompanied by concomitant migration of rural Sikhs to urban areas in Punjab will erode the existing divide between rural Sikhs and urban Hindus, and, in the process, will create conducive material conditions for the growth of secular Punjabi national identity. A point hinted in the paper that Sikh migration to urban areas may also lead to greater economic competition between Sikhs and Hindus and, therefore, to greater sectarian mobilisation on religious basis needs further investigation. It may be useful, on this point, to refer to Imran Ali's paper in the earlier section which examined the consequences of the migration of Sikhs and Hindus into Muslim majority areas in West Punjab during the canal colony phase for both Punjabi unity and the ferocious violence which followed when that unity was broken. It may also be necessary to point out here that ethnic polarisation and mobilisation is a very complex process and its relationship to any pattern of economic change is a very mediated and complex one.

Chaman Lal's paper explores the changes in Indian perceptions about the Sikhs after the 1984 events in Punjab and Delhi. He examines a few writings in Hindi to convey these changed perceptions. This paper highlights the need for much more work on the role of literature and media in the construction of images of Punjab,

Punjabis and Sikhs in India and outside. Literature in the other national languages of India and in English also needs to be examined from this perspective.

Ikram Ali Malik's paper examines the 1988 elections in Pakistan with the focus on Punjab and explains the rather contradictory character of the voting pattern that brought Benazir Bhutto to power at the Centre and her opponent Nawaz Sharif to Punjab.

Tejwant Gill's paper interrogates the perceptions of Jawaharlal Nehru, the first Prime Minister of India, regarding the political tendencies among the Muslims, Hindus and the Sikhs in Punjab. Gill shows that before Partition, Nehru considered the Sikhs to be progressive and the Punjabi Muslims and Punjabi Hindus oriented more towards communalism and fascism but after Partition, he increasingly became more and more hostile not only towards the Sikhs but also towards Punjabi language. To extend the scope of this paper would raise many important questions about the change in the relationship between Indian national identity and Punjabi/Sikh identity after the transition from a colonial state to an independent Indian nationalist state.

Growth and Mobilisation of the Middle Classes in West Punjab: 1960-1970

Asad Sayeed

Introduction

Pakistan's first encounter with praetorianism was a watershed in the country's political, social and economic history. By the time the Ayub regime was overthrown, relations between the eastern and western wings of the country had deteriorated irrevocably, eventually culminating in the liberation of Bangladesh. On the economic front, the demise of the regime also coincided with the loss of legitimacy of the policies pursued during the much touted 'Decade of Development'. The disjunctures and continuities that have emanated from this particular phase of the country's history are well documented and researched. This paper intends to contribute to the existing literature by focusing on the processes through which the economic and political policies pursued by the Ayub regime were to change the configuration of dominant groups and classes in Pakistan. The economic rights granted by the state during the 1958-70 period and the political processes through which these rights were granted shall give us specific clues to some crucial elements which have been central to subsequent developments in Pakistan's political economy.

Our analysis reveals that the growth and political mobilisation of the middle classes, especially in the Punjab, was crucial to the demise of the Ayub regime and the rise of populist politics in what was then west Pakistan. This is also in consonance with the thesis put forth by Moore (1966) that the genesis of any structure of rights which underpin industrialisation have to be sought in the agrarian class structure and the process through which transformations in the country side occur. As such conflicts that emerge in the industrial sector are more deep rooted than might appear at first sight (Khan, 1989, p224).

Work on state and class in Pakistan has tended to be focused either on fissures within the ruling elite - consisting broadly of the bureaucratic-military oligarchy, the landed elite and the numerically small industrial bourgeoisie - of the country, or of class struggle across conventional cleavages, i.e. the propertied classes and the working classes. The virtual absence of peasant rebellions or mobilisation of the urban working class gives little room for actual explanations of change in class configurations and political alignments for the period by using the conventional framework of class struggle. While changing alignments within the ruling classes is crucial to such an explanation, the process through which such a change occurred has to be specified. More crucially, as our analysis will reveal, the role of the middle classes as part of the political balance of the regime as well as its importance in its demise requires analytical explanation.[1]

Section 2 briefly discusses the analytical framework we have employed to arrange the historical information on Pakistan's political economy. We conceptualise the Ayub regime as reaching a growth enhancing political settlement which constituted in its ability to specify rights within the ruling coalition. The subsequent unravelling of the regime in turn was based on a specific form of political mobilisation that we define as clientelist surplus appropriation.

Since any political and economic strategy will be based on the existing class structure of a society and the state-society relationship that constellation of forces brings about, sections 3 and 4 are devoted to historically tracing the class structure of areas that constituted west Pakistan, both before and in the immediate aftermath of the partition of the Indian sub-continent in 1947. Sections 5 and 6, which form the main body of the paper, analyse the particular policies pursued by the Ayub regime to bring about a growth enhancing political settlement and the manner in which these policies laid the basis for the subsequent unravelling of the settlement. In particular the role of the small towns of the Punjab in this process is identified as central to this unravelling. Finally in section 7 we conclude by alluding to some important implications of conceptualising the developments during the Ayub regime through the analytical framework employed in this paper and link it to the more enduring effects of the developments in the 1960s on Pakistan's political economy in the years to come.

Some Conceptual Clarifications[2]

Political Settlements

To understand the dynamics of the state-society relationship requires a framework which arranges the respective position of the two entities vis-a-vis each other. Since State policy will be conditioned by as well as depend on the existing structure of economic and political rights in society,[3] the empirical identification of the particular constellation of forces either at a point in time or over time is necessary. Furthermore, the state has to be viewed not merely as an institution which resolves conflicts that occur in society and protects a given structure of rights; but also as the arena where such rights are contested and challenged. The group or the coalition of groups that dominate the direction of state policy will thus depend on the relative power that these groups constitute in society. The framework that operationalises these concepts has been termed a 'political settlement'. A 'political settlement' is more precisely defined as:

> the political balance which constitutes the alignments and
> mobilisations behind an existing structure of economic rights---

> once a major political settlement is arrived at, the rights it
> supports are not infinitely variable, though marginal changes
> can and are attempted. (Khan, 1989, p221)

Thus depending on the particular alignment of forces at any juncture, a political settlement can either lead to growth enhancing economic outcomes or otherwise. Similarly the unravelling of a settlement can come about as a result of either exogenous shocks which change the relative political strength of groups or the social and economic outcomes that the rights structure generates, gives rise to new forces which successfully contest the existent structure of rights and thereby alter the alignment.

The efficacy of state action in LDCs has also been conceptualised in terms of the relative autonomy of the state (Alavi, 1972 and Bardhan, 1984). This view states that although deeply conditioned by the constraints posed by the proprietary classes (and/or international capital), the objective function of the state is largely reflective of national rather than class aspirations. Given our definition of the political settlement, we preclude the possibility of any abstract notion of state autonomy. Autonomy for state action will only be possible within the bounds set by the given alignment of rights at a particular juncture and as the above quote suggests, the room to manoeuvre beyond those bounds can only be marginal.

The political settlement reached by the Ayub regime was growth enhancing. However, in order to understand the precise nature of the alignments which made such an outcome possible, we have to see the evolution of the class structure from the colonial period. This will enable us to understand the room to manoeuvre that the regime had as well as the constraints it was facing.

Clientelist Surplus Appropriation

Some sociological literature has conceptualised the state-society relationship as one akin to that of a patron-client relationship (see for instance, Eisenstadt and Roniger, 1984).[4] Taking the clue form this literature, 'Clientelism' is defined as a particular form of patron-client relationships "where the client can bargain for resources on the basis of an organisational ability to disrupt the income flows enjoyed by the patron"(Khan, p58). Clientelism, therefore, arises in the case where rights are highly contested and thereby weakly protected. However, the contestation of rights does not necessarily come from a hitherto excluded proprietary class, but one that has the ability through political mobilisation to demand side payments for resources to flow to the existent rights holders. Typically such a class, at least in the south Asian context, is what can loosely be called a petty bourgeoisie; composed of state bureaucrats, professionals, political cadres, petty traders and the urban 'educated'. The historical evidence we present in sections 5 and 6 shows the emergence of political mobilisation of such a class in Pakistan as a result of the consolidation of the political settlement under the Ayub regime. Depending on the degree and extent of its prevalence in a polity, clientelism has serious implications for economic performance over time. If there is a class which appropriates resources (specifically the investible surplus generated in an economy) on the basis of its ability to disrupt flows to rights holders, then over time not only will the investible surplus of the economy be lower, but also the attainment of efficient use of resources will be affected.

At first sight, conceptualising the state-society relationship as one of clientelism will seem similar to that of rent-seeking as propounded in the economics literature (Krueger, 1974 and Bhagwati, 1982). In a nutshell, the theory of rent-seeking is a critique of state-intervention through licenses, quotas, etc., which creates specific rights for those who attain these licenses to the exclusion of others. More importantly, it is the bargaining for these rights which is considered to be most damaging as it gives rise to corruption and nepotism for the attainment of state created rents.

The utcomes of a rent-seeking bargaining process and one of clientelism are, however, different. Firstly, rent-seeking refers to state-created rights for the attainment of a given economic strategy.[5] In that sense it is a supply-side phenomenon borne out of misinformed economic models that state personnel work with. Clientelism, on the other hand, refers to rights that might be historically inherited by a typical post-colonial state and therefore, constitutes a set of demands made on the state which have to be responded to in order to maintain some viability of the political settlement. Clientelism can also come about as an unintended outcome in the process of creating countervailing forces deemed necessary to maintain a particular political settlement. More importantly if clientelism operates through contesting rights, then it is a process that will not only be confined to actions which deal with state created controls and subsidies but will also affect transactions that will take place in trade outside the ambit of the state.[6] Given the distinction of the origins of clientelist rights and those of rent-seeking implies that the outcome of the two processes will be different. Moreover, since rent-seeking will be the outcome of any interventionist measure instituted by the state, we should observe similar outcomes in economic performance and the ability of the state to allocate resources in countries which undertake such intervention. Even casual observation reveals that whereas state created rents were prevalent in both East Asia and South Asia, the economic outcomes have been different. Thus an explanation of state-society relationship has to come from a more historically specific account of the processes of class formation and particular forms of state society relationship in different countries and regions.

Class Formation in Areas Constituting West Pakistan During the Colonial Period

The British annexed the areas which eventually constituted West Pakistan much later than their colonisation of the South and South eastern parts of the subcontinent.

As a result it has been suggested that whereas colonisation altered the class structure in other parts of India to politically consolidate its rule, it did not do so in the north-western region of the sub-continent; which in turn were largely ruled through the intermediation of the indigenously evolved class structure in the region.[7] British rule in Sindh and the Frontier was carried out by giving legal cover to the property rights of the existent structure of land holdings.[8] In a stagnant agrarian economy there was no impetus for political mobilisation in these areas.

In the Punjab, however, the situation was different. Apart from the larger landlords - considered to be those who did not cultivate land themselves and owned more than 150 acres of land[9] - the British did create a new class in the form of the lambardar. The position of the Lambardar - which was hereditary was created for revenue collection, though it went much beyond that. Apart from retaining 5 per cent of the revenue collected, the Lambardars were also granted lands as well as control over the village commons *(shamliat)*. Hamid (1980, p70) reports that with the collaboration of the local administration, by the end of the 19th century, most of the *shamliat* land was controlled by the lambardars and brought under cultivation. Combined with its economic power through increased land holdings and the appropriation of the agricultural surplus, the Lambardar was also politically powerful in his role as the intermediary between the administration and the village (Alavi, 1976, p345).

While the functional role of the Lambardar is similar to that of the Jotedar in Bengal,[10] the subsequent dynamics of the development of this class in Punjab was significantly different. Whereas the jotedar class in Bengal transformed itself over time into an urban middle class with organisational power to demand resources from the state through a patron-client network (Khan, 1989, chap. 11), in the Punjab, while the modus operandi of this class was also based on a patron-client network vis-a-vis the state, its organisational formation was effectively checked by three different mechanisms. These were canal colonisation, recruitment to the bureaucracy and the military and finally the Land Alienation Act of 1900. These mechanisms are discussed below.

Canal colonisation in the Punjab was perhaps the biggest experiment of social and economic engineering carried out by the raj. Through the development of the canal colonies between 1885 and 1947, the total cultivated area in the province increased from 3 million to 14 million acres. This development was also accompanied by a massive resettlement of the population within the Punjab. Perhaps learning from its experience in the southern and eastern parts of the subcontinent and also from peasant riots in the Sikh wars against the Mughal empire, the British anticipated the mobilisation of the new propertied class to challenge its writ. For this purpose, the colonial state took meticulous care in granting land in the canal colonies so that the social structure of the area was amenable to its effective governance.[11]

While the 'landed gentry' received grants in accordance with its status, a special category was created for the lamberdar class in the name of 'Yeoman' grants.[12] Land grants in this category consisted of land between 50 to 150 acres. These grantees in turn were brought in from the older settled areas of Lahore and Rawalpindi Divisions. Thus the colonisation process not only reproduced the social structure but also absorbed those, including the lamberdar class, who were losing out due to demographic pressure in the older settled districts caused mainly by a long process of land fragmentation or as a result of serious economic downturns.[13] Since canal colonisation was a continuous affair between 1885 and 1947, it endowed the raj with resources that could be doled out to absorb and thereby co-opt many of those who could potentially challenge its writ in the province. In fact, it was the Punjabi bureaucratic and military personnel who were the main beneficiaries from the land resumed for agricultural purposes through the construction of Sukkur Barrage in neighbouring Sindh after 1932 (Ansari, 1991, p188 and Ahmad, 1984a, p157).

Another form of absorption came by way of a continuous increase in the size of the bureaucracy. Because of demands on collecting revenues for the land being brought under cultivation the size of the bureaucracy had to increase. While the upper echelons of this bureaucracy were taken up by the colonial administration and the scions of the larger landholders, expansion in the lower rungs of the bureaucracy went a long way in absorbing a class which could potentially develop into a political force similar to what constituted the core of the Congress and the Muslim League in other parts of India.[14]

Since the Punjab, particularly its north-western districts, were major recruiting grounds for the British Indian army this created another avenue for the state to absorb any dislocations that economic growth or population resettlements might have caused. Moreover, military personnel were also given a significant share in the colonies, with large areas of irrigated land in the colonies reserved for them (Ali, 1988, chapt 4).

Canal colonisation combined with the military element created absorptive mechanisms in the Punjab that were not present in other areas of the British Indian empire. With cycles of agrarian stagnation and the lack of industrial investments, the upwardly mobile rural classes in other parts of India mobilised to oppose imperialism, the continuing prosperity bestowed on the Punjab created a more compliant middle class whose demands could be met. Arguably class formation in the Punjab was more akin to the North American model, where those who stood to lose through limited economic opportunities and could potentially mobilise against the state were accommodated through further expansion.

Apart from the above mentioned fortuitous conditions that the British encountered in the Punjab, the political settlement of imperialism in this province was further stabilised by disrupting the possibility of an urban-rural nexus in the

Punjab. This was done through the Land Alienation Act of 1900 which prevented urban money lenders from acquiring land in lieu of non-payment of loans. Peasant indebtedness in the late nineteenth century was the central precipitator for enacting this Act. Whether this was an autonomous decision of the imperial state or a response to the pressure from the landed classes in the Punjab is difficult to disentangle. However, its consequences for the subsequent political economy of the province were profound. The Act created a cleavage within the emerging middle class in the hinterland with the existing bourgeois and petty bourgeois interests in the cities.[15] As a result an urban-rural nexus which typically gives organisational impetus to political mobilisation was also checked. Although the Land Alienation Act was a significant deterrent to the formation of a middle class, the relative underdevelopment of urban Punjab also played a role in this all important nexus coming together. As a result of Sikh rule in the Punjab from the mid eighteenth to mid nineteenth centuries, the urban areas, particularly Lahore, were virtually destroyed[16] (see Major, 1991). As such industry and commerce were rather underdeveloped in the province compared to some other cities of India. Evidence on industrial activity in the province shows that in spite of a growing prosperity in the agricultural sector, the province was industrially underdeveloped compared to the rest of British India. Bagchi (1972, pp435-36) reports that in 1930, only 0. 18 percent of the population in the Punjab was employed in industry compared to 1.73 and 1.00 percent in the Bombay Presidency area and Bengal respectively.[17] Although there is some evidence that some of the large landlords - the Noons and the Tiwanas for instance - diversified into industry, evidence on the middle peasantry going into industry is scarce.[18] While commercial activities as well as money lending was in the hands of Hindus and Sikhs, Alavi (1972) reports that at the time of the partition there were 52, 000 Muslims employed in the bureaucracy in the Punjab.

The lack of a politically mobilised class in the Punjab is clearly illustrated by the divergence in the politics of this province with that of other parts of British India. While in the first half of the 20th century the rest of the country was in the throes of a nationalist movement, the Punjab was ruled by a pro-British cross-communal alliance of landed interests under the banner of the Unionist Party. In both the 1937 and 1946 elections to the provincial legislature, the Unionist Party was able to form the government in the Punjab at the cost of both the Congress and the Muslim League.[19] Some have perceived the lack of politicisation in the Punjab to be the result of the prosperity generated in the agrarian economy of the province.[20] This view holds weight only so far as it is recognised that imperial policy was successful in bestowing prosperity only to the extent that it kept political opposition to its rule in check.

The degree to which the Punjab lacked a mobilised intermediate class, particularly a Muslim middle class, can be gauged from the fact that for the 1946 elections, the Muslim League had to call in middle class intelligentsia from the United

Provinces to campaign for its candidates in the Punjab (Sayeed, 1980). Thus at the eve of partition, like other areas of West Pakistan, the Punjab also lacked a politically mobilised middle strata and the landed elite was the only indigenous dominant group in the political structure of the new nation state. The crucial difference in the Punjab, however, was that an incipient, though unmobilised middle class did exist. As we have demonstrated above the formation of this class owes its existence to the particular form of social engineering that British rule undertook in the province in the form of canal colonisation.

To recapitulate: At the time of partition, in terms of class structure, areas that constituted west Pakistan were conspicuous by the absence of a middle class. Apart from the fact that the areas of west Pakistan had a low level of urbanisation, middle class occupations in these areas were dominated by the Hindus and Sikhs.[21] With the mass exodus of Hindus and Sikhs at the time of partition, whatever the rudiments of a middle class that was prevalent in Pakistan also disappeared. Since the urban middle classes were instrumental in the political struggles of both the Muslim League and the Congress (Misra, 1961, p13), the lack of this class was a significant feature of the new nation state.

The Post-Partition Upheavals

The first decade of Pakistan's existence was fraught with a series of multifarious crises. Given the massive migration of populations, the financial bankruptcy of the state, the separation of the two wings of the country by more than a thousand miles of hostile territory, the perception of a grave threat from a larger and economically better-off neighbour, the quintessentially agrarian nature of the economy and above all a stark divergence of political affiliations between the ruling party and the indigenous peoples of the country (particularly in the west), no wonder there was considerable pessimism about the viability of the new nation-state.[22] The death of Jinnah - regarded and revered as the founder of the nation - in 1948 further compounded the tribulations in way of state formation. In hindsight, therefore, it does not come as a surprise that the politics of the country would remain so unstable as to go through seven prime ministers in a period of eight years.

Population Transfers and the Emergent Class Structure

Between August 1947 and April 1951, when the open borders between India and Pakistan were closed, 8 million Muslims from India moved into Pakistan and an estimated 6 million Hindus and Sikhs emigrated from the areas constituting Pakistan (Burki, 1973). In a region where the only political force was the landed and tribal elite, this massive transfer of populations had a profound impact on the class structure of West Pakistan. Table 1 shows that immigrants from India constituted about half the population to inhabit the urban landscape of West Pakistan:

Table 1. Proportion of Refugees in the Population of Major Pakistan Cities, 1951(000s)

CITY	Total Population	Refugees	% of Refugees
Karachi	1065	608	57.1
Lahore	849	386	45.5
Hyderabad	242	156	64.5
Rawalpindi	237	95	40.1
Multan	190	83	43.7
Lyallpur	179	126	70.4
Sialkot	168	56	33.3
Peshawar	151	18	11.9
Gujranwala	121	62	51.2
Quetta	84	24	28.6
Sarghoda	78	53	67.9
Sukkar	77	42	54.5
Jhang	95	36	37.9
Mardan	78	3	3.8
Sahiwal	75	33	44.0
Kasur	74	12	16.2
Gujrat	60	7	11.7
Bahawalpur	84	21	25.0
Wah	37	7	18.9
TOTAL	3944	1828	46.3

Source: GOP, 1955. (Burki, 1980, p12)

It is significant that half the population to reside in urban Pakistan soon after partition was made up of migrants. It is also significant that the proportion of migrants is higher than the average in larger cities like Karachi, Lahore, Hyderabad and Lyallpur. With the exception of some migrants from East Punjab, the background of migrants from UP, Bihar, Gujrat, Maharashtra and Hyderabad reveals that they were predominantly urban and literate (Wright, 1974). In Pre-Partition times the urban professions in areas constituting Pakistan were largely dominated by the Hindu and Sikh communities. After their exodus from these areas, these occupations were taken over by the migrants. The immigrants to West Pakistan constituted people from all classes. At the upper reaches of the class structure, the migrating community 'claimed' the urban property left behind by the emigrating Hindu and Sikh communities.[23] At this end of the class spectrum is also located the traders primarily from Gujrat and Bombay who subsequently constituted the industrial class of Pakistan for two decades.[24]

Below the rich traders and those with appropriate bureaucratic connections to accumulate assets through claims on evacuee property, were the millions of lower middle class urban and semi-urban muslims of North, West and South India. The educated among them are what Alavi (1989) has termed as the 'salariat'. This class was partially absorbed by a state which was in the process of forming an administrative network virtually from scratch. While some of the poor and uneducated migrants were also absorbed at the lower echelons of the bureaucracy, others either went into petty retail trade, worked as labourers in industries or were unemployed. The population movements as a result of partition thus soon created an urban middle class in Pakistan, albeit it was composed generally of migrants. Given the dislocations it had suffered and the regional heterogeneity in its composition meant that political mobilisation of a migrant class would take a longer time.[25]

Social relations in the rural areas were, however, little affected by the transfer of populations. In fact, if anything they strengthened the position of the landed elite. The Punjab was the largest recipient of migrant population in the country.[26] According to one estimate the emigres left behind 350-420,000 acres of land. Of this land 350, 000 acres was given to the migrants whereas the rest was either occupied by Muslim tenants of Hindu and Sikh landlords or was gobbled up by the landlords in connivance with the bureaucracy (Jalal, 1990, pp78-81). The landed elite of the Punjab also filled vacuum in the service sector, which in the past was the preserve of non-muslim entrepreneurs. This interlocking of landed interests with the typically urban petty bourgeois activities after partition further eroded whatever rudimentary middle class that was formed in the hinterlands of the Punjab as a result of migration. The situation in rural Sindh was similar. Of the 1,345,000 acres abandoned by Hindus 800,000 were taken by Sindhi landlords (Jalal, 1990, pp87-89). However, the interlocking of commercial activity with landed interests as observed in the Punjab did not happen in Sindh. Instead it was the migrant middle class, especially in southern Sindh which entered into this arena.

The Unstable Political Settlement of the 1950s

It was on the above delineated class structure that those who were in a position to wield power, pulled the economy and politics of the country in different directions. The first contender in this power equation was the ruling Muslim League. Perhaps the most ironic feature of West Pakistan was that the political party which had successfully rallied for carving British India on communal lines landed in power in a country where it had scarcely any indigenous support base.[27] As we mentioned earlier, the landed elite of the Punjab successfully opposed the Muslim League and the demand for Pakistan up until the eve of partition. Similarly the Frontier was ruled by the opposition Congress Party.[28] Thus the Muslim League was in the unenviable position of not only governing over a precarious state of affairs as mentioned above, but also had to create a constituency for itself. Since the League had derived its support base primarily from the urban Muslim middle classes of the

Hindu majority areas, it sought to develop its constituency among this group.[29] There was a two-pronged strategy that the politicians in power attempted to wield. One was to develop an upper urban strata which would provide the party with resources and clout in the political and economic system. This was done firstly with the help of those Muslim traders who had financially supported Jinnah and his league during the period 1940-47.[30] More importantly, through exercising its control over distributing evacuee property, the League attempted to create a populist electoral base.[31]

The second and perhaps the central element in the power equation was the 'military-bureaucratic oligarchy'. These two institutions were able to establish their authority simply because their institutional structures were already established by the colonial state and merely needed some "minor revamping" (Jalal, 1990, P 297). The squabbles with India over sharing of the spoils in the aftermath of partition as well as the security threat from the militarily superior neighbour after the war in Kashmir in 1948 led the military to press for a larger share of resources for itself. In a state with a narrow base for revenue generation meant that this aspiration could not be realised in the long run unless the country was to be industrialised. Though differing with the military on matters of detail, the bureaucracy emerged as their natural ally.[32] The direct beneficiary of this particular alignment was the industrial sector. Extensive use of quotas and exceptionally high tariff barriers created adequate incentives for migrant traders from Bombay and Gujrat to invest in industry. The result was that the structural disequilibrium in the industrial sector that was created as a result of partition was virtually overcome with an impressive performance on import substitution.[33]

Up to this point we see the interests of the politicians, particularly those of the western wing and the state machinery converging. In fact till the assassination of Liaqat in 1951 we see a political settlement based on these considerations stabilising. However soon two forces, hitherto ignored by the ruling triumvirate, started to assert themselves. The first was the opposition of both politicians and society in general in the eastern wing over the increasing control of west Pakistan over resources as well as its cultural hegemony.[34]

Burki (1977 and 1980) has suggested the second contradiction raised its head when the landed elite re-grouped itself and attempted to stake its claim in the political and economic rights that the state was in the process of doling out. The dismissal of the Nazimuddin Ministry in 1953 marked the rise of the landed elite at the cost of the migrant politicians of the Muslim League. While the landed elite was partially successful in directing state resources towards itself,[35] as mentioned earlier the centralising imperative of other elements of the power structure meant that the terms of trade remained against agriculture, the policy of compulsory procurement of grains remained in place and though the rupee was devalued in 1955 under the pressure of the landed elite it remained far above the parity rate. The result was that during the decade the agricultural sector grew at a rate of a mere 1.6 per cent per annum, while the industrial sector grew at an impressive rate of 15.4 per cent per annum.

This three-way struggle - between the migrant politicians and the indigenous elite, the politicians and the bureaucratic military oligarchy, and between those representing regional interests - within the dominant coalition meant that there were severe horizontal fissures within the political settlement. The parliamentary squabbles between 1951 and 1958 - described by the *Economist* as ranging between the "grotesque and the macabre" - bear ample testimony to this struggle over the definition of economic and thereby political rights.

While the bureaucratic military oligarchy gained an ascendant position because of the political squabbling, with the parliamentary facade still in operation, it could not efficaciously implement its policies. By 1958 the bureaucratic-military oligarchy had firmly consolidated its hold over administrative and economic decision making while at the same time it had given the politicians enough rope to hang themselves with. As a result its direct intervention was welcomed by most sections of civil society.

Political Settlement under Ayub Khan

The *coup d'etat* by the military has been described by some as an 'autonomous intervention'(Khan, 1989), while others have termed it as the consolidation of the system in operation since the Iskandar Mirza-Ayub Khan nexus was formed after the dismissal of the Nazimiddin ministry in 1953 (Alavi,1983). In either case, the regime marked a structural break from the past by consolidating the economic rights of the ruling coalition.

As discussed before, because of the centralising imperative perceived by the military-bureaucratic oligarchy as well as the constituency-building ambitions of the Muslim League politicians, the agricultural sector had been neglected. This created a serious viability crisis for the state in a predominantly agrarian economy.[36] Also, the Ayub government had to develop a constituency for its rule. And again given that the strength of numbers was in the rural hinterlands, the most effective way for achieving this goal was to develop a constituency for itself among this group. This was the area where the erstwhile Muslim League politicians had no support base and any mobilisation of urban groups could be effectively challenged by a numerically larger and hitherto economically more powerful agglomeration. However, to develop a broad-based and numerically strong constituency the Ayub regime needed the support of the numerous medium and small peasant, especially in the Punjab. By bringing in the middle peasantry into the ruling coalition, albeit as a junior partner, the regime could not only checkmate the designs of urban interests but could also check the large landlords from acquiring inordinate power in the dominant coalition. Two Orders of the military regime in 1959 were to serve the purpose of creating a rural constituency for itself. One was the Land Reforms Order and the other was the Basic Democracies Order. We examine the implications of both these reforms separately below.

The land reforms of 1959 went some way in specifying economic rights in the agrarian economy. Given that land reforms was a rallying cry among the nonlanded elements of the dominant coalition, the reforms sent the signal to these elements that the landed elite was being cut down to size. However, not only were the land ceilings rather liberal and implementation of reforms slack,[37] but there were enough loopholes in the land reform order to ensure that the land holdings of the large landlords remained intact.[38] In fact it has been argued that because of the handsome compensation given for the uncultivated land vacated by the landlords, the reforms actually benefited this group (Noman, 1988, p40). In any case, the land reforms meant that the economic rights for the landed elite were not a bone of contention for some time to come.

The Basic Democracy system (henceforth the BD system) was to work through electing 40,000 basic democrats from each wing of the country to union councils and union committees in the rural and urban areas respectively. These union councils in turn would indirectly elect members to *Tehsil* councils in West Pakistan and *Thana* Councils in East Pakistan. That the BD system was clearly a means for constituency building on the part of the Ayub regime is illustrated by the fact that those elected under the system were to form the electoral college for presidential elections. While not given unbridled powers,[39] those elected through the BD system came into a position of not only distributing state largesse which was handed out through the Rural Works Programme, it also provided them an institutional position to bargain with the state to direct resources in their direction. The acquisition of transport licenses and permits for government ration shops provides some rudimentary evidence in this direction (Sayeed, 1980, p147). The incipient mobilisation of a clientilist class can be identified through the institution of Basic Democracies.

The development of a rural middle class should only be seen as a balancing act on the part of the regime. The dominant partners from the hinterland in the new settlement continued to be the landed elite. Apart from securing its rights through the fictitious land reforms of 1959, its dominant position was secured through the appointment of Nawab of Kalabagh as the Governor of west Pakistan. The scion of one of the largest landholding families of the Punjab, Kalabagh took several practical steps to ensure the interests of the landed elites,[40] especially since the Constitution of 1962 had delineated agriculture as a provincial subject.

The class position of the landed elite and the middle peasantry[41] has been a subject of debate between Alavi and Burki.[42] Burki claims that the middle peasantry cultivated through the BD system was a distinct class than the big landlords in that its economic outlook was distinctly capitalist rather than the 'feudal' form of production prevalent among the landed gentry. Alavi, on the other hand, argues that there is no 'structural' distinction that can be drawn between the aspirations of the middle peasantry with that of the landed elite as their demands on the state are similar as well as their class position vis-a-vis the landless peasants and the tenant farmers. While Alavi is correct about the class position of the two tiers of the agrarian structure to be similar, yet Burki's contention on the conflict of interests among the medium and small peasantry and the large landlords also holds in one important respect which is operationally significant. This is because through its political and economic clout the landed elite can divert resources to itself at the cost of both the small and the medium peasant. This is particularly true as far as water resources, access to loans for tubewells, and mechanisation is concerned. It is not our concern to go into the empirical detail about the degree to which the middle peasant was able to increase his clout with the state in bargaining for these inputs, the point is that once a larger section of the peasantry is mobilised - as it was through the institution of BDs - its political implications are very different. In demanding resources and rights from the state the middle and small peasantry employs the means of populist politics rather than a one to one patron client approach that the larger landlord employs. It is this very important implication for subsequent events in Pakistan's political economy that emanates if Burki's thesis is stretched further.

Now we come to the third important pillar of the dominant coalition. - i.e. the industrial bourgeoisie. By bringing about a settlement in the rural areas and repressing industrial labour, the regime could divert resources towards a small group of merchant capitalists for developing the industrial sector.[43]

Going against the grain of established consensus, Burki has claimed that the Ayub regime broadened the base of the industrial class.[44] Burki argues that the Bonus Voucher Scheme (BVS) dispersed industrial capital across regions and thus undermined the monopoly hold of the Karachi-Hyderabad nexus of industrialists. Investigating this hypothesis is crucial to our argument given our contention that the dominant coalition in the Ayub political settlement did not create much room for broadening the base of the industrial bourgeois.

Seen in a statistically static sense, Burki will have difficulty proving his point given that there is irrefutable evidence about the concentration ratios in the large scale manufacturing sector. Comparing the profile of industrial houses at the top of the corporate ladder between 1960 and 1970, Amjad (1983) shows that only three new houses appear at the pinnacle of the corporate ladder - Abbas Khaleeli, Ghulam Farouque and Ghandhara. Since the owner of the first two groups were retired bureaucrats while that of the last was a retired general, diversification seems to be more a case of state patronage within its own ranks rather than any attempt at broadening the base of industrial ownership. In terms of concentration also, there is a small and insignificant decline - whereas in 1961, 13 houses controlled 30% of privately owned industrial fixed assets and 20% of the output, the same houses controlled 27% of assets and 17% of the output in 1970. Even if we look at concentration in industries such as textiles and sugar, where investment outlays and gestation lags are smaller - typically industries where first time entrants will appear - concentration is high at the end of the 1960s. In textiles there was a decline from 50% of output coming from 9 industrial houses in 1960 to 40% in 1970. Burki has further argued that disinvestments through the PIDC broadened the base of industrial ownership. This assertion again is not supported by evidence. By the end of 1962, 71.7% of the disinvestments made by the PIDC were in favour of the industrial houses (see Amjad, 1983, p183). And after that period, the PIDC did not disinvest much of its assets and concentrated primarily on investments in East Pakistan.

Burki has further argued that for the spread of industrial ownership we have to look towards the sprouting of small scale industry rather than the large-scale manufacturing sector. Since data on small scale industry in the 1960s is virtually non-existent, unfortunately the hypothesis cannot be tested directly. Indirect evidence, however, does lend credibility to his thesis. For instance in 1971-72, 55% of cotton cloth and 48.4% of all cloth was being manufactured in the unorganised and typically small scale sector.[45] It can be conjectured that at least some of this investment in the small scale industry would have been generated in the 1960s. Burki may be right about the spread of small scale industry in the 1960s, though for the wrong reasons. To say that the BVS spurred this process assumes that the small scale industrialisation that did take place was import intensive in terms of both machinery and raw materials. Studies on the small scale sector for a much later period reveal that the hallmark of the small scale sector is that both in terms of machinery as well as raw materials used, it is indigenously based (Nadvi, 1990). In that case the causative mechanism for small scale industrialisation can be better explained by investments from the agrarian surplus and the demands for spare parts and repair services that an increasingly mechanised agrarian economy would need. In that sense, small scale industrialisation developed in spite of the policy framework of the regime.

Burki's hunch might, however, find empirical support in figures for industrial financing. Whereas PICIC catered almost exclusively to the large industrial houses, only 20 per cent of IDBP's allocations went to the industrial houses. Although the rest of the 80 per cent of IDBP's allocations went to non-industrial houses, 66% of these allocations were those of over 1 million rupees and went to a mere 9.2% of the borrowers (see Amjad, 1983, pp196-97). Thus we still do not see any significant spread in industrial ownership being attempted by the regime. However, the point is well taken that the tool of state financing did attempt at broadening the base of industrial ownership albeit at the lower rung of industrial investments. While it is possible that the momentum of growth experienced in the period might have laid the basis for a new class of entrepreneurs to emerge in the late 1970s and the 1980s, the post Ayub political environment and the resulting policy structure provides a better explanation for this phenomenon to occur. Indeed the political settlement of the Ayub regime had little room to allocate resources to small scale industry as the urban middle class was not part of the dominant coalition of the Ayub political settlement. The political settlement thus reached under Ayub Khan resulted in specifying property rights to the dominant proprietary classes in Pakistani society. Internal feuds within the dominant coalition were kept at bay by creating a countervailing constituency through selective mobilisation of the rural middle classes.

As was mentioned earlier, urban west Pakistan was bereft of groups with much political weight. The urban petty bourgeoisie was largely un-mobilised. The Ayub regime for some time was able to circumvent the organisation of this bourgeoisie by using both the carrot and the stick. With healthy economic growth and the increasing role of the state in both the economic and social aspects of life, the Ayub regime was able to co-opt the migrant petty bourgeoisie, mainly based in large cities, through jobs in government departments and the numerous public and semiautonomous institutions that were created during the period. Since the numbers were relatively small in the earlier decades, the absorption of this class was manageable. On the other hand, through a series of oppressive legislations the development of a civil society was kept at bay. The press was gagged, the academic community was kept under a tight leash, formation of political parties was made increasingly difficult and trade union activity was dealt with ruthlessly. For some time the regime's policies made it increasingly difficult for the urban middle classes to mobilise against the regime (see Noman, 1988 and Ali, 1970).

The urban strategy of the regime was also extended to East Pakistan. With a markedly different social structure in the region, available evidence suggests that the carrot and stick policy was applied in the region with impunity. Also because of the existence of an already mobilised middle class in the region, clientelist political dealings were more frequently used than in the west (Khan, 1989, chapt 13).

It was on this edifice of political and economic rights that the impressive growth performance of the economy in general and the industrial structure in particular needs to be interpreted. It is also important to remember that the political settlement reached in turn was dictated by the existent class structure in society. That the Ayub political settlement was achieved at the exclusion of a large segment of the population (i.e. the entire East Pakistan as well as the large urban agglomerations of the western half of the country) did make it fragile. Given the sheer numbers of those who were excluded, a strategy of spreading industrial resources more thinly to create a small scale dominated industrial structure, akin to the one in Taiwan, could have made the settlement less exclusionary and hence more durable. As has been demonstrated above, the lack of mobilisation of an urban middle class as well as its smaller numbers in the western wing of the country coupled with the confidence of the regime to contain its mobilisation through a carrot and stick policy seemed to pay dividends for some time. The crucial gap in the Ayub political settlement was its presumption that its urban strategy would be equally successful in the eastern wing of the country also where the level of mobilisation was historically much stronger.[46] The domination of the western wing in both the civil and military leadership as well as its expressly dismissive and at times racist attitude towards East Pakistan seems to be the only tentative explanation for this crucial disregard of the aspirations of the majority of the populace of united Pakistan. However, so far as the economic implications of the settlement are concerned, the growth performance of the regime (on both wings of the country) demonstrates its undeniable success in protecting allocated rights at least for some time. Arguably, it is only with the benefit of hindsight that one can more clearly appreciate the inherent unsustainability of the settlement.

Unravelling of the Political Settlement

The unravelling of this balance of political forces came about as an unintended consequence of the agrarian transformation in the Punjab as well as a conjuncture of events which unleashed a new dynamic in Pakistani society. Tracing the sequence of events which led to the mass mobilisations against the regime will enable us to decipher the class back ground of those who were at the forefront of the resistance to the Ayub regime. With the help of data on riots/ arrests, Burki (1971 and 1972) shows that agitation against the regime started in the small towns of the Punjab as early as the spring of 1967.[47]

Table 2. Proportion of Students and Lawyers Arrested in Town of the Punjab Under Preventive Detention Ordinances in the Second Quarter of 1967

TOWN	Number of Arrests	Students	Percentage (%)	Lawyers	Percentage (%)
Gujar Khan	13	7	53.8	4	30.8
Gojra	17	8	47.1	5	29.4
Jaranwala	28	15	53.6	11	39.3
Kot Radha Krishan	6	2	33.3	1	16.7
Kamoki	24	11	45.1	7	29.2
Daska	11	4	36.4	4	36.4
Pasrur	6	3	50.0	1	16.7
Burewala	19	11	57.9	8	42.1
TOTAL	130	63	48.4	41	31.5

Source: Burki (1971, p477)

Table 2 brings to the fore two important phenomena. One that the riots started in small towns rather than large cities and two that those at the forefront of the riots belonged to the middle class. The population growth rate of towns[48], both large and small, was 4.7% per annum between 1961 and 1972 whereas that of the cities was 4.1% during the same period (Burki, 1974, p754). This growth was a result of both push and the pull factors generated by the growth and transformation of the agrarian sector. With agricultural output increasing at the rate of 5% between 1960-70, the towns developed to provide for the marketing and other services that the agrarian economy needed. Also mechanisation in agriculture and the increasing use of tubewells created additional demands on the agrarian service sectors. Though sparse, there is also evidence of manufacturing activity catering to the technological requirements of the agricultural sector coming on stream in these towns. For instance, the towns of Burewala and Daska are known to have specialised in the production of diesel pumps, strainers and various spare parts for tube wells and employed 8.3 and 21.1 per cent of the workforce in industry. (Burki, 1974, pp 758-59).[49]

This middle class in the small towns of the Punjab came together directly as a result of the agrarian transformation in the rural areas. The increasing use of tubewell water for irrigation, tractors for ploughing and later the use of High Yielding Variety seeds transformed the agrarian sector in the central and northern districts of the Punjab in profound ways. The first spur to agriculture in the Punjab came through increasing private and public investment in tubewells. Since the cash resources for such an endeavour were high, this phenomenon meant that those small landholders, between the categories of 12.5 acres to 25 acres were not able to benefit from this occurrence. As a result, many of these landholders found it profitable to either lease or sell their land and move to urban areas.

While the move to tubewell technology displaced the small and medium landowners, increased tractorisation resulted in displacing landless workers. It has been estimated that in the 1960s each tractor displaced between 9 to 12 workers. Given that in 1971 21,000 tractors were operating in this area means that a large number of landless workers and tenant farmers were made redundant in the agrarian sector.

A survey conducted between 1967-69 on rural out-migration in the Punjab corroborates the above argument in that the proportion of landless workers who migrated is the highest followed by tenant farmers and landowners respectively (see Burki, 1974). More interestingly, the survey also reveals that 72.2 per cent of the out-migrating landowners preferred to go to the towns rather than large cities while a larger proportion of landless workers (58.3%) went to the larger cities. Burki has argued that whereas the landless workers have a tendency to move to larger cities, those who are relatively more prosperous have tended to move to towns. This he contends is because the former tend to seek wage labour in the manufacturing sector, the latter with some capital at their disposal can set up small businesses in towns.

This seems a plausible explanation given that entry barriers to investments in larger cities are more formidable than in smaller towns.

The towns also consisted of a large number of the kindred of the small and medium landowners in search of upward mobility through education. As a result of fragmentation of land over time, particularly in the older settled districts of Lahore and Rawalpindi, those with enough cash to send their children to school and then for higher education also increased (Alavi, 1976, pp325-26). This factor accounted for a precipitous increase in the number of lawyers, the salariat and students whose base was the small and large towns in the Punjab. It was this class, created both as a result of the push and pull of agrarian transformations as well as the ambitions for upward mobility among the small and medium landowners that swelled the ranks of the middle classes primarily in the Punjab and to a lesser extent in Sindh and the Frontier.

The critical issue, however, is not the existence of a class 'in itself', but its mobilisation to become a class 'for itself'. As we saw earlier, the rural middle class was given political voice through the BD system and that the basic democrats diversified their economic activities through a patron-client network with the bureaucracy. A similar outcome was sought by the agitators in towns to challenge the existent structure of property rights, though their impact was different from that of the basic democrats or even the landed elite because of the larger size of this class. However, like the basic democrats, political mobilisation rather than the personalised dealing with the state was the channel to be used for this purpose. It needs to be stated that this particular form of bargaining with the state - what we call clientelism- is a mechanism which is a consequence of governance adopted by the post colonial state in traditions it inherited from the policies of what Washbrook (1981) has called the strategy of the 'high colonial state'.

At this juncture it is appropriate to draw a parallel between the Pre-Partition political settlement in the Punjab with that of the 1960s. The important difference was that the expansionary possibilities for accommodation of an upwardly mobile class - done earlier through canal colonisation - were not present any more. As a result any economic downturn or a significant change in technology would activate a hitherto latent class. As was shown above, the green revolution technologies did create an upheaval in the rural areas, and the migration that it engendered also had its effects on the urban and semi-urban landscape of the country.

A conjuncture of events contributed to the mobilisation of this class in the second half of the 1960s which eventually led to the demise of the Ayub regime. The first was a drought that afflicted the agrarian sector. This affected the agricultural service sector as well as the small time lawyers in the areas (Burki, 1971, p475). The drought also coincided with aid cut-off as a result of the 1965 war. The combined effects of these two phenomena created a severe economic downturn. The regime also lost a considerable amount of legitimacy as a result of Ayub Khan's perceived capitulation to India through the Tashkent agreement after the 1965 Indo-Pakistan war. The most important catalyst, however, was the resignation of Bhutto from Ayub's cabinet and his active search for a populist base for politics subsequently. Bhutto in 1967 travelled through the length and breath of the Punjab and sought the support of the middle classes, especially in smaller towns.[50] The process of mobilisation of the small town middle classes was thus fostered.

The sequence of events that transformed the movement from the small towns of the Punjab to the larger cities serves to illuminate the eventual mobilisation of the middle and lower middle classes at a national level. It is this linkage with the urban economy in the larger towns which has direct relevance to its impact on the industrial sector. Following the pattern of agitation in the towns, it was the students who initiated agitation against Ayub Khan and his government in the larger cities. With many of them coming from small towns they were aware of and identified with the mass discontent that was brewing in these small towns. The ranks of the students was soon joined by women's groups, trade unions, teachers, doctors, and bar associations to organise massive demonstrations which outnumbered and outmanoeuvred the law enforcing agencies (see Sayeed, 1980, pp 144-152 and Ali, 1970, pp 156-186 for a detailed account of urban demonstrations). While the mobilisation of the working classes which virtually brought industrial activity in the country to a halt is important in its own right, the more significant effect of these demonstrations was that

> ---for the first time white-collar workers like the clerical staff of banks,--- doctors, engineers and central government employees staged strikes. On March 6 (1969), the clerical staff of the National Bank of Pakistan in Karachi resorted to *gherao* with the result that the president and the managing director were confined to their offices until midnight when they accepted the demands of the striking staff. Similarly demands for better pay scales, better opportunities for promotion from a lower class to a higher class, and better working conditions were put forward by the Income Tax Inspectors association, All Pakistan Attached Departments Superintendents Association, the Central Government Servants Association and the West Pakistan Railway Workers Union (Sayeed, 1980, p150)

The hitherto unmobilised middle class in the larger cities, dominated by the migrants from India, forged an alliance with the emerging middle classes in the towns of the Punjab to concretise the class formation of a group which could exert political pressure on the state to challenge the existent property rights structure.

Conclusion

We have traced demise of the Ayub regime through the development and eventual mobilisation of a clientelist class during the period. Compared to other parts of British India, West Pakistan did not inherit a clentelistically mobilised class at the time of its inception. Apart from the feudal lobby, there were no other groups in society with well-entrenched economic rights. In that situation, once a political settlement was consolidated, the state went about not only specifying economic rights which were contested but in creating new ones. The chief beneficiaries of such state created rights was the industrial class. This political settlement started faltering as a result of structural changes that the economy went through and the emergence of a politically mobilised class which challenged the existent structure of economic rights that were granted by the state. This challenge came mainly in the form of political mobilisation by what we loosely identify as the petty bourgeoisie. Whereas in other parts of British India, notably in Bengal, we can trace the evolution of this class from the early days of British rule (see Khan, 1989), in Pakistan, while existing in an incipient form, its numbers were swelled by the agrarian transformation that occurred in the Punjab during the Ayub regime and it was given organisational impetus by the Ayub regime's political strategy of creating a countervailing class to the dominant coalition. The importance of the transformations that took place in the towns of the Punjab during the period was seen as the first indicator of this phenomenon.

Following from the argument developed above, it is clear that the industrial strategy of the Ayub regime fell into disrepute only as part of the increasing contention of economic rights endowed by the state. However, much of the rhetoric employed against the Ayub regime during the agitations centred around the beneficiaries of industrial rights. This class was particularly vulnerable to such an onslaught because of two interrelated reasons. One that it was the only proprietary class that the state had created and as such did not have any autonomous political base. Secondly, given that it was composed largely of migrants, it was not rooted within the country, which further eroded its legitimacy, particularly since the contention of rights initiated due to convulsions in the country side. With the rise of clientelism, the resources which could be devoted to a small class of industrialists was no longer possible as clientelist groups were powerful enough to demand progressively increasing side-payments for the process of industrialisation to continue. Subsequent developments in Pakistan's political economy was dominated by these concerns.

Though it is beyond the scope of this paper, the important role played by the middle class in both the Bhutto and Zia regimes, the rise of Nawaz Sharif as representing the interests of the small town bourgeoisie of the Punjab and increasingly of Sindh, points to the political importance of a middle class. In the economic sphere, the fact that the Zia regime did not dismantle the public sector in spite of professing an explicitly right wing ideology, the recent controversies in Pakistan over loan defaults, the yellow cab scheme and the cooperative scam alludes to the clientelist process steadily impinging on the country's economy.

NOTES

1. Burki (1971, 1972, 1976 and 1980) and Alavi (1976 and 1989) have alluded to the importance of the middle classes in Pakistan's political economy, albeit from different vantage points. While using secondary information, our analytical framework leads us towards different implications of the importance of this class than the above mentioned authors.

2. These concepts have been elaborated in greater depth in Sayeed, A. (forthcoming).

3. Rights are defined as politically defended claims over assets and resources (Khan, 1989).

4. In the case of South Asia patron-client relationships have been modelled in terms of 'factionalism', particularly in the analysis of electoral politics in India. See Brass (1990)

5. The literature particularly refers to protection regimes instituted in developing countries for the purposes of import substitution.

6. The policy implication which is particularly topical is that of liberalisation and privatisation. Whereas a state can withdraw rights conferred to groups through dismantling controls, if the controls were in place because of clientelist pressures the effect of liberalisation and privatisation will be merely to shift the inefficiencies of the public sector into the private realm.

7. Regions comprising north-western India were 'non-regulation' areas. This meant that the bureaucrat had complete writ over the administrative process with minimum interference from the central or provincial headquarters (Ahmed, 1980b, pp. 34-35).

8. See Ahmad (1984a) for the NWFP and Ahmad (1984b) and Arif (1990) on the agrarian structure of Sindh. With the construction of the Sukkur Barrage in 1932, nearly three million acres of land was resumed in Sindh. But, unlike the Punjab where the land resumed was handed over to indigenous groups, in Sindh, no such resettlement of the indigenous populations took place. Discussion below on canal colonisation in the Punjab will serve to clarify this point.

9. See Ali (1988, pp.71-73) for the distinction between the 'large' landlords and the yeoman groups who formed the bulk of the lambardar and zaildar classes.

10. See Khan (1989, chapt 1) and Ray (1979) for a description of the emergence of the jotededar class in Bengal.

11. See Ali (1988, chapts 2&3) for the process through which land grants in the new colonies were made.

12. There were three classes that were delineated for land grants in the colonies: the 'capitalists', the yeomans and smaller peasant holdings. While the bulk of the lamberdar class was accommodated under yeoman grants, the capitalist grants accommodated the larger landlords, but it was "meant also as a reward for persons who had served the government well" (Ali, 1988, p.24). Gilmartin (1988, pp.25-26) also gives evidence

to the importance of 'score of influence' along with aristocratic lineage in doling capitalist grants.

13.   See Alavi (1976) for a description of the agrarian structure of the older settled districts.

14.   Ali (1988, chapt 5) shows that the colonial government turned a blind eye to corruption and irregularities of the revenue collecting bureaucracy in the Punjab. He also goes on to argue that whereas the revenue collecting machinery could have been made more efficient, the state chose not to do so. This clearly reveals that the bureaucracy was used as an absorptive tool by the colonial state.

15.   Other cleavages within the body politic of the Punjab were also sharpened because of this Act. Since the majority of the money lenders were Hindus while a great number of agriculturists were Muslims, the religious divide was also brought to the fore by the Act. Similarly, the delineation of agricultural 'tribes' from other groups created much controversy regarding those whose status overlapped, particularly as landholders as well as urban based money lenders. See Gilmartin (1988, pp.26-38) for a detailed discussion on these issues.

16.   One illustration of the magnitude of destruction in the Punjab during the Sikh interregnum is that prior to the Sikh invasions the population of Lahore was around half a million, but by the time the British annexed the Punjab it was reduced to a mere 100,000 (Ali, 1988, p.40).

17.   Obviously a proportion of the work force would be a more accurate indicator of industrial activity. In the absence of which, this evidence should be considered merely illustrative.

18.   The cotton weaving industry was given a boost by increased agricultural production, but the lack of any entrepreneurial base in the province and its tied relationship with the industrial heartland of British India, i.e. Bombay and Gujrat meant that the area remained primarily a supplier of raw materials to the rest of the country. See Bagchi (1972, pp.199-216, 435-436).

19.   One has to note, however, that the Muslim League gained ground after 1940 and did well in the 1946 elections, though for other reasons.

20.   For instance in 1936 Nehru remarked:

         "The Punjab has some political immaturity indeed but then the Punjab has a special feature and that is its youthfulness which is both good and bad. (One) cause which, in my opinion, has its direct effect on the Punjab's political situation is that the peasants here are living in a slightly better position so that there cannot be much impetus for a national agrarian movement like the one we have in U.P; and then that discontent which is so common among the pedantry elsewhere is not to be found in that terrible form in the Punjab ..." (quoted in Low, 1991, p.21).

21.   For the occupational caste structure in north western India, See Papanek (1972)

22.   See Jalal (1990, chapt 2) for a vivid description of the proportions of this crisis.

23.   The process of 'claiming' property on the basis of producing two witnesses vouching for the claimant's assets left behind in India was extremely arbitrary. Ayub Khan (1967, p.94) aptly called it "a perfectly ridiculous formula: it meant that if a person could produce two witnesses that he owned half of India, then the Government of

Pakistan will have to accept this!"

24. See Papanek (1972) for occupational and regional background of the merchant capitalists who migrated to Pakistan.

25. The formation and subsequent mobilisation of the Muhajir Qaumi Movement (MQM) in Sindh was the ethnic manifestation of this class in the 1980s.

26. An estimated 5.5 million out of 8 million muslims who came to Pakistan settled in the Punjab (Jalal, 1990, p.79).

27. Of the three provinces in West Pakistan at the time, the Muslim League had control over only the Sindh legislature. The Frontier and Punjab assemblies were in control of the Congress and the Unionists respectively.

28. See Sayeed (1980, chapt 1) and Low ed. (1991) for detailed descriptions of the political tribulations of the Muslim League between the promulgation of the Government of India Act 1935 and Independence in August 1947.

29. Conventional wisdom has it that the muslim league was dominated by landlords (see for instance Ali, 1970). While this view is true for the league from the time of its inception to 1937 when Jinnah again took over at its leader, its character changed to mobilising the muslim middle classes from the 1937 elections onwards. The only exception to this rule perhaps was Bengal (Zaidi, 1970). Especially after the creation of Pakistan, 60 percent of the League's Working Committee came from the urban professional classes (Burki, 1980, p.19).

30. Prominent among them were Ispahani, Rahimtoola, Habib and Adamjee. See Papanek (1972).

31. In fact it is also alleged that the League deliberately engineered riots in Karachi which led many Hindus to flee from the city so that property could be distributed among its potential constituents (Jalal, 1990, p.88).

32. Jalal (1990, pp.235-252) documents the controversies that would arise within the oligarchy on the issue of consumption vs investments. Some bureaucrats, with the responsibility of running the day to day affairs of the state were more weary of large scale investments while others would be pushing for such measures.

33. The above paragraph is a description in a nutshell of Pakistan's industrial history through the 1950s which we have covered in considerable detail elsewhere. See Papanek (1967) for a detailed description.

34. The language riots in Bengal in 1952 and the dismissal of the Krishak Proja Party after its electoral victory in the 1954 elections were some events which gave initial impetus to this perception.

35. By facing the government to increase the extensive irrigation network, the landed elite was able to bring more area under cultivation and thus increase its political influence also (Burki, 1976, pp.301-304)

36. In 1959-60 the share of agriculture in GDP was 45.8 per cent. As a result of its sluggish performance, per capita GNP was virtually stagnant at 0.6 per cent per annum.

37. The ceilings were fixed at 500 acres of irrigated and 1000 acres of unirrigated land. A total of 5064 landowners declared excess land and land was acquired by the government from only 763 of the declarers, which comes to 15.06% (Nulty, 1972, p.31).

38. The ceilings on ownership were fixed on the basis of individual rather than family holdings. Another provision that allowed the landlords to retain lands above the ceilings was that additional area was allowed for orchards (Hussain, 1989, p.61).

39. As chairmen of the union councils, the basic democrats were only ex-officio members of the tehsil councils, which in turn were presided over by the subdivisional magistrate or the tehsildar, who in turn were bureaucrats (Alavi, 1976, p.46).

40. Most important among these was the institution of the Agricultural Development Bank, which provided finance to landowners. Also the support price of wheat was kept 'excessively high' despite strong opposition by the Planning Commission (Alavi, 1983, p.61).

41. The middle peasantry is classified by Burki as those owning between 50-100 acres of land (1976, p.307).

42. See Burki (1976, 1977, 1980) and Alavi (1976, 1983).

43. That this strategy was successful is clear from the high growth rates in the manufacturing sector during the 1960-70 period as well as the high degree of concentration in the industrial sector during the period.

44. See Burki (1977, 1980, 1993).

45. Data for cotton cloth is from GOP (1990) and for the cloth sector as a whole from World Bank (1987).

46. I am grateful to Mushtaq Khan for drawing my attention to this important point.

47. Most other accounts of agitation against the Ayub regime go back to the autumn of 1968. See Sayeed (1980), Feldman (1972), Ziring (1971) and Ali (1970).

48. The size classification for the urban areas used is as follows: Large cities with a population of 500,000 or more, medium cities between 100,000 and 500,000, large towns between 50,000 and 100,000, and small towns between with a population of more than 5000 and less than 50,000 inhabitants.

49. Also as stated earlier there was a spurting of powerlooms in the small scale sector, though it is not clear what proportion of it was situated in the small towns rather than the bigger cities.

50. For some accounts of Bhutto's mobilisation of the middle classes in towns, see Sayeed (1980), Feldman (1972), Burki (1980) and Syed (1992).

REFERENCES

Ahmad, F. 1984a "Transformation of the Agrarian Structure in the Northwestern Frontier Province of Pakistan," *Journal of Contemporary Asia*, Vol 14, No.1.

Ahmad, F. 1984b "Agrarian Change and Class Formation in Sindh," *Economic and Political Weekly*, Vol 19, No.39.

Ahmed, Emajuddin 1980 *Bureaucratic Elites in Segmented Economic Growth: Pakistan and Bangladesh*, University Press Limited, Dacca.

Alavi, H. 1972 "The State in Post-Colonial Societies: Pakistan and Bangladesh," *New Left Review*, No.74.

Alavi, H. 1974 "Rural Bases of Political Power in South Asia," *Journal of Contemporary*

Asia, Vol 4, No.4

Alavi, H. 1976   "The Rural Elite and Agricultural Development in Pakistan," in Stevens,
                    R.D., Alavi, H. and Betocci, P. (eds). *Rural Development in Bangladesh
                    and Pakistan,* The University Press of Hawaii, Honolulu.

Alavi, H. 1983   "Class and State in Pakistan," in Gardezi, H. and Rahid, J. (eds). *Pakistan:
                    The Unstable State,* Vanguard Books, Lahore.

Alavi, H. 1989   "Politics of Ethnicity in India and Pakistan," in Alavi, H. and Harriss, J.
                    (eds) *Sociology of Developing Societies: South Asia,* Macmillan, London.

Ali, I. 1988   *The Punjab Under Imperialism: 1885-1947,* Princeton University Press,
                    Princeton, New Jersey.

Ali, I. 1991   "The Punjab and the Retardation of Nationalism", in Low, D.A. (ed). *The
                    Political Inheritance of Pakistan,* Macmillan, London.

Ali, T. 1970   *Pakistan: Military Rule or People's Power,* William Morrow and Co., New
                    York.

Amjad, R. 1983   "Industrial Concentration and Economic Power", in Gardezi, H. and
                    Rahid, J. (eds). *Pakistan: The Unstable State,* Vanguard Books, Lahore.

Ansari, S. 1991   "Political Legacies of Pre-1947 Sind," in Low, D.A. (ed). *The Political
                    Inheritance of Pakistan,* Macmillan, London.

Arif, Z. 1990   "Mehnat Kash Nazariya: Qaumi Inquilabion Ki Nauiyat va Mahiyat,"
                    Research Forum, No. 10.

Bagchi, A.K. 1972   *Private Investment in India: 1900-1939,* Cambridge University Press,
                    Cambridge.

Bardhan, P. 1984   *The Political Economy of Development in India,* Basil Blackwell, Oxford.

Bhagwati, J. 1982   "Directly Unproductive Profit Seeking (DUP) Activities," *Journal of
                    Political Economy,* Vol 90, No.4.

Brass, P. 1990   *Politics of India Since Independence,* Cambridge University Press,
                    Cambridge.

Burki, S.J. 1971   "Social and Economic Determinants of Political Violence: A Case Study
                    of the Punjab", *The Middle East Journal,* Vol 25, Autumn.

Burki, S.J. 1972   "Ayub's Fall: A Socio-Economic Explanation", *Asian Survey,* Vol 12,
                    No.3.

Burki, S.J. 1973   "Migration, Urbanisation and Politics in Pakistan", in Wriggins, H. Guyot,
                    J. (eds) *Population, Politics and the Future of Southern Asia,* Columbia
                    University Press, New York.

Burki, S.J. 1974   "Development of Towns: The Pakistan Experience", *Asian Survey,*
                    Vol 14, No.8.

Burki, S.J. 1976   "The Development of Pakistan's Agriculture: An Interdisciplinary
                    Explanation", in Stevens, R.D., Alavi, H. and Betocci, P. (eds). *Rural
                    Development in Bangladesh and Pakistan,* The University Press of Hawaii,
                    Honolulu.

Burki, S.J. 1977   "Economic Decision-making in Pakistan", in Ziring, L., Braibanti, R. and
                    Wriggins, H. (eds) *Pakistan: The Long View,* Duke University Press,
                    Durham, N.C.

Burki, S.J. 1980   *State and Society in Pakistan: 1971-77*, Macmillan, London.

Eisenstadt, S.N. and Roniger, L. 1984 *Patrons, Clients and Friends*, Cambridge University Press, Cambridge.

Feldman, H. 1972 *From Crisis to Crisis: Pakistan 1962-69*, Oxford University Press, London.

Gilmartin, D. 1988 *Empire and Islam: Punjab and the Making of Pakistan*, University of California Press, Berkeley.

GOP, 1990   *Pakistan's Textile Statistics*, Textile Commissioner's Organisation, Islamabad.

Hamid, N. 1980   "Process of Agricultural Development," Unpublished Doctoral Dissertation, Stanford University.

Husain, A. 1989   "Pakistan: Land Reforms Reconsidered", in Alavi, H. and Harriss,J.(eds) *Sociology of Developing Societies: South Asia*, MacMillan, London.

Jalal, A. 1990   *The State of Martial Rule: The Origins of Pakistan's Political Economy of Defence*, Vanguard, Lahore.

Khan, Ayub 1967   *Friends Not Masters: A Political Autobiography*, Karachi.

Khan, M.H. 1989   "Corruption, Clientilism and Capitalist Development," Unpublished Ph.D. Dissertation, Faculty of Economics and Politics, University of Cambridge.

Krueger, A. 1974   "The Political Economy of the Rent-Seeking Society," *American Economic Review*, Vol. 64, No.3.

Low, D.A. 1991 (ed). *The Political Inheritance of Pakistan*, MacMillan, London.

Major, A.J. 1991   "The Punjabi Chieftains and the Transition from Sikh to British Rule", in Low, D.A. (ed). *The Political Inheritance of Pakistan*, Macmillan, London.

Moore, Barrington 1966 *Social Origins of Dictatorship and Democracy*, Beacon Press, Boston.

Misra, B.B. 1961   *The Indian Middle Classes*, Oxford University Press, London.

Noman, O. 1988   *The Political Economy of Pakistan: 1947-85*, KPI, London.

Nulty, L. 1972   *The Green Revolution in West Pakistan*, Preager, N.Y.

Papanek, H. 1972   "Pakistan's Big Businessmen: Muslim Separatism, Entrepreneurs and Political Mobilisation", *Economic Development and Cultural Change*, Vol 2 1, October.

Papanek, G. 1967   *Pakistan's Development: Social Goals and Private Incentives*, Harvard University Press, Cambridge, Mass.

Ray, R. 1979   *Change in Bengal Agrarian Society*, Manohar, Delhi.

Sayeed, K.B. 1980 *Politics in Pakistan: The Nature and Direction of Change*, New York.

Syeed, A. (forthcoming) *Political Alignments the State and Industrialisation in Pakistan*, Oxford University Press, Karachi.

Syed, A.H. 1992   *The Discourse and Politics of Zulfikar Ali Bhutto*, MacMillan, London.

Washbrook, D.A. 1981 "Law, State and Agrarian Society in Colonial India," *Modern Asian Studies*, Vol 15, No.3.

World Bank, 1987 *Overview of Issues and Development Strategies: Pakistan's Textile Sector.*

Wright, T. 1974   "Indian Muslim Refugees in the Politics of Pakistan", *Journal of Commonwealth and Comparative Politics*, Vol 12, March.

Zaidi, Z.H. 1970   "Aspects of the Development of Muslim League Policy", in Phillips, C.M.
                    and Wainwright, M.D.(eds) *The Partition of India: Policies and
                    Perspectives, 1935-47*, MIT Press, Cambridge, Massachusetts.
Ziring, L. 1971   *The Ayub Khan Era: Politics in Pakistan, 1958-69*, Syracuse University
                    Press, Syracuse, N.Y.

Development Process and Problems of
Punjabi Identity in Indian Punjab

Sucha Singh Gill

Introduction

After reorganisation of Indian Punjab on linguistic basis it was expected that Punjabi national/subnational identity will be strengthened. For a short while signs of its growing strong appeared on the scene following Akali-Jan Sangh and Akali-Janata Party coalitions in the state. But during the last one and a half decade, Punjabi national identity has suffered a set back. In its place religious identity of Punjabi Sikhs and Punjabi Hindus had been articulated by the political process. In fact the two major religious communities were drifting apart till this process was halted with the return of peace in the state. To understand the question of Punjabi identity in a multi-religious and multi-caste society of Indian Punjab one need to investigate its three major aspects. They are: (1) its historical process and context; (2) its material base/objective reality; and (3) the role of subjective forces and factors. The first and the last aspects are beyond the scope of the present paper. Here our basic concern is to investigate into the material reality which lays basis for the emergence of national identity.

Economic Growth and Structural Change

The developing economy of India has experienced uneven spatial pattern of development in the post independence period. The states of Punjab, Haryana, Maharashtra, Gujarat and West Bengal have emerged as islands of development in the vast areas of the backward economy. In per capita income the Punjab was ranked at number two in 1950-51 but was pushed to third position in 1955-56 and fourth position in 1961-62. Maharashtra overtook Punjab in 1955-56 and Gujarat in 1961-62. In 1964-65 Punjab (and Haryana) surpassed Maharashtra, Gujarat and West Bengal, all the three states ahead of it (Bhardwaj, 1982). The state has maintained this position till 1990-91. The Punjab has not only maintained its lead but has increased its distance from all India average and from both the advanced states as well as the backward states during 1970-71 to 1986-87. Per capita income of the state at constant prices of 1970-71 increased from Rs.1070 in 1970-71 to Rs.1896 in 1990-91 compared to Rs. 633 and Rs. 942 in case of all India average in the corresponding years (Table 1). This is because of the fact that the state has been growing at a higher rate (except for the decade of 1980-81 to 1990-91) compared to all India average (Table 2). Besides the state has the lowest incidence of poverty among the major states of the country (Minhas et. al. 1991). When economic development is measured in terms of physical quality of life index (Morris and Mcaplin 1979 and Karkal and Rajan 1991) taking into consideration life expectancy at the age of one, infant mortality rate and literacy, the state was ranked at number 3 in 1971 and 1981. The high and sustained rate of economic growth for several years and high initial level of per capita income has placed the state on high pedestal so far as the level of economic and social development is concerned. Though overall growth rate of the state has improved between 1980-81 and 1990-91 compared to that of between 1970-71 and 1981-82 yet it has slightly become lower than the all India average. This is explained by disturbed conditions in the state adversely affecting the tertiary sector growth rate and also due to a rise in the share of non-development expenditure particularly on law and order which has been at the cost of development expenditure. High growth rate of the state's economy has been caused by a set of several complex factors and is accompanied by diverse changes in social and economic life of the society. The state has become a symbol of economic prosperity in the country and the model to be emulated in other less developed parts of the country.

Sustained economic development in a particular region leads to changes in economic structure. The basic elements of economic structure are taken to be goods and services of different kind, and the employment provided by the production of such goods and services. Data relating to percentage distribution of net state domestic product originating from different sectors are presented in Table 3. To avoid the effect of relative price changes data are taken at constant prices with base of 1970-71. Data reveal that the share of primary sector in the net State domestic product of the Punjab has declined from 59.33 per cent in 1960-61 to 58.37 per cent in 1970-71 to 50.04 per cent in 1980-81 and 47.94 per cent in 1990-91. This shows loss of this sector in the net state domestic product by 11.3 percentage points over 30 years period. During this period the share of secondary sector has improved from 14.85 in 1960-61 to 15.31 in 1970-71 to 16.69 per cent in 1980-81 and 21.62 per cent in 1990-91. During these corresponding years the share of manufacturing (both registered and unregistered) increased from 7.37 percent to 8.00 percent to 11.04 percent to 16.60 per cent. The improvement in the share of this sector as a whole has been 6.77 percent points while that of manufacturing by 9.23 points. Within the secondary sector there is considerable decline in the share of construction activities from 6.99 per cent of the net state domestic product in 1960-61 to 6.53 per cent in 1970-71 to 4.41 percent in 1980-81 and 2.21 percent in 1990-91. The case of tertiary sector is slightly different. Its share of net state domestic product increased from 25.82 percent in 1960-61 to 26.32 percent in 1970-71 and to 33.27 percent in 1980-81 but declined to 30.44 percent in 1990-91. Thus, going by contribution of various sectors to net state domestic product Punjab has entered in the decade of the eighties, in the stage of positive growth where the share of both the primary and tertiary sectors has started declining and that of the secondary sector has begun to rise. Though changes in sectoral distribution of income took place between 1960-61 and 1970-71 but percentage change was very low. The changes in subsequent decades are sharp and pronounced.

Distribution of workforce (Table 4) in the state has given a trend similar to the distribution of net state domestic product. 62.67 percent of the total workers were engaged in agriculture in 1971 which declined to 58.03 percent in 1981 and 56.14 percent in 1991. The proportion of workers engaged in manufactures (both in household industry and registered factories) increased from 6.20 percent in 1971 to 6.82 per cent in 1981 and to 9.35 per cent in 1991. The proportion of other workers (which include workers in construction, electricity and workers in all variety of services) increased from 31.13 per cent in 1971 to 35.15 per cent in 1981 but declined to 34.51 per cent in 1991. Thus, shift in work force across sectors follows the shift in proportion of income among different sectors but the rate of workforce shift has been at a relatively slow pace. This is partly due to the arrival of migrant labour force from the backward states of Bihar, Orissa and Eastern U.P, and their employment in the relatively low paid jobs in various sectors. It is estimated that the migratory labour was 7.60 percent in 1978-79 and 9.57 percent in 1983-84 of the total workforce engaged in agricultural sector of the state (Gill, 1990). Assuming that the proportion of migrant workforce in the agriculture of the state remained the same in 1991 as it was in 1983-84 and deduct it from the total workforce of this sector then the proportion of work force in this sector of the total turns out to be 50.77 percent. This comes close to the share in income of agriculture and allied activities (47.74 percent). If movement of labour from slow growing states is separated from the flow of labour within the state then the lag between shift in sectoral income shares and corresponding workforce shares declines.

The spread of economic development and consequently structural change across different sectors is unequally distributed at spatial level. Some districts have experienced a shift in the level of distribution of workers in such a way that they demonstrate qualitative change in the level of economic activities. Three districts, namely Ludhiana (1981), Jalandhar (1981) and Ropar (1991) have more than 50 percent of workers engaged in secondary and tertiary sectors. In districts of Amritsar, Kapurthala, Hoshiarpur and Gurdaspur workers in these sectors were slightly above the state average of 41.97 percent in 1991. But districts of Ferozepur, Faridkot, Sangrur and Bathinda have high concentration of workers in primary sector in all cases above 68 per cent (Table 5). Leaving the case of Ludhiana, the higher share of workers in non-agricultural sectors does not go with higher per capita income in the various districts (Kaur, 1993). This is explained by relatively higher level of productivity in agriculture among the districts with high concentration of workforce in primary sector and particularly in agriculture and allied activities.

Changes in sectoral share of income and shift in distribution of workforce takes place in response to changes in real income and labour productivity. The shares of resources in the agricultural sector declined largely because capital is sent out and labour migrates out of it. Models of development and transformation of dual economy explain at the theoretical level the transfer of agricultural surpluses and migration of workforce as two most important and integrated ingredients initiating development process in the advanced sector in the initial phases and for its subsequent sustained growth. In fact, the growth and modernisation of agriculture through out-migration of labour and the transfer of economic surplus to modern manufacturing is the pre-requisite for the transformation and modernisation of the economy (Lewis 1954, Ranis and Fei, 1961 and Jorgenson, 1961).

Table 1: Per capita income in selected states in India (at constant prices of 1970-71) in rupees

State	1970-71	1980-81	1990-91
1.Andhra Pradesh	585	647	853
2.Assam	535	558	770
3.Bihar	402	441	606
4.Gujarat	829	904	1245
5.Haryana	877	1060	1488
6.Himachal Pradesh	651	711	914
7.Karnataka	641	687	899
8.Kerala	594	621	872*
9.Madhya Pradesh	484	516	763
10.Maharashtra	783	957	1396
11.Manipur	390	506	620**
12.Orissa	478	477	603
13.Punjab	1070	1354	1896
14.Rajasthan	651	535	815
15.Tamil Nadu	581	584	791**
16.Uttar Pradesh	486	519	657
17.West Bengal	722	797	998
All India	633	698	942

Source: *CSO, Estimates of Net State Domestic Product*, New Delhi, 1989 *and Statistical Abstract of Punjab 1992*, Chandigarh, 1993.
* 1989-90
** 1988-89

Table 2: Average annual compound growth rate of state/national income (per cent per annum)

Sector	Punjab 1960-61	India 1965-66
Primary	2.4	-0.9
Secondary	6.0	6.9
Tertiary	4.5	5.6
All sectors	3.6	2.7
	1965-66	**1968-69**
Primary	9.9	4.5
Secondary	6.7	2.9
Tertiary	6.8	3.9
All Sectors	8.4	4.0
	1970-71	**1981-82**
Primary	3.6	1.7
Secondary	6.2	4.1
Tertiary	6.8	5.3
All Sectors	4.9	3.4
	1980-81	**1990-91**
Primary	4.8	4.6
Secondary	6.4	6.3
Tertiary	5.0	5.2
All Sectors	5.2	5.7

Source: *ESO, Statistical Abstract of Punjab* 1979, 1989 and 1992, Government of Punjab, Chandigarh (1980, 1989 and 1992).
Note: Growth rates between 1960-61 and 1968-69 are at constant prices of 1960-61 and those between 1970-71 and 1981-82 are at constant prices of 1970-71 and those between 1980-81 and 1990-91 are at constant prices of 1980-81.

Table 3: Percentage distribution of net state domestic product at factor cost in Punjab at 1970-71 prices (in percentage).

Sector	1960-61	1970-71	1980-81	1990-91
Agriculture	48.62	43.26	36.56	34.69
Livestock	10.47	14.87	13.21	13.05
Forestry and logging	0.18	0.20	0.22	0.14
Fishing	0.05	0.04	0.04	0.04
Mining and Quarrying	0.01	0.03	0.01	0.02
1. Sub Total (Primary Sector)	59.33	58.37	50.04	47.94
Registered manufacturing	3.29	3.95	5.65	9.02
Unregistered manufacturing	4.08	4.05	5.39	7.58
Construction	6.99	6.53	4.41	2.81
Electricity and water supply	0.49	0.78	1.24	2.21
2. Sub Total (Secondary Sector)	14.85	15.31	16.69	21.62
Transport, communication and storage	3.69	3.50	4.19	4.75
Trade, hotels and restaurants	11.52	12.56	16.88	12.99
Banking and insurance	1.44	1.61	2.30	3.65
Real estate and ownership of dwellings	2.46	1.60	1.44	1.20
Public administration	1.57	2.20	3.52	4.24
Other services	5.14	4.85	4.94	3.61
3. Sub Total (Tertiary Sector)	25.82	26.32	33.27	30.44
Total (1+2+3) net state domestic product	100.00	100.00	100.00	100.00

Source: *ESO, Statistical Abstract of Punjab*, 1974, 1982, 1991, Chandigarh.

Table 4: Percentage distribution of main workers

S No Category of workers	1971*	1981	1991
1. Cultivators	42.56	35.86	32.83
2. Agricultural labourers	20.11	22.17	23.31
3. Household industry workers	3.17	2.58	2.93
Workers in registered factories	3.03	4.24	6.64**
4. Other workers	31.13	35.15	34.29
Total	**100.00**	**100.00**	**100.00**

* In 1971 census no distinction was made between main and marginal workers.
** This is based on estimated number of workers in registered factories in 1991.

Source: Census of India 1971, 1981 and 1991.
Note: Due to definitional problem of workers, data pertaining to 1961 census are not comparable.

Table 5: Share of workers in Secondary and Tertiary Sectors in various districts of Punjab in 1991

S No	Name of district	Percentage Share
1.	Ludhiana	60.95
2.	Jalandhar	52.83
3.	Ropar	52.17
4.	Kapurthala	45.77
5.	Amritsar	44.38
6.	Hoshiarpur	43.44
7.	Gurdaspur	42.37
8.	Patiala	42.03
9.	Ferozepur	31.87
10.	Faridkot	31.24
11.	Sangrur	31.24
12.	Bathinda	30.18
	Punjab	41.97

Source: *Census of India 1991*

Migration flows of labour in the Punjab economy have been more complex than the one way migration explained in these models. This is modified on account of the state acquiring the position of an advanced region among the slow growing backward states sending unchecked supply of labour to the Punjab in response to higher wages. There has been a massive inflow of labour in the state both in agriculture, small industry and odd activities in secondary and tertiary sectors. In fact Punjab has been sending a large number of migrants to various states of India and abroad but at the same time receiving large number of migrants from other states of India. Up to 1971 the state was experiencing net out-migration but between 1971 and 1981 it turned out to be net in-migrant state. The net in-migration amounted to 182,526 persons. Though the 1991 census data on migration is not yet available it is expected to show that the same trend has continued between 1981 and 1991.

Migration flows within the state have been much more powerful. There has been large migration of population from rural to urban areas (Table 6). Between 1951 and 1961 the share of migration to total increase in urban population was 27.00 percent and in the subsequent three decades of 1961-71, 1971-81 and 1981-91 it was 15.75 percent, 49.13 percent and 30.32 percent respectively. As a result of net out-migration from the rural areas the proportionate distribution of workforce in rural and urban areas of the state has changed in favour of the latter. The share of urban workers was 23.05 per cent in 1971 which increased to 26.25 per cent in 1981 and 28.87 per cent in 1991. There was a fall in the share of rural workers from 76.95 per cent in 1971 to 73.79 per cent in 1981 to 71.13 percent in 1991. The extent of migration of workers to urban areas was 164,356 during 1971-1981 and 166,637 during 1981-1991. This migration is caused largely on account of inter sectoral differences in per worker income (Table 7). In 1971 per worker income in agricultural and allied activities was 91.69 percent of the state average compared to 114.54 percent in case of non-agricultural activities. This was changed respectively to 80.85 per cent and 130.65 per cent in 1981 and 82.67 per cent and 123.90 per cent in 1991. Though in relative terms these differentials have declined between 1981 and 1991 compared to 1971 and 1981 yet in absolute terms these differences have increased over period of time from Rs. 830.68 in 1971, Rs. 2158.65 in 1981 and Rs. 2535.71 in 1991. These differences in per worker income can be used as proxy of rural urban income differentials to explain migration of workforce from rural to urban areas and from agriculture and allied activities to non-agricultural activities. Migration from the state is largely explained by pull factors rather than the push factors.

Movement of population from rural to urban areas has resulted in some changes in the religious composition of rural and urban population. This is due to the association and the concentration of population of various religious groups with respect to certain occupations and their distribution in rural and urban areas. Sikh population has high concentration in the rural areas and employment in agriculture and allied activities. The Hindu population has high concentration in urban areas and employment in non-agricultural activities. 87.86 per cent of the Sikh population and 58.02 per cent of the Hindu population was distributed in the rural areas of the Punjab in 1971. The respective share declined to 84.87 per cent and 51.91 per cent in 1981. This shows that increasingly Hindu population is shifting to urban areas where there is concentration of non-agricultural activities. Hindu population is also showing greater inter-state out-migration to cities like Delhi. This has led to decline in the share of Hindu population both in rural areas as well as in urban areas and also its share in total population. The share of Hindu population in rural areas declined from 28.56 per cent to 26.51 percent, in urban areas from 66.39 per cent to 64.15 per cent and in the total population from 37.54 per cent to 36.93 per cent during 1971 and 1981. The share of Sikh population increased in rural areas from 69.37 percent to 71.30 per cent, in urban areas from 30.79 per cent to 33.19 per cent and in the total population from 60.21 per cent to 60.75 per cent. This pattern is generally reflected across the various districts of the state except for a marginal reversal in Gurdaspur, Hoshiarpur and Jalandhar (Table 8). The exceptional case of Ferozepur showing major reversal is explained by reorganisation of this district in the intervening period resulting in separation of Sikh dominated Tehsil of Moga into a newly created district of Faridkot.

The process of rural-urban migration of population along with changes in the distribution of workforce across various sectors of the economy show that there is a sharp decline in the share of cultivators and increase in the proportion of workers in the secondary and tertiary sectors. This implies that a large number of Sikh peasants and their progenies are joining non-agricultural occupations in the urban areas. Concentration of religious groups across various sectors and changes over period of time have implications for the question of Punjabi national identity.

Implications for Punjabi Identity

Commonality of material interests and unity in struggle create a sound base for emergence and growth of nationalism among the people of a region with common culture and language. Unity in struggle is a necessary condition for development of consciousness of national identity particularly in the multi-religious groups.

The segregation of the major religious groups, Sikhs in rural and Hindus in urban areas is a first barrier in the unity in struggle. When Sikh farmers struggle for redressal of their grievances and promotion of their interests, the urban people remain indifferent. This is evident from the long history of peasant struggles and also from the recent phase of farmers' movement led by Bhartiya Kisan Union (BKU) and the Akali Dal Dharamyudh Morcha before operation Blue Star. Similarly when merchants and traders indulge in mobilisation (occasionally), the Sikh farmers remain indifferent.

Table 6: Growth of population and migration to urban areas of Punjab

| Year | Population (in lakhs) | | Percentage of urban population | Decadal percentage growth | | Migration in urban areas (in lakhs) | Percentage of migration to total increase |
	Total	Urban		Total	Urban		
1951	91.57	20.42	22.3				
1961	111.35	25.81	23.2	21.56	29.10	1.45	27.00
1971	135.51	32.16	23.7	21.73	25.27	1.00	15.75
1981	167.89	46.49	27.7	23.89	44.51	7.04	49.13
1991	201.91	60.01	29.72	20.26	29.11	4.10	30.32

Source: Census of India

Note: Migration into urban areas is calculated on the basis of difference between decadal growth of urban population minus decadal growth rate of the total population multiplied by total urban population in the base year.

Table 7: Distribution of workers, net state domestic product and per worker income of agricultural and non-agricultural workers in Punjab state

Sector	1971			1981			1991		
	No of workers	Sectoral income (Rs crores)	Per worker income (Rs)	No of workers	Sectoral income (Rs crores)	Per worker income (Rs)	No of workers	Sectoral income (Rs crores)	Per worker income (Rs)
1. Agricultural and allied activities	24,89,210	837.76	3365.57 (91.69)	32,53,875	1141.03	3506.68 (80.85)	36,80,146	1870.87	5083.68 (82.67)
2. Non-agricultural activities	14,23,322	598.40	4204.25 (114.54)	20,34,037	1152.35	5665.33 (130.63)	26,68,179	2032.99	7619.39 (123.90)
3. Overall of Punjab State	39,12,532	1436.16	3670.67 (100.00)	52,87,910	2293.38	4337.02 (100.00)	63,48,325	3903.86	6149.43 (100.00)

Note:1. Workers data of 1981 and 1991 include marginal workers and they are proportionately distributed among cultivators, agricultural labourers, allied agricultural workers and household industries.

Note:2. Income data relate to 1970-71, 1980-81 and 1990-91 at constant prices at 1970-71.

Note:3. Figures in parentheses are in percentage.

Table 8: District wise distribution of Hindu and Sikh population in Indian Punjab (1971 and 1981) (in percentage)

District	Urban Hindu		Urban Sikh		Rural Hindu		Rural Sikh		Total Hindu		Total Sikh	
	1971	1981	1971	1981	1971	1981	1971	1981	1971	1981	1971	1981
Gurdaspur	75.90	76.71	20.38	20.11	40.90	40.21	51.03	51.42	48.02	48.13	44.82	44.43
Amritsar	60.31	54.91	33.65	43.55	8.23	6.54	89.29	91.37	23.43	22.49	74.22	75.68
Hoshiarpur	74.65	75.34	23.23	22.96	57.13	56.75	41.60	41.86	59.25	59.43	39.38	39.16
Jalandhar	75.49	75.11	24.04	23.29	44.19	45.39	54.73	53.54	53.91	55.89	44.90	42.83
Ropar	67.46	60.80	30.51	36.87	39.21	36.61	60.10	64.69	33.58	44.32	65.07	54.26
Ludhiana	63.82	61.74	34.34	36.45	16.88	10.88	82.47	88.31	32.22	32.25	65.71	66.52
Patiala	63.92	63.64	34.93	35.14	37.49	33.34	61.03	64.69	33.58	44.32	65.07	54.26
Sangrur	50.25	50.00	34.33	34.03	21.25	15.87	75.20	80.15	27.14	23.66	66.90	69.63
Bathinda	61.13	61.75	37.96	37.26	12.92	11.56	86.67	87.69	22.56	23.00	76.93	76.26
Faridkot	-	57.52	-	41.55	-	9.02	-	90.38	-	20.62	-	78.70
Ferozepur	72.22	76.91	25.69	20.60	24.02	34.70	74.82	64.19	33.58	44.32	65.07	54.26
Punjab	66.39	64.16	30.79	33.19	28.56	26.61	69.37	71.30	37.54	36.93	60.21	60.75

Source: Census of India, Punjab Series 1971 and 1981.

Besides areas of exclusive mobilisation and struggle, there is a basis of conflict in economic interests of the Sikh farmers and the traders. This leads to the conversion of economic conflict into communal divisions in the society. In the situation of scarcities, this factor is likely to assume greater significance. As indicated earlier there is an increase in the proportion of Sikh population in the urban areas and consequent involvement of the Sikhs of rural origin in the occupations of traditional dominance by the Hindus. Though sometimes it can generate a communal divide yet it has created a basis of unity in struggle. This is evident in the middle class trade union movement which is quite strong in the region.

It is also observed that the Sikhs engaged in trading and manufacturing sectors have the tendency to stay away from the struggles launched by groups and parties dominated by the rural interests. They are, rather, more interested in their own economic interests. They join hands with members of other communities with common economic interests and work in the common organisations. This explains the failure of the strong conscious propaganda and pressure of division of the society on communal lines in the last decade of turmoil in the state.

The strength of the development process is generating greater flow of rural-urban migration leading to greater mixing of population from the two major religious communities. The involvement in new and growing occupations in the secondary and tertiary sectors will further create a basis for unity in struggle on common issues. But as yet there remains considerable areas of exclusiveness creating emotional and psychological indifference to each others' needs. This has provided a strong base for lack of emergence of Punjabi national identity.

The sustained political mobilisation before the formation of Punjabi Suba on religious lines often clashing with each other and subsequent political events have led to a situation of fractured Punjabi identity (Bombwall, 1985). For healthy development of Punjabi national identity, a sustained development process must be accompanied by a positive political process involving large masses of people from different religious communities in common struggles. This requires changes in the perspective of political leadership in the state. The compulsions of electoral process based on universal franchise are likely to generate pressure in this direction. Political parties in the state involved in power politics are already showing signs of communal accommodation in spite of continued mobilisation in terms of religious idiom.

REFERENCES

Bhardwaj, Krishna (1982), "Regional Differentiation in India: A Note", *Economic and Political Weekly*, Annual Number, February.

Bombwall, K.R., "Ethno-Nationalism" in Abida Samiuddin (Ed), *The Punjab Crisis: Challenge and Response*, Intellectual Publishing House, New Delhi, 1985.

Census of India, 1971, 1981 and 1991, Punjab Series, Government of India. C.S.O., *Estimates of Net State Domestic Product*, Government of India, 1989.

E.S.O.,   Statistical Abstract of Punjab (various issues), Government of Punjab, Chandigarh.

Gill, S.S. (1990),   *Migrant Labour in Rural Punjab*, Mimeo, Department of Economics, Punjabi University, Patiala.

Jorgenson, D.W. (1961), "The Development of a Dual Economy", *Economic Journal,* June.

Karkal, Malini and Rajan, S. Irudaya (1991), "Progress in the Provision of Basic Human Needs in India 1961-1981", *Economic and Political Weekly*, February 23.

Kaur, Varinder (1993), *Economic Development and Changes in Distribution of Workforce in Punjab since 1971*, M.Phil. dissertation, Department of Economics, Punjabi University, Patiala.

Lewis, W.A. (1954), "Economic Development with Unlimited Supply of Labour", *Manchester School of Economic and Social Studies*, May.

Minhas, B.S. et. al. (1991), "Declining Incidence of Poverty in the 1980s: Evidence Vs. Artefacts", *Economic and Political Weekly,* February 23.

Morris D. Morris and Mcaplin, Michale B. (1979), *Measuring the Economic Condition of World's Poor*, Pergman Press, New York.

Ranis, G. and Fei, J.C.H. (1961), "A Theory of Economic Development", *American Economic Review*, No. 3.

Productivity, Competitiveness, and Export Growth in a Less Developed Economy: A Study of Indian Punjab

Lakhwinder Singh

Introduction

Total factor productivity, competitiveness, and economic growth are linked in complex ways. Industries that have, from whatever source, higher rates of growth of output per unit of factor input are usually considered to be increasing in competitiveness, since their costs, in terms of real factor inputs, are rising less fast than are those of their competitors. An intrinsic characteristic of productivity is that it grows at a different rate in different industries, thus creating, as it rises, a dynamic change of the industrial structure, accompanied by parallel changes in the structure of its comparative advantage.

The empirical studies on manufacturing industries of less developed countries are a clear evidence of stagnating or slow growth of productivity in import-substitution industrialization which seems to have reduced comparative advantage of these countries in an international market (Chenery et al, 1986). An alternative way to achieve faster and efficient industrialization obviously suggested is the outward-oriented industrialization through which the East Asian success story can be emulated. Analysts who have studied these countries closely (Pack, 1994) give credit to East Asian governments for making the miracles happen, not by getting out of the way of private entrepreneurs, but by actively nurturing and protecting infant industries. They have stressed how learning and purposive R&D activity drive economic growth through the creation of new products and improvement in the quality of existing ones. India's industrial development compared with East Asian countries is rather dismal (Ahluwalia, 1985). Keeping in view its massive size, differential performance of industrial sector of different regions/states is expected. Therefore, this paper examines the relation of growth, competitiveness and export performance of the industrial sector of Indian Punjab since the mid-sixties.

Overview of Punjab Economy

Punjab economy has undergone a varied pattern of growth and structural change since the mid-sixties. During the period 1965-90, the State Domestic Product (hereafter SDP) increased by 5.45 per cent per annum (Table 1). Punjab has emerged as the most developed state of the Indian Union in terms of per capita income. When economic development is measured in terms of life expectancy, infant mortality rate, literacy at the age of 15 and above and per capita income, it is ranked at number

2(only next to Kerala). Besides, the state has the lowest incidence of poverty among the major states of the country. The high and sustained rate of economic growth for several years has placed the state on a high pedestal so far as the level of economic development is concerned.This has been caused by a set of several complex factors and is accompanied by diverse changes in social and economic life of the society.

Table 1 Trends in net State Domestic Product at 1970-71 Prices (per cent per annum)

Sector	Relative Share		Growth Rates				
	1970	1990	65/66 to 90/91	65/66 to 74/75	75/76 to 90/91	75/76 to 84/85	85/86 to 90/91
Agriculture	58.37	47.94	4.65	3.85	5.16	4.13	4.76
Industry	08.78	18.81	7.96	7.05	7.69	6.33	7.16
Manufacturing	08.00	16.60	7.65	6.71	7.45	5.68	11.03
Reg. Manufacturing	03.95	09.02	8.55	5.70	9.22	7.71	9.57
Unreg. Manufacturing	04.05	07.58	6.87	7.69	5.69	4.01	10.28
Construction	06.53	02.81	2.16	1.63	1.47	1.86	3.43
Services	26.32	30.44	5.75	5.99	4.40	7.02	4.94
Total	100.00	100.00	5.45	4.94	5.10	5.17	5.11

Source: C.S.O., Estimates of State Domestic Product, New Delhi: GOI, Various Issues

The dynamics of fast growth of the state economy can be seen from the differential performance of different sectors. The agricultural production increased at an average annual rate of 4.65 per cent during the period 1965-90. While dividing the whole period into early green revolution (1965-74) and after, agricultural production increased at lower rate (3.85 per cent) in the first period compared with second period (5.16) that is, 1975-90.It is worth mentioning that the industrial sector of the state has grown at a faster rate as compared to the other sectors of the economy. The rate of growth was 7.96 per cent per annum during 196590.Decomposing the overall growth rate of different sectors into sub-period shows better performance of Punjab economy except for unregistered industrial sector, services and construction, where the growth rates have been slowed down.It can be seen from Table 1 that the performance of the economy significantly improved in the late eighties (the only exception being services sector), the impact of political turmoil on the growth of the economy visible in the early eighties notwithstanding.

The varying growth rates of agriculture, industry and services sectors have resulted in noticeable changes in their share in the SDP. For instance the share of agriculture sector dwindled from 58.37 per cent in 1970-71 to 47.94 per cent in

1990-91. This decline is the gain of industrial sector. It is significant to note that the role of non-agricultural income was dominant in the eighties compared with the early seventies when agricultural sector was prominent (58.37 per cent income was being generated in this sector). Labour force diversification across sectors has also shown almost similar but slower trends as have been experienced in the SDP. Despite the fast economic growth and diversification, Punjab economy has still a long way to go to develop infrastructure and basic industries sufficient to meet the increasing demands of a growing economy.

Economic prosperity in Punjab is mainly associated with the phenomenal growth of the agricultural sector since the mid-sixties, and its contribution to the SDP has been widely acknowledged. The industrial sector which has also grown at a fast rate and has improved its share substantially in the SDP (10 percentage points),has been characterised as being woefully inadequate and backward both by social scientists and political leadership. But the fact is that with the ushering in of the green revolution, agriculture and industrial growth have gone hand-in-hand. The growth and structural changes that have been taken place within the industrial sector since the mid-sixties are described in following section.

Growth and Structural Change in the Industrial sector of Punjab

On the eve of independence Punjab was relatively industrially backward. The position of the industrial sector further worsened when some parts of the territory of Punjab went to Pakistan as a result of partition and 90 per cent of the skilled labour force migrated. This led to the closure of 40 per cent of the working industrial units in the state of Punjab (Pandit,1985). After independence India embarked upon an ambitious programme of transforming its economy from a low-income agricultural to a well developed industrialized one.This strategy was based on massive public investment, especially in the industrial sector. But the industrial sector of Punjab was virtually by-passed so far as public investment was concerned and the private corporate sector did not come forward to the desired extent (Banerjee and Ghosh,1985). In this process the industrial economy of Punjab remained deficient in so far as the location of large-sized industrial units are concerned. Thus its industrial structure is mainly constituted of small and medium-sized industries.

The industrial sector of the state produced goods and services worth Rs.12,875 crores and provided employment to 9,16,000 workers constituting 9.35 per cent of total workforce in 1990. As described earlier, this sector has grown at a rate of 7.65 per cent per annum during the period 1965-66 to 1990-91 which is quite high by Indian standards (Table 1). When we split this sector into registered and unregistered manufacturing, the registered sector has grown at a higher rate (8.55 per cent) than that of the unregistered sector (6.87 per cent).The average rate of growth for such a long period can conceal many facts related to the short term. We have,therefore, divided the whole period into two sub-periods and then the second sub-period further into two sub-periods. The rate of growth for the first sub-period (1965-66 to 1974-75) was 6.71 per cent which was a little lower than the overall rate of growth. During this period Indian industry was under severe depression. India's industrial sector has picked up since the mid-seventies, though on 'luxury-led' model of growth (Chandrasekhar,1988). Unlike Indian industry, Punjab's industrial sector has grown at a much more rapid rate during 1975 to 1990 which is considered to be the period of turnaround in growth in Indian industry (Table 2). But during 1975-76 to 1984-85, there was a slowdown in the growth rate of Punjab industry mainly because of the slowdown of the agricultural growth in the same period. Another important reason was that the rural elite of Punjab were becoming quality conscious and their consumption pattern underwent a change. The resultant effect is a decline in the demand for goods produced by the small industrial sector (Dhar,1990). The impact of this kind of change can be seen in the falling share of the unregistered sector sharply after the mid-seventies (Singh,1992). The unregistered industrial sector has become the victim because of its linkages with the larger industrial sector of the state. Punjab has been going through a turmoil,since the early eighties which has further contributed to the decline of unregistered sector. The registered industrial sector, though, reached a higher orbit of growth (11.03 per cent) in the late eighties due to the following reasons. First, the agriculture sector has grown at higher rate,and has generated more demand for industrial goods. Second, the industrial entrepreneurs have learnt to survive in crisis. Technological progress supported by domestic R&D expenditure with a liberal import policy resulted into higher rate of growth.

Table 2: Growth Rates of Manufacturing - Punjab and India

Years	Punjab	India		
		(a)	(b)	(c)
1965/66 to 1974/75	7.65	3.7	4.3*	-
1975/76 to 1984/85	5.68	4.8	-	4.6**
1985/86 to 1990/91	11.03	-	-	6.7***

Where: a stands for Sandesars's (1992) estimates.
        b stands for Ahluwalia's (1985) estimates.
        c stands for Worlds Bank's (1992) estimates.
  * 1966/67 to 1979/80 ** 1970-80 *** 1980-91

The other important structural change which is taking place in the industrial economy of the state is that a tendency towards the establishment of large-sized units has set in the industrial sector is oligopolistic but paternalistic in nature. There is a pattern of ancillarisation where sub-contracting emerges to be a dominant mode between parent plant (large one) and ancillary (small sub-contracting) units. This pattern is found both in their traditional industries like hosiery and sports, and modern industries like bicycle, tractor, and electronics. Patronage to the ancillaries is provided both by the government as well as by the large units. There have been cases of workers becoming workshop/small unit owners and small units are becoming medium range, in the due course of time (Gill, 1991).

Productivity, Competitiveness and Export Growth

The impact of technological progress on reduction in the cost of production and raising the competitiveness of an economy in international market has been widely acknowledged in economic growth literature. Therefore, sustained higher rate of economic growth can only be achieved if the resources are being utilized efficiently. The question of optimization of growth potential through resource use pattern have been posed and empirically tested in the case of Punjab in 1983 (Dhesi and Ghuman,1983). This study brought out the disturbing fact that during the early green revolution period, the growth of the industrial sector in Punjab was characterised by inefficient use of resources. A more careful and comprehensive analysis of the factor use pattern (both aggregative and disaggregative) of industrial sector of Punjab covering the period 1967 to 1981 has shown that factor inputs have been used highly inefficiently (Singh,1985). The higher growth rate in this period was mainly associated with capital deepening which have resulted in high cost of production structure. Measuring technological progress in twenty-one three-digit census sector industries covering the period 1973-82, in another study(Singh,1990) reported however, differential performance of industries. Industries such as fertilizer and pesticides; agricultural machinery and parts; electrical apparatus, appliances and parts; and bicycle and cycle rickshaw and parts have shown a significantly positive growth in total factor productivity. The falling trend in total factor productivity has been noted in rest of the industries. Therefore, it was concluded that except a few industry groups, the manufacturing sector of Punjab is utilising employed resources inefficiently and resulted into a high unit cost of production. Keeping in view the findings of earlier studies and their limitations in terms of exploitation of data, Bhalla(1991) has computed the Solow residual for the factory sector as well as two-digit industries excluding electricity covering the period 1979-86. His study showed significant technological progress by this sector. In his own words, "these relationships seem to have undergone a radical change during the eighties". However, he has not attempted to seek out the factors which are responsible for reversing the earlier trends.

To allocate the growth of output among the contribution of capital and labour inputs and changes in productivity both for factory sector as a whole and two-digit factory sector industry groups, we have used a translog index of productivity growth. This index is the difference between the growth rate of output and of capital, and labour inputs. Weights are given by average shares of each input in the value of output. The rate of growth of output is the sum of the contributions of capital and labour inputs and the rate of productivity growth. The contribution of each input is the product of average value share of input and its growth rate. Tables 3 and 4 compare the average annual growth rate of output at aggregate and in each industry with the average annual contributions of each input and the rate of productivity growth. The combined contribution of capital and labour inputs is the predominant source of growth of output for the factory sector as a whole. It is significant to note here that combined contribution of factor input declined in the eighties and contribution of productivity growth has improved substantially. The factory sector as a whole includes both electricity and repair services which may have reduced the contribution of productivity growth to output. The notorious performance of public sector units especially in electricity is a well known phenomenon.

Table 3: Growth of Output, Inputs, Total Factor Productivity and Real Wages in Punjab's Factory Sector

	1967-90	1979-90
Growth of Value added	9.04	8.43
Contribution of		
(a) Capital input	6.07	4.64
(b) Labour input	2.43	1.90
Growth of TFP	0.54	1.89
Growth of Labour Productivity	3.74	-
Growth of Real Wages	3.02	

Higher growth of output of Punjab's factory sector is also accompanied by higher growth both in wages and labour productivity.However,with respect to unit labour cost, these effects tend to counteract each other.The matching rise of real average wages with productivity may be due to the labour legislations,higher level of skills and well organised labour force especially in electricity industry.However,the trade union movement is quite weak in other manufacturing industries (Bhangoo and Singh,1988). During the decade of eighties, due to Punjab turmoil, the trade union activities virtually halted because of an emergency kind of situation created by both the state and militant groups.

During the period 1979-90, the changes in productivity is a more important source of growth in ten two-digit industries than that of the factor inputs(Table 4). For rest of the seven manufacturing industries, factor inputs have contributed predominantly to output growth. Our overall conclusion is that the contribution of capital input predominate over labour growth in accounting for output growth in manufacturing industries. Continuously rising trend of productivity growth experienced by the manufacturing industries during the eighties was mainly due to state policy of technological upgradation, modernisation and liberal import of intermediate inputs.

It is known to us through economic theory that an increase in productivity translates into lower cost per unit of output, thus increasing the firm's or industry's ability to compete successfully in domestic and international markets. We have employed the primary measure of international competitiveness, that is, the increase in the ratio of exports to SDP. The share of manufacturing exports in SDP has increased to 3.81 per cent compared with 1.77 per cent in 1971-72 (Table 5). It is also significant to note here that the share of exports in the manufacturing value added is 24.45 per cent. This seems to be a better measure of improved performance in international market compared with share of exports in SDP because agriculture sector's contribution in SDP is still predominant. Therefore, it can be inferred that the industrial economy of Punjab is highly integrated with the international economy. Although commodity composition of exports have been diversified over the period, yet exports remain concentrated to few items like hosiery, bicycle, sports and machine tools (Table 6).

Table 4: Growth of Output and Contribution of Factor Inputs and Total Factor Productivity of Manufacturing Industries of Punjab (1979-90)

Ind. Code	Ind. Name	Value added	Inputs Capital	Labour	TFP
20-21	Food products	10.13	3.58	1.54	5.01
22	Beverages, tobacco and tobacco products	11.96	3.48	1.96	6.53
23	Cotton textiles	5.36	4.40	0.42	0.54
24	Wool, silk and synthetic fibre textiles	11.81	2.71	1.96	7.15
26	Textile products	14.71	9.67	3.05	1.98
27	Wood & wood products furniture & fixture	0.33	2.51	-8.60	6.42
28	Paper and paper products	21.08	-2.74	10.67	13.14
29	Leather and fur products	11.53	3.86	4.40	3.27
30	Rubber, plastic, petroleum and coal products	26.72	17.23	3.90	6.40
31	Chemical and chemical products	7.48	-12.76	1.90	18.33
32	Non metallic mineral products	5.71	-2.20	2.72	5.20
33	Basic metal and alloys industries	6.57	0.23	0.40	6.30
34	Metal products and parts	2.65	3.82	-0.13	-1.09
35	Machinery, machine tools and parts	5.11	0.56	0.38	4.17
36	Electrical machinery apparatus, appliances	11.86	8.83	2.66	0.37
37	Transport equipment and parts	12.59	3.31	2.13	7.14
38	Other manufacturing industries	9.33	3.32	-1.43	7.44

The relationship between productivity growth and export growth is a very close one. The industries which have significantly contributed to exports have also observed higher growth in productivity. A noteworthy feature of manufacturing industries of Punjab is that the mean output growth is found to be more correlated with productivity growth across industries. This implies that domestic competitiveness of the manufacturing have increased significantly over time.

Table 5: Share of Industrial Exports in State Domestic Product and Manufacturing Value added

Year	Per cent OF SDP	Per cent of manufacturing value added
1971-72	1.77	19.93
1975-76	2.51	22.92
1980-81	2.95	23.23
1985-86	2.57	18.39
1990-91	3.81	24.45

Table 6: Changes in the Composition of manufacturing Exports and Growth

Ind. Code	Name of Industry	1975-76	1990-91	Growth
20-21	Food products	4.93	2.19	-1.21
23	cotton textile	1.88	3.82	18.92
24	Wool, silk and synthetic fibre textiles	7.74	2.95	0.52
26	Textile products	37.24	37.77	11.19
29	Leather and fur products	0.37	3.90	12.89
30	Rubber, plastic, petroleum and coal products	0.26	1.80	3.64
34	Metal products and parts	3.97	4.14	-0.19
35	Machinery, machine tools and parts	0.75	0.81	6.88
36	Electrical machinery, apparatus and parts	5.28	4.52	13.48
37	Transport equipment and parts	26.89	10.02	3.54
38	Other manufacturing industries	6.62	25.44	14.64

Impact of Domestic R&D on Total Factor Productivity

Technological progress, analysed in the previous section, have been treated by the neoclassical theory as an exogenous process and mainly focused on capital accumulation as an endogenous source of output expansion. Recent studies on technological progress view innovation effort as a response to economic incentives (Romer, 1990; and Coe and Helpman, 1993). The innovation process have been treated by these studies as a by product of knowledge which results from cumulative R&D expenditure. Empirical evidence on cumulative domestic R&D shows that it is an important determinant of productivity and have supported the above mentioned progress in theory (Griliches, 1988). Furthermore, recent studies on fast growing economies like South Korea have also supported the argument that domestic capability to adapt and further develop technology is more important than external factors (Pack, 1994). However, external interaction of an economy through trade, direct foreign investment, and spillovers of external R&D are considered to be an important source of growth for a small open economy but domestic R&D is more important for large economies (Coe and Helpman, 1993).

In what follows an attempt has been made to examine factors that explain variations in total factor productivity. The variations in productivity growth have been explained and tested through the following regression equation:

$$LogTFP = a + b \, LogSD + c \, LogE + U$$

In this equation the elasticity of total factor productivity(TFP) with respect to the domestic R&D capital stock equals b while the elasticity of TFP with respect to exports is equal to c. Estimates of these elasticities obtained through OLS procedure are as follows:

$$LogTFP = -0.2023 + 0.1468 \, Log \, SD + 0.3473 \, LogE$$

$$F(2,9)=0.2418 \qquad DW=1.7118 \qquad R^2=0.8431$$

During the period 1979-90, the elasticity of TFP with respect to domestic R&D capital stock is positive which shows that recent technological progress in manufacturing industries of Punjab has been achieved through incurring both domestic institutional and in-house R&D by the government and the firms respectively. However, the elasticity of trade have shown a positive trend but is insignificant. Our result on the positive contribution of domestic R&D capital stock is also supported by a study examining the success of firm level in-house R&D expenditure on reduction of production cost for the bicycle industry of Punjab (Chadha and Dhawan, 1993).

The process of innovation described in theory are of two kinds. One emphasized the aspect of demand induced process (Schmokler, 1966) and the other stressed on technology opportunity and hence on quality and quantity of resources devoted to innovation (Freeman at al, 1982). Our results is a pointer towards the latter factor. However, the R&D expenditure is mainly adaptive in nature and successful adaptation happens to be based on local resources, expertise and inputs, which obviously resulted in lower costs and higher productivity. It has also been pointed out in a study (Chadha and Dhawan,1993) that large and medium-sized enterprises were more successful in adapting technology than smaller ones. The overall conclusion which emerges from the foregoing analysis of technological progress is that internal factors are more important than the external ones in the case of Punjab.

Conclusions and Policy Implications

Punjab's industrial sector has grown rapidly after the ushering in of the green revolution. However, industrial growth of the state does not match keeping in view its growing problems. The situation demands restructuring of the industrial pattern and a process which can help in resolving the structural problems of the existing model of growth.

Small and medium scale industry, based on the traditional organizational pattern,can not afford heavy in-house R&D expenditure. The need therefore, is to build up institutional R&D on the basis of a cooperative organizational pattern,which can provide not only a resource base for technology upgradation but also ensure the integration of the industrial units with these institutions.The resource endowment of the state has to be kept in mind while restructuring the industrial process. The new enterprises have to be based on local materials and local demands. This kind of industrialization will be able to generate both production and expenditure linkages in the state's economy. It is relevant to recognise here that Punjab can not be industrialized along conventional lines. Priority should be given for setting up of the sunrise industries which produce skill-intensive, high-tech and high value-added items. In these industries the human resource factor is an important input in production relative to physical resources.

While deciding about the location of new enterprises, priority should be given to rural areas and that too for sufficiently large-sized units. This is contrary to the suggestions of the Eighth Five Year Plan.The suggestion is relevant because the small scale industrial units in the state are not only unable to attract and absorb the labour being displaced from the agricultural sector, but also because of the financial and technological non-viability of many small-sized units. Large sized-enterprises are subject to enforcement of labour legislation and, therefore, provide attractive working conditions. The attractive working conditions and rural location of units will not only ensure the participation of the peasants and local labour but also save them from costly urban living conditions. This process will also enable realisation of the dream of converting farmers into part-time farmers on the Japanese pattern.

Beyond that, there is the whole question of the integration of agricultural surpluses to finance industrial growth. This question enables us to look at the need to restructure the organizational pattern of the industrial sector. It needs to be mentioned here that the existing organizational pattern of the industrial structure is incapable of building up linkages between the modern industrial sector and agricultural capital. Thus, it appears to us that the most suitable organizational setup is a cooperative one. Even if cooperatives had failed in the past, their vital place in development strategy requires that they be made to succeed in the future. The suggested cooperatives as an organizational pattern for industrial development have the capacity to integrate the modern industrial sector and the vast hinterland and they can set in motion the dynamic process of the overall increase of income, consumption, employment and production as the core of self-sustaining economic growth.

REFERENCES

Ahluwalia, I. J. (1985) *Industrial Growth in India: Stagnation since the Mid-Sixties*, New Delhi: Oxford University Press.

Banerjee, D. and A. Ghosh (1985) 'Indian Planning and Regional Disparities', in A.K. Bagchi (ed.) *Economy, Society and Polity*, Calcutta: Oxford University Press.

Bhalla, G.S. (1991)'Agricultural Growth and Industrial Development: A Case Study of Punjab', New Delhi: ISID (mimeo).

Bhangoo, K.S. and U.C. Singh (1987) 'Trade Unionism in Punjab: A Decadal Analysis', Paper Presented in the *National Seminar on Trade Unions and Industrial Relations*, Allahabad: MONIRBU.

Chadha, V. and S. Dhawan (1993) 'Technology Adaptation by Cycle Industry', *The Tribune*, June 3.

Chanderasekhar, C.P. (1988) 'Aspects of Growth and Structural Change in Indian Industry', *Economic and Political Weekly*, Annual Number.

Chenery, H. et al. (1986) *Industrialization and Growth: A Comparative Study*, New York: Oxford University Press.

Coe, D.T. and E. Helpman (1993) 'International R&D Spillovers', *NBER* Working Paper No.4444.

Dhar, P.N. (1990) *Constraints on Growth: Reflections on Indian Experience*, New Delhi: Oxford University Press.

Dhesi, A.S. and B.S. Ghuman (1983) 'Productivity Trends and Factor Substitutability in the Manufacturing Sector in Punjab: Implications for Planning', *PSE Economic Analyst*, vol.III & IV.

Freeman, C. et al. (1982) *Unemployment and Technical Innovation*, London: Frances Pinter.

Gill, S.S. (1991) 'Development Experience of a Fast Growing Region in a Slow Growing Backward Economy', Patiala: Dept. of Economics, Punjabi University (mimeo).

Griliches, Zvi (1988) 'Productivity Puzzles and R&D: Another Non Explanation', *Journal of Economic Perspectives*, 2.

Pack, H. (1994)   'Endogenous Growth Theory: Intellectual Appeal and Empirical Shortcomings', *Journal of Economic Perspectives*, 1, Winter.

Pandit, M.L. (1985) *Industrial Development in Punjab and Haryana*, Delhi: B.R. Pub. Corporation.

Romer, P.M. (1990) 'Endogenous Technical Change', *Journal of Political Economy*, 98.

Sandesara, J.C. (1992) *Industrial Policy Planning 1947-1991*, New Delhi: Sage Publications.

Schmookler, J. (1966) *Invention and Economic Growth*, Cambridge: Harvard University Press.

Singh, L. (1985)   *Productivity Trends and Factor Substitutability in Punjab Industry*, Patiala: Punjabi University, unpublished M.Phil. thesis.

Singh, L. (1990)   *Industrial Growth in Punjab: An Analysis of Growth of Productivity and Structure of Wages*, Patiala: Punjabi University, unpublished Ph.D Dissertation.

Singh, L. (1992)   'Aspects of Growth and Structural Change in Industrial Sector of Punjab', *Man and Development*, June.

The Image of Punjabi Community in Hindi Literature:
Post 1984 scenario

Chaman Lal

The image of Punjabi community has come out differently in Hindi, Punjabi and other languages literature after 1984. The social events of 1984 in Punjab, Delhi and elsewhere in the country have been such that they made writers perceive Punjab reality and image of Punjabi community in different fashion than they used to perceive it prior to 1984.

Punjab was perceived as a fertile land and its people easy going and hard-working. This was reflected in creative literature as well as in social science writing. During the British period, a large number of Punjabis, particularly Sikhs, were attracted to the Army and Fauji has a different character in writings related to Punjab. Thus in Chander Dhar Sharma Guleri's immemorable story 'Usne Kaha Tha': ('It was her wish'), Lehna Singh Fauji dies in the war while keeping the word given to her adolescent age love, who was now married to his office.

Amongst Punjabis, Sikhs have been depicted more colourfully, whether these are Balwant Singh's novels on Punjabi life or many other writings. Krishana Sobti has focused on Punjabi women's zeal and lust for life and her women characters belong to all Punjabi communities be it Sikhs, Muslims or Hindus. Thus published in 1980, her 'Zindaginama' presents a panoramic scene of pre-partition Punjabi rural society.

The partition of Punjab in 1947 and tragic human suffering related to this event was also depicted in Punjabi, Hindi, Urdu, and English literature, but the characteristics of Punjabi community were usual except that they could also be led by communal frenzy and could kill and torture each other in frightening scale. Centuries old prejudices played an extended role in organising this frenzy.

The year 1984 again proved to be a traumatic year for Punjabi life and all people. Though the event culminated into flash point in 1984 in the form of 'Operation Blue Star' in Golden Temple Amritsar, 'Operation Woodrose' in rural Punjab and Anti-Sikh riots in Delhi and elsewhere. The background of these events were in progress since 1978, with the Akali-Nirankari clash in Amritsar, then during the Asiad 1982, misbehaviour with Sikhs in Haryana, killings in 1983, gathering of arms and ammunition by various groups at religious places, the Machiavellian policies of major political parties of Punjab, notably Akalis and Congress(I), ultimately resulted in Operation Blue Star, assassination of Prime Minister Smt. Indira Gandhi followed by massacre of innocent Sikhs in Delhi and elsewhere in the country. George Orwell's '1984' was proving to be to true at least in context of India, (later Bhopal Gas Tragedy also struck in the same year).

Thus, the year 1984 proved to be a sort of watershed not only in Punjab but in Indian society as a whole and the writers of almost all languages including that of Punjabi, were rather confused, of course pained, at the sharp turn of events. Myths about Punjabi life and its community were shattered and to reconstruct reality from a given social situation was a rather difficult task for the writers of any language, yet writers did recreate reality of Punjabi life and its community in various languages.

It was but natural that the bulk of such writings, would have been produced in Punjabi language. So it was and continues to be so till date. There have been a number of novels, short stories, plays, poems and other writings in Punjabi, trying to recapture the ongoing movement of society, whether negative or positive. Paash and Patar have proved to be outstanding in poetry, Waryam Sandhu in short story.

In Hindi also, here have been a number of novels, short stories and plays and poems written on the theme of changing patterns in Punjabi life. There have been novels like 'Veh Mehra Chehra' (Thats my face [identity]) by Tejinder, 'Jalta Hua Gulab' (The Burning Rose') by Tarsem Gujral, Gurbachan Singh's 'Sabhe Ghat Ram Bole'(The God Speaks in each soul) etc.

The number of short stories is quite high - Bhisham Sahni's "Zhutputa" and "Nausikhua", Giri Raj Kishore's "Lalghar", Swayam Prakash's `Kya Tumne Koi Sardar Bhikhari Dekha Hai", Arun Prakash's "Bhaiya Express", Amrik Singh Deep's "Kharkoo" and number of other stories deal with this changed situation. Bhisham Sahni's latest short play "Muavze" also depicts the post 1984 Delhi reality. Udai Prakash, Gorakh Pandey, Rajesh Joshi, Laltu, Vinod Kumar Shukl, Vishnu Naagar, Biren Dangwal and so many other poets are affected by Punjab's suffering and it comes out very sensitively in few of their poems.

Thus one can see that writer's sensitivity does depend on whatever situation he or she is faced with. Hindi writers have watched the massacre of innocent Sikhs from close quarters, the killing of innocent Punjabi Hindus or Sikhs by terrorists or security forces, other forms of torture have also been felt and observed by writers and depicted in their writings as per their talent.

The complex part of this whole scenario is the changed inter-personal relations of the communities and even the popular perception about communities have undergone sea-change during this period. Hindus and Sikhs were perceived almost as single unit as Punjabi community outside Punjab. Hindus and Muslims or Sikhs and Muslims, though Punjabis were not perceived as a single unit, even when their language was the same. This has been due to centuries old prejudices, against each other at religious level which were further strengthened and exploited during British Colonial rule in India. During the 1947 massacres, Hindus and Sikhs were on one side and Muslims on the other.

And the Sikh community was projected as a martial race by Britishers, as brave, patriotic and saviour of Hindu religion by Hindu religious leaders and dare-devil romantics by popular sayings. The Sikhs were also projected as somewhat idiotics by joke makers. In totality, somewhat super-human touch was given to their identity, which was strengthened by their own religious ballads etc. This identity came into crisis during this whole period and writers except the very realist ones, were also at a loss to understand and grasp the changing pattern of Punjabi identity in Indian society. The myths were being shattered, new myths were not being created, the reality was very crude and also complex and the challenge before writers was rather tough. There are few writers in any language, who come up equal to such challenges. But it is satisfying to see Hindi creative writing coming up to expectations, as we shall see in the next part of this paper. Tejinder's novel "Veh Mera Chehra" ("That my Face" [Identity]) does project the complex reality of the given time in a very sensitive manner, so does few other writings.

There have been number of poems in Hindi creating such immemorable characters like Ram Singh by Biren Dangwal, Sucha Singh Driver by Udai Prakash etc. In post eighty-four Hindi poetry also, there are flashes of Punjab reality as we see in Kumar Vikal's poem 'Identification':

>'The blood which is flowing on the road
>smell it
>And try to identify
>Whether it is of a Hindu or of a Muslim
>or of some Sikh or of a Christian
>of a sister or of a brother.'[1]

The innocent blood has flown so much in Punjab of all its people that the poet cries in pain over this totally unwanted bloodshed. How the easy going Punjabi community got divided into religious symbols, the poet says loudly in his poem 'Cry':

>'Whether I am killed by a 'Kirpan' (Sword)
>or by a 'Trishul' (The weapon used by Hindu Communalists)
>or by a Police bullet
>But before I die
>I will cry
>It is religion
>which teaches enmity with each other
>To Change the man into
>'Kirpan' or 'Trishul'[2]

In the same way Laltu puts the question 'whether sleep is also Hindu or Sikh in his poem of same the title. How the identity of Punjabi community has undergone change in the minds of common people outside Punjab, is brought out very sensitively and sharply in Vishnu Naagar's poem 'Harminder Singh': I introduce myself

> Sir, I am called Harminder Singh
> I am a Sikh
> 'from where'
> They ask
> from Delhi I tell
> Earlier I used to be in Trilokpuri
> now I live in Tilak Vihar'³

Here is the irony of the poem. It is a direct reference to the 1984 Anti-Sikh riots of Delhi. The innocent Sikhs in Trilokpuri and so many other localities of Delhi were massacred, maimed, tortured by criminal gangs patronised by their political bosses. After the massacre, those who survived were shifted as refugees to Tilak Vihar in refugee camps. And the 'brave' 'patriotic' 'outspoken', community was reduced to 'insulted and humiliated' meek ones like 'Harminder Singh'.

Punjab which was considered to be a friendly place and its people warm and affectionate ones, now creates uneasy feelings among non-Punjabis. Rajesh Joshi in his poem 'Anxiousness' depicts this situation:

> I never thought even in my dream
> that a day will come in life
> A childhood friend will invite me
> and I will not be able to go
> shall be uneasy to go to Punjab
> Which enemy of mine is sitting in Punjab
> I do not even have any property in Punjab
> why should anyone harm me in Punjab.⁴

Here again the certain image of Punjabi community seems to be giving place to an uncertain one. Vinod Kumar Shukal's poem 'In any village of Punjab' does reflect deep faith about Punjabi community, although the change in its character has also been underlined, but the poet perceives this change as a shortlived one and the real character to be a sustainable factor. The recent year seems to be proving the poet's faith as true. The poem begin on a simple note:

> In any village of Punjab
> someone keeps on coming
> The killers never came before
> they also came
> *ultimately they will not come,*
> friends do come

> friends will come again
> The dear ones come
> And they will come[5]

In short stories, Bhisham Sahni's 'Zhutputa' (The Dawn) focuses on the aftermath of a November 1984 riot scene in Delhi. Here the traditional image of Punjabi or more particularly the Sikh community has been relived in spite of all odds. At a milk booth, there is a long queue of people waiting for the milk to come, but all the drivers of Delhi Milk Scheme are Sikhs, and they are not likely to move out of their homes. But the Sikh driver proves his dare-devil do good image by driving the milk van for the sake of children- 'Baba, the children have to take milk! I told my mind, whatever may happen. Let the milk reach the people.'[6] In his other story 'Nausikhua'(The Apprentice) Bhisham Sahni exposes the contradictions in the Sikh terrorist movement itself. Thus the two conflicting images of Punjabi Sikh community emerge in the story. One, that of a fundamentalist and terrorist, who is cruel even to his fellow follower in the movement, another that of traditionally liberal devout Sikh youth, who can not kill an innocent person and is killed by his mentors.

Bhisham Sahni's play 'Muavze' focuses on corrupt official machinery and also on some person's weakness for gold or money. Hence one can see that Sikh or Punjabi Community is no different from any other community.

Giriraj Kishore's story 'Lalghar' (The Red House) deals with the situation on a psychological plane. What has been popularly called the 'Hurt Sikh Psyche' in the media, has been creatively constructed in his story 'Lalghar'. Vineet has come from America in India to see his parents. His friend in America Parminder has asked him to see his parents as well. He has told a lot of things to him about his family, his father being a Gandhite, having a white house. But when Vineet reaches in Parminder's parents house, everything is topsy-turvy. The house is not white, it is red. He is not welcomed there and is almost insulted by Parminder's father who is in a western suit and talking in chaste English. What Parminder told Vineet about his family, its traditions, the year 1984 has destroyed it all. The elder brother of Parminder has been killed, so is his Hindu friend and fiance of his sister who was trying to save him. Parminder has not been informed of the sufferings of the family. Sodhi Sahib, Parminder's father has undergone such psychological trauma that he lost faith in everything he believed earlier.

Giriraj Kishore's story deals with the crisis a certain community faces at a given time in social history . He has somewhat dramatised the agonising experience of the family while providing justification to the transformation of his characters, but actually in the process his main character Sodhi Sahib is rather loosing his identity and not changing.

Arun Prakash's story 'Bhaiya Express' became very popular due to its human concerns. 'Bhaiya Express' is a story of inter-community economic and human relationship. A large number of agricultural labourers have been coming to Punjab every year during the harvest period. Punjabi peasantry need their labour and they need the better wages in Punjab, so the mutually beneficial relationship. While they have to work very hard in Punjab, they are given much more humane treatment by Punjabi peasants than by their own landlords. They are treated as almost a part of family by Punjabi peasant women. But the terrorist movement cast its shadows over their relationship also. There were massacres of Bihari migrant labour at one or two places, but largely this relationship continued although somewhat strained by the fear of terrorists. The trains coming from Bihar to Punjab have become popularly known as 'Bhaiyya Express' as Bihari Labour is called 'Bhaiyyas' in Punjab. The story is sensitive in its depiction of tensions, fears and inter-community relations, yet it confirms the traditional friendly image of Punjabi community, particularly of rural Punjabi character, which is friendly, helpful and warm towards even strangers. Bishun Dev from Bihar, who was working near border village of Attari was killed by terrorists, his brother Ram Dev has come in his search. Going through fearful experience, he does reach his destination and is helped by the village Sarpanch. He even spends his curfew days with them and is paid Bishun Dev's wages in full. This is a touching story at the human level.

Vijay Kant's 'Koi Mehfooz Nahi' (No one is safe) though also deals with the theme of Bihari labour - Punjabi peasant relationship, is a different story altogether. It relates the inter-community relationship to class relationships. At that level Bihari Zamindar and Punjabi Zamindar come at one level and Bihari Labour and Punjabi Labour share another level of human relationship. The Bihari moneylender makes the labourers go to Punjab and never allows them to get out of his clutches, Phul Chand comes to Punjab and is killed, he is son-in-law of seventy year old Master Tileshwar Sharma, who is a class conscious person. Phul Chand has joined leftists in Punjab to fight against communal terrorists and Master Tileshwar knows that the real enemy of working class of Bihar are not Punjabis but the moneylenders and landlords in Bihar itself. The regional identities in this story are transformed into class identities. Phul Chand, a Bihari is a martyr for secular Punjabis as well. Vijay Kant, like Kumar Vikal, declares that the religion itself has terrorist moorings, it showed its terrorism in 1947 and now showing in 1987.

Amrik Singh Deep's story 'Kharkoo' (The Militant) brings out the common fears created by terrorists of Punjab. The Sikh youth with flowing beards, yellow turbans, though may be most gentle, do scare common middle class people, particularly at night time. In the story this situation is depicted in a somewhat tragi-comic manner. In some city locality, the 'Jagrata' (Whole Night religious singing) is going on when four Sikh youth with flowing beards, yellow turbans and hands in pockets enter the place, everyone including Sikhs are scared, number of incidents regarding bravery of Mohalla Sikhs are recollected by the characters present there. The youth come and pay tribute and the gathering there is relieved. This story, though simple, brings out the identity of Panjabi community into a sharp focus. The terrorist movement did change other than Sikh's perception of Sikhs in general, in the same way, the excesses did change Sikh's perception of other communities as well. But the stories like 'Kharkoo' try to restore the balance and traditional perception of communities about each other.

'Veh Mera Chehra' ('Thats my face' [Identity]) by Tejinder is the most important literary writing in Hindi to delineate the post 1984 problem of identity crisis of Punjabis settled outside Punjab. This is somewhat of an autobiographical novel by Tejinder who was born in Punjab, brought up and educated in Madhya Pradesh, where he is presently working.

Sardar Shaminder Singh is the central character of this novel, who is working as an editor in the Social Welfare department of Madhya Pradesh Government based in Bhopal. His colleagues in the office are all non-Punjabis - Nandita, Pandya, Singh and Mehtaji. The novel begins with the depiction of typical atmosphere of 'gapshap' in our offices and the table talk shifts immediately to Punjab. The novel was first published in 1990 and is focused on post 1984 social scenario. What is 'Tankhaiya' Shaminder is asked by his colleagues. Shaminder is himself not aware of many such words, which came into vogue in those days -'Hukamnama', 'Karseva', 'Ghallughara', 'Sarbat Khalsa' etc. - yet he was expected to know these, as he was a Sikh. Shaminder reacts - 'why these bloodies are after me and Punjab. They have no concern with the basic issues of life'.[7]

There are typical Khushwant Singh jokes repeated in the office, but for Shaminder Singh, the situation is an existential one. Though with his office colleagues and many people around, he has excellent relations. He himself is a thoroughly secular minded person. He considers himself part of Madhya Pradesh society just like any other person but the social milieu around him does not allow him to enjoy the feeling of 'natural part of that society.' The milieu around keeps on making him feel a 'different person'. Just because he has a beard and a turban on his head, his identity becomes different. What is his identity then?

Shaminder recollects his childhood. His father has migrated from Kapurthala in Punjab, where he was a clerk, to Kanker in Bastar district of Madhya Pradesh, to try his luck as Truck owner and Jungle contractor. Earlier Shaminder's grand father had migrated from Lahore to Kapurthala, due to partition. Shaminder's grandfather is a Hindu and he shaves daily, yet he knows Gurbani, more than Shaminder or many bearded Sikhs. Shaminder's father migrated trusting his friend Gurdeep, from whom he is disillusioned after a little time. Shaminder's grandfather, a retired teacher was never in favour of migrating to Kanker, knowing well the consequences of migration, yet when his son desires to return to Kapurthala, he opposes by saying that one should try to get stable in life at some place and he settles down where he gets his two sons and a daughter educated. They later shift to Raipur, where Shaminder during his college education, gets the practical training of Journalism and later gets his present job in Bhopal, by the time, the traumatic year of 1984 has stung their lives.

Shaminder has a first and only friend in Kanker, namely, Kiran with whom he shared the best of his childhood. Both of them used to venture out in Jungle, caves and mysterious places around Kanker. Shaminder's beard and headgear used to give him different look from other school children. In common perception, the Sikhs are brave people and Kiran asks Shaminder in one situation 'what yaar, you are so scared even being a Sardar?'

In replying to Kiran's query, Shaminder or rather his creator, Tejinder reflects beautifully on the folk-beliefs and constructed perceptions regarding communities. Tejinder reflects:

> "This, I could neither understood then nor till date I can understand that what things one can do and what things one can not do being a Sardar. After all, every person carries a kind of personal fear, which has nothing to do with the caste or, community, in which one was born. And why fear alone? All the abstract things are personal only. In fact, your past is not that, about which you have listened only proud stories, but is that, which you yourself see or listen.[8] (p. 14-15)

The question before the author is that what is it which not only binds one with his past, but it establishes one's identity also.

No other author among contemporary Hindi or Punjabi writers is as conscious about the question of community identity, as is Tejinder. In fact, Tejinder in his novel, struggles throughout with this question. What kind of childhood 'Samskaras' Shaminder acquires. He gets the best of Gurbani teachings, from his grand father and mother, yet he is not particularly community conscious of his identity. The deepest impression, he gets in his childhood is that of an Adivasi woman who saves him from a frenzied male buffalo in Jungle. Shaminder is a school going child when this incident happened. The kind of security he felt in those moments leaves an indelible impression on his personality for the rest of his life and in his later insecure post-1984 life, he remembers Sukhna Bai, the Adivasi woman. He feels "How life was truly simple and spontaneous among those tribals of Kanker. They never asked that Shaminder, why you are having such long hair on your head? Shaminder why you have worn an iron ring in your wrist? And Shaminder, why twelve are struck to you people?"[9]

For Shaminder, Kanker was as homely and secure place, as Lahore was for Shaminder's grand parents and parents. In spite of being born and brought up in Sikh family, knowing Panjabi language and Gurbani, he could not relate himself to Punjab or just the community. For him, Kanker, Raipur and Bhopal were just such places, where he has his identity. What was his identity? A Panjabi, a Sikh or an Indian or a Madhya Pradesh Wallah? Shaminder could not narrow down his personality to these regional or religious identities. He just wanted to feel spontaneous like tribals of Bastar. He wanted to feel and live like a natural, warm, affectionate human being, feeling equally about his fellow human beings, without super-imposing religious or regional or community identities over them. There are interesting incidents in his childhood. They have heard a lot of prejudicial and negative things about Muslims in context of 1947 partition from their parents, yet when they go to see a Muslim teacher in a very curious mood, they are unarmed by the teacher's simplicity and affection.

In fact, Tejinder is no less worried and pained by the innocent killings at the hands of terrorists in Punjab. Equally he is agonised by the innocent Sikhs being killed in the 1984 anti-Sikh riots. He is an admirer of Satya Pal Dang like leftists in Punjab, who were and are in the forefront in struggle against terrorist violence, as well as against state repression. Shaminder is his own representation in the novel, 'Veh Mera Chehra' but the social milieu around does not understand his concerns and sometimes, he is insulted in public places like coffee houses, being abused as 'A Khalistani' etc. But his colleagues in the office and many more people do understand and respect him which gives him strength.

Tejinder exposes the selfish and unscrupulous people of communal overtones of any community. Thus Balbir Singh Rai in Raipur, tries to gobble up people's donations for the riot victims of 1984, for his personal ends. He makes use of Gurdwara politics for his business interests. He keeps government officials as well as Khalistanis, in good cheer, but tries to trap Shaminder by lodging false complaints as being 'close to Khalistanis', whereas Shaminder is thoroughly opposed to Khalistanis. In one situation Shaminder's father gives up and decides to return to Punjab. Shaminder is also in conflict, but his colleague's affection and an unknown auto-rikshaw driver saving him after an accident makes him firm in his resolve not to leave the place of his identity:

> 'All the doubts and confusion of my mind were clear in one shock. I believed that if this battle is fought on the street tomorrow, I am not alone....I will tell Papa, if you people have to go to Punjab go. I shall stay here only.
> I did not remember the face of Autowallah. His face was mingled into the light with the sunrise. I thought I shall once again try to locate his face, getting up tomorrow early in the morning'[10]

Tejinder is a poet himself and in his dedication poem he has dedicated this novel to the innocent people who were killed by the cruel murderers. He has also Kumar Vikals's poem 'Myth' to convey the message that he is coming out of his shell to find a secure place for existence.

In the process of creating this novel, Tejinder has shattered many myths, such as Sikhs being a martial race or a specially brave people. Every group of people, according to their life conditions, develop certain characteristics in their group personality. During the phase of terrorist killings or state repression, how many people are able to resist?' This is the collective strength of a class or a society, which is really able to resist oppression.

The social events in 1984 have been tragic and traumatic. The events in 1947 were even more tragic and traumatic. Compared to European literature and art created in response to first and second world wars the creative Indian literary response (which includes Pakistan's literary response also) to the human suffering was inadequate, to say the least. The literary response to the social events of 1984, also, has not been highly satisfactory, still some of the creative works do focus on the human predicament. In this sense, Tejinder's 'Veh Mera Chehra' can be termed as an outstanding novel.

With the passage of time a more objective assessment of the reality may be made by creative writers of Punjabi and Hindi. More mature literary responses may then come up and those writings may prove to be more insightful and illuminating. Till then, the essential humanist concern of the writers, reflected in novels like 'Veh Mera Chehra' are welcome to keep the faith in creativity alive. The image of the Panjabi community as been reflected in post 1984 Hindi literature is realist at one level and somewhat idealist at another.

NOTES

1.   Vikal, Kumar, 'Pehchaan', *Nirupma Dutt, Main Bahut Udaas Hoon*, 1993, 1st ed., Panchkula, Aadhaar Prakashan, p. 28.
2.   Ibid , p. 34.
3.   Naagar, Vishnu, 'Harminder Singh', *Bache Pita aaur Maa*, 1992, 1st ed., Delhi, Apurv Prakashan, p. 56.
4.   Joshi, Rajesh, 'Ghabraaht', *Nepathy main Hansi*, 1994, 1st ed., Delhi, Rajkamal Prakashan, p. 45.
5.   Shukal, Vinod Kumar, 'Punjab Ke Kisi Bhi Gaon mein', *Sab Kuchh Hona Bacha Rahega*, 1992, 1st ed., Delhi, Rajkamal, p. 79.
6.   Sahni, Bhisham, 'Jhutpata', *Pali*, 1989, 1st ed., Delhi, Rajkamal, p. 56.
7.   Tejinder, *Veh Mera Chehra*, 1990, 1st ed., Delhi, National Publishing House, p. 6.
8.   Ibid, p. 14-15.
9.   Ibid, p. 26.
10.   Ibid, p. 157.

1988 Elections in the Punjab (Pakistan):
A Retrospective Analysis

Ikram Ali Malik

The Elections of 1988 were the third general elections in Pakistan and fourth in the Punjab. After independence, the first elections to the Punjab Assembly were held from 10 to 20 March 1951, followed by those in 1970 and 1977. The other elections were conducted on indirect and restricted franchise while those of 1985 were held without participation of political parties. The elections of 1988 were made possible due to General Zia-ul-Haq's death on 17 August 1988. Though, a month earlier he had announced date of the elections, he had expressed his intention to hold them on party-less basis.[1] The Acting President, Ghulam Ishaq Khan and the Chief of Army Staff General Aslam Beg declared their determination to maintain the date of the elections.[2] They also braved the demands of caretaker chief ministers of Punjab and Sindh and a few federal ministers for postponement due to September floods in Punjab and eruption of violence in Sindh.[3] The Supreme Court in its judgment on 2 October, directed the Government to allow participation of political parties and to expeditiously fix the date for provincial elections.[4] Though upholding the Lahore high Court's ruling for declaring Zia-ul-Haq's dissolution of assemblies on 29 May 1988, as illegal, it did not reinstate Junejo Government and the assemblies.[5] Earlier it had also condemned Martial Law regime's Political Parties Registration Act. The ground was thus laid for election of the National Assembly on 16 and that of Provincial assemblies on 19 November 1988.

Punjab enjoys a pre-eminent position in national politics and economy. According to the census of 1981, it had a population of 47,292,441 while the number of its registered voters in October 1987 was 28,850,735. The latter included 28,251,525 Muslim and 599,210 non-Muslim voters.[6] It was represented by 115 Muslim and women's seats in the National Assembly while Punjab assembly consisted of 240 Muslim, 16 non-Muslim and 12 women members. The non-Muslims were represented by 10 members in the National Assembly. The Muslim seats were allocated to districts according to their population and the election was held on the basis of simple majority and single-member territorial constituency.[7] For non-Muslim members in national assembly the whole of Pakistan excluding FATA (Federally Administered Tribal Areas) and those in the Punjab assembly, the whole of province formed one constituency with as many seats as were allocated to them in the national and provincial assemblies.[8] The seats reserved for women were filled through indirect election by members of the national and provincial assemblies respectively. Besides these, women could also contest from general seats.

The Punjab had been experiencing rapid progress in urban and rural economy, over the preceding 10 to 15 years, resulting in the growth of a politically conscious and articulate middle class. The employment of a large number of Pakistanis in Arab countries also considerably contributed towards this process. Zia-ul-Haq's confidence-building measures encouraged industrialists to invest their capital in development of urban land and agro-based industries. A new class consisting of traders, craftsmen, transporters and middle men also grew up in rural areas. The Punjab had a higher literacy ratio i.e. 27.42%, over 26% for the whole country, while in the urban areas it was 46.72% for men and 36.72% for women. It had been more peaceful and possessed a greater cultural harmony than other provinces. Zia-ul-Haq's efforts at depoliticization and successive non-party elections for local bodies created a growing desire for power among traders, biraderis and religious groups.[9] The traditional feudal families had also benefited and adequately regained their position during the elections of 1985.[10] All these forces provided the background and affected political conditions leading to the elections of 1988.

With the announcement of Supreme Court's judgement on 2 October 1988, the political parties began hectic efforts for electoral alliances and election campaign. Such alliances had been formed earlier, the most notable being Pakistan National Alliance against Zulfiqar Ali Bhutto's government in 1977. In 1981 the M.R.D (Movement for the Restoration of Democracy), consisting of nine parties, had been established for the revival of 1973 constitution. After Zia-ul-Haq's death it had lost its vitality due to the lukewarm attitude particularly of Pakistan People's Party. Though efforts were made for its revitalization, yet the component groups could not agree on the distribution of electoral seats, with the result that People's Party decided to pull out and contest the elections from its own platform.[11] Its co-chairperson, Mrs. Nusrat Bhutto, however, held talks with Maulana Fazal-ur-Rehman, Secretary General of Jamiat-i-Ulema-i-Islam (Fazal-ur-Rehman group), Sher Baz Mazari of Pakistan National Party, Malik Mohammid Qasim, President of Muslim League (Qasim group) and Nawab Mohammad Akbar Bugti of Balochistan, for electoral understanding.[12] On 6 October, eight right-wing parties formed Islami Jamhoori Ittehad (Islamic Democratic Alliance). It included Pakistan Muslim League (Fida group), National People's Party (Fakhar Imam group), Jamiat-i-ulema-i-Islam (Darkhawasti group), Markazi Jamiat Ahl-i-Hadith, Nizam-i-Mustafa group, Jamiat-ul-Mashaikh.[13] Four days later, it was also joined by Jamaat-i-Islami.[14] On 6 October Maulana Shah Ahmed Noorani, President of the Muslim League (Junejo group) and Air Marshal (Retd) Asghar Khan of Tehrik-i-Istaqlal established Pakistan Peoples' Alliance for five years. The same day six left-wing parties i.e. Quami Mahaaz-i-Azadi, Mazdoor Kissan Party, Watan Dost Inqilabi Party, Communist Party, Awami Fikri Mahaz and Socialist Party announced the formation of Left and Democratic Front. It was followed by National Democratic Alliance of Muslim League (Zehri group), Pakistan Muslim Mahaaz, Tehrik-i-Tameer-i-Pakistan, Pakistan Liberal Party and Jeeway Pakistan.[16] The leaders of Pakistan Muslim League which had been divided into two main camps i.e. Junejo and Fida groups, after Zia-ul-Haq's action on 29 May, also tried to re-unite themselves. Their efforts bore fruit when Mohammed Khan Junejo announced to join the Islamic Democratic Alliance on 14 October.[17] He tried to maintain an understanding with Pakistan People's Alliance but could not succeed due to differences over allocation of seats.[18] Thus the main contesting parties or groups were Pakistan People's Party, Islamic Democratic Alliance and the Pakistan People's Alliance. Though some components held different views on policy matters and other issues they joined for fear of the other groups coming into power.[19]

Nearly all the political parties issued formal manifestos or intent of reforms for the country. These were drafted without consideration of available means.[20] The People's Party in its fifty-page document proposed to strictly implement all previous land reforms, distribute state lands to farmers, restrict public control only to heavy industries, improve labour and tax laws, increase expenditure on education, remove all discriminatory laws against women and minorities, revive the 1973 constitution and give freedom of artistic expression.[21] It did not lay stress on socialism or its old slogan of "roti, kapra and makaan" i.e. bread, clothing and shelter. In foreign policy, it favoured implementation of Geneva Accords on Afghanistan and normalization of relations with India.[22] The Islamic Democratic Alliance laid stress on Islamization of laws, deregulation of economy, safeguarding of women's rights, inexpensive and expeditious justice, equality of economic opportunities and proprietary rights of lands for occupants of more than forty years. Its leaders particularly Nawaz Sharif, care-taker Chief Minister of Punjab, promised to obliterate terrorism, unemployment and exploitation. They also assured to provide food, shelter and employment to everyone. Though favouring the Geneva Accords, the Alliance pledged full support to Afghan Jehad and to the liberation of Kashmir.[23] The other right wing parties like National People's Party, Tehrik-i-Istaqlal and Jamiat-i-Ulema-i-Pakistan also announced similar programmes with slight modifications. For example, the Tehrik proposed limitation of land-holding to 25 acres, fixed taxes on traders and the establishment of confederation with Bangladesh. The Jamiat called for enforcement of the Islamic system, distribution of all state lands to peasants and compulsory military training and service for all able-bodied persons. The left wing parties like Awami National Party and Pakistan National Party, on the other hand, supported greater provincial autonomy, further land reforms, nationalization of important industries, establishment of Saraiki province in southern Punjab and friendly relations with neighbouring countries.[24]

These manifestos were mere formalities or paper work and were generally not dilated upon during the election campaign.[25] Firstly, they were issued late and thus failed to generate public attention. Secondly, the candidates mostly talked in general and audience-pleasing terms, spending more time on the demerits of opponents rather than on the good points of their own programme.[26] The political parties also expressed opinions on different issues confronting the country. All except the left wing parties, though condemning Zia-ul-Haq's measures, called for further

Islamization. Similarly, they all supported, with slight variations, the restoration of the 1973 constitution and the annulment of the Eighth Amendment. They, particularly the left wing parties, agreed upon allocation of only four subjects to the centre. They also called for tax reforms and increased expenditure on public welfare. Some, particularly the Islamic Alliance, promised to provide allowance for the unemployed. The nuclear programme also came under heated discussion during the election campaign. The Islamic Alliance accused the PPP leadership of offering, under American pressure, to allow foreign inspection of the Kahuta plant. It also expressed its determination to increase the nuclear capability for defence purposes. The PPP vehemently refuted the charge and pledged to protect the programme at all costs. The other right-wing parties like Jamaat-i-Islami, Jamiat-i-Ulema-i-Pakistan, National People's Party and Tehrik-i-Istaqlal also supported further development of the programme whereas the left wing parties called for an end to the nuclear race between India and Pakistan.[27]

The People's Party and Islamic Alliance both had to face considerable difficulties in allocation of party tickets. Several members of Pakistan Muslim League and defunct assemblies joined People's Party in order to reassure their place in the new assemblies. They also included members of feudal families who had regained their strength in the 1985 elections. The party workers who had suffered imprisonment and whips during the Martial Law regime, known as Korra (whip) group as against the Pajero group of the former, also applied for nomination as party candidates.[28] According to Mrs Nusrat Bhutto the party received as many as eighteen thousand applications from all over the country.[29] It had, therefore, to face an uphill task particularly in Punjab. Both the groups exerted utmost pressure and at times created tumultuous scenes during meetings of the Parliamentary Board. The result was a compromise list in which the Pajero group gained ascendency.[30] On 14 October, the party announced 99 candidates for 115 Punjab seats in the National Assembly and two days later, the list of candidates for the Punjab assembly. The former included fifty nine landholders and ten businessmen and industrialists, while thirty belonged to the middle class. The same ratio was visible in nominations for the provincial assembly.[31] The party leaders explained that they had decided on merit and nominated only those candidates who were most likely to succeed. This, however, did not satisfy a very large number of workers who reacted strongly and blamed the leadership for having surrendered and sold the party to the opportunists. This dampened their enthusiasm as they had to compromise their ideological convictions to support and work for the new entrants and Zia-ul-Haq's former companions. This also cast its shadow and prevented to produce any issues during the election campaign.[32]

The Islamic Alliance announced its candidates a week after the PPP. Its biggest problem was to conciliate the demands of its nine component parties. It was also hindered by the efforts of Mohammed Khan Junejo to forge a bigger group with Pakistan People's Alliance. The result was the delayed and discordant list of its candidates for Punjab seats in the National Assembly and members of the provincial assembly. Nearly every party, particularly the Junejo group and Jamiat-i-Islam (Darkhawasti group) complained of diminished representation.[33] Several workers of Pakistan Muslim League protested against the ascendency of Jamaat-i-Islami.[34] Many applicants, when denied of party ticket, refused to withdraw and decided to contest as Independents.[35] A lady from Jhang and an industrial tycoon from Faisalabad each demanded a nomination from two national assembly constituencies. After rejection, the lady contested as an independent from both the areas while the tycoon participated as Alliance candidate in one and as independent in the other constituency.[36] Due to the delay in announcements many candidates failed to get the party symbol printed against their names on the ballot paper while in several areas more than one candidates claimed to hold party nomination.[37] The situation was further confounded by later adjustments particularly on the eve of provincial elections.[38]

The Pakistan People's Alliance announced 129 names for the Punjab assembly on 20 October. For several constituencies various leaders were empowered to nominate candidates.[39] Despite its high sounding principles it embraced dissidents from any party.[40] In fact, this lack of conviction and ethics afflicted the whole body politics, perhaps more so in the Punjab. Many persons changed parties without the slightest pricking and were also accepted by the "graced" party without hesitation.[41] Quite a few members of Junejo cabinet joined People's Party after its dissolution on 29 May. A former Junejo minister from Sahiwal was described as his right-hand man and a few days later as Benazir Bhutto's brother on wall-chalkings.[43] For many politicians particularly from the rural Punjab, power posed as the biggest attraction.[44] Another interesting feature was their representation in different political parties. If the father was in the Muslim League, one of his sons, brothers or other close relative would be in the People's Party, so that the power was retained whichever party was elected. That is why a few Punjab families have been dominating politics under the garb of one or the other political party.

The election campaign was conducted through processions, public meetings, rallies, door-to-door canvassing, posters, banners, hoardings and newspaper advertisements. The two major political parties held mammoth public meetings preceded by long processions. Besides, the candidates also arranged big and small meetings within their constituencies. Both the People's Party and Islamic Alliance held their finale in Lahore with miles-long processions and public addresses on the last two days of the campaign.[46] Their leaders also toured and addressed public meetings in various towns. Mrs. Benazir Bhutto undertook a train journey and addressed big gatherings on route from Karachi to Rawalpindi. Similarly the leaders of Islamic Alliance headed by Qazi Hussain Ahmed, the Amir of Jamaat-I-Islami travelled from Karachi to Lahore by train and thereafter to Rawalpindi by road. The Alliance also organized cycle rallies in order to popularize their election symbol. The Pakistan People's Alliance held public meetings but these were not very largely attended.

The political parties and candidates also published millions of posters and hand bills, which were distributed and pasted on every available space. They also hoisted party flags in similar numbers and erected big hoardings on thoroughfares. According to one estimate nearly ten million rupees were spent daily in Lahore on the election campaign. Beside other effects, it resulted in price hikes and dearth of paper, cloth and other related items.[47] Most of the candidates believed that they were caught in a vicious circle by the induction of capitalists and smugglers, and that such expenditure was necessary to impress voters and demoralize opponents. They thus far exceeded and violated the limits fixed by the Election Commission.[49]

The election was generally marked by a lacklustre public enthusiasm.[50] Though a large numbers of people participated in processions and meetings, they were less motivated by any ideology or issues other than to listen to the 'ladies' and other speakers. The candidates also generally played with words and spent more time on discrediting the opponents.[51] The Islamic Alliance presented the PPP as a party opposed to Islam, country and democracy.[52] Its leaders accused Benazir for having influenced America to stop supply of F-16 and her late father for dismembering the country.[53] They also tried to vilify the Bhutto ladies by printing their objectionable pictures.[54] They also claimed that Islam did not permit a lady to become a head of the state. The PPP on the other hand, presented the Alliance as a group of reactionaries and as members of Zia-ul-Haq's team. It recounted acts of repression and brutality perpetrated against students, women and general masses under the Martial Law regime. It also blamed Zia-ul-Haq for political regression, Siachen debacle and failure to acquire the French reprocessing plant.[56] Thus in several Punjab's constituencies, the contest, irrespective of candidates' character and background, was described as a battle between Islam and secularism, true and disloyal Pakistanis or between continuity and change.[57] The Pakistan People's Alliance on the other hand condemned both the People's Party and the Islamic Alliance as opportunists and exploiters.[58] The Islamic Alliance vehemently propagated against Benazir's alleged statement in Sahiwal that she would not accept a Punjabi prime-minister. On the eve of provincial elections it also called upon the people of Punjab to protect 'their own government'.[60] The candidates, while on tour, generally promised to improve the physical conditions of their constituencies. The Punjab care-taker government provided, for this purpose, large development grants to its candidates. It also announced several amenities for workers, landless farmers and occupants of *kachi abadies* (unauthorised ghettoes).[62] Similarly *Zakat* and *Jahez*, (dowry) funds were used to influence the voters. The rich, in addition, spent their own money or used influence to instal Sui gas connections, repair streets and other means of public health. Some also distributed sewing machines and necessities of life to endear themselves to the poor and the needy.[64] These elections, therefore in many areas, assumed the character of those for local bodies.[65]

The elections for national and provincial assemblies were conducted in a peaceful and orderly manner. The Government and Election Commission had made elaborate arrangements for this purpose. The judiciary and army units were inducted to supervise and assist local administration in case of an emergency. Every voter was obliged to present their National identity card in order to prevent bogus voting. Except for a few minor clashes, both the days passed off peacefully and without complaints of planned riggings. The turn-out of voters varied in different localities and towns. In affluent areas, it was generally slow in the morning but picked up pace in the afternoon Voters of lower and middle classes came out in gay dresses and generally in larger numbers.[66] The turn-out for National assembly was 46.49% while in most of the constituencies it varied between 40 and 45%. It was the highest i.e. 57.96% in NA 45 (Jhelum) followed by 57.88% and 57.59% in NA 56 and 55 (district Bhakkar). It was lowest i.e. 34-35% in Rahim Yar Khan and Dera Ghazi Khan districts.[67] The turn-out for the Punjab assembly was slightly lower i.e. 45.82%. It was again highest i.e 63 % in far the flung district of Bhakkar.[68] Close contests were fought in several constituencies of Lahore, Rawalpindi, Multan, Okara, Gujranwala, Gujart, Chakwal, Sargodha, Faisalabad, and Mianwali.[69] Nawaz Sharif contested from four constituencies i.e. two each for National and Punjab assemblies. General (Retd) Tikka Khan the Secretary General of People's Party contested against Sheikh Rashid Ahmad from NA 38 of Rawalpindi while Begum Abida Hussan fought against two religious scholars i.e. Maulana Haq Nawaz Jhangvi and Maulana Rehmat Ullah from Jhang. In some areas, close relatives were pitched against each other notably in Muzaffargarh and Dera Ghazi Khan Districts.[70] Thirteen candidates contested from more than one constituency, as a result of which eight successful candidates had to vacate National and five their Punjab assembly seats.[71]

The People's Party secured 62 seats for National Assembly with 39.18% of the polled votes, whereas it had won 62 seats with 41.7% votes in 1970. The Islamic Democratic Alliance whose components got eleven seats and 13.4% votes in 1970 considerably improved with 45 seats and 37.50% votes. The Pakistan People's Alliance received only three seats (including two from Mianwali) while its component, Jamiat-i-Ulema-i-Pakistan, had alone achieved four seats with 4.9% popular votes in 1970. The number of independent members increased from 5 in 1970 to 11 in 1988. The highest popular swing compared to 1970 in favour of PPP was 29.3 % in Dera Ghazi Khan and Rajanpur followed by 17% in Bahawalpur and Attock and 16.9% in Rahim Yar Khan, while it registered 21% fall in Sialkot. Except for the odd result in Sialkot, all these areas comprised a belt of low to medium prosperity. The moderate swing (6 to 15%) in favour of PPP was in Jhang (13.7%) Mianwali and Bhakkar (11.6%) and Gujrat (14.3%) but it decreased by 12.6% in Rawalpindi, 11.1% in Faisalabad and Toba Tek Singh, 9.1% in Jhelum and Chakwal 8.3% in Lahore and Qasur and 8.15% in Sahiwal and Okara. In the areas of middle to high prosperity i.e. Multan, Vehari, Khanewal, Sargodha and Khushab districts it registered increase of less than 5% while it fell by the same ratio in Gujranwala, Sheikhupura, Muzaffaragarh, Layyah and Bahawalnagar. The Islamic Democratic Alliance considerably improved its position in sixteen of the twenty nine districts, the highest by 30.1% in Dera Ghazi Khan, followed by Jhang (29.3%) and Sialkot (25.9%). Its notable losses were in Attock, (35.45%) Mianwali and Bhakkar (24.50%) while it fell by 10.7% in Gujrat, 7.4% in Bahawalnagar, 4.9% in Sargodha and Khushab and 1.5% in Jhelum and Chakwal. In big cities like Lahore, Faisalabad and Multan (with the exception of Rawalpindi), the PP got 71% seats. It secured 69% of the seats in small and medium sized industrial belt comprising Gujrat, Gujranwala and Sheikuprara. It won all the seats in Attock and Sheikhupura, 86% seats in Multan, 75% in Lahore and Faislabad, 66% in Gujranwala and Dera Ghazi Khan and 60% in Jhang districts but only 33% seats in the affluent rural heartland of Sahiwal, Sargodha, Vehari, Okara and Toba Tek Singh.

The Islamic Alliance, on the other hand, got all the seats in Chakwal, 86% seats in Sahiwal, 66% in Khanewal and Vehari and 60% in Sargodha districts thus showing a clear cleavage between rural and urban bases of the followers of the two main political contestants. In the Punjab assembly, the Islamic Alliance improved its position by winning 108 seats with 34.98% of the votes cast while PPP got 94 seats with 34.17% votes. The Pakistan People's Alliance and Pakistan Democratic Party received two seats each followed by Jamiat-i-Ulema- Islam (Fazalur Rehman) and National People's Party (Khar group) with one seat each. Thirty-four independent candidates were returned successfully bagging 22.85% of the votes thus becoming the third largest power in the Punjab assembly. As compared to the figures for the National assembly the popular vote for the People's Party fell in Chakwal, Jhelum, Bhakkar, Jhang, Mianwali, Faisalabad, Qasur, Layyah, Dera Ghazi Khan, Vehari and Sheikhupura while it gained only in Bahawalnagar district. The Islamic Alliance, on the other hand, improved its vote bank in Jhelum, Sargodha, Qasur, Muzaffargarh and Layyah districts.[73] The election of 1988 put the country back on its democratic path. These also gave enough testimony to the political forbearance and realistic approach of the Punjab's people. The long period of Martial law rule had failed, despite its best efforts, to obliterate their political ideas and likings. They did not succumb to feudal pressure, personality cult or religious fanaticism. They were also not moved by character-assassination and tall talk by the candidates. The results exposed various myths regarding *pirs* and *waderas* and cut several parties down to their actual size. The split decision for Central and Punjab assembly also showed their political realism and distaste of uncontrolled power. A new class of traders and industrialists emerged who challenged the traditional ascendency of the landed aristocracy. Adversely affected by economic policies of the first PPP government, they organized and considerably strengthened their position during the elections of local bodies and those of 1985. This, to a large extent, explains the emergence of Nawaz Sharif as leader of the Islamic Democratic Alliance.[74] The election of independent candidates though augmenting badly for political stability, was the result of peculiar conditions and confusion proceeding selection by political parties. The Punjab's Administration, judiciary and law-enforcing agencies also showed their admirable capability in organizing and holding the elections in a peaceful and orderly manner. The people of the Punjab thus by voting Benazir Bhutto to the centre and Nawaz Sharif to the Punjab assembly showed their liking for young, liberal and energetic administration.

REFERENCES

1. *Jang* (Urdu daily) Lahore, 14 August 1988.
2. *Jang* 2, 4, 11 October 1988; *The Muslim* (daily) Islamabad, 11 October, 1988.
3. *Jang* 7 October 1988; *The Muslim* 11 October and 2 November 1988.
4. *Jang* 3, 5 October 1988.
5. *Jang* 6 October 1988.
6. *Report on the General Elections*, 1988, vol II, Islamabad.
7. *Report on the General Elections*, 1988, vol I, Islamabad, pp.55-57.
8. *Ibid* p.207.
9. 'Provincial Profile: Punjab - The Price of Prosperity', *The Herald (monthly) Election Special 88*, Karachi, pp.50-52; Daud, Zafar Nadeem: *A Study of National Assembly Constituency No.85 in 1988 Elections* (Urdu), Unpublished M.A. dissertation in Political Science, Punjab University, Lahore, 1988, pp. 347-353.
10. 'The Ruling Class', *The Herald Election Special 88*, p.112.
11. *Jang* 7, 8, 10 October 1988.
12. *Jang* 8 October 1988.
13. *Jang* 7 October 1988.
14. *Jang* 11 October 1988.
15. *Jang* 9 October 1988.
16. *Jang* 11 October 1988.
17. *Jang* 15 October 1988.
18. *Jang* 15, 19 October 1988.
19. Rasul B., Rais: 'Pakistan in 1988: From Command to Conciliation Politics', *Asian Survey*, Vol XXIX, No. 2, February 1989, p.202.
20. *Jang* 7 November 1988.
21. 'Parties', *The Herald Election Special 88*, pp.14-15.
22. 'Issues', *The Herald Election Special 88*, p.26.
23. *Jang* 28 October and 1, 5, 6, November 1988; *The Muslim* 2 November 1988; 'Issues', *The Herald Election Special 88*, p.26.
24. 'Parties', *The Herald Election Special 88*, pp.14-21, 26.
25. Kausar, Naheed: 'Elections of 1985, 1988 and 1990: A Study of Gujrat District' (Urdu), Unpublished M.A. dissertation, Political Science, Punjab University, Lahore, 1990, pp.114-115.
26. Rasul, B. Rais: *op. cit.*, p.203; Sabuhi, Sameena: *Elections of 1985 1988 & 1990 - A Study of Faisalabad District*, Unpublished M.A. dissertation, Political Science, Punjab University, Lahore, 1990, p.97.
27. *Jang* 2,1, 31 October and 13, 6, 13, 14 November 1988; 'Issues', *The Herald Election Special 88*, pp.26-31.
28. Ismail, Tariq: *Election 88* (Urdu) Lahore, 1989, pp.36-41; 'The Ruling Class', *The Herald Election Special 88*, p.112.
29. Ismail, Tariq: *op. cit.*, p.42.
30. 'The Ruling Class', *The Herald Election Special 88*, p.112.
31. *Jang* 15, 16 October 1988.
32. 'Lahore Campaign Diary', *The Muslim* 2 November 1988; Kardar, Shahid: 'Is PPP Making a Strategic Error?', *The Muslim* 3 November 1989.
33. *Jang* 15-19, 21, 24 October 1988; *The Herald Election Special 88*, p.112.

34. 'Bureau Report and Lahore Campaign Diary', *The Muslim* 2 November 1988; Ismail, Tariq: *op. cit.,* p.42.
35. *Jang* 20 October 1988; Ismail, Tariq: *op. cit.,* pp. 121-122, 144-145, 175-176.
36. Ismail, Tariq: *op. cit.,* pp.135, 151-153.
37. *Ibid* pp.102, 114-115; *Jang* 21 October 1988.
38. Farooq, Umar: 'What the IJI Did to Win Punjab Polls', *The View Point* (Weekly), Lahore, 24 November 1988.
39. *Jang* 21 October 1988.
40. Ismail, Tariq: *op. cit.,* pp.97, 105-106, 119.
41. Kardar, Shahid: *op. cit.*
42. Ismail, Tariq: *op. cit.,* pp.36-41, 256-257; *Jang* 15 November 1988.
43. Ismail, Tariq: *op. cit.,* p.276.
44. Kausar, Naheed: *op.cit.,* p.116.
45. Eirabi, Ghani: 'Democracy Hijacked by Feudal Families', *The Muslim* 5 November 1988.
46. *Jang,* 13-15 November 1988.
47. *Jang* 22, 30 October 1988; Bangash, Naushina: *General Elections of 1985, 1988, 1990 in Sargodha District: An Estimate* (Urdu) M.A. dissertation Political Science, Punjab University, Lahore, 1991, p.94.
48. Kausar, Naheed: *op. cit.,* pp.131, 134, 233; *Jang* 9 November 1988.
49. Jabeen, Farhat: 'Election Process in Chakwal 1970-1990' (Urdu) Unpublished M.A. dissertation Political Science, Punjab University, Lahore, pp.97-98; Kausar, Naheed: *op. cit.,* p.131.
50. Akbar, S: 'Why is Election so Soulless', *The Muslim* 2 November 1988.
51. Kausar Naheed: *op. cit.,* pp.117-119, 121; Jabeen, Farhat: *op. cit.,* p.92; Daud, Zafar Nadeem: *op. cit.,* p.80.
52. *Jang* 1, 2, 7, 9, 12 November 1988; *The Muslim* 2 November 1988.
53. *Jang* 4, 12, 14 November 1988.
54. Daud, Zafar Nadeem: *op. cit.,* pp.79, 92.
55. *The Muslim* 2, 3 November 1988.
56. *Jang* 3, 12 November 1988.
57. *Jang* 2 November 1988.
58. *Jang* 4, 5 November 1988; *The Muslim* 4 November 1988.
59. *Jang* 30 October 1988.
60. *Jang* 19 November 1988.
61. Kausar, Naheed: *op. cit.,* pp.131-132; Sabuhi Sameena: *op. cit.,* pp. 62, 101-102, 111.
62. *The Muslim* 2 November 1988.
63. *Jang* 6, 7 November 1988.
64. *Jang* 2 November; Sabuhi, Sameena: *op. cit.,* pp.101-102.
65. Rehman, I.A.: 'Elections: The Verdict of History', *The Herald Election Special 88,* p.7; Kausar, Naheed: *op. cit.,* pp.131-132; Sabuhi, Sameena: *op. cit.,* pp.101-102.
66. *The Dawn* (daily) Karachi; *The Muslim* 17 November 1988.
67. *Report on the General Elections 1988* Vol II, pp.103-110.
68. *Ibid* pp. 221-235.
69. *Report on the General Elections 1988* Vol III, pp.13-46, 77-167.
70. 'District Profile and Families', *The Herald Election Special 88,* pp.79-117.
71. *Report on the General Elections 1988,* Vol I, p.245.
72. 'The Swinging Punjab', *The Herald,* December 1988, pp.67-69; *Report on the General Election 1988* Vol III, pp.13-46.
73. *Report on the General Elections 1988* Vol II, pp.74-88, 172-193; *The Muslim* 21 November 1988.
74. Ahmed, Aqil: 'Polls: Some Old Myths Destroyed, *The Dawn,* Karachi, 6 Dec. 1988.

Jawaharlal Nehru and the Punjab

Tejwant S. Gill

Just a mention of the Punjab in the context of Jawahar Lal Nehru's policies and programmes before and after independence brings to mind a relationship that was intricate from the very beginning. As becomes evident from the corpus[1] of his writings speeches, interviews and statements, Nehru began to reflect on the Punjab from the twenties onward. These reflections show that religious composition of the people along with its political complexion, was the primary concern of Nehru. For regarding religion as coextensive with politics, their denotation was progressive to begin with. Their connotation could not be so in the absence of other factors i.e. class, gender, common sense and good sense.

No wonder the ambiguity between their denotative and connotative aspects got embedded in the very origin of Nehru's reflections. He did not feel the urge to ponder over the nature and culture of the Punjab while acclaiming it as fertile land inhabited by brave and virile people. This acclaim did not reckon with what the earlier epithets *Panch-nad* in the ancient Indian classics or *pentapotamia* in the ancient Greek manuscripts and *panj-aab* in the Persian chronicles evoked with regard to its natural habitus. This also did not reckon with Nehru's historiography, the poetic paradigm of which was nurtured upon male-female or lover-beloved syndrome. For example, the male-female aspect of this syndrome impelled him to write about India as nobility-incarnate with a "strong and serene face-strong and yet calm and determined, that ancient face which is ever young and vibrant." In the same strain, it was the lover-beloved aspect of this syndrome that led him to glorify the service of the motherland as "a unique experience... such an experience as though full of turmoils and hardships is good for a nation."[2]

Nehru's reflections on the Punjab were in fact occasioned by another paradigm of his historiography. Being ideological, he was impelled to take note of the diversity marking the unity of the country. It was under the burden of this impulse that he sought to relate the problems of the people to the economic, social, political and religious factors of their life. Literacy, planning, industrialisation and socialism were the measures which he suggested for their growth as against communalism, parochialism and linguism which kept them underdeveloped and backward. The second paradigm owed its inception to this impulse.

These two paradigms operated in converging parallelism in Nehru's mind when he reflected upon India as a civilisational unity. It was usually the first paradigm that transported him for heralding and glorifying her achievements in the fields of spirituality, literature and culture. Drawn to her poverty at the present historical juncture, he employed the second paradigm to frame policies and programmes for ameliorating the condition of the vast multitude of her people. Impelled to describe the natural beauty of his native land i.e. Kashmir, he invariably took recourse to the poetic means of the first paradigm. Through these means he would evoke the protuberances, curvatures and apertures of its mountainous region as if it were identical with the female body. While reflecting upon other regions of India particularly Bengal and the Punjab which nurtured feelings of identity and self-identity, he found only the second paradigm relevant for his purpose.

Under the burden of this paradigm, Nehru found three religious communities marking the composition of the Punjabi people. They were the Muslims, the Hindus and the Sikhs in order of percentage. Nehru felt that with the largest percentage though, the Muslims were not the addressees whom as an addressor he could address his message. They were not even the recipients whom as a speaker he could have the disposition to forward his discourse. To all intents and purposes, his address or discourse sought to exclude them as the Other though not with the rigour that the post-structuralist/ post-modernist dispensation holds veritable now. For without any involvement of the sort, the Muslims could formally be his listeners. The large-scale killing of the Muslims particularly in the erstwhile Patiala state in the aftermath of the partition did trouble him a lot. The expression that he gave to his troubled state of mind was also agonising. Its significance at that juncture was only gestural or gesticulative however. In face of the large-scale killing of the Hindus and the Sikhs in the Western part, deferral was its only alternative.

The exclusion of the Muslims as the addressees of his message and the recipients of his discourse, was valid because Nehru felt that they aligned themselves politically either with a feudal party as the *ithaad* party under the leadership of Sir Sikander Hyat Khan, Sir Sunder Singh Majithia and Sir Chotu Ram etc. or a communal organisation as the Muslim League led by the cohorts of Muhammed Ali Jinnah. This provoked his ire so much that to guarantee their separation from the Hindus and the Sikhs, he started approving the partition of the country that he had earlier opposed with vehemence. The rationale that he provided was that for the health and survival of the body, it is advisable to amputate the diseased or the paralytic limb. The use of disease imagery that he employed in this regard in the writings, statements, speeches and interviews included in the second to fifth volumes of *The Selected Works* in the second series is evident enough. On the basis of this evidence, he thus expostulated his consent to the partition of the country: "We agreed because we felt that India's political and social life was being undermined and poisoned by continuous inner conflict and we wanted to put an end to this so that people may consider the questions facing us dispassionately".[3] That this sought to invert the norms of the paradigm drawing sustenance from the male-female or lover-beloved syndrome, did not visibly exasperate him. He treated the Hindus of the Punjab as the addressees for whom his address was of significance or the recipients for whom his discourse carried meaning. They were addressees or recipients of the passive sort. This was albeit his position till the time of the partition, the rationale for which he drew from the suppression to which they in the course of history were subjected by the Muslim invaders. Though their invasions made the Hindus aware of the Islamic message of equality and fraternity, they were so caste ridden that it elicited no positive response from them. As Nehru recorded in The *Discovery of India*, the new approach forwarded by Islam "produced powerful psychological reactions among the people and filled them with bitterness." He was constrained further to remark, "There was no objection to a new religion but there was strong objection to anything which forcibly interfered with and upset their way of life."[4]

The Sikhs at this juncture were the fittest people to whom in the active sense of the word Nehru wanted to be the addressees for his message and the recipients of his discourse. So they remained till the partition of the country. Nehru first came into close contact with them when as an observer of the 'Guru Ka Bagh morcha', he was arrested at Jaitu in 1923. During his short internment he prepared a statement which he proposed to read in his self-defence in the court at Nabha. The text of the proposed statement is available in a volume of the first series of *The Selected Works*. It is an eloquent expression of Nehru's admiration for the Sikhs, their indomitable courage and selfless sacrifice. In its concluding paragraph he rejoiced that he was being tried for a cause that "the Sikhs had made their own." He marvelled at "the courage and sacrifice of the Sikhs" and wished for an opportunity to show his "deep admiration for them by some form of service". Now when the opportunity was there he hoped to prove worthy of "their high tradition and fine courage".[5] To impart a proper climax to his enthusiastic admiration, he ended his statement with the traditional salutation of 'Sat Sri Akal' which signifies the Sikhs's faith in the invincibility of truth and its praxis.

The event convinced Nehru of the need to bring into the national fold the religious morcha launched by the Sikhs under the hegemony of the Akalis. It was at his suggestion that a publicity-cell was set up at Amritsar for this purpose. He recommended the names of A.T. Gidwani and K.M. Pannikar for conducting the affairs of the publicity-cell. Their reports bore testimony to the fact that the basic hindrance in the way of the Sikhs' espousal of the national cause under the leadership of the Congress Party was the strain that prevailed between the Hindus and the Sikhs.

Nehru's perception of the communal strain revealed to him the negative feature of the Sikh-Hindu relationship. He realised that the Sikhs were obdurate and had no generous word or gesture for people of the other community. This perception of the obduracy of the Sikhs was fair enough but the historical reasons for the Sikhs adopting such an attitude were not articulated anywhere in his writings. He did not take adequate note of the fact that in the 18th and 19th centuries the Sikhs had waged relentless struggle both against the Delhi Sultanate and the Persian/Afghan invaders. This relentless struggle bore fruit in the form of Maharaja Ranjit Singh's kingdom. It was for the first time that the Punjab felt itself as a sovereign entity. For all the open-endedness claimed by history, this was perhaps the last time as well for Punjab's sovereignty to show itself. This sovereignty also laid claim to the fact that the Muslims and the Hindus comprising 90 percent of the population accepted the political hegemony of the Sikhs. Likewise the Sikhs had no compunction in consenting to their cultural supremacy.

In his *The Glimpses of World History*, Nehru had words of praise, for Maharaja Ranjit Singh and his achievements. To his engaged mind Ranjit Singh's kingdom was "a great Sikh state" that "weakened and began to break up soon after his death". Ruefully recollecting that it was not possible even for the later Mughals to suppress the Sikhs when they were a hunted minority group he commented that this was illustrated by the old maxim: "one rises in adversity and falls after a success is attained".[6] By the time he came to write *The Discovery of India* his mind had got reflective enough. In this new state of mind he found Ranjit Singh's kingdom "a marginal state not affective in the real struggle for supremacy against the British."[7] Both these observations are profound but they do not encompass the whole problematics of the Sikh kingdom and the traumatic impact of its end on the Sikh psyche. Rather than dialectical and historical, these observations entailed a positivistic and empirical perception.

For all the defining and redefining involved, he did not articulate how this traumatic impact resulted in a sort of disorientation for the Sikhs. Howsoever vague, he had an inkling of this disorientation. That is why he felt that Sikh nationalism that arose from the end of the 19th century was only a 'sectional nationalism' working for a more distinct and separate existence. At the same time its negative aspect was offset by what he viewed positive in it i.e. "an amazing exhibition of courage and endurance."[8] Thus an element of criticism, albeit a mild one, was added to his enthusiastic admiration for the Sikhs. As compared to this criticism, it was condemnation, though compassionate, that he reserved for the Hindus at this historical juncture. In the second volume of the first series, he recorded the bitterness that the Hindus had invariably nurtured for the Muslims and the Sikhs. Characterising it as an essential feature of the Hindu psyche, he found that "this bitterness of the Hindu against the Sikh and the Muslim" was chiefly due to "the realisation of his utter weakness and humiliation." The irony of the situation was that this bitterness, instead of urging him to better himself or make himself stronger, turned to "hatred and curses."

That this criticism did not get the better of Nehru's admiration for the Sikhs was proved by the deep regard that he had for their organising capacity. As compared to the Hindus and Muslims, the Sikhs formed a minority, marginal in number to the multitude of the two majorities. All the same he found them invulnerable not because the Hindus and the Muslims were considerate but because the Sikhs were well-organised and even ready "to defend themselves from unrighteous attacks." He felt that the fissure in the Hindu-Sikh relations had deprived the Congress "of much of the good of the Akali civil disobedience." Since the Akali civil disobedience was something to be emulated so he wanted this fissure to end. He found that both the communities wanted this undesirable divide to go but nothing could be done because "each was afraid of lowering its prestige by taking the first step."[9]

The organising capacity of the Sikhs he thought, could be useful both at the national and the international level. The national purpose could be served by bringing the morcha launched by the Sikhs under the hegemony of the Akalis into the broad framework of the *satyagraha* espoused and initiated by the Congress Party. To serve the international purpose however, it was desirable to associate the Sikhs with the movement against imperialism. In the third volume of the first series there is a letter by Nehru to the organiser of 'The Sikh League' presumably S. Mangal Singh Gill suggesting, "it will suit the Sikh League better to become an associate body...of the League against Imperialism." He conveyed this information to V. Chattopadhyaya who was then the most important Indian working for that organisation. At the same time Nehru expressed the fear that the leaders concerned were "hardly likely to pay much attention" to the matter because they seemed "to have developed a very strong communal outlook."[10]

For all his scepticism, Nehru cherished the hope that the Sikhs would advocate the cause of anti-fascism at the international level. That he had no such hope from the Hindus and Muslims, is evident from the double spectre of fascism that he found lurking over India an the eve of the partition. In the first volume of *The Selected Works* in the second series, he confirmed the growth of fascist tendencies amongst the Hindus and the Muslims. It was his conviction that "the two-pronged Indian fascism threatened to wipe out the proud culture and civilisation" of the country.

Regarding them as two opposing forces, he believed that the components of this "two-pronged Indian fascism" mutually contributed to the growth of each other. Placed at equi-distance in theoretical perspectives they did not provoke him to confront them in an equal measure. It was the Muslim fascism under the leadership of the Muslim League that in the first instance he was led to oppose after the formation of the Interim Government. He believed that "the best manner in which the existing situation" could be improved was "by educating the Muslim peasantry against the poisonous communal propaganda of the League."

However he failed to embark on this ideological programme on account of communal riots in several parts of the country. He felt any compromise with the Muslim League as impossible because of his considered view that its leaders had "intellectual and mental affinity with senior Government officials like Governors." In the event, "mass slaughter, arson, burning of human beings, rape, abduction on a

large scale, forcible conversions and all manner of other things" extremely exasperated
him. At the most, he could hold out such a general threat as "if anybody has mistaken
my silence, he does not know me" or give a sermon in appreciation of "courage and
strength" along with the advice that they had to be "directed to proper channels and
not frittered away in outbursts of communal frenzy."[11]

The deteriorating situation in the country made Nehru so helpless that he felt
like putting the whole blame on Hindu fascism. It seemed to him that "the
responsibility for the disturbances lies on the Hindus as they are in a majority." He
remained fraught with doubt, disillusion and agony. Caught in a predicament he
either condemned such psychic factors as animality, fear and "anarchy of the mind"
or invoked self-sacrifice almost as a metaphysical panacea. Urging the students to
do relief work, he solemnly remarked, "I will congratulate the students if a few of
them have to die in their endeavour to restore confidence."[12]   That Nehru did not
apprehend the growth of fascist tendency among the Sikhs is a factor of which the
members of this community can be proud even at the present historical juncture. It is
also a tribute to his secular outlook that is extremely difficult, if not impossible to
maintain in India even now. More so, it was difficult to maintain such a secular
outlook before independence when political activity was disposed to derive vital
impulse from communal and religious consideration.

After independence when Pakistan became a separate country and the Muslims
claimed to have realised their destiny, Nehru's perception changed with regard to the
Sikhs as well. Either his priorities changed or a deep disillusionment set in his mind
about their intentions. From now onwards, he began to address the Hindus as his
addressees of the active sort, with the Sikhs feeling themselves rendered passive
recipients of his discourse. It was Nehru's perception perhaps that in the emergent
situation the Sikhs were no longer imperative for countering the Muslim communalism
as they earlier had been before independence. Feeling themselves thus reduced in
significance, the Sikhs became self-centred and in this self-centredness Nehru decoded
their disposition to imitate the Muslims. This decoding was not without encoding as a
result of which he magnified it beyond measure, and felt that the Sikhs posed a danger
to the edifice of secularism that he sought to build so assiduously in the country.

No wonder in Nehru's perception every claim forwarded by the Sikhs became
sceptic. Even their genuine claims of which the one for the linguistic reorganisation
of the Punjab was incontrovertible, became controversial of which no viable resolution
was possible. So much so that he got sceptic about the linguistic veracity of even the
Punjabi language. In the thirteenth volume of the second series, he pointed out to
Bhim Sen Sachar, the then Chief Minister of the Punjab, that "Gurmukhi was not
advanced to be a medium of instruction after the matriculation." Here the substitution
of Gurmukhi the name of the script for Punjabi the language was rather intriguing.
Then in a letter to C.M. Trivedi, the then Governor of the Punjab, he passed an

inexcusable stricture on the Punjabi literature itself. Without entertaining any doubt on his misinformation verging on disinformation he wrote, "There is hardly any literature in Gurmukhi, so far as I know except some sacred literature."[13] How one wishes that he should have avoided the subterfuge that the modest claim made through the immodest intervening clause! In his speech in the Lok sabha delivered on August 30, 1961, he gave expression to his scepticism in a circumlocutory way. Reiterating that Punjabi was the language of Punjab, he referred to the usage of Persian script. He forgot in the process that the Persian script was common with the Muslim writers whereas the non-Muslim writers had invariably employed the Gurmukhi script. Then he claimed that Punjabi was "a home language."[14] It was an ambiguous way of calling it a dialect. He forgot in the process that Dogri, a dialect to which his Government awarded the status of language, was actually a spoken form of Punjabi. Besides that it had under its ambience several other dialects in the eastern and the western parts of the Punjab.

For all that, Nehru ardently championed Punjab's claim to literacy and progress. Perhaps he visualised some sort of a common culture to grow in Punjab. Maybe the Regional Formula was a measure in the same direction. The Regional Formula identified a Punjabi and a Hindi region. In the former region Punjabi was to be the primary language with Hindi as the secondary one. Likewise in the latter region Hindi was to be the primary language with Punjabi as the secondary one. Both the regions were to be administered by two regional committees claiming substantial powers. Nehru believed that with the implementation of the Regional Formula no further question would be left out from the language point of view. This was rather wishful thinking because in recalcitrance he had to confess that what to speak of problems relating to power politics between the Hindus and the Sikhs, it did not even solve the language question. Symptomatic of it was the census of 1961 in which the Hindus settled in the Punjabi region were instigated to declare Hindi as their mother-tongue. In all candidness Nehru felt that "it was not a truthful statement and it did a lot of harm."

Holding the Akali party and certain Hindu organisations as equally guilty for causing this strain, the Congress had recourse to the policy of deferral and difference. Such a policy smacking of manipulation in the vulgar sense of the word, provided the Congress political space for rule in the Punjab. The damage this rule caused to the social and cultural fabric was tremendous. Nehru, with all his subtlety and sobriety failed to award hegemonic meaning to his own value-based strategy as distinct from the opportunistic policy of his party. As a result his vision of the Hindus and the Sikhs as "interwoven like the warp and woof of a fabric" proved to be an illusion. No less illusory proved his commitment he so candidly articulated in the following words:

> What troubles me is that if we separate them applying the
> principle of division, we shall be tearing a finely woven tapestry
> into two bits and spoil it. Such a tearing process will have awful
> consequences. Tearing up an integrated community into two is

a terrible thing. With all my desire to be flexible, I find it
impossible to adapt myself to the idea."[15]

Rather than grow into a resilient strategy to resolve the issue this sort of
thinking resulted in a diffident policy, meant to complicate it further. No wonder, the
Akalis, got extremely desperate, launched one morcha after the other. They even
talked in a vein sounding secessionist to the chauvinistic ears. So the issue lingered
on till Mrs.Indira Gandhi made it explosive on the one hand by granting a truncated
Punjabi Suba and on the other hand by dispossessing it of its resources. Now after so
much of bloodshed if any veritable resolution of the issue is to be found, it can only
be which Nehru visualised through the Regional Formula. The revisualised
implementation of its clauses (a) the Punjabi in the Gurmukhi script, as the official
language in the Punjabi Suba with its secondary status in Haryana, Delhi, Himachal
Pradesh and Jammu (b) the prospective integration of those areas into the Punjabi
Suba which the Regional Formula had retrospectively recognised as Punjabi speaking
(c) Hindi as the second language in the re-organised Punjabi Suba (d) continuance of
English as link-language with the West and (e) provision for the study of the dialects
of Punjabi aspiring to become languages, may replace the feelings of difference and
deferral with those of filiation and affiliation so essentially required under the new
historical ambience.

NOTES

1.   Jawaharlal Nehru's corpus comprises *Glimpses of World History, An Autobiography,
        The Discovery of India, A Bunch of Old Letters, Jawaharlal Nehru's Speeches (4
        Vols.), The Selected Works of Jawaharlal Nehru (10 Vols.),* first series, *The Selected
        Works of Jawaharlal Nehru,* second series, of which 14 volumes have appeared so far.
        Meticulously edited by the distinguished historian Dr. S. Gopal they will hopefully be
        more than 50 in number. The writer of this paper has published 20 review articles in
        The Tribune on these volumes and other writings which have appeared on Jawaharlal
        Nehru during the last ten years.
2.   *Jawaharlal Nehru's Speeches,* Volume IV (1957-63) Publications Division, New Delhi,
        1964, p.20.
3.   *The Selected Works of Jawaharlal Nehru,* Volume IV, second series, Jawaharlal Nehru
        Memorial Fund, Teen Murti House, New Delhi, 1986, p.269.
4.   *The Discovery of India,* Signet Press, Calcutta, 1945, p.248.
5.   *The Selected Works of Jawaharlal Nehru* Volume 1, first series, Orient Longman,
        New Delhi, 1976 (Reprint), p.375.
6.   *Glimpses of World History,* Asia Publishing House, Bombay, 1967 (Reprint), p.424.
7.   *The Discovery of India,* p.290.
8.   *Glimpses of World History,* p.747.
9.   *The Selected Works,* Volume 2, first series, pp.138, 151.
10.   *The Selected Works,* Volume 3, first series, pp.137, 148.
11.   *The Selected Works,* Volume 1, second series, pp.26, 51, 53.
12.   Ibid, pp.57, 87.
13.   *The Selected Works,* Volume 13, second series.
14.   *Speeches,* p.15.
15.   Ibid., pp.16, 17, 18.

Section IV

International Migration, Globalisation and Punjabi Diaspora

Editors' Introduction

The papers in this section deal with the 'third Punjab' - the Punjabi diaspora created through the process of international migration and bringing into full force the impact of globalisation on Punjabi identity at home and abroad.

The paper by Parminder Bhachu emphasises the globalising influence of economy and culture on the forms in which ethnicity is negotiated in newer contexts. It explores the experience of the Punjabi women in their engagement with the economy and culture of Britain in different regional, local and class contexts. The range of these Punjabi women's experiences and backgrounds - direct migrants from rural Punjab, twice migrants from the metropolitan contexts of East Africa and thrice migrants to America -is brought into analysis. There may be some who are "quadrice" migrants - first after the Partition, then to East Africa and Britain and finally to America. Bhachu highlights some of the continuities in ethnic identity markers - especially wedding gifts - and some discontinuities. The active transformatory role played by women in cultural reproduction of their identities is especially emphasised.

Arthur Helweg in his paper uses five 'etics' or 'building blocks of ethnicity' viz membership, history, tradition, land and language to analyse the character of Punjabi identity in a global context. While he identifies the solid foundations of a common Punjabi identity, he also refers to the recent sectarian conflicts to point out the cracks in these foundations which, if not repaired quickly and effectively, can destroy the foundations irreparably.

Bruce La Brack in his paper views the recent contestations on Punjabi/Sikh identity in America as a result of the reaction to the events in Punjab since 1984 as nothing unique to Sikhs; he refers to the similar contestations within Irish, Jewish, Nicaraguans and Salvadorean groups in America to highlight the general phenomenon of such contestations. He also provides evidence to argue that in the beginning of the century, Punjabi identity was more dominant than religious identities among the migrant groups from the Punjab. Recent events have shifted the emphasis to religious identities and the future, like the past, 'is likely to be replete with multiple interpretations and contested identities' but "the difference is that this process will now be obscured, and commented upon, by outsiders and played out upon a world stage."

Narindar Singh's paper has two parts. In the first part, he offers a description of his views on Sikh identity and in the second, he describes very briefly some aspects of the history of Sikh immigration into Canada and their efforts to retain their religious and cultural identity.

Raminder Kaur and Virinder Singh Kalra attempt an exploration of the arena of music and cultural identity, and venture into terminological innovations to capture the fluidity of identity in a globalised musical space. The authors look at Bhangra music and Punjabi identity from this perspective. The Bhangra music form constructed by the diaspora Punjabi youth played the role of a vital input in transforming the Bhangra music in Punjab. Their paper is particularly interesting because it explores the dimension of the cultural impact of the diaspora on the homeland community in a globalised space.

Multiple Migrants and Multiple Diasporas:
Cultural Reproduction and Transformation
among British Punjabi women in 1990s Britain

Parminder Bhachu

This paper has two main themes. Firstly, I want to refer to the complex nature of migration and settlement to point to the variation in migration and settlement trajectories, that produce a range of diasporic cultures in which South Asian women are situated internationally. The vast majority of literature in the academy and that available to and utilized by policy makers mostly treats migration as single first movement of direct migrants to their destination economies. Yet there are direct, twice, and thrice migrant women, many of whom are further involved in fourth movements, especially in the 1990's. I myself am involved in such a process and movement. These multiple migrations are important to the ways in which different migrants and settlers view themselves, their orientations to a homeland and the impact of this on cultural reproduction in local, regional, and transnational settings.

I focus on South Asian women of Punjabi Sikh descent from the Indian subcontinent and its diaspora, especially in Britain. These migrant women have different histories of migration and settlement in Britain and the US. I want to propose a more complex conceptualization of their economic and cultural locations than is conveyed in the literature and by the media images, where Asian women are frequently represented as "working class victims" forced to struggle with what are constructed as their "oppressive cultural systems". Yet, Asian women actively engage with the British and American economies and occupy a range of class niches which is further reflected in their cultural systems and consumption styles.

Secondly, I want to point to the *transformative* role of diasporic Asian women in choosing the cultural patterns they engage with, and in engaging with their "ethnic" cultural base in the context of their local, regional, and national cultures and class codes, they *transform* them to generate new cultural forms. By examining their consumption patterns and cultural styles through an analysis of the wedding economy, in particular the dowry system, I want to emphasize their role as *cultural entrepreneurs*, who choose their cultural forms and create new ones. Migrants women's agency and their self-defining roles are largely ignored in the literature and common sense sensibilities of them, which portray them as passive recipients of their cultures. I will also explore the construction and reconstruction of their ethnicity and diasporic identities to show that they are contextualized products of time and space occupied by these women in the migration process. Their marriage and dowry patterns are like their identities, continuously negotiated and determined not only by their migration histories but powerfully filtered through by the codes of their local and national cultures and also by their class positions. Equally important are the international forces which have a strong impact on their engagement with global economies and on their cultural patterns that are negotiated in these contexts. I want to point to the elastic and plastic nature of their ethnicities in the diaspora.

Direct, twice and thrice migrant women

Direct, twice, and thrice migrant women represent different histories of migration and settlement in the diaspora. In previous work (Bhachu 1985, 1988, 1992) on the *twice migrant* British Asians who migrated from the Indian subcontinent to East Africa, thence to Britain in the late 1960's, I have demonstrated that migrants and settlers have differential skills and experiences of migration and settlement. This is further reflected in their destination economies in cultural reproduction, in economic participation rates, and in the varying speeds with which the infrastructures of their communities are established.

In previous publications on British Punjabi Sikh women (1985, 1988, 1992), I have explored the dynamics of migration through an analysis of their cultural base as it is reproduced through the axis of race, caste, and class on the British scene. Experienced settlers, twice (i.e. in the British context) and thrice migrant women (in the US context) possess considerable expertise in the management of their minority status, in the reconstruction of their ethnicities, and in the negotiation of their cultural systems. Their communities migrated from rural India in the latter part of the nineteenth century to East Africa where they urbanized and established defined East African Asian identities. From Africa, they migrated to metropolitan Britain in the late '60's, after their jobs were Africanized in post-independent East Africa. Many of them further migrated to the US, Australia, and other European countries in the '80's and '90's. As relatively prosperous twice migrants in Britain with great command over mainstream skills, in comparison to the less experienced direct migrants who are less skilled at the "game of migration", they also occupy separate class as well as caste positions and also maintain exclusive marriage and community circuits. These are precisely some of the people who constitute the thrice migrants in the US. As expert migrants, they were able to enhance their already considerable migration skills initiated and developed in Africa, established and refined in Britain, and further reproduced very efficiently in the US and in other tertiary destination economies in the diaspora.

Twice, thrice and "quadrice" (if there is such a term) migrants possess very powerful communications networks which have been greatly facilitated and enhanced by global communications. Their command over "western" bureaucratic skills and the English language has given them considerable expertise at reproducing their cultural bases and community infrastructures in a range of countries. Such a scenario is in complete contrast to that of the less "culturally and ethnically skilled" direct migrants, who are often characterized by home orientation and "a myth of return". An important consequence of the latter characteristic is that the resources they generate in their destination economies, are frequently remitted to a country of origin where their positive or for that matter negative reference groups and status hierarchies lie. Unlike direct migrants, for whom migration especially in the initial stages is frequently a temporary economically goal-orientated move, for twice and thrice migrants, migration is not a sojourn but a more permanent move to settle. They lack home-orientation and are geared towards staying in their destination economies right from the point of entry and of maintaining their capital and resources within them. For these multiple migrants, the phases of settlement that apply to direct migrants of initial bachelor all-male households to the later reconstitution of their communities, through family unification often many years later, are greatly telescoped. Twice and thrice migrants often migrate with three-generational family units or are united with their families within a year or two of settlement. Their communities possess a balanced age-profile unlike the directly migrant who often have a much younger age profile and only two generational nuclear families.

This pattern of migration involving a series of moves, is widely applicable to a whole range of groups in the US, like for example, the Vietnamese, the Armenians, the Iranians, etc. It also applies to migrants in other continents, especially, in recent times, like Canada, Australia, New Zealand, and also to other prosperous European and Asian countries like Germany and Japan. Situated as these experienced migrants are in an international milieux, migration in the 1980's and 1990's is for them no longer a first move, but a second, third, or even fourth movement, thus, constituting transnational people with established international, national, and local connections. These features are critical to the reproduction of their cultural bases and ethnicities and to their engagement with the economies and polities of their countries of settlement. In all these processes of the construction and reconstruction of their identities and the reproduction of diasporic cultures, migrant women are the key actors.

Female Economic Activity and Recent Labour Market Profile

The cultural patterns and identities generated by these diasporic women are contextualized products of the time and space they occupy in the migration process. These new cultural forms are analyzed here by examining their consumption patterns, as viewed through the wedding economy in which they play a much more significant economic and cultural role as a result of migration. This wedding gift exchange system has been elaborated upon since the early migration especially as a result of women's entry into the waged labour market in Britain. These working women have translated their earnings into it, thus, transforming and also "traditionalising" a "traditional" cultural arena. A reason for this is greater control over cash by young Asians than ever before, due to their more active engagement with the British economy as wage earners. This is obvious from some of the recent labour market figures, though, the complexity of their class position is not a new phenomenon. It has existed as long as the Indian presence in Britain (Bhachu 1988, 1991, 1993, 1994).

In the present day (as in the past), their labour market profile and their engagement with the British economy has further implications for the reproduction of facets of their cultural systems and a strong impact on their cultural reproduction. Contrary to the stereotype of Asian women, they actively engage with the British economy. In certain cases they have higher economic activity rates than locally born, indigenous white women. The consequences for ethnic entrepreneurship of this active engagement of migrant women with the British waged economy are explored elsewhere (Westwood 1988 and Bhachu, 1988), though they are also critical to the elaboration of the wedding economy.

For example, a higher proportion of Afro-Caribbean and non-Muslim women, including Sikh women, are in the labour market in full time employment, than white indigenous women born in the U.K. who are economically active in the mid to late 80s. Of women between 25-44, 66 per cent of white indigenous origin are economically active as are 77 per cent of West Indian origin, 62 per cent of Indian origin, and only 17 per cent of Pakistani/Bangladeshi origin. These latter categories constitute mostly directly migrant women from the subcontinent. The rather low officially recorded figure should be higher for Pakistani/ Bangladeshi women. This latter rather low figure does not capture the paid homework/ home sewing done by Muslim women: they are more economically active than this recorded figure (Brah 1987: 41). The reasons for the considerably lower rates of entry into waged labour by Pakistani and Bangladeshi women are not clear and really need further research. In the case of Bangladeshi women, they are certainly amongst the last group of South Asians to reconstitute their families by joining their husbands in Britain in the 1970's, a number of whom had migrated in relatively early days of the 1940's and 50's. They have come mostly from rural areas and occupy a different class position from that of the experienced and highly metropolitan East African Asian women. However, the class position of Pakistani Muslim women is really complex. There are many women from metropolitan Pakistan and who occupy a range of class groups and whose engagement with the waged labour market is likely to differ from rural direct migrants. It is also possible that they have labour histories of much less involvement in the waged market sectors than the twice and thrice migrant women, though Muslim women of the latter category and there are many of them, may have shared similar labour participation rates. However, there are many queries to be made of the low officially recorded figure of Pakistani/Bangladeshi economic activity. Islamic religious ideologies, especially, as played out in the 80's also must have a considerable impact on the construction of what are considered to be "masculine" and "feminine" roles. Such factors are important in determining their labour market histories and their current engagement with the waged economy.

Twice migrant East African Asian women have higher rates at 69% than both indigenous white women and the directly migrant Indian and Pakistani women (*Employment Gazette* 1987). The higher rate of economic activity amongst East African Asian women in Britain is a product of their urban experiences in formal employment sectors in Africa, in comparison to the mainly rural background of the majority of the directly migrant women from the subcontinent, and also to the continuation of the employment trends established prior to migration from metropolitan Africa to metropolitan Britain. For example, the number of Asian female employees in Kenya had risen from 600 in 1948, to 3,750 in 1962, then comprising 10% of the total Asian Labour force in that country (Ghai 1965:95). By 1967, this had risen to 18 per cent (Ghai 1970). This period coincides with the most intense amount of Asian migration to Britain from Africa after the full impact of the Africanisation policies on them in the mid '60s. This was very different from the directly migrant women's experiences, most of whom came either from rural areas or from places where there were fewer opportunities for female waged employment, or from traditions in which waged employment for women was discouraged.'[1]

The differences between white and Asian women in managerial and professional groups are slight, in fact proportionately the same in the case of the twice and thrice migrant East African Asian women - 7% for white women, 7% for African Asian women and 1% for West Indian women (Brown - Policy Studies Institute Survey 1984:198). As Sheila Allen (1987:182) points out "The difference in types of jobs and earnings found among black and white women are much less than those found among men. There are proportionately almost as many Asian women in professional, employer to management sectors (6%) as white women (7%) and the percentage of white women in unskilled jobs at 11% is higher than either West Indian (7 %) or Asian women (2%)." The implications of this greater overlap between women's earnings and jobs, is that their expenditure and consumption patterns are also more likely to share a common ground regardless of ethnicity and class - than that of men, who are much more unequally distributed.

There are significant regional differences in the economic participation rates of Asian women depending on the opportunity structures. Until recent times of recession which has hit the South East of Britain particularly badly, the South East was characterized by very high rates of economic activity and lower unemployment rates, a situation applicable to whites and blacks alike. This is an important area for Asians, since over half the Indian population (54%) and three-fifths of the East African Asian population is based in the South East of Britain (especially in London), in comparison to 31% of whites. Thus, there are considerable differences in the number of economically active women (and men) in the South East, who were in full time employment than anywhere else in the country (Employment Gazette 1988). Also in the South East, there are many more Asian women in white collar/clerical and managerial/professional jobs than anywhere else. There was an increasing amount of waged employment for Indian women in the Midlands in the late '80s filling in the jobs created by the mushrooming "anorak industry", the rapid growth of the clothing manufacturing sectors. There are significant regional differences in the economic niches and employment opportunities of British Asian women.

It should by now be clear that the labour market profile of Asian women is much more complex than presented in most literature. They are more widely distributed in a range of economic niches and employment structures than I have actually outlined here. Their occupational profile is, therefore, determined by local economies and the opportunity structures in them. However, I want to reiterate that this should not detract from their predominantly working class locations. However, it should equally be emphasized that they also occupy a number of non-working class sectors, that they have had different histories of participation in the labour market prior to settlement in Britain and also since settlement in different regional economies in Britain. These varied economic histories are further played out in the reinterpretation and reproduction of the wedding gift exchange system in the diaspora.

Migrant and Diaspora Dowries

It is to this important role of cultural reproduction by British Punjabi Sikh women that I will focus on, in particular, on the impact of the economic on the cultural, and on the formulation of identities which are responsive to the local cultures in which they are situated. I want to explore this variation through an examination of one facet of their culture, which reflects their British consumption styles and class locations and which encodes reflections of their identities. Dowries - *daajs* - which represent the legitimate and recognized property rights of women and have been elaborated since migration to Britain, as a result of women's entry into the waged labour market. Young Punjabi women play a central role in manufacturing them because the arena of dowry in the '80s and '90s in Britain, has become amongst other dimensions, a more important arena of creative consumption and re-interpretation than ever in the past (Bhachu 1985; 1986 and 1988). It is a cultural idiom that has always been relevant to them and which has seen significant inflation, its commoditization is determined by the specificities of their class positions and sub-cultural consumption styles, especially in the 1980s and 1990s, when most of the brides and younger Punjabi women are either locally born or have arrived as youngsters, and are therefore educated and socialized to regional and local British cultures. Firstly, some brief background (detailed elsewhere Bhachu 1985 and 1986) on the development of the dowries as related to the migration process and settlement.

There is a close similarity between Punjabi Sikh notions of dowries - *daajs* - and those of high status North Indians. The high caste status North Indian ideology of *kanyadaan*, the pure gift of a maiden for which no return in expected and the accompanying *stridhanam* - exclusive female property - in the form of movable goods, presented as pre-mortem inheritance from the patrimony (Goody 1985: 1), also applies to Punjabi Sikhs regardless of their place within the migration chain and the diaspora. However, even though the same complex of beliefs as that of the high caste Brahmans is widely accepted, sanskritic terms rarely used by the Punjabi Sikhs. The four components of the *daaj:* clothes, and gold for the bride, household goods including utensils, furniture, linen, quilts, kitchen gadgets, crockery, and consumer items etc; and finally affinal gifts are always presented. Money payments like bridegroom price are non-existent, though the groom, his mother and father are receivers of substantial wedding gifts.

These four major components, constituting the external framework of *daajs,* have remained stable with migration and diasporic cultural reproduction, though, there have been internal content changes in the gifts presented. The designation of wedding gifts has also shifted according to the various phases of migration and in response to structural changes in the household and power relations within families. For example, the *daajs* of the 1920s, 30s and 40s presented in India and Africa were designated for the mother-in-law, the most powerful and senior female decision-maker of expenditure and consumption choices within the domestic domain. She could redistribute the *daaj*, often using it for further gift-giving. The brides of this period only had direct control of their *muklawa* which was received from her parents at the consummation of the marriage, often anything from 3-5-7 years after the wedding ceremony and the presentation of the original *daaj*. It was after this rite-de-passage that she took up permanent residence in her affinal home.

The *daajs* of the 1950s and 1960s in Africa, and the 70s, 80s and 90s in Britain and U.S., in the case of the twice and thrice migrant women, have acquired a different meaning. Affinal gifts had been separated so that the mother-in-law had little control over bridal clothing items and gold, though household goods in the 1950s and 1960s were often absorbed into extended family households which were then quite prevalent. By this stage, bridal control over her sectors of the *daaj* increased, undermining the redistributive authority over them of the mother-in-law. This development coincides with the late 40s and 50s *daajs* presented in Africa. The previous *daajs* belonged to brides whose marriages had taken place in India where the joint family system was stronger and when families were less fragmented by migration. None of these Indian-married brides had their own separate households, though an increasing number were establishing nuclear residences in urban Africa, a trend reproduced by the vast majority of twice and thrice migrant brides in the 70s, 80s and 90s in Britain and in the US.

By the 1970s, the British *daajs* - unlike the African Punjabi and Indian Punjabi ones - contained fewer heavier household goods (like the bedroom, dining, and sitting room furniture), because there has been an increase in expensive easily movable consumer items. There was around this time, a total separation of the affinal goods from those reserved for the bride. This trend of earmarking affinal gifts initiated in 1950's Africa, was the norm by the 1970's among twice migrant brides in Britain. This separation of affinal and bridal gifts partly reflected household changes but were also a consequence of changing residential patterns, which facilitated the establishment of a separate residence immediately after marriage. The quite dramatic increase in the earning powers of the brides in Britain catalyzed this process, being contributors to house mortgage payments and sometimes initiators of house purchases. Also, since they helped to make the *daaj*, they also expected to control it. Few (in fact, I did not record any case) of the pre-1970s brides who could exercise such options. Their command over economic resources, if any, was considerably lower.

Thus, changes in the structure and control of the *daaj* is a product of the migration process. Of course, some of these trends are also obvious among urban households in India and are a consequence of changing female employment patterns and residential patterns. In East Africa, these processes had already begun, although they have become far more fully established in Britain, as families have separated into nuclear units and as women have become cash contributors to family incomes. Also, the erosion of control by the affine over the redistribution of bridal gifts and of the residential choices of couples, is a result of the increased couple-orientation as opposed to kinship group-orientation characteristic of the previous phases of migration. Spouse-selection criteria have also shifted to take more account of couple suitability and personal demands rather than extended family expectations (See Bhachu 1985).

To summarize: Dowries which consisted of minimal items both for the bride and her affinal kin in the earlier phases in the late '50s and '60s, have escalated in the '70s and '80s. The three components of the *daaj* -the elaborate traditional garments and some "western" clothes, household goods including luxury consumer items and gold ornaments in the form of "sets" that are designated specifically for the bride herself and the fourth component of affinal gifts for the groom and his close kinsmen and women are always adhered to rigidly for caste endogamous East African Asian marriages. Hence, the structure of the *daaj* has not changed over time, even though, there have been internal changes in the items presented reflecting the move to urban Britain. The designation of the *daaj* has also shifted reflecting structural changes in the organization of the household and the various power relations within it. Migration, changing residential patterns and increased female economic activity in the diaspora from the late 1960s onwards has favoured the brides.

Commoditized Wedding Economies

The varied economic profile of British Asian women is reflected in their different positions in the class hierarchy and their various cultural and regional locations in Britain especially in the late '80s, a period which has the most number of British born or British raised women. This regionality is reflected in the consumption and cultural styles that they adopt, even though, patterns that emerge from London are the most influential because they are products of the dominant minority community' The wealth generated through their own relationship with the labour market is deployed and expended in accordance, with their sub-class styles and related consumption values. These specificities are reflected in their marriages and dowries - *daajs*.

I am presenting here only a brief summary of the escalation of the dowry system since migration to Britain, not so much to detail the process of elaboration within it (Bhachu 1985; 1986 and 1988), but to point to the significant inflation within it of those spheres that directly concern the brides themselves. This elaboration of the dowry system is just one facet of the cultural and religious effervescence that has taken place amongst the Sikhs in the settled phases of the '70s and '80s in Britain. I have discussed these processes elsewhere (Bhachu 1988 and 1991), in relation to the various phases of settlement in Britain, to highlight the important role of women as agents and catalyzers of cultural reproduction and as generators of symbolic capital (Andizian 1986:265) for their communities.

The spheres within the wedding economy that have been most significantly inflated in Britain, especially since the late 70s, concern the brides themselves. The wedding economy has been greatly elaborated since the 1970s as the twice migrants increasingly settled. This inflation applies both to the ritual/wedding procedure and to the dowry system, to which young brides are significant contributors. A consequence of their direct engagement with the waged economy is that their wages are transferred into building their dowries which are interpreted with a great deal of their own input even though, the content of the daaj has remained highly conservative throughout the various migrations. (Bhachu 1988,1991).

For example, as mentioned above, dowries have increased from 11-21 clothing items in the '50s and '60s in Attica, to 21 items in Africa and Britain, to anything from 21-51 items in the 70s, 80s and 90s in Britain and the US. Some of these are very high quality silk saries and prestigious designer clothes, which are designed by leading European and Bombay based Indian designers, and which are accompanied by expensive Gucci and Bally shoes and bags, especially, in the case of high earning professional brides. The "standard" East African Punjabi Sikh dowry of 21 cloth items and a whole range of accompanying accessories and prestigious consumer items for the bride are always presented in Britain. This norm persists regardless of the standing of the families involved and has been further reproduced in Britain and also US. Twenty-one clothing items are commonly presented in the Indian subcontinent and Pakistan and among the diaspora Indians.

However, even though, a 21-itemed *daaj* constitutes the "British/ American/

East African Sikh" pattern, there are major qualitative differences in its content, according to the earning powers of the brides themselves. A bride who has not earned in her own right before marriage, invariably has a basic 21 -itemed *daaj*, in comparison to the earning brides whose are much more elaborate and voluminous. The latter *daajs* are characterized by the inclusion not only of higher quality garments and personal accessories but also a more vast range of consumer durables - china sets, silver cutlery, electronic music equipment, exclusive linen etc. - that the brides have themselves purchased from their own earnings and which they themselves are likely to utilize and also control.

In the late 80s and early 90s, British sub-cultural/regional styles have become more influential in the interpretation of not only the "traditional" garments/goods/ gifts but also of their class-encoded consumption patterns. So, that there are *daajs* that are Sloane Rangerish[2] in their interpretation - reflecting the "London S.W. 1,3,5,/ Knightsbridge/ Sloane Square" consumption patterns of some of the high earning and professional brides, just as there are prestigious `Designer Ethnic/European" *daajs*, the Middle/Lower Middle Class "Oxford St. Marks and Spencerish/Mass Produced-Departmental Store" types, Working Class "East Ender" types, provincial "Liverpudlian Sikh" and "Mancunian types" etc. Different regional styles are quite clearly discernable. For example, a Midlands *daaj* is interpreted differently from those of London brides of an equivalent class group, despite the similarity in the content of the *daajs* and the persistence of the external framework -its three main spheres for the bride and fourth component for the affine. These regional patterns are also obvious from the marriage circuits of an informal metropolitan hypergamy - which operates in Britain. London girls tend not to marry outside London and the South East. If they are married out, in a majority of cases they move back to London to set up a nuclear residence within a couple of years of marriage.

In the above, I have simplified a much complex procedure (see Bhachu 1985, 1986 and 1992) mainly to point to the elaborations in the bridal spheres which have seen the most significant inflation. Punjabi Sikh women's increased command over productive resources and the translation of their wages into a cultural idiom which has existed for centuries and survived their two migrations from India to Africa and to Britain, and then to North America. Traditional structures have not only been reproduced, but also enhanced in the changed circumstances since their entry into the British labour market as wage earners.

Much more than the 1970s dowries in Britain and earlier ones in Africa, the late 80s and 90s dowries of the British-born and raised Asian women, are particularly reflective of the British sub-cultural/regional styles, especially in the interpretation of their "traditional" ethnic garments. So that there are dowries that are "very London" emerging form the various areas and subcultures of the capital and according to the class positions occupied by the brides and their kinship groups. Similarly, there are dowries that reflect the various regional styles and cultures and in accordance with dominant consumption choices of the areas in which the brides have been brought up in the local cultures and to which they have been socialized. They are, therefore, class- and region-coded consumption patterns of particular phases of settlement and migration and this is asserted in the content of the dowries. All this also applies to the identities and ethnicities negotiated and generated by these diaspora Asian women. They too have their specificities and these are activated differently according to the various contexts.

Conclusion: Cultural Reproduction and Multiple Migrations

Twice and thrice migrant, indeed transnational women, interpret and reinterpret their cultural systems in the context of their local and national localities being the *cultural entrepreneurs* that they are in the multiple diasporas they occupy, internationally. By engaging with their cultural frameworks in the context of their local and national codes and the international forces that impact on women internationally, they transform them to manufacture *new cultural forms and diasporic spaces* which take from their ethnic traditions and which are continuously formulated in the context of their class and local cultures. Yet, there is little perception of these migrant women as active agents and as negotiators of their cultural values, which are frequently presented as non-negotiable entities enforced on them as passive victims by patriarchies and capitalist producers. Indeed, the latter agencies are powerful in determining their cultural patterns and cultural reproduction. However, these women also have agency which plays an important role in their choice of lifestyles, their role as innovators and originators of new cultural forms and new diasporic spaces. Their agency as actors in multiple migrations is one that is largely absent in the literature.

The assumptions in the literature are that the crucial determinants of their identities and cultural bases, especially in the context of migration and settlement are: the nurturing forces of a homeland cultures (which at least in the early stages of migration and settlement) provides cultural reinforcement, the maintenance of ethnic boundaries through the exclusionary forces of racism, confrontations that are said to lead to identities of resistance and defiance, and the desire of migrants/ settlers/ diaspora Asians to emulate and aspire to particular "white" class cultures and their symbols. There is a great deal of emphasis on boundary maintenance and on the perpetuation of what are presented as clearly worked out, homogeneous and fixed cultural values. Importance is attached to the impact of rejection, racism and discrimination as the fundamental forces in structuring their identities and cultural locations in diaspora. In all this, ethnicity is presented as a thing that has fixed components and symbols and is considered to be the primary agent controlling and generating their various identities and migrant cultures. Indeed, all these are important social mechanisms in structuring their lives and in determining their life chances.

However, my concern is that there are a number of other forces that are equally important in framing their experiences and for diasporic cultural reproduction.

These include international forces which have a strong impact on their engagement with global economies and on the cultural patterns they negotiate in local and international economies. Thus, particular ethnicities and identities are not stable, despite a common core of key fundamental religious and cultural values that constitute their cultural roots, but which shift according to the forces that operate on them. In the case of these direct, twice and thrice migrant women, these are not just products of confrontation and rejection, and the wholesale transference of homeland culture, but they emerge out of vibrant and changing cultures in which Asian women are situated in Europe and in international contexts over which they have genuine unselfconscious command.

NOTES

1.   Nearly half of the ethnic minority labour force lives in London (Employment Gazette 1987:18), an area (in common with the South East in general) characterized by the most amount of economic activity and least amount of unemployment for them (Employment Gazette 1988:175). There are very significant differences between London and the South East and the rest of the few, though, major urban centres that Asians are settled in.

The interesting development in the late 80s concerning the Bangladesh/Pakistani officially recorded figure, especially as related to the younger women of this group, is that there is much higher rate of entry into the labour market of women between 16-24 at 23%. These younger women, presumably are benefitting from greater length of stay in Britain or are ones who are locally born or raised. This shift will in years to come have particular cultural and social implications for this group, which is currently the worst off economically of the directly migrant groups. This occurs at a time and for an age group that is twice or more likely to suffer unemployment for Pakistanis and Bangladeshi. The unemployment situation during a time of severe recession in 1990's Britain is, of course, affecting all British Asian and Blacks intensely. Labour market figures for the current period are not available yet, though, they are sure to have made a major impact on consumption patterns.

However, in the 80s, this group also had "young Indian women most likely to be students ... at 27% in comparison to the general figure of 13% of all women in this age group (Employment Gazette 1987:22) This interest in female education is also borne out of the Inner London Education Authority 1987 report on examination results and performance, which showed that Asian women are not only entering examinations in considerable numbers but are also outperforming the boys. This report states: "The average performance score obtained by girls was 17.7 compared with 13.7 for boys.

In all ethnic groups, girls did better than boys (1987:7) I will not elaborate the implications of this here, because I have discussed their educations choices and the changes both current and potential elsewhere (Bhachu 1986 and 1989, Gibson and Bhachu 1986, 1989).

2.   I refer to "Sloane Rangerish" styles as those that emanate from the Sloane Ranger set, which were popularized by the "Super Sloane" Princess Diana, prior to her current "queenly style". There are "Asianized" and "Punjabized" versions of Sloane Ranger fashion trends. These are particularly obvious from the interpretation of the "ethnic garments" like the Punjabi suit (worn by a cross-section of North Indian women) which is put together using Sloane Ranger accessories and in accordance with the Sloane Ranger style codes. Although the Punjabi suit has been worn by Punjabi women for centuries, over the past decade it has acquired particular significance for younger South Asian women in diaspora communities internationally, and also on the subcontinent, as a high fashion dress form that is being very creatively interpreted both by them and by leading Indian, Pakistani, and also British designers like Zandra Rhodes. It has become very much part of transnational South Asian culture and increasingly available through mushrooming mail-catalogues and also through fashion magazines like *Libas, Connections, Rivaz* etc.

REFERENCES

Allen, S. 1987. "Gender, Race and Class in the 1980's." In Charles Husband (ed), *Race in Britain: Continuity and Change,* London: Hutchinson.

Andizian S. 1986. "Women's Roles in Organizing Symbolic Life: Algerian Female Immigrants in France." *International Migration: The Female Experience*, New Jersey: Rowman and Allanheld.

Ballahatchet K.A. 1980. *Race, Sex and Class Under the Raj: Imperial Attitudes and Policies and their Critics, 1793-1905*, London: Weidenfeld and Nicolson.

Bhachu, Parminder. 1985. *Twice Migrants: East African Sikh Settlers in Britain,* London and New York: Tavistock.

1986. "Work, Marriage and Dowry among East African Sikh Women in United Kingdom." *International Migration: The Female Experience*, New Jersey: Rowman and Allanheld Publishers.

1988. "Home and Work: Sikh Women in Britain. *Enterprising Women: Ethnicity Economy and Gender Relations*, London and New York: Routledge.

1988. "Ethnicity and School Performance: A Comparative Study of Sikhs in Britain and the United States." *Ethnic and Racial Studies*, 11 (3): 239-262.

1989. "Ethnicity Constructed and Reconstructed: The Role of Sikh Women in Cultural Elaboration and Educational Process in Britain". *Gender and Education* (3):147-62.

Punjabi Identity:
A Structural/Symbolic Analysis

Arthur Helweg

Who is a Punjabi? What does it mean to be a Punjabi? These are issues that have not been extensively researched. Although works on the Sikhs have been numerous[1] few Punjabi village studies have been done,[2] works of a general nature have been sparse[3] and inquiry concerning the Punjabi diaspora[4] are lacking. However, as this brief article will show, being a Punjabi not only has many consequences and, the ethnic dynamics of Punjabis identity differ from the ethnic process of some other communities. Thus, answering the questions, 'Who is a Punjabi'? or 'What does it mean to be a Punjabi'? are not only important in understanding the ethnic dynamics of Punjabis, it is a crucial but unstudied aspect concerning ethnic processes, for it deals with a people who claim a common identity, but that identity encompasses a great deal of cultural diversity and subcategories.

Studies, like this one, are significant because ethnicity may well be the most powerful social force in the world today. It is a basis on which nations are formed, wars are fought, and social unrest instigated. The nature and dynamics of ethnicity vary from people to people, place to place and time to time. To aid in developing a conceptual framework to understand ethnic processes, this paper will set forth a means to analyze the ethnic structures, meanings and processes.

The Nature of Ethnicity

The Ethnic Process

> Cultures have destroyed other cultures; resisted destruction; exploited other cultures; resisted exploitation; competed with one another; influenced, accommodated and created one another.[5]

Crucial to understanding ethnic behavior is the realization that it is a historical process.[6] Kathleen Conzen recognized this in her 1991 Presidential Address to the Immigration History Society. In her presentation she proposed the analogy of a river to understand ethnic dynamics. Ethnicity, like a river, can have many sources. So it flows, it can merge with others and separate again, it can take different forms and meanings, depending on the development, time and context, and, move at different speeds. Like a river, ethnicity is also a process. Others have recognized the dynamics of ethnicity and have set forth other analogies such as the boiling cauldron[7] and the simmering cauldron.[8] The point is, however, that ethnic identity is not a list of traits, as bureaucrats and policy makers would like to think, it is a process that is continually merging, dividing and evolving.[9]

An outsider may not know the criteria that determines membership in a particular community, but the members do, and they define themselves in opposition to other groups by, among other things, establishing ethnic boundaries.[10] However, the nature of the boundaries and the boundaries themselves can change over time.[11] For example, when people of India entered England during the time of colonial rule, many wanted to be perceived as Englishmen — the English were a reference group[12] of imitation -- it was prestigious to be an overseas English gentleman. By the 1970s, the people of South Asia had achieved independence and felt discriminated against by the English. Thus, the English became a negative reference group to the people of South Asia. The nature of the ethnic boundary between English and some people from India had changed.

Next, the meaning of being a member of an ethnic group can vary, even though the same term may be used. What it means to be a Sikh for a practicing member of that community who is a professional, Ramgarhia and part of a family that migrated from Punjab to Kenya and then on to England, is very different from a Sikh Jat who was born, raised and has lived in a Punjabi village all his life. They both call themselves Sikhs and use many of the same words when they speak of their faith. What the term Sikh means, what membership entails, and the same words in the scriptures can mean something entirely different. In fact, for some Kenyan Sikhs, it is not feasible to live in a Punjabi Sikh village.[13]

It must be kept in mind that people have different identities and compartments in which they live,[14] and the identity chosen changes from time to time, place to place and circumstances. Asian Indians in the United States, at the turn of the century, claimed to be Aryans. Now they ascribe to an Asian identity. They still claim India as their place of ethnic origin, but what that means is different from what it meant at the turn of the century. Also, an Asian Indian may claim Punjabi identity when at a party with Punjabis, choose Sikh identity while attending a Gurdwara, yet claim to be Asian Indian when working at his job. The identity he chooses and behavior he ascribes to differs according to time, place and context.

One of the problems in dealing with ethnic issues is the lack of recognition concerning the complex configurational aspects of identity. For example, many government policies are based on the notion that ethnic identity is a fixed criteria that makes members of a group identifiable. Ethnic group identification and formation is not so simplistic. A man like Khushwant Singh can wear all the Sikh symbols and claim to be a practicing Sikh while other members of that same community will assert that 'he is not a true Sikh'. Yet the Government of India, for census purposes, classifies Khushwant Singh as a Sikh. However, John Jacobson, an individual of Caucasian origin, who adopted all the beliefs and practices of the Sikh religion is not likely to be classified as a Sikh, Punjabi or Indian by a Government of India Census.

Second, a researcher simply cannot study people only quantitatively to arrive at theories concerning ethnicity. Quantitative analysis certainly has its place,[15] but many ethnic indicators are not easily isolated to statistical verification; and in some cases, it is not a factor but a configuration of components that set forth a group's ethnicity. In the case of John Jacobson and Khushwant Singh, their behaviors and dress may be similar, but their beliefs, values and interpretations are likely to differ. The astute observer and local members of the community identify criteria for membership, but concepts like beliefs and values are not statistically verifiable. The only thing that can be measured is what can be observed and what people claim. These observable and testimonial aspects may be very different from what people actually are.

The concept of ethnicity is like the notion of a game. A game can be every thing from football, to monopoly, to marbles. Game, as a concept, encompasses such diversity that, when one game is compared with one another, they may have little in common. Yet, all know that they are games.[16] The concept of ethnicity is similar. Ethnicity can have a great deal of diversity according to components, configuration and process.

The practical implications of understanding ethnic dynamics are important. As this article will show, ethnic processes vary. Different situations require different solutions. A realization of the diversity in ethnic processes helps avoid blunders being made by administrators that do not understand the ramifications of policies they impose on others -- good intentions do not necessarily yield proper and intended results. An understanding of the particular situation is imperative if progress is to be made in developing any kind of multiethnic society.

Importance of Ethnicity

Ethnic identity is important for three, and possibly more, reasons. It enables people to belong to a group, it provides a culture, and it establishes ties to the eternal. Belonging to a group enables a person, family or community to obtain social, economic and emotional support. Support functions may vary in nature and degree in different ethnic communities. It may be support in time of conflict, or a sense of commonality with others. It may be just feeling comfortable and 'at ease' with a people because the symbols and norms of behavior are accepted and familiar. Being part of a group, however, enhances the emotional stability of the individual. Second, having a culture enables people to communicate, have meaning in their lives and make order out of their experiences. This is important for meaning, order and understanding are crucial for human existence.[17]

All ethnic communities adhere to a cultural system. As Kroeber and Parsons point out, culture is an abstract symbolic system which is composed of values, meanings and beliefs.[18] Beliefs are those assumptions on which we justify our values. Concepts such as capitalism, democracy or gender equality are principles that cannot be proved of disproved; but, they are the foundation that members of the ethnic community agree on -- what they mean, however, can vary from culture to culture and time to time. Thus, when a person ascribes to a culture, which the individual does as a member of an ethnic group, the individual also ascribes to the beliefs of the community, or at least behaves as if he did.

The culture sets forth the rules to regulate behavior, bases for establishing values, means for ranking goals, criteria enabling members to evaluate themselves, framework for making moral choices and means for evaluating behavior of themselves and others. It is these beliefs and values that provide meaning in life. Without the culture, a state of anomie exists which results in alienation and marginality.[19]

Culture, by assigning meanings to symbolize enables members to communicate. This can be the establishment of meaning for words, situations or, along with the beliefs, order and understanding of what is happening around them. This is because members of a group agree on the meanings of symbols. It must be kept in mind that cultural concepts may be established, but that does not mean that people always obey or live by them. Like in a game, people may disobey rules so they can win, if it is likely that they won't get caught or have to pay a price. Members in a community may claim adherence to cultural principles but in actual behavior, deviate from them if they deem it to their advantage.

Third, identification with a group gives members a past on which they can build to make a contribution for future generations. Thus, ethnic membership links members to something timeless where they can build on a tradition to endow future members with something better. It helps provide a meaning and timelessness to one's existence.

Structural Components of Ethnicity

One of the early thinkers concerning the structuralist approach to understanding human behavior is Kenneth Pike who compared analyzing human behavior to the study of linguistics.[20] All languages have common components. Phonemes and morphemes are two; but there is also a grammar, syntax and so on. The configuration of each unit has meaning according to the particular context. The same phonemes can have different meanings in different cultures or within different contexts or at different times within the same socio/cultural unit.[21]

As the recent literature on ethnic dynamics is analyzed[22], five *etic*[23] units or building blocks of ethnicity become evident: membership (this includes adherence to the cultural and social systems of the group), history, tradition, land, and language.[24] As will be illustrated below, these five *etic* units can be compared cross-culturally. As I will show below, this structural approach is one formulation by which the diversity of ethnic development can be compared and analyzed.[25]

Punjabi Ethnicity

Comparing the *etic* units of ethnicity (membership, history, tradition, land, and language) within the Punjabi situation, a configuration of ethnic development becomes manifest. Although there may be exceptions, the generalities set forth below indicate a general pattern taking place now. Thus, in explaining the different ethnic processes below, the *etic* concept will first be set forth; then its applicability and influence on the ethnic development of Punjabis.

Membership

Generally, ethnic membership can be based on principles of blood, land, or adherence to abstract principles.[26] A people like the Japanese or Germans are an example of membership by blood. If one's racial origins are considered to be Japanese, it makes no difference where or for how long they or their progenitors have lived outside of Japan, they are considered Japanese. Membership in the Japanese community uses racial criteria only. A Korean whose ancestors have lived in Japan for numerous generations can never be a Japanese. The same principles apply to Germans. However, an individual born in the United States is considered an American regardless of his or her racial origins.[27] Membership is by principle of land, not blood.

A third category is adherence to a set of principles. Some argue that an American is a person who adheres to certain principles such as democracy, freedom and/or the 'American Dream'.[28] However, groups like the Mormons obtain membership by conversion, that is claiming a particular belief system. It must be kept in mind that like the situation of Khushwant Singh and John Jacobson narrated above, membership may not be agreed on by all.

To be Punjabi, membership is determined by claiming ancestral origins in the geographical region of Punjab and claiming the Punjabi language as their tongue of identification. Geographical Punjab is different from the political boundaries of Punjab. Geographical Punjab is located in the extreme northwest corner of South Asia. It is an hour glass shaped region bridging both India and Pakistan -- the axis of which intersect at Lahore. It is bounded on the north by Kashmir and the Northwest Frontier Provinces on the north, Afghanistan and Baluchistan on the west, Sind and Rajasthan on the south and Uttar Pradesh on the east.[29]

Since 1947, geographical Punjab has been divided politically between India and Pakistan, and within India, the states of Haryana and Himachael Pradesh have been created. In the last decade, the people of Haryana have emphasized their distinctiveness because they are Hindus and do not want to be subordinated to the Sikhs, who claim Punjab as their homeland. However, when regional differences are manifest in an Overseas Indian Community, the people of Haryana are generally considered Punjabis, although the people of Haryana may be in the process of creating a new ethnic community.   The people of Himachael Pradesh are different. They may have been part of geographical Punjab, but they claim ethnic unity with the Paharis of the hills. Thus, since Punjabi is not their language of ethnicity and they identify with the hill people, they are not considered Punjabi.

Within Punjabi ethnicity there is a great deal of diversity. Religious orientation can vary, ethnic Punjabis include Hindus, Muslims, Sikhs and Christians. Although Jats dominate, a Punjabi can be of any caste, nationality and religion.[30]

In spite of this diversity, Punjabis share a common dress (*salwar-kameez*, with men wearing turbans[31] and the women a *dupata*),[32] history,[32] tradition,[34] family and kinship pattern,[35] village political structure (especially the *panchayat*),[36] arts, literature,[37] ritual and cultural concepts.[38]

Membership also entails concerns and perceptions. The cultural framework that a group's members adhere to concerns explaining the 'whys' of concerns. One way of understanding this is to look at the literature of a people. People read and enjoy those writings that set forth ideas and concepts they agree with. Of course, like any society, there is variation among the membership. When a work, be it a poem, story or novel, is popular, it is popular because it communicates things to the people they agree with. Punjabi literature is one area where the changing concepts are manifest in Punjabi identity, not only the changes over time, but the variation between those in Punjab and those living abroad.

Surindar Singh Kohli[39] classifies Punjabi literature into six periods: pre-Nanak, (9th to 15th centuries); Age of the Gurus (1469-1708); Later Mughal Period (1709-1798), Ranjit Singh Period (1799-1849); British Period (1850-1947); and Period of Independence (1947-Present). Each period builds on the previous phase by accepting, rejecting or modifying aspects. The seventh category, Literature of the Punjabi Diaspora, has some unique qualities.

During the pre-Nanak period, Punjabi literature was emphasizing ideas of yogic discipline, heroic poetry that exemplified valor in combat and Muslim mysticism. Yogic ideas were propagated through the Naths and Yogis. They claimed to attain mystic powers through yogic discipline. Heroic poetry resulted partly from Punjab being located on the invasion route into South Asia. Because of the continual incursions, poetry, songs, and stories exemplified heroics in battle.

Muslim mysticism was communicated through Sufi poetry and literature. It resembled the Bhakti movement where their concepts, like that of Allah, resembled Brahman and many Hindu practices, such as meditation, were incorporated into their belief and ritual systems. Thus we see the basis of three Punjabi traditions; the exemplification of valor, the blending of Muslim and Hindu concepts and the toleration of other communities.

The period of the Gurus built on the previous themes and combined them into a new belief system. Guru Nanak, for example, conceived of God as Ultimate Reality and One, not a combination of deities with specialized places. Each Guru added to the beliefs of the Sikhs, and even though Sikhs may not even be a majority in the geographical region of Punjab, much of their literature is as much a part of Punjabi culture as Christian and Greek concepts are part of the Western Civilization.

The Moghal Period that followed the Sikh Gurus brought a return to emphasizing Muslim ideology. Some, like the religious poets of the Sufis and lyric poetry of Qissa writers, exemplified the pre-Guru ideology, the Maulvis inculcated Persian concepts in Punjabi culture. It was a rich amalgamation of Persian and Sanskrit works being translated into Punjabi with themes of love and valor in combat being exemplified alongside the ideas of meditation, other worldliness and being part of the world. Sometimes the concepts were contradictory, but they existed side by side, sometimes in mutual toleration, sometimes not. In spite of the diversity, Punjabis perceived of themselves as a unified whole with a love for their homeland, Punjab. This love for Punjab, with its descriptions of the countryside, customs and behavior of its people, became an ongoing theme.

Under Ranjit Singh, Persian remained the language of the court, as it had been under Mughal rulers. Indian folklore, Muslim ideas, and Qissa literature with its ideas of romance with its rich descriptions of human emotions concerning trials, tribulations, heroics and valor, were prominent.

Under the British however, Punjabis began to identify themselves in opposition to the British. Most Punjabis felt threatened by the British Christian missionaries with their Greek philosophy, logic and political domination. Thus movements like the Singh Sabha sprang up where education and writings were designed to combat Christian and Western ideas and concepts. Urdu and Punjabi poets became more popular as Punjabi and Urdu became the popular medium of communication. It was also a time when Punjabi culture was extolled as being superior to British ideas and the valor of Punjabi heros was taught in poem, song and stories. After 1900, the themes turned to the struggle for freedom from British rule.

With independence and partition, faith in traditional Punjabi institutions and concepts was challenged. Thus, some leaned towards Marxist and Socialist ideals which created a social consciousness of equality and a rejection of the romanticism of the past. Internationalism, world peace and nationalism became prominent themes.

However, the Punjabi community in North America and Britain developed a different theme in their Punjabi identity. Twentieth century Punjabi writers emphasize love and security for being at home in the Punjab. After the partition of Punjab, with its emphasis on Marxism and humanism, themes in the literature of the Punjabi diaspora began to develop. For example, Ishwar Chitarkar's awareness of difficulties in Punjab are by the way of happiness. In England, he sees the distinction between harsh reality and human fulfillment as being very stark. Some use old poetical types, like the *ghazal,* and give them new meaning. Others write about the pain and departure from their homeland, along with a loss of fulfillment and direction in life. Themes of internationalism, despair of corrupt politicians in their homeland, and humanistic concerns are emphasized.[40]

It can be seen through literature that there has been a gradual change of what it means to be a Punjabi. At each stage, their world view has changed. A sweeping generalization would be that it has changed from seeing their world in romantic and mystical terms to a greater orientation to Marxism and internationalism. For those residing in Great Britain and North America, alienation and loss of purpose in life are more pronounced.

History

History influences ethnicity in two ways. Actual events make their impact, but equally important is how people interpret happenings and what incidents they emphasize and what they ignore. History is used to reinforce the ideology of the people of that particular time. As one reads the history of Punjab, four themes are evident: antiquity, invasions, birth of the Sikh faith and success.

The word 'Punjab' is a combination of two Persian words *Panj* which means five and *Aab,* which means water -- the land of the five rivers. This land contains the Harappan and Mohenjo-daro civilizations that date from around 2500 BC to 1500 BC. Aryan invasions brought that era to an end -- Punjabis claim Aryan ancestry.

Starting with Darius of Persia in 522 BC, Punjab became the invasion route into South Asia. It has continually been over-run by invading Armies. Alexander the Great of Macedonia, Chandragupta of the Mauryan Empire, Scythians, Parthians and Kushans. Starting in 712 AD, Muslim invasions began with Punjab experiencing the worst of these incursions. Except for a few minor rulers between the 5th to the 7th centuries AD, Ranjit Singh (1780-1839) was the major Punjabi (and a Sikh who tolerated all faiths) who ruled the region. Upon the death of Ranjit Singh, the region was annexed by the British and in 1947, divided between India and Pakistan. Both countries created political units but altered the boundaries so that the political units did not correspond to the geographical unit. It is from this turbulent history that a community of diverse cultures have forged the ethnic entity 'Punjabi'.

From their history, Punjabis emphasize their Aryan origins as well as their prowess in conflict and ability to survive in hostile environments and situations. Considering their history and what they emphasize, it is not surprising that Punjabis of all religions dominate in the military of both India and Pakistan.

Tradition

A tradition is a set of opinions or beliefs a people have about themselves. They may change or be created but are used to

> facilitate readily definable practical operations, and are readily modified or abandoned to meet changing practical needs, always allowing for the inertia which any practice acquires with time and the emotional resistance to any innovation by people who have become attached to it.[41]

In other words, a tradition can be created and changed, but it is treated as if it were permanent and has ancient origins. Tradition is usually comprised in a people's history, and long established customs. The value of traditions and history are in the belief of their permanency and ancient origins. However, traditions change, are invented or rewritten to suit the belief and values of the contemporary situation.[42] It must be kept in mind that the validity of the tradition is not important, the crucial factor is that the people believe it.

Since Punjab has experienced numerous invasions, it has not established structures, like the temples of South India (except for the Sikh Golden Temple) or rituals such as British royalty. The traditions of Punjabis lie in self concepts and abstract ideas. Thus, the traditions follow from their history and encompasses at least four general themes: having ancient origins, unity, self confidence, exchange, mobility and adaptability. Punjabi claims of Aryan origins provides them with an antiquity and ties to a dominant race of people. The Aryans spread from Central Europe both East and West, and Punjabis perceive of themselves as not only descending from these ancient people, but from a people of an ancient philosophy and religion from whom they draw their roots.

Second, Punjabis see themselves as a diverse people who are united, which embodies for them a 'Unity in Diversity'.[43] Until 1947, when the region was partitioned between India and Pakistan, four religious communities and numerous caste groups lived harmoniously together. It was not unusual for a Hindu, Sikh, Christian or Muslim to consider the other a brother or sister;[44] and, such is still often the case among Punjabi overseas communities.[45] Also, the traditions are not mutually exclusive. Muslims are part of and practice the Hindu caste system, Sikhs have Muslim writers in their scriptures; and, Punjabi Hindus are not as strict in their adherence to concepts of purity and pollution as are some other communities in South Asia.[46] In rural areas, it is not unusual for Sikhs in a village to pay homage to a Muslim saint or a Sikh to be part of the caste system.

Unity is also manifest in family and kin group relations. Much has been written about factionalism and infighting among Punjabis and their families.[47] However when a Punjabi family or group is threatened by an outsider, the conflicting groups forget their differences and unite against the external challenge. Families will unite against other families, caste groups will unite against other caste groups and villages will unite in the best interest of their village. Punjabis perceive of themselves as maintaining or achieving solidity when an outside force is challenging.

Self confidence is part of Punjabi tradition.[48] The harvest dance of the *Bhangra*, with its prominent beat and bright colors, communicates a self confident air for both men and women. Punjabi literature emphasizes romance, using wits, and overcoming adversity.[49] The region has been the pathway for invaders and the local people have had to overcome external oppression. Having survived oppression for hundreds of years has given Punjabis a tradition of confidence and determination to overcome adversity. It is a theme in conversation and it is a theme in their literature.

The unique Punjabi tradition concerning exchange is one way of maintaining relationships, especially in a culture that has minimal political control. Among Punjabis, the custom of *Vartan Bhanji* is the institution for gift giving and receiving. Initially it was practiced within the family where a mother gave her daughters gifts and help. It was expanded out where elders helped out younger members of the kin group. Now, as Punjabis become more international, it is a form of exchange where gifts are given to establish a kin type of relationship. For example, it is common in North America for Punjabi women to help each other in providing food in times of need, and the exchange becomes part of the two women becoming 'sisters', meaning that they have a sister-like relationship. Yet, giving a gift to a person who is not worthy elicits scorn. For example, when Kamala Singh gave gifts to her sisters upon returning home from America, her sister Nima chastised her saying, 'Why give gifts of such value to your other sisters, what have they done for you'? By giving equal presents to all sisters, Kamala Kaur was discrediting the special treatment she had received from her sister Nimi.

When gifts are given for a wedding present, the parents of the recipient should respond in kind for the marriage of the givers offspring. Or, they can give a better more expensive present to indicate superiority. Yet, for a boss, for example gifts are given for holidays or auspicious occasions. The rules of exchange are close to those indicated by Mauss[50] and Sahlins.[51] But, in essence, it is an institutionalized means of establishing and maintaining relationships between individuals or kin groups.

Last, Punjabis have a tradition of being mobile and adaptable. They are not bound to a locality. They move to where opportunity is present for they perceive of themselves as being able to deal with most situations, even if they are very adverse. Thus, Punjabis are found all over India and the world. They will leave their homeland when opportunities present themselves elsewhere. Not bound by the strict concepts of maintaining purity, as is the case in other parts of South Asia, they are traders and administrators in Africa, skilled craftsmen in the Middle East and Great Britain, and farmers and professionals in North America and Great Britain. Where ever they reside, their traditions of unity, self confidence, determination and adaptability accompany them.

Land

The symbolic meaning of land is part of the ethnic configuration.[52] Most nations have a homeland, which has a sacred connotation of being their place of origin. Having a homeland is crucial in maintaining the eternal character of the ethnic community. Claim can be made to it as being the first to settle on it, being awarded by god, or developing it. For communities like the Jews or Sikhs, having an ethnic homeland is considered essential for ethnic survival, even for the expatriate population who may never reside or even visit their homeland.

The symbolic meaning of a homeland for Punjabis is different from groups like the Jews, Sikhs, or even much of Europe. For the Punjabi, Punjab is the tie to the eternal, but political control does not have to be under Punjabis. Unlike the Jewish community who feel that controlling the land that they believe God gave to them is essential for survival. Punjabis have their homeland, but political control is not crucial.

It is important to be able to return and visit the homeland however. For example, Punjabis who were expelled during Partition in 1947 never felt at home in their new abode. My wife's family is a good example. They lived in Lahore before Partition and, like many Punjabis of that time, lived in a community where Muslims, Sikhs and Hindus lived in close harmony, considering each other as brothers and sisters. Having to evacuate and move to Delhi in 1947, my wife's father always dreamed of Lahore as his home and longed to return to his home in that city -- a dream that was never fulfilled. But, the fact that they could not return to Lahore never placed the future of Punjabi ethnicity in doubt. At present, however, religious divisions between Sikh, Hindu and Muslim have become exacerbated, thus Punjabi unity may be threatened because of one group claiming Punjab as being exclusively their homeland. Such a claim, even if the ruling group is tolerant, may destroy Punjabi unity.

Language

Language is an ethnic marker. Like dress or physical features, it distinguishes the ethnic group from others. Language embodies that uniqueness. Like culture it marks the community apart from all others. To some, however, language is more than a marker, it is crucial in the tie to the eternal, the building on the past to contribute the future. Besides, a group's language is tailored to the cultural configurations of the group. One Punjabi lady put it well when she said, 'our language is like the trunk of a tree from which all ideas and concepts branch out'. To many, language maintenance is symbolic of ethnic survival.

The Punjabi language, like the people, goes back to ancient times. But, Punjabi emerged as an independent language in the 11th century from the *Saucraseni Apabhramsa*, although *Paisachi* has contributed to its modern form. The Punjabi language has changed over time. It was a successor to the Vedic period and influenced by Arabic and Persian. Its use as poetry dates back to the 13th century when Baba Farid, a Muslim mystic, who used it in composing *sloks* and hymns. Its golden period in use as literature was during the Sikh Gurus and is preserved in the *Adi Granth*. But, its use and development for religious (Muslim, Hindu, Sikh and Christian) and secular poetry and literature continues to the present day.[54]   Punjabi is a very graphic language that expresses the confidence, frustration, pride, faith and challenges of Punjabis, especially in the villages.

Conclusions

Ethnicity is one of the most powerful social forces in the world today. It is a dynamic force that is continually changing as to goals, meanings and composition. One way to chart its course is to focus on the etic concepts of membership, history, tradition, land and language. This analysis has not been exhaustive, but it shows how ethnic dynamics can vary from group to group and place to place. Some scholars have given different emphasis concerning the etic components. Driedger[55] emphasizes territory, institutions, culture, symbols, ideology and leadership. Nash[56] emphasizes kinship, dress, language, physical features, religion and land. The methodological point, however, is that by using etic concepts along with their contextual meanings,[57] a better comparative understanding of ethnic processes can be developed.

However, one must be careful in the etic concepts used. Nash[58] maintains that religion is an etic concept in understanding ethnicity. As this papers shows, religion is not a etic category to understand Punjabi ethnicity for Punjabi culture contains various religious communities and diverse traditions. Punjab is an outstanding example of a ethnic community that has tolerated diversity. How and why this is the case deserves further study from which modern societies may profit.

Each ethnic group's behavior is strongly influenced by the symbolic meaning for each etic category. The meaning attached to each category may change from time to time. Concerning the meaning of land, for example, Punjabis seem unique in that political control is not considered crucial in their tie to their homeland for survival as Punjabis. If a group or groups claim exclusive control of the region, it would seem that the survival of Punjabis as an ethnic category may be in jeopardy. However, Punjabis have survived such challenges before.

NOTES

1.   Recent examples include J. S. Hawley and G. S. Mann, *Studying the Sikhs: Issues for North America* (State University of New York Press, 1993); H. Izmirlian, Jr., *The Politics of Passion: Structure and Strategy in Sikh Society* (South Asia Books, 1979); M. Leaf, *Information and Behavior in a Sikh village* (University of California Press, 1971); J. T. O'Connell, M. Singer, W. G. Oxtoby, W. H. McLeod and J. S. Grewal, *Sikh History and Religion in the Twentieth Century* (University of Toronto, Centre for South Asian Studies, 1988); J. Pettigrew, *Robber Noblemen: A Study of the Political System of the Sikh Jats* (Clarendon Press, 1975).

2.   Examples of village studies include Z. Eglar, *A Punjabi Village in Pakistan* (Columbia University Press, 1960); T. G. Kessinger, *Vilyatpur 1848-1968: Social and Economic Change in a North -Indian Village* (University of California Press, 1974); M. W. Smith, 'Social Structure in the Punjab', in M. N. Srinivas (ed.), *India's Villages* (Asia Publishing House, 1955).

3.   Some works of a general nature include M. L. Darling, *The Punjab Peasant in Prosperity and Debt* (Oxford University Press, 1925); S. Dulai and A. Helweg, *Punjab in Perspective: Proceedings of the Research Committee on Punjab Conference 1987* (Asian Studies Center, Michigan State University, 1991); P. H. M. van den Dungen, *The Punjab Tradition: Influence and Authority in Nineteenth Century India* (George Allen and Unwin, 1972); P. Tandon, *Punjabi Century, 1857-1947* (Chatto and Windus, 1961).

4.   A. Helweg, 'Punjabi Immigrants in America: Focus on the Family', in S. Dulai and A. Helweg (eds.), *Punjab in Perspective: Proceedings of the Research Committee on Punjab Conference, 1987* (Asian Studies Center, Michigan State University, 1991).

5.   C. R. Stimpson, 'On Differences: Modern Language Association Presidential Address 1990', in P. Berman (ed.), *Debating P.C.: The Controversy Over Political Correctness on College Campuses* (A Laurel Trade Paperback, 1992).

6.   K. Verdery, *Transylvanian Villagers: Three Centuries of Political, Economic and Ethnic Change* (University of California Press, 1983).

7.   M. Nash, *The Cauldron of Ethnicity in the Modern World* (The University of Chicago Press, 1989).

8.   R. Takaki, *A Different Mirror: A History of Multicultural America* (Little, Brown & Company, 1993).

9.   For a more complete theoretical treatment of ethnic dynamics that form the theoretical framework of this article, see B. Anderson, *Imagined Communities* (Verso, 1991); E. Hobsbawm, T. Ranger, *The Invention of Tradition* (Cambridge University Press, 1983); and Nash, *Cauldron of Ethnicity*.

10.   F. Barth, 'Introduction', in F. Barth (ed.), *Ethnic Groups and Boundaries: The Social Organization of Cultural Difference* (George Allen & Unwin, 1969).

11.   A. Helweg, *Sikhs in England* (Oxford University Press, 1986), 242, 90-2, 175-6, 209-10; A. Helweg, 'Sikh Identity in England: Its Changing Nature', in J. T. O'Connell, M. Israel, W. G. Oxtoby, W. H. McLeod and J. S. Grewal (eds.), *Sikh History and Religion in the Twentieth Century* (University of Toronto Centre for South Asian Studies, 1988).

12.   Reference Group Theory, as used here, begins with Robert Merton's assertion that a community's relationship to other groups influences behavior; see R. Merton, *Social Theory and Social Structure* (The Free Press, 1968), 335-40. Owen Lunch added to Merton's ideas by identifying three of many possible reference groups, which are: 1) reference group of imitation (group emulated), 2) reference group of identification (community in which people claim membership), and 3) negative reference group (people they have animosity toward or have animosity toward them); see O. Lynch, 'The Politics of Untouchability: A Case Study from Agra, India', in M. Singer and B. Cohn (eds.), *Structure and Change in Indian Society* (Aldine Publishing Company, 1986) 209-40. For a more complete treatment of reference group theory as applied to Sikhs in England, see Helweg, *Sikhs in England*, 90-2, 175-6, 209-10; and Helweg, 'Sikh Identity'.

13.   P. Bhachu, *Twice Migrants: East African Sikh Settlers in Britain* (Tavistock Publications, 1985); Helweg, *Sikhs in England*, 152-208.

14.   A. Helweg and U. Helweg, *An Immigrant Success Story: East Indians in America* (C. Hurst, 1990), 108-45; M. Singer, *When a Great Tradition Modernizes: An Anthropological Approach to Indian Civilization* (Pall Mall Press, 1972).

15.   R. Alba, *Ethnic Identity: The Transformation of White America* (Yale University Press, 1990).

16.   C. Mahmood and C. Armstrong, 'Do Ethnic Groups Exist?: A Cognitive Perspective on the Concepts of Cultures', *Ethnology* 31, 1 (1992), 1-14.

17.   V. Frankl, *Man's Search for Meaning* (A Touchstone Book, 1986).

18.   A. Kroeber and T. Parsons, 'The Concepts of Cultural and Social Systems', *American Sociological Review*, 582-3.

19.   E. Durkheim, *Suicide* (The Free Press, 1951).

20.   K. Pike, *Language in Relation to a Unified Theory of Human Behavior* (Mouton, 1954).

21.   See R. Naroll, 'Introduction', in R. Naroll and F. Naroll (eds.), *Main Currents in Cultural Anthropology* (Prentice-Hall, 1973), 2-4.

22.   Anderson, *Imagined Communities*; L. Driedger, *The Ethnic Factor* (McGraw-Hill Ryierson Limited, 1989); Hobsbawm and Ranger, *Invention of Tradition*; and Nash,

Cauldron of Ethnicity.

23.   'Etic' is a general concept, as opposed to 'emic' which is something peculiar to a particular culture; see Naroll, 'Introduction', 22.

24.   With modifications, the building blocks used here are based on Anderson, *Imagined Communities;* Driedger, *Ethnic Factor,* and Nash, *Cauldron of Ethnicity.*

25.   These etic units are the author's summary and adaptation of the literature. Writers on ethnicity are not agreed as to what etic units should be used; if a commonality is necessary.

26.   There may be other criteria for determining ethnic membership, but according to my knowledge, these are the only three.

27.   This is an ideal situation. Some ethnic groups may feel that they are not accepted by the host society; but, those born in the United States are, according to US law, citizens of the United States with all the rights and privileges thereof. Also, by going through a certain process, any individual can become a citizen of the United States. Membership is by the principle of land, not race or genetic heritage.

28.   G. Spindler and L. Spindler, *The American Cultural Dialogue and its Transmission* (The Falmer Press, 1990).

29.   H. A. Rose, *A Glossary of the Tribes and Castes of the Punjab and Northwest Frontier Provinces* (Languages Department, Punjab, 1883), 4; J. Schwartzberg, *A Historical Atlas of South Asia* (Oxford University Press, 1992), Plate TX. A. 4.

30.   Helweg, *Sikhs in England,* 4, 5.

31.   The turban is considered part of Punjabi dress and is part of their traditional formal attire.

32.   The *kameez,* is a long tunic top and the *salwar* is baggy trouser with a draw string around the waist. A *dupata* is a two meter length of cloth draped over the head or shoulders.

33.   S. M. Latif, *History of the Panjab* (Eurasia Publishing House (Pvt.) Ltd., 1964ʃ, I. A. Malik, *The History of the Punjab, 1799-1947,* (Lahore Publishing, 1970).

34.   Dungen, *Punjab Tradition.*

35.   P. Hershman, *Punjabi Kinship and Marriage* (Hindustan Publishing Corporation, 1981).

36.   A ruling council composed of five members. There can be caste or village panchayats. See Hershman, *Punjabi Kinship and Marriage,* 35-6; Helweg, *Sikhs in England,* 7, 14; Izmirlian, *Politics of Passion,* 33, 36; Kessinger, *Vilyatpur,* 18, 20, 207, 112.

37.   S. Dulai, 'The Severed Kite: Punjabi Writing in Great Britain and America', in S. Dulai and A. Helweg (eds.), *Punjab in Perspective: Proceedings of the Research Committee on Punjab Conference, 1987* (Asian Studies Center, Michigan State University, 1991); S. S. Kohli, *History of Punjabi Literature* (National Book Shop); R. C. Temple, *The Legends of the Punjab,* Vols. I, II, III (The Languages Department, Government of Punjab, reprinted 1962); V. N. Tewari, *Punjab: A Cultural Profile* (Vikas Publishing House Pvt. Ltd., 1984).

38.   Eglar, *Punjabi Village in Pakistan;* Helweg, *Sikhs in England,* 12, 13.

39.   Kohli, *History of Punjabi Literature.*

40.   S. Dulai, "The Severed Kite'.

41.   Hobsbawm and Ranger, *Invention of Tradition*, 3.

42.   Hobsbawm and Ranger, *Invention of Tradition*, 1-14.

43.   V. N. Tewari, *Punjab*, 47.

44.   Although it was not publicized in the news, there are many stories of Hindus protecting Sikhs and Sikhs protecting Hindus, each at the risk of their own lives, during the period immediately after the assassination of Mrs. Gandhi and the subsequent violence that went on in Punjab. The tradition of Punjabi brotherhood is still prominent in India and abroad.

45.   I personally experienced this many times. But when I was doing my first field research, I and my family were helped by Punjabi Sikhs because, Mala, my wife, of Hindu origins and born in Lahore and family now in New Delhi, was a 'Punjabi sister'. I had never experienced such unquestioned acceptance and help before or since.

46.   This, of course, is illustrative and not an exhaustive list of the merging of traditions in the Punjab.

47.   Hershman, *Punjabi Kinship and Marriage;* Pettigrew, *Robber Nobleman.*

48.   F. Colon, *'Peoples'. The Cambridge Encyclopedia of India, Pakistan, Bangladesh, Sri Lanka* (Cambridge University Press, 1989), 47.

49.   The classic folk story of *Heer Ranjha and Sohni Mahiwal* typifies romance and the · poem *Mirza Sahiban* mystic aspects.

50.   M. Mauss, *The Gift* (W. W. Norton & Company).

51.   M. Sahlins, 'On the Sociology of Primitive Exchange', in M. Banton (ed.), *The Relevance of Models for Social Anthropology* (Tavistock Publications, 1965).

52.   Anderson, *Imagined Communities,* 1-22.

53.   Nash, *Cauldron of Ethnicity,* 12.

54.   K. Mathew, *Manorama Yearbook 1991* (Malayala Manorama, 1991), 462.

55.   Driedger, *Ethnic Factor,* 143.

56.   Nash, *Cauldron of Ethnicity,* 4-19.

57.   Pike, *Language in a Unified Theory of Human Behavior;* Naroll, 'Introduction', 2-4.

58.   Nash, *Cauldron of Ethnicity,* 4-19.

California's "Punjabi Century":
Changing Punjabi/Sikh Identities

Bruce La Brack

The premise behind this paper is simple: in the nearly 100 years of Punjabi presence in North America major shifts in what it meant to be "Sikh" have occurred. However, to document these changes and locate historically the sources of these shifts is a complex task. What "Sikh" meant in 1904 and what it means now are quite different.

I contend that for nearly a half-century, at least until the mid-1940s, the identity which predominated among overseas Punjabis in North America was just that...Punjabi. Inheritors of a late 19th and early 20th century South Asian social identity based upon shared homeland, language, history, opposition to British rule, and even intermarriage, the Punjabis who came to Canada and the United States at the turn of the century tended to stress their South Asian cultural commonalities and their disadvantaged corporate status in the West rather than their religious differences. It is not that Punjabi Hindus, Muslims, and Sikhs did not practice their faiths individually or that such distinctions were irrelevant, but rather that a more secular Punjabi identity tended to transcend religious particularism. This was essentially a continuation of the reality of village life in the Punjab of that era and not a new or adaptive strategy precipitated by migration.

This ecumenism continued in North America until Partition in spite of the ferment in India over Sikh identity and political roles which included some of the most momentous events in recent Sikh history including, but not limited to, the continuation of the Sikh Sabha/Tat Khalsa movements into the 1920s, Jallianwala Bhag, the rise of the Akalis, the establishment of the Shiromani Gurdwara Prabandak Committee, the Gurdwara Reform Act, and the negotiations prior to Partition... not to mention the Sikh participation in World Wars I and II and the Independence movement.

Beginning in the 1950s and continuing to the present this transcendent and incorporative Punjabi identity was slowly but surely replaced by a more self-conscious, increasingly militant, and exclusive Sikh identity. This second half-century is characterized in North America by exponential population growth, establishment of over one hundred *gurdwaras* in the United States alone, and in the ability of overseas Sikhs to influence not only domestic and international policy in their adopted countries but to become a significant factor in South Asian politics.

Simultaneously, in India, events transpired which would impact Diaspora Sikhs world-wide. These included several Indo-Pakistani wars, the Punjabi Suba movement, creation of Punjab as a linguistic state, the Emergency, the invasion of the Golden Temple, the assassination of Indira Gandhi and the subsequent Delhi Riots, and the continuing, if waning, Khalistan movement. All these events had the general impact of stimulating Sikh political activity and intensifying (if not unifying) Sikh identity.

Moreover, in the past two decades the kind of theological debates about Sikhism and Sikh identity which once took place almost exclusively in Indian contexts have become highlighted in America. This came about for many reasons such as: *goras* converting to Sikhism; the increase of Western scholarship on Sikhism and the establishment of Sikh Studies in 'university' contexts; the reaction to events since 1984; continuing legal issues centring on the maintenance of the *panch kakka*; and the contradictions and tensions involved in raising Sikh children abroad.

Thus, as we near the centenary of Sikh presence in North America, which essentially brackets the whole of the 20th century, it seems appropriate to attempt a retrospective evaluation of such identity shifts and the history behind them as well as the myriad of mutual impacts this period has had on Sikhs in America and abroad. Such an analysis may serve three purposes. First, to record and review the record of critical events over the entire immigration span. Second, to act as a corrective to certain emerging contemporary evaluations and perceptions about the meanings and motivations of Sikhs in the Pioneer generation. Third, to put some of the current debates into a historical framework, at least as concerns North American Sikhs. We begin with an historical overview.

"Sikhs" in Diaspora

Since the late 19th century Punjabis from northwestern India have been going abroad for a variety of reasons, although financial gain and new opportunities were primary. The majority of these Punjabi migrants are designated as Sikhs. By the mid-20th century they formed communities and enclaves all over the world, including the South Pacific, Caribbean, East and South Africa, North America, throughout South and Southeast Asia, and Great Britain. This outmigration increased exponentially in the post-World War II era after Indian Independence, and Sikh communities world-wide have been engaged in significant socio-religious and political activity since the Indian events of 1984.

In the colonial period South Asians abroad were often international only in the sense of living overseas, and most did not intend to settle permanently. Their involvement in local government was often limited, and they frequently found themselves encapsulated minority groups in stratified Anglodominated societies. Likewise, the migrants' effect upon social, religious, and political affairs back in

India was usually minor. The only exceptions to this were the economic impact of remittances and the revolutionary activity of overseas Indians particularly in World War I and II.

Since 1945 South Asians have been establishing permanent residence, acquiring citizenship, raising families, building businesses, and practising their faiths outside Asia. This shift from economic migrants to new members of many societies has resulted in new patterns of adaptation and many changes; some occurred largely *within* the Indian overseas communities located in the West, some have effected the larger, outside, non-Indian populations in the host society, while other activities have reverberated all the way back to India.

What I wish to focus upon here is an analysis of how and why Punjabi Sikh identity has changed over the course of nearly a century of residence in North America and how events in Canada, the United States, and even India impacted (or failed to impact) the self-conceptions Sikhs had, and have, of themselves. There are some presuppositions that I should make clear immediately. First, I believe all social identities are constructed and undergo alteration over time as circumstances change. While the rate and direction of change may vary, over time local interpretations and practices are likely to diverge somewhat from both Great Tradition/textual prescriptions and traditional behavioural norms. This naturally results in a multiplicity of perspectives.

Second, there will always be areas of "contested identities" within and between communities as social and doctrinal heterodoxies and religious orthodoxies work out their agendas in vastly different regional/national contexts. Third, the communication and utilization of these identities will be differentially employed over time as Sikhs respond to circumstances both in the new countries-of-residence and back in South Asia.

These issues are important today as they lie at the heart of a great deal of current agitation and discussion among overseas Sikhs. They are manifested in a wide variety of Sikh activities and concerns ranging from: fundamental issues about "Who is a Sikh"; what are the legitimate sources of authority in religious affairs; what is the proper role, if any, of Western academic research on Sikhs and Sikhism; what version of Sikh history and culture is to be transmitted to the second and third-generations abroad; and what are the most core and central continuities (dogma?) of Sikh identity which must be preserved and what beliefs and behaviours are subject to individual conscience and can be altered or selectively applied? Are the "Sikhs" a single "people"; a "race", a "nationality" (with or without a "nation"), a "minority group", a "religious designation", "South Asians", hyphenated-Americans or some kind of "Punjabi". Or, more likely, do they move in and out of multiple identities depending upon time, place, and circumstance? Robin Jeffrey has called a certain kind of modern Sikh history "rhetorical" while Harjot Oberoi has termed similar historical conceptualizations as "therapeutic history". In the first case because it contains claims which are useful to groups promoting a Sikh nation-state, in the latter, because such history builds "self-esteem" in the same way hagiographic accounts of major figures, bolsters commitment and enhances pride in tradition.

Just as Sikhism itself has become transformed and transnationalised from a parochial, regionally-based faith associated almost exclusively with South Asian Punjabis towards a more inclusive, global religion, there have been similar shifts of identity for Sikhs in North America over the past century, particularly in the last twenty-five years. Some attention will be given to the continual interplay between three areas which have concerned Sikhs since their earliest encounters in North America: first, the interplay of regional and national events in South Asia as they impact upon Sikhs in Punjab and throughout South Asia: second, the internal relations between and among South Asian groups in California; and third, the American socio-political-legal context as it affected South Asians generally and Sikhs in particular. It is in these areas that Sikh identity was interpreted and acted out over the last century. Of course, this is just one of a dozen major Sikh Diaspora sites around the world.

Each such population can be expected to have somewhat distinct adjustment patterns, and to exhibit specific adaptive strategies. They have all had to deal simultaneously with recent tragic events in Punjab while continuing their lives in a relatively new environment. Let us begin at the beginning in America.

Punjabi Male Dominance in Identity to World War II

From 1904 to the end of World War II the history of South Asians in North America was largely a Punjabi male affair, 90% of whom are now designated as Sikhs, the majority of which were Jats. In the New World, all South Asians found themselves as political orphans with no external support in their fights over racism, alien land laws, or immigration laws. Simplified, the first fifty years of Punjabi history in North Amerida is a woeful tale which begins with being in the "wrong place at the wrong time" (i.e. arriving on the West Coast at the height of anti-Asian agitation) and continues through a series of discriminatory legal acts. The Alien Land Laws (1910) , the "Barred Zone" (1917), and the "Thind Decision" of Supreme Court (1923) resulted in closing off immigration from Punjab, making trips back to India impossible (as re-entry would not be permitted), rendering many South Asians "stateless persons", and generally encapsulating the communities within rural California contexts. The popular press compounded these insults by dubbing all Punjabis "Hindoos", or "East Indians" regardless of their faith.

Deprived of preferred marriage partners from abroad or unable to reunite with wives already in Punjab, at least 400 Punjabi men formed bi-cultural, bi- and tri-lingual marriages with women largely from Mexican backgrounds beginning in the first decade of their arrival. As Karen Leonard will be addressing this conference much more thoroughly on the identity issues raised by these marriages, I will not duplicate her data here, except to say that the Sikh-Mexican intermarriages spoke eloquently to a religious orientation which was flexible and practical, although far from what would be considered acceptable orthodoxy today.

The men maintained their personal faith through daily prayers and occasional visits (four or five times a year) to the gurdwara in Stockton. Built in 1915 (following the founding of the Pacific Coast Khalsa Diwan Society in 1912), the temple in Stockton seldom had a trained *granthi* and the more literate would rotate the position. For fifty years, life-cycle rites, with the exception of funerals, were rarely performed there as there were no Punjabi couples who needed marriages performed, few children requiring naming ceremonies, and a few *pahul* initiations requested. The majority of the Punjabi's American-born children were raised Catholic. Few Sikhs maintained the turban and beard.

Two situations centring on the gurdwara in Stockton can be said to be emblematic of the prevailing attitudes. In the first, according to the oldest informants, until the 1940s it was commonplace for Punjabi Muslim labourers travelling through Stockton to stay at the gurdwara for days or weeks between agricultural cycles. They were apparently allowed to place their prayer rugs in the temple for daily prayer so long as they did not turn their back to the Guru Granth Sahib. This was not a problem because the raised dias in which the Sikh holy book is enshrined faces east.

In the second situation, prior to World War II and into the 1950s, the Stockton gurdwara began using folding chairs for the *sangat* to sit on and allowed worshippers and guests to enter the temple with shoes on and hats removed (heads uncovered). It is only when *keshadari* Sikhs from newly-independent India arrived and were disturbed by these practices that the sex-divided, floor-seating and headcovering/ shoe removal more common in India were re-instituted. In both of these earlier cases the motivation for the deviations seemed to derive from a spirit of accommodation. The first instance was based on common Punjabi heritage and a monotheistic doctrine of deity. Punjabi Hindus also used the social services of the gurdwara and participated actively in Gadhr politics throughout the period of 1914-1947. In the second, there often was a "When in Rome" attitude expressed towards days of worship and location, dress, and other matters not deemed core to one's identity or contrary to matters of faith.

While externally it could have been (and was) viewed at this time as a community in decline, internally it often exhibited a solidarity and sense of common purpose. From work gangs, to shared resources, participation in the Gadhr movement, farming partnerships, and even worship sites, Punjabis saw themselves as a group with similar roots and suffering under the same discriminations in America. As non-Christian, dark-skinned, sometimes illiterate and/or non-English speakers from an Asian country under British colonial rule, the Punjabis realized their collective disabilities and disadvantages in the larger Anglo-dominated society. It intensified their hospitality and natural tendency towards mutual aid among themselves.

Compared to the gross (and unfair) discriminations they were subject to outside of Punjabi circles, the internal (religious and cultural) differences between them paled. Whatever ferment was brewing in India, the most, if not the only, salient fact for California Punjabis, Sikhs included, was the overriding fact of the British Raj and their commitment to its overthrow. Another indication of the Punjabi "unity in diversity", is found on the masthead of several Gadhr revolutionary vernacular publications in which the various names of god are written out in Urdu (Allah), Hindi (Ram), and Punjabi (Ek Onkar), regardless of the script of the following text.

By 1947 there were less than 1,500 ageing South Asians left in America out of a total of around 10,000 immigrants, including 3000 illegals after 1910. The majority were generally labourers or small farmers who had little education or capital. Although there were small clusters of students, professors, businessmen, and professionals throughout urban America, the state of California had at least half of the U.S. total by 1947 with about half of that total in the Yuba City/Marysville region of the Northern Sacramento Valley.

The majority of these were Sikhs who owned a total of some 1000 acres of farm land and were to form the centre of Post-World War II immigration to California. They were to eventually serve as an important nucleus of a resurgent and much more strident Sikh identity which was to arise in the late-1960s, intensify in the 1970's, and become hardened after 1984. This area remains a centre of strong pro-Khalistan sentiments and is seen by many urban California Sikhs as a more conservative and traditional community than counterparts in Punjab itself. This is a complete reversal of the situation prevailing in the first fifty years after initial emigration.

Recent Events and Identity Questions

In the first three quarters of this century, when ethnic, racial, religious, or communal violence occurred in South Asia it was usually considered by most Western nations as an internal, national matter. Unless it provoked border disputes, threatened to destabilise an ally, or was perceived as part of a Communist plot, little diplomatic attention was paid to internal repression, particularly in the last century of British colonial administration. Over the last twenty-five years, this attitude towards events in Asia has changed in American political circles and more dramatically yet for Sikhs in America since 1984. The Sikh situation in India has become far more than a regional or communal issue between the Indian government and the Sikhs living in India. It has had ramifications in the economic, political, religious, legal, and humanitarian spheres of dozens of nations and there is currently no reason to believe the impact will decline.

However, perhaps the most obvious result of Operation Blue Star and the invasion of the Golden Temple was the instant emotional unification of the majority of Sikhs in the belief that sacrilege had been done and that, once again, the Panth and the Khalsa was under attack and endangered. In India, to the extent that the GOI actions were seen as coterminous with Hindu chauvinism and majority disregard for minority civil and religious rights, it divided Sikhs from Hindus, Punjabi or not. To the extent "Sikh" became identified with "terrorist", it divided Hindus and Muslims from Sikhs, Punjabi or not. Some rather unusual permutations resulted from these events. They ranged from the "I (heart) Bhindranwale" and "Khalistan" bumper stickers appearing across America, from rural California to Detroit, Los Angeles, and New York... and further to Montreal, Manchester, and Sydney. Sikhs formed a political party called Akali Dal, U.K. in London while Babbar Akalis created political action groups in Vancouver. Let me make two points here. Neither the transnationalisation of religion nor conflict is anything new: in religion, we can consider the sweep of Christianity and Islam since their inception; for European/ American political links consider the Boston Irish and "the troubles" in Northern Ireland or the American Jewish community and the State of Israel. What is relatively new is the injection of South Asian issues arising out of regional conflict into the foreign policy arenas and national media of the United States as a result of activity by domestic South Asian Sikhs who are U.S. citizens. This could be extended to include a consideration of Tamils in the U.S. reacting to the situation in Sri Lanka or Punjabi Muslims over Kashmir, among others.

The Punjab Conflict and North American Sikhs

There are four areas of reciprocal interaction which can be fruitfully pursued. First, the impact of Punjab events on overseas Sikhs in America and elsewhere. Second, the impact on inter-group relations between Sikhs and other South Asians in the U.S. Third, the impact of Sikh activities on U.S. local, state, and national politicians and the media. Fourth, the impact of the expatriate Sikh community on the Punjab situation in India. All of these have influenced Sikh identity, but I will outline only the first and second areas here. First the desecration of the seat of the Sikh religion and the perceived threat to the Panth by a Hindu chauvinist majority and the Congress Party galvanized Sikh public opinion and rage, within and without India. Suffice it to say that it threatened primordial loyalties and mobilized furious, widespread Sikh opposition to the government of India. Inexorably, over time, the factionalism which often characterizes Sikh politics arose, causing moderates to feel intimidated and the more radical to engage in bitter internecine feuds. By late 1993 the GOI had restored a degree of normalcy to Punjab, although the brutality with which it was done will linger for generations. In one sense, the estrangement which had been felt between Sikhs and the central government in the aftermath of the Partition was simply geometrically re-enforced.

Prior to 1984 the bulk of Sikh-sponsored political activities in North America had been directed towards such religious freedom issues as: maintenance of the 5 K's (either the retaining of the turban in the military, transport, construction or educational contexts or the size and concealment of a *kirpan*); immigration or naturalization statutes; or discrimination/minority issues. There were exceptions such as response of Sikhs to the declaration of the Emergency in India, the Indo-Pakistani conflicts, and similar focused concerns. These have not ceased. For example, there was a legal suit against Burger King for their insistence that a female Sikh worker remove her *kara*. Also, the A.C.L.U. has taken up the case of three California San Joaquin valley Sikh school children denied access to school because of "concealed weapons" (i.e. kirpan). In contrast, many American Sikhs' current activities seem to me to be much more international, impacting several national and world regions simultaneously, and in the process raising issues of identity revolving around inclusivity vs. exclusivity, incorporation vs. fission, multiplistic vs. monolithic doctrine, traditional vs. modern, and conformity vs. open debate.

Khalistan as a Symbol Overseas

In the aftermath of the Golden Temple invasion and subsequent events, many Sikhs abroad felt the only answer was not simply to defend the faith and relatives back in India, but to fight back, even to the extent of supporting the secession of Punjab from the Indian Union to form a theocratic Sikh state. It was (and remains) difficult to tell the actual levels of support by Sikhs abroad for the concept, but it was certainly the most aggressively promoted position and visible symbol of Sikh discontent. Achievement of Khalistan (which remained largely undefined) was the platform many Sikh organizations were dedicated to. Although Sikhs since Ranjit Singh have always desired a secure homeland where they might hopefully form a majority Punjabi-speaking population, many felt it might be obtained within the Indian Union, at least until the 1980s. Serious pursuit of the Khalistan option was recent, slowly evolving between the late 60s to early 80s, mostly abroad, and accelerating in the wake of 1984.

I first heard of it in 1974 when I drove Jagjit Singh Chohan from a Yuba City gurdwara to the UC-Berkeley campus. To be honest, it seemed at the time an unnecessary extreme and unworkable proposition (but then so did Pakistan and Bangladesh in the early stages). Moreover, I had heard that many Sikhs, in the Northern Sacramento Valley at least, were unhappy with his message and presence. The measure of how things change is that a decade later there were debates in the

U.S., U.K., India, the United Nations on the subject of Khalistan. One group set up a government-in-exile and created a flag, currency, stamps, and passports ... powerful symbols all.

In sum, the reactions of overseas Sikhs to events in Punjab was immediate and visceral. More conservative and moderate voices found themselves isolated, although an inter-group dialogue of sorts continued. Perhaps as disturbing was that similar divisions arose in overseas South Asian inter-group discussions and have remained problematical.

Hindu/Sikh Estrangement and Muslim Friendship Associations

Since 1984, as the Khalistan option became more attractive to many overseas Sikhs and terrorism in Punjab became endemic, considerable consternation between moderate and radical overseas Sikh groups surfaced, eventually becoming an issue between overseas Sikh and Hindu groups. Events in India, aided by yellow journalism and propaganda on both sides in India and abroad, and by some increasingly anti-Brahmanical/anti-Hindu propaganda, have resulted in a Hindu/Sikh estrangement in many overseas communities. For example, on U.S. college campus and even high school campuses what had been "Indian" student associations were fragmented, Sikhs forming their own associations and refusing to participate in traditional pan-Indian celebrations as Indian Independence Day or Diwali. These feelings were not helped by the eruption of Hindu-Muslim violence in 1992 in Ayodya (Ramjambhoomi/Babri Masjid controversy).

Conversely, the formation of a number of Sikh-Muslim, or Sikh-Pakistani Friendship associations in California, New York, and Chicago remains one of the more unusual manifestations of overseas political realignment brought about by events in India. It seems to me that both sides must be cultivating deliberate historical amnesia given their recent past interactions. This situation is certainly not unrelated to the supportive role of the late Pakistani President Zia in arming and training Sikh insurgents before his mysterious death and the continued role that state may play in cross-border support of militants in Punjab and Kashmir. The sympathy, if not support with which some overseas Sikhs greeted Ayatollah Khomeini's death sentence on Salman Rushdie over *Satanic Verses* and further agreement that banning and complete censorship was reasonable seemed part of this pattern.

Once again, this is not a new kind of response by American groups towards events in their country of origin. Consider the pro/anti Sandinista groups of U.S. Nicaraguans, the Salvadoran factions of the 1980s, and the ongoing, intractable debates by Irish Americans on the Catholic/Protestant conflict in Northern Ireland. However, for Sikhs in the U.S. this climate of reasonable paranoia and "minority" oppression appears to have resulted in intensifying the question of what it means to be a Sikh and created some unnecessarily rigid lines of division within the community while simultaneously resulting in some unusual (and probably quite temporary) alliances with groups not normally part of the institutional or organizational structures within Sikhism or Sikh culture. All of this is in extraordinary contrast to the first half-century of Sikhs in North America.

Revisionist History in the 1990s

There appears to me to be a link between recent political events in India and North America that have sparked debates about Sikh identity and the study of Sikhism in North American universities. It seems to have had at least one additional effect that I view as largely negative. Specifically, the tendency of certain groups of Sikhs to reinterpret aspects of early Sikh history (up to 1960 or so) in ways not historically inaccurate, but obviously more reflective of contemporary sensitivities and political alignments than past realities. We might expect such revisionism on the part of non-Punjabis when viewing certain aspects of Sikh history (i.e. characterizing early Sikh immigrants and other Asian labourers as having few skills and making marginal contributions to say, California agriculture, when the reality was they possessed not only agricultural expertise but entrepreneurial ambitions and made significant technical and economic contribution). When the sources of similar retrospective re-interpretations are Sikh, it seems more destructive. For example here are five aspects of early Sikh history that have consistently and systematically been misinterpreted:

Claim
1.   Sikh identity was paramount among early Punjabi immigrants
2.   Pioneers were lone sojourners with few social supports
3.   Intermarriages with Spanish women unimportant or considered aberrant
4.   Practice of Sikhism was orthodox if orthopraxy somewhat variable
5.   Ghadar was a Sikh run and led organization which united community

Reality
1.   Identity was dominated by Punjabi sensibilities and language
2.   Often travelled with kin or village mates. Formed "gangs".
3.   Marriages formed the backbone of the social networks in California for at least forty years
4.   Few Keshadari Khalsa Sikhs among early Punjabis and practice of religion was often highly personal and quietistic
5.   Ghadar was not Sikh run until after 1917 and support, although wide, was not universal.

One can see why such viewpoints would be expressed. If for no other reason, the new interpretations, if widely accepted, would give North American Sikh history a sense of continuity, traditional-orientation, unity, and cohesion that is not present in the testimony and written records of the time, but that would be useful for contemporary reasons. All identity is contested and all history is subject to multiple interpretations; however, when the basic facts are distorted beyond supported documentation the construction of the past becomes a largely political act and not simply the presentation of a plausible alternative reading of events.

As we move toward the centenary perhaps this tendency may increase as a result of the desire to make the past relevant to the present. I find the Sikh past, particularly in North America, exhibited enough drama, courage, achievement, and religious commitment without unwarranted attempts to improve this history by biased and backward projections of current sentiments and affairs. The ongoing debate about "Who is a Sikh", and "what a good Sikh believes" and "how he or she behaves" is necessary, generally healthy, and bound to continue. But like the past, the future is likely to be replete with multiple interpretations and contested identities. The difference is that this process will now be observed, and commented upon, by outsiders and played out upon a world stage.

REFERENCES

Akbar, M.J.   *India: The Siege Within*. Harmondsworth, Middlesex: Penguin Books, 1985.

Appadurai, Arjun.   "Disjunction and Difference in the Global Cultural Economy," *Public Culture*, Vol. 2, No. 2 (Spring), 1990.
"Global Ethnoscapes: Notes and Queries for a Transnational Anthropology," in *Recapturing Anthropology*, Richard G. Fox, ed. Santa Fe: School of American Research, 1991.

Ballard, Roger.   "The Context and Consequences of Migration: Jullundur and Mirpur Compared," *New Community*, Vol. 11, No. 4, 1983.
The Context and Consequences of Emigration from Northern Pakistan. Report on ESRC Funded Research Project, January 1986a.
The Political Economy of Migration: Britain, Pakistan and the Middle East. Paper for presentation at the Association for Social Anthropologists Conference, April 1986b.

Buchignani, Norman L. and Dorreen M. Indra. *Continuous Journey: A Social History of South Asians in Canada*. Toronto: McClelland and Steward Ltd., 1985.
"Key Issues in Canadian-Sikh Ethnic and Race Relations: Implications for the Study of the Sikh Diaspora," in *The Sikh Diaspora*, N. Gerald Barrier and Verne A. Dusenbury, eds. Columbia, Missouri: South Asia Publications, 1989.

Das, Rejani, K.   *Hindustani Workers on the Pacific Coast*. Berlin: Walter de Gruyter, 1923.

Dusenbery, Verne A. *Straight>freak>yogi>Sikh*. M.A. thesis, Anthropology, University of Chicago, 1975.

"Punjabi Sikhs and Gora Sikhs", *Sikh History and Religion in the Twentieth Century*, O'Connell et al., South Asian Studies Papers, No. 3, Centre for South Asian Studies. Toronto: University of Toronto, 1988.

"The Sikh Person, the Khlasa Panth, and Western Converts," in *Religious Movements and Social Identity*, Bardwell L. Smith, ed. Leiden: E.J. Brill, forthcoming.

"On the Moral Sensitivities of Sikhs in North America," in *Divine Passions*, Owen M. Lynch, ed. Berkeley: University of California Press, 1990.

"A Sikh Diaspora? Contested Identities and Constructed Realities," *Nation and Migration: The Politics of Space in the South Asian Diaspora*, Peter van der Veer, ed. Philadelphia: University of Pennsylvania Press, 1994.

"The Poetics, and Politics of Nationalism and Multiculturalism: Diasporan Sikhs in Pluralist Polities", Unpublished manuscript, 1994.

Fox, Richard G.   *Lions of the Punjab: Culture in the Making*. Berkeley: University of California Press, 1985.

Gibson, Margaret A. *Accommodation Without Assimilation: Sikh Immigrants in an American High School*. Ithica: Cornell University Press, 1988.

Hawley, Jack Stratton and Gurinder Singh Mann. *Studying the Sikhs*. Albany, New York: State University of New York Press, 1993.

Helweg, Arthur W. "Emigrant Remittances: Their Nature and Impact on a Punjabi Village", *New Community*, Vol. 10, 1993.

"Emigration and Return: Ramifications for India," *Population Review*, Vol. 28, Nos. 1-2, 1984.

Sikhs in England. New Delhi, Bombay, Calcutta, Madras: Oxford University Press, 1986.

"Sikh Identity in England: Its Changing Nature," in *Sikh History and Religion in the Twentieth Century*, Joseph T. O'Connell et. al., eds. Toronto: University of Toronto, Centre for South Asian Studies, 1988.

Hess, Gary R.   "The Hindu in America," *Pacific Historical Review*, Vol. 38, 1969.

Jacoby, Harold S. *A Half-Century Appraisal of East Indians in the United States*. Stockton: University of the Pacific, 1956.

Jeffrey, Robin.   *What's Happening in India? Punjab, Ethnic Conflicts, Mrs. Gandhi's Death and the Test for Federalism*. Hampshire and London: MacMillan Press Ltd., 1986.

Jensen, Joan M. *Passage from India: Asian Indian Immigrants in North America*, New Haven: Yale University Press, 1988.

Josh, Sohan Singh. *The Hindustan Gadar Party: A Short History*, 2 vols. New Delhi: People's Publishing House, 1977, 1978.

Jurgensmeyer, Mark. "The Ghadar Syndrome: Nationalism in an Immigrant Community," *Punjab Journal of Politics*, 1 (October), 1977.

Kerr, Ian J.   "Fox and the Lions: The Akali Movement Revisited," in *Sikh History and Religion in the Twentieth Century* (S. Asian Studies Papers, 3), (Joseph T. O'Connell, Milton Israel, Willard G. Oxtoby, eds.), University of Toronto,

Toronto, 1988.

Kessinger, Tom G. *Vilyatpur, 1848-1968: Social and Economic Change in a North Indian Village.* Berkeley: University of California Press, 1974.

Kondapi, C. *Indians Overseas.* New Delhi: Oxford University Press, 1951.

La Brack, Bruce. "Sikhs Real and Ideal: A Discussion of Text and Context in the Description of Overseas Sikh Communities", *Sikh Studies: Comparative Perspectives on a Changing Tradition*, M. Juergensmeyer and G. Barrier, eds. Berkeley Religious Studies Series, 1979.

"Immigration Law and the Revitalization Process: The Case of California Sikhs," *Population Review*, Vol. 25, No. 1 & 2. (Jan.-Dec.), 1981.

"Occupational Specialization Among Rural California Sikhs." *Amerasia*, 21:2, Los Angeles, California, 1982.

and Leonard, Karen. "Conflict and Compatibility in Punjabi Mexican Immigrant Families in Rural California; 1915-1965, 11 *Journal of Marriage and the Family,* Vol. 46, No. 3, 1984.

"Sants and the *Sant* Tradition in the Context of overseas Indian Communities", *The Saints: Studies in a Devotional Tradition of India*, Berkeley Religious Studies Series, Berkeley, 1987.

The Sikhs of Northern California: 1904-1986, AMS (American Migration Series) Press, Series 2, New York, 1988.

"The New Patrons: Sikhs Overseas," *The Sikh Diaspora* (N. Gerald Barrier and Verne A. Dusenbery, eds.), New Delhi, Manohar, 1989.

Leonard, Karen. "The Pioneer Sikhs: Religious Tolerance," in *Sikh Samachar*, Vol. VIII, No. 3 (November), 1984.

"Ethnicity Confounded: Punjabi Pioneers in California," in *Sikh History and Religion in the Twentieth Century,* Joseph T. O'Connell, et. al. Toronto: University of Toronto, Centre for South Asian Studies, 1988.

"Pioneer Voices from California: Reflections on Race, Religion, and Ethnicity." in *The Sikh Diaspora*, N. Gerald Barrier and Verne A. Dusenbury, eds. Columbia, Missouri: South Asia Publications, 1989.

Making Ethnic Choices: California's Punjabi Mexican Americans, Philadelphia: Temple University Press, 1992.

Madhaven, M.C. "Indian Emigrants: Numbers, Characteristics, and Economic Impact," *Population and Development Review*, Vol. 11, No. 3 (September), 1985.

McLeod, W. H. *The Evolution of the Sikh Community.* Oxford: Clarendon Press, 1976.

The Punjabis in New Zealand. Amritsar: Guru Nanak Dev University Press, 1986.

The Sikhs: History, Religion, and Society. New York: Columbia University Press, 1989.

Who is a Sikh? The Problem of Sikh Identity. Oxford: Clarendon Press, 1989.

Miller, Allan P. *An Ethnographic Report of the Sikh (East) Indians of Sacramento Valley.* Unpublished mss. University of California, Berkeley, South/Southeast

Asia Library, Berkeley, California, 1950.

Nayer, Kuldip and Khushwant Singh. *Tragedy of Punjab: Operation Bluestar & After*. New Delhi: Vision Books, 1984.

Oberoi, Harjot.   *The Construction of Religious Boundaries: Culture, Identity, and Diversity in the Sikh Tradition*. Delhi: Oxford University Press, 1994.

Puri, Harish Kumar. *Ghadar Movement: Ideology, Organization and Strategy*. Amritsar (Punjab): Guru Nanak Dev University Press, 1983.

Saran, Parmatma.   *The Asian Indian Experience in the United States*. Massachusetts: Schenkman Publishing Company, Inc., 1985.

Singh, Iqbal.   *Punjab Under Seige*. New York. London. Sydney: Allen, McMillan and Enderson, 1986.

Singh Jane et al.   *South Asians in North America: An Annotated and Selected Bibliography*. Occasional Paper No. 14, Centre for South and Southeast Asia Studies. Berkeley: University of California Press, 1988.

"Pioneer Voices from California: Reflections on Race, Religion, and Ethnicity" in *The Sikh Diaspora*, N. Gerald Barrier and Verne A. Dusenbury, eds. Columbia, Missouri: South Asia Publications, 1989.

Tinker, Hugh.   *A New System of Slavery: The Export of Indian Labour Overseas, 1830-1920*, London, 1974.

The Banyan Tree: Overseas Emigrants from India, Pakistan, and Bangladesh. London: Oxford University Press, 1977.

Tully, Mark and Satish Jabob. *Amritsar: Indira Gandhi's Last Battle*. London: Jonathan Cape, 1985.

Wood, Ann.   *East Indians in California*. M.A. thesis (Anthropology), University of Wisconsin, Madison, 1966.

Canadian Sikh Identity

Narindar Singh

Introduction

Guru Nanak laid down the foundations of a universal world religion. His spiritual experiences revealed as *Gur-bani* (divine poetry) formed the basis of Sikhism. His teachings constituted the fundamental principles of the Sikh faith which also became the foundations of his thought on social reform. Sikh identity emerged from the teachings of Guru Nanak. The succeeding Gurus carried out his mission and elaborated upon social and religious structures.

Guru Nanak used the concept of *Sachiara* (the enlightened, emancipated individual) to create a future world order, which became the desired symbol of change simultaneously invested with divine qualities. It is the saint-soldier concept of Guru Gobind Singh - an individual who combines moral and physical discipline and is in tune with the Supreme Being. Guru Nanak wanted his Sikh to be Sachiara transformed into a saint-soldier - internally solid, standing on moral principles and thereby attaining supremacy in other areas of life.

The Gurus organized people outside the unjust Hindu caste order and oppressive political state by creating parallel Sikh institutions, separate religious centres, a separate script and a scripture of their own to build a new society. The growth of theology along with historical experiences associated with *Kakkar* (Sikh symbols) of the order of the *Khalsa* shaped the Sikh identity.

The Sikh scripture embodied with radical doctrines, the divine mission of the ten Gurus, the persecution of the Sikhs for a century, their revolt, making extreme sacrifices to maintain Sikh identity, and finally the Sikh struggle triumphed into the Sikh Raj (Sikh rule).

Elements of Sikh Identity

A. The Concept of God

1. Sikhism is uncompromising monotheism, the creed embodied in *Guru Granth Sahib*. The Creator God being the sole entity.
2. The Supreme Being is the upholder of the moral spirit of the universe and is the foundation of all existence. He is the manifestation of the divine essence and the source of all values and virtues. God created the world and permeated it with his

Light. He is the controller of *Hukam* (the moral order of the cosmos), retributor of deeds and awarder of *Karam* (grace). This conception of God forms the core of Sikh faith.

3.   The phenomenal world is not *Mithya* (illusion) or suffering, it is real, but its reality is transient and one must not form attachment to it.

B.   Spiritual Foundations

1.   Guru Nanak disapproved of monasticism, ascetism and withdrawal from the concerns of life and recommended the life of a householder with social responsibility.

2.   Guru Nanak recommended life affirmation in all areas of life instead of life negation.

3.   The woman was looked upon as inferior, evil, impure and a temptation, why slander her from whom are born great ones. He recommended a householder's life and advocated equal status for women with men in all spheres of life.

4.   The householder must engage in beneficent activity, keeping his mind absorbed in contemplation and devotion combining spiritual with the empirical. The individual is to engage in righteous action that may further God's plan of righteousness in the world.

5.   In Sikhism there is overwhelming presence of compassionate attitude towards all humanity. It weighs against cruelty and injustice and aims at the establishment of a just society. 6. Guru Nanak's call for playing the game of love and sacrifice was repeated by Guru Gobind Singh at the time of *Amrit* ceremony to which five piaras offered their heads.

6.   The introduction of the institution of martyrdom by Sikh Gurus over a period of two hundred years is virtually unknown in Indian society.

C.   Sikh Ideals

1.   In Sikhism the highest ideal is to carry out the Will of God.

2.   Sikhism is completely a new thesis, to ensure the Sikh identity Guru Arjan authenticated the Sikh scripture.

3.   Sikhism is a whole life system.

4.   The creation of the new society by Guru Nanak is based on Miri-Piri (temporal and spiritual) system.

5.   Sikhism being a Miri-Piri system could not accept an extreme theory of either *Ahimsa* or violence. Instead it promoted an integrated balanced approach of justice under which both violent or non-violent means were historically employed in order to protect, nourish and encourage freedom and justice.

6.   Guru Nanak created the system of succession to ensure the implementation of his thesis.

7.   In Sikhism, God is never born. *Guru Granth Sahib* strictly denies the doctrine

of incarnation avtarhood (God taking human form).

8. Guru Hargobind wore two swords conveying the significance of spiritual and empirical unity in the Sikh system.

9. Guru Gobind Singh's creation of the order of the *Khalsa* (the doctrine of Sikh initiation) is the formalization of saint-soldier concept thus instilling spirituality into human action a people imbued with the ideal of *Miri-Piri* - the concept of Guru Nanak's *Sachiara*. He abolished succession by heredity, and restored to the people both spiritual and temporal sovereignty, spiritual to *Guru Granth Sahib* and temporal to the *Khalsa*.

10. Every thing laid down in the *Guru Granth Sahib* is final and unalterable.

11. Guru Gobind Singh's Nash doctrine made it absolutely clear that plurality of beliefs signifying one's identity has no place in Sikhism. Amrit ceremony clearly defines the Sikh.

12. *Guru Granth Sahib* pronounces a distinct and independent Sikh identity.

13. By stopping the line of succession of *Guruship*, Guru Gobind Singh made it clear that not a word could be added or altered in the *Guru Granth Sahib*.

D.   Sikh Ethics

1. During Guru Nanak's time there were two malignant growths - the prevalent Hindu caste system and the oppressive political system. The Guru forcefully condemned these institutions. He accepted equality of all men. He raised his voice in divine indignation at Mughal ruler's aggression of India for the suffering caused to innocent humanity.

2. Although Sikhs had a long history of struggle with the Muslim rulers but once the Sikhs came to power, they never tried to convert either Hindus or Muslims to the Sikh faith.

3. The Sikh armies gave a unique treatment to their vanquished adversaries that bear an unparalleled conduct of contemporary or modern army.

E. Oppression

The military clashes between the Sikhs and Mughal armies demonstrate that the Mughal rulers considered the Sikh society an unwanted political entity which had to be curbed or destroyed.

Canadian Sikh Identity

Around the turn of the century the Sikhs arrived in Vancouver in search of livelihood and entered a tense racial atmosphere. Their industrious, adaptive nature and willingness to work hard enabled them to find work quite easily. They were soon absorbed into the Canadian labour force, but this did not last very long. Sikhs ran up against racial intolerance, discrimination, and legal barriers. They faced problems of cultural conflict, difficulties within their own community, and with their neighbours. Soon the exclusionist forces were successful in shutting the door against Sikh immigration into Canada. There was an era of relative tranquillity when Sikhs were accepted and tolerated, though as inferior members of the community. The exclusionary forces fanned anti-Asiatic feeling which led to the anti-oriental riots of 1907. The government moved to stop immigration of Sikhs. In 1908, the door was shut to further immigration from Punjab, for the next half century.

Salient Features of the Sikh Struggle in Canada

The ban on immigration and the discriminatory practices provoked great resentment among the Sikh pioneers, which was expressed in the form of a liberation struggle to free India. The Sikhs resolved to fight:

a)   racial discrimination
b)   the immigration ban and the imposition of continuous Journey
c)   exclusionary laws.
d)   removal of Sikhs to British Honduras.
e)   the ban on Sikh families. Sikhs took the case to British Indian Government in London and to Viceroy in Dehli.
f)   in the Ghadar movement to liberate India.
g)   oppression and surveillance, Sikhs offered martyrdom when *Gurdwara* sanctity was trampled.
h)   retention of Sikh identity by maintaining traditions.
i)   the Citizenship rights and the vote.
j)   retention of Sikh symbols in Bhinder versus Canadian National Railway
k)   for Sikh symbols versus RCMP
l)   for Amelie Sikh refugees (a ship load of 174 refugees)

The Sikhs set up Sikh institutions such as the *Khalsa Diwan Society* (Sikh organisation) in 1907, and built the Vancouver Gurdwara in 1908. The *Gurdwara Management Committee* within it was the principal organization acting in the interest of not only Sikhs but also spoke on community concerns for all Indians. The Gurdwara served as a gathering place for Hindus, Muslims, and Sikhs, and all discussed their grievances and mutual problems in these meetings. They promptly provided Punjabis with a sense of place, identity, order, continuity, and community pride. The Sikhs rapidly established *Gurdwaras* everywhere in British Columbia. Religious institutions brought the Sikhs together and provided an organizational focus for collective action on several issues. Virtually every aspect of the ongoing battle against the immigration ban was planned, supported, and orchestrated through the Gurdwara organization.

Sikh pioneers came to Canada with a strong identity. Despite the hardship, discrimination, and social isolation, they rarely doubted the worthiness and correctness of their firmly held point of view. They united together under threat and went on the defensive.

By the end of 1908 the Sikhs were politically neutralized as a voting force in Canada. Immigration had been effectively terminated. Economically, a racial line had been drawn: Punjabis were forced to become unskilled blue-collar workers if they were to work at all. They were generally the last hired and first fired. They were therefore integrated into the economy but as a subordinate labour force. Routine discrimination in all other aspects of life contributed to nearly total isolation for the Sikhs in British Columbia. The Sikhs developed community institutions, mutual aid and leadership. As the community turned increasingly religious and culturally homogeneous, Sikh institutions became central to community life. The *Gurdwara* and the *Khalsa Diwan* Society were the main Sikh institutions engaged in holding the Punjabi community together.

British Honduras Scheme

The Canadian government did not stop at the continuous passage restriction. Instead it attempted to remove Sikhs already in Canada. In 1908, the Canadian government devised a scheme to remove the Sikh settlers in Canada as indentured labourers to British Honduras. The Sikhs of British Columbia strongly resisted the government scheme. The *Khalsa Diwan Society* conducted negotiations with the minister of the interior, and provided a forum at which the idea was emphatically rejected.

Mr. J.B. Harkin, assisted by William Charles Hopkinson, was assigned to approach Vancouver's Punjabi community in this regard. The Sikh community allowed to send Satnagar Singh and Sham Singh as delegates to Belize (British Honduras). They were accompanied by Harkin and Hopkinson. On arrival in Belize the Punjabi delegation found the conditions were far inferior to those in Vancouver. The delegation also found thirty Indians in Belize who had immigrated as indentured labourers about a generation before - all thirty wanted to return to India.

By this time Professor Teja Singh, had joined the Vancouver Punjabi community. He told the representatives of the Canadian government that Sikhs strongly objected to their being packed off to Central America. If the government still forcibly sent the Sikhs to British Honduras, it would clearly be a gross injustice. The Sikhs unanimously rejected the proposal of settling in British Honduras. They refused to be indentured labourers in a colony where there were low wages, and they decided to remain free men in Canada.

Challenging Exclusion

The Sikh community did not expect that the "continuous passage" rule would be enforced against them. In November, 1909, the Sikh community sent Teja Singh and Hari Singh to England to solicit the support of Liberal British circles, where Teja Singh spoke to a number of sympathetic audiences. Around this time a small party of Sikhs left for India to bring their wives and children. President Raja Singh and priest Balwant Singh of the Vancouver *Gurdwara* joined the party. They brought their wives and children along with them to Canada. They were denied entry on the basis of the "continuous passage" rule. The immigration issue generated nationalist feelings in the local Sikh community. Anti-British sentiments arose. From 1910 on, it led an agitation against immigration laws, raised funds to fight individual cases, and focused attention on the fact that Sikhs settled in Canada should be allowed to bring their wives and children from India.

The Canadian government imposed unbearable restrictions on Sikh immigrants who were British subjects. The forcible separation of the wives and children from their husbands and fathers annihilated Sikh immigration into Canada. This compulsory separation of families was punitive. Sikhs found it impossible to comply with such a devious regulation and demanded its immediate abolition. Seeing that their efforts bore no fruit in Canada, Sikhs decided to have their case represented before the British and the British Indian government. On the 22nd of February, 1913, the *Khalsa Diwan Society* appointed Nand Singh Sihra, Balwant Singh and Narain Singh as a delegation to approach the Home government in London and the Indian government to help remove restrictions on immigration. The delegation met with the Viceroy in Delhi on December 20, 1913, and he agreed to press for the partial removal of the continuous passage restriction only as it applied to wives and children of Sikh immigrants.

The fight for the independence of India became a great moving force in 1913. *Khalsa Diwan* leadership became actively involved in the struggle for liberation of the motherland from British rule. The British Indian government, apprehensive of the situation, requested the cooperation of Canadian Government, and sought the assistance of their officials to keep a close watch on the movements of Indian activists in North America. When war with Germany broke out, in late summer of 1914, the Ghadar Party urged all Punjabis to return to India to prepare for an armed uprising. Hundreds of Sikhs in British Columbia responded to the call.

Komagata Maru

For several weeks prior to the arrival of *Komagata Maru,* Vancouver newspapers carried stories from Hong Kong that a boat load of Punjabis were headed for British Columbia's shores. On the night *Komagata Maru* reached Vancouver, Premier McBride was quoted as saying: "To admit Orientals in large numbers would mean in the end the extinction of white people, and we always have in mind the necessity of keeping this a white man's country." Hate mongering articles began to appear in the newspapers on a daily basis.

Gurdit Singh's bold attempt to bring the *Komagata Maru* to Vancouver on May 23, 1914, threw the Canadian bureaucracy in disarray. The Canadian government immediately placed an armed guard in a launch which continued to circle the ship day and night. Gurdit Singh stayed a prisoner, and was not allowed to make contacts with the Vancouver Sikh community. The ship was turned back from Vancouver, and forced to return to Asia. When the passengers were ordered to board a special train to take them to Punjab they refused, were fired at, and a massacre ensued.

Martyrdom of Mewa Singh

Bela Singh and Harnam Singh were loyal informers of Hopkinson, who spied on the Ghadar nationalists fight for the liberation of India. On August 17, 1914, Harnam Singh vanished; his body was found at the end of the month. Arjan Singh, another spy of Hopkinson, was accidentally shot dead. On September 5, Bela Singh turned up for Arjan Singh's funeral at the *Gurdwara*. Priest Bhag Singh started offering Ardas (supplication). Bela shot Bhag Singh twice in the spine when the priest was kneeling forward, then systematically fired into the Sangat (congregation). Bhag Singh and Battan Singh were mortally wounded and seven others were shot. These killings enraged the Sikh community. Since the murders took place in the *Gurdwara* premises by Bela, a government agent, it implied that the government was behind Bela's rampage. Bela was arrested.

The trial was slated for October 21. No informer had yet been successfully prosecuted, although informers had been brought to court many times. Hopkinson publicly stated that he intended to give evidence to substantiate Bela's claim that he shot in self-defence. In the wake of Bhag's death Mewa Singh concluded that Hopkinson had to be stopped from taking the witness stand. Mewa Singh Lopoke volunteered to kill him. Mewa strongly believed Hopkinson and Malcolm Reid were behind the desecration of the sacred Gurdwara premises at the hands of Bela. On the morning of Bela's trial, Mewa Singh caught up with Hopkinson in Vancouver court house corridors. When he was within a foot of Hopkinson, Mewa Singh pulled a pair of .32 caliber revolvers and without saying a word he shot him dead. Mewa surrendered quietly. He was convicted and hanged on January 11, 1915. Mewa Singh's courageous action was a classic example of the Sikh tradition of martyrdom.

Surveillance

The British were engaged in political surveillance of Punjabi immigrants on the West Coast from 1908 on. They carried out vigilance either directly, through their own agents, by way of Canadian agents, or via United States officials. In the first months of the First World War, the Ghadar Party leaders tried to stage a rising in

Punjab. They encouraged immigrants to return to India and take part in the insurrection. Their efforts were ill organized and attracted little support from the Sikh population in Punjab. The refusal of the Honduras scheme in 1908, prompted the first surveillance by Canadian government. This led to the appointment of William Charles Hopkinson for vigilance by the Laurier government. In 1915, under Ghadar organization, an estimated 3,125 Punjabis from the United States, Canada, as well as other parts of the world poured into Punjab to liberate India. Many of the Ghadar Party's liberation plans met with disaster however. German efforts to supply ship loads of arms and ammunition had been bungled.

Ghadar

In and around San Francisco a small group of Indian intellectuals arose to become the nucleus of a revolutionary independence movement. The vehicle for this was the *Hindustan Ghadar* Party. Though it originated in the United States, it was also active in Canada since the time it was established. Since the vast majority of immigrants were Sikhs, the earliest immigrant organizations centred around *Gurdwaras*. The difficulties faced by Sikhs put them in the lap of revolutionaries. The traditional Sikh response against domination was to fight back. Since *Gurdwaras* were the only public places where Punjabis could meet, they became the storm centres of political activity. The *Ghadar* Party was formally organized to promote national independence of India. *Ghadar* leaders in America started organizing a revolt in India. Several ships were commissioned to transport Sikh revolutionaries to mainland India from the United States, Canada and several other countries from the Far East. Germany came forward to render substantial financial assistance and arms to the *Ghadarites* for their rousing a revolt in India. Important Ghadar leaders left the United States shore to engage their fight in different countries. On arrival in India the Ghadarites discovered that the Indians were not conducive to revolution. The carefully laid plans were foiled by the police. The Ghadar uprising was smashed. Despite the Ghadar movement one hundred thousand Sikhs from Punjab donned army uniforms and fought with loyalty and exceptional gallantry along with Canadian and British soldiers against Germany in World War I. Sikh soldiers established a sterling record on European, Turkish, and African battlefronts. Sikhs won fourteen Victoria crosses.

Dwindling Numbers

After the departure of the *Komagata Maru* in 1914, the Sikh population dwindled in size. The immigration ban left Vancouver's Sikh community virtually isolated from the rest of the Sikh world. In such a situation a number of possibilities were open to the Sikhs. They could have either given up and left Canada in search of greener pastures, or remained as an isolated, predominantly-male community carrying on a bachelor-like existence. Or they could have assimilated through inter-marriage with the western society. Quite a few chose the first alternative and left. Some, however, remained and stayed as an isolated community as inter-marriage with the Anglo or Euro-Canadians was not acceptable to them. The population dropped from its peak of six thousand around the First World War to about one thousand one hundred just before the Second World War. Yet, those who did remain apparently retained kakkar (Sikh symbols).

Impact of Outside Influences

The Jallianwala massacre on April 13, 1919, sent shock waves to the Sikh communities all over the world. Canadian Sikhs were strongly affected by these events. The financial contribution from Canadian Sikhs continued to flow towards the *Gurdwara* reform movement in Punjab in 1921. In 1924, a Jatha (organized Sikh group) of eleven Sikhs from Canada led by Mit Singh Pandor (one of the pioneers) joined the reform movement in Punjab.

The Depression

An extensive system of mutual aid among Sikhs helped them survive the Depression during the 1930s. A Sikh was never found in a soup kitchen line up; they considered it too humiliating, even if some were poor. In spite of these hardships they never went on unemployment assistance and despite economic hard times Sikhs pursued their fight for the removal of restrictions on their rights, the ability to vote, and the immigration ban.

The Vote

During World War II, the Sikhs also opposed the draft stating that a country which does not allow some of their citizens to vote could not ethically ask them to fight. The Sikh community kept up the pressure in 1943 although most Sikhs were willing to serve if the vote issue could be resolved. Probably there were too few of them to justify the formation of special units. Perhaps they were excused from compulsory military service because one hundred thousand Sikh soldiers from Punjab fought along side British and Canadian soldiers on all fronts with exceptional gallantry and loyalty. A few hundred recruits from Canada would presumably not have made any difference.

Basic legal restrictions against Sikhs persisted until 1947. Sikhs continued the opposition. The *Khalsa Diwan Society* endeavoured to solicit greater public support for their cause. A united front was attempted with the Chinese who were also pressing for the vote. The Election Committee agreed to recommend the necessary changes in the voting laws. The changes were unanimously passed by the province on April 2, 1947, which in turn, automatically brought the federal vote and ended legal restrictions on Sikhs.

Pioneer's Contributions

During the "Quiet Years"(1919-47), immigration dropped very low. The population was a little over a thousand. The community was faced with the retention of their ethnic identity. They went through the struggle of unequal pay for equal work and ineligibility to vote. The continuity of traditions was their primary task. Extensive literature has been written by Sikhs and on Sikhs in Canada since their arrival. The pioneers wrote poetry, published newspapers, journals and articles. Literature was fostered through an increasing number of *Gurdwaras*, publications (newspapers and journals) , and cultural organizations. Singing and music being an integral part of Sikh religious practice meant poets had their works included in musical presentations. The practice of poetry reading on the *Gurdwara* stage helped poets and writers address the audience.

Ethical Conduct and Pursuit of Identity

Although Sikhs have been in Canada for ninety years, few have been assimilated into Canadian society. Sikh professionals and workers in practice have left an imprint as a result of their work ethics, which speaks volumes about their agility and admirable adaptation to the adopted country. Non-Sikh and Sikh Canadians have influenced and often creatively adapted to each others value system. Sikhs have continued to instill their culture in their children. Third and fourth generation Sikhs still understand Punjabi. Punjabi is the spoken language at home, and is backed by the strong religious conviction of parents and well-established 18 religious institutions. Children generally become believers of the Sikh faith. Sikh parents have been conscious of differences in outlook between themselves and their children raised in North America. They feared the influence of North American cultural values which conflict with Sikh values.

The Sikhs struggled hard to maintain their ethnic identity through community institutions such as *Gurdwaras* religious organizations, national organizations, institutes,, schools, language classes, newspapers, television and radio programs, community-oriented business, arts, and ethnic associations. North American culture predominates at work, in the schools, in government, and in the media. Community institutions are the only organizational responses to the non-Sikh cultural values to which the growing child is exposed.

Democratically elected Sikh religious organizations have existed in Canada for more than four generations. The first Sikh *Gurdwara* (Sikh church) was built in 1908, in Vancouver. Now there are close to seventy *Gurdwaras* across the country. There are numerous Sikh organizations with more being founded all the time.

Provincial funding for language promotion has been of great benefit to the community. In 1981, Sikhs were able to set up a Sikh national organization, the

Federation of Sikh Societies of Canada, and received the federal funding for its activities. For Sikhs, the establishment of religious institutions is quite an accomplishment.

Education of Children

Parents have few resources to ward off the impact of those Western values which are incongruent with Sikh values on Sikh children, with the exception of teaching at home and weekend schooling. At home, parents attempt to establish parent-child relationships on traditional lines, such as strict obedience to their authority, and try to keep their children from social situations that could threaten Sikh values, particularly the girls from dating. The dating restrictions are enforced rigidly.

Sikhs have started administering Kirtan (devotional singing) through music classes in *Gurdwaras* or community centres. Parents facilitate better understanding of subjects by teaching children at home. Two to three week youth camps provide religious orientation ranging from history of the Sikh Gurus, to history of Canadian Sikhs, fundamentals of Sikh religion, music, Kirtan, Punjabi sports, and several motivating incentives to the Sikh children and youth. Many young Sikhs have taken Amrit (Sikh initiation). *Khalsa* (Sikh) schools are being set up for Sikh children. Chairs of Sikh studies have already been set up at the University of British Columbia and at the University of Toronto. Several Sikh Studies conferences were organized in the past five years in North America.

The range of activities pursued by the community to preserve Sikh identity is merely the measure of awareness of a long struggle ahead for generations to come. It is not going to lead them successfully through the stormy ocean when odds against their survival are enormous, however the struggle must go on.

Several community-based programs aimed at language retention, religious instructions, Punjabi music, and dance have had a major impact on inculcating Sikh values in the sphere of religion and culture on Canadian-born Sikh children. Sikhs are conscious of their ethnicity and heritage, and they know that they are a visible minority. In spite of rigorous indoctrination of their children, there is a strong feeling that in the long run their cultural values would be difficult to preserve in North America. They are fighting against enormous odds.

Bhinder Versus Canadian National Railways

Mr. Bhinder K.S., an employee of the Canadian National Railway since April 1974, had worked for more than four years as a maintenance electrician in its Toronto coach yard. Canadian National adopted a policy which required all employees in the Toronto coach yard to wear a hard hat when at work. Bhinder, a Sikh refused to wear a hard hat. The Canadian National Railway terminated his services on December 5, 1978.

Bhinder filed a complaint with the Canadian Human Rights commission and was awarded compensation for loss of salary and ordered his reinstatement with the Canadian National Railway with an exemption from the hard hat requirement. Canadian National applied to the Federal Court of Appeal for a judicial review to set aside the decision of the Human Rights Tribunal. On April 13, 1983, the Federal Court of Appeal allowed the application to be set aside. The case was then appealed to the Supreme Court of Canada by the Canadian Human Rights and Bhinder. The appeal was dismissed. The Sikhs lost the hard hat case.

Sikh Symbols Versus RCMP

Sikhs have donned turbans and Sikh symbols in police forces in the U.K., Singapore, Malaysia, Thailand, Hong Kong, and India. Sikhs in turbans have served in the British Indian Army in World War I and World War II, and in the United Nations Peace-keeping Force. For those of the Sikh faith, the wearing of the turban, growing a beard, keeping unshorn hair and other Sikh symbols are essential part of their religious requirement and tradition. Any initiated Sikh was unable to join the RCMP if he was not allowed to wear the turban. Therefore, the existing dress code became an infringement of their rights under the Charter.

Around mid-1987 the RCMP Commissioner, Norman Inkster, came up with recommendations for necessary dress code changes to RCMP uniform to facilitate entry of initiated Sikhs into the force. It provoked opposition in Western Canada.

On March 14, 1990, the Canadian solicitor general declared in the House of Commons that the Canadian Sikhs would be able to serve in the RCMP without having to compromise their religious requirement to wear turbans and Sikh symbols. All Canadian Sikhs of different affiliations were united on the RCMP turban issue, and they joined hands toward successful realization of this objective.On May 11, 1991, Baltej Singh Dhillon, an initiated Sikh, made history when he was decorated as an RCMP officer wearing a turban and other Sikh symbols at a colourful graduating ceremony from the Regina Police Academy.

Amelie Sikh Refugees

On July 12, 1987, 174 Sikh refugees from Punjab landed at Charlesville near Halifax. The Amelie passengers were detained by the RCMP without a hearing and without access to lawyers. The Canadian Sikhs demanded an immediate release. Several Sikhs offered to assist the new arrivals and were willing to cover all would-be immigrants' settlement costs. There was a storm of public protest over immigration laws that will allow one hundred seventy-four Sikh refugees to remain in Canada. Canadian Sikhs were offended by the depth of public outrage and lack of public sympathy. Alarmed by the depth of public reaction about Sikh refugees, Prime Minister Brian Mulroney ordered a recall of Parliament to deal with the perceived abuse of Canada's refugee system. Most of the Sikh refugees settled in Toronto and Vancouver. The hard working refugees soon established themselves and became self supporting.

REFERENCES

Ashworth, Mary. *The Forces Which Shaped Them: A History of Education of Minority Group Children in British Columbia.* Vancouver: New Star Books, 1979.

Brown, Emily C. *Har Dayal: Hindu Revolutionary and Rationalist.* Tucson: University of Arizona Press, 1975.

Buchignani, Norman and Indira, Doreen M. *Continuous Journey: A Social History of South Asians in Canada.* Toronto: McClelland and Stewart, 1985.

Canadian Sikhs' Studies Institute, "Presentation to Hon. Pierre Blais, Solicitor General: A Signature Campaign and 90 minute Discussion on the Turban Issue and Sikh Symbols," Those Present: Dhillon, Balbir S. Dr., Dhillon, Bikar S. Sara, Iqbal, and Singh, Narindar. February 1, 1990.

Chadney, James G. "The Vancouver Sikhs: An Ethnic Community in Canada," Ph.D. thesis: Michigan State University, 1976.

Chair of Sikh Studies. A booklet. Ottawa: Federation of Sikh Societies of Canada, 1985.

Cole, Owen W. and Sambhi, Piara Singh. *The Sikhs: Their Religious Beliefs and Practices.* New Delhi: Vikas Publishing House Pvt Ltd., 1978.

Dhillon, Gurdarshan Singh. "The Sikhs and the British 1849-1920," Paper Presented at International Conference on Sikh Studies University of Toronto, Nov. 24-25, 1990.
          "Sikh Identity: A Continuing Feature," Paper presented at the International Conference on Sikh Studies, University of British Columbia, Vancouver, Dec. 2, (1990).

Dilgeer, Harjinder Singh. and Takhar, Sardool Singh. "The Sikh Turban (Dastar)," *The Sword,* Spring/Summer, (1990).

Ferguson, Ted. *A White Man's Country: An Exercise in Canadian Prejudice.* Toronto: Macmillan, 1975.

Finlayson, Ann. "A Canadian Minority in Turmoil," Maclean's, July 9, 1985.

Gessell, Paul. "IRCMP Dress Code Headache for Minister: Turbaned Officer Problem Difficult Blais Admits," *The Ottawa Citizen,* February 23, 1990.

James, Alan G. *Sikh Children in Britain,* London: Oxford University Press. For the Institute of Race Relations, 1976.

Janigan, Mary with Mackenzie, Hilary and Gessell, Paul. "A Harrowing Story," Maclean's, August 17, 1987.

Janigan, Mary with Mackenzie, Hilary. "A Wary Welcome For a Human Cargo," *Maclean's*, August 3, 1987.

Jensen, Joan M.   *Passage From India: Asian Indian immigrants in North America.* Toronto: Yale University Press, 1988.

Johnston, Hugh.   *The Voyage of Komagata Maru: The Sikh Challenge to Canada's Colour Bar.* Delhi: Oxford University Press.

Canadian Historical "Patterns of Sikh Migration to Canada, 1900-1960," *Sikh History and Religion in the Twentieth Century.* ed. O'Connel Israel, Oxtoby, Mcleod, Grewal. University of Toronto, 1988.

"The Surveillance of Indian Nationalists in North America 1908-1918," *B.C. Studies,* Number 78 Summer (1988).

Josh, Sohan Singh. *Hindustan Gadar Party: A Short History.* 2 Vols. New Delhi: People's Publishing, 1977-1978.

Tragedy of Komagata Maru. New Delhi: People's Publishing, 1975.

Kanwaljit Kaur.   "Sikh Women". *Fundamental Issues in Sikh Studies.* Chandigarh: Institute of Sikh Studies, 1992.

Kashmeri, Zuhair and McAndrew, Brian. *Soft Target: How the Indian Intelligence Service Penetrated Canada.* Toronto: James Lorimer, 1989.

Mansukhani, Gobind Singh. *The Quintessence of Sikhism.* Amritsar: Shiromani Gurdwara Parbandhak Committee, 1985.

"The Tradition of Miri and Piri in Sikhism," *Miri Piri da Sidhant,* Singh, Lal, Ahluwalia, Jasbir Singh. Chandigarh: Guru Gobind Singh Foundation, 1977.

"A Survey of Sikh Studies and Sikh Centres in the West," in *Harbans Singh Commemoration Volume* Published by *Harbans Singh Commemoration Committee,* New Delhi, 1988.

"Impressions of the Canadian Sikhs," *The Sikh Review,* September 1970.

Mayer, Adrian C.   *A Report on the East Indian Community in Vancouver.* Vancouver: University of British Columbia, 1959.

Purl, Harish K.   *Ghadar Movement: Ideology, Organization and Strategy.* Amritsar: Guru Nanak Dev University, 1983.

Sandhu, Ranbir S. "Sikhs in America: Stress and Survival," Paper presented at the International Conference on Sikh Studies, George Washington University, December 8, 1990.

Scanlan, T. Joseph. *The Sikhs of Vancouver: A Case Study of the Role of Media in Ethnic Relations.* Ottawa: Carleton University, 1975.

Singh, Avtar.   *Ethics of the Sikhs.* Patiala: Punjabi University, 1983.

Singh, Baba Gurdit. *Voyage of the Komagata Maru or: India Slavery Abroad,* first edition. Calcutta: Arya Press, 1920.

Singh, Daljeet.   "Naam in Sikhism," in *Advanced Studies in Sikhism.* ed. Mann, Jasbir Singh and Saraon, Harbans Singh. Chandigarh: Published by Sikh Community of North America U.S.A., 1989.

"Sikh Identity", in *Fundamental issues in Sikh Studies.* ed. Mann, Kharak

Singh, Mansukhani, Gobind Singh, Mann, Jasbir Singh. Chandigarh: Institute of Sikh Studies, 1992.

Sikhism: A Comparative Study of its Theology and Mysticism. New Delhi: Sterling Publishers Ltd., 1979.

Essays on the Authenticity of Kartarpuri Bir and the integrated Logic and Unity of Sikhism. Patiala: Punjabi University, 1987.

Singh, Darshan. *Japuji Sahib: Context and Concerns of Guru Nanak.* London: Sikh Education Council UK, 1992.

Singh, Ganda. *Amrika Vich Hindustani.* Vancouver: Keser Singh Khalsa, 1976. (P)

Singh, Gopal. *Guru Gobind Singh.* New Delhi: National Book Trust, 1966.

The Religion of the Sikhs. Delhi: Asia Publishing House, 1978.

Singh, Harbans. *The Heritage of the Sikhs.* New York: Asia Publishing House, 1964.

Singh, Jagjit. *The Sikh Revolution.* New Delhi: Bahri Publication, 1981.

Singh, Narindar. *The Canadian Sikhs: History Religion and Culture of Sikhs in North America.* Ottawa, Ontario: Canadian Sikhs' Studies Institute, 1994.

Singh, Preetam. Dr. Q.C. "Canadian Sikhs," *The Sikh Messenger,* Autumn/Winter, (1988).

Singh, Saint N. "The Sikhs in Canada or Grievances of East-Indians," *The Canadian Magazine,* Toronto: 30 (November 1907), 57-60.

Singh, Teja. *Jeevan Katha: Gurmukh Piayre Sant Attar Singh ji Maharaj.* Patiala: Director Bhasha Bibhag, Punjab, 1946-1981. (P)

Sugunasiri, Suwanda H.J. *The Search for Meaning: The Literature of Canadians of South Asian Origin.* Multiculturism, Department of the Secretary of State of Canada, 1988.

Supreme Court of Canada Decision. *Bhinder, K.S. and the Canadian Human Rights Commission Appellants Vs. the Canadian National Railway Company Respondent and Attorney General of Canada.* December 17, 1985. Canadian Human Rights Reporter, Vol. 7, Decision 488. January, 1986.

Talib, Gurbachan Singh. *Sri Guru Granth Sahib.* In English Translation Vol. 1, 2 & 3. Patiala: Punjabi University, 1991.

The Canadian Human Rights Act. *Bhinder K.S. Complainant Vs. Canadian National Railways Respondent,* Decision rendered on September 22, 1981.

"Turban and the RCMP, *World Sikh News.* n.d.

"Turbans in the RCMP: How the Sikhs Were Permitted to Wear Turbans", in *Canadian Police.* "A Report to the Sikh Nation," *The Sword,* Spring/ Summer, 1990.

Wood, Chris, with Surette, Ralph. "The Newest Boat People," Maclean's, July 27, 1987.

Brazen Translations: Notes for a New Terminology

Raminder Kaur and Virinder Singh Kalra

Me say me gone to make a movie mon over India plane a where me catch a Indian air-liner
Place a where me land, dat a Amritsar, who meet me no de Prime Minister
Who a rush me baggage no a fe her father, who kiss me Gandhi daughter
Me there in de country like a big movie star jump pon a taxi dem call a rikshar
Pass Bombay and a Kalistania, de people meet me dem a no de producer
Make one film with de one Amitabh make another one with de one Rekha
Who sing de song Lata-Mangeshka, who play de music no Ravi-Shanka
Come take it from de youth baro-back rider, me chatta pon de mic like you could of never
So each and everyone mon come follar me mon dip your knee cork out your botty
De style a where you do are Bhangra jockey...
Your pound and dollar say dat a rupee your firewater say dat a desi
You want a glass a water say dat a parnee, me want me chalice say dat a hookie
Me pull out me rizzla and me sensi, dey say Wild Apache mon you a umalee
Come take it from de youth mon fe everybody, you no say dis a youth have de authority
Me play it fe de White, de Indian and de Yardy.
(Movie over India, Apache Indian, *1993)*

Despite much recent theorisation on the role of Black youth cultures in the shaping of British identities, particularly by Paul Gilroy and Stuart Hall, one aspect of the complex which has not been sufficiently considered is the position of British Asian minorities. In this paper we intend to propose a conceptual vocabulary in the hope of addressing the experiences of South Asians in Britain whilst also accounting for global movements and re-settlements. In order to pursue this argument, we will foreground musical cultures. We concentrate on the arenas inhabited by diasporic artistes and consumers of South Asian background, in the process of which we attempt to destabilise rigid terms of identifications.

Problems in the conceptualisation of Asian identities

The purpose of this paper is to begin a debate around the field of Asian identities which has hitherto not been satisfactorily explored. There are many reasons, both within and outside of academia, which can account for this lack of theoretical depth. However, for present purposes, the development of the discursive fields of race and ethnic studies is mainly responsible for the present impasse. In the race field, the notion of Asian was subsumed in the all encompassing category Black. It is important to note that since this particular use of the term Black has gone out of fashion (Hall

1992), a satisfactory terminology to describe those occasions when racism actually does unite disparate cultural and social groupings in a resistive way has not yet emerged. Our present concern is to tackle what the dissolution of the homogeneous Black subject may have left in its wake. Here the ethnic studies school of thought is also lacking. An assessment of a wide range of literature (particularly the works of M. Anwar, P. Bhachu, R. Ballard, A. Dahya, V-S. Khan, A. Shaw, P. Werbner) reveals that group definition is often taken to the anthropological extreme, where priority is given to the smallest social unit which is inevitably *biraderi/kin* based. When representation in a public situation is considered identification is ascribed to national origins, thus the use of terms such as Pakistani and Indian, which are analytically, perhaps even less useful than Black. To look further afield, when considering Indology, Sociology and Anthropology preference is given to the term South Asian, Diaspora or as in this book the Punjabi diaspora, privileges the perspective of the country of 'origin'. However, in the description of popular culture and social movements the most frequently used term is 'Asian' or sometimes 'British Asian'.

While the debate over the use of the term Asian raged in Commision for Racial Equality circles (Modood, 1990) it attracted scant academic attention, annoying those race theorists who saw it as another example of false consciousness and of no relevance to the ethnic studies school as it was still too general. The most thorough attempt to justify the use of the term Asian is given in the works of Tariq Modood (1990, 1992, 1994) who argues that Asian is far more appropriate than Black to describe the experiences of people from the Indian sub-continent. However, Sharma, Hutnyk and Sharma (1996) expose the essentialist tendencies of Modood's use of the term and in that sense find a certain tautology in his argument.

From Br-Asian to Tranl-Asian

Due to corresponding experiences between migrants to Britain from its former colonies of Africa, the Caribbean, and Asia, sociological race theorists have, and continue to unify them in the socio-political category of black. The socio-political circumstances of blacks, as understood, are ones that locate them in the margins when compared to the Euro-American centres. This is not to say that there is not an in-between dual motion between the two, but their primary positions locate them towards one end of the centre-margin continuum. In asserting that there are various junctures where these two routes from the margins overlap in terms of strategies of resisting dominant European discourses and practices we note that there is also a good deal of difference between the two to which consideration should be given. These differences are largely to do with a lack of familiarity with each others' linguistic and cultural traditions - their nuances rhythms, mores and transformations.

Therefore, when considering musical productions, we wish to propose the contingent term defining those of African and Afro-Caribbean backgrounds in Britain as Blak (Gilroy 1993:81), and those of South Asian backgrounds resident in Britain as Br-Asian. This latter term refers to the complex subject positions of migrants and their offspring settled in Britain with links both imagined and material to South Asia. It is intended to be an open term, beginning the exploration of shifting identifications and representations. The over-used and poorly defined category, British Asian, is problematic as it essentialises both terms, as well as hierarching the former against the latter. Further, it does not fully convey the various and sliding subjectivities which come into play in response to historical, social and political vicissitudes. While acknowledging the impossibility of complete categorisation in theory and in practice, Br-Asian is intended to be disruptive of the centre-margin relationship and to destabilise fixed notions of Asian identities, stressing their contingency on historical and spatial movements.

We recognise that for any particular situation there are two basic opposing vectors to trends of identity formations. One is that of correspondence, where ideas of a shared past, similar backgrounds or comparable present-day circumstances are stressed. The other is that of difference where either through antagonism, resistance or cultural superiority complexes, particularities are stressed. These need not be rigid dimensions. We might find a complicated entwining of the vectors as personal inclination and situation emphasise one more than the other - latticed identities that might be rigid for one situation but loosen up for others. Thus we find an oscillation of the one and the many, the fixed and the unfixed, the essentialised and the de-essentialised, the particular and the hybrid, in constant processes of suturing and fracturing.

To take us out of the locality of Britain, there is a need to account for the shifting centres within the South Asian diasporas, in the process of which, exposing the limitations of the very notion of diaspora. We note that technological innovations, amongst its other usages, have had a key part in allowing minority group cultural productions to transgress nation-state boundaries and communicate with others. Global media, telecommunications, and the flow of sound-structures divorced from their place of manufacture have provided for a greater interconnectedness and interdependency for minority groups. To begin the exploration of this phenomena, we propose the imagined spatial arena of transl-Asia. Our contention is that diaspora privileges the space of 'origin', which is of an unchanging and stable nature, whereas Transl-Asia is intended to prioritise the notion of space, which 'highlights histories of domination and the production of difference and hierarchy, as well as imaginative social practices' (Axel 1994:17). We note parallels with Bhabha's comments:

> 'Culture as a strategy of survival is both *transnational* and *tranlational*. It is transnational because contemporary postcolonial discourses are rooted in specific histories of cultural displacement. It is translational because such spatial histories of displacement... now accompanied by the territorial ambitions

of global media technologies....make the question of *how* culture
signifies, or what is signified by *culture*, rather complex issues.
It becomes crucial to distinguish between the semblance and
similitude of the *symbols* across diverse cultural experiences -
and the social specificity of each of these productions of
meaning as it circulates *as a sign* within specific contextual
locations and systems of value.' (Bhabba, 1992:47, his italics)

The constellation of spaces within the concept of Transl-Asia might include
changing configurations between parts of South Asia, Europe, North America, the
Caribbean, East Africa, Australia and the Far East. The localisation of *symbols,* in
our case musical forms, might take on variant associations according to the social,
geographical and historical contexts. Our paper considers this phenomena mainly in
relation to South Asian and Br-Asian musical forms.

Musics on our Doorsteps

The above arguments will now be bought to bear on the musical scene in Britain.
There is a criss-cross mesh of appropriative devices not only with the centre and the
margin, but also within the margins. These are sliding points on a continuum to the
point of interchangeability depending upon the perspective taken and subject covered.
To simplify the mass of complex trajectories, we will consider the triangular positions
of White, Blak, and Br-Asian in the music industry with the particular emphasis on
the latter due to it having received scant attention. As in the previous account, the
dominant partner remains, on the, whole, White, whereas Blak and Br-Asian each
have a pendulum relation with this centre. Each of these sites of identification, in
turn, have a complex relation with their respective global configurations. Whereas
in the 1990s black can begin to be identified as the centre, particularly when it comes
to international musical productions, Blak has a more ambiguous relation - sometimes
veering towards the centre, but more often locatable in the margins.

This triad of subject positions and their interactions has provided the fertile
ground from which Bhangra and related Br-Asian youth musical creations began to
emerge from the 1980s onwards. This is to acknowledge that music has been an
integral part of domestic and public life amongst Br-Asians since migration, but not
in wider arenas. Here we present a summary account of the musics. Broadly, while
we have not seen Bhangra bands with their Punjabi lyrics and musical style on *Top
of the Pops,* for instance, what we can perceive is that the centre has began to receive
and transmit the music through channels such as Radio One and mainstream venues
like the Hammersmith Palais in West London. Therefore, neither has the centre
totally opened up, nor has Bhangra totally remained in the margins, but new spaces
have began to emerge where those two sites overlap to a greater or lesser degree.

The ferment of modernised Bhangra began to be felt in Southall (West London) with bands like *Alaap* who began musical experimentations with synthesizers and drum machines. They were instrumental in setting the ball rolling in terms of providing a new blend of Bhangra sounds which were appreciated for the quality of their musical sound alone rather than being tied to any particular celebratory occasion - beginning the process of the commoditisation of music into a sound-object. Hindi film song also had a strong influence on this new British style; which represents a reversal of the post-1950s phenomenon, where Hindi film culture parodied regional musics. Now, it appeared that Bhangra bands, Br-Asian offsprings of Punjabi musical performances, cannibalised Hindi film tunes as well as the latest sounds in Western dance music. This dynamic is not surprising if one also considers that the Bhangra bands tapped into a cassette industry already providing Hindi film music. The ground was prepared by these 'grandfathers' of Bhangra, such as *Alaap, Premi, Heera, D.C.S.*, and *Golden Star* for Br-Asian youth to capitalise on the musical scene and attempt to break into mainstream music circles. One example is *Culture Shock*, who revelled in House Bhangra, in which Punjabi lyrics and dholak (drum) sounds were fused with the racy rhythm and sounds of House music popular in mainstream dance circuits. Other younger groups include *Shaktee* and *The Sahotas* who specialised in heavily synthesised electro dance music.

Modernised Bhangra particularly filled a demand among Br-Asian youth, enabling them, to enjoy a musical genre that was at once modern, yet different from mainstream pop such as to express their identities in innovative ways. At first the young audiences identified more with the music and lyrics than with the performers. Whilst enjoying the music, many youth began to express a disaffection with the Hindi filmi costuming - usually sequins, spangles, and white trousers - of these generally middle-aged performers. Consequently, band's with younger members whose ages and tastes were closer to those of their audiences began to emerge, as was the case with *Anaamika, The Sahotas*, and *Achanak*. Many of these group members correlated Black music with that of mainstream Western music, for which Vijay's comments are representative:

'We have always kept the Bhangra *beat*. With that we've added
a lot of Western influence, like ragga, rap, house.... whatever
is going down in the club seen". (Vijay - lead singer of Achanak,
Rhythm and Raag 1992)

Although it has been argued that the Bhangra scene allowed for a modern pan-Asian form of identification particular to Britain (Bauman and Banerji 1990) in many cases this gradually dissipated into complaints about its untrendiness, linguistic barriers and the lack of socially meaningful lyrics. In addition, there was an ambivalence towards Bhangra when it was assumed that all that Br-Asian youth listened to performed was Bhangra. Let us consider two cinematic depictions of Bhangra bands: in Gurinder Chadda's film, *I'm British But...* (1989), a Bhangra band is performing in a Southall street, singing lyrics relevant to Br-Asian life. This contrasts starkly with the later film script written by Harwant Bains, *Wild West* (1991), in which a parody of a Bhangra band is hissed off the stage, followed shortly by the welcome reception of a country and western band, the *Honky Tonk Cowboys*, fronted by Br-Asian boys. In this film the message is clear: music is music for anyone's taking, defiant of any links between skin colour and expected cultural associations.

One of the most recent examples of cut 'n' mix (Hebdige 1987) - to describe the sound editing procedures as well as the relations between identities and music - is the way Bhangra traits of Punjabi lyrics, antiphonal styles and dholak sounds have been mixed with the dance hall chat known as Ragga. It is noticeable that the dynamics of musical interchange in Blak and Br-Asian margins have resulted in the likes of Bally Sagoo's remixes with Bhangra tracks, Ragga patois and other dance sounds. The creolisation between the two musical forms is commonly referred to as Raggabhangra and the performers, Ragga/Bhangramuffins. They cannot be simply inserted as derivative of black musics for they have their own musical histories and reference points. Various languages of tradition are used as inspirations and as resources to play with the mainstream, and sometimes as resistance to selling out to a vision of white mainstream culture. These two stylistic strategies of periodic embracement or critique exist in a creative turmoil in the contemporary Br-Asian musical scene. Equally important, new textual spaces have been created for both Blak and Br-Asian listening audiences.

It is instructive to consider this position in relation to Br-Asian, Blak, Transl-Asian, and Black as explained in our above argument. Let us consider the example of Apache Indian's music as a narrative text of oscillating subjective positions. Multifarious cultural and personal histories and experiences might be represented in terms of at least three inter linked subjective stances:

(i)   Br-Asian evoked by (a) an association with centres of Br-Asian concentration and activities in place such as Bradford, Southall and Handsworth, and effectively serving as a mouthpiece relevant to the experiences of Br-Asian youth, and (b) a sense of Britishness, brought into relief by the cultural incomprehension encountered whilst visiting India, pertinent in the song, *Movie over India,* and overall the creole of music he has created which is specific to British musical landscapes.

(ii)   The second broader position is that of Transl-Asia as highlighted with references to (a) a sense of Punjabi ethnicity, occasionally further particularised to the caste, Jat - this is represented by the musical and lyrical references to Bhangra, dhols, Jallandar city, Amritsar, Khalistania and use of the Punjabi language and idioms like *Chakde phatte* and *Balle Balle*; and (b) India in general, as evoked with the terms "Indian ragamuffin possie", "my India" his song *Come Follow Me* involving a tour of India with mention of the Taj Mahal, Bombay city and so forth; use of symbols like Gandhi and the Indian flag (the latter on Apache's *No Reservations* album cover cleverly juxtaposed with the colours of Rastafarian Africa leads on to the next area):

(iii)   Blak/Black as invoked in Apache's Ragga patois, mention of, and work in, Jamaica, and his Reggae affiliations.

These polychromatic subject positions have opened up the ambiguity of the categorisations Br-Asian, Transl-Asian and Black in that the single artiste, Apache, parades through each of these various locations. This is further exemplified by firstly, Apache's duet with Maxi Priest, *Fe Real* (1993), in which Maxi sings some lines in Punjabi as a gesture to some kind of mutual appropriation in the creation of new textual spaces for Blak and Br-Asian youth, while at the same time being a chart success. Secondly, the oscillation between Br-Asian and Transl-Asian is conveyed by the following example where Apache bridged issues of caste inequities both in India and Br-Asian communities in his song, *High Caste, Low Caste*. In addition, his song *Moving On* about communalism in India was swiftly altered to expose racism in Britain two days after a British National Party candidate was elected into power in Tower Hamlets, London, 1993. Thirdly, Apache's recognition of the marginality of Transl-Asian cultural productions are illustrated when he represents himself a the musical pioneer who is breaking through into the global manistream at a Indian Press conference:

> 'One, thing I am trying to do for the whole of the Indian people
> and the whole of the Western people and the White press in
> England and America is [to show] that Indian people have got
> a lot of talent. But the problem is that people like Michael
> Jackson, Elvis Presley and Whitney Houston are stars for the
> whole world. Indian stars, Indian singers and Indian actresses
> and actors should be stars for the whole world, not just Indian
> people! (Apache Indian, 1993)

Transl-Asian Centres

In recognising the relationship between the mainstream 'stars of the world' and the periphery 'only for Indian people', Apache Indian reproduces global hegemonic relations in the interview above. This denies the major importance of Hindi films and musics in the "Third World", where they are a dominant form of entertainment from South East Asia to West Africa, including the former Eastern bloc countries. This angle prompts a refocusing of hegemonic relationships, centring what is considered marginal, and in the process, revealing new interstices and conjunctures.

To appreciate the changing waves created by Br-Asian musical productions we have to trace the travelogues of both artists and consumables (cassettes, records and C.D.s). It becomes apparent that Br-Asian musical developments have placed

Britain at the centre of Transl-Asia. However, this is not a fixed centre but one which is in oscillation with other centres such as Toronto (Canada), Bombay (India), Jallandar (India) and California (USA). In each case as musical innovation develops, technology interacts with and dissipates it to the four corners of Transl-Asia.

One can find parallels with the triangular dynamics as delineated by John Storm Robert's (1973) description of the musical round-trip between Africa, the Caribbean and South American countries. Roberts notes that musical styles originally from Africa were creolised in places like Cuba due to the presence of communities of African backgrounds and then went 'home' so as to influence the development of popular music on the African continent. Similarly, Br-Asian Bhangra music went to South Asia influencing the development of popular music in the subcontinent. This resulted in the signing of Indian film music contracts for Br-Asian groups such as *Alaap, D.C.S. and Golden Star* and is just one facet of a complex series of loops happening at a transnational level.

Conclusion

In conclusion we wish to raise some of the possibilities for the development of the terminology that we have proposed today. Firstly, we may be accused of cowardice when we make the statement that our suggestions primarily refer to musical culture. However, this decision is based on historical contingency as it is mainly in the field of music and related expressive cultures that the conditions have existed for the emergence of Br-Asian. There are many other situations in which this terminology may become applicable, but this is open to further debate and development. Secondly, identifying groups of people as Punjabi, Putohari, or Pakistani even with the hyphenated British is insufficient in both analytical and descriptive terms as it leaves out the development of crucial hybrid forms. It is in these situations that the term Br-Asian takes on greatest relevance.

Br-Asian in itself is not able to account for the total story. Here the history of political mobilisation in Britain highlights many of the problems: if we consider the last ten years, some of the major events that have affected Br-Asians have been the storming of the Harimandir Sahib (Golden Temple in Amritsar) in 1984, the Rushdie affair in 1989 and the destruction of the Babri Masjid in 1992. The stark truth of the matter is that these events managed to mobilise more people in Br-Asian communities than any demonstration against racism and racial attacks. This point is not meant to defend the politics which have created this state of affairs but more to raise the issues under consideration. It is in the need to describe and explain this type of political mobilisation that terms such as Transl-Asia can become of critical relevance. The previous examples are part of a two-way flow with the centre located primarily in the subcontinent. This does not however always remain the case as is best illustrated by the fact that the Jammu and Kashmir Liberation Front was founded in Birmingham and the self-styled leader of Khalistan is a resident of London.

We would like to end on a lighter note and one which perhaps shows the greatest need for some new concepts. A Br-Asian friend of ours was in Pakistan recently and was faced with an intransigent bureaucrat on a visa issue. During the conversation the bureaucrat continually mumbled a word and then went on to say something about people from overseas. When pushed by our friend as to what he was saying, he told them that he was calling him an 'abroadee' as they were obviously not English and somehow not Pakistani. For want of a better term, that bureaucrat encapsulated the debate which we wish to begin today.

BIBLIOGRAPHY

Axel, B. (1994)   *Place and Displacement or Have Trope... Will Travel*. Unpublished paper. University of Chicago.

Bhabha, H. (1992) 'Freedom's Basis in the Indeterminate.' October [61] Summer.

Bhabha, H. (1994) *The Location of Culture*. London and New York: Routledge.

Bauman, G. and S. Banerji (1990) 'Bhangra 1984-8: Fusion and Professionalization in a Genre of South Asian Dance Music'. *Black Music in Britain: Essays on the Afro-Asian, Contribution to Popular Music*. P. Oliver (ed.). Oxford: Oxford University Press.

Decker, J. L. (1993) 'The State of Rap: Time and Place in Hip-hop Nationalism' in *Social Text* [34].

Gilroy, P. (1993)   *The Black Atlantic: Modernity and Double Consciousness*. London: Verso.

Hall, S. (1992)   'The Question of Cultural Identity'. *Modernity and its Futures*. Hall, Held and McGrew (eds).

Hebdige, D. (1987) *Cut'n'mix: Culture, Identity and Caribbean Music*. London: Methuen

Sharma, S., J. Hutnyk, and A. Sharma (1996) *Dis-Orienting Rhythms: The Politics of the New South Asian Dance Music*. London: Zed Books.

Jameson, F. (1984) 'Post-modernism, or the Cultural Logic of Late Capitalism.' *New Left Review* [146].

Modood, T. (1990) 'Muslims, Race and Equality in Britain: Some Post-Rushdie Reflections', *Third Text*, Summer, 11: 127-134.

Modood, T. (1992) *Not Easy Being British*. London: Trentham Books.

Modood, T. (1994) 'Political Blackness and British Asians' in *Sociology*, 28, 4: 859-876.

Roberts, J. S. (1973) *Black Music of Two Worlds*. London: Penguin Books .

Slobin, M. (1993)   *Subcultural Sounds: Micromusics of the West*. Hanover and London: University Press of New England.

Spivak, G.C. (1987) *In Other Worlds*. London: Methuen.

West, C. (1989)   'Black Culture and Postmodernism'. *Remaking History*. B. Kruger and Mariani (eds.). Washington: Bay Press.

DISCOGRAPHY

Apache Indian (1993) *No Reservations.* Island ICT 8001 514 112-4.
Apache Indian (1993) *Nuff Vibes.* Island ICT 862 537-4.
Fun^da^mental (1993) *Sista India.* Nation Records.

FILMOGRAPHY

Birthrights (1993)   B.B.C.
Maine Pyar Kya (1988) dir. Sooraj R. Barjatya.
I'm British But.. (1990) dir. Gurinder Chaddha.
Rhythm and Raag (1992) Interface Video Productions
Rapido (1993)   Channel 4.
Wild West (1991)   dir. David Attwood; screenplay by Harwant Bains.

Index